Cornwall, Connectivity and Identity
in the Fourteenth Century

Cornwall, Connectivity and Identity in the Fourteenth Century

S. J. Drake

THE BOYDELL PRESS

© S. J. Drake 2019

All Rights Reserved. Except as permitted under current legislation no part of this work may be photocopied, stored in a retrieval system, published, performed in public, adapted, broadcast, transmitted, recorded or reproduced in any form or by any means, without the prior permission of the copyright owner

The right of S. J. Drake to be identified as the author of this work has been asserted in accordance with sections 77 and 78 of the Copyright, Designs and Patents Act 1988

First published 2019
The Boydell Press, Woodbridge
Paperback edition 2022

ISBN 978-1-78327-469-7 hardback
ISBN 978-1-83765-008-8 paperback

The Boydell Press is an imprint of Boydell & Brewer Ltd
PO Box 9, Woodbridge, Suffolk IP12 3DF, UK
and of Boydell & Brewer Inc.
668 Mt Hope Avenue, Rochester, NY 14620–2731, USA
website: www.boydellandbrewer.com

A catalogue record of this publication is available from the British Library

The publisher has no responsibility for the continued existence or accuracy of URLs for external or third-party internet websites referred to in this book, and does not guarantee that any content on such websites is, or will remain, accurate or appropriate

For Annie

Contents

List of Illustrations	ix
Acknowledgements	xi
List of Abbreviations	xiii
Author's Note	xvi
Preface: a Little Understood Land	xvii

PART I
CORNWALL: ITS GENTLEMEN, GOVERNMENT AND IDENTITY

1.	The Very Ends of the Earth: an Overview of Fourteenth-Century Cornwall	3
2.	Office-Holding in a Wild Spot	21
3.	Since the Time of King Arthur: Gentry Identity and the Commonalty of Cornwall	41
4.	An Extraordinary Folk: the Cornish People	68

PART II
DISTANT *DOMINIUM*: COMITAL, DUCAL AND REGNAL LORDSHIP

5.	The Final Tempestuous Years of the Earldom, 1300–36	111
6.	The Black Prince and his Duchy, 1337–76	135
7.	Richard of Bordeaux: Duke of Cornwall and King of England, 1376–99	152

PART III
CONNECTIVITY: CORNWALL AND THE WIDER REALM

    Communication, Movement and Exchange: Connectivity Frameworks   169

8. Sovereign Kings and Demanding Subjects: Regnal Connectivity   171
9. Pillagers with Long Knives: Military Connectivity   183
10. Formidable Lords and True Tenants: Lordly Connectivity   205
11. Gold, Tin and Terrible Ale: Commercial Connectivity   215
12. Lawless Judges and Litigious Cornishmen: Legal Connectivity   235
13. God and Cornwall: Ecclesiastical Connectivity   255
14. Of Shipmen, Smugglers and Pirates: Maritime Connectivity   278

    Connecting Cornwall   303

Conclusion: Cornish Otherness and English Hegemony?   311
Epilogue: Contesting Cornwall   315
Appendices
    I. Cornwall's Office-Holders, c. 1300–c. 1400   318
    II. Cornish Men-at-Arms and Mounted Archers who Served the King between c. 1298 and c. 1415   393
    III. Cornish Ports that sent ships to Royal Fleets between c. 1297 and c. 1420   425
Bibliography   431
Index   463

Illustrations

MAPS

1. A Sketch-Map of Later Medieval Cornwall	xxi
2. The Hundreds and Stannaries of Cornwall	xxii

TABLES

1. Cornishmen with Incomes of £40 or more p.a. Summoned to a Great Council of 1323–4	13
2. Cornish Gentry Paying the 1450 Income Tax	14
3. The Locations of County Peace Sessions in Richard II's Reign	27
4. The Black Prince's Cornish Itinerary of 1354	141
5. The Black Prince's Cornish Itinerary of 1362–3	144
6. Petitions Submitted by the Residents of Cornwall, 1300–1420	178
7. Cornwall's Assessment in the 1440 Alien Subsidy	280

This book is produced with the generous assistance of a grant from Isobel Thornley's Bequest to the University of London

Acknowledgements

In writing this book I have incurred a great many debts to a great many people. First and foremost, my deepest thanks go to Professor Nigel Saul, who has provided endless help, advice and encouragement. His clear-sighted suggestions about a first draft of this study added greatly to its quality. Dr Oliver Padel has also been very generous with his time and expertise about Cornwall, welcoming me into the small but loyal group of medievalists who have made the county their special study. He, too, very kindly read through parts of this book. I am just as grateful to Professor Jim Bolton and Professor Anthony Musson for reading through earlier drafts of my work. The many discussions that I have had with Dr Hannes Kleineke about medieval Cornwall were equally invaluable to my research and thinking. Dr Jo Mattingly and Professor Nicholas Orme have been generous with their thoughts too. Providing many morale-boosting cups of tea, Dr Clive Burgess has been another great source of encouragement. Both Professor Caroline Barron and Professor Peregrine Horden also kindly offered me advice about my project. Indeed, discussions with the convenors, presenters and attendees at the Institute of Historical Research's Late Medieval and Medieval and Tudor London Seminars have been invaluable. There is nothing to equal researching in such a dynamic environment.

I am very grateful to Caroline Palmer and the team at Boydell & Brewer for their advice and help in publishing this book. I also owe a great debt to the University of London, which kindly awarded me funding for parts of this project, and to the Art and Humanities Research Council for footing some of the bill. I am very grateful to the Institute of Historical Research (IHR) and the Royal Historical Society for awarding me a fellowship, and to Professor P. J. Marshall for funding the post. Both the Q-Fund from Cornwall Council and the Cornwall Heritage Trust kindly awarded me bursaries for my research. The help and patience of the staff at the National Archives, the IHR, the Cornish Record Office and the Royal Institution of Cornwall must also be acknowledged, as their aid and diligence were essential to my research.

Last, but by no means least, stand the many debts that I have incurred to my family and friends during these years, especially to Annie, Emma, Avril, David, Liz and Jon. Without them, and many more people besides, I simply could not have written this book.

Sam Drake

Abbreviations

BL	British Library, London
BRUO	A. B. Emden, *A Biographical Register of the University of Oxford to 1500*, 3 vols (Oxford, 1957–9)
Carew	R. Carew, *The Survey of Cornwall by Richard Carew*, ed. J. Chynoweth, N. Orme and A. Walsham, Devon and Cornwall Record Society, n.s. 47 (Exeter, 2004)
CChR	*Calendar of Charter Rolls, 1226–1516*, 6 vols, HMSO (London, 1903–27)
CCR	*Calendar of Close Rolls, 1296–1454*, 38 vols, HMSO (London, 1892–1947)
CFR	*Calendar of Fine Rolls, 1272–1452*, 18 vols, HMSO (London, 1911–39)
CIM	*Calendar of Inquisitions Miscellaneous, 1219–1422*, 7 vols, HMSO (London, 1916–68)
CIPM	*Calendar of Inquisitions Post Mortem, 1272–1427*, 20 vols, HMSO (London and Woodbridge, 1908–2003)
Cornish Wills	*Cornish Wills, 1342–1540*, ed. N. Orme, Devon and Cornwall Record Society, n.s. 50 (Exeter, 2007)
CP	G. E. Cokayne, *The Complete Peerage…*, ed. V. Gibbs et al., 12 vols in 13 (London, 1912–59)
CPMR	*Calendar of Plea and Memoranda Rolls*, ed. A. H. Thomas and P. E. Jones, 6 vols (Cambridge, 1924–61)
CPR	*Calendar of Patent Rolls, 1292–1477*, 42 vols, HMSO (London, 1893–1916)
CRO	Cornwall Record Office, Truro
CS	*The Caption of Seisin of the Duchy of Cornwall (1337)*, ed. P. L. Hull, Devon and Cornwall Record Society, n.s. 17 (Torquay, 1971)

DCNQ	*Devon and Cornwall Notes and Queries*
DCO	Duchy of Cornwall Office, London
DCRS	Devon and Cornwall Record Society
EcHR	*Economic History Review*
EETS	Early English Texts Society
EHR	*English Historical Review*
Escheators	*List of Escheators for England and Wales*, compil. A. C. Wood, List and Index Society, 72 (London, 1971)
FA	*Inquisitions and Assessments Relating to Feudal Aids, 1284–1431*, 6 vols, HMSO (London, 1899–1920)
FF	*Cornwall Feet of Fines*, ed. J. H. Rowe et al., 2 vols, Devon and Cornwall Record Society (Exeter and Topsham, 1914–50)
GL	Guildhall Library, London
HA	*The Havener's Accounts of the Earldom and Duchy of Cornwall, 1287–1356*, ed. M. Kowaleski, Devon and Cornwall Record Society, n.s. 44 (Exeter, 2001)
HOP	*The History of Parliament, The House of Commons 1386–1421*, ed. J. S. Roskell, L. Clark and C. Rawcliffe, 4 vols (Stroud, 1993)
HW	*Calendar of Wills Proved and Enrolled in the Court of Husting, London 1258–1688*, ed. R. R. Sharpe, 2 vols (London, 1889–90)
JRIC	*Journal of the Royal Institution of Cornwall*
LB	*Calendar of Letter Books of the City of London, A–L*, ed. R. R. Sharpe, 11 vols (London, 1899–1912)
LMA	London Metropolitan Archives, London
MPs	*Return of Members of Parliament*, 2 parts in 4 vols (London, 1878–91), i part 1
NCMH	*The New Cambridge Medieval History, VI, c. 1300–c. 1415*, ed. M. Jones (Cambridge, 2000)
ODNB	*The Oxford Dictionary of National Biography*, ed. H. C. G. Matthew and B. H. Harrison, 60 vols (Oxford, 2004)
PROME	*The Parliament Rolls of Medieval England*, ed. and trans. P. Brand, A. Curry, C. Given-Wilson, R. E. Horrox, G. Martin, W. M. Ormrod and J. R. S. Philips, 16 vols (Woodbridge, 2005)
RBP	*Register of Edward the Black Prince*, 4 vols, HMSO (London, 1930–3)

Reg.Brantingham	*The Register of Thomas de Brantyngham, Bishop of Exeter (1370–1394)*, ed. F. C. Hingeston-Randolph, 2 vols (London, 1901–6)
Reg.Grandisson	*The Register of John de Grandisson, Bishop of Exeter (1327–1369)*, ed. F. C. Hingeston-Randolph, 3 vols (London, 1894–9)
Reg.Stafford	*The Register of Edmund Stafford (1395–1419): An Index and Abstract of its Contents*, ed. F. C. Hingeston-Randolph (London, 1886)
Reg.Stapeldon	*The Register of Walter de Stapeldon, Bishop of Exeter (1307–1326)*, ed. F. C. Hingeston-Randolph (London, 1892)
RESDCornwall	J. Hatcher, *Rural Economy and Society in the Duchy of Cornwall, 1300–1500* (Cambridge, 1970)
SCKB	*Select Cases in the Court of King's Bench*, ed. G. O. Sayles, 7 vols, Selden Society, 55, 57, 58, 74, 76, 82, 88 (London, 1936–71)
Sheriffs	*List of Sheriffs for England and Wales*, List and Index Society, 9 (London, 1898)
TCO	'Thomas Chiverton's Book of Obits', ed. P. L. Hull, *Devon and Cornwall Notes and Queries*, 33 (1974–7), pp. 97–102, 143–147, 188–193, 236–239, 277–282, 337–341; 34 (1978–81), pp. 5–11, 52–55.
TRHS	*Transactions of the Royal Historical Society*
YB	*Year Books 30 and 31 Edward I to 7 Richard II*, ed. M. S. Arnold et al., Ames Society, Rolls Series and Selden Society (London and Cambridge, MA, 1863–1989)

All unpublished documents to which reference is made are preserved in the National Archives of the UK unless otherwise stated.

Author's Note

With non-standard spelling the norm in the middle ages, the majority of personal names used in this book follow the most common form found in the documents.

Preface: a Little Understood Land

On 17 June 1497, the massed forces of Henry VII charged into an army of Cornishmen that had marched in rebellion from the furthest south west of the realm to Blackheath, just outside London.[1] Proving deadly effective, the king's troops were to break the Cornish line and rout those men who had taken up arms over the burden of royal taxation. Many died in the melee and ensuing chaos, with the government capturing the two Cornish rebels-in-chief, Thomas Flamank of Bodmin and Michael Joseph of St Keverne, later sentencing them both to be hung, drawn and quartered. They suffered their gruesome fate at Tyburn soon after. So it was that by *force majeure* the Crown put down the first Cornish Rebellion of 1497, and these events hold a potent place in Cornwall's collective memory to this day. While it cannot be doubted that the rebels were profoundly dissatisfied with the king, however, all was not as it seemed. For a start, the insurgents were actually by no means all Cornish, the rebels having garnered support from across southern England.[2] Neither did the Cornish contingent of the rebellion seek to sever their county from the realm, as this was no war of liberation. On the contrary, after centuries of royal rulership Cornwall's residents believed so implicitly in the king's government that they were willing to march hundreds of miles to petition their sovereign for reform.

Indeed, a contradiction lies at the heart of Cornish history and identity. By some, this idiosyncratic peninsula is seen as a shire of England and an integral if distinctive part of the country at large. But to others, it exists – or deserves to exist – as a country unto itself: one rendered distinct by language, law, culture, genetics and even nature, by the whole length of the river Tamar. Celtic Cornwall, so this logic runs, was subjugated by a rapacious English state in the tenth century, inaugurating millennia of political and cultural domination. Despite some measure of 'accommodation' afforded by its English overlords,

---

[1] For the classic account, A. L. Rowse, *Tudor Cornwall: Portrait of a Society* (London, 1941), pp. 114–128.
[2] Below, pp. 102–103.

and despite its isolation, Cornwall formed a conquered and colonised land.[3] By 1497 the county's residents could supposedly tolerate their servitude no longer, especially after suffering heavy-handed Tudor government, rising in revolt under the leadership of the 'Cornish Braveheart' Michael Joseph.[4] As with all grand narratives, however, we may well wonder about the accuracy of this construct.

Stretching out into the wild Atlantic, Cornwall actually remains a little understood land. In the later middle ages, the long and slender Cornish peninsula held a place on the very edge of the known world. Within its boundaries some Cornish men and women even spoke Cornish, a language entirely different to that of the rest of England, with these folk believing in a rich range of local myths and saints. To many of them King Arthur was a real-life historical Cornishman and they believed that their natal shire had once been the home of mighty giants. The trope of an isolated, self-contained 'little land' certainly found favour among older generations of scholars and antiquaries.[5] According to them, medieval Cornwall could 'be likened to a backwater' left 'self-contained and serenely apathetic', only 'awakening' from 'the long sleep of the middle ages' with the coming of the Tudors.[6]

While fourteenth-century Cornwall stood out as strikingly distinctive, at the same time the peninsula was powerfully integrated into the wider realm. More recent scholarship has considered aspects of the county's government, economics, religious practices and so on, showing how the affairs of the peninsula were influenced by its place in the kingdom.[7] The Celtic influences on

---

[3] P. Payton, *The Making of Modern Cornwall: Historical Experience and the Persistence of 'Difference'* (Redruth, 1992), pp. 43–70.
[4] P. Payton, *Cornwall* (Fowey, 1996), p. 125.
[5] For example, A. L. Rowse, *The Little Land of Cornwall* (Guernsey, 1986); Rowse, *Tudor Cornwall*; L. E. Elliott-Binns, *Medieval Cornwall* (London, 1955); also, W. Borlase, *Antiquities, Historical and Monumental, of the County of Cornwall*, 2nd Edition (London, 1769); other historians of the county were not so sentimental, see C. Henderson, *Essays in Cornish History*, ed. A. L. Rowse and M. I. Henderson (Oxford, 1935); J. Maclean, *The Parochial and Family History of the Deanery of Trigg Minor*, 3 vols (London, 1873–9).
[6] Elliott-Binns, *Medieval Cornwall*, p. 70; Rowse, *Tudor Cornwall*, p. 16.
[7] Politics: H. Kleineke, 'Why the West Was Wild: Law and Order in Fifteenth-Century Cornwall and Devon', *The Fifteenth Century: III, Authority and Subversion*, ed. L. Clark (Woodbridge, 2003), pp. 75–93; M. Page, 'Royal and Comital Government and the Local Community in Thirteenth-Century Cornwall' (Unpubl. Univ. Oxford D.Phil, 1995); C. Tyldesley, 'The Crown and the Local Communities in Devon and Cornwall from 1377 to 1422' (Unpubl. Univ. Exeter PhD, 1978); Economics: H. S. A. Fox, 'Devon and Cornwall', in *The Agrarian History of England and Wales: III, 1348–1500*, ed. E. Miller (Cambridge, 1991), pp. 152–174, 303–323, 722–743; J. Hatcher, *Rural Economy and Society in the Duchy of Cornwall, 1300–1500* (Cambridge, 1970); J. Hatcher, *English Tin Production and Trade before 1550* (Oxford,

Cornwall have also received some attention, with the Cornish language and the county's place-names prominent among these subjects.[8] Yet even here the peninsula's English credentials are recognised as significant. At the same time, however, Cornish ethnicity and otherness have increasingly been emphasised as forces that marked the peninsula out as a 'land apart', explaining the tumultuousness of 1497 and thereafter.[9] Although there have been many recent contributions to Cornish history, each of them has – to a greater or lesser extent – had a narrow focus. No overarching study of medieval Cornwall has been written for over sixty years. It also true that the peculiarities of the peninsula often loom larger in the existing scholarship than its links with the rest of the realm. Appearing simultaneously both detached and yet integrated, Cornwall's dual aspects come across as seemingly contradictory and never reconciled.

The main aim of this book, therefore, is to present an account of how fourteenth-century Cornwall cohered with the rest of the kingdom while remaining a quite remarkable place. Beginning as an internal study of the peninsula before broadening its perspective to encompass the county's interactions with the wider realm, this book opens by looking at the gentlemen, government and identity of Cornwall. Once the county's distinctive but still integral place in the kingdom is established, consideration will be given to the way in which the earldom-duchy and the Crown together rendered the politics of Cornwall part and parcel of the collective politics of England. Attention is then directed away from Cornwall as defined by its boundaries to study connectivity with the wider realm: the movement of people, goods and ideas brought about by the needs of the Crown, warfare, lordship, commerce, the law, the Church and maritime interests. By virtue of placing Cornwall at the centre of the latest debates about centralisation, devolution and regional and national identities, it will be possible to add to our understanding of both the county itself and the regional and social operation of the kingdom at large.[10] The unity of the

---

1973); G. R. Lewis, *The Stannaries: A Study of the Medieval Tin Miners of Devon and Cornwall* (Truro, 1908); *The Havener's Accounts of the Earldom and Duchy of Cornwall, 1287–1356*, ed. M. Kowaleski, DCRS, n.s. 44 (Exeter, 2001); The Church: N. Orme, *Victoria County History of Cornwall: II, Religious History to 1560* (London, 2010).

[8] For instance, O. J. Padel, *A Popular Dictionary of Cornish Place-Names* (Penzance, 1988).

[9] M. Stoyle, *West Britons: Cornish Identities and the Modern British State* (Exeter, 2002).

[10] For some other regional studies: M. Bennett, *Community, Class and Careerism: Cheshire and Lancashire Society in the Age of Sir Gawain and the Green Knight* (Cambridge, 1983); C. Carpenter, *Locality and Polity: A Study of Warwickshire Landed Society, 1401–1499* (Cambridge, 1992); R. H. Hilton, *A Medieval Society: The West Midlands at the end of the Thirteenth Century* (London, 1966); C. Liddy, *The Bishopric of Durham in the Late Middle Ages: Lordship, Community and the*

period rests on the fourteenth-century expansion of royal government and the resultant growth of source material, both of which prove revealing of the changing nature of Cornish integration. At one and the same time Cornwall was distinctive and integrated, with these twin strands of its history and identity indivisibly tied together and not mutually contradictory.

Cult of St Cuthbert (Woodbridge, 2008); S. J. Payling, *Political Society in Lancastrian England: The Greater Gentry of Nottinghamshire* (Oxford, 1991); A. J. Pollard, *North-Eastern England during the Wars of the Roses: Lay Society, War, and Politics, 1450–1500* (Oxford, 1990); N. Saul, *Knights and Esquires: The Gloucestershire Gentry in the Fourteenth Century* (Oxford, 1981); *idem.*, *Scenes from Provincial Life: Knightly Families in Sussex, 1280–1400* (Oxford, 1986); S. Wright, *The Derbyshire Gentry in the Fifteenth Century* (Chesterfield, 1983).

Map 1. A Sketch-Map of Later Medieval Cornwall

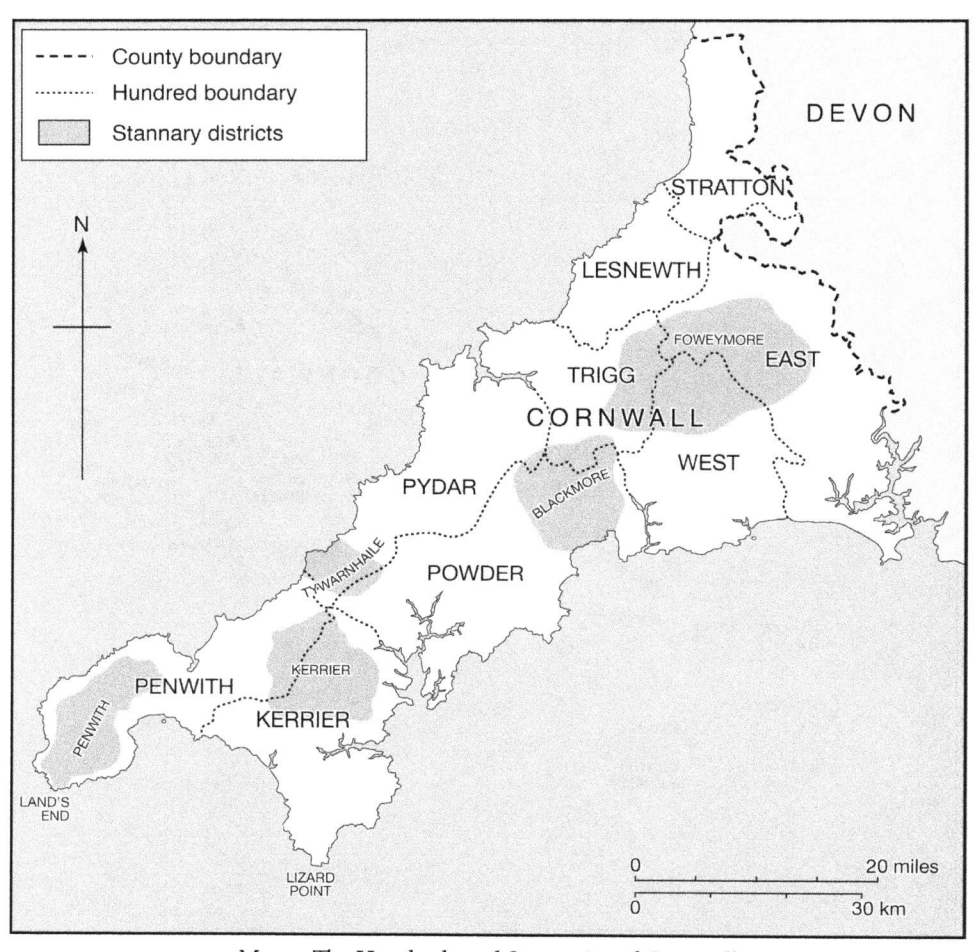

Map 2. The Hundreds and Stannaries of Cornwall
N.B. The area of the stannary districts should only be regarded as a rough approximation, as their exact boundaries were never defined in the middle ages.

I

Cornwall: its Gentlemen, Government and Identity

1

The Very Ends of the Earth: an Overview of Fourteenth-Century Cornwall

'Not only the ends of the earth', so goes Bishop Grandisson's lament of Cornwall in 1327, 'but the very ends of the ends thereof.'[1] The bishop's bewailing of the county as an isolated wilderness, scarcely integrated into the realm, typifies many interpretations of the medieval peninsula. So remote was Cornwall that Richard II's government even employed Tintagel Castle as a place of exile for John Northampton, the demagogue mayor of London.[2] Standing in the furthest south-western corner of the kingdom, Cornwall is undoubtedly distant from the heartlands of England. On three sides the sea envelopes the Cornish peninsula, with the Tamar demarking the greater part of its border on the east. In this way, the county forms a defined geographic space.

Yet Cornwall also contains striking topographical variation between the granitic moorland and sub-tropical valleys, being by no means perfectly uniform. Neither was the county completely isolated. 'Much frequented by travellers', the county's major road artery, the *Via Regalis Cornubiensis*, ran from the far west of the peninsula along its spine to Launceston and across Polston Bridge into Devon, whence it charted a course via Exeter to London.[3] A busy main southern route linked Fowey, Looe and beyond, crossing the Tamar by ferry at Little Ash, near Saltash; while yet another busy route, this

---

[1] *Reg.Grandisson*, i, 97–98; *RESDCornwall*, 1.
[2] *CCR 1381–1385*, 485; also, *CCR 1396–1399*, 161.
[3] *Reg.Stafford*, 258; W. Worcestre, *Itineraries*, ed. J. H. Harvey (Oxford, 1969), pp. 13, 38–39; C. Henderson and H. Coates, *Old Cornish Bridges and Streams* (Truro, 1928), pp. 11–12; CRO, BLAUS/42; G. B. Grundy, 'Ancient Highways of Cornwall', *Archaeological Journal*, 98 (1941), pp. 165–180.

time running from Padstow to Fowey, connected the north and south coasts.[4] Vessels also thronged the sea that enveloped Cornwall, for all Bishop Grandisson's bemoaning its rarely navigable nature. Ships from places as diverse as the Mediterranean and the Baltic were to land on the peninsula, while many vessels sailed from county harbours on to London and elsewhere. Although storms and the rocky Cornish coast could challenge seafarers, while the county's narrow lanes and branching estuaries could slow journeys on land, a heavily used and increasingly dense 'transport system' connected Cornwall to the rest of England and beyond.

For all these journeys, however, a fleeting glance suggests that the county remained relatively impoverished. Recording movable wealth varying from less than £5 per square mile up to £9, the 1334 lay subsidy shows that comparable figures for parts of East Anglia stood at over £30.[5] The government excluded tinners' operations from parliamentary taxation, however, making the county appear over-poor, particularly as these privileges were sometimes abused. So as to limit their tax liabilities, for example, in 1343 'rich men and others' had allegedly asserted 'that they are stannary men when they are not'.[6] Since smuggling was also rife, we may well wonder whether the county's residents had perfected the art of undervaluation.[7] While there can be little doubt that Cornwall did not enjoy the honour of being the wealthiest shire, it was more prosperous than these tax assessments suggest and this wealth was to burgeon across the later middle ages.[8]

Resting on farming, mining, fishing and shipping, the late-medieval Cornish economy was strong and diversified.[9] As with every shire of England, agriculture was essential to Cornwall's wealth. The peninsula's mild climate extended growing seasons and the coasts proved reasonable for the production of wheat and barley, with the result that Cornish foodstuffs were exported to London and elsewhere.[10] In 1361 one John Treeures even claimed that his land 'bore wheat, barley, oats, hay and peas, and is as good and fair as any

---

[4] *Reg.Stafford*, 245; Worcestre, *Itineraries*, pp. 30–33; CS, 118.
[5] *The Lay Subsidy of 1334*, ed. R. Glasscock (London, 1975), p. xxvii.
[6] *CPR 1343–1345*, 165.
[7] Cf. W. M. Ormrod, 'The Crown and the English Economy, 1290–1348', in *Before the Black Death: Studies in the 'Crisis' of the Early Fourteenth Century*, ed. B. M. S. Campbell (Manchester, 1991), pp. 149–183 at 155–157.
[8] N. G. Pounds, 'Taxation and Wealth in Late Medieval Cornwall', *JRIC* (1971), pp. 154–167.
[9] J. Hatcher, 'A Diversified Economy: Later Medieval Cornwall', *EcHR*, 22 (1969), pp. 208–227; *RESDCornwall, passim.*; P. Schofield, 'The Arundell Estates and the Regional Economy in Fifteenth-Century Cornwall', in *Town and Countryside in the Age of the Black Death: Essays in Honour of John Hatcher*, ed. M. Bailey and S. Rigby (Turnhout, 2012), pp. 277–297.
[10] For example, *CPR 1313–1317*, 447.

soil in Cornewaille'.[11] Far less suited to arable agriculture, however, granitic moorland covered large tracts of the peninsula. Farmers typically employed these 'zones' for rough grazing or simply left them as wasteland, resulting in a 'patchwork pattern' of cultivation.[12] If Cornish land use stood out as distinctive, then so too did the organisation of its estates. By the fourteenth century it is 'questionable' whether the seventeen manors of the earldom-duchy 'can be called manorialised at all', demesne agriculture having been replaced by conventionary tenure.[13] Such a tenurial arrangement involved the earl-duke leasing out land for seven years at a time, with the price of the lease being determined at the court of assession, comprising an annual fixed rent and a fine, the value of which fluctuated depending on demand. While this estate management practice yielded the greatest seignorial profits, the peninsula was by no means ideally suited to agriculture.[14]

Instead, maritime interests and the metals which lay under the county's craggy moors were perhaps more significant than cultivation on these hillsides. A great richness of copper, lead, silver, gold and other metallic minerals occur in Cornish rocks, with tin standing pre-eminent among these ores. The county's prosperity in no small part rested on this internationally significant metal. Thousands of folk were involved in extracting and processing tin, while yet more people were employed in supporting industries, not least the production of peat charcoal for smelting.[15] As complex credit networks helped fund the tinning industry, it is unsurprising that merchants from within and without Cornwall transported large amounts of the metal to London, the Low Countries and elsewhere.[16] With the great majority of tin being shipped from the county, maritime industries naturally formed another pillar of the peninsula's wealth. A skilled bunch, Cornish seafarers transported commodities as varied as hides, salt and wine to ports ranging from Chester down to Bordeaux and across to Bruges.[17] The county's fisheries also expanded in this period, while 'piracy', smuggling and wrecking could yield considerable profits at times.[18] Together, these tinning, maritime and agricultural interests contributed to the

[11] *RBP*, ii, 178.
[12] Fox, 'Devon and Cornwall', pp. 307–308, 152, 159–161.
[13] *RESDCornwall*, 52–54; J. Hatcher, 'Non-Manorialism in Medieval Cornwall', *Agricultural History Review*, 18 (1970), pp. 1–16; it remains unclear whether other manors employed conventionary tenure, *The Cornish Lands of the Arundells of Lanherne, Fourteenth to Sixteenth Centuries*, ed. H. S. A. Fox and O. J. Padel, *DCRS*, n.s. 41 (Exeter, 2000), p. lviii.
[14] *RESDCornwall*, 9.
[15] Hatcher, *Tin*, p. 47; Fox, 'Devon and Cornwall', p. 162; *CPR 1461–1467*, 482.
[16] Hatcher, *Tin*, p. 51; below, Chapter 11.
[17] Below, Chapter 14.
[18] M. Kowaleski, 'The Expansion of South-Western Fisheries in Late Medieval England', *EcHR*, 53 (2000), pp. 429–454; H. S. A. Fox, *The Evolution of the Fishing*

county's economy and character while linking the peninsula into extended networks of exchange.

By no means impoverished, many Cornish boroughs formed hubs of commercial activity. The county saw the 'proliferation' of small boroughs within its midst, the government taxing eighteen of these thirty or so settlements in 1334 alone.[19] 'Plants of exotic growth... fostered by great landholders as profitable sources of revenue', many new towns stood out.[20] The earldom-duchy owned nine of these, while the local gentry oversaw many others and the bishops of Exeter enjoyed lordship over Penryn.[21] Most urban settlements stood astride the county's main roads or at sites advantageous for shipping, these towns generally representing the convergence of mercantile and seigniorial interests. Whatever the case, the county played host to a striking density of urban centres which in 1334 accounted for over a fifth of its tax yield. The government reckoned Bodmin to be the richest of these places, with some £200 of movable property; Truro came second, having over £120 to its name; but the Crown assessed Camelford at a mere £4.[22] Despite such contrasts in size and wealth, each settlement and its burgesses relied on royal charters securing their tenurial and commercial practices, as trade in Cornwall carried on in much the same way as every other part of the realm.[23]

But how many people lived in the peninsula? Unfortunately, overall figures for the county's late-medieval population remain notoriously unreliable. Although scholars have employed the 1377 poll tax returns to suggest that some 51,411 people inhabited Cornwall at this time, more recent studies have pushed this number higher.[24] Even these revised figures do not represent the high watermark of the peninsula's medieval population, the Black Death having ravaged the county by the late fourteenth century. In Bodmin alone the friars

---

Village: Landscape and Society along the South Devon Coast, 1086–1550 (Oxford, 2001); C. L. Kingsford, *Prejudice and Promise in XVth Century England* (Oxford, 1925); *A Calendar of Early Chancery Proceedings Relating to West Country Shipping, 1388–1493*, ed. D. Gardiner, DCRS, n.s. 21 (Torquay, 1976); *RESDCornwall*, 32–35.

[19] *Lay Subsidy*, p. 29; M. Beresford and H. Finberg, *English Medieval Boroughs: A Hand-List* (Newton Abbot, 1973), pp. 76–83; A. Preston-Jones and P. Rose, 'Week St Mary: Town and Castle', *Cornish Archaeology*, 31 (1992), pp. 143–153.

[20] Henderson, *Essays*, p. 19.

[21] M. Beresford, *New Towns of the Middle Ages: Town Plantation in England, Wales and Gascony* (London, 1967), pp. 399–414.

[22] For all urban figures, *Lay Subsidy*, pp. 29–35.

[23] *Placita de Quo Warranto*, ed. W. Illingworth and J. Caley (London, 1818), pp. 108–111; *Gazetteer of Markets and Fairs in England and Wales to 1516*, compil. S. Letters, 2 vols, List and Index Society, Special Series, 32–33 (Chippenham, 2003), i, pp. 76–85; J. Mattingly, 'The Medieval Parish Guilds of Cornwall', *JRIC* (1989), pp. 290–329.

[24] J. C. Russell, *British Population History* (Albuquerque, 1948), p. 132; J. Hatcher, *Plague, Population and the English Economy, 1348–1530* (London, 1977), pp. 11–15.

reckoned that some 1,500 folk succumbed to the 'great plague throughout the world'.[25] Outside the county's urban centres the death toll was still high, for Cornwall's dispersed settlements did not mitigate the plague's effects, as once believed.[26] The contraction and subsequent stagnation of the county's population was of concern to the Black Prince himself, who in 1359 complained that the stannaries were suffering 'partly owing to the lack of workers since the pestilence'.[27] As in the rest of England, the plague exercised great influence on the county, but charting its full effects remains fraught with difficulties.

When we turn from the county's economic to its political history, we find a story marked by instability and at least a degree of turbulence. Although King Stephen had created Alan de Bretagne earl of Cornwall back in 1140, he then stripped the dignity from him soon afterwards. No single family was to dominate the earldom subsequently. The title often reverted to the king who then recreated the dignity for another favourite, as did Henry III for his younger brother, Richard of Cornwall, king of the Romans from 1257.[28] Enjoying great influence over Cornish affairs, Earl Richard and his son held the lordship in 1225–72 and 1272–1300 respectively, but Edmund was to die without issue at the turn of the century. Reverting to his cousin and heir, King Edward I, the earldom for the next thirty-seven years bounced back and forth between the Crown and its supporters. In 1337, however, Edward III chose to elevate the lordship to a dukedom and vest it upon his eldest son, Edward of Woodstock, better known to posterity as the Black Prince. The prince then governed the county punctiliously for nearly four decades, but on his demise in 1376 his son, Richard of Bordeaux, succeeded him as duke. All honours then merged with the Crown on Richard's accession to the throne as Richard II, remaining there until his deposition in 1399. Following the Lancastrian Revolution, however, the title devolved to Henry of Monmouth, who was later to rule the duchy directly as Henry V. Throughout the late-medieval period, the lordship had close connections with the Crown.

Not only did he enjoy a direct link with the king, the earl-duke had the good fortune to oversee a county that was neither truncated by any significant liberties nor one which saw another lay magnate hold noteworthy lands within its bounds.[29] He actually held as many as seventeen manors spread across Cornwall, along with nine boroughs and a host of advowsons. Giving him

[25] Worcestre, *Itineraries*, pp. 94–95.
[26] *RESDCornwall*, 102–104; for the county's dispersed settlements, M. Beresford, 'Dispersed and Grouped Settlement in Medieval Cornwall', *Agricultural History Review*, 12 (1964), pp. 13–27.
[27] *RBP*, ii, 157–158.
[28] *CP*, iii, 427–439; G. Ellis, *Earldoms in Fee: A Study in Peerage Law and History* (London, 1963), pp. 113–116; N. Denholm-Young, *Richard of Cornwall* (Oxford, 1947).
[29] *Quo Warranto*, pp. 108–111; *FA*, i, 208–218.

extensive powers over the peninsula, the earl-duke's prerogatives included the right to appoint the sheriff and take the profits of the county court, all while holding eight and one third of the peninsula's nine hundreds. The earl-duke also enjoyed the position of chief lord of every knight's fee in Cornwall, standing out as the universal landlord.[30] All these rights yielded great profits, with the duchy's gross income in 1337 standing at over £4,500.[31] In this year Edward III codified ducal rights in the so-called Great Charter of the duchy, which first stipulated that the duchy's estates never be dismembered and then set out how the title was to devolve to the eldest son of the sovereign at birth, reverting to the Crown in the absence of a rightful duke.[32] By the terms of its descent, the king forever bound together the duchy and the Crown.

Yet despite the earl-duke's great authority over the peninsula, his perennial absenteeism was one of the most significant aspects of the history of Cornwall's lordship. This non-residency influenced the operation of every part of his lordly rulership, but it by no means removed the county from the exercise of his seigniorial power. On the contrary, the structures of the earldom-duchy formed a network of control across the length and breadth of Cornwall. Standing at the administrative heart of the earl-duke's Cornish estates, the 'duchy palace' in Lostwithiel housed his exchequer, the coinage and shire halls and the chief gaol of the stannaries.[33] Combined with seigniorial castles, these formed physical manifestations of lordly power, the source of which resided hundreds of miles away. With comital-ducal officials, they enabled the earl-duke to administer his estates and uphold his rights throughout the county.[34]

As lordly rights to tin were by far the most valuable of all the earl-duke's prerogatives, it is no surprise that the fiscal importance of this metal also resulted in extensive royal concessions to tinners. Back in 1201 the earliest surviving stannary charter had confirmed ancient tinning rights to free bounding, the right freely to search and dig for tin, releasing tinners from manorial justice in all cases save 'life, limb, and land'.[35] Issuing a further charter in 1305, Edward I exempted tinners from normal taxation while formalising a tax on tin itself

---

[30] *RESDCornwall*, 5–6; *Ministers' Accounts of the Earldom of Cornwall, 1296–7*, ed. L. M. Midgley, 2 vols, Camden Society, Third Series 64, 68 (London, 1942–5).

[31] *CS*, lviii.

[32] *CChR 1327–1341*, 399–400, 436–437; *RESDCornwall*, 5–6.

[33] N. G. Pounds, 'The Duchy Palace at Lostwithiel, Cornwall', *Archaeological Journal*, 136 (1979), pp. 203–217; A. Saunders, 'Administrative Buildings and Prisons in the Earldom of Cornwall', in *Warriors and Churchmen in the High Middle Ages: Essays presented to Karl Leyser*, ed. T. Reuter (London, 1992), pp. 195–216.

[34] Cf. G. Holmes, *The Estates of the Higher Nobility in Fourteenth-Century England* (Cambridge, 1957), pp. 58–84.

[35] Hatcher, *Tin*, p. 48; Lewis, *Stannaries*, pp. 137–138, 158–159.

known as coinage duty.³⁶ Across the thirteenth century this had become fixed at 40s. per thousandweight (1,000 lb.). While the authorities did not actually define what constituted a 'tinner' until as late as 1376, when Edward III classified these men as labourers in tin workings themselves, all these folk enjoyed a direct line of communication to the earl-duke and king through the institutions of the stannaries.³⁷ In this way, the structures and personnel of the lordship helped to draw Cornwall into the kingdom.

For all the earl-duke's mineral wealth, it is a truth self-evident that land held the main key to wealth and power in medieval England. In the case of Cornwall, the bulk of that land was held by those lesser landholders whom we term the gentry, a group loosely defined 'as all lay, non-baronial landholders who enjoyed an income of £5 per annum or more from freehold property'.³⁸ When considering these proprietors, royal levies on knights' fees provide some of the best listings of the county's landed lineages.³⁹ For the first of these imposts in 1303, Edward I was to levy an aid at 40s. per fee for the marriage of his daughter, with the surviving lists for Cornwall recording some eighty-one tenants-in-chief paying this tax.⁴⁰ If we exclude the Religious, the nobles and the king, who were lords of a different sort, we are then left with a figure of seventy-five Cornish landholders. Forty-three years later, the returns of an aid for the knighting of the Black Prince give a list of no fewer than seventy-eight proprietors, revealing few changes of family names.⁴¹ Excluding the prince himself, the only nobles to make an appearance were the earls of Warwick and Gloucester. Such levies show that gentlemen owned nearly 73 per cent of Cornwall's taxed manors, with just under 17 per cent in the hands of magnates and a little over 10 per cent under the control of the Religious.

Turning to a different class of documents, a list drawn-up in 1344–5 for the extension of military service may be considered among the most useful sources for gauging the size of the Cornish gentry. Naming as many as 128 *homines ad arma* aged between sixteen and sixty who owed service in the county, the return lists a considerably greater number of landholders than the levies on knights' fees.⁴² While we should be mindful of the fact that underassessment

---

[36] *CChR 1300–1326*, 53–54; Hatcher, *Tin*, p. 48; J. F. Willard, *Parliamentary Taxes on Personal Property, 1290–1334: A Study in Medieval Financial Administration* (Cambridge, MA, 1934), pp. 118–120.
[37] Lewis, *Stannaries*, pp. 96–99; *PROME*, v, 347–348.
[38] Payling, *Nottinghamshire*, p. 3; P. Coss, *The Origins of the English Gentry* (Cambridge, 2003), pp. 9–11.
[39] In 1303, 1306, 1346 and 1428.
[40] *FA*, i, xxii, 195–202; M. Jurkowski, C. L. Smith and D. Crook, *Lay Taxes in England and Wales, 1188–1688* (Richmond, 1998), p. 26.
[41] *FA*, i, xxiv–xxvi, 208–218; Jurkowski et al., *Lay Taxes*, pp. 47–48.
[42] C47/2/39/12; *CPR 1343–1345*, 414–415; M. Powicke, *Military Obligation in Medieval England: A Study in Liberty and Duty* (Oxford, 1962), pp. 190–199.

was rife even here, this figure of 128 folk provides a benchmark for the size of the entire Cornish gentry. Whether all these individuals resided west of the Tamar, however, remains another matter. Licences to crenellate manors are perhaps the surest way of identifying Cornish residency, but only six such for the county survive.[43] Of these, one permitted Sir Ralph Bloyou to crenellate his 'dwelling places' in Cornwall and Dorset, with the Crown conceding the others to Sir Ranulph Blanchminster, Sir William Bassett, Sir John Dauney and Sir John l'Ercedekne. In 1478, however, William Worcestre listed as many as thirty-two castles in the peninsula, among them Sir John Basset's 'tower' at Carn Brea and the Botreaux family's *castrum vocatum Botreaux Castel* at Boscastle.[44] These sorts of castellated residences could proclaim in stone the status of their owners; 'at the hed of [Lanihorne] creeke', according to John Leland, 'standith the Castelle of Lanyhorne sumtyme a castle of a 7. tourres, now decaying for lack of coverture. It longgid as principal house to the archdeacons', the l'Ercedeknes.[45] At times these structures had to earn their keep, with Elizabeth Treffry forced to 'repell the French out of her house [Place House, Fowey] in her housebandes absence' during a raid in Henry VI's reign.[46]

Another clue to residency is to be found in licences for household chapels or oratories. The bishops of Exeter conceded *licencie celebrandi* to Cornishmen and women who wished to celebrate mass in their own household chapels or private residences, with these licences serving as markers of both gentility and residency.[47] Although lists are by no means exhaustive, evidence survives of Bishops Stapeldon, Grandisson, Brantingham and Stafford between them conceding over 250 licences of this sort to local proprietors.[48] Generations of leading Cornishmen sought these written permissions, including scions of the families of Arundell, Beaupel, Beville, Bloyou, Bodrugan, Botreaux, Carminow, Chenduyt, l'Ercedekne, Petit, Peverell, Reskymer, Sergeaux, Soor, Trenewith, Trevarthian and Whalesborough. While leading proprietors sometimes received *licencie celebrandi* for one residence alone, Cornish knights are often to be found seeking permission for chapels in numerous manors. This was because these prominent gentlemen itinerated around their Cornish

---

[43] CPR 1327–1330, 541; CPR 1313–1317, 262; CPR 1334–1338, 75, 77, 79, 238.
[44] Worcestre, *Itineraries*, pp. 20–23.
[45] J. Leland, *The Itinerary of John Leland in or about the years 1535–1543*, ed. L. T. Smith, 5 vols (London, 1907–10), i, p. 199; also, G. Beresford, 'The Medieval Manor of Penhallam, Jacobstow, Cornwall', *Medieval Archaeology*, 18 (1974), pp. 90–145.
[46] Leland, *Itinerary*, i, p. 204.
[47] K. Rawlinson, 'The English Household Chapel, c. 1100–c. 1500: An Institutional Study' (Unpubl. Univ. Durham PhD, 2008), pp. 69–77.
[48] *Reg.Stapeldon*, 299–302; *Reg.Grandisson, passim.*, although Bishop Grandisson's register records no licences after 1332, he evidently conceded them after this date, CRO, AR/27/1; *Reg.Brantingham*, ii, 947–955; *Reg.Stafford*, 270–283.

estates, while proprietors of lesser means more often sought oratories in what was probably their only residence.[49] Despite these variations in landed wealth, the Cornish gentry were undoubtedly numerous, well-established and locally influential.

We find that some Cornish estates, however, were held by lords who did not dwell west of the Tamar. It is illustrative of this that Tregony Castle, 'a building of the Devonshire Pomeroys', even made an appearance on William Worcestre's list of castles.[50] Another landed family, the Dinhams of Hartland, also resided principally in Devon, despite the fact that they held considerable estates in Cornwall.[51] Men largely resident in Devon owned numerous manors in Cornwall; equally, it can be said that men largely resident in Cornwall had interests across the county boundary.[52] There is evidence that a few dynasties at least were active in both shires, among them the Huishs and Chaumpernouns, who held lands and offices on either side of the Tamar.[53] The ties enjoyed by the peninsula's landholders stretched far beyond the county's near neighbour, however, and the Wylintons, for example, oversaw two Cornish manors from their seat in Gloucestershire. Evidently the peninsula's propertied society was by no means hermetically sealed, and yet it is striking that the majority of those lords who owned land in the county resided principally or solely in Cornwall.

Although we group all these proprietors together as 'the gentry', contemporaries referred to landholders of this sort by a variety of terms in any one of four languages.[54] While the French *chivaler* could be translated into the Latin *miles* and the English knight, *gentil homme* had no clear Latin counterpart until the fifteenth-century *generosus*. Below the *miles* stood the *armiger* and *valletus*, terms that in 1300 were generally used as if synonymous. Across the fourteenth century, however, the two diverged. On the one hand, it seems that *valletus* came to be rendered as *yoman* in English, but a lowly *yoman* could not be considered a *gentil homme*.[55] On the other hand, esquire became the preferred English translation of *armiger*, with these men holding a place in gentle society. As the men termed knights (*milites*) and esquires (*armigeri*) made up the mounted elite, contemporaries grouped them together as men-at-arms

---

[49] *Reg.Brantingham*, i, 332, 340; *Reg.Stafford*, 282.
[50] Worcestre, *Itineraries*, pp. 20–21.
[51] *CPR 1334–1338*, 558; H. Kleineke, 'The Dinham Family in the Later Middle Ages' (Unpubl. Univ. London PhD, 1998).
[52] Page, 'Comital Government', p. 129; BL, Harley MS 1192 f. 46.
[53] *CCR 1337–1339*, 387; Appendix I.
[54] Saul, *Gloucestershire*, p. 30; K. B. McFarlane, *The Nobility of Later Medieval England* (Oxford, 1973), pp. 268–278; T. B. Pugh, 'The Magnates, Knights and Gentry', in *Fifteenth Century England, 1399–1509: Studies in Politics and Society*, ed. S. B. Chrimes, C. D. Ross and R. A. Griffith (Manchester, 1972), pp. 86–128 at 86, 96.
[55] Saul, *Gloucestershire*, pp. 6–7, 16–17; Coss, *English Gentry*, pp. 216–238.

(*homines ad arma*). Even in the far south west, the *Ordinalia* Cornish-language play *Origo Mundi* had knights (*marrouggyoun*) and esquires (*squyerryon*) serve together.[56]

A combination of magnate absenteeism and Earl Richard's dispersal of Cornwall's two baronies, of Cardinan and Vautort, left county leadership in the hands of the richest and most important resident knights.[57] While Mark Page found that thirty-five knightly families were active at any one time in thirteenth-century Cornwall, by the latter years of Edward I's reign this number had dwindled somewhat.[58] A military summons of 1300 named only twenty-eight Cornishmen who enjoyed yearly incomes of £40 or more, a figure which by Edward II's reign had come to represent the minimum required for knighthood.[59] This much is shown by a royal summons to a Great Council of 1323–4, in which the sheriff testified that all twenty-five named Cornishmen enjoyed annual incomes of at least £40. By this time economic difficulties 'had slimmed the ranks of those who could afford to be *milites*'.[60] Since knights formed but the pinnacle of gentle society, however, it is no surprise that in 1352 Edward III found that some forty-seven Cornishmen were in receipt of yearly incomes of £20 or more.[61] These forty-seven represented both the knights and greater esquires of the county, its leading proprietors. When all the information from these documents is pulled together, it seems that before 1348 around twenty-five knights (*milites*) stood at the head of Cornish landed society. Below this group was a squirearchy, those referred to as *armigeri*, of at least 128 families and probably many more, around thirty of whom enjoyed annual incomes of £20 and upwards.

Propertied society, however, did not for long maintain its earlier shape and structure. By the fifteenth century it was changing. In 1413 we find that the Statute of Additions recognised the existence of gentleman as the lowest gradation of gentility, the structure of which henceforth comprised knights who enjoyed yearly incomes of £40 or more, esquires with £10 or more to their names and gentlemen with incomes of £5–10.[62] Below the rank of gentleman there also came to exist those wealthy freeholders who had assumed the 'airs and graces' of gentility, those whom we term the 'parish gentry'. Many scholars

---

[56] *The Ancient Cornish Drama*, ed. and trans. E. Norris, 2 vols (Oxford, 1859), i, OM, lines 1639–1640, 2004.
[57] M. Page, 'Cornwall, Earl Richard, and the Barons' War', *EHR*, 115 (2000), pp. 21–38 at 33.
[58] Page, 'Comital Government', pp. 122–123.
[59] C47/1/6/7-8, excluding the Religious and Devonians.
[60] Saul, *Gloucestershire*, p. 10.
[61] BL, Harley MS 1192 f. 50; *Carew*, 52, three more were Devonians; C47/1/12/26; C47/1/13/15-16.
[62] Saul, *Gloucestershire*, pp. 18–20, 29; Coss, *English Gentry*, pp. 216, 237.

Table 1: Cornishmen with Incomes of £40 or more p.a. Summoned to a Great Council of 1323–4

The Knights	The Men-at-Arms
1. William Botreaux	1. John Dinham
2. Reginald Botreaux	2. Ranulph Bloyou
3. Ranulph Blanchminster	3. William Basset
4. Richard Chaumpernoun	4. Oliver Carminow
5. Henry Chaumpernoun	5. Henry Pengersick
6. .... le Petit	6 Roger Reskymer
7. Thomas l'Ercedekne	7. John Lambourne
8. John Alneto [Dauney]	8. John le Soor
9. John Tynten	9. Richard Sergeaux junior
10. William Ferrers	10. John Pyne
11. Robert Beudyn	11. Roger Prideaux
12. Reginald Mohun	12. Ranulph Beaupel
13. Robert Fitz William	
14. John Carminow	n.b. Dinham and Ferrers were Devonians.
15. Otto Bodrugan	

Source: Parliamentary Writs, ed. F. Palgrave, 2 vols in 4 (London, 1827–34), ii part 2, p. 655.

have argued that the Black Death formed the principal agent of change here.[63] Increasing the rate of familial extinctions, the plague and its subsequent visitations inaugurated a period of high mortality that led to the fragmentation of estates. It followed that 'new' proprietors were able to accumulate estates of their own and emulate their social betters, redrawing the broadened bounds of gentility.

Unfortunately, the discontinuous nature of our source material renders quantifying these changes impossible. The returns to a feudal aid levied in

---

[63] C. Dyer, *An Age of Transition? Economy and Society in England in the Later Middle Ages* (Oxford, 2005), pp. 126–172, especially 132–139; Coss, *English Gentry*, pp. 233–237; Saul, *Gloucestershire*, pp. 25–29; S. J. Payling, 'Social Mobility, Demographic Change, and Landed Society in Late Medieval England', *EcHR*, 45 (1992), pp. 51–73; J. L. Bolton, '"The World Upside Down", Plague as an Agent of Economic and Social Change', in *The Black Death in England*, ed. W. M. Ormrod and P. F. Lindley (Stamford, 1996), pp. 17–78 at 48, 62–63.

1428 list as many as 800 landowners in Cornwall, pointing to a very considerable expansion of landed society.[64] It is virtually impossible, however, to say whether these 800 represent new landowners or landowners whose families had always existed but which had not been recognised in previous surveys. The problem is that we cannot be sure that we are comparing like with like, and it seems that the aid of 1428 lists under-tenants as opposed to tenants-in-chief. We encounter similar difficulties when considering the returns to a parliamentary subsidy in 1450, which list some seventy-five Cornishmen who enjoyed incomes qualifying them as gentle. While this roll-call purports to name every county proprietor in receipt of an annual landed income of £2 or more, a great many people resisted paying this 'novel' subsidy.[65] Although the difficulties of the evidence means that we cannot precisely measure the changes, among the gentry of fifteenth-century Cornwall were many proprietors who enjoyed the newly recognised rank of gentleman.[66] 'Cornish gentlemen', so Richard Carew was to write, 'can better vaunt of their pedigree, than their livelyhood'.[67]

Table 2: Cornish Gentry Paying the 1450 Income Tax

Yearly Income	Number of Cornishmen
£40 or more	6
£20	8
£10–£20	23
£5–£10	9
£5	29

Sources: E179/87/92; Royal Institution of Cornwall, HC/43.

Since many leading local lineages suffered the misfortune of failing in the male line, by 1450 it seems that the peninsula played host to a mere six knightly families.[68] It was naturally the case that familial extinctions saw some

[64] FA, i, xxvii–xxviii, 220–243; Jurkowski et al., Lay Taxes, pp. 85–86; Richard Carew preserved a partial copy of a feudal aid of 1401, Carew, 39r–44v.
[65] R. Virgoe, 'The Parliamentary Subsidy of 1450', Bulletin of the Institute of Historical Research, 55 (1982), pp. 125–138; Jurkowski et al., Lay Taxes, pp. 102–104.
[66] For instance, CPR 1429–1436, 198.
[67] Carew, 63r.
[68] E179/87/92; the numbers of knights declined across the realm, A. Bell, et al., The Soldier in Later Medieval England (Oxford, 2013), pp. 83–84; Powicke, Military Obligation, p. 178.

estates dismembered or carried by heiresses into the hands of new families. K. B. McFarlane, however, has identified the other side to this phenomenon, which was that the fewer and fewer dynasties who survived amassed greater and greater landholdings through inheritance.[69] The latter process is visible in Cornwall too. Of the thirty-eight proprietors whom the sheriff assessed for military service in 1346, the heads of the houses of Botreaux and l'Ercedekne were reckoned to enjoy yearly incomes of £100 apiece; the next six wealthiest lineages – the Arundells, Blanchminsters, Carminows, Reskymers, Sergeauxs and Soors – were each in receipt of £60; the Ingepennes enjoyed £50 a year and the Chaumpernouns £40.[70] A century later, however, the families of Arundell and Colshull were thought to enjoy annual incomes of £200 and £120 respectively; the Bonvilles were in receipt of £66; and the Bodrugans, Courtenays and Whalesboroughs were each in possession of £40.[71] For all the dangers latent in comparing taxes, it does appear that wealth had coalesced into fewer hands.

Although roughly twice as many knightly families failed in the male line in the century after 1350 than in the century before, these changes were not wrought by the plague alone as the vagaries of chance and genetics had a role to play here. In years around 1400, for example, the Bodrugans experienced a crisis with no direct legitimate heir in the male line, giving rise to a great deal of litigation; the Bodrugan estate passed to a legitimate grandson through the female line instead of to an illegitimate son, William Bodrugan.[72] Another knightly family, the Carminows, suffered an even greater crisis when in 1396 their heiress, Joan, died while still a minor, extinguishing the main family line.[73] As a result, the Carminow patrimony was then shared between their in-laws from houses of Arundell and Trevarthian. Following the Carminows into extinction at around this time was yet another knightly lineage, the Sergeauxs, while in the late fourteenth century Sir Warin l'Ercedekne's four daughters stood out as his heiresses.[74] Naturally enough, by 1402 these four eligible women had carried the l'Ercedekne lands into the hands of their husbands from the houses of Arundell, Trevarthian, Courtenay and Lucy. As elsewhere in England, families were always rising and falling in Cornwall.

[69] McFarlane, *The Nobility*, p. 59.
[70] C47/2/41/5, Blanchminster appears in the £60 'group' without an income.
[71] E179/87/92.
[72] *FF*, ii, 13, 29–31, 34–35; H. Matthews, 'Illegitimacy and English Landed Society, c. 1295–c. 1500' (Unpubl. Univ. London PhD, 2012), pp. 113–114; J. Whetter, *The Bodrugans: A Study of a Cornish Medieval Knightly Family* (Gorran, 1995); for the landholdings of the Bodrugans, see their early fourteenth-century cartulary, CRO, ME/595.
[73] CRO, AR/1/192; *Catalogue of Ancient Deeds in the Public Record Office*, 6 vols, HMSO (London, 1890–1915), iv, pp. 552–553; *Arundells of Lanherne*, p. xvi.
[74] *CIPM*, xviii, 15; *HOP*, ii, 506–507; *Ancient Deeds*, v, p. 470; *CP*, i, 187–188.

While part of the gentry of England, the county's proprietors stood out as distinctive. Ranging from £100 downwards, their similar levels of wealth rendered them a group of flattish composition in the fourteenth century. As no local lord was able to dominate the peninsula with influence derived from his landed wealth alone, this 'Cornish homogeneity' influenced every aspect of county life from the nature of office-holding to the workings of dispute resolution. Even the assets that supported gentle lifestyles in the far south west stood out as distinctive. Some local proprietors were salt-water lords who had invested in shipping, while others possessed tin workings and enjoyed toll tin, the right to take a percentage of the value of metal found beneath their estates, and others again grew fat on the combined profits of their landed, mineral and maritime interests.[75] Yet despite these different sources of income, it seems that the peninsula's relative poverty meant that an estate yielding £50 yearly, for example, required the exercise of a more exacting and geographically expansive lordship than one in the wealthier Thames Valley. Reflecting Cornish topography and demography, the estates of leading county proprietors were spread across the peninsula. In the lower echelons of landed society we may well wonder if gentility itself started at a reduced level of income. This was because the county's modest prosperity resulted in families of comparatively slender resources standing out as the richest folk in their locality, perhaps securing their *de facto* gentility.[76] And yet for all the idiosyncrasies of the Cornish gentry, the whole range of county society knew that land remained the key to wealth and power in the peninsula.[77]

Sharing the gentry's universal interest, local proprietors constantly sought to defend and augment their estates. There is evidence that a land market operated west of the Tamar, as elsewhere, a fact well-illustrated by Sir Robert Tresilian's rapid accumulation and even more rapid loss of estate.[78] Tresilian stands out first and foremost as a successful lawyer. It seems that he acquired much of his property, however, by a favourable marriage to the heiress Emmeline Huish. In Cornwall, again as elsewhere, marriage emerges as 'the most common way in which substantial areas of land changed hands'.[79] The

---

[75] CRO, AR/15/1; *CPR 1381–1385*, 405; *West Country Shipping*, pp. 80–84; S. J. Drake, 'The Michelstow Family (*per. c.* 1350–c. 1454)', *ODNB* (2016), http://www.oxforddnb.com/view/article/107361?docPos=1 (accessed 15 May 2016); *Arundells of Lanherne*, p. xciv.

[76] Cf. J. Chynoweth, *Tudor Cornwall* (Stroud, 2002), pp. 32–61; P. Contamine, 'The European Nobility', in *The New Cambridge Medieval History: VII, c. 1415–1500*, ed. C. Allmand (Cambridge, 1998), pp. 89–105.

[77] For example, *Cornish Drama*, i, OM, lines 2395–2400; ii, RD, lines 1701–1702.

[78] Below, pp. 248–249.

[79] Cf. C. Given-Wilson, *The English Nobility in the Later Middle Ages: The Fourteenth-Century Political Community* (London, 1987), p. 10.

rise and rise of the Arundells of Lanherne certainly bears testament to this. It was Remfrey Arundell's marriage to Alice de Lanherne before June 1268 that brought the manor of Lanherne itself to the family. A series of good matches thereafter increased their holdings, connecting them with leading Cornish lineages including the Carminows, Lambournes, l'Ercedeknes, Luscotes, Nandsladrons and Soors.[80] The Carminows could likewise boast of relations with the Arundells, Beaupels, Botreauxs, Heligans, Glynns and Pomeroys to name but a few, while the Lambournes enjoyed links with the Bevilles, Sergeauxs, Reskymers, Whalesboroughs and others.[81] Seemingly all Cornish gentlemen were cousins, as Richard Carew was later to claim.[82]

In medieval England local marriages were common enough, however, constituting 'insufficient proof that the Cornish were a breed apart'.[83] Indeed, many county nuptials can be found yielding links to other parts of the realm. The Arundells were one family that acquired extensive lands in Devon through marriage, while ties created through matches could introduce major new figures into Cornwall itself. For example, the London vintner John Colshull became a leading proprietor overnight through his marriage to Sir Robert Tresilian's widow.[84] Numerous Cornish dynasties are also found owning property to east of the Tamar, including the families of Blanchminster, Botreaux and Sergeaux, who held lands in Yorkshire, Hampshire and Oxfordshire respectively.[85] In this way, common bonds of blood, chivalry and landed interest linked all these Cornishmen both to each other and to their fellow gentry from across England. The author of the *Ordinalia* even had 'trusty', 'proud and strong' knights raise troops and swear that they are no cowards by their 'order of knighthood', all while serving their king.[86] Here especially we see how the Cornish gentry comprised a distinctive group while maintaining a wealth of connections with other parts of the realm.

Standing out as the county's other great landholder was the Church. Since Cornwall was encompassed in the diocese of Exeter, it is unsurprising that the bishop owned estates across the county. In 1346, for example, he was found to hold fees in no fewer than ten Cornish manors, from Lanisley, outside Penzance, to Lawhitton, right on the Tamar.[87] As the priors of Bodmin and Tywardreath exercised lordship over the boroughs of Bodmin and Fowey

---

[80] CRO, AR/1/192/1; AR/20/11; *Arundells of Lanherne*, pp. xiii–xxiv, clvi.
[81] J. L. Vivian, *The Visitations of the County of Cornwall, Comprising the Heralds' Visitations of 1530, 1573, and 1620* (Exeter, 1887), pp. 72–75; *TCO, passim*.
[82] *Carew*, 64v.
[83] Page, 'Comital Government', p. 14.
[84] *FF*, ii, 44, 49; *HOP*, ii, 633–635; Maclean, *Trigg Minor*, ii, pp. 504–505.
[85] Appendix I.
[86] *Cornish Drama*, i, OM, lines 2150–2167, 2199–2224.
[87] *FA*, i, 208–218.

respectively, Cornwall's religious houses also possessed lands and advowsons throughout the peninsula.[88] While none of these small houses rivalled the wealth and political clout of the abbeys of south-eastern England, among them St Albans and Canterbury Cathedral Priory, possession of assets gives a narrow view of the Church's activity as religion was interwoven with every aspect of medieval life. To support orthodoxy in the far south west, the bishops of Exeter administered Cornwall as an archdeaconry of its own, overseeing a peninsula divided into parishes devoted to many local saints. It follows that the county was an integral part of the diocese of Exeter, the *Ecclesia Anglicana* and a wider Christendom, one that still followed many local practices.[89]

Through their many interactions with the county's residents, diocesans became only too aware of Cornish peculiarities. So it was that in 1329 Bishop Grandisson observed that 'a language, too, exists in the furthest parts of Cornwall, known not to the English-speakers but to the British-speakers'.[90] When in dialogue with the parishioners of St Buryan in 1336, for example, Grandisson relied on one Henry Marsely, the rector of St Just-in-Penwith, to translate his words for those parishioners who knew only Cornish.[91] In responding to the bishop, 'the majority' of the parishioners did so 'in the English and French language; but others, who knew only the Cornish language' naturally did so in Cornish. Cornwall was unique in England as possessing its own native tongue, a Celtic (Brittonic) language similar to Welsh and even closer to Breton. By the fourteenth century, however, only half the county's residents are thought to have spoken Cornish. The Fowey–Padstow isogloss linguistically transected the peninsula, with English spoken by those who resided east of this divide, while most of those who lived to its west, in the 'furthest parts', were bilingual, speaking both Cornish and English.[92] Although there can be little doubt that the Cornish language was a significant local marker, linguistics emerge as no impediment to county folk seeking their fortunes elsewhere in the realm. We must also remember that multilingualism was the norm in medieval England, with French and Latin current and English itself heavily

---

[88] *Quo Warranto*, pp. 108–111; SC6/816/11 m. 13; DCO 4; see, Orme, *Religious Houses*.
[89] Below, Chapter 13.
[90] *Reg.Grandisson*, i, 98; my thanks to Oliver Padel for his advice about this point; M. F. Wakelin, *Language and History in Cornwall* (Leicester, 1975), p. 88.
[91] *Reg.Grandisson*, ii, 820–821; my thanks to Oliver Padel for his advice about this point.
[92] M. Spriggs, 'Where Cornish was Spoken and When: A Provisional Synthesis', *Cornish Studies*, 11 (2003), pp. 228–269; O. J. Padel, 'Where was Middle Cornish Spoken?', *Cambrian Medieval Celtic Studies*, 74 (2017), pp. 1–31.

regionalised.[93] Even in the extremities of Cornwall, only a minority of people were monoglot Cornish speakers.

Yet the churchmen of the day still stand among the most critical observers of Cornwall and its people. Bishop Grandisson's lament of the county as 'the very ends of the earth' serves as a prime example of this. These sorts of complaints came to form a veritable genre of their own, but the circumstances of these comments should not be overlooked.[94] By no means were all assessments of the peninsula critical either, for in 1481 Richard Germyn was to write to his employer, William Stoner: 'as to your tenaunts in Cornwale, thei be as trew unto you as y can understand as any tenauntes that ye have'.[95] We see here how external observers perceived the peninsula as a coherent whole, with the Cornish themselves having a powerful notion of Cornwall existing 'since the time of King Arthur'.[96] Despite being hallowed by history, however, and for all its idiosyncrasies, the county and its residents also depended on their place in the kingdom of England.

While the earl-duke wielded great influence over fourteenth-century Cornwall, nearly all the offices of local government remained directly accountable to the king.[97] At the same time the common law regarded the county's inhabitants as English. In the *Quo Warranto* proceedings of 1302, for instance, leading Cornish lay and spiritual proprietors secured royal confirmation of their liberties, an act which implicitly recognised their acceptance of the county's place in the kingdom.[98] Throughout the later middle ages Cornwall was also obliged to contribute to parliamentary taxation, with the Crown levying tenths and fifteenths in the peninsula just as in other English shires. The county was exceptionally well-represented in parliament, typically returning two shire MPs and a further twelve representatives from its six enfranchised boroughs. As thousands of Cornishmen fought in the wars of this period, the peninsula's residents owed military service to their king too.[99] All these processes of interaction had a powerful integrative effect, drawing the county into the kingdom.

But what of the realm in which Cornwall held a place? The truism bears repeating that England played host to one of the most sophisticated and

---

[93] J. A. Jefferson and A. Putter, 'Introduction', in *Multilingualism in Medieval Britain (c. 1066–1520): Sources and Analysis*, ed. J. A. Jefferson and A. Putter (Turnhout, 2013), pp. xi–xxiv.
[94] Below, Chapter 4.
[95] *The Stonor Letters and Papers, 1290–1483*, ed. C. L. Kingsford, 2 vols, Camden Society, 3rd Series 29–30 (London, 1919), ii, p. 120.
[96] Below, Chapter 3.
[97] Below, Chapter 2.
[98] *Quo Warranto*, pp. 108–111; D. W. Sutherland, *Quo Warranto Proceedings in the Reign of Edward I, 1278–1294* (Oxford, 1963), p. 30.
[99] Below, Chapter 9.

powerful governments of the European later middle ages.[100] From its focal point at Westminster, the king's central government – the chancery, exchequer and so on – oversaw the collection of royal dues from across the kingdom while conveying the sovereign's commands far and wide. Firmly linking the king and the Westminster-based bureaucracy to the wider realm, the royal government was represented in the shires by a host of local office-holders – sheriffs, justices of the peace and so on. Outside Cheshire and County Durham, the kings of England enjoyed universal jurisdiction throughout their lands. Their mighty fiscal machine was similarly all-pervasive, raising funds for extensive royal warfare. In levying taxes, however, kings were compelled to summon parliament to give consent to these subsidies. Representing the commonalty of the whole realm, the House of Commons was to speak with an increasingly powerful voice. Since England was a much-governed country, the workings and uniformity of its judicial, fiscal and representative structures helped to pull the polity together. All this led Mark Ormrod to conclude that England was 'one of the very few medieval kingdoms that deserve to be called "states"'.[101]

Such a picture, however, proves by no means complete. R. R. Davies has criticised the concept of the medieval state, providing a powerful corrective.[102] He placed emphasis on the fact that the surviving evidence chiefly concerns the workings of royal government, making the king appear all-powerful when he was most certainly not. Royal authority was neither absolute in Cornwall nor anywhere else in England for that matter, as many 'private' administrations operated in every locality. Yet, in contrast to the voluminous archives of the Crown, the records of these many other lords have long since disintegrated. Losses of this sort and scale greatly distort our vision of the realm. Wielding limited coercive might of his own, the king instead relied on other agents of power, among them earls, knights, bishops and mayors, to enforce his writ across the land. At the same time as playing host to the mighty apparatus of royal government, the realm contained many powerbrokers and sentiments beyond that of the king's administration and regnal solidarity. When set within a powerfully governed and yet more heterogeneous kingdom, Cornwall's contradictory existence as a place simultaneously distinctive and integrated appears less irreconcilable.

---

[100] For the best introductions, G. L. Harriss, *Shaping the Nation, England 1360–1461* (Oxford, 2005); J. R. Maddicott, *The Origins of the English Parliament, 924–1327* (Oxford, 2010); W. M. Ormrod, *Political Life in Medieval England, 1300–1450* (Basingstoke, 1995).
[101] Ormrod, *Political Life*, p. 1.
[102] R. R. Davies, 'The Medieval State: The Tyranny of a Concept', *Journal of Historical Sociology*, 16 (2003), pp. 280–300.

2

Office-Holding in a Wild Spot

According to the Venetian ambassador, Cornwall was 'a wild spot where no human being ever came, save the few boors who inhabited' the desolate place.[1] It is clear that in the county and everywhere else the intermeshing of local interests, traditions and lordships moderated the impact of royal rulership. Yet it is just as clear that by the fourteenth century the tendrils of royal government had long stretched into every corner of the kingdom, with the men who held the main county offices serving as the Crown's agents in the locality.[2] In the far south west, the intertwined offices of the royal shire and the comital-ducal franchise simultaneously helped to bestow coherence upon Cornwall itself while integrating the county into the kingdom.

The Sheriff-Stewards

The sheriff was the oldest shire office with the broadest responsibilities. Although shrieval authority had been eroded since the Anglo-Norman period, the post still retained an impressive range of powers. Within his bailiwick

---

[1] *Calendar of State Papers Venetian*, 38 vols in 40, HMSO (London, 1864–1940), i, p. 312.
[2] The Sheriff: W. A. Morris, *The Medieval English Sheriff to 1300* (Manchester, 1927); R. Gorski, *The Fourteenth-Century Sheriff: English Local Administration in the Late Middle Ages* (Woodbridge, 2003); The MPs: *HOP*; Maddicott, *English Parliament*; The JPs: B. H. Putnam, 'The Transformation of the Keepers of the Peace into the Justices of the Peace', *TRHS*, 4th series, 12 (1929), pp. 19–48; A. Musson, *Public Order and Law Enforcement: The Local Administration of Criminal Justice, 1294–1350* (Woodbridge, 1996); The Escheator: S. T. Gibson, 'The Escheatries, 1327–41', *EHR*, 36 (1921), pp. 218–225; The Coroner: R. F. Hunnisett, *The Medieval Coroner* (Cambridge, 1961); also, *The English Government at Work, 1327–1336*, ed. J. F. Willard et al., 3 vols (Cambridge, MA, 1940–50); R. Gorski, 'A Methodological Holy Grail: Nominal Record Linkage in a Medieval Context', *Medieval Prosopography*, 17 (1996), pp. 145–179.

the sheriff enjoyed administrative omni-competence, with the preservation of royal rights forming the mainspring of his duties.[3] The earl-duke held the shrievalty of Cornwall in fee, however, even though that the county had paid King John and Henry III for charters enshrining shrieval elections, charters that Earl Richard was later to repudiate.[4] It followed that until 1376 the earl-duke appointed a deputy to act as sheriff on his behalf, also employing this man as his steward in Cornwall.[5] Standing at the apex of the local administration of comital-ducal prerogatives, the steward oversaw the lordship's manors, stannaries and boroughs, along with the county court itself.[6] While the sheriff-steward received a handsome annuity for his labours, some £60 under the earldom and £40 during the Black Prince's tenure, those who held the post perennially failed to raise the enormous dues required of them.[7]

Although lordly rights to the shrievalty marked Cornwall out as distinctive, the county was by no means the only shire to be overseen in this way by a seigniorial sheriff.[8] In the north west, for example, successive earls and dukes of Lancaster appointed the sheriff of Lancashire to defend their local interests.[9] Enjoying yet greater powers over the shrievalty in his palatinate of Durham, the bishop there concurrently bestowed the shrievalty and escheatorship on the same man.[10] Yet in this county palatine both offices accounted to the bishop alone, whereas in Cornwall the sheriff-steward rendered account to the exchequers of both the earl-duke and the king.[11] In this way, the sheriff of Cornwall was a simultaneously lordly and royal official. Long terms and the regular appointment of 'outsiders' were characteristic of all seigniorial shrievalties and Cornwall proved no exception. Between 1300 and 1376 some twenty-four men are found holding the shrievalty-stewardship, with Thomas de la Hyde of Staffordshire and John Dabernon of Bradford, Devon, serving for some sixteen years apiece.[12] Just under half of those who held the office hailed from east of the Tamar, with 'incomers' serving as sheriff-steward for fifty of these seventy-six years.[13]

---

[3] Morris, *English Sheriff*, chapters 7–9.
[4] Page, 'Barons' War', 22, 27–28.
[5] SC6/811/3 m. 1r; *Ministers' Accounts*, i, pp. xxix–xxx; *RESDCornwall*, 5; aside from in 1336 and 1342–7.
[6] *RESDCornwall*, 42–45.
[7] *CIM 1307–1349*, 83; *CCR 1333–1337*, 399–400; *RBP*, ii, 62, £20 as sheriff and £20 as steward; many former sheriff-stewards were indebted, for example, E372/177 m. 23v.
[8] Gorski, *Sheriff*, pp. 33–34.
[9] R. Somerville, *History of the Duchy of Lancaster, 1265–1603*, 2 vols (London, 1953–70), i, pp. 10–11, 45, 59.
[10] Liddy, *Durham*, pp. 132–139.
[11] For example, *RBP*, iv, 34–35, 88.
[12] Albeit not continuously; for individual biographies, see Appendix I.
[13] Gorski, *Sheriff*, pp. 46–47; Liddy, *Durham*, pp. 133–135.

Across the fourteenth century the parliamentary Commons requested repeatedly that the king change his sheriffs annually. At the same time the Commons sought the appointment of men who resided in the county in which they held office and were in enjoyment of an annual freehold income of at least £20.[14] Presenting a combined petition concerning the shrievalty and escheatorship in 1371, the Commons were finally to achieve their ambitions. Three years earlier the Crown had conceded that the escheator should enjoy an annual landed income of at least £20, and once this was accepted of the escheator 'it seemed reasonable' to expect the same of the sheriff.[15] Using concessions related to the former office to force the Crown's hand over the latter, the Commons at the same time secured the introduction of annual shrieval appointments. In Cornwall, however, the implementation of these changes was delayed until 1376. It was only after the death of his father, the Black Prince, that Richard II divided the two offices, replacing the sheriff annually while retaining seignorial control of the stewardship. This was because Richard sought to use the shrievalty to draw leading Cornishmen into the magistracy, securing their acceptance of his rule. Between 1376 and 1405 a further twenty-two men held the post, two of whom served three times, seven held the office twice and the rest served once only. All but three originated from Cornwall, although of these exceptions all possessed a stake in the county through marriage. It certainly seems fair to talk of a 'shrieval elite' from 1376 onwards, for scions of leading local lineages, men such as Sir Richard Sergeaux and Sir Ralph Carminow, are often found holding the post.

Whether they were knightly proprietors, minor gentlemen, or 'outsiders', the shrievalty elevated all these men to a leading position in the county. Each of these office-holders served as the foremost local representative of his king and earl-duke, defending royal and lordly interests to the west of the Tamar. Although the powers of the sheriff-stewardship also presented countless opportunities to advance local agendas, the office still proved essential to the county's commonweal.[16] Holding a leading position in Cornwall's administration and collective life, while simultaneously forming a lasting point of contact between the county and the wider realm, the sheriff-stewardship was an influential and desirable post.

The MPs

Since the 1290s the Crown had issued writs instructing each sheriff to cause to be chosen two knights from his shire and two burgesses from each borough to attend parliament with authority to speak for their

[14] Saul, *Gloucestershire*, pp. 107–111.
[15] Saul, *Gloucestershire*, p. 110.
[16] Cf. Gorski, *Sheriff*, pp. 102–125.

locality.[17] For the period from 1295 to 1405 some ninety-seven returns for Cornwall have come down to us.[18] Just under a hundred men are known to have represented the county in this time, and whereas many served on multiple occasions, half sat only once. Perhaps as many as sixteen parliaments were attended by two county MPs who had never sat in the House before, with this becoming less prevalent as the century went on. At least nine knights of the shire had prior experience through attendance as parliamentary burgesses, notably Sir John Treiagu, who had represented Truro in 1304–5.

Although the majority of those who sat for Cornwall were Cornish, some fifteen MPs can be identified as hailing from east of the Tamar. It seems that Richard Bakhampton, John Moveroun and John Kentwood, for example, were officials in the comital-ducal administration who owed their election to their posts in the lordship. While there is no evidence of a concerted lordly policy to pack parliament, this does not necessarily imply an absence of coercion.[19] It should be noted, however, that the great majority of those returned were well-qualified by Cornish birth, landownership, or both, including the six-times elected Sir Thomas l'Ercedekne. Knightly lineages were to achieve no stranglehold on the county's representation, however, as a steady stream of less prominent gentlemen can be identified as also making their way to parliament. Over two-thirds of Cornwall's MPs held other posts in local administration, attesting to their active involvement in county affairs. Believing that parliamentarians who enjoyed the support of their fellow Cornishmen possessed the clout to defend royal interests locally, the Crown often appointed men who had sat in the House to other county offices.[20]

To concentrate on the knights of the shire alone, however, presents only a limited view of the county's representation as Cornwall contained one of the highest densities of parliamentary boroughs in the kingdom: Bodmin, Helston, Launceston, Liskeard, Lostwithiel and Truro. Each of these boroughs returned two men to the House, resulting in as many as fourteen Cornish spokesmen sitting in a typical parliament.[21] Across the period as a whole the names of over 400 burgesses who sat for Cornwall's towns have come down to us, even though returns remain incomplete and writs of expenses are sparse.[22] Nonetheless, we know enough about the urban members to offer some general

[17] Saul, *Gloucestershire*, p. 119.
[18] Only one member each are recorded in 1340, 1352, 1353 and 1371.
[19] Cf. Saul, *Gloucestershire*, p. 123; J. R. Maddicott, *Thomas of Lancaster, 1307–1322: A Study in the Reign of Edward II* (Oxford, 1970), pp. 51–52.
[20] Tyldesley, 'Local Communities', p. 36.
[21] At least on paper; *HOP*, i, 295–317; in 1295 Tregony replaced Lostwithiel; in 1298 neither Launceston nor Lostwithiel sent returns.
[22] M. McKisack, *The Parliamentary Representation of the English Boroughs during the Middle Ages* (Oxford, 1932), p. 75.

observations. Those who sat for Cornish boroughs were mainly of lesser substance than the county's MPs. Some were men of commerce, while others made their living at the law and others again were minor local gentry. Burgesses could enjoy long parliamentary careers, pre-eminent among them the nineteen-times returned John Cokeworthy, a busy lawyer who sat for multiple boroughs.[23] The county's towns emerge as willing to look beyond their own residents for their MPs, with the result that during his career one man might well sit for several Cornish boroughs. Again, there appears to have been no magnate policy to manipulate returns.

Since parliament served as the greatest political forum in the kingdom, its burgeoning influence was to secure continued attendance by the most influential Cornishmen.[24] Despite being a fusion of fact and fiction, the *Modus Tenendi Parliamentum*, a tract written in the 1320s, recorded widespread co-operation between the various strata of parliament.[25] The once rigid divisions between the knights and the burgesses began to break down in the early years of the century, and after that time the two groups often collaborated.[26] In Cornwall, the actual membership of these two groups of county and urban representatives overlapped. At least a tenth of Cornwall's MPs first entered the House as burgesses, while a minimum of five men sat for the county's towns after being returned as knights.[27] So it was that parliamentary meetings encouraged the peninsula's residents to think in terms of both collective Cornish concerns and kingdom-wide interests, not least when considering the maintenance of law and order.

The JPs

Forming an essential cog of shire administration, the office of keeper of the peace had acquired a quasi-judicial role by the fourteenth century.[28] Accordingly, Edward II empowered commissioners to 'enquire by sworn inquest of felonies and trespasses, and to arrest and imprison the indicated' until the case could be brought before royal justices.[29] Pressure from the parliamentary Commons and the desire to enforce order across the realm resulted in the

---

[23] *HOP*, ii, 620–621.
[24] Saul, *Gloucestershire*, p. 126; Maddicott, *English Parliament*, pp. 352–366.
[25] *Modus Tenendi Parliamentum*, ed. T. D. Hardy (London, 1846), pp. 20–21.
[26] Maddicott, *English Parliament*, pp. 335, 342–343.
[27] Cf. Tyldesley, 'Local Communities', p. 54; H. Kleineke, 'The Widening Gap: the Practice of Parliamentary Borough Elections in Devon and Cornwall in the Fifteenth Century', *Parliamentary History*, 23 (2004), pp. 121–135.
[28] Cf. A. Harding, 'The Origin and Early History of the Keepers of the Peace', *TRHS*, 5th series, 10 (1960), pp. 85–109 at 102, 106; Coss, *English Gentry*, pp. 167–168.
[29] Saul, *Gloucestershire*, p. 128.

Crown conceding a range of extra powers to the keepers from 1327, notably the ability to determine cases.[30] Although the gentry had performed many judicial functions in the shires before the 1360s, the permanent acquisition of the determining power by the keepers at this time established these officers as justices of the peace, with wide judicial authority.[31] Even after this decade, however, peace commissioners enjoyed no monopoly on the local dispensation of justice. This was because the county bench remained linked to itinerant circuits of royal assize and gaol delivery staffed by justices of the central courts, who brought with them national practices and precedents in civil and criminal matters.[32] As a devolved system of justice operated across England under royal supervision, it is unsurprising that the Crown included Cornwall on the south-western assize circuit.

To promote law and order, the Crown issued peace commissions for Cornwall at the same time as commissions for every other part of England, although between times their membership might be altered as and when circumstances required. The trend across the fourteenth century was for the commissions to grow slowly in size, and this was the case in Cornwall too. Until 1338 no Cornish commission can be found containing more than four men, but in this year the pressures of war prompted the Crown to appoint thirteen members to the bench, with numbers falling back to five or six for the next thirty years or so. From 1369 commissions were again to expand, however, averaging nine members until 1405. A very similar picture emerges for the shire of Gloucestershire, whereas in the semi-autonomous palatinate of Durham the bishop alone issued commissions 'sporadically'.[33]

Since no great lords resided west of the Tamar, it is unsurprising that noblemen rarely headed the Cornish bench. The gentlemen and lawyers of the county instead dominated Cornish commissions. Upwards of 120 men are known to have served between 1300 and 1405, with perhaps eighty hailing from Cornwall itself. Many of these folk were local gentry who held numerous other posts but, as ever, a mix of the richly and poorly endowed appear, with the latter gaining in prominence. Local lawyers were especially well represented from the 1370s onwards, undertaking most of the day-to-day work. All these Cornish folk were also joined by numerous 'outsiders'. Across the century as a whole no fewer than twenty-one comital-ducal stewards served as JPs, and in

---

[30] Putnam, 'Keepers of the Peace', 25–45; Saul, *Gloucestershire*, pp. 128–131; B. Post, 'The Peace Commissions of 1382', *EHR*, 41 (1976), pp. 98–101.
[31] Musson, *Public Order*, pp. 79–82.
[32] E. Powell, 'The Administration of Criminal Justice in Late-Medieval England: Peace Sessions and Assizes', in *The Political Context of Law*, ed. R. Eales and D. Sullivan (London, 1987), pp. 49–59; Musson, *Public Order*, pp. 95–122.
[33] Saul, *Gloucestershire*, pp. 133–134; Liddy, *Durham*, p. 141.

Table 3: The Locations of County Peace Sessions in Richard II's Reign

Bodmin	The sessions were held most often in these three towns
Launceston	
Lostwithiel	
Helston	The JPs met on several occasions in each of these six settlements
Lelant	
Liskeard	
Marizion	
St Columb Major	
Truro	
Camelford	There are single references to proceedings in each of these seven locations
Grampound	
Penryn	
Saltash	
Stoke Climsland	
St Colan	
St Germans	

Source: Tyldesley, 'Local Communities', p. 76.

1349 the king even issued a commission 'by bill of the [Black] prince' himself.[34] Naturally, the king made his judicial authority felt on the county bench. It is illustrative of this that in 1344 Edward III appointed Justice William Shareshull to the quorum, one of the earliest appointments of an inner circle of royal justices to a commission.[35] To secure royal interests, in the last quarter of the century the Crown routinely appointed central court justices of this sort to the county bench.

As a result of all this judicial activity, Cornwall's peace commissions formed an arena for both 'local' and 'national' rivalries.[36] A prime example of the former is to be found in February 1381, when Richard II removed all Cornishmen from the bench in an attempt to end the virulent Sergeaux–Carminow–Trevarthian

---
[34] CPR 1348–1350, 383.
[35] B. H. Putnam, *The Place in Legal History of Sir William Shareshull, Chief Justice of the King's Bench, 1350–1361: A Study of Judicial and Administrative Methods in the Reign of Edward III* (Cambridge, 1950), pp. 25–26.
[36] Cf. Saul, *Gloucestershire*, p. 131; R. Virgoe, 'The Crown and Local Government: East Anglia under Richard II', in *The Reign of Richard II*, ed. F. R. H. Du Boulay and C. M. Barron (London, 1971), pp. 218–241.

feud.[37] The high politics of the realm can also be found intruding on Cornish commissions: notably in 1312, 1314, 1330, 1381, 1387–8 and 1397–9. While nobles and kings regularly interfered in such appointments elsewhere, the scale of intervention in Cornwall is striking.[38] There are a number of possible reasons why this was so. Perhaps most significant was the earl-duke's perennial absenteeism, which meant that local office held a more important key to power in the peninsula. Since the Cornish bench can be shown to have sat in as many as sixteen different locations across the county, this mobility further increased its reach, workload and local importance.[39] From all this we can see that royal peace commissions were essential to the authority of the Cornish magistracy, the earl-duke and the king himself, enabling these various powerbrokers to influence county affairs.

The Escheators

In contrast to that of the JPs, the power of the escheator was to wane in the later middle ages. The escheator's post was concerned with the collection of those feudal prerogatives arising from the king's position as lord paramount.[40] For the purposes of collection, in 1300 the country was divided into two great escheatries north and south of the Trent, with Cornwall and Devon overseen in the 1310s by the sub-escheator Richard de Clare.[41] In 1323, however, Edward II reorganised the office by creating eight bailiwicks, one of these comprising the western counties of Cornwall, Devon, Dorset and Somerset.[42] Sir Robert Bilkemore, a Bedfordshire-man, held the west country post from 1323 to 1327 when the Crown appointed him escheator south of the Trent. In this year the government had chosen to re-establish the northern and southern bailiwicks.

Embarking on a fresh major reform of the office, in 1341 Edward III decided to align the escheatries with the shrievalties. To this end, he appointed as

[37] Tyldesley, 'Local Communities', p. 139.
[38] Cf. Saul, *Gloucestershire*, pp. 131–132; Virgoe, 'East Anglia', p. 234; S. Walker, *Political Culture in Later Medieval England*, ed. M. J. Braddick (Manchester, 2006), pp. 83–85; idem, *The Lancastrian Affinity, 1361–1399* (Oxford, 1990), pp. 245–246.
[39] Tyldesley, 'Local Communities', pp. 68–78; *Quo Warranto*, pp. 108–111.
[40] S. L. Waugh, 'The Origins and Early Development of the Articles of the Escheator', *Thirteenth Century England, V*, ed. P. R. Coss and S. D. Lloyd (Woodbridge, 1995), pp. 89–113; S. L. Waugh, 'The Escheator's General Inquest: the Enforcement of Royal Lordship in the Late Fourteenth Century', in *Foundations of Medieval Scholarship: Records Edited in Honour of David Crook*, ed. P. Brand and S. Cunningham (York, 2008), pp. 11–24; also, *The Fifteenth-Century Inquisitions Post Mortem: A Companion*, ed. M. Hicks (Woodbridge, 2012).
[41] SC8/275/13734.
[42] Gibson, 'Escheatries', 218–219; *English Government at Work*, ii, pp. 163–165; *CFR 1319–1327*, 251–252.

escheator of Cornwall one John Dabernon, the Black Prince's feodary. While some tensions were to arise early on over royal and ducal rights, until 1368 the king and the prince always bestowed the offices of escheator and feodary on the same man.[43] In that year, however, the prince appointed one Henry Cokyn as feodary while the king retained in the office of escheator a certain Robert Wisdom. Three years later the king again combined Cornwall and Devon in one escheatry, a unit that was to remain in place until 1395. Fourteen men held the post over the period from 1368 to 1395, only four being Cornish, the rest coming from Devon. In 1395, however, Richard II once again made Cornwall a bailiwick in its own right, although in 1401 Henry IV recoupled the post with that of Devon. It seems that competing demands on the escheatries produced this complex history.[44] Petitioning the king repeatedly concerning corruption, qualifications and the annual appointment of escheators, the parliamentary Commons received few royal remedies for such grievances.[45] So far as personnel is concerned, the office in Cornwall was a less prestigious one than that of sheriff or JP, virtually all the local gentlemen holding the post being of comparatively humble stock: men such as the tin-merchant Roger Juyl.

The Coroners

Mirroring the escheatorship, the office of coroner was subject to repeated reorganisation. The post had been created back in 1194 by Richard I 'to keep the pleas of the crown', duties which turned principally on the holding of inquests on dead bodies and the organising of outlawries promulgated in the county court.[46] To secure the enforcement of these royal rights, the government regularly divided the peninsula into four districts under four separate coroners.[47] As these officials were elected in the county court, Cornwall's coroners were answerable to both the Crown and the commonalty in much the same way as every other shire.[48] Showing rather less concern about coroners than about the posts that we have already discussed, the parliamentary Commons complained only periodically about qualifications for office and the execution of duty.[49] As many as sixty-three men are known to have served as coroner in Cornwall between 1298 and 1409, fifty-two of whom held no other county office. Virtually all these folk were of modest means, with the

---

[43] CCR 1346–1349, 447, 565; Cf. Liddy, *Durham*, pp. 132–139.
[44] Gibson, 'Escheatries', 219.
[45] Saul, *Gloucestershire*, pp. 136–137.
[46] Hunnisett, *Coroner*, pp. 1–4, 100–115; for example, JUST3/120 m. 23.
[47] Tyldesley, 'Local Communities', p. 111.
[48] Hunnisett, *Coroner*, pp. 150–151; Cf. Liddy, *Durham*, pp. 155–156.
[49] Saul, *Gloucestershire*, p. 141.

Crown on no fewer than thirty-two occasions ordering the removal of a coroner because they held insufficient estates.[50] The coronership was an office seemingly little sought after. This much is indicated by the fact that although the government had ordered Noel Paderda's removal in 1379, he remained in post until after 1386.

Leading proprietors evidently valued elections to parliament and appointments to the shrievalty and the county bench, with the escheatorship and coronership exerting far less appeal to them.[51] The Crown's need for these lesser officials, however, meant that relatively minor figures of comparatively few means such as William le Poer were drawn into royal service, in his case as a coroner and parliamentary burgess. Extending the magistracy, such recruitment of gentry into administrative service created a yet denser mesh of links between the county and the rest of the kingdom. Shire administration actually had even deeper roots than this survey has shown, as many of the more substantial officers employed deputies to help them execute their commissions. One such underling was Odo Ude, whom we find in 1384 serving as under-sheriff of Cornwall.[52] All these men were involved in the collaborative business of government.

The Taxers, Arrayers and Minor Officers

In addition to these main offices, a variety of fixed-term offices and commissions had the effect of drawing even more proprietors into involvement in the royal administration. The office of tax collector can be taken as a case in point. Like their peers in every other part of the realm, the residents of Cornwall were obliged to contribute to parliamentary taxation.[53] Every time the parliamentary Commons made a grant of the levy on movable property to the king, a group of commissioners was appointed in each county to collect the sums approved. The numbers of gentry nominated to these panels steadily increased in the course of the century. We can chart these developments in Cornwall, where the king appointed two chief taxers to collect the 1327 lay subsidy but called on as many as six men to collect the poll tax of 1379.[54] Since the Cornish peninsula formed part of the frontline when hostilities erupted with France, commissions of array were equally important to county life.[55]

---

[50] *CCR 1343–1346*, 198.
[51] For example, *CCR 1392–1396*, 315.
[52] *CPR 1381–1385*, 499.
[53] The stannary-men were exempted, Willard, *Taxes*, pp. 21–22, 118–120; Jurkowski et al., *Lay Taxes*, pp. 36–37.
[54] *CPR 1327–1330*, 173; *CFR 1377–1383*, 144.
[55] Below, pp. 199–200.

Before 1370 the Crown had appointed two or three Cornishmen to each array, nominally mobilising every sixteen- to sixty-year-old capable of bearing arms. After this date, however, the commissions grew in size to contain as many as thirteen proprietors. Looking beyond these offices, the Crown can regularly be found appointing commissions of oyer and terminer to investigate specific grievances raised by county folk. Not only did Cornishmen sit on these many royal commissions; they often requested that such investigations be launched in the first place. In this way, 'consumer demand' and royal ambition between them saw the royal administration grow increasingly pervasive. As shire and franchise were tightly interwoven in Cornwall, this created a yet thicker web of government across the peninsula.

The Stewards

Concerning himself with the management of his master's prerogatives, the steward stood at the head of the earldom-duchy's local administration. Accordingly, it was the earl-duke himself who appointed the steward to the shrievalty until 1376.[56] From this year, however, the duke separated the two posts and Edward III divided the duchy's estates between Richard of Bordeaux and the latter's mother, Princess Joan.[57] During Richard II's turbulent reign the king and his adversaries alike sought to secure the appointment of their own candidates to this office. We therefore find as many as nine different stewards active between 1377 and 1405, six of whom held other county offices. Three were Cornish while another one, John Colshull, possessed a stake in Cornwall through marriage. Aside from Sir Robert Tresilian who served from 1377 to 1378, it was only in 1402 that another Cornishman attained the office, but this man, Sir John Arundell of Lanherne, continued in post until 1430. On top of their general duties as steward, all these men served on a range of seignorial and regnal commissions for the simple reason that lordly and royal government overlapped in Cornwall.

The Receivers

Jointly pre-eminent with the steward stood the receiver, whose 'cardinal duty' was to account for the money due from lordly reeves and bailiffs.[58] He also oversaw the payment of fees, handling thousands of pounds a year. While the division of work between the steward and receiver remains unclear, after 1337

---

[56] Aside from in 1336 and 1342–7.
[57] *RESDCornwall*, 47, 137–138, until Joan's death in 1385.
[58] *RESDCornwall*, 44.

the latter's name looms large in the accounts and he received a £20 salary for his labours.[59] From this year, some sixteen men are known to have served as receiver, seven of whom held other offices in the county. Of these sixteen only three were Cornishmen, among them the local powerbroker Ralph Trenewith. Two more were Devonians, but the rest hailed from further afield and one John Kendale, who served between 1348 and 1365, came from as far off as Westmorland. The earl-duke generally appointed people with financial expertise to the receivership, for raising dues from across the Cornish peninsula was an unending challenge.

The Haveners

Collecting the profits arising from the lordship's maritime prerogatives, the havener was one of the officials who rendered account to the receiver. As a reward for his services, the earl-duke paid him a 10-mark salary and granted him a robe worth 13s. 4d., with the king annexing the office of weigher of tin and keeper of the tinners' gaol to this post in 1396.[60] No fewer than twenty-one men served as havener between 1300 and 1400, four of them holding the office jointly. Only four of these officials originated from Cornwall, however, including William Talcarn, as the great majority of these office-holders held places in the households of the king or earl-duke. Rarely visiting their bailiwick, as many as seventeen haveners sat on no other commissions in the county. There is evidence, however, that Thomas Fitz Henry served the Black Prince 'on the ground' for some thirty-six years, even acquiring the epithet Thomas 'Havener'.[61]

The Stannaries

Since the coinage of tin yielded over £2,600 in 1337 alone, the stannaries were of paramount importance to the earl-duke.[62] It seems that the chief stannary official in Cornwall was interchangeably titled 'controller of the stannaries', 'keeper of the stannaries', 'controller of the stampage of tin' and 'controller of the coinage'.[63] Such designations stemmed from the physical stamp used to

---

[59] *RBP*, ii, 213.
[60] S. M. Campbell, 'The Haveners of the Mediaeval Dukes of Cornwall and the Organisation of the Duchy Ports', *JRIC* (1962), pp. 113–144; *HA*; *RBP*, ii, 186–187.
[61] *CPR 1385–1389*, 585.
[62] *CS*, lvi.
[63] *CCR 1313–1318*, 178, 396–397; *CPR 1330–1334*, 54, 494; *RBP*, i, 71; *CPR 1389–1392*, 83; E101/263/28; Lewis has suggested that a warden oversaw the stannaries, *Stannaries*, pp. 38, 86–87; but there is little evidence of this office in the 1300s (except *PROME*,

mark the tin presented at coinage sessions, proving that tax had been paid.[64] Throughout the thirteenth century the position had normally been held by the steward, but after 1300 the earl-duke more often separated the offices and appointed his own household men as controllers.[65]

Overseeing all aspects of stannary administration, the controller of the stannaries was responsible for promulgating mining laws and supervising the payment of coinage duty.[66] For the better enforcement of these rights, he appointed a bailiff apiece to supervise Cornwall's four stannary districts: Blackmore, Tywarnhaile, Penwith and Kerrier, and Foweymore. The bailiffships were principally the preserve of the sub-gentry, with their duties involving the collection of toll tin and the supervision of the stannary courts.[67] Concerning themselves chiefly with disputes arising from tin production, in 1337 the latter tribunals yielded just over £17 in fines.[68] While the Black Prince intermittently employed a receiver of the stannaries, the earldom-duchy played no direct part in tin production.[69] This was because the lordship earnt its money by levying coinage duty on tin, not by directly extracting the metal itself. As the steward and receiver enjoyed oversight of the stannary administration, these institutions formed part of the intertwined shire-franchise structure.[70]

The Castles

Towering over the county, Cornwall's chief castles – Launceston, Restormel, Tintagel and Trematon – formed a network of administration, control and defence ruled by the earldom-duchy.[71] The earl-duke appointed a constable to each, and in the case of Launceston this man generally managed the gaol, while the constable of Restormel often also held Restormel Park.[72] All these castellans received livery robes to the value of 13s. 4d. along with an annuity

---

v, 347–348); Elliott-Binns has argued that the warden and controller were one and the same, *Medieval Cornwall*, pp. 126–127, and while *CCR 1405–1409*, 447 seems to support him, the earl-duke may have served as overall warden, deputising the role of controller.

[64] *CCR 1318–1322*, 254.
[65] *Ministers' Accounts*, i, p. xxiv.
[66] Lewis, *Stannaries*, pp. 86–87.
[67] For instance, DCO 4; SC6/817/4 m. 15r; *Ministers' Accounts*, i, p. xxiv; Hatcher, *Tin*, p. 52; below, pp. 238–239.
[68] CS, lvi; E101/264/2.
[69] *RBP*, ii, 56, 187.
[70] *RBP*, ii, 149; Cf. Lewis, *Stannaries*, p. 86; Elliott-Binns, *Medieval Cornwall*, p. 127.
[71] I. D. Spreadbury, *Castles in Cornwall and the Isles of Scilly* (Redruth, 1984), pp. 14–35; Trematon's ownership was disputed, Elliott-Binns, *Medieval Cornwall*, pp. 161–162.
[72] *RBP*, ii, 186; SC6/816/11 m. 1r; *CPR 1334–1338*, 383.

in recompense for their service, some 20 marks for Launceston but only 50s. 8d. for the others.[73] While at times the lordship can be found spending considerable sums maintaining these fortifications, Tintagel was particularly dilapidated.[74] No fewer than forty-two men are known to have served as castellans of these four fortresses, only fourteen of whom were Cornish. The rest hailed from outside the county, most being loyal retainers of the earl-duke or the king himself. Whether Cornish or not, however, the majority of castellans served on other royal and lordly commissions in the county.

The Feodaries and Minor Estate Offices

A remarkable range of minor offices are to be found in the administration of the earldom-duchy, and it may be helpful to touch on some of these briefly. The officer responsible for collecting the feudal incidents pertaining to the duke was the feodary, who received a fee of 4d. a day from his employer.[75] The office encompassed both Cornwall and Devon, although the Black Prince expanded the commission of one holder, a certain Robert Wisdom, to include the whole west country. To protect both their prerogative rights, from 1341 to 1368 the prince and the king always bestowed the offices of feodary and escheator on the same man.[76] The earl-duke also appointed a bailiff-errant to assist with raising the large sums yielded by his privileges, employing Cornishmen and lordly dependants alike here.[77] As he held numerous parks to west of the Tamar, it was natural that the earl-duke had a parker manage each of these valuable assets and intermittently appointed a 'keeper of the prince's game'.[78] There is evidence that numerous stannary officials also served in the earldom-duchy, among them the chief pesage (weigher) of tin and the keeper of the tinners' gaol.[79] With lordship an exacting discipline, seigniorial administration depended on deputies and temporary commissioners to support its efforts. When serving as sheriff-steward, for instance, Sir John Dabernon appointed the Cornishman John Treveri as his lieutenant, while the Cornish lawyer John Tremayne is found holding a varied collection of temporary lordly commissions.[80] For the better management of all these officials, comital-ducal clerks recorded their financial endeavours in the ministers' accounts and the earl-duke then had

---

[73] SC6/811/7 m. 2r; E372/152B m. 9; SC6/1094/13; *CIPM*, iii, 548; Tintagel was held without fee for a time, *RBP*, ii, 14.
[74] SC8/327/E796; SC6/811/12 m. 1r; SC8/327/E818; *RBP*, ii, 2, 9.
[75] *RBP*, ii, 164.
[76] *RBP*, ii, 184.
[77] *RESDCornwall*, 45–46; *RBP*, i, 11; *RBP*, ii, 209.
[78] *RBP*, ii, 14, 65; *RESDCornwall*, 46
[79] SC6/811/18 m. 1r; *RBP*, ii, 185.
[80] *RBP*, i, 92; *RBP*, ii, 57, 116, 207; *RESDCornwall*, 45–46.

these documents thoroughly audited.[81] Such a well-developed administrative structure enabled the lordship to influence every part of Cornwall.

The Hundreds

For the purposes of local administration Cornwall was divided into nine hundreds: Eastwivelshire (East), Kerrier, Lesnewth, Penwith, Powdershire (Powder), Pydershire (Pyder), Stratton, Triggshire (Trigg) and Westwivelshire (West).[82] The earldom-duchy held eight and one third of these administrative divisions, with the remaining two-thirds of Penwith in the possession of the Arundells of Lanherne.[83] A bailiff headed the administration of every hundred, units comprising a number of frankpledge tithings whose members were mutually responsible for good order.[84] We find hundredal officials playing a vital administrative and military role for the Crown, even helping to keep the king's peace in Cornwall by levying fines on felons and indicting alleged criminals for trial before the justices of gaol delivery.[85] Each hundred also possessed its own court, an institution organised by the sheriff and overseen by the hundredal bailiff. During these monthly sessions cases were held between private parties and by tithing, with cases of trespass and suits of debt-detinue accounting for most of the business.[86] Although each suit was enacted without the royal writ, the Crown still supervised hundredal government when twice a year the sheriff undertook his tourn, during which he received the view of frankpledge.[87]

Justice, as ever, was to yield an income from fines and in 1337 Cornwall's hundreds are recorded generating over £130.[88] Each bailiff paid the earldom-duchy a farm for his office in the expectation of making a profit from the levying of these fines, a practice which encouraged racketeering.[89] In an attempt to

---

[81] RESDCornwall, 46–47.
[82] O. J. Padel, 'Ancient and Medieval Administrative Divisions of Cornwall', *Proceedings of the Dorset Natural History and Archaeological Society*, 131 (2010), pp. 211–214.
[83] CIPM, iii, 457–458; CChR 1327–1341, 399–400; Ministers' Accounts, i, p. xxiii; SC8/18/900; 'Three Courts of the Hundred of Penwith, 1333', ed. G. D. G. Hall, in *Medieval Legal Records*, ed. R. F. Hunnisett and J. B. Post (London, 1978), pp. 170–196 at 171; P. A. S. Pool, 'The Penheleg Manuscript', *JRIC* (1959), pp. 163–228.
[84] See, H. M. Cam, *The Hundred and the Hundred Rolls: An Outline of Local Government in Medieval England* (London, 1930); H. M. Jewell, *English Local Administration in the Middle Ages* (Newton Abbot, 1972), pp. 162–164.
[85] For example, KB27/241 m. 103r; JUST3/121 m. 13.
[86] SC2/161/74 mm. 12–23v; SC2/161/75; 'Three Courts', pp. 173–174; Cam, *Hundred Rolls*, p. 181.
[87] For example, CPR 1330–1334, 527.
[88] CS, lviii.
[89] Cam, *Hundred Rolls*, p. 143; CRO, AR/2/463 m. 5r.

prevent such extortions, the Statute of Lincoln in 1316 stipulated that hundreds should be managed by 'suitable people', that bailiffs should have sufficient land and that hundred farms should be 'reasonable'.[90] Since the parliamentary Commons petitioned repeatedly regarding oppressions and over-large farms, this legislation presumably remained a dead letter.[91] In the case of Cornwall, each of the county's hundreds was held in fee. From 1337 the ministers' accounts regularly recorded the names of the bailiffs, chiefly Cornishmen who generally appointed Cornish under-bailiffs, but 'incomers' often made an appearance. The earl-duke at times can be shown to have granted out whole hundreds to his favoured retainers.

When considering the public or private nature of hundreds, G. D. G. Hall has argued that this distinction turned on the rights to take profits, the rights to hold court and whether or not a hundred enjoyed additional judicial responsibilities.[92] Although Cornwall's hundreds enjoyed no extra powers, the earldom-duchy's prerogatives initially make them all appear private. In 1334, however, there is evidence that Michael Trenewith the elder mainprised one Odo de St Colan, the bailiff of Penwith, guaranteeing that Odo would faithfully serve the king and John Arundell, the chief bailiff, paying the profits of the hundredal court as fully as either the sheriff or Arundell required.[93] Here we see how hundredal government formed an essential component of the combined shire-franchisal administration that was rooted deep in Cornwall.

Conclusion

There can be little doubt that Cornwall ranked among the great seigniorial enclaves of late-medieval England. It is equally clear, however, that the county still held a place within the kingdom as a whole, contrasting with the position in both the Marcher lordships and principality of Wales. Within the Welsh March, for example, the king's writ simply did not run in the lordships, as each lord enjoyed nearly unlimited jurisdictional power in his own 'soveraigne' lordship.[94] Only once in the later middle ages did the magnates of the March consent to paying a tax to the king, sending no representatives to sessions of parliament and even defending their right to wage private war itself. The prince of Wales, normally the king's eldest son, enjoyed similarly unfettered powers

---

[90] *The Statutes of the Realm*, ed. A. Luders et al., 11 vols (London, 1810–28), i, pp. 174–175; *PROME*, iii, 209.
[91] *PROME*, v, 377; also, SC8/102/5080.
[92] 'Three Courts', p. 172.
[93] CRO, AR/3/115; *Quo Warranto*, pp. 108–111.
[94] R. R. Davies, *Lordship and Society in the March of Wales, 1282–1400* (Oxford, 1978), pp. 217–228.

in his principality.[95] He alone appointed the officials of his lordship, overseeing courts that divided his subjects along English and Welsh ethnic lines in a way which simply did not exist in fourteenth-century Cornwall. Wales and the Welsh stood outside the realm, Cornwall and the Cornish did not.

Neither did Cornwall constitute a county palatine, a parcel of the kingdom of England that had been elevated to the status of an immunity. The 'purest' form of palatinate possessed immunity from royal taxation, which meant that the lordship did not return members to parliament. In a franchise, all officials owed their allegiance to the lord of the liberty, not to the king, with each palatine possessing its own chanceries, exchequers and courts. Indeed, the courts of the palatinate enjoyed jurisdictional finality, with the lord himself acting as the judge of last resort. As his rights were grounded in territorial authority, the lord also served as the universal landlord of his county palatine. Judged by these parameters Durham, Chester and, from 1351, Lancaster all formed palatinates.[96] What, however, was the case in Cornwall?

While fourteenth-century Cornwall possessed some of the attributes of a county palatine, franchisal powers in the earldom-duchy fell short of full palatinate status. In the years of the earldom and duchy, Cornwall remained fully enfranchised and paid parliamentary subsidies just like any other shire.[97] No court in the peninsula enjoyed jurisdictional finality in civil or criminal matters either, as the county was included on the royal assize and gaol delivery circuits.[98] At the same time the central common law tribunals adjudicated over many Cornish suits and cases heard in the county could be reviewed in the court of king's bench through writs of *certiorari* and writs of error.[99] In contrast to Durham and Cheshire, the king also continued appointing nearly all local government officials. Although Edward III issued the Great Charter of 1337 elevating the earldom of Cornwall to a dukedom held by the Black Prince, the clause stating that no 'minister of the king's shall enter therein' was more honoured in the breach than the observance.[100] At the core of the

---

[95] R. R. Davies, *Conquest, Coexistence and Change: Wales 1063–1415*, Oxford History of Wales, vol. II (Oxford, 1987), pp. 364–369, 391–411.

[96] G. Barraclough, *The Earldom and County Palatine of Cheshire* (Oxford, 1953); H. M. Cam, 'The Evolution of the Mediaeval English Franchise', *Speculum*, 32 (1957), pp. 427–442; Liddy, *Durham*, pp. 1–24; P. Morgan, *War and Society in Medieval Cheshire, 1277–1403* (Manchester, 1987), pp. 11, 100–102; Pollard, *North-Eastern England*, pp. 146–147; J. Scammel, 'The Origin and Limitations of the Liberty of Durham', *EHR*, 81 (1966), pp. 449–473; K. Stringer, 'States, Liberties and Communities in Medieval Britain and Ireland', in *Liberties and Identities in the Medieval British Isles*, ed. M. Prestwich (Woodbridge, 2008), pp. 5–36.

[97] For example, E179/87/7; E179/87/37.

[98] For example, JUST1/1349 mm. 13r–18r; JUST1/1390 mm. 10r–11r; JUST3/120 m. 23.

[99] Below, Chapter 12.

[100] *CChR 1327–1341*, 399–400, 436–437; *RESDCornwall*, 5–7.

duchy's semi-regalian powers were those of the ancient earldom, which had not enjoyed palatinate status. It remained the case after 1337, for instance, that the county held a place on the royal assize and gaol delivery circuits.[101] It was therefore the king, not the duke, who acted as the judge of last resort in Cornwall. The king also continued to appoint nearly all the officials of local government, issuing many commands to these local representatives of the Crown.[102] While the Great Charter codified and extend the earldom's prerogatives, Cornwall under the fourteenth-century duchy was by no means excluded from the realm.

None of this is to suggest that the prerogatives and powers of the earldom-duchy were insubstantial. On the contrary, the lordship held rights to the shrievalty, minorities and many other prerogatives besides.[103] So as to protect his many rights and privileges, the earl-duke appointed a great many officials of his own in the county who then defended his interests there with force if necessary.[104] Even offices not directly in the earl-duke's power were still susceptible to his lordly influence, with the king often appointing comital-ducal dependents to Cornish posts in his gift. By dispensing a form of equitable justice from his council, the earl-duke also played an important judicial role in the county.[105] The lordship enjoyed great authority over Cornwall, but all these powers were locally intermeshed with those of the Crown. As the earldom-duchy was generally held by royally appointed lords, moreover, it was common for the personnel and practices of the Crown and the lordship to overlap. All this activity necessarily drew the county into the kingdom.

Not sustained by charters alone, franchises were only effective when lords and subjects both had a vested interest in upholding the rights of the franchise. The residents of Cheshire, for example, constantly sought to defend 'Cheshire law' by refusing to be brought before royal justices.[106] This was not the case in fifteenth-century Durham, however, where the local elite waged a sustained campaign to bring about royal intervention between the Tyne and Tees. It seems that Durham's liberties were more susceptible 'to serious challenge from within than without'.[107] In contrast to the 'true' palatinates, in Cornwall the local populace were in the habit of regularly calling on royal justice and

---

[101] For example, JUST1/1426A m. 21r; JUST1/1476 m. 70r; JUST1/124 m. 3; JUST3/9/2 m. 3; JUST3/153 m. 7.
[102] *RBP*, iv, 88.
[103] *CIPM*, iii, pp. 456–458, 475–477; *Ministers' Accounts*, i, pp. xxiii–xxxi.
[104] *RBP*, ii, *passim*.; *CCR 1346–1349*, 203, 565, 466.
[105] Below, pp. 178, 212–213; Cf. A. Musson, 'Queenship, Lordship and Petitioning in Late Medieval England', in *Medieval Petitions: Grace and Grievance*, ed. W. M. Ormrod, G. Dodd and A. Musson (York, 2009), pp. 156–172.
[106] Barraclough, *Cheshire*, p. 22.
[107] Liddy, *Durham*, pp. 208–211, 235.

grace, as were the earl-dukes themselves. While all parties were aware of the extensive prerogative rights of the earldom-duchy, they were equally cognisant of the fact that Cornwall held a place among the shires of England. In the far south west franchise and shire complemented and drew strength from each other, with 'Cornwall' forming an amalgam of the two. This much is indicted by a petition of c. 1338, in which the Commons of Cornwall requested that Edward III order the duke and his council, along with the chancellor and treasurer of England, to appoint a more suitable sheriff.[108] We see here how the officers of Cornwall had many overlapping loyalties, being accountable to the king and his ministers, as well as to the duke and his household, while also having a 'public' responsibility to the county commonalty. In this way, the earldom-duchy's privileges were less sharply defined in reality than rhetoric.

The Cornish peninsula comprised no land apart, as the structure of royal officialdom provided a framework of power enabling the Crown to project its might into the furthest corners of the county. Since the local residents of Cornwall sought the same royal assurances concerning local office as their fellows from across the realm, these posts naturally gave rise to the same concerns as elsewhere in England. While the earldom-duchy nuanced every aspect of county governance, the earl-duke's close involvement in the high politics of the realm rendered the lordship another channel connecting the peninsula into the kingdom. All these earls, dukes and kings, however, did not simply impose their rulerships on Cornwall. Quite the reverse, in fact, for Cornishmen and woman depended on the workings of shire-franchisal administration, requesting lordly and royal intervention in their affairs through petitions, commissions and so on. At the same time the 'private' influence of Cornish proprietors proved essential to the county's 'public' administration. In appointing Sir Ranulph Blanchminster to the county bench in the 1330s, for instance, the Crown bestowed public authority on him while harnessing his private power to the king's cause. Making him locally mighty, Blanchminster employed his own seigniorial constable on the Scilly Isles, a certain William Daundely in c. 1348, and maintained twelve men-at-arms to keep the islands' peace and garrison his castle of Evor.[109] In much the same way, generations of the Botreaux family held county offices while their residence at Boscastle was known locally as 'the Courte', containing 'the diversified roomes of a prison' that evidenced in stone their 'large jurisdiction'.[110]

Every leading office-holding gentleman in Cornwall, as elsewhere in England for that matter, brought the clout and nous derived from his own lordships to the royal commissions on which he sat. Such an intertwining of

---

[108] SC8/193/9648.
[109] CPR 1301–1307, 538; *Cornish Wills*, 28.
[110] *Quo Warranto*, pp. 108–110; Leland, *Itinerary*, i, p. 176; *Carew*, 120v.

personal and public power meant that the king and the earl-duke depended on the local influence of these Cornish lords to carry their government effectively to west of the Tamar, just as Cornish proprietors relied on royal and comital-ducal might to magnify their own authority. As the century went on, office-holding was to tie together all these powerbrokers the more tightly. It is illustrative of this that in 1300 some fourteen officials can be identified as heading the administration of the shire-franchise, while by a century later this figure had grown to twenty-four. On those occasions when the government summoned a parliament, levied a subsidy and issued a commission of array those figures would rise to thirty-two and fifty-two at the beginning and end of the century respectively. For all the points of possible friction, the Cornish gentry, the king and the earl-duke formed a triumvirate of common interest for the great preponderance of the time.[111]

Throughout the fourteenth century we find that the county's pre-eminent dynasties, among them the Bodrugans, Carminows and l'Ercedeknes, maintained a leading presence in Cornwall's administration. Many gentlemen of lesser means also joined them, drawing a considerable and growing body of Cornishmen into the magistracy. It was certainly not the case, however, that the office-holding elite and the gentry class were co-existent. Some knightly lineages served rarely, the Soors for example, while lesser gentlemen attained only a few leading posts. Yet in Cornwall the personnel of local administration sharply contrasted with the staffing of the lordships in the March and principality of Wales, where the higher administrative posts were nearly exclusively reserved for 'outside Englishmen'.[112] Neither did the operation of magnate patronage result in a 'fractured office-holding community' in Cornwall, as in Durham, where leading posts remained the preserve of episcopal candidates only.[113] While 'outside' men more often staffed the earldom-duchy, Cornishmen remained well-represented in county administration and were to rise to prominence from the 1360s onwards. In reasserting themselves in this way, they emulated their peers in every other shire of England – it was in the gentry's nature to rise.[114] By creating a point of social and political convergence for the whole range of county society, the locally intermeshed posts of the earldom-duchy and the Crown helped to bestow coherence on Cornwall itself while drawing the county into the kingdom. Cornwall was a shire of England, one that played host to a most powerful lordship.

---

[111] Cf. Coss, *English Gentry*, pp. 165–201.
[112] Davies, *Wales 1063–1415*, p. 415.
[113] Liddy, *Durham*, p. 172.
[114] Cf. J. C. Holt, *The Northerners* (Oxford, 1961), p. 60.

3

Since the Time of King Arthur: Gentry Identity and the Commonalty of Cornwall*

Identity is a construct forged by people and in polities through a two-way interaction between pressures from above or outside and appreciation of ties established more locally. It is a subject essential to understanding the actions and lives of individuals and groups. Yet, paradoxically, identity emerges as intangible, ever-changing and 'hardly ever totally knowable'.[1] While historians can employ a variety of sources, including wills and manuals outlining proper behaviour, to tease out self- and group perceptions, assessing the way in which these influenced identities is no simple task. For those who study the later medieval gentry, the absence of personal correspondence and diaries, which perhaps contain the most eloquent statements of self-perceptions and communal loyalties, renders this difficult subject all the more challenging. As bloodless administrative documents provide scant evidence for such a multifaceted phenomenon, so gentry identity remains a vexing and highly contested subject.[2]

---

* This chapter builds on my, 'Since the Time of King Arthur: Gentry Identity and the Commonalty of Cornwall, c. 1300–c. 1420', *Historical Research*, 91 (2018), pp. 236–254.
[1] M. Rubin, 'Identities', in *A Social History of England, 1200–1500*, ed. R. Horrox and W. M. Ormrod (Cambridge, 2006), pp. 383–412 at 383.
[2] For the county model, Bennett, *Cheshire and Lancashire*, pp. 21–40; Saul, *Gloucestershire*, pp. 106–167; R. Virgoe, 'Aspects of the County Community in the Fifteenth Century', in *Profit, Piety and the Professions in Later Medieval England*, ed. M. Hicks (Gloucester, 1990), pp. 1–13; for social network theory, C. Carpenter, 'Gentry and Community in Medieval England', *Journal of British Studies*, 33 (1994), pp. 340–380; for judicious overviews, Walker, *Political Culture*, pp. 68–80; Coss, *English Gentry*, pp. 202–215.

Until the 1990s the prevailing orthodoxy among those working in medieval and early-modern local studies maintained that there was such a thing as the 'county community'. Although there is no pithy definition of this entity, it assumes a range of solidarities across the county shaped by networks of kin, local government, parliamentary representation and so on. With each revolving around the county, interactions of this sort contributed to a marriage of gentry and county identity. In 1994, however, Christine Carpenter offered a substantial critique of this concept, instead suggesting a model based on 'social network theory': an analysis of the relative strength and density of links between different members of the gentry, nobility and agents, such as lawyers.[3] Inviting us to believe that for hundreds of years the shire stood unchallenged, all but unchanging and largely self-contained, the county model undoubtedly needed nuancing. Since it was through the shire structure that the Crown governed England, it was naturally the case that shires figured prominently in all royal administrative documents. Yet despite this, the county did not merit total destruction. It seems that Christine Carpenter's reasoning for utterly abandoning the idea of the county rested upon her work on Warwickshire, a fissiparous shire with no defined natural borders and a powerful resident magnate.[4] It needs to be stressed that Warwickshire constituted a by no means typical county, if such a thing existed. To analyse the shape and density of Warwickshire's social networks she also relied heavily on deed evidence, a class of documents with an uncertain survival rate.[5] We simply have no way of knowing the completeness of the networks constructed from deed-based evidence of this sort, nor can we quantify the full density of links within the confined world of a county's landed society. Evidently the material that has been lost is more important than that which has survived the passage of time.

Since Cornwall contrasts greatly with Warwickshire in all sorts of ways, we may well question the extent to which deed-based social network theory illuminates the identity of the peninsula's landed lineages. Correspondence hints at possibilities of interaction that deeds by themselves do not reveal. Consider, for example, two letters sent by the Black Prince in 1351 to Sir John Trevaignon and Sir John Arundell.[6] In both of these the prince made clear that he would not countenance these gentlemen accompanying him on campaign as their 'bearing has been and still is so outrageous and offensive to us, our subjects, ministers, and tenants, as well as to your neighbours in the parts of Cornwaille, as to be improper and unsuitable for a man of your order'. We see

---

[3] Carpenter, 'Community', 366–368, 377–380.
[4] Carpenter, *Warwickshire*, pp. 25–28, 345, 360–398.
[5] Carpenter, *Warwickshire*, pp. 281–346, especially 291–292; Carpenter, 'Community', 360.
[6] *RBP*, ii, 9–10.

here some hint of social complexities now lost. Informal interactions which took place during hunting trips or when proprietors called on friends and relations have left virtually no trace, with Richard Carew writing that Cornish gentlemen 'converse familiarly together, & often visit one another'.[7] For this reason, it proves impossible to quantify and qualify networks based on the analysis of deeds alone. More seriously still, there is a danger that in vesting social networks with absolute authority we impose an interpretation on the evidence that fails to consider the complexities of medieval society. Although network theory should not completely replace the county model, the case for studying social networks remains compelling because these formed one strand of gentry identity. Comprising 'a cluster of co-existing attributes', identity emerges as multi-layered and ever-changing, with these different 'boundaries of the mind' all influencing the self-perceptions of Cornish proprietors.[8]

If we bear in mind the limitations of network theory, and if we remember too the great differences between Warwickshire and Cornwall, we may find it worthwhile to return to the county model. It must be admitted that this too has limitations. The Latin *communitas comitatus* has often been rendered as 'county community' by historians, but the notion conjured by this anglicised idiom is so vague as to be devoid of meaning, while at the same time suggesting a strikingly coherent common interest. Perhaps the crux of the issue is the form of community envisaged. On the one hand, some communities, such as those of certain peasant villages, were tightly tied together, yet on the other the county was more expansive and diffuse.[9] The county still had a meaning, however, forming a permanent institution influencing the lives of those who lived under its auspices.

In acknowledging the different forms of community, we should perhaps employ a different terminology. Leaving 'community' for small groups, we should cautiously favour the term 'commonalty' for the more expansive form of collective interactions represented by the county, a term that contemporaries often employed. 'Commonalty' in this respect suggests a sense of shared values, a collective sense of purpose and a common organisation embracing the entirety of the Cornish gentry and the local earldom-duchy officials. It also encompassed their families, the web of mutually supporting public and private connections that bound all these folk together. Remaining only shorthand for a neither perfectly defined nor definable organism, 'commonalty' embraces

---

[7] Carew, 64v.
[8] Rubin, 'Identities', p. 410; Cf. S. Reynolds, *Kingdoms and Communities in Western Europe, 900–1300*, 2nd Edition (Oxford, 1997), pp. 234–236, 335.
[9] Reynolds, *Kingdoms*, p. 219; Virgoe, 'County Community'; M. Rubin, 'Small Groups: Identity and Solidarity in the Late Middle Ages', in *Enterprise and Individuals in Fifteenth-Century England*, ed. J. Kermode (Stroud, 1991), pp. 132–150 at 134–135; Walker, *Political Culture*, pp. 70–71.

the gentry more loosely and abstractly than the 'county community' of old. At the core of the commonalty of Cornwall stood the leading Cornish proprietors and local administrators who interacted in the face-to-face world of the county, finding identity and fulfilment in its structures.

The county was by no means the sole call on the loyalties of the local elite, however, for wider and narrower solidarities operated simultaneously. Beginning with the former, a case can certainly be made for south-western regionalism in this period. Although this region's boundaries remain nebulous, bonds strengthened from Exeter westwards. Forming a 'zone of common human activity', this loosely defined area comprised 'a flow of ideas and people, gossip... and influence'.[10] Neither watertight nor perfectly homogeneous, many regional solidarities still operated. Considerable economic ties were to link this region together, for instance, as tin occurred under the craggy moors of both Cornwall and West Devon.[11] Since Cornishmen and Devonians were often found engaging in joint trading ventures and 'piracy' alike, shipping concerns also connected these two counties.[12]

Many links stretched sinuously across the Tamar. Several trans-county dynasties, among them the Huishs and Chaumpernouns for example, can be found holding estates and offices on both sides of this river, while numerous Cornishmen and Devonians served in the administration of each other's shires. There is evidence that Cornwall and West Devon also shared a penchant for lawlessness that took little account of formal borders.[13] As both counties shared many interests, not least fear of French activity, it is no surprise that the two of them can be shown to have jointly lobbied parliament at times.[14] The Crown appreciated their interconnected nature, grouping the two together for the escheatory and for some other administrative functions.[15] Seigniorial power leached across this supposed frontier as well, with the earldom-duchy's lands stretching deep into Devon. Providing yet greater coherence to this area, both counties were brought together in one diocese, centred on Exeter.[16] In many ways these two shires shared an outlook and way of life that faded into each other. The degree of regional cohesion, however, should not be overstated. With little to gather these strands together, the south west remained a diffuse society. Exeter proved too small and too distant from Cornwall to act as a provincial capital, and neither lordship nor royal government drew this

---

[10] E. Royle, 'Introduction: Regions and Identities', in *Issues of Regional Identity, in Honour of John Marshall* (Manchester, 1998), pp. 1–13.
[11] Hatcher, *Tin*, pp. 2–3, 21.
[12] For example, C241/172/3; C131/207/25; *CPR 1385–1389*, 165.
[13] Kleineke, 'Why the West Was Wild'.
[14] *PROME*, iii, 389.
[15] Tyldesley, 'Local Communities', p. 3.
[16] Below, Chapter 13.

amorphous and expansive area together.[17] Perhaps inevitably, south-western regionalism was to exercise little pull on the imaginations of its inhabitants, having less meaning than, for example, the 'North Country' at the opposite end of England.[18]

At the other end of the spectrum stood a profusion of lesser solidarities, for sub-county localism was a potent force in every shire. Powerful individual sentiments remained significant and in 1346 we find the burgesses of Padstow claiming that John Billioun 'bears himself as king in the county of Cornwall'.[19] One's family name and patrimony also weighed on personal sentiments, with John Leland commenting on the Bodrugans' 'auncient stok'.[20] After allegedly committing a murder, Sir Ralph Bloyou even refused to plead before the county assize in 1301 because he feared that his family estates would be forfeit if he lost the case.[21] He was therefore sentenced to death, with his sacrifice remembered in an obit recording that he was 'killed in prison with a copper key, 1302'.[22] These kinds of familial relations were closely connected to social networks and neighbourliness, shaping the outlook and identity of the county elite.

As the stannaries of Devon operated under a lighter regime than those of Cornwall, the burden of taxation helped to create varying solidarities and identities among these folk. Being administered as four bailiwicks, even the stannaries in Cornwall did not form a monolithic entity; tinners west of Truro were to lobby Edward I separately in 1302, and the endorsement on the petition ordered the barons of the exchequer to investigate their grievances.[23] In much the same way, the county's maritime character helped to foster marine cultures of various forms and strengths. Both tin and sea fashioned distinctive ways of life, with the gentry emerging as tin-owning gentlemen and salt-water lords. At the same time many petty boroughs created smaller urban societies in the county, which were themselves sub-divided between different guilds, streets and so on. Deeply localised factors greatly influenced Cornish identities. So it was that in 1361 a dispute between the tenants of Carnedon and Rillaton manors concerning boundaries was 'so high' that the sheriff found himself unable to achieve a settlement.[24]

---

[17] Below, Chapter 11.
[18] Cf. Walker, *Political Culture*, pp. 73–74.
[19] *CPR 1345–1348*, 235–236; A. Black, 'The Individual and Society', in *The Cambridge History of Medieval Political Thought, c. 350–c. 1450*, ed. J. H. Burns (Cambridge, 1988), pp. 588–606.
[20] Leland, *Itinerary*, i, p. 201.
[21] Elliott-Binns, *Medieval Cornwall*, pp. 233–234.
[22] *TCO*, 33, 189.
[23] *CPR 1301–1307*, 539; SC8/315/E168; Lewis, *Stannaries*, pp. 85–90.
[24] *RBP*, ii, 180.

More substantially, the county's nine hundreds – and their constituent tithings – played a significant role in regulating daily life. We see this in 1416, when the Commons of Penwith and Kerrier petitioned the king separately, and the endorsement on the petition empowered the king's council to investigate extortions committed there under the authority of parliament.[25] Since geographical divisions reinforced Cornwall's hundreds, these units could exercise considerable influence on the sentiments of their inhabitants. Inevitably, the county's immensely varied topography and geology proved of great consequence to its identity. Both features rendered the Lizard and Penwith particularly distinctive areas, but branching estuaries sub-divided large parts of the county while sharply contrasting granitic moorland and sub-tropical valleys created units of quite different characters.[26] On an even grander scale, the peninsula's sheer length diluted the shire identity, rendering interactions between those who resided at opposite ends of Cornwall the more challenging. In this way, Cornish topography encouraged sub-county localism by creating distinctive areas within the county's boundaries.

It was also the case that the Fowey-Padstow isogloss linguistically transected Cornwall, with English spoken by those who resided east of this divide, while most of those who lived to its west were bilingual, speaking both Cornish and English.[27] In the *Ordinalia, Passio Christi* the jailor's servant even complained:

From here to Trigg,	alemma bys yn tryger
upon my faith, a worse master	war ow fay lacka mester
I could not encounter him!	ny alsen y thyerbyn![28]

Some folk, then, may be assumed to have identified with western Cornish-speaking Cornwall. When we turn to the peninsula's ecclesiastical organisation, we find that the bishopric of Exeter administered the county as an archdeaconry in its own right. Even though parishes were more cohesive entities, these were typically sub-divided between different guilds and chapelries, while many gentlemen possessed their own household chapels.[29] Such sundry sentiments powerfully and immediately affected the lives and identities of the

---

[25] SC8/104/5161.
[26] H. S. A. Fox, 'Urban Development', in *Historical Atlas of South-West England*, ed. R. Kain and W. Ravenhill (Exeter, 1999), pp. 400–407 at 402; P. Herring, 'Multiple Identities in Cornwall', in *Recent Archaeological Work in South-Western Britain: Papers in Honour of Henrietta Quinnell*, ed. S. Pearce (Oxford, 2011), pp. 159–167.
[27] Above, pp. 18–19.
[28] *Cornish Drama*, i, PC, lines 2274–2276; correspondence with Oliver Padel, 2 February 2016.
[29] Mattingly, 'Parish Guilds'; D. C. Harvey, 'Territoriality, Parochial Development and the Place of 'Community' in Later Medieval Cornwall', *Journal of Historical Geography*, 29 (2003), pp. 151–165.

Cornish – this is Nigel Saul's 'county of communities'.[30] Each formed a different 'boundary of the mind', and yet neither supra- nor sub-shire solidarities robbed the county altogether of significance.

Surrounded on three sides by the sea, Cornwall was better defined geographically than virtually any shire, coherently fusing county with topography. Water in the form of the Tamar even delineated its eastern border, and while this river proved far from impassable it was psychologically significant, creating a bounded territorial space. The author of the so-called *Charter Fragment*, the only surviving secular work of Middle Cornish, thought in terms of the whole county and highlighted this river's importance when promising a wife without equal 'from here to Tamar Bridge!'.[31] In crossing the Tamar, 'the most famous river in Cornwall', William Worcestre was very conscious that he was entering 'the county and province of Cornwall' (*comitatus provincie Cornubie*); or, as John Leland put it, 'the rvyer of Tamar… almost from the hed of it to the mouth devidith Devonshir from Cornewaule'.[32] The riverine boundary of Cornwall was truly ancient, having been fixed at the Tamar back in the tenth century by Athelstan.[33] Since the peninsula had been absorbed into the Anglo-Saxon kingdoms even before Athelstan's reign, it is no surprise that Domesday demonstrates the way in which Cornwall formed a functioning shire by as early as 1086.[34] In the fourteenth century the county had achieved institutional longevity and legitimacy.

Institutionally the shared responsibility of all its members, Cornwall, like other counties, had a corporate personality and could legally sue and be sued.[35] By far its most important institution was the county court, which typically met in the great shire hall within the 'duchy palace' in Lostwithiel.[36] Although legislation passed in 1278 was to result in debts larger than 40s. being pursued elsewhere, the judicial importance of this body was augmented by Cornwall's distance from the central common law tribunals.[37] The county court remained

---

[30] Saul, *Sussex*, pp. 60–61; Coss, *English Gentry*, p. 209.
[31] *The Middle Cornish Charter Endorsement*, ed. L. Toorians (Innsbruck, 1991), pp. 6, 28; correspondence with O. J. Padel, 2 February 2016.
[32] Worcestre, *Itineraries*, pp. 24–25, 22, 30; Leland, *Itinerary*, i, p. 174.
[33] W. of Malmesbury, *Gesta Regum Anglorum*, ed. R. Mynors, 2 vols (Oxford, 1998–9), i, pp. 216–217; S. Foot, *Athelstan: The First King of England* (London and New Haven, 2011), pp. 81–82, 164, 253.
[34] Foot, *Athelstan*, p. 164; *Domesday Book, X, Cornwall*, ed. C. and F. Thorn (Chichester, 1979).
[35] Walker, *Political Culture*, p. 70.
[36] CS, 4–5; R. Palmer, *The County Courts of Medieval England, 1150–1350* (Princeton, NJ, 1982), pp. 8–9.
[37] Palmer, *County Courts*, pp. 31, 237–261; J. R. Maddicott, 'The County Community and the Making of Public Opinion in Fourteenth-Century England', *TRHS*, 5th series, 28 (1978), pp. 27–43 at 41–42.

the most prestigious tribunal in the fourteenth-century peninsula, having an 'immutable schedule' meeting every twenty-eighth Monday.[38] With the great majority of local proprietors and sundry other folk besides engaged in litigation there, the court roll of 1333 reads like a Cornish gentry 'Who's Who'.[39] Not simply an institution in which folk sued and counter-sued, the county court also acted as the forum for selecting Cornwall's MPs. With parliament's burgeoning influence, this articulation of collective Cornish interests grew increasingly significant.[40] Although fourteenth-century election turnouts are impossible to chart, we know that in 1411 at least sixty-six men drawn from the whole range of local society were to attend, including many landed gentlemen, the mayors of five boroughs, the priors of Bodmin and Launceston and even a few 'pirates'.[41] The county sent petitions to the House regarding everything from justice to defence, with parliamentary lobbying of this sort demonstrating the breadth of interests represented that drew the commonalty together.[42]

It is a mistake to underestimate the court, for it was there that 'statutes were proclaimed, petitions drafted, county rates fixed, and visiting justices of assize informed of the disposition of the county'.[43] It followed that the chief local office-holders regularly attended its sessions, acquiring considerable influence over its deliberations. In 1313 one John Bedewynde even chose this venue to denounce Edward II's evil policies relating to tin, showing how the court could act as a forum for making public complaint.[44] Evidently the decline in its judicial function did not impinge on the court's role as a channel for the two-way transmission of information between the king and his Cornish subjects.[45] Yet for all this activity, county opinion was not made in the court alone. As no 'single locus' of the shire existed, a great deal of administrative and other business occurred in varying 'public' and 'private' venues across the peninsula.[46]

There can be little doubt, however, that the county underwrote many aspects of local administration, with the result that the unit impinged on the consciousness and sentiments of the main administrators.[47] It was through the county that the king taxed the realm, an exercise that by its very nature proved communal as the county was assessing itself. The Crown also organised

---

[38] *PROME*, iii, 100; Palmer, *County Courts*, pp. 22–24.
[39] SC2/161/74 mm. 1–11.
[40] Maddicott, 'County Community', 39, 42; Coss, *English Gentry*, p. 202.
[41] C219/10/6 m. 9; Tyldesley, 'Local Communities', p. 54; *HOP*, i, 294; lists of those attesting the return were only compiled from 1406, Carpenter 'Community', p. 347.
[42] Below, p. 178.
[43] Walker, *Political Culture*, p. 72.
[44] Below, p. 117.
[45] Maddicott, 'County Community', 34; Coss, *English Gentry*, p. 210.
[46] Maddicott, 'County Community', 43; Carpenter, 'Community', 346.
[47] Above, Chapter 2.

defence by shire, fostering an *esprit de corps* among the local elite and many other Cornishmen besides. Fear of France made this particularly pressing, as the peninsula formed part of the frontline when conflict erupted from 1337 onwards. Every major local office was defined by a county identity and the officials were often Cornishmen, with the sheriff of Cornwall in particular 'a symbol of the shire's identity'.[48] Across the fourteenth century the Crown's increasing governmental demands actually enhanced the institutional significance of the county. In Cornwall, this is best demonstrated by the county bench. From modest beginnings, by the last quarter of the century this tribunal had amassed wide judicial powers, being manned by a considerable number of greater and lesser gentlemen who sat in as many as sixteen different locations across the county.[49] In serving in the sessions of the peace these proprietors acted in one sense as the 'embodiment' of their shire and, along with quarter sessions, such tribunals played a significant role in articulating county sentiment.[50] Fusing the aspirations of traditional powerbrokers and the newly gentrified alike around the county, the expansion of government drew an increasing proportion of the landed elite into the magistracy. Even the peasantry were made aware of the power of this entity when the sheriff undertook his tourn. We see here how, on the one hand, pressure from above helped to forge 'Cornwall' into a collective project, for people acted together in response to government.[51]

On the other hand, 'Cornwall' formed a joint-stock enterprise in which all the peninsula's powerbrokers held a stake. At the core of this group stood the shire establishment of leading local lineages, known as the *buzones* in the thirteenth century, who took the 'lion's share' of local office.[52] The generation to generation service of these knightly dynasties fostered a long-established social solidarity, a 'backbone' of personnel in the county and an outlook both within these families and without which saw familial might and shire service as intertwined. While extinctions and 'new blood' prevented these proprietors achieving an absolute monopoly, many dynasties can be found holding office throughout the century: the Arundells, Bevilles, Bodrugans, Botreauxs, Carminows, l'Ercedeknes, Peverells, Reskymers, Sergeauxs, Trenewiths and Trevarthians.[53] Local service was a matter of duty, a *cursus honorum*, with offices much sought after; there is little evidence of eligible gentlemen taking measures to avoid service, the Crown only granting six exemptions between

---

[48] Harriss, *Shaping the Nation*, p. 164.
[49] Tyldesley, 'Local Communities', pp. 75–76; for office-holding solidarities, Bennett, *Cheshire and Lancashire*, pp. 21–40; Coss, *English Gentry*, p. 210.
[50] Walker, *Political Culture*, pp. 72, 94.
[51] Cf. Reynolds, *Kingdoms*, pp. 229, 244, 319.
[52] Walker, *Political Culture*, p. 71.
[53] Cf. Saul, *Gloucestershire*, pp. 160–161.

1295 and 1405.[54] Service of this kind extended in time a commonalty anchored in place, tying together gentry and county identity.

Considering harmonious collectivism alone, however, presents a restricted view of the shire. The county's true strength lay in its quasi-coercive powers. The shire played a powerful role in restraining and attempting to resolve tensions generated by 'a diverse collection of lesser groupings in its midst'.[55] Formalised in the county court as 'the will of the whole "community of the county"', the shire establishment played an important regulatory and mediatory role. To this end, these men brought their moral and practical authority to bear on malefactors and victims alike, with the aim of effecting a settlement. At times physical force might prove necessary, as in 1309, for example, when the conservator of the peace Sir Thomas l'Ercedekne had to employ the structures of the shire to mobilise a 'great *posse*' to rescue the sheriff-steward, who had been besieged by 'divers' stannary-men who sought to murder him.[56] This cohesive and coercive duality was to endow the notion of 'Cornwall' with authority in the minds of its residents.

Yet administrative documents provide few clues to county sentiment; small wonder, considering that the type of material which has survived by no means lends itself to the study of identity. A rare example of a clue in such a document is to be found in the thirteenth century, when the county paid thousands of marks to King John and Henry III for charters securing rights to elect their own sheriff, emphasising the concern felt for local office.[57] In 1302 the county was again to petition the king for the honouring of these charters, Earl Richard and his successors having repudiated the documents.[58] Here we are afforded striking evidence of the collective memory of the county. Equally suggestive is a border dispute between Cornwall and Devon in 1386. After the residents of both counties had complained that 'dissensions' had arisen as the boundary between the two was 'in places not ascertained', the government appointed a commission to determine the county's 'metes and bounds'.[59]

Some twenty-six surviving petitions from the 'Commons of Cornwall' provide the strongest evidence for county identity.[60] Seeking to defend the peninsula's collective concerns, supplications of this sort claimed that the 'people of Cornwall' would be destroyed unless the government embarked on reform. Although these petitions may actually represent sectional inter-

---

[54] *CPR 1330–1334*, 456; *CPR 1334–1338*, 169; *CPR 1340–1343*, 44; *CPR 1345–1348*, 82; *CPR 1354–1358*, 141; *CPR 1391–1396*, 187; Saul, *Gloucestershire*, p. 150.
[55] Walker, *Political Culture*, p. 74.
[56] *CPR 1307–1313*, 173.
[57] Page, 'Barons' War', 22, 27.
[58] SC8/323/E562.
[59] *CPR 1385–1389*, 255.
[60] For example, *PROME*, v, 347; *PROME*, vi, 89–90; SC8/102/5080.

ests, their phrasing leaves little doubt that the county existed in the minds of contemporaries.[61] Numerous petitions tell us about 'those political issues that still tended to unite, rather than divide' and show that the shire elite 'were thinking and acting precisely in these county terms'.[62] It followed that the county was a unit of both collective government and shared grievance. Writing in the fourteenth century, John Trevisa, the Cornish-born translator of Ranulph Higden's *Polychronicon*, stated overtly that 'Cornewayle is a schere of Engelond'.[63] His writings reiterate the substance of the county and demonstrate the way in which contemporaries thought in terms of shires. Founded in part on the sheer antiquity of its origins and diversity of functions, the county resonated with its inhabitants.

The notion of 'Cornwall' was rendered yet more coherent by the absence of many private franchises within its midst. Indeed, the one significant franchise which operated in the county, namely the earldom – later the duchy of Cornwall – actually reinforced the county identity by overlapping with it. When the Black Prince journeyed to the peninsula in 1354, for example, he was met at the county border by the local landholder John Killigrew who, 'by custom', had to 'carry with the prince at the prince's entry into Cornewaille'.[64] Killigrew's duties marked the county's symbolic submission to its lord and master. All the inhabitants of Cornwall owed homage and fealty to the earl-duke, their feudal lord. With rights over stannary, hundredal and county court jurisdictions, along with the shrievalty itself, the earl-duke's power was commanding. At the same time, however, he stood responsible for the good condition of all in Cornwall, with duke and duchy mutually dependent.

While liberty, lordship and community did not overlap as fully in Cornwall as in the marcher lordships of Wales for example, the earldom-duchy further enhanced county solidarities.[65] Lordly influence empowered the county court, which was overseen by both the king and earl-duke, rendering it a more important arbiter of justice and perhaps resulting in it serving as an embryonic

---

[61] Coss, *English Gentry*, p. 212; Cf. Walker, *Political Culture*, p. 73.
[62] W. M. Ormrod, 'Murmur, Clamour and Noise: Voicing Complaint and Remedy in Petitions to the English Crown, c. 1300–c. 1460', in *Medieval Petitions: Grace and Grievance*, ed. W. M. Ormrod, G. Dodd and A. Musson (York, 2009), pp. 135–155 at 155; G. Dodd, *Justice and Grace: Private Petitioning and the English Parliament in the Late Middle Ages* (Oxford, 2007), pp. 254–266 at 266.
[63] J. Trevisa, trans., *Polychronicon Ranulphi Higden…*, ed. C. Babington and J. A. Lumby, 9 vols, Rolls Series (London, 1865–86), ii, p. 91; J. Beale, 'Mapping Identity in John Trevisa's English *Polychronicon*: Chester, Cornwall and the Translation of English National History', *Fourteenth Century England, III*, ed. W. M. Ormrod (Woodbridge, 2004), pp. 67–82 at 72.
[64] *RBP*, ii, 69.
[65] Stringer, 'Liberties and Communities', pp. 26–27; Davies, *March of Wales*, pp. 220–221.

parliament. As it met regularly in the 'duchy palace', the court allowed for an initial airing of complaints that could, if necessary, be referred to parliament proper. Providing a powerful selection of posts which along with the offices of the shire were essential to county governance, the lordship extended the local *cursus honorum*. Until 1376 the shrievalty and stewardship actually remained fused, with the men who held this combined post standing out as the personification of the county-franchise itself. Magnifying the importance of these offices, the earl-duke's perennial absenteeism heightened lordly dependence on these positions. Such was their prominence in Cornish life that the officials themselves appeared as characters in the 1504 Cornish-language play *Beunans Meriasek*, with the 'duke's steward' informing and advising his master about the peninsula.[66] Exercised on a territorial basis, partly through the shire's structures, comital-ducal might rendered the notion of Cornwall yet more powerful.

Physical manifestations of comital-ducal authority might also prove significant. Castles, parks, mills and hedges were all planted on the Cornish landscape, serving as perpetual and palpable reminders of the county's lordly connections.[67] Standing as material testament to lordly eminence in the county, the physical apparatus of the earldom-duchy's power was of great importance. A large complex, the 'duchy palace' in Lostwithiel served as the lordship's institutional heart; and towering over the borough, set within a diadem of seigniorial parkland, loomed Restormel Castle, the grandest in the peninsula and home to the earl-duke's steward. Every Easter the burgesses of Lostwithiel staged an elaborate pageant, selecting one of their number to play the part of duke and robing him in majesty 'to sett fourth the Royaltyes of *Cornwall*, and the honor of that Dukedome'.[68]

While the architectural setting of the earldom-duchy emerges as grand and imposing, it was actually fused with the physical structures of the shire, for the county court regularly met in the great hall within the 'duchy palace'.[69] Shire and franchise shared the most important administrative space west of the Tamar, the grandest building in Cornwall, a bond between them immortalised in stone. Playing an important role in the county's judicial and tinning affairs too, the 'duchy palace' often played host to visiting royal justices while serving as the centre of stannary administration. Within the imposing

---

[66] *Beunans Meriasek: The Life of St Meriasek, Bishop and Confessor*, trans. W. Stokes (London, 1872), lines 2224–2229.
[67] *RESDCornwall*, passim.; Cf. Liddy, *Durham*, pp. 17–19, 233–234
[68] J. Norden, *A Topographical and Historical Description of Cornwall* (London, 1728), p. 41.
[69] CS, 4–5; Pounds, 'Duchy Palace'; *HOP*, i, 311; Cf. A. Musson, 'Court Venues and the Politics of Justice', *Fourteenth Century England, V*, ed. N. Saul (Woodbridge, 2008), pp. 161–177.

structure royal, lordly and local power and personnel were fused together, to the mutual benefit of all.[70] Housing many documents relating to the shire, the earldom-duchy and perhaps even private muniments, this complex was also a repository of shared Cornish memory.[71] All the county's residents appreciated its significance, with the burgesses of Lostwithiel in 1315 claiming of their town and the 'duchy palace' that:

> because the said town was in the middle of the country, earl Edmund had a large hall provided and built at great expense, to be used to hold the county courts, and for the assemblies of people coming and repairing to the same town, and likewise another great building to store the tin coming from the mines in Cornwall, and to be weighed and coined in the said building there.[72]

The 'duchy palace' was the physical embodiment of shire-franchisal power, of 'Cornwall' itself.

In the light of all this, it is unsurprising that seigniorial power can be shown to have influenced Cornish identities. To the Black Prince, for example, 'the county of Cornwall' and 'his duchy of Cornwall' were one and the same.[73] A petition to Edward III's parliament of 1376 from the *commune del counte de Cornewaylle* was followed just two years later by another one to Richard II's – who directly held Cornwall – from *voz communes de duche de Cornewaill*.[74] So it was that the county commonalty and seigniorial government were strikingly interdependent. A sense of place underpinned both, with the petition in the latter year claiming that the French and Spanish threatened to 'return next season to the said duchy... and seize and claim the said land as their own'. In *Beunans Meriasek* we find the duke's character parading in splendour while proclaiming:

I am duke in all Cornwall	*Me yv duk in oll kernow*
as was my father	*indella ytho ov thays*
and high lord in the land	*hag vhel arluth in pov*
from Tamar to Land's End.	*a tamer the pen an vlays*[75]

For all the earl-duke's authority, however, seigniorial power could both wax and wane depending on the abilities of the particular lord. Tensions could also erupt between the lordship and the commonalty. It is illustrative of this that in 1347 'the people of the duchy' complained that there were more 'under-bailiffs

[70] Cf. Musson, 'Court Venues', 169, 177; it sometimes required repair, *RBP*, ii, 18.
[71] *RBP*, ii, 48–49.
[72] *PROME*, iii, 69–71.
[73] For example, *RBP*, ii, 9, 16, 18, 49.
[74] *PROME*, v, 347; *PROME*, vi, 89–90.
[75] *Beunans Meriasek*, lines 2205–2208; correspondence with Oliver Padel, 29 January 2016.

and others' who meddled in the prince's name than necessary.[76] No model of perpetual acrimony locally is sustainable, however, as the commonalty often called on the intervention of their lordly master, in relation to matters varying from the conduct of his officials to storm damage. Individual Cornish petitioners, from leading gentlemen such as Sir John l'Ercedekne right down to 'poor liege tinners' including John Skeweyk, also requested that the earl-duke personally intercede on their behalf.[77] Even Cornish prayers helped propagate belief in lordly power, for hermits, friars, canons, parishioners and castle chaplains all requested divine intercession for the soul and success of earl-dukes past and present.[78] The underlying strength of lordship cannot be doubted, nor can the shared commitment of the Cornish elite and county magnates to the fused structures of shire and franchise.

Rendering this indissoluble franchise-shire all the more potent was the nature of Cornish society itself. The absence of any great boroughs or cities in the peninsula, and the resultant absence of urban economic and political muscle, created a vacuum which was filled by the institutions of lordship and county. Magnate absenteeism and the modest means of the Cornish gentry also proved significant, as even the greatest men in fourteenth-century Cornwall enjoyed yearly incomes of no greater than £100. Since proprietors found themselves unable to dominate the county with influence derived from landed wealth alone, it was inevitable that local office held a more important key to power in the peninsula. This lack of 'distance' between their grandest members and those of minor means rendered the Cornish elite a homogeneous group by influence, wealth and outlook. Indeed, the shared foundations of their landed, maritime and tinning prosperity fostered formidable collective interests in the defence of which they often mobilised their county-franchise.[79]

However, this fairly flattened social pyramid was to result in scions of leading local lineages trying to differentiate themselves from petty gentlemen. As the 'shire was the arena where local status was confirmed and augmented', so this too strengthened the county's structures. For the shire establishment, their ability to 'bear the rule' of the county proved their credentials, while for lesser gentlemen involvement in county administration marked them out as superior to the mere parish gentry.[80] The Black Prince's letters to Sir John Arundell and Sir John Trevaignon informing them that their conduct was unacceptable for men 'of your order' demonstrate the way in which prominent proprietors were expected to lead local society, even if they fell short of this ideal. Local office was

---

[76] *RBP*, i, 151.
[77] *RBP*, ii, 19, 28–29; below, pp. 178, 212–213.
[78] Worcestre, *Itineraries*, pp. 84–87, 92–93; *RBP*, ii, 38, 75, 185, 194; *Reg.Grandisson*, ii, 1173, 1190.
[79] For example, *PROME*, vii, 217–218, 269–270.
[80] Walker, *Political Culture*, p. 75.

essential to the maintenance of both the commonweal and the gentry's collective authority, something suggested by the fact that in 1340 the commonalty of Cornwall requested that Edward III launch an investigation after malefactors had prevented Sir Ralph Bloyou 'doing what pertained to his office' as keeper of the peace.[81] Since the great majority of Cornwall's leading dynasties only held land in the peninsula, with their properties spread widely across the county, these folk enjoyed a feeling of traditional 'place' in Cornish affairs.[82]

In medieval England, where public and private authority were often fused together, these administrative functions were entwined with lateral bonds of neighbourliness, kinship and association. Such a triumvirate often proved more powerful than government. As Richard Carew's claim that 'all Cornish gentlemen are cousins' certainly had substance, the Cornish cousinage created a web of associations stretching across the county.[83] Although not exclusively confined to the peninsula, these links provided the county with added coherence. There is evidence that many proprietors itinerated around Cornwall, often visiting one another and conversing 'familiarly together', with Lady Joan Arundell receiving a chapel licence in 1339 for her household 'and guests'.[84] Family celebrations and feasts could result in yet more interactions, something suggested by the fact that the Treverbyns were staying with Sir Henry Bodrugan when his son, Otto, was born, while Joan Treviur 'especially' loved the same Otto as her godson.[85] Gentlemen often hunted and hawked together, with Sir Ralph Carminow, while out on a hunt in 1386, even 'pulled over a cliff' to his death 'by a brase of Greyhounds'.[86] Such dangers notwithstanding, these shared pastimes resulted in further interactions and actual friendships.[87] While waiting to embark from Fowey to his family estates in Ireland, for example, Reginald, the fourth son of John, Lord Mohun of Dunster, went hawking to pass the time. He had some luck when he made a kill in the garden of the manor of Hall in Lanteglos-by-Fowey, and in retrieving his prize he by chance met Elizabeth, daughter and heiress of Sir John Fitz William. Elizabeth and Mohun fell in love and were married soon after.[88]

Less romantic although not less significant is the fact that Cornish proprietors are often to be found holding joint assets, regularly witnessing each

---

[81] CPR 1338–1340, 486; Cf. Coss, *English Gentry*, pp. 180, 186–187.
[82] Cf. Wright, *Derbyshire*, pp. 6–7.
[83] Carew, 64r.
[84] Carew, 64v; CRO, AR/27/1.
[85] CIPM, v, 168, proofs of age may be fictitious, but they provide evidence of the type of interactions that were commonplace.
[86] Reg.Brantingham, ii, 627–628, 634; HOP, ii, 489–490.
[87] CIM 1377–1388, 101.
[88] Elliott-Binns, *Medieval Cornwall*, p. 240; the match was unsuccessful; *Reg.Grandisson*, ii, 701–702, 721–722, 727.

other's property transactions and frequently serving each other as feoffees and executors.[89] The county commonalty grew out of these endless informal interactions, much more than it did from all these individuals coming together in one fixed place at one fixed time. When contracting his marriage to Elizabeth Whalesborough in 1452, for example, John Trevelyan was in no doubt that he was organising his personal affairs in the 'shire of Cornwayle'.[90] Office-holding also contributed to this interconnectedness. This was because once an individual had entered into the burden of county administration, he was likely to meet all Cornwall's notables and many more folk besides. Evidently kindred, neighbourliness, office-holding and wealth bound together the shire establishment at the core of the county. All holding a stake in their commonalty, the Cornish gentry had a strong vested interest in the sound administration of their county, their *home*. Even in death these folk remained interlinked, something suggested by the fact that a list of obits celebrated in fourteenth-century Cornwall named nearly every local knightly lineage and many lesser gentlemen besides.[91] Such extended genealogical networks helped to bestow a collective sense of memory and identity on the Cornish elite.

For all the cohesive forces of county society, the gentry were the most fractious part of the local populace, regularly resorting to violent self-help. Although disorder of this sort had the potential to weaken the solidarity of Cornish society, a countervailing influence was provided by the informal ties which held local proprietors together.[92] Max Gluckman has argued that the number and variety of such bonds determined the cohesion of a group as a whole. In Cornwall, these ties stand out as legion. This made it all but impossible for the commonalty to mobilise into two permanently hostile camps, for 'people who are friends on one basis are enemies on another'.[93] With many folk simultaneously 'allies' of both plaintiff and defendant, these cross-ties and divided loyalties exerted great pressure on the protagonists to reach a settlement. 'Peace' involved more violence than we would expect, but the potential for cohesiveness still existed as there was 'peace as well as war in the threat of a feud'.[94]

---

[89] For instance, C131/11/11; C131/215/4; C241/118/288; CRO, AR/4/415; AR/15/1; AR/20/2; AR/20/11; ME/529; *Cornish Wills, passim*.

[90] *Trevelyan Papers*, ed. J. P. Collier et al., Camden Society, o.s. 67, 84 and 105 (London, 1857–72), i, p. 38.

[91] TCO; my thanks to Oliver Padel and Nicholas Orme for their advice about these obits.

[92] M. Gluckman, 'The Peace in the Feud', *Past and Present*, 8 (1955), pp. 1–14; M. Gluckman, *Politics, Law and Ritual in Tribal Society* (Oxford, 1971), pp. 109–116; N. Saul, 'Conflict and Consensus in English Local Society', in *Politics and Crisis in Fourteenth-Century England*, ed. J. Taylor and W. Childs (Gloucester, 1990), pp. 38–58.

[93] Gluckman, 'Peace', 2.

[94] Gluckman, 'Peace', 13.

Paradoxical as it might seem, in one sense disorder encouraged cohesion, in that it forced the commonalty to come together in applying pressure or arbitration for a settlement. It is illustrative of this that in 1402 no fewer than seven proprietors, among them Geoffrey St Aubyn, are found arbitrating a dispute between William and Otto Bodrugan.[95] Back in 1388, Sir Richard Sergeaux and three other gentlemen had even mainprised the prior of St Germans 'that he shall do or procure no hurt or harm' to Oliver Wysa.[96] The structures of the county had a role to play here too. Not only were local offices used corruptly and malevolently, so encouraging disputes, but the county's coercive powers also helped achieve peace by forcing a resolution. We find one case of this sort in 1333, when several Cornish gentlemen investigated the former sheriff-steward Sir John Treiagu for 'oppressions by colour of his office'.[97] Driving both fission and fusion in its society, the shire was rendered all the more important.

When we turn from inter-gentry dealings of this sort to Cornish myths and customs, we find that local legends and traditions provided 'Cornwall' with yet further meaning. Perhaps most significantly, in Geoffrey of Monmouth's mythical twelfth-century history of Britain Corineus, brother in arms of Brutus, the reputed founder of Britain, is credited with establishing Cornwall, 'calling the region of the kingdom which had fallen to his share Cornwall, after the manner of his own name, and the people who lived there he called Cornishmen'.[98] Since this collective origin myth bound people and place together, the Cornish could all claim a common descent from Corineus, their progenitor. Establishing the extent to which courtly pseudo-historical literature shaped the outlook of contemporaries is difficult, but it undoubtedly influenced Johannes de Hauvilla's twelfth-century *Architrenius* (the arch-weeper), a narrative satire in 4,361 lines of Latin hexameter. In this, Hauvilla sought to flatter his Cornish-born patron, a certain Walter of Coutances, who 'like spring itself, dispels the winter, Walter, in whom flourishing Cornwall makes good the loss of Troy'.[99] Hauvilla also wrote of how King Arthur and Sir Gawain had fought the forces of Avarice, claiming that 'noble Cornwall traces its ancestry to the blood of the Phrygians'.[100]

Yet Geoffrey of Monmouth's contribution to Cornish sentiment, whether intentional or not, went far beyond this foundation myth. As the county and its fictional Cornish dukes played an important role in the *Historia*, Monmouth

---

[95] CRO, ME/580.
[96] *CCR 1385–1389*, 490.
[97] *CPR 1330–1334*, 440.
[98] G. of Monmouth, *The History of the Kings of Britain*, trans. L. Thorpe (London, 1966), p. 72; below, pp. 86–88.
[99] J. de Hauvilla, *Architrenius*, trans. and ed. W. Wetherbee, Cambridge Medieval Classics 3 (Cambridge, 1994), ix–xi, book 1 lines 135–136.
[100] Hauvilla, *Architrenius*, book 5, lines 385–393, 430–431.

afforded Cornwall a place of significance, subtle though it was, with most of the 'action' taking place elsewhere, that many medieval writers were to identify.[101] Enjoying great popularity, stories of this sort circulated widely and evolved with time. It seems that they influenced men as varied John Trevisa in the fourteenth century, William Worcestre in the fifteenth and Richard Carew in the sixteenth; these 'ancient' dukes even appeared in some Cornish saints' lives, among them that of St Mylor, supposedly the 'only sonn' of Duke Melianus of Cornwall.[102] Here especially we see how the duchy's actual history became seamlessly fused with its fictional past, deftly grafting the lordship onto Cornwall and vesting the shire-franchise with greater legitimacy. Richard Carew was to write that *'Cornwall,* as an entire state, hath at divers times enjoyed sundry titles, of a Kingdome, Principality, Duchy, and Earldrome', being the 'farthest shire of England westwards'.[103] Tintagel's stony bulk loomed as monumental testament to this illustrious past.

It was King Arthur himself, however, who stood out as the legendary figure who most caught the Cornish imagination. Although Arthur was a pan-Brittonic hero, Geoffrey of Monmouth had both his conception and his death as occurring in Cornwall and the far south west was referred to as *terra Arturi*.[104] There is reason to suppose that there was widespread Cornish belief in the historical reality of Arthur, an outlook increasingly influenced by international literary culture. For example, while contesting a series of flytings, an exchange of insults in verse, with Master Henry d'Avranches in the mid-thirteenth century, Michael of Cornwall, sometimes known as Michael Blaunpayn, claimed that 'King Arthur was the first of our Cornishmen', honouring Cornwall as invincible.[105] Another of the county's sons, Richard Carew, was to write that Arthur was 'a Cornishman by

---

[101] O. J. Padel, 'Geoffrey of Monmouth and Cornwall', *Cambridge Medieval Celtic Studies*, 8 (1984), pp. 1–28; J. Gillingham, *The English in the Twelfth Century: Imperialism, National Identity and Political Values* (Woodbridge, 2000), pp. 19–39.

[102] Trevisa, trans., *Polychronicon*, v, pp. 337–339; Worcestre, *Itineraries*, pp. 20–21, 94–95; *Carew*, 76v–79r; N. Roscarrock, *Nicholas Roscarrock's Lives of the Saints: Devon and Cornwall*, ed. N. Orme, DCRS, n.s. 35 (Exeter, 1992), p. 88.

[103] *Carew*, 76v, 1r.

[104] *De Miraculis Sanctae Mariae Laudunensis*, ii, 15–16, ed. J. P. Migne, *Patrologia Latina*, 156 (1880), cols. 961–1018 at 983; O. J. Padel, 'The Nature of Arthur', *Cambrian Medieval Celtic Studies*, 27 (1994), pp. 1–31 at 5; S. M. Pearce, 'The Cornish Elements in the Arthurian Tradition', *Folklore*, 85 (1974), pp. 145–163; J. Wood, 'The Arthurian Legend in Scotland and Cornwall', in *A Companion to Arthurian Literature*, ed. H. Fulton (Oxford, 2009), pp. 102–116.

[105] 'Eine mittellateinishe Dichterfehde: *Versus Michaelis Cornubiensis contra Henricum Abrincensem*', ed. A. Hilka, in *Mittelalterliche Handschriften: Festgabe zum 60. Geburtstag von Hermann Degering*, ed. A. Bömer and J. Kirchner (Leipzig, 1926), pp. 123–154, line 207; A. G. Rigg, *A History of Anglo-Latin Literature 1066–1422* (Cambridge, 1992), pp. 193–198.

birth, a king of Britaine by succession', and in 1478 William Worcestre had recorded Arthur's conception in Tintagel and the slaying in Castle-an-Dinas of Cadoc, duke of Cornwall and husband of 'the mother of Arthur'.[106] Fighting his last great battle beside the 'river Camblan' in Cornwall, a site long identified as the river Camel, Arthur was 'mortally wounded' there and handed over 'the crown of Britain' to his cousin, Constantine, son of duke Cadoc of Cornwall.[107] In the sixteenth century, John Leland recorded that 'by this ryver Arturte fowght his last feld, yn token wherof the people fynd there yn plowyng bones and harneys'.[108]

More pertinently, in the fourteenth century when the Carminows discovered that they bore the same arms as the Scropes, in the resulting case the Carminows claimed that they had borne them 'since the time of King Arthur' (*depuis le temps de roy Arthur*) and that Cornwall formed 'a large land long ago bearing the name of a kingdom' (*un grosse terre et jadys portant le noun dune roialme*).[109] Even John Trevisa believed in this legendary king, leaping to his defence in the face of Ranulph Higden's questioning of Monmouth's *Historia*: 'meny noble nacious speketh of Arthur and his nobile dedes', although 'it may wel be that Arthur is ofte overpreysed, and so beeth meny othere'.[110] Identifying with these stories, Trevisa sought to defend Merlin from claims that he had been fathered by an incubus by emphasising the fact that as he had died, and as death could not slay fiends, 'Merlyn was ergo no gobelyn'.[111]

Merlin was proud of his links with Cornwall in the *Historia*, prophesising that although the 'Red Dragon' of the Britons would be overcome by the 'White Dragon' of the Saxons, 'the Boar of Cornwall' would bring 'relief from these invaders'.[112] Probably composed in the 1150s, John of Cornwall's *Prophesy of Merlin* reworked this prophesy into Latin hexameters and provided an extended marginal commentary containing a few Cornish phrases and names.[113] At the

---

[106] *Carew*, 61v; Worcestre, *Itineraries*, pp. 20–21, 94–95.
[107] G. of Monmouth, *Kings of Britain*, pp. 259–261; but see, A. Breeze, 'The Battle of Camlan and Camelford, Cornwall', *Arthuriana*, 15 (2005), pp. 75–90.
[108] Leland, *Itinerary*, i, p. 314.
[109] *De Controversia in Curia Militari inter Ricardum le Scrope et Robertum Grosvenor...*, ed. N. H. Nicolas, 2 vols (London, 1832), i, pp. 50, 214.
[110] Trevisa, trans., *Polychronicon*, v, p. 339; Beale, 'Mapping Identity', pp. 78–81.
[111] Merlin Ambrosius, Trevisa, trans., *Polychronicon*, i, p. 421.
[112] G. of Monmouth, *Kings of Britain*, p. 171; cf. O. J. Padel, 'Geoffrey of Monmouth and the Development of the Merlin Legend', *Cambrian Medieval Celtic Studies*, 51 (2006), pp. 37–65.
[113] O. J. Padel, 'Evidence for Oral Tales in Medieval Cornwall', *Studia Celtica*, 40 (2006), pp. 127–153 at 147–148; M. J. Curley, 'A New Edition of John of Cornwall's *Prophetia Merlini*', *Speculum*, 57 (1982), pp. 217–249.

other end of our period Richard Carew recorded a Cornish-language prophesy about a Spanish raid in 1595 on Penzance and its environs:

| Those who shall land upon Merlin's Rock | *Ewra teyre awar meane Merlyn* |
| Who shall burn Paul, Penzance, and Newlyn. | *Ara lesky Pawle Pensanz ha Newlyn*.[114] |

This 'rock' was at Mousehole, with the Cornish supposedly putting up little resistance as they believed the sacking pre-ordained. Written accounts of Arthur's life and Merlin's magic can be shown to have to circulated in fourteenth- and fifteenth-century Cornwall, with Sir Ranulph Blanchminster in 1348 bequeathing to Alice Huish a copy of the Brut Chronicle containing the mythical Arthur story.[115] Bodmin friary also held a copy of the 'ancient chronicles of the Britons in French', recounting Arthur's Cornish ancestry and Corineus' founding of the county.[116] At the same time the friars celebrated obits for dozens of local proprietors, tying together the memory of all these gentle and pseudo-historical folk.

Arthurian legend proved particularly powerful in Cornwall as these courtly romances interlocked with oral folkloric traditions and local landmarks. On Goss Moor, for example, one rock was said to show the hoofprints of his horse, while a nearby megalith bore the name Arthur's Quoit, linking this 'huge stone with Arthur's gigantic strength'.[117] Another great rock, King Arthur's Bed on Bodmin Moor, supposedly bore the indentation that he had created when he had slept there during a hunt.[118] Uniquely in the western canon, Arthur appeared as a character in a fifteenth-century Cornish-language drama about the life of St Kea, proclaiming:

Peace! Since I command wild and tame,	*Peysyth yhot wyld and tam*
man and four-footed beast,	*den ha best peswar trosak*
I say Arthur is my name,	*I say Arthur is my nam*
a great and powerful king	*myghtern bras ha galosak*
and a conqueror.	*ha conquerior*.[119]

Wielding Excalibur and having St Kea mediate between him, Mordred and Guinevere, Arthur was presented in the play as a 'mild and generous' king who was the 'best hero who ever came from Cornwall', unforgettable until

---

[114] *Carew*, 158v–159r; Padel, 'Oral Tales', 146.
[115] *Cornish Wills*, 28.
[116] Worcestre, *Itineraries*, pp. 92–97.
[117] Padel, 'Oral Tales', 132; Padel, 'Arthur', 26–29.
[118] Padel, 'Oral Tales', 132.
[119] *Bewnans Ke, The Life of St Kea: A Critical Edition with Translation*, ed. G. Thomas and N. Williams (Exeter, 2007), lines 1397–1401.

doomsday itself.[120] Combined with its complex staging, this drama presented a powerful image of King Arthur the Cornishman.[121]

It seems that stories about Arthur circulated widely to the west of the Tamar. According to Nicholas Roscarrock, writing in c. 1600 what 'olde people speaking by tradition doe report', Arthur had been the godfather of St Endellion and had slayed a local lord who had killed the saint's cow, although St Endellion later 'miraculously revived' the man.[122] Back in 1113 a conversation had arisen in Bodmin between some visiting canons of Laon and a Cornishman over whether or not Arthur had died. The Cornishman maintained that he was alive while the Frenchmen unwisely scoffed at the suggestion, resulting in a near riot *cum armis*.[123] All this points to the existence of a county-wide belief in a Cornish King Arthur. By the later middle ages, however, Arthurian lore had declined into 'an impoverished allusion' in Cornwall, sustained by local landmarks and international literary culture.[124] Nonetheless, belief in the legend of this most illustrious monarch provided the Cornish with a unifying figure, a shared hero and a powerful imagined solidarity. A 1428 copy of the *Brut* even claimed that the 'Cornysch seyeth thus, "that [Arthur] leuyth... And schall' come & be a kyng again"', although Trevisa believed that 'mad men' told this 'magel tale'.[125]

These many Arthurian stories were by no means the only legends to circulate in the peninsula. Although *Beunans Meriasek* placed the castles of the duke of Cornwall at Tintagel and Castle-an-Dinas, these fortresses were as much connected with King Mark and the Tristan Stories as with King Arthur.[126] Legend had it that Mark, 'king of Cornwall and England', held court at Tintagel, and the county formed the backdrop to the story of Tristan and Iseult's love affair. Perhaps originating from the far south west, the Tristan stories stand out as 'Cornwall's most significant, and best-known, gift to the literary world' – it was the Cornish versions of the Tristan stories that provided the basis on which

---

[120] *Bewnans Ke*, lines 1336–1390, 1569, 1657–1659, 1914–1915, 2487, 2650, 3268–3269; O. J. Padel, 'Christianity in Medieval Cornwall: Celtic Aspects', in N. Orme, *Victoria History of the County of Cornwall, II, Religious History to 1560* (Woodbridge, 2010), pp. 110–125 at 114.

[121] Cf. *Records of Early English Drama: Cornwall*, ed. S. L. Joyce and E. S. Newlyn (Toronto, 1999); A. J. Fletcher, 'The Staging of the Middle Cornish Play *Bewnans Ke* ('The Life of St Kea')', *Yearbook of English Studies*, 43 (2013), pp. 165–173.

[122] Roscarrock, *Lives of the Saints*, p. 71.

[123] *Sanctae Mariae*, col. 983.

[124] Padel, 'Oral Tales', 152.

[125] *Arthur: A Short Sketch of his Life and History in English Verse*, ed. F. J. Furnivall, EETS, o.s. 2 (London, 1864), p. 19; Trevisa, trans., *Polychronicon*, v, p. 339.

[126] *Beunans Meriasek*, lines 2209–2215; O. J. Padel, 'The Cornish Background of the Tristan Stories', *Cambridge Medieval Celtic Studies*, 1 (1981), pp. 53–81 at 71–72.

the Continental romancers built their own narratives.[127] The county's folklore was rich indeed, and William Worcestre recorded that at St Michael's Mount:

> An appearance of St Michael at the Mountain tomb, formerly called the Hoar Rock in the Wood; and there were both woods and meadows and ploughland between the said mount and the Scilly Islands and 140 parish churches were drowned between the mount and Scilly.[128]

Also recounting this myth, John Leland noted that the sea had 'devourid' these lands, with Richard Carew and John Norden asserting that this sunken realm was none other than Lyonesse, a name derived from the Tristan legend.[129] The Cornish families of Trevelyan and Vyvyan actually claimed descent from a lord who had escaped from this inundated land with the aid of his horse swimming him to safety. Both dynasties chose to commemorate this event on their armorial bearings, while a Vyvyan family tradition has it that 'for many centuries a white horse was kept in the stables, saddled and ready for just such another emergency'.[130] Another legend had it that the city of Langarrow or Langona, once the largest and richest in England, had stood between Gannell and Perranporth until it was smothered by wind-blown sand during a storm that God had sent as punishment for its sins.[131] All these stories helped to propagate a notion of Cornwall, with its extraordinary past.

Naturally enough, the county's linguistic and cultural distinctiveness enhanced its collective group identity. The Cornish language, despite being spoken in only half the county by the fourteenth century, marked the peninsula out as unique in England. Leading gentlemen were undoubtedly alive to the distinctiveness of their shire, with some families, among them the Carminows and Reskymers, employing Cornish in their family mottos.[132] Others employed canting heraldry, as did the Arundells for example, who included a depiction of a wolf on their seal, punning on the name of their manor of Trembleath, 'the farmstead of the wolf'.[133] Since many gentry families enjoyed toponymic surnames, in some measure Cornish naming practices contributed to the marriage of people and place: 'By *Tre*, *Pol*, and *Pen*, You shall know

---

[127] Padel, 'Tristan Stories', 80.
[128] Worcestre, *Itineraries*, pp. 98–99.
[129] Leland, *Itinerary*, i, pp. 189, 320; *Carew*, 3r; Norden, *Description of Cornwall*, p. 9; Padel, 'Oral Tales', 141–142.
[130] Padel, 'Oral Tales', 139–141.
[131] Padel, 'Oral Tales', 141.
[132] R. M. Nance, 'Cornish Family Mottoes', *Old Cornwall*, 1, i (1925), pp. 18–21; *idem.*, iii (1926), p. 29; *idem.*, iv (1926), pp. 26–27; *idem.*, vii (1928), pp. 27–28.
[133] CRO, AR/20/3; AR/20/7; AR/20/18, my thanks to Oliver Padel for these references; D. E. Ivall, *Cornish Heraldry and Symbolism* (Perranwell, 1987), pp. 72–75.

the *Cornishmen*'.[134] Many local customs reinforced this picture, with a specific Cornish husbandman way of riding, numerous parcels of land measured in Cornish acres and coarse grains grown on these that were used to brew a distinctive 'thycke' ale 'lyke wash as pygges had wrestled dryn'.[135] While the division between the Cornish gentry and the peasantry stood out as a chasm, as it did in every shire for that matter, gentry-distinctiveness and the distinctiveness of the folk whom they governed bolstered belief in 'Cornwall'.

Closely allied to these local practices were the myriad cults of saints in the county. Although Bishop Grandisson thought little of these people, the saints stand out as a distinctly Cornish phenomenon. Proprietors attended and presented to churches dedicated to them, and a remarkable tenth of these sacred sites contained the body of its saint.[136] Often joining these holy men and women in death, the elite too were buried in these churches and in 1433 Sir John Arundell of Lanherne bequeathed 40s. 'to the parishioners of Perranzabuloe to enclose the head of St Piran honourably'.[137] Cornish 'relickes', after all, 'might haue power' so that Bodmin Priory kept long calendars of these saints' holy days.[138] Keeping a record of St Illogan's burial in Illogan Church, Truro Friary at the same time commemorated the deaths of numerous Cornish proprietors.[139] All these gentle and holy folk were united in death west of the Tamar.

With churches, crosses and holy wells strewn across the county, everywhere reminders of Cornwall's saints punctuated the landscape. In St Mawes, for example, the residents regarded the well of St Mawes and 'a Seat of hard stoane which the inhabitan*tes* called St Mawes chayre, in which hee vsed to sitt' as part of the physical fabric of their lives.[140] In much the same way, in 1448 Reginald Mertherderwa of Camborne left money for the erection of nine new stone crosses in his natal parish 'where the bodies of the dead being carried to burial are laid down for prayers'.[141] The county's many holy wells also formed physical manifestations of saintly power, with St Madron for example believed to perform miracles at his, especially on the feast of Corpus Christi.[142] As Oliver Padel has written, 'the physical geography of early Christianity caused

---

[134] *Carew*, 54v–55r; Fox and Padel, *Arundells of Lanherne*, pp. cxxiv–cxxxvii; Chynoweth, *Tudor Cornwall*, pp. 56–61.

[135] *Carew*, 36r, 66v; CRO, AR/3/5; AR/1/192; A. Boorde, *The First Boke of the Introduction of Knowledge*, ed. F. J. Furnivall, EETS, extra series 10 (London, 1870), pp. 122–123.

[136] *Reg.Grandisson*, i, 585; ii, 819; N. Orme, *The Saints of Cornwall* (Oxford, 2000); Padel, 'Christianity', pp. 111–112.

[137] *Cornish Wills*, 67

[138] Roscarrock, *Lives of the Saints*, pp. 54, 64; Worcestre, *Itineraries*, pp. 86–89.

[139] Worcestre, *Itineraries*, pp. 98–99.

[140] Roscarrock, *Lives of the Saints*, p. 87.

[141] *Cornish Wills*, 77.

[142] Roscarrock, *Lives of the Saints*, p. 86.

the names of many of the obscure saints to become fixed in the later patterns of parishes and settlements'.[143]

While no all-powerful saint oversaw the county, no equal of St Cuthbert and the *Haliwerfolc* in Durham, these holy men and women served as a sacred source of Cornish identity.[144] It is illustrative of this that St Hermes or St Erme was believed to have been a *confessor gentis de Cornubia*, while St Piran held the office of *episcopus de Cornubia*.[145] In some measure, then, Cornwall was the land of the saints. Using the county as a point of reference, the Cornish-language *Ordinalia* had a Marazion smith who was forging nails for the Cross itself employ the rhetorical flourish:

I do not know a smith in all Cornwall	*ny won gof yn ol kernow*
who may blow with bellows,	*a whytho gans mygenow*
certainly, any better!	*certan byth wel!*[146]

Combined with ancient hill forts, inscribed stones and megaliths, along with more recent memorials and crosses, these ageless stories and markers served as a powerful reminder of Cornwall's different past and distinctive present. With its collective mythology, hagiography and customs, this romantic Cornwall of imagination had true meaning to its inhabitants.

Woven within the mutually supporting structures of shire and franchise was the world of imagination, a sense of shared past and present that enhanced county sentiment. Forming no mere administrative division, 'Cornwall' enjoyed an historic identity of its own that helped it resonate with the local gentry. Such an entity was never perfectly crystalline in its form, however, for the local elite varyingly termed it a *pays*, *terre*, *counte*, *schere* and *duche*, with these proprietors speaking at certain times for the *hominibus*, *gentz*, *bones gentz*, *commonalty* and *communes* of Cornwall.[147] A notion of the county nonetheless existed, at the core of which stood the local gentry and lordly officials who found identity and employment in its structures.

Although we should favour the idea of a commonalty of Cornwall, this entity was by no means static. On the contrary, Simon Walker has argued for the three-stage development of 'county communities' in England. The first ran from c. 1300–50, when the shire gained both definition and authority by its acquisition of a range of new administrative powers. Following this came

---

[143] Padel, 'Christianity', p. 125.
[144] Cf. Liddy, *Durham*, chapter 5; Rubin, 'Identities', pp. 405–406.
[145] Worcestre, *Itineraries*, pp. 82, 102.
[146] *Cornish Drama*, PC, lines 2712–2714; correspondence with Oliver Padel, 2 February 2016.
[147] *PROME*, v, 347; *PROME*, vi, 89–90; *PROME*, iii, 100; *inter Ricardum le Scrope et Robertum Grosvenor*, i, p. 214; Trevisa, trans., *Polychronicon*, ii, p. 91; SC8/102/5080; CPR 1338–1340, 486.

a 'social phase' from c. 1350–1430, in which high levels of mortality enabled some families to accumulate sufficient landed wealth to establish themselves as the undisputed leaders of the county. In the final stage from c. 1430, pressure from the polarisation of national politics resulted in shires emphasising their independence and neutrality.[148] For Cornwall, however, a somewhat different picture emerges. Throughout the later middle ages, the lordship of the earl-duke provided coherence of a slightly different form in the county. As the person of the lord himself and the institutions of his rulership furnished an additional framework which helped the county to cohere, so the overlap of shire and franchise proved mutually supporting in the peninsula.

As a result of these many strands of Cornishness, we may well wonder if 'Cornwall' exercised a stronger pull on the sentiments of its residents than any other shire. Even in the far south west, however, the county commonalty remained only one rung on a hierarchy of associations. Many wider and narrower calls were made on the loyalties of the local elite, and while occasional tensions could erupt between each one, for a great part of the time they all existed harmoniously. It follows that layered identity perhaps holds the key to an understanding of this complex subject. A whole array of identities could co-exist, with different ones coming to the fore at different times and locations.[149] While individual sentiment stood at the core of all self-perceptions, this quickly faded into one's kindred, lineage and social network. It is clear that gentry identity in particular was founded on a territorial and collective identity, in our case revolving around the county.[150] Since the phrasing of petitions suggests that 'the shire existed in the minds of contemporaries', the notion of Cornwall emerged most clearly when the county perceived itself as threatened.[151] Such an entity could weigh on the considerations of local proprietors in many circumstances, however, as for example in 1402, when William Brewer chose to define himself as a 'Cornyshman' in London, rather than adopting the more common label 'of Cornwall'.[152] Even when these many nested strands of identity were in mutual opposition, tensions between each served to sharpen the notion of the whole and its constituent parts.

Perceiving neither themselves nor their county as separate from the body politic, the Cornish gentry also viewed themselves simultaneously as English. This point is evident from the twenty-four surviving petitions that they submitted to the parliamentary Commons, in which the 'county of Cornwall' was to make its voice heard. Those who drafted these petitions perceived Cornwall

---

[148] Walker, *Political Culture*, pp. 75–77.
[149] Cf. Rubin, 'Identities', pp. 383, 390–391, 410.
[150] Cf. Coss, *English Gentry*, p. 202.
[151] Coss, *English Gentry*, p. 212; Rubin, 'Identities', p. 410.
[152] *CCR 1402–1405*, 362.

as a whole, one forming an essential part of the wider realm. Urban members viewed the county as holding a place in England too, while in 1391 the parliamentary Commons stated unequivocally that 'in Cornwall there accrues a great commodity of the kingdom of England, that is tin' (*en le conte de Cornewaille crest un grant commodite du roialme d'Engleterre, ceo est esteem*).[153] Evidently the belief that Cornwall had long ago formed a kingdom unto itself in no way detracted from its integration into fourteenth-century England, for the Cornish gentry believed that they were essential partners in government with the Crown, a charmed circle.

A proud Cornishman, it was John Trevisa who most clearly articulated this opinion. In one of his longest interpolations in the *Polychronicon*, he wrote that Cornwall formed 'oon of the chief parties of this Bretayne', which consisted of England, Wales and Scotland. But Cornwall was 'nought in Wales, for there is a grete see bytwene, nother in Scotlonde, for there beeth many hondred myle bytwene. Than Cornwayle is in Engelond'.[154] He went on: 'Cornwayle is in Engelond, and is departed in hundredes, and is i-ruled by the lawe of Engelond, and holdeth schire and schire dayes, as othere schires dooth'. To complete his case, he emphasised the contribution made by Cornishmen to the English language and highlighted the fact that the county had held a place in the episcopal jurisdiction of the West Saxons.[155] Placing Cornwall firmly within England territorially, administratively, legally, ecclesiastically, historically and linguistically, Trevisa viewed the structures of the shire as the bedrock of this integration.

The Crown held the same opinion, treating Cornwall's residents as English in every sphere of its activities. Forging a powerful sense of regnal solidarity, the king and 'England' also commanded Cornish loyalties. This was because regnal solidarity overlaid all others, sustaining both the county and the kingdom, the local administration being in some sense 'self-government at the king's command'.[156] Such a mutuality of interests made kings and subjects alike contributors to the common good.[157] Since the royal government and the earldom-duchy together meshed the peninsula into the wider realm, Cornish politics was much more than simply the stuff of marriages and local rivalries. As a result, Cornish and English identities were intertwined, with 'the reciprocal

---

[153] *PROME*, iii, 61, 69–71; *PROME*, vii, 217–218.
[154] Trevisa, trans., *Polychronicon*, ii, p. 91.
[155] Trevisa, trans., *Polychronicon*, ii, pp. 121, 159–161.
[156] A. B. White, *Self-Government at the King's Command: A Study in the Beginnings of English Democracy* (Minneapolis, 1933).
[157] Reynolds, *Kingdoms*, pp. 251, 262–270, 292, 337; J. Watts, *The Making of Polities: Europe 1300–1500* (Cambridge, 2009), pp. 201–286; W. M. Ormrod, '"Common Profit" and "The Profit of the King and Kingdom": Parliament and the Development of Political Language in England, 1250–1450', *Viator*, 46 (2015), pp. 219–252.

relationship between the part and the whole' resulting in 'a creative tension that ultimately strengthened the identity of both'.[158] It is illustrative of this that in 1378 the Commons of Cornwall were to petition the king concerning their exposure to enemy raids.[159] While this supplication implicitly reaffirmed the place that the peninsula held in England, the county's representatives went further than this when they presented Cornwall's security as vital to the defence of 'our lord the king and the kingdom'. By identifying Cornwall's collective interests with those of the wider realm, the petitioners demonstrate how connections beyond the Tamar spread an awareness of the county's place in the kingdom while sharpening a sense of Cornishness in the peninsula itself.

*

Naturally enough, 'Cornwall' meant different things to different people. The county was not only sustained by the external force of the Crown, nor even by the institutions of lordship, but also by a powerful sense of place, the interconnectedness of its inhabitants, their shared commitment to the shire's structures and their collective belief in the peninsula's communal history and traditions. Each and all of these interlocked, vesting the name and notion of Cornwall with meaning. Yet county sentiment still emerges as looser and more abstract than that of the 'county community' of old; we should think instead of a neither perfectly defined nor definable 'commonalty'. A shared notion of Cornwall was only one of a hierarchy of associations, ranging from sub-county localism through supra-shire regionalism to kingdom-wide loyalties. Wider and narrower solidarities such as these represent different layers of Cornish identity, rendering the county one of many calls on the loyalties of its elite. Fully appreciating their place in a wider realm, the Cornish gentry at the same time enjoyed a pride and dignity of their own while believing that Cornwall had existed since the time of King Arthur.

---

[158] A. Ruddick, *English Identity and Political Culture in the Fourteenth Century* (Cambridge, 2013), pp. 95–97.
[159] *PROME*, vi, 89–90.

4

An Extraordinary Folk: the Cornish People

'The folk (*populus*) of these parts', so Adam de Carleton wrote in his resignation letter from the archdeaconry of Cornwall in 1342, 'are quite extraordinary (*valde mirabilis*), being of a rebellious temper, and obdurate in the face of attempts to teach and correct'.[1] Within and without the boundaries of the county, Cornwall and its people have long provoked strong feelings. Since contemporaries believed that God had divided humankind into 'peoples' (*gentes*), the ethnographic origins of such collectivities proved essential to medieval understandings of the world.[2] With a mythical founder, many shared customs, a powerful lordship and a strong identity of their own, the Cornish could supposedly join the English, the Irish, the Scots and the Welsh as a people in their own right.[3] Yet although the county's residents enjoyed a shared identity that proved potent in practice and imagination, notions of Cornishness were far more complex than simple peoplehood.[4]

---

[1] *Reg.Grandisson*, ii, 957–958; *RESDCornwall*, 2.
[2] R. R. Davies, 'The Peoples of Britain and Ireland, 1100–1400: I. Identities', *TRHS*, 6th series, 4 (1994), pp. 1–20; R. R. Davies, 'The Peoples of Britain and Ireland, 1100–1400: II. Names, Boundaries, and Regnal Solidarities', *TRHS*, 6th series, 5 (1995), pp. 1–20; R. R. Davies, 'The Peoples of Britain and Ireland, 1100–1400: III. Laws and Customs', *TRHS*, 6th series, 6 (1996), pp. 1–23; R. R. Davies, 'The Peoples of Britain and Ireland, 1100–1400: IV. Language and Historical Mythology', *TRHS*, 6th series, 7 (1997), pp. 1–23.
[3] Stoyle, *West Britons*; Payton, *Cornwall*, pp. 86–118.
[4] For imagined identities, see B. Anderson, *Imagined Communities: Reflections on the Origins and Spread of Nationalism* (London, 1983); see also P. J. Geary, *The Myth of Nations: The Medieval Origins of Europe* (Oxford, 2002); G. Heng, *The Invention of Race in the European Middle Ages* (Cambridge, 2018), especially pp. 37–42.

A Shared Name and Land

A great deal is in a name, according to R. R. Davies.[5] Whereas Cornwall's residents stand out as highly varied by status, descent and so on, under the label of 'Cornish' all these folk were drawn together into one local collectivity. In many ways it was this communal epithet that made the Cornish. Yet although they might appear unchanging and almost primeval, convincing people of unbroken continuity, names were in constant flux, meaning different things at different times. With the peninsula's Cornish-speaking residents calling their land *Kernow* in the fifteenth century, the assumption of a name formed a potent part of self-definition.[6] Such a definition could be imposed by others, however, the Cornish being known by the Anglo-Saxons as the *Corn-Wealas*, the Corn-*foreigners*.[7] Becoming imbedded in the county's name itself, this pejorative appellation had lost its meaning and negative connotations by the later middle ages. In 1402 one William Brewer actually chose to define himself as a 'Cornyshman', but it is actually only in the mid-fifteenth century that the word 'Cornish' is first attested in Middle English, with little known about how the term was used before this date.[8] When medieval scribes and authors employed the Latin *Cornubicus* and *Cornubiensis* or the Anglo-Norman *Cornewailleis*, it seems that they used these terms in a geographic rather than ethnic sense, with scant evidence for how and when these words came to mean someone 'Cornish'.[9] While a collective name bestowed coherence upon the peninsula's inhabitants, at the same time such an appellation emerges as mutable and masks the every-changing and many-layered nature of Cornishness.

Indivisibly tied to Cornish nomenclature was the name and territory of Cornwall itself. According to John Norden, the county's sixteenth-century residents articulated the name of their native land in Cornish, Latin and English, as *Kernauia*, *Cornubia* and *Cornwall* respectively, to which we might add the French *Cornouaille*.[10] Derived from the tribal appellation *Cornowii*, 'the horn-people', the county's name proclaimed its geographical position at the end of the 'horn' of Britain.[11] It followed that late-medieval and early-modern Cornishmen and women thought in terms of a well-measured and

[5] Davies, 'Names, Boundaries', 3; also, H. Pryce, 'British or Welsh? National Identity in Twelfth–Century Wales', *EHR*, 116 (2001), pp. 775–801.
[6] *Cornish Drama*, i, PC, line 2712.
[7] Padel, *Cornish Place-Names*, pp. 72–73.
[8] *CCR 1402–1405*, 362; *Middle English Dictionary*, ed. H. Kurath and others (Ann Arbor, MI, 1956–2001), ii, p. 608.
[9] *Dictionary of Medieval Latin from British Sources*, ed. R. E. Latham and others, 4 vols (London and Oxford, 1975–2013), i, p. 494; *Anglo-Norman Dictionary*, ed. W. Rothwell and others (London, 1992), p. 116.
[10] Norden, *Description of Cornwall*, p. 8.
[11] Padel, *Cornish Place-Names*, pp. 72–73.

well-defined territorial space, one 'cast out into the sea' and stretching right up 'to Tamar Bridge', near Launceston.[12] Inviting stories about towering moorland and sheltered bays that proclaimed Cornish links with their land, the peninsula's terrain added to this connection between people and place. Everyone knew that below the 'hills, Rockes, and craggye mountaynes' of mid-Cornwall stretched rich seams of tin, the quintessentially Cornish metal.[13] The extraction of these ores left a landscape riddled with 'old mynes, wrought yn tymes past', physically anchoring the Cornish to Cornwall.[14] Since the sea enveloped the peninsula on three sides, the county's maritime character was also significant. In the fifteenth-century play that bore his name, St Kea sailed from Brittany to Cornwall in a boat hewn from rock and declared: 'My vessel was a slab of stone/ over deepest sea'.[15] Even the county's tenurial arrangements reflected the peninsula's landscape, with the fourteenth-century Scilly Isles held for either an annual rent of half a mark or 300 'puffins'.[16] Many folk believed that the coming together of tin, tide, topography and climate influenced the character of the Cornish themselves, contributing to their strength and roughness.[17] In this way, Cornwall's sea-girt wildness helped to fashion a powerful image of the land west of the Tamar, but one that varied across the county's many contrasting landscapes.

Inevitably, 'outside' observers commented on the county's geography, some none too favourably. Bishop Grandisson's 'not only the ends of the earth, but the very ends of the ends thereof' stands out as the pithiest of these.[18] In the sixteenth century Polydore Vergil simply wrote that Cornishmen 'dwell in a part of the island so restricted in area as it is poor in resources', while the Venetian ambassador recorded the peninsula's place in the 'extremity of the island'.[19] It was natural that medieval cartographers depicted the county on the edge of the realm, with the fourteenth-century Gough Map showing the peninsula stretching out into the western sea, the limit of the known world.[20] 'On account of the distance and difficulty of the roads', the abbot of Beaulieu Abbey in Hampshire even refused to travel down to fourteenth-century Cornwall,

---

[12] Carew, 1v; Charter Endorsement, pp. 6, 28.
[13] Leland, Itinerary, i, p. 315; Norden, Description of Cornwall, p. 8; Carew, 5v–7v.
[14] Leland, Itinerary, i, p. 316.
[15] Bewnans Ke, lines 94–95.
[16] CIPM, ix, 100–101, of Sir Ranulph Blanchminster (d. 1348).
[17] For example, Norden, Description of Cornwall, p. 22.
[18] Reg.Grandisson, i, 97–98.
[19] P. Vergil, The Anglia Historia of Polydore Vergil, 1485–1537, trans. D. Hay, Camden Society, 3rd Series 74 (London, 1950), pp. 89–90; State Papers, Venetian, i, p. 312.
[20] N. Millea, The Gough Map: The Earliest Road Map of Britain? (Oxford, 2007), p. 75.

and the Black Prince himself thought that the county, his own lordship, comprised 'such distant parts'.[21]

Yet by no means were all contemporary assessments of Cornwall's place in the world negative. In an attempt to flatter his Cornish-born patron, Johannes de Hauvilla wrote in the twelfth century that Cornwall stood out as the 'uttermost threshold of the west wind', rendering the county's liminality a source of authority.[22] Along with a great many other county folk, Richard Carew was to revel in the fact that the peninsula formed the 'farthest shire of England westwards' in the sixteenth century.[23] We see here how the county's remoteness formed an essential strand of Cornishness. Such a trope, however, was not anathema to medieval English writers and geographers. Forming an essential part of the kingdom's identity, England's position on the 'edge of the world' premised 'both the exaltation and the marginalization of England during the Middle Ages'.[24] The margins enjoyed a certain social authority. And while Cornwall's position on the edge of the edge helped to define the county, it also linked the peninsula to the rest of England, as together they shared the same challenges and opportunities of peripheral life.[25] We should also note the context in which writers chose to denigrate the county's location. Polydore Vergil, for one, was carefully prefacing an account of Cornish rebellion by maligning the county, while Bishop Grandisson was simply employing a convenient cliché. Despite the impression they gave of the peninsula's wildness, many travellers can be shown to have journeyed down the county's rocky windswept spine, colouring their views of Cornwall as a whole.[26]

For all the miles between Cornwall and the heartlands of England, as we have seen, the county still held an integral place in the kingdom. Contemporaries were only too aware of this, with William Worcestre, for example, in the fifteenth century commenting that St Just-in-Penwith stood in the 'westernmost part of England' and Edward II in the fourteenth claiming that Cornwall was situated 'in the more remote parts of the realm'.[27] Even noting the distances involved, the Gough Map depicted the peninsula as linked to the rest of England by a network of routes and by geography itself. It was the fourteenth-century Cornishman John Trevisa, however, who provided the most powerful statement of medieval Cornwall's geographic inclusion.[28] For

[21] *CPR 1327–1330*, 328; *RBP*, ii, 22.
[22] Hauvilla, *Architrenius*, book 5, lines 420–425.
[23] *Carew*, 1r.
[24] K. Lavezzo, *Angels on the Edge of the World: Geography, Literature, and English Community, 1000–1534* (London, 2006), p. 8
[25] Cf. Lavezzo, *Edge of the World*, p. 74.
[26] A point I owe to Oliver Padel.
[27] Worcestre, *Itineraries*, pp. 96–97; *CFR 1319–1327*, 300.
[28] Trevisa, trans., *Polychronicon*, ii, p. 91; above, p. 66.

him, the county's land-links to the rest of the realm formed an essential part of Cornish integration and identity. Fostering a powerful notion of the peninsula as a whole, Cornwall's geographic position and contrasting landscapes at the same time encouraged sub-county localism while connecting the county closely into the kingdom.

Governmental Solidarities

While royal government, lordship and the law encouraged yet greater internal coherence in Cornwall, this administrative triumvirate neither established the county's residents as a separate *gens* nor their home as a land apart. On the contrary, governmental solidarities of this sort simultaneously integrated the county into the kingdom while endowing 'Cornwall' with meaning in the minds of its inhabitants. Although it was not until Athelstan's reign in the tenth century that the peninsula was absorbed fully by the Anglo-Saxons, from this time on it formed an integral shire of the realm. Accordingly, a sense of regnal solidarity saw the royal writ often welcomed by the peninsula's fourteenth-century residents, who owed homage and loyalty to the king of England himself, their most dread sovereign lord. At the same time the royal administration of the shire created a governmental structure that pulled this peninsula together.[29] Such an institutional corset helped to foster a practical and imagined sense of Cornishness, one that saw itself as both distinctive and integrated at one and the same time. Claiming in the fourteenth century that Cornwall formed 'a large land long ago bearing the name of a kingdom', the Carminows demonstrate how the county had come to hold a place in the wider realm while retaining a strong identity of its own.[30]

Forming another institution that helped to bind Cornwall together and into the kingdom, the earldom-duchy overlapped and interlocked with the shire structure in the peninsula. With lordly agents enforcing seigniorial rights in the name of the earl-duke himself, the lord's prerogatives encompassed the whole peninsula. All this activity spread awareness of the lordship's influence over every Cornishman and woman. In the early sixteenth-century play *Beunans Meriasek* the character of the duke even declared his position of 'high lord' in 'all Cornwall', evidencing the way in which the earldom-duchy encouraged a sense of Cornishness 'from Tamar to Land's End'.[31] The lordship, and especially the fame of the duke himself, who also held the principality of Wales, being the eldest son of the king, can be shown to have influenced external views of Cornwall. It seems that Froissart's comments about the violent nature of Cornish

---

[29] Above, Chapter 3.
[30] *inter Ricardum le Scrope et Robertum Grosvenor*, i, p. 214.
[31] *Beunans Meriasek*, lines 2205–2208.

and Welsh soldiers after the battle of Crécy in 1346, for example, arose from the fact that the Black Prince ruled both lordships.[32] Framing interpretations of the county, this lordly link explains a case that cropped up in 1402.[33] In this year, Henry IV heard how a certain John Sparrowhawk of Cardiff had spread scurrilous rumours derived from a tailor's wife in Hertfordshire. Emerging as fantastical, the most serious of these stories claimed that the earl of March was the rightful king of England and that the Welsh rebel Owain Glyn Dŵr was 'the legal prince of Wales and of Cornwall'. Yet while the earldom-duchy marked out the county's identity, this semi-royal lordship helped to draw Cornwall into the realm by supporting the king's rulership in the far south west.

Together, the Crown and the earldom-duchy enforced the universal common law of England in the county, for by the later middle ages this had come to form the law of Cornwall.[34] As laws protected the practices that fostered a collective identity among a *gens*, contemporaries were highly concerned about the maintenance of judicial customs. We see this in the *Quo Warranto* proceedings of 1302, in which leading Cornish lay and spiritual proprietors secured royal confirmation of their liberties, accepting their inclusion in the realm.[35] In Cornwall the peace was the king's peace, with the common law regarding all Cornishmen and women as English. There were no separate courts for Cornish and English people in the peninsula, or anywhere else for that matter, while no tribunal west of the Tamar enjoyed any jurisdictional finality. Although the stannaries incorporated some ancient laws regarding free bounding and the like, they did not constitute a separate Cornish legal system because their jurisprudence simply proved too narrow.[36] Since Cornish cases can be shown to have informed the practices and precedents of the wider English legal system, so the county formed an essential part of a juridical England.

In all this Cornwall contrasted with the position in parts of Ireland and Wales, where distinct native and English law codes and tribunals operated for the different peoples who inhabited these lands. It was a central tenet of Welsh law-texts, for example, that these laws were the birthright of all Welshmen; while Irish laws sought to secure the practices and jurisdictional rights of all Gaelic Irishmen; and English laws aimed to regulate along English lines the settlers who lived cheek by jowl with these other peoples.[37] These judicial customs could exercise considerable influence on the sentiments of contemporaries,

---

[32] J. Froissart, *Chronicles*, ed. and trans. G. Brereton (Harmondsworth, 1968), p. 93; below, p. 189.
[33] *SCKB*, vii, 123–124.
[34] Below, Chapter 12.
[35] *Quo Warranto*, pp. 108–111.
[36] Below, pp. 238–239.
[37] Davies, 'Laws and Customs', 1–12.

with Llywelyn ap Gruffudd in 1279 seeking to protect his jurisdiction before Edward I's judges thus:

> Each province under the empire of the lord King has its own law and customs according to the habit and usage of the parts in which it is situated – for example, the Gascons in Gascony, the Scots in Scotland, the Irish in Ireland and the English in England.[38]

Cornwall is notably absent from this list for the simple reason that it did not possess its own law codes, and there is no evidence that the county's residents made comparable claims themselves in the later middle ages. This was because they accepted the role of the common law in the peninsula, choosing to bringing cases before the king's courts.

At times the division between separate peoples and laws were less sharply defined than the authorities expected. Passed in 1366, the Statutes of Kilkenny sought to erect a *cordon sanitaire* between the English and native Irish populations of Ireland, for although the English of Ireland had once:

> used the English language, mode of riding and apparel, and were governed and ruled... by the English law... now many English of the said land forsaking the English language, fashion, mode of riding, laws and usages, live and govern themselves to the manners, fashion, and language of the Irish enemies; and also have made divers marriages between themselves and the Irish enemies.[39]

As fears of degeneracy were prevalent, the theory and practice of separate *gentes* were two different things. No legislation of this sort was either needed in or passed for Cornwall, however, because no laws or courts divided the peninsula's residents along ethnic lines. Chief Justice Sir John Fortescue (d. 1479), who ought to have known, his legal career having actually brought him in to contact with the county's residents, wrote that Scotland had 'grown into a kingdom political and regal' while implicitly accepting Cornwall's place in the realm of England.[40] Having 'united' England 'into one', the role of the common law in the county was so secure that it required no comment.[41]

---

[38] *The Welsh Assize Roll, 1277-1284*, ed. J. C. Davies (Cardiff, 1940), p. 266; Davies, 'Laws and Customs', p. 1.

[39] *Statutes and Ordinances and Acts of the Parliament of Ireland: King John to Henry V*, ed. H. F. Berry (Dublin, 1907), pp. 430–431; R. Frame, 'Ireland', in *NCMH*, pp. 375–387; Feng, *Invention of Race*, p. 40.

[40] CRO, AR/3/314; J. Fortescue, *De Laudibus Legum Anglie*, ed. S. B. Chrimes (Cambridge, 1942), pp. 32–33.

[41] Fortescue, *De Laudibus Legum Anglie*, pp. 30–31.

The Customs of the County

Medieval folk always twinned together laws and customs, as the 'law was but the customs which regulated those social relationships which had been brought within the ambit of judicial procedures and regulations'.[42] Here, too, Cornwall's English credentials are once again confirmed. In contrast to native Welsh practices of social castes, partible inheritance and so on, English customs of primogeniture, comparative freedom in the alienation of land and wealth-determined social status were integral parts of the county's life.[43] There is evidence that dress served as a racial marker in native Wales and Gaelic Ireland, but not in Cornwall, with the Welsh characterised as 'bare-footed rascals' and the Irish sporting haircuts and moustaches that marked them out from the English – sartorial determinism.[44] Attitudes towards marriage, expectations of rulership and so on varied just as much among all these peoples.

Yet, if Cornwall does not emerge as divided from England by laws and customs, at the same time the county played host to some striking traditions of its own. Naming practices certainly formed significant local markers. Although patronymic surnames were common across Western Europe, by the mid-fifteenth century the great majority of people in England enjoyed hereditary surnames.[45] The fact that in 1549, however, one John Roberd is recorded as holding land near St Columb Minor with his sons Henry John and Richard John, suggests that some Cornish folk at least continued employing patronymics well into the sixteenth century.[46] Since occupational and 'nickname' surnames were equally widespread across western Christendom, it is no surprise that county folk can be found bearing these appellations too. As a distinctively Cornish nuancing of this wider practice, some names of this sort were couched in the Cornish language itself, including the fourteenth-century John *Gwycor* 'merchant', Richard *Lagadek* '(big) eyed' and Richard *Pencogh* 'red-head'.[47] As the Cornish-language surnames of the 1300s were nearly exclusively confined to west Cornwall, however, not all local adaptations of wider naming practices were so distinctive. There was certainly no equivalent of the Welsh patronymic *ap* or *map*.[48] In terms of forenames, a certain Minawe Carminow was active in the county in the mid-fourteenth century and one Launcelot Glynn of Cornwall appeared in London in 1402, but no widely employed Cornish Christian

---

[42] Davies, 'Laws and Customs', 12.
[43] Davies, *Wales 1063–1415*, pp. 115, 120, 420–421.
[44] Davies, 'Laws and Customs', 14–15.
[45] For the wider context, *The Oxford Dictionary of Family Names in Britain and Ireland*, ed. P. Hanks, R. Coates, P. McClure and others, 4 vols (Oxford, 2016), i, p. xxiv.
[46] Fox and Padel, *Arundells of Lanherne*, pp. cxxv–cxxxvii.
[47] Padel, 'Where was Middle Cornish Spoken?', 112.
[48] Fox and Padel, *Arundells of Lanherne*, p. cxxvii.

name existed as an equivalent to Madoc, Llewelyn and the like in Wales.[49] Virtually no county folk shared their forenames with local saints, for example, as a remarkable 1,373, 652, 513, 359 and 336 of the 6,000 people taxed in 1327 bore the names John, William, Richard, Robert and Roger respectively.[50] Here we see how the county's naming practices did not render the peninsula totally different from the rest of the realm.

But what about the link between social status and ethnicity? It is clear that patronymic forms among the peasantry proclaimed the pride that some of the richer sorts took in their lineages and extended kinship groupings.[51] Non-manorialism and the use of conventionary tenures in parts of the county had a role to play here, fostering relative freedom – tenurially, socially and geographically – within the Cornish peasantry. And yet Richard Carew could 'say little' about the differences between 'the yeomanrie of Cornwall' and 'those of other shires'.[52] While a chasm always existed between the gentry and the rest of the populace in the county, as elsewhere in England, a great many points of contact linked all these folk together. There were certainly no courts in the far south west that operated on the different ethnicity of the Cornish gentry and peasantry. In this, Cornwall was very different from the parts of Wales where an English elite ruled over a native population divided by blood and administration.[53]

If not establishing the county's residents as a separate people, a rich range of customs still marked out the Cornish as highly distinctive. Especially in the sixteenth century, there is evidence that the county's residents employed their own water- and land-measures for goods sold in the peninsula, measuring Cornwall itself in Cornish acres.[54] Local tastes ensured that farmers grew coarse grains on these lands, making 'bread and dryncke' that some thought tasted 'smoky and ropye' being 'spylt for lacke of good ordring'.[55] Distinguishing some Cornishmen and women, the 'apparell' of husbandmen was 'course in matter, ill shapen in manner'.[56] Supposedly leaving 'their legges and feet naked and bare', these folk could 'hardly... abide to weare any shooes; complaining how it kept them over hote'.[57] Some county residents, especially in the

[49] *RBP*, ii, 78; *CCR 1402–1405*, 123.
[50] E179/87/7; E179/87/37.
[51] Cf. Stoyle, *West Britons*, p. 16; J. W. Armstrong, 'Concepts of Kinship in Lancastrian Westmorland', in *Political Society in Later Medieval England: A Festschrift for Christine Carpenter*, ed. B. Thompson and J. Watts (Woodbridge, 2015), pp. 146–165.
[52] *Carew*, 66r.
[53] Cf. Davies, *March of Wales*, pp. 302–318; Davies, *Wales 1064–1414*, pp. 283–285, 391–392, 419–421; despite Stoyle's suggestion, *West Britons*, p. 19.
[54] *Carew*, 54r, 36r.
[55] Boorde, *Knowledge*, p. 123.
[56] *Carew*, 66v.
[57] *Carew*, 66v.

west, employed slings as their weapons of choice into the sixteenth century, another important local practice, while Chaucer's fourteenth-century translation of the French allegorical poem the *Romaunt of the Rose* referred to the 'discordance' of 'hornpipes of Cornwaile'.[58] Even in the late 1500s the 'meaner countrie wenches of the westerne parts' supposedly still rode their horses 'astride, as all other English folke used before R. the 2 wife brought in the side saddle fashion'.[59] Writers in the sixteenth century also characterised the 'baser sorte' of Cornwall as highly litigious, being 'muche inclined to lawe-quarrels for small causes'.[60]

Despite writings of this sort, however, we should be careful of accepting comments made by the elite as evidence of ethnic difference rather than social snobbery, not least because these observers sought to emphasise such traits in order to entertain their audiences. Neither were the lower orders of Cornwall alone in being so denigrated, as poor Northerners were often written about in similar terms.[61] As critical comments of this sort formed part of a wider genre, and one that clearly blossomed in the sixteenth century, this should caution us not to accept their words at face value. In practice customs and traditions varied considerably from the Tamar westwards as well, with different weights and measures employed in east and west Cornwall.[62] At the same time the county's residents can be found inviting 'national' standards into their natal shire, reckoning value, for example, in the king's coinage. All these practices rendered the peninsula strikingly distinctive but neither excluded from the wider realm nor uniform and unchanging.

As equally prominent aspects of county life, Cornish wrestling and hurling were important local pastimes. 'Wrestling', so Richard Carew was to write, 'is full of manlinesse', enjoying great popularity across both Cornwall and Devon.[63] Squaring up, each of the two wrestlers aimed to 'overthroweth his mate in such sort, as that either his backe, or the one shoulder, and contrary heele do touch the ground', a so-called 'fall', employing many named 'sleights and tricks'.[64] Since Bishop Quinel of Exeter had banned wrestling from south-western churchyards back in 1287, this sport was of great antiquity.[65] It

[58] *The Cornwall Muster Roll for 1569*, ed. H. L. Douch (Bristol, 1984), p. iii; 'The Romaunt of the Rose' in *The Riverside Chaucer*, ed. F. N. Robinson, 3rd Edition, ed. L. D. Benson (Oxford, 1988), pp. 687–767, lines 4250–4251.
[59] Carew, 66v.
[60] Norden, *Description of Cornwall*, p. 22.
[61] H. M. Jewell, *The North–South Divide: The Origins of Northern Consciousness in England* (Manchester, 1994), pp. 120–122.
[62] Carew, 54r.
[63] Carew, 75v.
[64] Carew, 75v–76r; Norden suggested that there were two types of wrestling, *Description of Cornwall*, p. 23.
[65] *Early English Drama*, pp. 463–464, 579–580.

even influenced the writings of Geoffrey of Monmouth in the twelfth century, who had Corineus choose Cornwall as his own because he loved wrestling the giants who inhabited the peninsula, especially Gogmagog.[66] At the other end of our period, Michael Drayton's 1627 *The Battaile of Agincourt* had the county's soldiers at this victory include 'two wrestlers' on their banner, this sport being an important marker of identity.[67]

Although hurling was supposedly a Cornish 'peculiaritie, because elswhere it is not in manner used', this handball game was actually well-known in Devon.[68] With an earlier game called 'soule' played across these two shires in 1284, the earliest reference to the game of hurling comes from as late as 1529.[69] Hurling saw two teams compete for a silver ball, with the game also existing in two forms; one of which was played to 'goales' and the other played to 'the countrey'.[70] In-hurling saw two teams of fifteen to thirty or more players assemble, with each team member paired with an opposing player and played man to man. A pitch was laid out with two bushes placed at either end 'some eight or ten foote asunder', these being the goals through which 'whosoever can catch' the ball 'and cary through his adversaries gaole, hath wonne the game'. As gentlemen assigned their homes or villages some miles apart as the targets, out-hurling saw whole parishes compete against each other. Making their way over 'hilles, dales, hedges, [and] ditches', the whole affair was 'like a pitched battaile'. It seems that wrestling formed an essential part of both forms of hurling, with players fighting for possession of the ball. These two sports then, hurling and wrestling, while contributing to the county's life can be shown to have evolved with time and proved popular on either side of the Tamar. As the county's medieval residents also enjoyed hunting, hawking, shooting and even playing some form of football, they were not opposed to these more mainstream pastimes either.[71]

From martyred zealots through to dragon healers, the county's many saints and their cults stood among the most prominent markers of Cornwall's distinctiveness. Many Cornish parishes had a patron saint found nowhere else. Since physical reminders of these holy men and women were spread across the county, and local hagiography and relic processions were commonplace, it is no surprise that local belief in their efficacy was widespread.[72] Consider, for example, how in 1477 St Merthiana of Minster Church supposedly performed

---

[66] G. of Monmouth, *Kings of Britain*, pp. 72–73.
[67] M. Drayton, *The Battaile of Agincourt...* (London, 1893), p. 29.
[68] Norden, *Description of Cornwall*, p. 23; J. Mattingly, 'One Game or Two? Wrestling and Hurling in Cornwall in 1700', *JRIC* (2012), pp. 57–74.
[69] Mattingly, 'Wrestling and Hurling', 63–64.
[70] *Carew*, 73r–75v; the east–west division suggested by Carew cannot be substantiated.
[71] *YB 30 & 31 Edward I*, xxxviii; *Carew*, 72r–73v.
[72] For example, Roscarrock, *Lives of the Saints*, p. 107.

a posthumous 'miracle concerning a man out of his senses and a woman and a certain girl'; or how the burgesses of fourteenth-century Fowey felt such a strong affinity with the patron saint of their town, a certain St Fimbarrus, that they christened some of their ships 'Barry' after the diminutive of his name.[73] With the wholesale rebuilding of the county's churches undertaken during the latter half of the fifteenth century and the first half of the sixteenth, people from across Cornwall lavished money on their local parishes.[74] In Bodmin alone the churchwarden accounts record no fewer than 460 burgesses subscribing to the rebuilding of the church there between 1469 and 1472, while the parishioners of St Neot commissioned an elaborate glazing scheme that survives to this day.[75]

Although some of these saintly sites were imposing, such as 'the beautiful shrine' of St Petroc in Bodmin Church, no saint can be said to have prompted pan-Cornish devotion the equal of St Cuthbert in Durham.[76] Quite the reverse, in fact, for local Cornish communities preferred 'their saints to be different to one another'.[77] This much is shown by Nicholas Roscarrock's writings in the sixteenth century, which recounted the lives of numerous holy men and women from the county and beyond but made scant reference to many others, even from places near to his home in the parish of St Endellion.[78] Belief actually varied by social status and gender, with the gentlemen donors of St Neot commissioning images of international saints to which they attached their heraldic arms, while the wives of the parish chose to commemorate the local St Mabena, among others. These saintly cults also changed with the passage of time, as some late-medieval parishes invented a '"Celtic" context' for their patron saint when none had existed before, such as a certain holy Ludewan of Ludgvan.[79] 'New' saints could certainly find a following in the county, among them Edmund Lacy (d. 1455), the saintly bishop of Exeter, and even the archetypally English St George, while all these cults existed alongside devotion to the great international saints such as Mary.[80] In some measure propagating a sense of collective Cornishness, the county's holy men and women simultaneously

---

[73] Worcestre, *Itineraries*, pp. 28–31; E101/30/29 m. 5; E101/40/40 m. 2.
[74] P. Beacham and N. Pevsner, *Cornwall: The Buildings of England* (New Haven and London, 2014), p. 28.
[75] 'Receipts and Expenses in the Building of Bodmin Church A.D. 1469 to 1472', ed. J. J. Wilkinson, in *The Camden Miscellany*, viii, Camden Society, n.s. xiv (London, 1875); J. Mattingly, 'Stories in the Glass – Reconstructing the St Neot Pre-Reformation Glazing Scheme', *JRIC* (2000), pp. 9–55.
[76] Worcestre, *Itineraries*, pp. 86–87.
[77] Orme, *Saints of Cornwall*, p. 23.
[78] Roscarrock, *Lives of the Saints*, p. 22.
[79] Orme, *Saints of Cornwall*, pp. 22, 44.
[80] Roscarrock, *Lives of the Saints*, p. 71; *Early English Drama*, p. 412.

helped to foster many localised identities while spreading awareness of the county's links with Wales, Ireland, Brittany, England and all Christendom.

Naturally enough, Cornish hagiography, myths and folklore may be considered as closely connected. We can see this in the life of St Agnes, a fourth-century Roman martyr who became a 'local' saint by settling in the county, turning the devil himself into stone and destroying the local giant, one Bolster, by throwing him over a cliff near the settlement to which she gave her name.[81] Legend had it that many craggy Cornish hills had once played host to a giant, with their identities preserved in the names of the great granite boulders that they hurled at each other.[82] In one step striding some seven miles, however, the giant of Carn Brea in his last manifestation was none other than John of Gaunt himself.[83] It seems that Gaunt had made a grant to the Basset family of nearby Tehidy which became imbedded in local culture. Emerging as both traditional and dynamic at the same time, all these myths were as mutable as Cornishness itself. Folk even refashioned sixteenth-century accounts of St Buryan's life so that the 'Watch Towre' that she built was 'erected against that of Spaine'.[84] Folkloric tales concerning the natural and human wonders of the county – among them Rat Isle in the Scillies, on which 'so many rattes' dwelt that they would 'devore' any 'lyving best', and the Hurlers Stones on Bodmin Moor, which had supposedly once been 'men, and for their hurling upon the Sabboth, so metamorphosed' – created a Cornwall both deeply conservative and endlessly reimagined.[85]

It was inevitable that the county's miracle plays drew upon and nourished these beliefs. Each performance was probably staged in an open-air amphitheatre called in Middle Cornish a *plen-an-gwarry* or 'playing place', with placename evidence suggesting that over thirty of these sites existed.[86] Designed for performance over three consecutive days, the *Ordinalia* cycle of three Middle-Cornish dramas dates from c. 1400. Taking redemption and the defeat of the devil as their unifying themes, together these plays weave their way from the creation of the world through the Passion of Christ and then on to the Resurrection, while also recounting the story of the Holy Rood and the death of

[81] Orme, *Saints of Cornwall*, p. 60; also, Roscarrock, *Lives of the Saints*, p. 63; G. of Monmouth, *Kings of Britain*, pp. 72–73.
[82] B. C. Spooner, 'The Giants of Cornwall', *Folklore*, 76 (1965), pp. 16–32; W. Camden, *Britannia: or a Geographical Description of the Flourishing Kingdoms of England, Scotland, and Ireland...*, trans. R. Gough, 4 vols (London, 1806); i, p. 3.
[83] Spooner, 'Giants', 22.
[84] Roscarrock, *Lives of the Saints*, p. 61.
[85] Leland, *Itinerary*, i, p. 318; *Carew*, 129v.
[86] *Early English Drama*, pp. 559–563.

Pilate.[87] In rendering these holy stories into Middle Cornish, and augmenting them with other accounts of the sacred, the playwright created a definitively Cornish biblical narrative. He also tied these plays closely to Cornish topography, having characters as varied as King Solomon and Pontius Pilate grant county properties to their followers.[88] Interpolating local myths into his dramatic verse, the author of the *Ordinalia* explained Christ's nature thus:

He might be well	*ef a alse bos yn ta*
Half man and half God	*hanter den ha hanter dev*
Human is half the mermaid,	*den ya hanter morvoron*
Woman from head to the heart;	*benen a'n pen the'n colon*
So is the Jesus.	*yn della yw an iheus.*[89]

Forming no stolid theology lessons, these dramas were designed to be entertaining. In one scene Pilate's body was so evil that the ground rejected it, causing the man burying him to flee flatulating in terror.[90] Performances were intended as important social occasions too, with the *Resurrexio Domini* closing with the lines: 'Now minstrels, pipe up diligently,/ That we may go to dance.'[91] Evidently the *Ordinalia* cycle stands as a powerful testament to fourteenth-century Cornish distinctiveness. And yet these plays were composed for the Cornish-speaking residents of west Cornwall alone, almost certainly being penned by churchmen associated with Glasney College in Penryn to educate the laity. Since they referred to pan-English institutions in French, Latin and English, the plays spread awareness of the county's identity as a distinctive place in a wider realm and yet wider world.

Constituting the other surviving Middle-Cornish miracle plays, *Bewnans Ke* and *Beunans Meriasek* were composed to recount the lives of their respective saints. Probably performed 'in the round' as well, these dramas required complex staging with raised scaffolds and so on.[92] The prosody of their dramatic words incorporated Brittonic-style lines of verse – strict syllable-count and end-rhyme regardless of stress – with complex English stanzaic structures in a genre probably borrowed from Brittany, a revealing mix of cultures.[93] Only recently discovered, *Bewnans Ke* probably dates from between 1450 and

---

[87] B. O. Murdoch, 'The Cornish Medieval Drama', in *The Cambridge Companion to Medieval English Theatre*, ed. R. Beadle (Cambridge, 1994), pp. 211–239 at 216–217; J. A. Bakere, *The Cornish Ordinalia: A Critical Study* (Cardiff, 1980); also, B. O. Murdoch, *Cornish Literature* (Cambridge, 1993).
[88] For example, *Cornish Drama*, ii, RD, line 673.
[89] *Cornish Drama*, i, PC, lines 1740–1744.
[90] *Cornish Drama*, ii, RD, lines 2081–2092.
[91] *Cornish Drama*, ii, RD, lines 2645–2646.
[92] Fletcher, 'The Staging of *Bewnans Ke*'.
[93] My thanks to Oliver Padel for his advice on this point.

1500 and narrates how St Kea journeyed to Cornwall to preach, finding the county under the rule of the tyrant King Teudar whom 'not many people love' on account of his 'evil ways'.[94] Soon getting into a theological dispute, Teudar resorted to having St Kea assaulted. Despite – or perhaps because of – this thuggery, the saint went on to perform a series of miracles, including raising a holy well in St Kea parish itself, with the king later seeking his forgiveness. Such a story proclaimed parochial pride, securing this holy life for posterity. In the second half of the play, however, the deeds of King Arthur himself were recounted, these being derived in no small part from Geoffrey of Monmouth's work. Contemporary political themes also appeared in the drama, with Mordred promising his messenger 'the livery of Gaunt', that is of the Lancastrians, but the messenger preferring the 'blue and murray' of the Yorkists.[95]

Composed in 1504, *Beunans Meriasek* bears some striking resemblances to *Bewnans Ke*. Again, the drama seeks to glorify a saintly life and parish, in this case that of St Meriasek and the parish of Camborne.[96] St Meriasek also journeyed to Cornwall to minister, finding the peninsula under the yoke of the evil tyrant Teduar, 'a graceless pagan', who sought to impose his beliefs on the county:

Teudar I am called	*Tevdar me a veth gelwys*
Lord reigning in Cornwall.	*arluth regnijs in kernov*
That Mahound be honoured	*may fo mahum enorys*
Is my charge without fail,	*ov charg yv heb feldov*
Near and far.	*oges ha pel*
Whosoever worship another god	*penag a worthya ken du*
They shall have keen pains,	*y astevt peynys glu*
And likewise a cruel death.	*hag inweth mernans cruel.*[97]

Persecuting the saint for his beliefs, Teudar drove him back to his native Brittany where the play itself was originally penned, although without the Cornish material.[98] With the themes of salvation, conversion and right belief pervading the drama, this complex play also included an account of St Silvester and the *Donation of Constantine*, tying these stories to St Meriasek and the intercessionary power of the Virgin.[99] As the drama made directions for 'a gonn yn y dragon ys mouthe aredy & fyr', the staging would have been quite spectacular.[100] The nominative similarities between Teudar and Tudor have prompted

---

[94] *Bewnans Ke*, lines 1064–1065.
[95] *Bewnans Ke*, lines 3058, 3064.
[96] *Beunans Meriasek*, lines 644–645, 687.
[97] *Beunans Meriasek*, lines 2242, 759–766.
[98] Murdoch, 'Medieval Drama', p. 234.
[99] Murdoch, 'Medieval Drama', pp. 212, 230.
[100] *Beunans Meriasek*, between lines 3947 and 3948.

the suggestion that *Beunans Meriasek* formed a piece of subversive theatre, composed after Henry VII had crushed the rebellions of 1497.[101] In the light of the recent discovery of *Bewnans Ke*, however, such an interpretation looks increasingly strained. The archetypal villain, Teudar was an ancient Cornish folkloric figure. While his character may have acquired some seditious overtones as a result of 1497, the fact that both plays were concerned with royal government, tyranny and church–state relations demonstrates the extent of Cornish integration. Concerns of this sort were common to all England.

From all this we can see that the county's late-medieval culture was time-honoured, vibrant and adaptable all at once, with these many traditions helping to propagate a shared notion of Cornwall itself. Yet for all the importance of these collective customs and interactions, none of this activity marked the county's inhabitants out as a separate race. Instead, practices varied considerably across the peninsula and evolved with time, all the while being influenced by Cornwall's involvement in the wider realm. A two-way cultural diffusion over the Tamar even saw Robin Hood dramas performed throughout late-medieval Cornwall and the rest of kingdom.[102] So it was that Cornish customs intermingled with wider English and European practices, rendering the county all the more distinctive but not a land apart.

The Cornish Language

The miracle plays of Cornwall can lead us on to consider the Cornish language itself. Although forming a defining feature of a *gens*, language was less significant than it at first appears. This was because contemporaries believed differences in language divinely ordained, being 'so much a part of social life, at different levels, that they were hardly worthy of comment, let alone the focus of loyalty or hostility'.[103] Multilingualism in fourteenth-century England was in fact the norm, as French and Latin were the languages of both elite lay and spiritual interaction and administration. It was also the case that English was fragmented into many regional dialectics, or, as John Trevisa put it in the late-fourteenth century, there were 'dyvers manere Englische in the reem of Engelonde'.[104] This Oxford-educated Cornishman went on: 'the weste men of

---

[101] P. Payton, 'a... concealed envy against the English': a Note on the Aftermath of the 1497 Rebellion in Cornwall', *Cornish Studies*, n.s. 1 (1993), pp. 4–13; see Cooper's criticisms made before the discovery of *Bewnans Ke*, J. P. D. Cooper, *Propaganda and the Tudor State: Political Culture in the Westcountry* (Oxford, 2003), pp. 72–83.
[102] *Early English Drama*, pp. 397–400.
[103] Davies, 'Language and Historical Mythology', 3; Geary, *Myth of Nations*, pp. 33, 38.
[104] Trevisa, trans., *Polychronicon*, ii, pp. 160–163; Cf. D. C. Fowler, *The Life and Times of John Trevisa* (Seattle, 1995).

Englonde sownde and acorde more with the men of the este... than the men of the northe with men of the sowthe', admitting that 'we southerne men' may scarcely 'understonde' those of the north. Without universal education or a standardised print-culture, it was naturally the case that many different English dialectical forms thrived.[105] In such circumstances, it is little wonder that notions of a 'national language' and a 'single linguistic community' remained embryonic.[106] Although in 1344 Edward III claimed that the French threatened to destroy 'the English language and occupy the land of England', even here language emerges as one of a bundle of the kingdom's identifiers and not the most important of these.[107] The king's claims were actually recorded in French.

Use of the Cornish language rendered the linguistic map of Cornwall yet more complex. Spoken throughout the peninsula in the early-twelfth century, this Brittonic tongue prompted Gerald of Wales (d. 1233) to comment that in 'both Cornwall and Brittany they speak almost the same language as in Wales', and although 'rougher and less clearly pronounced' it was 'probably closer to the original British speech'.[108] In a more official capacity, in 1155 Henry II issued a charter to 'all his sworn men' in Cornwall, 'French, English, and Welsh (*Wallencibus*)', that is Cornish, addressing everyone who spoke these different tongues.[109] By the fourteenth century, however, it is thought that Cornish was confined to the west of the county alone, with the Fowey–Padstow hundredal boundary marking the linguistic divide.[110] As Bishop Grandisson observed in 1329, 'a language, too, exists in the furthest parts of Cornwall, known not to the English-speakers but to the British-speakers'.[111] Even by this time speaking Cornish and a pan-Cornish identity and culture simply did not prove synonymous.

While not rendering the county a coherent linguistic whole, the distinctive local language of parts of the peninsula could still be significant in the late middle ages. It is illustrative of this not only that Cornwall's miracle plays were powerful statements of local identity and language, but also that a knowledge of the existence of the Cornish tongue had spread far and wide in England.

---

[105] For example, *A Linguistic Atlas of Late Mediaeval English*, ed. A. McIntosh et al., 4 vols (Aberdeen, 1986); *Regionalism in Late Medieval Manuscripts and Texts*, ed. F. Riddy (Cambridge, 1991).

[106] Davies, 'Language and Historical Mythology', 3–4.

[107] *PROME*, iv, 362.

[108] G. of Wales, *The Journey through Wales and the Description of Wales*, trans. L. Thorpe (London, 1978), p. 231.

[109] *The Cartulary of Launceston Priory: A Calendar*, ed. P. L. Hull, DCRS, n.s. 30 (Torquay, 1987), p. 9; discussed in R. Sharpe, 'Addressing Different Language Groups: Charters from the Eleventh and Twelfth Centuries', in *Multilingualism in Medieval Britain*, pp. 1–40 at 12–13.

[110] Padel, 'Where was Middle Cornish Spoken?', 26–27.

[111] *Reg.Grandisson*, i, 98.

When Europe's ecclesiastics converged on Constance in 1414 to try to heal the schism that had riven Christendom since 1378, delegates were to form *nationes principales* for the purposes of voting.[112] Among these 'nations' were France and England, although in practice such groupings were broader than their titles suggest. Disputes also erupted about the order of precedence and England's representative, a certain Thomas Polton, sought to secure English voting rights:

> Where the French nation, for the most part, has one vernacular which is wholly or part understandable in every part of the nation, within the famous English or British nation, however, there are five languages, you might say, one of which does not understand another. These are English, which English and Scots have in common, Welsh, Irish, Gascon and Cornish. It could be claimed with every right that there should be representation for as many nations as there are distinct languages.[113]

It should be noted, however, that Polton made no claims for Cornwall enjoying a special political situation as a result of its language. His comments instead reveal the way in which the Cornish language could be used to make political points for the whole realm, as it had been in 1347. After his capture of Calais in this year, Edward III signed a truce with France that some of his more bellicose subjects resented. In a twenty-six-line poem, the *Anonymous of Calais* mocked the French and Scots and warned against a truce: 'For "truce" in Cornish tongue spells out "dismay"' (*Lingua Cornubica designat treuga dolores*).[114]

It should also be noted that by the fourteenth century nearly all west Cornwall's residents were bilingual, speaking both Cornish and English.[115] In this, Cornwall contrasted sharply with Wales, a society of two or more separate languages.[116] Even by 1300 it was English, French and Latin that enjoyed currency across the whole county, not Cornish. Trevisa's comments about the English dialect of 'we southerne men' demonstrates how this helped to integrate the county into the fourteenth-century realm.[117] He went on to emphasise the role that Cornishmen had played in the English language itself, claiming that John

---

[112] A. Ruddick, 'The English 'Nation' and the Plantagenet 'Empire' at the Council of Constance', in *The Plantagenet Empire, 1259–1453: Proceedings of the 2014 Harlaxton Symposium*, ed. P. Crooks, D. Green and W. M. Ormrod (Donington, 2016), pp. 109–127.

[113] C. M. D. Crowder, *Unity, Heresy and Reform, 1378–1460: The Conciliar Response to the Great Schism* (London, 1977), p. 121.

[114] *Political Poems and Songs Relating to English History*, ed. T. Wright, 2 vols, Rolls Series (London, 1859–61), i, p. 57; Rigg, *Anglo-Latin Literature*, pp. 264–265; O. J. Padel, 'Cornu-Latin treuga "griefs"', *DCNQ*, 40 (2007–11), pp. 118–121.

[115] Padel, 'Where was Middle Cornish Spoken?', 27.

[116] Davies, 'Language and Historical Mythology', 6.

[117] Trevisa, trans., *Polychronicon*, ii, p. 163.

of Cornwall had changed the 'construccioun of Frensche in to Englische' in 'the gramere scoles of Engelond' and that Richard Pencriche had then spread this 'manere [of] techynge'.[118] Undoubtedly exaggerated, Trevisa's writings nonetheless show us that English had come to form an essential part of the county's linguistic identity. The Cornish tongue remained a powerful local marker, one that to 'outsiders' unfamiliar with its distribution in the county coloured their views of Cornwall as a whole. Yet by the later middle ages Cornish was confined to the western parts of the peninsula alone and co-existed with English, neither rendering fourteenth-century Cornwall a coherent linguistic collectivity nor the Cornish a separate *gens*.

Mythical Foundations

Every people worthy of the name could claim a progenitor of their own, a founding figure from whom they had all descended. According to Geoffrey of Monmouth, the Britons were established by none other than Brutus, who after his escape from the sack of Troy came upon an island named Albion: 'then called the island Britain from his own name, and his companions the Britons. His intention was that his memory should be perpetuated by the derivation of the name'.[119] When writing in the twelfth century, however, Geoffrey of Monmouth acknowledged that five 'races' now inhabited Britain: 'the Norman-French, the Britons, the Saxons, the Picts, and the Scots', as the 'vengeance of God' had forced the Britons to submit to the Picts and Saxons.[120] By a 'mythological sleight of hand', English chroniclers and historians could claim that as divine judgement had replaced the Britons with the Saxons, the English could lay claim to the ancient heritage of the Britons.[121] Britain now formed England, so that Brutus stood out as the founding father of the English.

At the outset, however, Geoffrey of Monmouth marked out the Cornish as different. In his twelfth-century pseudo-history he instead recounted how Corineus, Brutus' brother-in-arms, had founded the county and named the people there Cornishmen.[122] From his text Cornwall emerges as at one and the same time both entwined with the founding of Britain and yet strangely distinct within it, a condition subtly magnified by the role that he assigned to his fictional Cornish dukes and by his placing of King Arthur's conception

---

[118] Trevisa, trans., *Polychronicon*, ii, pp. 159–161.
[119] G. of Monmouth, *Kings of Britain*, p. 72.
[120] G. of Monmouth, *Kings of Britain*, p. 54.
[121] R. R. Davies, *The First English Empire: Power and Identities in the British Isles, 1093–1343* (Oxford, 2000), p. 49; Ruddick, *English Identity*, pp. 171–172.
[122] G. of Monmouth, *Kings of Britain*, pp. 72–73.

and death in the county.[123] For whatever reasons – maybe he was inspired by tensions in the twelfth-century peninsula, or perhaps the county formed a 'safe' Brittonic area that constituted no threat to the kingdom – Geoffrey of Monmouth composed an immensely entertaining story that was to frame interpretations of Cornwall for centuries to come.

It did so because the *Historia* was recounted as historical truth by chronicler after chronicler, providing 'the base on which later chroniclers built their accounts of England's past'.[124] Since hundreds of manuscripts containing this mythical story survive from across Christendom, 'the matter of Britain' entered the historical consciousness of the English people and many more folk besides.[125] To take but two examples drawn from three centuries apart, Gerald of Wales (d. 1223) stated as a matter of fact that Corineus had founded Cornwall.[126] When writing his account of pre-Conquest England some three centuries later, Polydore Vergil (d. 1555) similarly drew upon chronicles recounting this pseudo-history, and although at times he questioned their validity such stories influenced his views:

> The whole contrie of Britaine (which at this daie, as it were in dowble name, is called Englande and Scotlande)... is divided into iiij. partes; whereof the one is inhabited of Englishmen, the other of Scottes, the third of Wallshemen, the fowerthe of Cornishe people. Which all differ emonge them selves, either in tongue, either in manners, or ells in lawes and ordinaunces.[127]

He went on to write that England is 'limited' on 'the Weste parte with the bowndes of Cornewall and Walls', and that in Cornwall 'continueth the nation of Britons'.[128] Such comments have been taken as proof of Cornish separation.[129] In fact, however, they arose from Vergil's reading of Galfridian narratives. Although accounts of a mythical past sharpened an idea of Cornishness in both the county and the rest of the kingdom, the repetition and embellishment of Geoffrey of Monmouth's writings also enshrined an authoritative and

---

[123] Padel, 'Geoffrey of Monmouth and Cornwall'; also, J. S. P. Tatlock, *The Legendary History of Britain* (1950).
[124] C. Given-Wilson, *Chronicles, The Writing of History in Medieval England* (London, 2004), p. 158; P. C. Ingham, *Sovereign Fantasies: Arthurian Romance and the Making of Britain* (Philadelphia, 2001), pp. 25, 33.
[125] A. Gransden, *Historical Writing in England*, 2 vols (London, 1996), i, pp. 201–207; Given-Wilson, *Chronicles*, pp, 4–5.
[126] G. of Wales, *Journey through Wales*, p. 220.
[127] P. Vergil, *Polydore Vergil's English History: The Period Prior to the Norman Conquest*, ed. H. Ellis, Camden Society, 36 (London, 1846), p. 1; Gransden, *Historical Writing*, ii, pp. 430–443.
[128] Vergil, *English History*, pp. 4, 14.
[129] Cf. Stoyle, *West Britons*, pp. 31–32.

long-lasting literary ideal of Cornwall as a 'land apart' that fits ill with its later-medieval integration.

It is perhaps unsurprising that writings of this sort did not even present a coherent picture of Cornwall. While Geoffrey of Monmouth recounted Corineus' endeavours, for example, he did not actually write that the Cornish formed a people or a political entity in their own right. Once he had killed off Brutus, Geoffrey of Monmouth instead had Britain divided between his three sons, a tripartite division that made no mention of Cornwall.[130] Thereafter the narrative made no other allusion to the county's political status, implying that the peninsula formed part of the kingdom of Britain. Here we see evidence of Cornwall's distinctive but not distinct existence. Even Polydore Vergil wrote later in his sixteenth-century history that 'Coornewall' formed one of the 'Shires' of England, holding a place in the episcopal jurisdiction of the bishops of Exeter.[131] Recounting the ancient history of the Britons, the *Brut* Chronicle was one of the most widely circulated texts in later-medieval England.[132] In its many continuations, however, later writers extended the narrative into the fourteenth century and beyond, recording the political and administrative history of the kingdom. In this way, accounts of Cornwall's remarkable past continued to circulate widely while the peninsula's place in the realm also came to be emphasised.[133] The *Brut* helped to propagate an idea of England, one in which Cornwall held an idiosyncratic but still integral place.[134] In much the same way, Ranulph Higden's *Polychronicon* and its fourteenth-century English translations by John Trevisa reproduced the Galfridian stories at some length.[135] Circulating equally widely, the *Polychronicon* also helped to spread awareness of Cornwall's distinctive place in the realm.[136]

The deeds of King Arthur himself comprised a major part of the *Historia*. Forming the 'main conduit' of Arthurian literature throughout the middle ages and beyond, Geoffrey of Monmouth's writings marked out Cornwall as the place of Arthur's conception and the setting of his last battle to folk from across Christendom.[137] When the Black Prince journeyed to the peninsula in 1354, for example, it seems that he travelled to Tintagel, the most Arthurian

---

[130] G. of Monmouth, *Kings of Britain*, p. 75.
[131] Vergil, *English History*, pp. 1-2.
[132] A. Galloway, 'Writing History in England', in *The Cambridge History of Medieval English Literature*, ed. D. Wallace (Cambridge, 1999), pp. 255-283 at 273.
[133] For example, *Cornish Wills*, 28.
[134] Ruddick, *English Identity*, pp. 177-178.
[135] P. Brown, 'Higden's Britain', in *Medieval Europeans: Studies in Ethnic Identity and National Perspectives in Medieval Europe*, ed. A. P. Smyth (Basingstoke, 1998), pp. 103-118; Given-Wilson, *Chronicles*, p. 165.
[136] Galloway, 'Writing History', p. 275.
[137] H. Fulton, 'Introduction: Theories and Debates', in *A Companion to Arthurian Literature*, ed. H. Fulton (Oxford, 2009), pp. 1-11 at 4; see the other essays in this

of castles.[138] During the Barons' War of 1264-7, the Welsh even composed a political song to rally support against the weakened English:

> The Cambrians, who are used to slay Saxons, salute their relations the Britons and Cornish-men (*Britones et Cornubienses*); they require them to come with their sharp swords to conquer Saxon enemies... The Soothsayer Merlin never said a thing that was vain... If our valiant predecessor, King Arthur, had been alive, I am sure not one of the Saxon walls would have resisted him.[139]

Whether such a ballad actually sought to elicit Cornish aid or simply employed Galfridian myths to rally Welshmen around a unifying dream is uncertain. It should be noted, however, that during the revolt that he led in Wales against English rule in the early 1400s, Owain Glyn Dŵr composed letters to the Scottish King and the Irish lords seeking their support against the English, our 'mortal enemies the Saxons', but sent no correspondence to garner Cornish backing.[140]

Portraying Cornwall as slightly distinct from the rest of England, medieval cartographers and their *Mappa Mundi* were greatly influenced by Galfridian stories. 'Representations of reality', however, were 'not foremost in mapmakers' minds'.[141] Relying on textual descriptions, world maps were philosophical, religious and historical documents that sought to tell a story, one that firmly set 'geography in the context of history'.[142] Such 'historical atlases' naturally sought to emphasise the county's Arthurian credentials rather than accurately portray its contemporary situation. It is illustrative of this that Cornwall was afforded a significant position on a late-fourteenth century *Mappa Mundi* in a copy of the *Polychronicon*, but that the county was still shaded red along with the rest of Britain.[143] Even Matthew Paris' map of Britain from 1250, that actually sought to depict the physical appearance of the country, marked out Cornwall and Tintagel Castle for all to see; while the Gough Map afforded this Arthurian inspired fortress a position of prominence out of all proportion to its fourteenth-century significance.[144] Mapping King Arthur in particular and

---

excellent volume and those in *The Arthur of the English*, ed. W. R. J. Barron (Cardiff, 1999).
[138] *RBP*, ii, 120–121.
[139] *Thomas Wright's Political Songs of England: From the Reign of John to that of Edward II*, ed. P. Coss (Cambridge, 1996), pp. 56–58.
[140] A. Usk, *The Chronicle of Adam Usk 1377–1421*, ed. C. Given-Wilson (Oxford, 1997), pp. 148–153.
[141] E. Edson, *Mapping Time and Space: How Medieval Mapmakers viewed their World* (London, 1997), p. 2.
[142] Edson, *Medieval Mapmakers*, pp. 15, 18, 135, 164.
[143] BL, Royal MS 14.C IX ff. 1v–2r.
[144] BL, Cotton MS Claudius D.vi, f. 12v; Millea, *Gough Map*, p. 75.

the pseudo-historical past in general were highly important cartographical tasks, determining depictions of Cornwall as a whole.

Inevitably, Galfridian traditions exercised just as much influence on chroniclers and romancers. We see this clearly in the writings of Peter Langtoft, who composed a chronicle in the romantic tradition in late-thirteenth-century Yorkshire.[145] In his history of Britain from Brutus to 1307, he sought to vilify the Welsh and Scots while glorifying Edward I and Arthur, directly linking these two kings:

> *Of the union of England and Scotland.*
> Ah, God! how often Merlin said the truth
> In his prophecies, if you read them!
> Now are two waters united in one,
> Which have been separated by great mountains;
> And one realm (*realme*) made of two different kingdoms (*regnez*)
> Which used to be governed by two kings.
> Now all the islanders are joined together,
> And Albany reunited to the royalties
> Of which king Edward is proclaimed lord.
> Cornwall (*Cornewaylle*) and Wales are in his power,
> And Ireland the great at his will.
> There is neither king nor prince of all the countries (*cuntrez*)
> Except king Edward, who has thus united them;
> Arthur had never the fiefs so fully.[146]

Langtoft, who it should be noted had no known connections with the south west, placed Cornwall here among the non-English parts of Edward's domains. His account, however, was inspired by Arthur's legendary kingship over the whole of Britain and Edwardian imperial ideology, not by the actual territorial divisions of the British Isles. Much ambiguity is also apparent between England, Britain and these other lands, for Langtoft praised Edward the Elder, king of Wessex, thus:

> He had all England; never by his folly
> Did he lose a foot of land, he ruled well Albany,
> Cumberland, and Wales, and all Cornwall,
> Lindsey and Kent, Dorset and Surrey.[147]

---

[145] Gransden, *Historical Writing*, i, pp. 440–441, 476–485.
[146] P. Langtoft, *The Chronicle of Pierre de Langtoft*, ed. T. Wright, 2 vols, Rolls Series (London, 1866–8), ii, pp. 264–267.
[147] Langtoft, *Chronicle*, i, pp. 322–323; Ruddick, *English Identity*, p. 71.

The status of all these territories is even more unclear here, whether as sub-divisions of England or as distinct political entities. Since Geoffrey of Monmouth's writings so influenced Cornwall's place in medieval discourse, we should be careful not to read works composed to entertain as historical fact.

A great chivalric hero, King Arthur existed in many literary forms and Sir Thomas Malory's fifteenth-century *Le Morte d'Arthur* attempted to pull together these Arthurian romance traditions into one narrative. Drawing upon numerous English and French versions of the Arthurian myth, Malory succeeded in creating the 'most comprehensive, coherent, and consecutively ordered Arthurian story until the modern age'.[148] The narrative he wove returned again and again to Cornwall, as did the many stories on which he drew. Malory even chose to open his book with an account of 'a myghty duke in Cornewaill that helde warre ageynst' Uther Pendragon, 'kynge of all Englond'.[149] He also told us that during King Arthur's reign:

> there were many kynges that were lordys of many contreyes, but all they helde their londys of kynge Arthure; for in Walys were two kynges, and in the Northe were many kynges, and in Cornuayle and in the Weste were two kynges; also in Irelonde were two or three kynges, and all were undir the obeysaunce of kynge Arthure.[150]

Although Cornwall's position fluctuated throughout the *Morte*, the county always remained worthy of mention. For example, Cornish knights serving in the retinue of King Mark of Cornwall were often besmirched; 'Cornyssh knyghtes... ar nat called men of worship', with one 'the shamfullist knyght' and a 'grete enemy to all good knyghtes', while another was 'the moste orryble cowarde that ever bestrode horse'.[151] This 'othering' was part of a literary device that denigrated the court of King Mark so as to make Camelot appear all the more virtuous. Yet although 'the honour of both courts be nat lyke', the two chivalric centres parallelled each other and King Arthur himself hailed from Cornwall.[152] Perhaps in some measure the *Morte*'s treatment of the peninsula arose from Malory's knowledge of fifteenth-century Cornish distinctiveness. It

---

[148] D. Armstrong, 'Mapping Malory's *Morte*: the (Physical) Place and (Narrative) Space of Cornwall', in *Mapping Malory: Regional Identities and National Geographies in Le Morte Darthur*, D. Armstrong and K. Hodges (Basingstoke, 2014), pp. 19–43 at 19.

[149] Thomas Malory, *The Works of Sir Thomas Malory*, ed. E. Vinaver, rev. P. J. C. Field, 3 vols (Oxford, 1990), i, p. 7.

[150] Malory, *Works*, i, p. 371.

[151] Malory, *Works*, ii, pp. 504, 580, 586; K. J. Harty, 'Malory and the Cowardly Cornish Knights – "'The strangest races [that] dwell next door'", *Études Anglaises*, 66 (2013), pp. 379–387.

[152] M. W. Anderson, '"The honour of bothe courtes be nat lyke": Cornish Resistance to Arthurian Dominance in Malory', *Arthuriana*, 19 (2009), pp. 42–57.

stands as a more powerful testament, however, to the influence that the Arthurian image of Cornwall exercised on later-medieval discourse. By publishing on his new-fangled printing press the *Morte*, the *Brut* and the *Polychronicon*, William Caxton (d. 1492) disseminated both the romantic and chronicle Arthurian construct of Cornwall to a yet wider public.[153] All these works presented a specific literary interpretation of the county, so that even *Don Quixote* was to recount how Arthur did not die but 'by magic art' was turned into a Cornish chough.[154]

None of this is to deny that the county's residents shared a powerful notion of a Cornish King Arthur.[155] As late as 1428 a copy of the *Brut* even claimed that the peninsula's inhabitants believed that Arthur would 'be a king again'.[156] These beliefs spread awareness of Cornish solidarity and the county's place in the wider British Isles, with the duke of Cornwall's character in the fifteenth-century *Bewnans Ke* serving with King Arthur and commanding 'young and grey, Irish and Scot!' (*yonk ha loys, Gothal ha Scot!*).[157] Views of this most illustrious monarch changed with time, however, as international literary culture permeated the peninsula, reshaping belief in the king. Drawing upon these romances at the same time as emphasising Arthur's Cornish credentials, the author of *Bewnans Ke* introduced his character with the lines: 'ARTHUR KING OF BRITAIN (*which is now called England*)'.[158] The playwright deftly exploited the 'mythological sleight of hand' that enabled English chroniclers to claim that Britain was now England to show how a Cornishman had once ruled over the kingdom of England itself. While King Arthur's many manifestations came to form part of an elaborate pseudo-historical narrative, such writings do not prove that Cornwall stood apart from the kingdom.

Stories about Corineus and King Arthur were tied closely to the Saxon conquest of Britain, the point at which the *Historia* ended. Naturally enough, notions of Anglo-Saxon annexation have long held a place in the county's collective memory. Forming an independent polity for the century or so following the conquest of Devon in the late 600s, Cornwall had been left 'as the surviving tail-end of the earlier British kingdom of Dumnonia'.[159] In 815, however, King Egbert was said to have 'ravaged Cornwall, from east to west',

---

[153] Gransden, *Historical Writing*, ii, p. 467.
[154] R. Hunt, *Popular Romances of the West of England* (London, 1903), pp. 308–309; Wood, 'Arthurian Legend in Scotland and Cornwall', p. 112.
[155] Above, Chapter 3.
[156] *Arthur: A Short Sketch of his Life*, p. 19.
[157] *Bewnans Ke*, line 1259.
[158] *Bewnans Ke*, between lines 1396 and 1397.
[159] O. J. Padel, 'Slavery in Saxon Cornwall: the Bodmin Manumissions', *Kathleen Hughes Memorial Lectures*, 7 (Cambridge, 2009), pp. 4–5; also, M. Todd, *The South West to AD 1000* (London, 1987), pp. 267–275.

conquering the whole peninsula by 838.[160] Although under Saxon suzerainty, the peninsula retained its own sovereign until the death of King Dungarth, the last king of Cornwall, who drowned in 875–6.[161] It was only in the mid-tenth century that King Athelstan fully assimilated the peninsula into the English shire structure. Before this time the Cornish had indeed formed a people, one that prompted Aldhelm (d. 709) to write an amusing poem describing a journey through Cornwall, a place 'devoid of flowering vegetation'.[162] In a period of embryonic government and nascent customs, however, the Cornish people were less sharply defined than it would first seem.

Spreading awareness of Anglo-Saxon aggression for centuries to come, accounts of these events continued to circulate in numerous works. According to Gerald of Wales the Britons, who had 'retreated to the southern corner of the kingdom' in the face of Saxon expansionism, 'could not continue their resistance, for their territory [had] no natural protection'.[163] It was William of Malmesbury's twelfth-century account of Athelstan's south-western policies two centuries earlier, however, that enjoyed the widest currency. His work came to form one of the principal foundations on which later chroniclers constructed their own narratives of England's past.[164] Writing of Athelstan, Malmesbury claimed that 'he turned towards the Western Britons who are called Cornish (*Cornewalenses*)', attacking them 'vigorously' before expelling them from Exeter and setting the 'boundary of their territory (*provintiae*) at the river Tamar'.[165] Having thus 'purged the city by sweeping out an infected race (*contaminatae gentis*)', Athelstan then 'fortified it with towers and surrounded it with a wall'. While the Saxon invasions were undoubtedly destructive, what appears to be a definitive statement of Cornish oppression is in fact a foundation myth for Exeter, distorting how it presents these events to glorify the city. Rather than attacking Cornwall, it seems that Athelstan organised proper religious provision in the peninsula.[166]

Regardless of Athelstan's actual activities in the far south west, William of Malmesbury's writings helped to foster a long-lasting idea of repression of the Cornish. Writing in the sixteenth century, Richard Carew directly based the parts of his *Survey of Cornwall* concerned with Athelstan's activities on the *Regum Anglorum*, while in his *Lives of the Saints* Nicholas Roscarrock relied on

---

[160] *The Anglo-Saxon Chronicle*, ed. D. Whitelock (London, 1961), p. 39.
[161] *Annales Cambriae, A.D. 682–954: Texts A–C in Parallel*, ed. and trans. D. N. Dumville (Cambridge, 2002), pp. 12–13.
[162] Aldhelm, *The Poetic Works*, trans. M. Lapidge and J. L. Rosier (Cambridge, 1985), pp. 177–179.
[163] G. of Wales, *Journey through Wales*, p. 220.
[164] Given-Wilson, *Chronicles*, p. 158.
[165] Malmesbury, *Regum Anglorum*, i, pp. 216–217.
[166] Foot, *Athelstan*, p. 165.

both Carew's and Malmesbury's accounts of this king's campaigns.[167] It seems that oral folkloric traditions in the county also preserved some memory of general Anglo-Saxon aggression, or at least invented one. We find evidence for this in Richard Carew's writings, although he felt compelled to create a fictitious chronicler, a certain Matthew of Westminster, to lend authority to his words:

> one point of their former roughnesse, some of the Westerne people doe yet still retaine... together with the Welsh, their aunceint countrimen: namely, how fostering a fresh memorie of their expulsion long agoe by the English, they second the same with a bitter repining at their fellowship; and this the worst sort express, in combining against, and working them all the shrewd turnes which with hope of impunities they can devise.[168]

In his 1586 mining treatise, the Cornishman Thomas Beare even claimed that the Saxons were 'heathen people... when they inhabited our Country'.[169] Everyone knew that Cornwall had once been conquered, and yet these writings perpetuated a fossilised sense of domination.

Whether real or imagined, notions of Cornish resistance to the Anglo-Saxons (read English) still exercised significance in the later middle ages. Some county folk are found employing these ideas to repudiate their English credentials, for a key strand of Cornishness was forged in the fire of opposition to Englishness. While the medieval evidence for this is scanty, the fact that in 1233 the county's residents were said to have fled into the woods to avoid an eyre, only being coaxed back with special proclamations of peace, at least shows an implicit rejection of royal authority at this time.[170] Another clue to such sentiments is to be found in *Bewnans Ke*, where Teudar – admittedly in a damaged section of this fifteenth-century play – seemingly employs the phrase 'filthy Englishman' (*lobbry Sous*) as an insult.[171] Other Cornishmen and women, however, embraced their Anglo-Saxon connections. One such group were the canons of St Buryan, who in the fourteenth-century prized their charter of foundation from Athelstan, while many county burgesses took pride in the Anglo-Saxon history of their towns.[172] Yet those who stridently rejected their place in England, and those who enthusiastically accepted it, did not form two discrete groups. Instead, Cornwall's Englishness emerges as both situationally and chronologically dependent. So it was that some people claimed 'English

---

[167] Carew, 96v; Roscarrock, *Lives of the Saints*, p. 62.
[168] Carew, 66v–67r.
[169] T. Beare, *The Bailiff of Blackmoor...*, ed. J. A. Buckley (Camborne, 1994), p. 1.
[170] *Annales Monastici*, ed. H. R. Luard, 5 vols, Rolls Series (London, 1864–9), iii, p. 135.
[171] *Bewnans Ke*, line 679, *lobbry* may be a corruption, as it is not attested anywhere else; my thanks to Oliver Padel for his advice about this point.
[172] *CPR 1391–1396*, 522; Leland, *Itinerary*, i, pp. 179–180.

oppression' at moments of discontent with the government, while at other times these same folk actually requested royal involvement in county affairs.

For all this complexity, however, Cornishness was still defined by some measure of blood. Writers as varied as Gerald of Wales in the thirteenth century and William Camden in the sixteenth recognised Corineus as the Cornish progenitor, with the fact that for 'the most parte' the county's residents were 'west Britons' descended 'of the British stocke' a common trope.[173] Such ethnographic origins supposedly gave rise to shared traits, with Cornishmen long-lived, 'verie stronge, actiue, and for the most parte personable', being 'hardye and nymble'.[174] Yet in reality there was no such thing as 'pure' Cornish stock. Even though the county was less heavily settled by the Anglo-Saxons than many other parts of the realm, the peninsula has always been open to seaborne and land-based migration.[175] People move, rendering pointless any attempt to identify genetically 'undiluted' Cornish folk. More significant still is the fact that the Anglo-Saxons and then the Normans absorbed the peninsula at an earlier date than English activities in Ireland and Wales. This meant that they lacked the more powerful bureaucracies of later centuries and were unable to establish the necessary governmental machinery to preserve the distinction between people of Cornish and English descent.[176] The two therefore intermixed over many centuries. Athelstan and his successors had succeeded in integrating Cornwall fully into their realm, with the Domesday Book showing how Cornwall was a functioning shire of England in 1086.[177] In this way, Englishness came to form another layer of Cornishness, an identity that was embraced and resisted in turn. Having Cornish blood certainly did not preclude the county's inhabitants being simultaneously English, for Cornishness and Englishness were not mutually exclusive concepts. Ethnicity emerges as both situational and strategic rather than a substantive construct, one of many identifiers that influenced the outlook and actions of contemporaries.[178]

While some genealogical dimensions of Cornishness were significant, as unwritten rules based on blood, birth and ancestry must have existed, the very question of what it meant to be Cornish had no firm answer. We may well wonder about the role that residency, mind-set and so on played in

---

[173] Norden, *Description of Cornwall*, p. 21; G. of Wales, *Journey through Wales*, p. 220; Camden, *Britannia*, i, p. 1.
[174] Camden, *Britannia*, i, p. 3; Norden, *Description of Cornwall*, pp. 22–23; Carew, 63r.
[175] Padel, *Slavery in Saxon Cornwall*, pp. 5–6.
[176] Cf. S. Reynolds, 'Secular Power and Authority in the Middle Ages', in *Power and Identity in the Middle Ages: Essays in Memory of Rees Davies*, ed. H. Pryce and J. Watts (Oxford, 2007), pp. 11–22 at 21.
[177] *Domesday Book, X, Cornwall*.
[178] R. Bartlett, 'Medieval and Modern Concepts of Race and Ethnicity', *Journal of Medieval and Early Modern Studies*, 31 (2001), pp. 39–56; Heng, *Invention of Race*, p. 27.

determining one's Cornish credentials, which were not defined by biology alone.[179] By the fourteenth century the peninsula's place in the realm generally sharpened notions of the county as a coherent entity within a wider kingdom, these layered identities being mutually supporting. A venerable literary tradition extolling Cornish otherness, however, has come to mediate our views of medieval Cornwall. Arising in part from the fact that the county stood out as idiosyncratic, such a trope contributed to this distinctiveness by creating a narrative of difference to which people within and without the peninsula could refer. This imagined literary Cornwall of simple separation, however, by no means reflected the complex reality of the county's fourteenth-century integration.

Cornishness and Englishness Interwoven

None of this is to suggest that a sense of Cornishness was unimportant in Cornwall itself. On the contrary, the county's residents often took great pride in their Cornish credentials, seeking to defend their collective concerns and shared identity in the 1300s and beyond. 'Outsiders' can be found commenting on them as a whole too. As far back as 1192 we find Richard of Devizes claiming that for the qualities of boorishness you 'should always look on Cornishmen as we in France consider our Flemings' (*Cornubienses* as *Flandrenses*).[180] In the thirteenth century Henry d'Avranches turned to stock stereotypes, prompting Michael of Cornwall's sharp rebuke: 'You call me Cornish goat, but the term suits Normans better.'[181] It seems that Cornishness could mark out the county's residents enough for their origins to be blamed when things went wrong. After two Cornish-born vicars had mismanaged the fourteenth-century living of Pelynt, for example, the monks of Newenham Abbey in Devon, who held the rights of presentment, claimed that 'posterity' should 'beware' the Cornish (*Cornubicus, qui malum fecit Domui; de quibus, posteri, caveatis*).[182] In much the same vein, in 1342 Archdeacon Carleton wrote that the peninsula's residents were *rebellis et difficilis*.[183] A political song from Henry VI's reign complained that the avarice of the well-connected Cornish esquire John Trevelyan, named 'the Cornysshe chawgh' on account of his armorial bearings, 'hathe made our Egull [the king] blynde'.[184] Even some administrative documents

---

[179] Cf. Heng, *Invention of Race*, p. 57.
[180] *Chronicles of the Reigns of Stephen, Henry II, and Richard I*, ed. R. Howlett, 4 vols, Rolls Series (London, 1884–9), iii, p. 438.
[181] Rigg, *Anglo-Latin Literature*, p. 194.
[182] *Reg.Stapeldon*, 241, the 'quibus' is intended for Cornishmen generally; J. Davidson, *The History of Newenham Abbey* (London, 1843), pp. 192–193.
[183] *Reg.Grandisson*, ii, 957–958.
[184] *Trevelyan Papers*, i, p. 67.

noted the identity of the county's sons, with the *Port Books of Southampton* in 1436 naming Richard Priest *i home de Cornewaille* and a government instruction some ninety years earlier about smuggling claiming that goods had been taken to 'Ireland, Cornwall, Wales, Berwick-on-Tweed, or elsewhere without the realm'.[185]

Context, however, is king. Forming part of a well-established literary convention, poetic abuse simply saw Michael of Cornwall and Henry d'Avranches turn to standard objects of satire, among them origins and physical defects.[186] Neither should we accept the embittered writings of defrauded monks nor the resignation letters of resentful archdeacons as universally accepted accounts of how the Cornish were viewed. And although a few administrative documents commented on Cornishness, the authorities can be shown to have treated the county's residents as English in nearly every circumstance, a condition generally welcomed by these folk. Other writers emphasised the peninsula's contribution to the common profit, as did the fourteenth-century chronicler Thomas Walsingham and the anonymous author of the fifteenth-century poem the *Libelle of Englysche Polycye*.[187] The twelfth-century poem the *Architrenius* even stated that it should be taken as 'law' that 'Cornwall can produce nothing rank', only giving 'birth to flawless fashioned creatures', and a very different source, the fifteenth-century *Stonor Letters*, recorded how 'trew' were 'tenaunts in Cornwale'.[188] There was certainly no Cornish stereotype equal to the endlessly repeated refrain, supported by legislation, of the 'Welsh Vagabonds' or 'Wild Irish Enemies'.[189] While comments about the county in some measure arose from its distinctiveness, each statement was made in a specific set of circumstances for a specific set of purposes. Sometimes the peninsula was admired, at other times it was looked down on, but for the greater part of the time 'outsiders' and county folk alike regarded Cornwall as a place both intrinsically Cornish and integrally English. Identities emerge as nested, not exclusive.

The nature of fourteenth-century England helps to explain how Cornwall existed as a place simultaneously distinctive and integrated. While England played host to one of the most powerful governments of the European middle

---

[185] *The Local Port Book of Southampton for 1435–36*, ed. B. Foster, Southampton Record Society, 7 (Southampton, 1963), pp. 76–77; *CPR 1343–1345*, 575.
[186] Cf. Rigg, *Anglo-Latin Literature*, p. 196.
[187] *The Chronica Maiora of Thomas Walsingham*, ed. J. Taylor, W. R. Childs and L. Watkiss, 2 vols (Oxford, 2003–11), i, pp. 289–293; *The Libelle of Englyshe Polycye...*, ed. G. Warner (Oxford, 1926), lines 89–90, 215–218.
[188] Hauvilla, *Architrenius*, book 5, lines 475–476; *Stonor Letters*, ii, p. 120.
[189] *Parliament of Ireland*, pp. 430–431; R. Frame, *Ireland and Britain 1170–1450* (London, 1998), pp. 131–150; *CPR 1399–1401*, 469–470; *PROME*, viii, 96–97; R. R. Davies, *The Revolt of Owain Glyndŵr* (Oxford, 1995), pp. 284–292.

ages, royal rulership still relied on the voluntary service of folk from across the kingdom to carry its writ into the localities. Such an intertwining of 'central' and 'local' power had the effect of both propagating a notion of a wider realm and of significant sub-kingdom solidarities. The medieval mind saw no problem in layered authorities and identities, with a political song that circulated in the aftermath of the battle of Bannockburn in 1314 lauding England as no less than the 'matron of many regions'.[190] In the palatinate of Chester, for example, where a powerful collectivity sought to defend local customs and practices 'against all England', the lordship's residents still believed that Cheshire should form a major force in English politics.[191] Since those born of English blood within the realm of England were considered English, territorial and ethnic dimensions chiefly determined fourteenth-century English 'nationality'.[192] On both these measures the peninsula's residents ranked as English, with none of this diminishing a sense of their own Cornish birth and ancestry. It is suggestive of the point that in 1389 one Richard Carver of Cornwall stood mainprise for a Fleming accused of spying in London, confirming Carver's status as both a Cornishman and an English subject of the king.[193] Spread across the realm, an overarching idea of Englishness existed alongside a great many other sentiments.

As the so-called Plantagenet Empire extended far beyond England, the king sought to foster an allegiant identity based on shared subjecthood among people from across his domains: in England, Gascony, Ireland, Wales and (at times) both France and Scotland.[194] More prevalent in the high middle ages, the view that kings were only powerful when they ruled over several peoples still enjoyed some substance.[195] We see this when the French courtier Philippe de Mézières in his *Epistre* of 1395 addressed the famously image-conscious Richard II as: 'King of Great Britain, Prince of Wales and North Wales, Lord of Great Ireland, and King of Cornwall (*roy de Cornuaille*)'.[196] While Mézières in part derived such lofty titles from Arthurian literature, they well-illustrate the

---

[190] *Wright's Political Songs*, ed. Coss, p. 262; T. Turville-Petre, *England the Nation: Language, Literature, and National Identity, 1290–1340* (Oxford, 1996), pp. 143–147.
[191] See, R. W. Barrett, *Against All England: Regional Identity and Cheshire Writing, 1195–1656* (Notre Dame, 2009).
[192] A. Ruddick, 'Ethnic Identity and Political Language in the King of England's Domains: A Fourteenth-Century Perspective', *The Fifteenth Century, VI*, ed. L. Clark (Woodbridge, 2006), pp. 15–31.
[193] *CCR 1389–1391*, 17.
[194] Ruddick, 'Ethnic Identity', 23–24; also, P. Crooks, 'State of the Union: Perspectives on English Imperialism in the Late Middle Ages', *Past and Present*, 212 (2011), pp. 3–42.
[195] Reynolds, *Kingdoms and Communities*, p. 257.
[196] P. de Mézières, *Letter to King Richard II...*, ed. and trans. G. W. Coopland (Liverpool, 1975), p. 101.

composite nature of the king of England's domains. It follows that the relationship between fourteenth-century national, ethnic and political identity was by no means fixed. Shared subjecthood did not dispel mutual ethnic hostility, and yet a great many more interactions went on between all these peoples than harsh stereotyped words and blunt government policy suggest – the 'line between English and non-English was not absolutely clear-cut', as various identities were shared and contested among all these folk.[197] In such a polity, Cornwall's existence as a place simultaneously integrated and yet distinctive was not as fraught as it first appears.

Across the later middle ages and into the sixteenth century, however, these shifting patterns of affiliation assumed harder lines. Containing a better-defined 'package of rights and privileges', subjecthood acquired a narrower definition that became the preserve of folk with English blood alone.[198] At the same time 'aliens' were more sharply marked out as excluded, with an increasing number of royal statutes seeking to regulate their activities in England.[199] More significantly still, a growing sense of a unitary realm increasingly came to replace notions of dominion over diverse people, lands and regions.[200] This growing focus on uniformity was supported by linguistic developments, for 'the triumph of English' saw the vernacular – in fits and starts – displace French and Latin as languages of elite interaction and administration, growing more standardised in the process.[201] It was also the case that political and popular thought increasingly yoked together language and national loyalty.[202] These many interlinked strands fostered a narrower, more assertive sense of

---

[197] R. Frame, 'The Wider World', in *Social History of England*, pp. 435–453 at 451; also, C. Sponsler, 'The Captivity of Henry Chrystede: Froissart's Chroniques, Ireland, and Fourteenth-Century Nationalism', in *Imagining a Medieval English Nation*, ed. K. Lavezzo (London 2014), pp. 304–339.

[198] R. A. Griffiths, 'The English Realm and Dominions and the King's Subjects in the Later Middle Ages', in *Aspects of Late Medieval Government and Society: Essays Presented to J. R. Lander*, ed. J. G. Rowe (London, 1986), pp. 83–105; Ruddick, 'Ethnic Identity', 24.

[199] K. Kim, *Aliens in Medieval Law: The Origins of Modern Citizenship* (Cambridge, 2000); B. Lambert and W. M. Ormrod, 'Friendly Foreigners: International Warfare, Resident Aliens and the Early History of Denization in England, c. 1250–c. 1400', *EHR*, 130 (2015), pp. 1–24.

[200] Davies, 'Laws and Customs', 22–23.

[201] B. Cottle, *The Triumph of English, 1350–1400* (London, 1969); J. Catto, 'Written English: the Making of the Language, 1370–1400', *Past and Present*, 179 (2003), pp. 24–59; W. M. Ormrod, 'The Use of English: Language, Law, and Political Culture in Fourteenth-Century England', *Speculum*, 78 (2003), pp. 750–787.

[202] Frame, 'Wider World', p. 444.

Englishness, one fuelled by the hatreds of war and the changes wrought by the Reformation.[203]

Throughout all these developments the county was still viewed as an integral part of the realm, but 'outside' disquiet grew about the Cornish language in particular, increasingly a marker of dangerous Cornish difference. We see this in the writings of the sixteenth-century polemist Andrew Boorde, who recorded that: 'In Cornwall is two speeches; the one is naughty Englyshe, and the other is Cornyshe speche', with many supposedly unable to 'speake one worde of Englyshe, but all Cornyshe'.[204] Linking language to a thoroughly unflattering assessment of the county's residents, with their bad habits and nasty ale, Boorde included this material in an appendix 'treating of Cornewall and Cornyshe men' rather than in his chapter on England proper. Another sixteenth-century writer, John Norden, also commented about the county's linguistics, but differently, as Cornish was supposedly easier to pronounce than Welsh because Cornishmen 'strayne not their words so tediously throowgh the throate'.[205] He went on to say that the peninsula's inhabitants had 'conformed themselves to the use of the Englsih tounge', with their English 'equall to the best'. For Norden the use of English helped to secure the county's integration into the realm, while for Boorde the Cornish tongue marked Cornwall out as different enough to warrant separating his writings about the county from those concerning England proper. Both writers, however, implicitly accepted that language had come to form a more important marker of identity and political affiliation.

Uniformity in the new language of religion, of English, formed a key strand of the English Reformation. Since Cornish was still spoken in parts of the county and Latin rites were so established, linguistic impositions of this sort provoked the rightly famous statement by the rebels of 1549 that 'we the Cornyshe men... utterly refuse this newe Englysh'.[206] In abolishing the religion of the saints, moreover, the government outlawed a major part of Cornish piety, a decision made all the more galling as the county's residents had just rebuilt

---

[203] For example, D. Green, 'National Identity and the Hundred Years War', *Fourteenth Century England, VI*, ed. C. Given-Wilson (Woodbridge, 2010), pp. 115–130; D. Pearsall, 'The Idea of Englishness in the Fifteenth Century', in *Nation, Court and Culture: New Essays on Fifteenth-Century English Poetry*, ed. H. Cooney (Scarborough, 2001), pp. 15–27; D. MacCulloch, *Reformation: Europe's House Divided 1490–1700* (London, 2003); B. Bradshaw, 'The Tudor Reformation and Revolution in Wales and Ireland: the Origins of the British Problem', in *The British Problem, c. 1534–1707: State Formation in the Atlantic Archipelago*, ed. B. Bradshaw and J. Morrill (Basingstoke, 1996), pp. 39–65.
[204] Boorde, *Knowledge*, p. 123.
[205] Norden, *Description of Cornwall*, p. 21.
[206] A. Fletcher and D. MacCulloch, *Tudor Rebellions*, 5th Edition (Harlow, 2008), p. 152.

so many of their parish churches to glorify these holy men and women. A case from 1543 nicely demonstrates the resultant tensions. When Cornish and Devonian pilgrims had travelled together to Windsor to pray to the shrine of Henry VI, to 'good king Henry of Windsor', the dean of the chapel admonished them for committing 'such great idolatry' and having 'vainly' spent 'their goods in coming so far to kiss a spur, and have an old hat set upon their heads'.[207] He lambasted them for so long that they promised never to go on pilgrimage again. In this more sharply defined world, there was less room for Cornish particularism. Even Shakespeare's *Henry V* had the character of Pistol enquire after the identity of the disguised king, with the incognito Henry V replying 'Harry Le Roy!' and Pistol responding: 'Le Roy? A Cornish name: art though of Cornish Crew?'.[208] Crew in this sense had derogatory undertones.

Interactions between the county and the rest of early-modern England were far more complex than simple antipathy, however, not least because of the limitations of our sixteenth-century evidence. One such problematic account is that of Andrew Boorde, who was undoubtedly critical of Cornwall but actually lampooned everyone so as to produce an amusing tome.[209] John Norden presented a different picture of Cornwall, one of a much more settled county. Even Richard Carew's claim that Cornish-speaking folk able to converse in English, when addressed in this tongue by outsiders, would respond 'Meea Navidna Cowzasawzneck', I can speake no Saxonage' is not unproblematic.[210] While demonstrating the rise of linguistic tensions, his comments also show that Cornishmen played to the gallery and emphasise the fact that Carew himself sought to present an engaging account of his natal shire. It has to be recognised that the concerns, language and perceptions of these sixteenth-century writers have come to dominate our image of pre-modern Cornwall. Configuring Cornwall's past to glorify the present, all these men wrote a particular type of history in a shared intellectual milieu. Richard Carew, for example, employed the writings of William of Malmesbury and Geoffrey of Monmouth to emphasise Cornish particularism, while also citing Polydore Vergil and discussing Cornwall with William Camden.[211] Camden, in turn, acknowledged his great debt to Carew's intellectual endeavours, with the latter's writings influencing John Norden, Nicholas Roscarrock and many others.[212] All these works tell us

---

[207] *The Acts and Monuments of John Foxe*, ed. S. R. Cattley, 8 vols (London, 1837–41), v, p. 467.
[208] Henry V, Act 4 Scene 1, discussed in Stoyle, *West Britons*, pp. 36–37.
[209] For example, Boorde, *Knowledge*, pp. 116–117.
[210] Carew, 56r.
[211] Carew, 96v, 2v, 78r, 54v; see, *Topographical Writers in South-West England*, ed. M. Brayshay (Exeter, 1996).
[212] Camden, *Britannia*, i, p. 9; Roscarrock, *Lives of the Saints*, pp. 90–91; Cooper, *Tudor State*, p. 256.

as much about their authors and their reasons for writing as about Cornwall itself. Their views were not universal truths and Cornish alterity was not nearly so exotic as they all suggested.

Loyal Rebellions

Neither did the Cornish rebellions which have come to dominate perceptions of the county's past simply erupt from a combination of long-term oppression and Tudor assertiveness. It seems that taxation was the main short-term cause of the first of these revolts in 1497, with the rebels supposedly unable to 'bear the weight of tax for the Scottish war', Henry VII's planned expedition north.[213] Although the king's stannary policies and the minority of the then duke also played some part in fomenting discontent, proving more important still was the degree of Cornwall's integration.[214] After contributing much to the war effort, the county's residents were dissatisfied that they had received so little in return. Viewing themselves as essential stakeholders in England, the rebels made no attempt to establish a Cornish kingdom unto itself. Instead, they marched on London to 'deliuer the King a strong petition', aiming to do 'the duety of true Englishmen, and good liege men' by 'delivering the King from such Wicked ones that would destroy both him and the Country'.[215] In avoiding placing the blame on the king himself, they were following a well-established tradition of popular English insurrection. The Cornish leaders who emerged, the smith Michael Joseph of St Keverne and the lawyer Thomas Flamank of Bodmin, actually focused on the legality of their actions, with the latter supposedly talking 'learnedly, and as if he could tell how to make a Rebellion, and neuer breake the peace'.[216] Among their number the insurgents counted people from the whole range of county society, all of whom sought to reform a government that enjoyed legitimacy in both Cornwall and the wider kingdom.[217]

On the march to London the rebels were certainly not treated as an 'alien invasion' by the inhabitants of southern England. Quite the reverse, in fact, as the 'Rebellis... were ffavourid of the people as they passid the Cuntrees' for 'they paid well for all thyng that they took', actually being joined by folk from

---

[213] Vergil, *Anglia Historia*, pp. 89–90; *Calendar of State Papers, Milan*, ed. A. Hinds, HMSO (London, 1912), p. 323.
[214] I. Arthurson, 'The Rising of 1497: A Revolt of the Peasantry?', in *People, Politics and Community in the Later Middle Ages*, ed. J. Rosenthal and C. Richmond (Gloucester, 1987), pp. 1–19 at 4.
[215] F. Bacon, *The Historie of the Raigne of King Henry the Seventh...* ed. M. Kiernan (Oxford, 2012), pp. 113–114; Vergil, *Anglia Historia*, pp. 89–91; *State Papers, Milan*, pp. 316–317.
[216] Bacon, *Henry the Seventh*, p. 113.
[217] Cf. Arthurson, 'Rising of 1497', pp. 5–6.

Devon, Dorset, Kent, Somerset, Surrey, Sussex and Wiltshire, not least Lord Audley in Somerset.[218] Although it began in Cornwall, this was no 'Cornish Rebellion' alone for it drew on universal strands of dissatisfaction with Henry VII. Being known as 'the Comons of Cornewayll', the Cornish rebels were directly linked by contemporaries with 'Jak straw, Jak Cade & othir Rebellis'.[219] Popular rebellions from 1381 to the mid-sixteenth century employed the political language of 'the commons' to emphasise the fact that they held a place in political society, for the link between commons and the well-being of the realm was widely appreciated.[220] All these rebels, the Cornish among them, viewed themselves as rightful political actors who sought to intervene in the realm's government so as to correct its wrongs.[221] While the bloody end of the revolt at Blackheath cannot be doubted, with Polydore Vergil stigmatising the rebels as a 'base Cornish horde' and Michael Joseph supposedly of 'such stowte stomake' that before his death he proclaimed that 'he should have a name perpetuall and a fame permanent', such critical assessments of a failed rebellion were to be expected from those who had prevailed.[222] In the aftermath, Henry VII issued a general pardon to all those who had taken up arms against his majesty, Cornish and non-Cornish alike, with no distinction made between these folk.[223] All these English subjects of the king were treated accordingly, with Polydore Vergil even claiming that the rebellion had been no less than a 'civil war'.[224]

If the first revolt of 1497 was no war of independence, then neither did the rebellions of later 1497 nor 1549 witness the Cornish seek self-government. The second rising of 1497 saw the pretender Perkin Warbeck proclaim himself King Richard IV at Bodmin, with the county's disturbed condition helping him garner Cornish backing.[225] Supporting a claimant to the throne of England, however, these Cornishmen did not proclaim Warbeck king of

---

[218] *The Great Chronicle of London*, ed. A. H. Thomas and I. D. Thornley (London, 1938), p. 276; Vergil, *Anglia Historia*, pp. 94–95; *Tudor Royal Proclamations*, ed. P. L. Hughes and J. F. Larkin, 3 vols (London, 1964–9), i, p. 39; Arthurson, 'Rising of 1497', pp. 6–7.
[219] *Chronicle of London*, pp. 275, 278.
[220] J. Watts, 'Public or Plebs: The Changing Meaning of "the Commons", 1381–1549', in *Power and Identity*, pp. 242–260.
[221] M. Bush, 'The Risings of the Commons in England, 1381–1549', in *Orders and Hierarchies in Late Medieval and Renaissance Europe*, ed. J. Denton (London, 1999), pp. 109–125.
[222] Vergil, *Anglia Historia*, p. 95; E. Hall, *Hall's Chronicle: Containing the History of England...* (London, 1809), *Henry VII*, f. 43.
[223] *Tudor Royal Proclamations*, i, pp. 39–40.
[224] Vergil, *Anglia Historia*, pp. 92–93.
[225] Vergil, *Anglia Historia*, pp. 104–111; I. Arthurson, *The Perkin Warbeck Conspiracy 1491–1499* (Stroud, 1994), pp. 182–188.

a newly established realm of Cornwall. After Henry VII had prevailed over this force, his government actually had to guard Warbeck 'well' so 'that the men of Cornwall may not murder him, as they are incensed since they have learned from the king that they have been worshipping a low born foreigner as their sovereign'.[226] Having more overtly religious causes, the Rising of 1548 and the so-called Prayer Book Rebellion of 1549 arose in no small part from the government's imposition of English rites.[227] Beginning first in Devon, the latter rebellion saw Cornish folk lend their support to those who had risen against the king, rejecting the new English-language service as 'but lyke a Christmas game' in the petition that they were to submit to the sovereign.[228] Yet the fact that both the Cornish and Devonian rebels referred to themselves as 'the commons', petitioning the Crown to affect change, shows how implicitly they believed in the kingdom's legitimacy. Even in the Great Civil War, when Cornwall declared overwhelmingly for the king and the parliamentarian pamphleteers denigrated the peninsula's residents as plundering 'Cornish Choughs' with 'much danger in a Cornish hugg', the county's sons were fighting to defend the royal position in the country at large and the harsh words of propagandists were not matched by equally violent action after parliament's victory.[229]

The supposed clash between Cornwall and England that these rebellions have come to epitomise was nothing of the sort. While there may have been some ethnic dimensions to the revolts, there were remarkably few mentions of racial tension. More localised concerns proved highly significant, as all Cornwall by no means spoke with one voice. We may also wonder if these revolts really represent a continuum of disorder, as each rising occurred in a different set of specific circumstances. Perhaps the most striking continuity is that none of these rebellions strived to sever the county from the rest of the country. Seeking to correct royal government so as to restore both Cornwall and the rest of the kingdom to good order, the Cornishmen who rose in revolt were willing to risk their lives to defend the county and its place in the wider realm.

In seeking to intervene in the rulership of the kingdom at large, all these rebellions sharply contrasted with the revolt that Owain Glyn Dŵr led in Wales from 1400 onwards.[230] Arising from deep-seated tensions between the English

---

[226] *State Papers, Milan*, p. 331.
[227] F. Rose-Troup, *The Western Rebellion of 1549* (London, 1913); M. Stoyle, '"Fullye Bente to Fighte Oute the Matter": Reconsidering Cornwall's Role in the Western Rebellion of 1549', *EHR*, 129 (2014), pp. 549–577; I. Arthurson, 'Fear and Loathing in West Cornwall: Seven New Letters on the 1548 Rising', *JRIC* (2000), pp. 68–96.
[228] Rose-Troup, *Western Rebellion*, pp. 220–222; Fletcher and MacCulloch, *Tudor Rebellions*, pp. 151–153.
[229] Cf. Stoyle, *West Britons*, pp. 37–38, 78–81.
[230] See, Davies, *Owain Glyndŵr*.

and Welsh inhabitants of Wales, along with more recent political disturbances, Glyn Dŵr's revolt rejected English overlordship and sought to drive out all English government from its native land. Rather than marching on London or petitioning the king for reform, Glyn Dŵr set about killing Englishmen in a guerrilla war and proclaimed himself prince of an independent Wales. He even sought an alliance with the French. In response to his actions in Wales, and again unlike in Cornwall, the Crown passed a raft of anti-Welsh legislation excluding Welshmen from positions of significance and 'restraining... bards and other vagabonds'.[231] Neither was there a Cornish equivalent of the so-called Declaration of Arbroath, a letter of 1320 supposedly from the 'whole community of the realm' of Scotland that sought to defend Scotland's right to exist as a sovereign kingdom.[232] Nor was there anything like the Remonstrance of 1317, another letter, this time professing to be sent by 'the Irish people' claiming that the English had denied them their freedoms. From all this we can see that Cornwall's late-medieval residents and even its rebels believed in their English credentials while also enjoying a strong sense of their own Cornishness.

The county's inhabitants long remembered these rebellions, however, and Cornish folk acquired something of a reputation for disorder.[233] One such instance is to be found in 1537, when the citizens of Exeter claimed to be 'half afraid of a privy insurrection of Cornishmen', as St Keverne was 'a very large parish where first stirred the Cornishmen to rise when they came to Blackheath; the blacksmith dwelt there'.[234] Another comes from 1538, when the French ambassador wrote that England 'contains Wales and Cornwall, natural enemies of the rest of England, and speaking a language which is French'.[235] Closer to home, the Elizabethan *Mirror for Magistrates* included a long account of 'the Blacksmith' Michael Joseph, who 'puft vp wyth pryde' resisted the king.[236] In the end, however, the *Mirror* had him repent because the whole piece was included 'to teach all people... obedience to the hyghest powers'.[237] For all the hyperbole, the authorities even regarded Cornish rebels as English. Also entering Cornwall's collective consciousness, the revolts supposedly saw 'the baser sorte of people' in the county 'retayne a kinde of conceyled envye agaynste the Englishe, whome they yet affecte with a desire of revenge for their

---

[231] *CPR 1399–1401*, 469–570.
[232] Discussed in M. Brown, *Disunited Kingdoms: Peoples and Politics in the British Isles 1280–1460* (Harlow, 2013), pp. 96–111.
[233] Cf. Stoyle, *West Britons*, pp. 40–45.
[234] *Letters and Papers, Foreign and Domestic, of the Reign of Henry VIII*, ed. J. S. Brewer et al, 23 vols in 35 (London, 1864–1920), xii part 1, p. 450 and part 2, p. 60.
[235] *Letters and Papers*, xiii part 2, p. 482.
[236] *The Mirror for Magistrates*, ed. L. B. Campbell (Cambridge, 1938), pp. 402–421.
[237] *Mirror for Magistrates*, pp. 419, 421.

fathers sake, by whome their fathers recvyved the repulse'.[238] At the other end of the social spectrum, Richard Carew thought these popular revolts shameful.[239] Evidently the memory of these rebellions divided county opinion.

While accusations of sedition could at times be levelled at Cornwall's residents, with these sometimes accepted by county folk and at other times rejected by them, they do not illustrate a place riven with racial hatred.[240] These sorts of claims were neither generally made nor accepted, as pre-modern Cornwall was not perpetually ready to explode into disorder. The county should not be judged on these rebellions alone. Neither were these revolts the inevitable result of the Anglo-Saxon conquest some 700 years earlier. There was no such thing as a long arc of repression that saw Celtic Cornwall perpetually subjugated by an Imperial England, finally rising to throw off the yoke of English domination. Such a judgement accords more closely to modern national assumptions than to the realities of medieval politics and attitudes. While frictions and tensions were always to abound, such is politics, with Cornishness and Englishness interacting west of the Tamar in many shifting ways. In the fourteenth century Cornwall was no colonised land and history should not be read backwards.

Conclusion

Perhaps the firmest conclusion we can draw is that Cornwall existed in the hearts and minds of its residents. Strikingly traditional and yet ever-changing, Cornishness emerges as highly varied, endlessly reimagined and time-honoured all at once. The idea of 'Cornwall' had to negotiate a rich range of sub-county localisms, with these many strands of self-perception informing what it meant to be Cornish. Although the peninsula's inhabitants articulated their collective identity most clearly when they felt that the county as a whole was threatened, even here the worthy few were more strident than the less biddable many. We may well wonder if in practice as many 'Cornwalls' existed in the minds of the county's residents as there were residents. While there were some ethnic dimensions to being Cornish, with a measure of blood and ancestry determining this status, no formal definition of ethnicity existed. Neither did such a thing as a *cordon sanitaire* divide the peninsula's residents from those of the rest of England. On the contrary, the county's inhabitants enjoyed both Cornish and English blood at one and the same time, these two strands representing different layers of identity. Rather than testifying to the county's exclusion from the realm, the literary construct of a separate Cornwall arose

---

[238] Norden, *Description of Cornwall*, p. 22.
[239] *Carew*, 97v–98r; Stoyle, *West Britons*, p. 41.
[240] Cf. Cooper, *Tudor State*, pp. 136, 144.

from the repetition of a specific history with common Galfridian roots. While in some ways this immortalised a sense of difference, a chasm existed between 'words and deeds', between the stock images of Cornish otherness and the practical relationships stretching sinuously across the Tamar.[241]

We have seen how notions of Cornishness were defined in no small part through the county's interactions with the rest of England, by Cornwall's Englishness. At times deploying a shared sense of Cornishness in resistance to 'England', the county's residents could at other times employ such oppositional identities to bestow greater coherence on the far south west. Often by the fourteenth century, however, the peninsula's place as an integral part of the realm simultaneously enhanced a sense of Cornishness and an awareness of the county's wider loyalties. The interweaving of kingdom-wide concerns with pan-Cornish sentiments and more localised solidarities rendered the peninsula all the more remarkable. Comprising many mutable, nested identities, Cornishness and Englishness themselves were palimpsest terms that over many centuries were endlessly renegotiated both east and west of the Tamar. Although enjoying a potent and polyglot identity of their own, one that in turn proved to be dynamic and conservative, deeply localised and strikingly outward-looking, the Cornish were not repressed or excluded from the kingdom. Being Cornish was never that simple.

---

[241] Cf. Frame, 'Wider World', p. 453.

II

Distant *Dominium*: Comital, Ducal and Regnal Lordship

5
The Final Tempestuous Years of the Earldom, 1300–36

Heralding the most tempestuous period in the earldom's history, the death of Earl Edmund in 1300 brought to an end the dynasty founded by his father, Earl Richard of Cornwall, king of the Romans. Edmund's patrimony was to pass to his cousin, Edward I himself, creating the link between the lordship and the Crown which endures to this day. For the next thirty-seven years the title bounced back and forth between the king, Piers de Gaveston, Queen Isabella and John of Eltham, before finally returning to the hands of Edward III. It was to this backdrop that in March 1337 Edward elevated the earldom to a dukedom, vesting it upon his son and heir, the Black Prince. In contrast to the previous years of instability, the prince then governed his patrimony assertively for forty years until his death in 1376. In this year, however, Richard of Bordeaux inherited the duchy from his father and in 1377 the lordship came to be vested in the Crown itself after he ascended to the throne of England as Richard II. Although the final disorderly years of the earldom, the punctilious supervision of the prince and Richard's turbulent reign contrast in many ways, together they emphasise the integrative role played by the lordship in Cornwall.

Before embarking on the fourteenth-century history of the earldom-duchy, however, it is worth considering what expectations contemporaries had of good lordship. According to Robert Boutruche, lordship, *dominium*, was the 'power of command, constraint and exploitation. It [was] also the right to exercise such power'.[1] The institution of lordship emerges as ubiquitous in medieval England. Even Cornwall's miracle plays were infused with the lordly language of fiefs and liege lords, with the character of Christ himself stating that lords

---

[1] R. Boutruche, *Seigneurie et Féodalité*, 2 vols (Paris, 1968–70), ii, p. 83.

enjoyed 'dominium over their people' (*myghterneth war aga tus*).[2] Yet despite the power of lordships great and small across England, a profound difference existed between the mere exercise of power and actual 'good lordship'.[3]

To aid this analysis we can separate the lord's perspective of good lordship from that of his dependants. The former can perhaps best be summarised as involving effective governance and correct behaviour. In his treatise on estate management, Walter of Henley recommended that a lord should thoroughly acquaint himself with his patrimony.[4] A good lord should fight constantly against the erosion of his rights, employing men of good report who would labour diligently in his service.[5] While he might assert his mastery over them, admonishing servants who 'loyter in theire woorke', he should also provide suitable rewards in recognition of their diligence. It followed that servants should learn to 'love theire maister and to feare him'.[6] Close control of tenants was equally essential, for the lord's 'wrath' should be unbearable but his concern for peace unequalled.[7] All this seignorial activity would secure the legitimacy which drew the potentially 'free' power of the locality around the 'reverence' of lordship, to the benefit of lordly might and coffers.[8]

When considering good lordship from the perceptive of dependants, it becomes apparent that this can best be characterised as involving the reciprocal relationships of protection and patronage.[9] Dependants orbited around their lord at varying distances, with those closest to him – his household and retainers – expecting to receive annuities, offices and gifts.[10] On the one hand, Bishop Brinton of Rochester eulogised the Black Prince's generosity to his followers; Walter of Henley, on the other hand, cautioned against giving 'to muche nor to little'.[11] Evidently material reward formed an essential component of good lordship, as did the quasi-judicial role of *dominium* because a

[2] *Cornish Drama*, i, PC, lines 785–790.
[3] R. R. Davies, *Lords and Lordship in the British Isles in the Late Middle Ages*, ed. B. Smith (Oxford, 2009), p. 7.
[4] *Walter of Henley and other Treatises on Estate Management and Accounting*, ed. D. Oschinsky (Oxford, 1971), pp. 312–313.
[5] Davies, *March*, pp. 176–177, 199; Davies, *Lords and Lordship*, p. 163; *Walter of Henley*, pp. 339–341.
[6] *Walter of Henley*, pp. 316–317, 340–341, 398–402; K. B. McFarlane, *England in the Fifteenth Century: Collected Essays*, with an Introduction by G. L. Harriss (London, 1981), p. x.
[7] *Bewnans Ke*, line 1264; *Beunans Meriasek*, line 2208.
[8] Davies, *Lords and Lordship*, pp. 158–178; McFarlane, *The Nobility*, p. 47; J. Watts, *Henry VI and the Politics of Kingship* (Cambridge, 1996), p. 69.
[9] Davies, *March*, pp. 223–224.
[10] McFarlane, *Fifteenth Century*, pp. xiv–xv, 17–18.
[11] *The Sermons of Thomas Brinton, Bishop of Rochester (1373–1389)*, ed. M. A. Devlin, 2 vols, Camden Society, 3rd Series 85–86 (London, 1954), ii, pp. 354–357; *Walter of Henley*, pp. 310–311.

seigniorial connection should yield advancement to lordly retainers.[12] At the same time, however, supporters required honourable leadership so as not to be loathed as agents of lordly extortion.[13] As tenants and all others within the ambit of seignorial authority sought protection and justice, it is unsurprising that in *Bewnans Ke* the duke of Cornwall's character can be found providing 'peace' to 'everybody, common and grand' (*Pes, tout gent, pedit et ground*).[14] Standing out as the arbiter of the common good, a good lord needed a strong sense of *noblesse oblige*.[15]

From all this we can see that mutual 'dependence, service, and reward' characterised good lordship for both lords and dependents.[16] Yet whereas some components of lordship emerge as mutually supporting, others were opposed. A lord had to be careful not to impoverish his tenants, for instance, while love and fear might sometimes prove incompatible. Neither did good lordship form an absolute quality, as contemporaries weighed lordship against the alternatives on offer and the regimes which had come before. It is illustrative of this that in the time of Queen Isabella's rule of Cornwall the commonalty harked back to Earl Richard's practices over forty-five years earlier.[17] A concept founded on subjective judgment, actual good lordship could only ever exist in the eye of the beholder, and even there but fleetingly. In both theory and practice, then, good lordship was a complex institution, indeed so complex as almost to appear paradoxical. While lordship was intensely personal, it was yet impossible to exercise personally because its exercise depended on the mediation of seigniorial administrators. It was still the lord's conscientiousness that provided his lordship with direction and momentum, however, with the result that lordship operated in a different manner depending on who happened to be lord.[18] In this sense lordship formed a personal affair, being refashioned in Cornwall each time the title changed hands.

*

Edmund's successor in the earldom, King Edward I, was keen to exploit his newly acquired rights for personal financial advantage. To this end, he ordered that all Edmund's muniments be brought to London and a grand set of ministers' accounts was produced for 1300-1.[19] While the impetus for all this activity came from the king, it also provided the Staffordshire-born Thomas de la Hyde,

---

[12] McFarlane, *Fifteenth Century*, p. xxi; Davies, *Lords and Lordship*, pp. 197–217.
[13] Davies, *Lords and Lordship*, p. 42; McFarlane, *Fifteenth Century*, p. 18.
[14] *Bewnans Ke*, line 1260.
[15] *Thomas Brinton*, pp. 355–356; *Walter of Henley*, pp. 310–311; Davies, *Lords and Lordship*, p. 175.
[16] Davies, *Lords and Lordship*, p. 197.
[17] SC8/40/1996, the petition probably dates from 1317.
[18] Cf. McFarlane, *The Nobility*, p. 47.
[19] *CCR 1296–1302*, 599; SC6/811/2–3.

sheriff-steward of Cornwall since 1296, with a chance to prove his mettle.[20] At the same time the king had Sir Reginald Beville and other local gentlemen enforce the reissue of Magna Carta in Cornwall.[21] He also set about rewarding his servants with posts in the earldom, in 1301 for example granting Launceston Castle to his yeoman, one Peter Burdet. Edward made the full force of his royal administration felt in the county, despatching justices of eyre, the most powerful royal justices, there in 1302. Once in Cornwall, these justices adjudicated over dozens of civil and criminal cases brought by folk from the whole range of county society, raising as much as £1,456 from fines.[22]

While the king's highly assertive justice and heavy fines risked alienating the county's residents, Edward emerges as receptive to Cornish concerns.[23] In October 1302, in response to a petition from the county commonalty about shrieval elections, he investigated their concerns and soon after replaced Hyde with Sir Roger Ingepenne.[24] Sir Roger counted as a compromise candidate. Although he hailed from Berkshire, he had served as Earl Edmund's sheriff-steward in 1285–6 and held some Cornish lands, later granting these to his nephew and heir, one Roger Ingepenne junior. Furthering his Cornish connections, the latter had acquired the hand of a certain Joan, the heiress of Sir John Halton of St Dominick. Presumably influencing the appointment too, Aymer de Valence, the earl of Pembroke, retained both nephew and uncle.[25] Sir Roger was to have a short tenure, however, being indicted before the eyre of 1302 for 'homicides, larcenies, felonies… trespasses' and appropriation of the king's money.[26] Pembroke's timely intervention secured his pardon, but as the king would not tolerate mendacity he chose to reinstate Hyde.

Since the Scottish Wars overshadowed the affairs of the realm at this time, fiscal considerations underlined Edward's actions in Cornwall.[27] Ordering that the earldom's issues be collected promptly, the king assigned over £900 of this income for wine consumed by his household.[28] He also loaned money to boost tin production and in 1305 granted a new and comprehensive stannary charter

---

[20] For all office-holders, see Appendix I.
[21] *CPR 1292–1301*, 516, 573; *CPR 1301–1307*, 42; M. Prestwich, *Edward I* (London, 1988), pp. 518–522.
[22] *YB 30 & 31 Edward I*, 74–291; D. Crook, 'The Later Eyres', *EHR*, 97 (1982), pp. 241–268 at 252.
[23] *CPR 1301–1307*, 350–351, 354, 406–407, 480; *CCR 1296–1302*, 594; JUST1/1330 mm. 1r, 47d–50; JUST1/119; KB27/171 m. 63; KB27/186 m. 12.
[24] SC8/323/E562; SC8/323/E561, these petitions probably date from 1302.
[25] J. R. S. Phillips, *Aymer de Valence, Earl of Pembroke 1307–1324: Baronial Politics in the Reign of Edward II* (Oxford, 1972), p. 296.
[26] SC6/816/9; KB27/171 m. 63; *SCKB*, iv, lxxiii; *CPR 1301–1307*, 122.
[27] Prestwich, *Edward I*, pp. 401–435, 537, 554–555.
[28] *CCR 1296–1302*, 460; *CPR 1301–1307*, 482; *CCR 1302–1307*, 372, 374, 396, 509–510; SC6/811/2–8; E389/55–58.

ad tranquillitatem et utilitatem stannatorium nostrorum.[29] Such concessions arose from the fact the county and the Crown were enjoying a new and direct line of communication.[30] Some of Cornwall's revenues were then assigned to Edward's sons, Thomas of Brotherton and Edmund of Woodstock, although the king is said to have torn out handfuls of his heir's hair when the youth suggested that Gaveston be created earl.[31] This was the situation in the earldom on his death in 1307, when his son, another Edward, inherited the throne.

One of Edward II's first acts as king was to grant his favourite, Piers de Gaveston, the earldom of Cornwall.[32] Over the next few years the favourite's egregious use of authority, like a 'second king, to whom all were subject and none equal', festered at the heart of English politics.[33] In Gaveston's own lordship, however, his rule was weak and ineffective. He reappointed Hyde as sheriff-steward because he paid so little attention to his earldom.[34] Gaveston had trouble simply taking possession of his lands, with the officials slow to respond to his instructions and the king admonishing them for their tardiness.[35]

Inevitably, Gaveston's aggrandisement and Edward's intransigence quickly resulted in tensions between the king and his nobility. These came to a head in 1308, and in a state of near civil war the king's opponents stripped Gaveston of his estates and exiled him to Ireland.[36] Edward, however, set his will on securing his favourite's return, achieving this the next year and returning the earldom to Gaveston.[37] Hyde had continued as sheriff-steward during Gaveston's exile, with the Gascon reappointing him on his return; earls might fail and fall, but Hyde did not. His fourth appointment to the same office stands as eloquent testament to Gaveston's complete lack of interest in Cornwall. Hyde's manifest failings make his employer's neglect all the more apparent. An episode that occurred in 1309 conveniently illustrates this point. After he had

---

[29] E159/87 m. 160; *CPR 1301-1307*, 326; *CChR 1300-1326*, 53-54; Lewis, *Stannaries*, pp. 239-241.
[30] E179/87/5; E372/161 m. 41; Hatcher, *Tin*, p. 67.
[31] *RESDCornwall*, 4; H. Johnstone, *Edward of Carnarvon, 1284-1307* (Manchester, 1946), pp. 123-124.
[32] *CChR 1300-1326*, 108; J. R. S. Phillips, *Edward II* (New Haven and London, 2010), pp. 126-128; J. S. Hamilton, *Piers Gaveston, Earl of Cornwall 1307-1312: Politics and Patronage in the Reign of Edward II* (London and Detroit, 1988); J. Burgtorf, "'With my life, his joyes began and ended": Piers Gaveston and King Edward II of England Revisited', *Fourteenth Century England*, V, ed. N. Saul (Woodbridge, 2008), pp. 31-51.
[33] *Vita Edwardi Secundi, The Life of Edward II...*, ed. W. R. Childs (Oxford, 2005), pp. 4-5.
[34] SC6/811/9-10; E389/59.
[35] Hamilton, *Gaveston*, p. 41.
[36] Phillips, *Edward II*, pp. 146-151.
[37] Hamilton, *Gaveston*, pp. 67-74; *CChR 1300-1326*, 131; *CCR 1307-1313*, 225-226.

confiscated some stannary-men's cattle in lieu of a debt, Hyde and his bailiffs were assaulted by these same men, who forcibly rescued their cattle. Pursuing him to Ralph Arundell's house, the tinners then besieged Hyde with the aim of murdering him, so that Sir Thomas l'Ercedekne with a 'great *posse*' had to rescue the erstwhile sheriff-steward.[38] The roots of such lawlessness were to be found in the neglect or abuse of their responsibilities by all three of Edward, Gaveston and Gaveston's sheriff-steward.[39] The absence of effective lordship emboldened local malefactors, and without effective supervision Hyde himself increasingly managed the county to his own advantage.[40] In the end, however, it was his inability to raise the earldom's dues that proved the greatest problem.

In the next few years events in the rest of the country were to put Hyde's personal failings into the shadows. In March 1310, the king agreed resentfully to the set of Ordinances imposed on him by Lancaster and the opposition lords, the general aim of which was to correct his misgovernment.[41] Gaveston was sentenced to perpetual exile.[42] Although rumours circulated that he remained skulking in Tintagel, this was not the case and Edward schemed to undo the affront to his majesty and secure the return of his favourite. To strengthen his hand, in November 1311 he ordered the sheriff to take control of Gaveston's Cornish lands.[43] Throughout all these events Hyde had still retained his position.[44] Flouting the Ordinances, Gaveston returned from exile in early 1312.[45] The king once again sought to secure the Gascon's position, despatching his own clerk, one John Bedewynde, with a mandate 'to attend to' Gaveston's Cornish affairs.[46] As Hyde's failings were outweighed in the short-term by the need for his loyalty, the king buttressed his power by appointing him a conservator of the peace and charging him with 'attending to the custody' of Restormel Castle.[47] Seeking to secure the loyalty of the county's proprietors and fortresses at this time, Edward appointed Sir William Botreaux and Sir Thomas l'Ercedekne to the county bench while replacing all Cornwall's castellans: Launceston now went to Botreaux, Tintagel to l'Ercedekne and Trematon to Odo l'Ercedekne.

---

[38] *CPR 1307–1313*, 173, 236–237.
[39] For some cases, *CPR 1307–1313*, 40, 85, 133, 365, 417, 537; JUST1/1349 mm. 13r–18r; JUST1/1351 mm. 8d–10d.
[40] *CPR 1307–1313*, 255–257.
[41] M. Prestwich, 'The Ordinances of 1311 and the Politics of the Early Fourteenth Century', in *Politics and Crisis*, pp. 1–18.
[42] Phillips, *Edward II*, pp. 173–182; *Vita Edwardi Secundi*, pp. 38–39.
[43] *CFR 1307–1319*, 117.
[44] *CCR 1307–1313*, 382.
[45] Phillips, *Edward II*, pp. 182–185.
[46] *CCR 1307–1313*, 457.
[47] *CPR 1307–1313*, 473; *CCR 1307–1313*, 454.

Despite all Edward's efforts on Gaveston's behalf, the dissident earls captured the favourite in June 1312 and beheaded him near Warwick.[48] A month after this bloody event the king chose to replace Hyde as sheriff-steward with Bedewynde, giving him the title of keeper of the late earl's lands in Cornwall and Devon.[49] While Hyde had still been raising considerable sums, delivering no fewer than 1,000 marks to Bedewynde, collection of dues had fallen behind schedule and the family account remained in the red in the 1330s.[50] The great survivor, Hyde had held office for some sixteen years, during which time his administration grew increasingly lax as a result of Gaveston's perfunctory lordship and Edward's failing kingship.[51]

On Gaveston's death the earldom once again reverted to the king, remaining under his direct control until 1317. Yet Edward chose to retire Bedewynde less than a year after his appointment, the keeper having committed the offence of announcing to the county court that the king had been evilly advised over the stannaries.[52] The complaint had focused on Edward's banker, a certain Antonio Pessagno of Genoa, who had loaned the king more than £140,000 between 1312 and 1319.[53] In October 1312, on the advice of the elder Despenser, who naturally secured a £320 cut, the king granted Pessagno rights to all Cornish tin, ordering tinners to bring this metal to Restormel, where Pessagno would pay them as Earl Edmund had.[54] Becoming deeply entrenched in stannary finance, Pessagno is recorded coining over 1.8 million lbs of tin between 1312 and 1314.[55] His interference, however, caused much resentment. It was alleged that he paid over 4½ marks less per thousandweight than other merchants and employed a 'false scale', with the result that many Cornishmen sold their tin to whomsoever they pleased and others 'assaulted and threatened' his servants.[56] Combined with petitions claiming that Pessagno's enterprises threatened to destroy Cornwall and 2,500 of its 3,000 tinners, these events led to Edward removing him from the stannaries in 1316.[57] The king's drive to raise money had nonetheless earnt him the enmity of many of his Cornish subjects.

---

[48] Phillips, *Edward II*, pp. 185–191.
[49] *CFR 1307–1319*, 139–140.
[50] *CPR 1307–1313*, 488; *CFR 1307–1319*, 156; E372/158 m. 46r; E372/179 m. 17v.
[51] For some cases, KB27/194 mm. 18r, 28r, 31r; KB27/202 mm. 44r, 108r.
[52] E159/86 m. 76; J. C. Davies, *The Baronial Opposition to Edward II* (Cambridge, 1918), pp. 28, 553–554.
[53] E. B. Fryde, 'Sir Antonio Pessagno', *ODNB*, xliii, pp. 859–860.
[54] SC6/811/12 m. 6r; E159/88 m. 129v; *CFR 1307–1319*, 147; *CCR 1307–1313*, 481; E159/86 m. 76v; *CCR 1307–1313*, 498.
[55] E101/261/1; E101/261/17; *CPR 1313–1317*, 205; *CCR 1313–1318*, 130.
[56] *PROME*, iii, 99–100; SC8/103/5129; *CPR 1313–1317*, 228, 413; KB27/218 m. 101r; KB27/221 mm. 113r, 118r, 122r.
[57] *CPR 1313–1317*, 572–573.

As a result of Bedewynde's criticisms, in 1313 the king had replaced him as sheriff-steward with Sir Thomas l'Ercedekne.[58] l'Ercedekne seemed eminently suitable since he already held Tintagel and possessed his own estates in Cornwall, qualities supplemented by his brother's constableship of Trematon. The l'Ercedeknes were a force to be reckoned with in these years. Although a treaty between the king and his baronial opponents in December 1312 somewhat defused tensions in the rest of the realm, mutual suspicions remained.[59] After just a year, the government stripped all l'Ercedekne's offices from him.[60] Bannockburn had shattered the fragile political consensus, with the earl of Lancaster and his allies enforcing the Ordinances in earnest by removing virtually every sheriff on charges of mendacity.[61] There is evidence that l'Ercedekne had indeed used the office forcibly to further his own ambitions, while his connection with the Crown was unacceptable to the king's opponents.[62]

The English defeat at Bannockburn cast a long shadow over the politics of the realm, and in this inauspicious year Richard Polhampton of Berkshire took up the reins of the sheriff-stewardship.[63] In May 1316, however, after barely a year, the king decided to grant the office to Sir Henry Wylinton, who held some lands in Cornwall despite being of Gloucestershire baronial stock. At the same time as appointing him sheriff-steward, Edward made him purchaser of tin and granted him the county's ports and castles.[64] While his many offices made Wylinton relatively powerful in the county, he faced serious challenges because the lordship had sunk into decline. In 1313–14, for example, wrongdoers had launched a wholesale assault on the earldom's maritime prerogatives, one of a large number of crimes.[65] Even the king's taxers in the county acted contrary to their commissions, while the keepers of the peace 'had ceased doing so'.[66] So poor were conditions that in 1315 Cornish MPs claimed that the king had ill-kept the peace.[67] Evidently Edward's 'poisonous politics' were having a damaging effect on the entire kingdom.

The rapid change in the earldom's personnel, however, can easily mask Edward's concerted policy to mobilise the peninsula's resources. The king

---

[58] *CFR 1307–1319*, 160–161; Phillips, *Pembroke*, p. 38.
[59] Phillips, *Edward II*, pp. 197–201.
[60] *CFR 1307–1319*, 221; *CPR 1313–1317*, 163.
[61] Phillips, *Pembroke*, p. 70; Maddicott, *Lancaster*, pp. 160–161; *CPR 1313–1317*, 208, 242–243.
[62] *CPR 1313–1317*, 313.
[63] SC6/811/13; E389/61; *CFR 1307–1319*, 221.
[64] *CFR 1307–1319*, 278–279, 314; SC6/811/17 m. 3r; SC6/811/15 m. 1r.
[65] KB27/215 m. 12r.
[66] *CFR 1307–1319*, 332; *CCR 1313–1318*, 205; Cf. C. Burt, 'Local Government in Warwickshire and Worcestershire during the Reign of Edward II', in *Political Society*, pp. 55–73.
[67] *PROME*, iii, 100.

sought to use his Cornish revenues to make up for the losses of income that he had suffered in the Ordinances. Pessagno's appointment was a means to this end. Even after Pessagno's fall the king continued packing the earldom with his creatures, in 1317 appointing his household men Stephen de Abyndon and John Pecok the Elder as purchasers of tin.[68] He did all this, however, to the backdrop of famine and incessant rain.[69] Although the king sought to marshal the earldom's gold, he showed little interest in transforming Cornwall into a citadel of royal power.[70]

Edward instead left it to others to amass power in the peninsula into their hands, chief among them Bishop Stapeldon.[71] The Stapeldons were a west country family with a seat in west Devon, and Walter had been appointed to the see of Exeter in 1307, later serving twice as treasurer of England.[72] During his years in the see, Stapeldon, although an able diocesan, devoted considerable energy to furthering the interests of his own kin. To this end, he and his brother, Sir Richard, both legally and illicitly acquired lands and advowsons across the peninsula.[73] Bishop Stapeldon sought out valuable wardships, including that of the Arundells in 1307, and even tried to marry his niece to John Arundell, a match that the latter resisted.[74] Closely supervising his officials and obtaining charters for weekly markets in his manors, the bishop can be found defending his rights vigorously.[75] All this activity, extensive as it was, presents only a limited view of Stapeldon's meteoric rise, as he also set about courting local powerbrokers in Cornwall. In 1308 he nominated Sir John Treiagu as steward of his Cornish lands, Treiagu being a wealthy and busy man who had the local clout to defend the bishop's interests.[76] Although he had avoided politics in the early part of the reign, the bishop's later career as treasurer of England provided the scope for this 'empire building'. As the reign went on, Edward increasingly delegated lordship in the area to his staunch ally, harnessing the

---

[68] *CPR 1313–1317*, 619, 627.
[69] Cf. W. C. Jordan, *The Great Famine: Northern Europe in the Early Fourteenth Century* (Princeton, 1996).
[70] For some cases, JUST1/1371 m. 4d; KB27/224 m. 22r; KB27/227 m. 73r.
[71] M. C. Buck, *Politics, Finance and the Church in the Reign of Edward II: Walter Stapeldon, Treasurer of England* (Cambridge, 1983); K. Edwards, 'The Political Importance of the English Bishops during the Reign of Edward II', *EHR*, 59 (1944), pp. 311–347.
[72] Buck, *Finance and the Church*, pp. 10–12, 38–47.
[73] C143/81/14; KB27/204 m. 55r; KB27/205 m. 52r; *CPR 1313–1317*, 382, 561; *PROME*, iii, 60; Buck, *Finance and the Church*, pp. 20–26.
[74] CRO, AR/16/1; *Reg.Stapeldon*, 33–34.
[75] *Reg.Stapeldon*, 146–147; *CChR 1300–1326*, 183, 409, 431; JUST1/109 mm. 3r–6d; KB27/241 m. 38r; *CIM 1307–1349*, 65; *CPR 1313–1317*, 696–697; *CPR 1307–1313*, 377
[76] *Reg.Stapeldon*, 411; also, *CCR 1318–1323*, 559.

bishop's power to his Crown. Having no desire to micro-manage the far south west, however, the king left Bishop Stapeldon with much freedom of action.

Edward's lack of interest in the earldom is further illustrated by the events of 1317. In this year, he granted the lordship to his queen, Isabella, as part of her dower, where it was to remain until 1324.[77] Although Queen Isabella's administration adopted a 'businesslike' approach, gold seems to have formed the limit of her vision.[78] For this reason, she kept Wylinton in office as there were to be few changes in personnel, with little attempt made to forge a robust lordship anchored in local support. Leasing-out five whole manors, the queen realised that the system of farming-out maximised revenue with minimum input. She exploited her rights to the full, even if this was to the detriment of the county.[79] Isabella employed one Robert Miles as her receiver, but he also served the king as his clerk, Edward believing in keeping a close watch on his wife.[80] Throughout her tenure the queen secured the issue of numerous royal commissions investing disorder in the county, with everyone from leading gentlemen right down to peasants having illegally hunted in her Cornish parks and felled her trees with impunity.[81] Neither the quality of local lordship nor kingship saw a marked improvement during Isabella's tenure.

The rapprochement between the king and Lancaster, forged in the aftermath of Bannockburn, was to bring only a temporary respite to political strife in the realm. Tensions built up again from 1316, culminating in the attacks on the Despensers' properties in Glamorgan in the summer of 1321.[82] By this stage Edward and Lancaster were irreconcilable, but the king had also succeeded in alienating the lords of the Welsh March, potentially powerfully allies. Disturbed conditions across the realm led Edward to empower Hugh Courtenay and William Martyn to attack anyone who rose against him in Cornwall and Devon.[83] At this time the government removed Wylinton from the sheriff-stewardship, replacing him with Sir John Treiagu, although Sir William Botreaux appears in the office a few months later.[84] While Botreaux's greater wealth perhaps provided him with the clout to secure the royal position west

---

[77] *CPR 1317–1321*, 5, 8–9, 223; the claims of Gaveston's widow, Margaret, were settled in 1318, *CPR 1317–1321*, 251.
[78] *RESDCornwall*, 85; CRO, AR/42/4; see P. C. Doherty, 'Isabella, Queen of England, 1296–1330' (Unpubl. Univ. Oxford D.Phil, 1977).
[79] E389/62 m. 1r; *CCR 1323–1327*, 90; SC8/40/1996.
[80] E389/62 m. 1r; *CFR 1319–1327*, 308.
[81] *CPR 1317–1321*, 94, 291, 293, 463, 473, 604–605, 609; *CPR 1321–1324*, 147, 251, 447, 457; JUST1/126; KB27/250 *Rex* m. 17r.
[82] Maddicott, *Lancaster*, pp. 190–239, 259–268.
[83] Phillips, *Edward II*, pp. 328–409; *CCR 1318–1323*, 507; JUST1/1385 mm. 9r–10d.
[84] E389/63 m. 1r.

of the Tamar, Edward showed little sign of pursuing a policy of packing local government across the realm.[85]

Having secured the return of the Despensers early in 1322, the king was faced by a rebellion by Lancaster and the lords of the Welsh Marches. It is illustrative of the times that Edward sent an order to his local officers to investigate whether the wives or children of the rebels had entered Cornwall, either to stay or to take ship overseas.[86] Proving their loyalty and value, Sir Thomas l'Ercedekne and Ralph Trenewith fought for the king in the Marches, almost certainly serving at his side again later in the year.[87] It seems that Cornwall, however, provided no other forces for Edward's great enterprise, the government later claiming that the 'men of the county' had not 'hitherto rendered aid to the king against his enemies'.[88] Marshalling his forces effectively, on 16 March Edward defeated Lancaster at Boroughbridge and had the earl executed.[89] A number of Cornishmen had been involved in the fighting against Edward, among them Sir Otto Bodrugan, Sir Reginald Mohun and Henry Tyes.[90] Later threatening 'severe penalties' unless the county furnished him with soldiers, the king considered Cornwall and Lancashire especially disaffected.[91] As punishment, Edward confiscated the estates of the contrariant Cornishmen who had opposed him, only restoring them to their holders after the latter had agreed to pay hefty fines.[92] Bodrugan was coerced into paying 1,000 marks, one of the largest penalties of any non-Lancastrian, while Henry Tyes was even less fortunate, being 'drawn and hung at London in the time of Edward II'.[93] Despite the fact that Edward's regime employed fear and debt as forms of political control, it is striking that more Cornishmen actively opposed than supported his cause.

With Lancaster and many of the Marchers removed, the king secured his *révanche* and the Despensers were established more securely than ever in power, holding sway until the end of the reign.[94] As both Hugh the elder and

---

[85] N. Saul, 'The Despensers and the Downfall of Edward II', *EHR*, 99 (1984), pp. 1–33 at 18, 21, 29.
[86] *CCR 1318–1323*, 417.
[87] *CPR 1321–1324*, 65.
[88] *CPR 1321–1324*, 93.
[89] Phillips, *Edward II*, pp. 406–408.
[90] SC6/1146/21; *CIM 1307–1349*, 124–125; *CCR 1323–1327*, 63, 111; *CFR 1319–1327*, 161; for the rebels that Edward pardoned on account of their military service in France, see Appendix II.
[91] N. Fryde, *The Tyranny and Fall of Edward II, 1321–1326* (Cambridge, 1979), p. 70; *CPR 1321–1324*, 93.
[92] SC6/1146/21; *CFR 1319–1327*, 149–150, 160–161, 173.
[93] *CCR 1318–1323*, 618; *CFR 1319–1327*, 155; *CPR 1321–1324*, 183; *TCO*, 33, 190; Fryde, *Tyranny*, p. 72.
[94] Phillips, *Edward II*, pp. 441–448.

Hugh the younger founded their overweening brutality on informal influence, this practice of exercising power obscures any direct control they exercised in Cornwall.[95] More significantly, Isabella's possession of the earldom effectively blocked their activities west of the Tamar. After 1322, however, the queen's relationship with her husband rapidly soured. In 1324 Edward actually confiscated Isabella's Cornish estates on the pretext of their vulnerability to invasion, holding them until the end of his reign.[96] Many contemporaries claimed that he did so on Bishop Stapeldon's advice, and it must be noted that the bishop seized and subsequently managed her prerogatives.[97] These events marked the beginning of the bishop's real ascendancy in Cornwall. Eight days after the confiscation Stapeldon nominated Treiagu, his own steward, to the sheriff-stewardship. Still taking a close interest in county revenues, the king on the same day employed as receiver his own clerk, a certain Roger Blacolvesle.[98] The bishop and his royal master together set about strengthening their position in Cornwall, with Edward granting Tintagel Castle and Bossiney to Stapeldon 'for good service' and a yearly rent of £40.[99]

Despite these royal and episcopal efforts, Treiagu experienced severe difficulties in carrying out his duties. In early 1326 the king had to launch an investigation after a chain of violence had been set off when Treiagu had impounded Sir William Botreaux's 'beasts' for a debt. Botreaux had responded by mobilising his 'confederacy', including Sir William Basset, which then marched fully armed into the county court. Once inside, it was alleged that they had brazenly assaulted Treiagu and for a prolonged period prevented him from holding court and keeping the king's peace. Also attacking the king's bailiffs, for two years hunting illegally 'by night and by day' in royal parks, and ambushing money destined for the exchequer, their activities show that the peninsula was riven from top to bottom by thuggery.[100] While the bishop was able to wield considerable power, his lordship was far from all-embracing as it had had insufficient time to take root. His machinations also made mockery of the law, something shown by the fact Cornwall and Devon petitioned unavailingly about his abuse of excommunications and his misuse of ecclesiastical courts for secular pleas.[101]

At the end of the reign developments elsewhere conspired again to influence Cornish affairs. Queen Isabella, alienated from Edward, fled abroad and

---

[95] Saul, 'Downfall of Edward II', pp. 19–22, 24–25; Fryde, *Tyranny*, pp. 106–118, 149–164.
[96] *CFR 1319–1327*, 300.
[97] *Vita Edwardi Secundi*, pp. 242–243; Buck, *Finance and the Church*, p. 152.
[98] E389/63 m. 1r; *CFR 1319–1327*, 302–303.
[99] *CFR 1319–1327*, 401; *CCR 1323–1327*, 591.
[100] *CPR 1324–1327*, 238–239.
[101] SC8/42/2100.

from the Low Countries, in September 1326 she returned with a small invasion force to England, removing her husband from the throne.[102] With her paramour, Roger Mortimer, the queen then appropriated the governance of the realm during the minority of her son, Edward III. A breadknife-wielding London mob likewise cut short Bishop Stapeldon's empire building, beheading him in Cheapside near St Paul's.[103] There can be little doubt that the unhappy regimes of this *lassiez-faire* king and his self-aggrandising bishop had had a profound effect on Cornwall.

With Edward II by now deposed and in prison, on 10 January 1327 Isabella, effectively the new ruler of England, secured the 'restoration' of the earldom with an enlarged income of 20,000 marks.[104] Treiagu, left powerless by the overthrow of his local protector, was replaced; the new sheriff-steward was Sir Robert Bilkemore. Although hailing from Bedfordshire, Bilkemore was already in possession of the office of escheator in Cornwall. While Isabella was to have her son, John of Eltham, created titular earl in 1328, she retained all comital lands and prerogatives herself.[105] Contemporaries were fully aware of her ascendancy, among them Sir William de Cornewaille, who petitioned her directly concerning Treiagu's seizure of his Cornish manor of Brannel.[106] Appointing castellans and stewards alike in her hard-won lordship, the queen was happy to exercise her rights.[107] Isabella's quest for riches resulted in her pursuing similar estate management practices to those of her first term in 1317–24.[108] Yet the queen also set about establishing her political position more securely this time than then. She punished Sir Thomas l'Ercedekne, who stood out as a supporter of the former king, by a delayed request that he submit accounts for his time as sheriff-steward.[109] By contrast, Isabella bought Sir Otto Bodrugan's loyalty by both pardoning him the fine that he had incurred from fighting against her husband and granting him Lundy Island.[110] Bodrugan became a trusted supporter of the queen, in July 1330 arraying men to resist rebels challenging her in the peninsula.[111] Securing the issue of a new

---

[102] Phillips, *Edward II*, pp. 502–519.
[103] Buck, *Finance and the Church*, p. 220.
[104] *CPR 1324–1327*, 346; *CPR 1327–1330*, 21–22, 66–69, 438, 442, her executors were to hold Cornwall for three years after her death.
[105] *RESDCornwall*, 5; S. L. Waugh, 'John of Eltham', *ODNB*, xxx, pp. 173–174; P. Dryburgh, 'Living in the Shadows: John of Eltham, Earl of Cornwall (1316–36)', *Fourteenth Century England, IX*, ed. J. Bothwell and G. Dodd (Woodbridge, 2016), pp. 23–48.
[106] SC8/41/2001.
[107] *Sheriffs*, 21.
[108] *RESDCornwall*, 85–86; *CPR 1327–1330*, 333.
[109] *CCR 1327–1330*, 414; E372/177 m. 23v.
[110] *CCR 1327–1330*, 20, 30, 157.
[111] *CPR 1327–1330*, 571.

peace commission containing Robert Aspel, her steward, Roger Blacolvesle, a royal clerk, and Robert de Seliman, the escheator south of the Trent, the queen asserted her mastery over Cornwall.[112]

Unfortunately for them, neither she nor her paramour chose to exercise this sort of political acumen in England at large. Isabella and Mortimer were just as grasping as the previous regime had been but, try as they might, they could not prolong Edward III's minority forever. In October 1330 Edward asserted his majority in a spectacular *force majeure* at Nottingham, arresting his mother and her lover.[113] Over the next few months the newly empowered king set about securing the arrest of the former regime's creatures, investigating Benedict Noght and John le Taverner of Mousehole for aiding the overseas escape of John Maltravers and Thomas Gurney, Edward II's suspected murderers.[114] More significant, however, was Edward's confiscation of the earldom from his mother, on 1 December 1330.[115] Three days after this he confirmed John of Eltham, his younger brother, who was aged just fourteen, in the title earl, while retaining the substance of power himself. Indeed, of the 1,000 marks in revenues he assigned for Eltham's support, a mere £20 came from Cornwall.[116] For the better management of the lordship, and to secure the loyalty of the county's powerbrokers, the king appointed Sir William Botreaux to the sheriff-stewardship in early 1331 and granted Sir John Carminow the keeping of Trematon and Restormel castles.[117] Simultaneously, Edward set about packing the earldom's hierarchy with his own men, appointing as havener, for example, one William de London, sergeant to the king and tailor to the queen.[118] Wishing to maximise his revenues, the king paid down his creditors with the earldom's issues.[119]

Unlike his mother and father, however, Edward endeavoured to provide the county with more effective governance. So much is evident from the king's appointment of Carminow and Treiagu to a new peace commission in 1331, replacing the one dominated by Isabella's men. Edward showed considerable concern for this office, in the following year adding the Cornishman and serjeant-at-law John Trevaignon to the bench.[120] Launching an investigation into oppressions by his parents' ministers, the king was keen to expunge the

---

[112] *CPR 1327–1330*, 567.
[113] C. Shenton, 'Edward III and the Coup of 1330', in *The Age of Edward III*, ed. J. S. Bothwell (York, 2001), pp. 13–34; for Edward III, see W. M. Ormrod, *Edward III* (New Haven and London, 2011).
[114] *CPR 1330–1334*, 144; Phillips, *Edward II*, pp. 572–574.
[115] *CFR 1327–1337*, 215–216.
[116] *CChR 1327–1341*, 198.
[117] After some confusion, *CFR 1327–1337*, 200, 222, 232, 247–248, 277; *CPR 1330–1334*, 106.
[118] *CPR 1330–1334*, 40, 43, 163; *CFR 1327–1337*, 221, 225, 261–262, 288.
[119] SC6/811/18 m. 1r; *CFR 1327–1337*, 242; *CCR 1330–1333*, 217; *CPR 1330–1334*, 209.
[120] *CPR 1330–1334*, 286, 294.

ancien régime.[121] This ongoing process saw the government investigate the hapless Treiagu in 1333 'for alleged oppressions... by colour of his office'.[122] The final stage of this administrative upheaval came in October 1331, when John of Eltham received the substance of his title from the king, being granted most of the earldom's lands, but not the stannaries. Two years later, after Edward had shattered the Scots in battle at Halidon Hill, the king was to expand the grant to his brother to some 3,000 marks.[123] Royal and comital power were by now tightly intermeshed in Cornwall, to their mutual benefit. In 1336, while the siblings campaigned together in Scotland, the king even issued a special peace commission to keep regnal-comital peace with the *posse comitatus* if necessary.[124]

For all this royal activity, Eltham still pursued policies of his own in the county, in 1333 replacing Botreaux as sheriff-steward with Henry Trethewey.[125] Actually devoting considerable attention to the staffing of his lordship, the earl employed the royal yeoman John Moveroun as constable of Launceston Castle and in 1336 appointed Richard Bakhampton as steward, separating this post from the shrievalty.[126] Eltham set about boosting his revenues, granting Helston and Grampound new charters, speculating in tin on a grand scale and reforming the assessionable system to create more profitable short-term leases.[127] His tenure of the earldom was a brief one, however, as he died at Perth of undisclosed causes on 13 September 1336, before coming of age. The earldom once again reverted to the Crown, remaining under the king's protection for six months.[128] 'In fulfilment of a promise... made by the king's brother', in February 1337 Edward appointed a series of the deceased earl's retainers to Cornish posts, with one Henry de Erth, Eltham's standard-bearer at Berwick, gaining the constableship of Trematon.[129] So it was that Edward III enacted the last instruction of the last earl of Cornwall.

A desire to maximise revenue probably proved the main principle informing John of Eltham's rule of the earldom, as it had been for every fourteenth-century earl. There is evidence, however, that he also strived to govern the county with an effectiveness not seen for decades, by all accounts closely supervising

---

[121] *CPR 1330–1334*, 133.
[122] *CPR 1330–1334*, 440, 350.
[123] *CChR 1327–1341*, 233, 302–303; *CPR 1330–1334*, 413, 463, 493; *CPR 1334–1338*, 23, 123, 245, 261; *CCR 1330–1333*, 439–440; *CCR 1333–1337*, 64–65.
[124] *CPR 1334–1338*, 287, 357, 367–371; Cf. Dryburgh, 'John of Eltham', p. 2.
[125] SC6/812/12; E372/177 m. 17r; *CFR 1327–1337*, 364, 369; *CCR 1333–1337*, 399–400.
[126] *CPR 1334–1338*, 336; *CPR 1340–1343*, 18–19; *RBP*, ii, 42; SC6/1094/13 m. 12.
[127] SC6/1094/13 m. 12; *CPR 1330–1334*, 537; *CPR 1334–1338*, 25; E101/262/25; Hatcher, *Tin*, p. 57; *RESDCornwall*, 74–77; *CFR 1337–1347*, 4.
[128] SC6/1094/13 m. 1; *CPR 1334–1338*, 426, 447; *CCR 1333–1337*, 612.
[129] *CPR 1334–1338*, 383, 392–393; *CFR 1337–1347*, 4.

Cornwall. This brings us to the question of agency, of who was really responsible for the changes. The earl's young age suggests that his successes cannot be assigned to him alone, and Edward III himself was probably a significant figure in Eltham's life and lordship.[130] To separate the work of the two brothers, however, is perhaps to misunderstand the relationship between them. In all likelihood the two sought to stabilise Cornwall and the kingdom together.

*

At this point we need to break off to consider a topic which has been mentioned in passing on a number of occasions: the matter of lawlessness. As violence was seemingly a ubiquitous phenomenon in fourteenth-century England, it is no surprise that its causes were many and varied. Remaining stubbornly persistent, the ancient code of vengeance had a role to play.[131] It is also clear that chivalry itself idealised a noble code of violence. Since many Cornishmen fought in the king's expeditions, the long-running wars of the time created a deep pool of brutalised men. In raising armies, the government regularly pardoned criminals in return for military service; after his efforts at the siege of Calais, for example, the Cornishman Oliver Rusculian received a royal pardon for two murders and for 'breaking out' of the Marshalsea.[132] In Edward II's reign conflict in the form of civil war also wracked the realm, resulting in widespread dislocation, embittered divisions and convenient cover for private quarrels.[133] Even during peacetime, lawlessness and officialdom emerge in these years as interwoven. There is plentiful evidence that local officials exacted a profusion of petty extortions in the name of kings and lords which their employers simply could not prevent. Edward II's rule in particular, being so inept, encouraged predatory officials and the corruption of justice.[134] We see this in c. 1321, when Sir Thomas l'Ercedekne allegedly abused his royal purveyance commission by not only failing to remunerate those folk whose goods he had requisitioned, but also by employing the powers of his position to extort ransoms under the threat of hangings.[135] Nature itself could cause disruption, with hunger and hardship forever persisting in medieval England.

Widespread lordly manipulation of the law also prevailed, in the form of what is known as the practice of maintenance. Local lords are often found

---

[130] Dryburgh, 'John of Eltham', p. 23.
[131] For the classic accounts, J. Bellamy, *Crime and Public Order in England in the Later Middle Ages* (London, 1973), pp. 37–68; R. W. Kaeuper, *War, Justice, and Public Order: England and France in the Later Middle Ages* (Oxford, 1988), pp. 134–145, 187–188.
[132] *CPR 1350–1354*, 37.
[133] Fryde, *Tyranny*, p. 69; Maddicott, *Lancaster*, pp. 161–162, 176–177.
[134] Maddicott, *Lancaster*, p. 186; Walker, *Political Culture*, pp. 24–26.
[135] SC8/99/4921.

meddling in legal process to secure the interests of their dependents. A good example of this comes from 1309, when the government outlawed Thomas Gevely in Cornwall for robbing Margery, the widow of Sir Walter Treverbyn, and raping her daughter, Sibyl.[136] Although he was later pardoned on account of his good service in Scotland, Gevely subsequently followed the women to London and with two accomplices broke down the door to their lodgings, allegedly raping Sibyl again. Margery then sued him for a second time, but the repugnant Gevely appeared in the company and protection of the war-captain and courtier Sir Henry de Beaumont. Nobody would therefore accuse him in court, nor attach him when Margery tried to raise the hue. 'Petty tyrannies' such as these drew down the ire of the parliamentary Commons. In 1377 their complaints were to coalesce around the badges and liveries that nobles distributed to their supporters, as these represented the least stable magnate-dependent relationship and were believed to fuel the twin evils of disorder and maintenance.[137]

Suing and counter-suing to promote their own interests, the gentry themselves often employed legal guile. A good example of such a case is to be found in 1310, when Thomas Tregonon alleged that Sir John Treiagu had robbed him of no less than 40 lbs of silver.[138] Treiagu, however, denied all charges. Gentlemen often employed the law as a means to exact vengeance, with Treiagu later complaining that many men had conspired to have him imprisoned.[139] Indeed, the propertied elite 'combined their litigation quite comfortably with a propensity for violence and self-help.'[140] Armigerous society's lawlessness was compounded by the fact that law enforcement was dependent on gentlemen themselves, seemingly the most fractious group in society. At the same time the legal system itself had a role to play in propagating disorder. Incapable of resolving by verdict the civil suits that came before them, the courts, slow and ineffective, were unable to 'serve as a realistic detriment to criminal activity.'[141] The punishments handed out often had a limited effect too, a point illustrated by Sir John l'Ercedekne's exploits of 1346. Despite being outlawed by the king in this year, l'Ercedekne had allegedly still rampaged across Devon 'with a large number of armed malefactors' in pursuit of his accuser.[142] Together, these many interlinked strands had the effect of undermining order across the realm.

---

[136] KB27/196 m. 40r; SC8/76/3756; *CPR 1307–1313*, 362.
[137] N. Saul, 'The Commons and the Abolition of Badges', *Parliamentary History*, 9 (1990), pp. 302–315.
[138] KB27/202 m. 108r.
[139] JUST1/109 m. 2d; Saul, 'Conflict and Consensus', p. 42.
[140] Kaeuper, *Justice*, p. 264; McFarlane, *The Nobility*, p. 115.
[141] Payling, *Nottinghamshire*, p. 186.
[142] For example, *CPR 1345–1348*, 113, 180.

The extent of lawlessness, however, is difficult to quantify, as we know only of recorded crime and not its totality, while at the same time not all the recorded cases may be true. In some sense medieval society emerges as litigious rather than lawless, seeing not so much an actual increase in disorder as an increase in the volume of legal documentation giving an impression of disorder. In the sixteenth century, indeed, it was to be alleged that Cornishmen resorted to the law 'for waggyng of a straw'.[143] It follows that legal records simply cannot be taken at face value, the Treverbyn–Gevely case among them.[144] Although Margery Treverbyn's initial case in the king's bench made mention of robbery along with breach of peace, she neither carried through the appeal of robbery nor made any mention of rape at this time. It was only in her subsequent petition that the Anglo-Norman term *ravistat* appeared, suggesting that the petition and subsequent litigation was aimed at forcing an out-of-court settlement of this abduction/ravishment case.[145] As litigation generally formed part of a complex process of dispute resolution, people from across the realm often entered pleas that overstated the levels of violence in order to compel the defendant to accept arbitration of the quarrel.

While we should bear all these points in mind, it is also true, however, that specific factors in Cornwall had the effect of undermining local order. In a ground-breaking article, Hannes Kleineke has argued that the fifteenth-century Cornish peninsula was particularly lawless, having a 'culture of violence'.[146] The county's rich geology had a significant role to play here. As tin provided large stores of movable wealth, tough miners and ample scope for disagreement over rights, it is perhaps unsurprising that in 1344 John Carminow and sixteen others supposedly 'assembled a huge multitude of evildoers' who assaulted dozens of the Black Prince's stannary-men, seizing £1,000 of tin.[147] At all levels of the stannaries fraud, coercion and semi-criminality abounded, and in 1358 one John Polper allegedly employed his bailiffship of Penwith and Kerrier itself to abduct Philip de Caerhays.[148] Since so many folk had tinning interests, criminality encouraged by the tin trade spread throughout the peninsula. The county's maritime character also emerges as a significant factor in causing crime. Full of rich prizes, the sea was a lawless watery frontier. After a storm of 1340 had wrecked the vessel of Raymond Maugnel of Cork on the Cornish coast, for example, some fifty-seven gentlemen, merchants, clergymen and

---

[143] Boorde, *Knowledge*, p. 122.
[144] Saul, 'Conflict and Consensus', pp. 41–42, 54; Harriss, *Shaping the Nation*, p. 198; see, *Crime, Law and Society in the Later Middle Ages*, trans. and ed. A. Musson with E. Powell (Manchester, 2009).
[145] My thanks to Anthony Musson for his advice about this case.
[146] Kleineke, 'Why the West was Wild', pp. 80–83, 93.
[147] *CPR 1343–1345*, 401.
[148] KB9/9 m. 39.

peasants 'cut the ship into little pieces and carried away the cargo'.[149] These sorts of thefts appear to have been commonplace. 'Piracy' also was rife, and with gentlemen engaging in seagoing larceny and 'pirates' active ashore, a two-way transmission of criminality operated between the county and the Channel.[150] Sea-fights of this sort in some sense comprised a form of border warfare, the maritime equivalent of raids and 'rieving' in the Anglo-Scottish marches.[151] To some extent Cornwall was a marcher county, a militarised frontier society.

Compounding county fractiousness, the peninsula's distance from the central courts further weakened these main common law tribunals. A petition of 1315 even claimed that the costs of travel had bankrupted numerous Cornishmen taking cases to courts, so that many folk were 'as happy to be ruined and stay at home as to struggle to court and be ruined'.[152] Although the county's MPs employed hyperbole to add weight to their supplications, the government still endorsed the petition with a promise to send justices to the county to inform the king about 'what is rightly to be done'. There is evidence that the complex bodies of law in Cornwall also indirectly promoted lawlessness. While the king stood at the apex of the pyramid, below him the earl-duke dispensed equitable justice from his council, while the stannaries, hundredal tribunals and so on all enjoyed jurisdiction in the far south west.[153] At times quarrels can be found erupting between each, as in the 1350s, when 'feigned suits' supposedly breached the privileges of the town of Liskeard.[154] The overlapping tribunals themselves could be employed to importune one's adversaries, as in the case of Matthew de Cornewaille, who in 1357 petitioned the Black Prince after allegedly having been 'wrongfully driven... from court to court, so that he is ruined and dare not remain' in Cornwall.[155] In the light of all this, it was perhaps inevitable that each local tribunal proved susceptible to 'jury packing' by litigants keen to secure their desired verdict.[156] Even if a case ran smoothly, in 1380 as many as eight criminals managed to escape from Launceston gaol in less than four months.[157] All these failings encouraged contempt for the law in Cornwall.

---

[149] *CPR 1338–1340*, 488.
[150] Below, pp. 291–293.
[151] Cf. C. J. Neville, 'The Keeping of the Peace in the Northern Marches in the Later Middle Ages', *EHR*, 109 (1994), pp. 1–25.
[152] *PROME*, iii, 100; Cf. P. Brand, 'The Travails of Travel: The Difficulty of Getting to Court in Later Medieval England', in *Freedom of Movement in the Middle Ages: Proceedings of the 2003 Harlaxton Symposium*, ed. P. Horden (Donington, 2007), pp. 215–228 especially 218.
[153] Below, p. 236–239.
[154] *RBP*, ii, 82–83.
[155] *RBP*, ii, 115–116.
[156] For example, *CPR 1345–1348*, 388.
[157] *CPR 1377–1381*, 454.

At the heart of the nature of Cornish lawlessness stood the composition of county society itself. Forming a group of flattish composition by wealth, the Cornish landholding class had no natural leader who could maintain stability. In the absence of such a figure, the local gentry were left free to pursue their 'fur collar crime'. Sometimes criminal activity is found running in families over the generations. Christopher Tyldesley has highlighted the virulent feud that erupted between the Sergeauxs, on the one hand, and the Carminows and Trevarthians, on the other, a vendetta that first comes to light in 1377 and which both parties were to pursue vigorously into the 1390s.[158] Yet Sir Richard and John Sergeaux had been introduced into disorder by their father, Sir Richard Sergeaux senior, all three having been hauled before the assize of 1351 for dispossessing Sir Richard Stapeldon of land.[159] Direct action was often an inter- and even intra-family affair, and with leading Cornish lineages strikingly interrelated and holding estates spread across the peninsula, many inheritances and property boundaries could be contested.

While not all dynasties proved nefarious in their deeds, feuds could develop easily and the local gentry's many familial connections drew an array of evenly matched confederacies into these conflicts.[160] If not comprising formally liveried retainers, these affinities still encompassed a 'multifarious collection of relatives, dependents, household servants, and hangers-on'.[161] In 1315, for example, it was alleged that one gang of gentlemen-criminals led by Sir John Treiagu and John and Reginald le Soor had seized Sir Thomas l'Ercedekne's son, another Thomas, at St Euny Church in Redruth and spirited him away to Penryn.[162] Such confederacies could employ the latest weapons of war, as in 1389 for instance, when John Trelawny, Roger Menywynnek and 'other evildoers' supposedly attacked Sir Humphrey Stafford with an 'engine called a gunne... so that his life was despaired of'.[163] With supernatural armaments proving significant, Sir Ralph Botreaux and his 'covin' procured three necromancers 'to subtly consume and altogether destroy' the body of William, Lord Botreaux.[164] Serving as bases from which attacks could be launched or resisted, the county's many fortified residences rendered these kinship groupings all the more formidable.[165] In some sense local society formed a crucible or commonalty of lawlessness, with Lady Elizabeth Botreaux alleging in 1381 that John Trevarthian 'and his adherents' were 'so powerful in the country that none

---

[158] Tyldesley, 'Local Communities', pp. 22–23; below, pp. 153–155.
[159] JUST1/1445 m. 51r.
[160] For gangs, Bellamy, *Public Order*, pp. 69–88; Saul, *Gloucestershire*, pp. 178–182.
[161] Tyldesley, 'Local Communities', p. 20.
[162] CPR 1313–1317, 411.
[163] CPR 1388–1392, 134.
[164] CPR 1422–1429, 363.
[165] Cf. Kaeuper, *Justice*, pp. 211–225.

can have common law or right against them'.¹⁶⁶ Among these 'crime lords', the highest circle of Cornish gangsterdom, the law was regarded as a force to be enforced, subverted and flouted in turn.

Inevitably, the structure and conduct of landed society undermined the effectiveness in office of county administrators. While those who held the sheriff-stewardship enjoyed impressive public powers, none of the Cornishmen or 'outsiders' who filled this office enjoyed the private clout required to achieve true mastery of the county. Institutionalising malpractice and official thuggery, numerous officials can be found employing county offices to pursue their own lawless agendas. As most of the populace engaged in smuggling or some other form of tax evasion, low-level law-breaking was also prevalent in the peninsula.¹⁶⁷ There can be little doubt that semi-criminal elements abounded throughout all strata of Cornish society as the culture of violence was so pervasive.¹⁶⁸ The archdeacon of Cornwall went so far as to claim that the Cornish were *rebellis et difficilis*, so commonplace was lawlessness in the far south west.¹⁶⁹

For all this skulduggery, however, we should not view corruption, mendacity and violence as uniquely Cornish phenomena. Every local office in later-medieval England depended on the service and diligence of local lords, voluntarily given, with all the associated dangers of vested interest and malevolent agendas. Disorder simply emerges as the corollary of governmental limitations across the land, with folk from every corner of England employing violence to supplement and supplant formal procedures in turn. As a result, self-help held an integral place in the workings of contemporary society and disorder is better seen as representing rational violence in pursuit of rational aims.¹⁷⁰ Even Gevely's seemingly mindless attacks on the Treverbyns probably had a clear ambition, that of securing Sibyl's marriage and dowry. To protect their patrimonies, leading Cornish gentry often chose to employ both martial might and legal process simultaneously. This is well demonstrated by a case from 1306, when Sir Ranulph Blanchminster had Edward I sue out on his behalf an oyer and terminer commission to investigate his allegation that William le Poer, the coroner of the Scilly Isles, and 'a multitude of malefactors' had attacked his property on Scilly, seizing a whale 'thrown upon the shore'.¹⁷¹ On the same day, however, Poer sought a comparable investigation into Blanchminster, who had allegedly caused him to be imprisoned 'by persons

---

[166] *CIM 1377–1388*, 101–102.
[167] *CPR 1391–1396*, 263; Hatcher, *Tin*, pp. 6, 110–111.
[168] Kleineke, 'Why the West was Wild', 93.
[169] *Reg.Grandisson*, ii, 958.
[170] Hilton, *West Midlands*, p. 251.
[171] *CPR 1301–1307*, 480; SC8/264/13182; SC8/264/13181.

unknown' on the islands.[172] In this way, the Cornish elite employed both direct action and royal commissions to defend their interests. With disorder forming one of a bundle of remedies used during disputes, lawlessness does not stand out as the aberration that it at first appears.

Indeed, lawfulness and lawlessness are best seen as inexorably bound together.[173] The dearth of 'good' lordship and effective kingship between 1307 and 1330 had the inevitable effect of leading to a decline of confidence in lordly and legal resolutions.[174] Resorting to solving disputes by violent means, the county's residents increasingly looked to their own resources as they had no other answer to their grievances. It seems that in the time of Gaveston's supine lordship the officials themselves engaged in large-scale personal freebooting, and Bishop Stapledon's regime proved little better, despite – or perhaps because of – all his efforts. Overlaying these many lordly failings loomed those of Edward II himself, whose ineffectual kingship compounded the problems. It was only under the combined attentions of Edward III and John of Eltham that lordship and kingship once again began to operate more effectively. Eltham was to closely supervise his officials, discouraging corrupt practices, while the king's own attentions to the county bench helped to promote better order. Order and disorder are best seen as interrelated, with periods of weak royal-lordly government resulting in Cornwall's residents more readily employing violence to solve their disputes.[175]

A many-faceted phenomenon, lawlessness had the additional effect of contributing to political discourse and popular protest. A good example is afforded by an episode that we have already looked at, when in 1312 Edward II granted all the tin in Cornwall to Antonio Pessagno, who then ruthlessly extracted as much money as he could from the stannaries. As the king's tinning policies provided the county's residents with a serious source of grievance against him and his banker, Cornishmen made their profound discontent known through parliament while also employing direct action, in the form of assaults on Pessagno's servants, to resist lordly-kingly machinations. Here we see how dissidence emerged as a direct response to Edward's maladministration, and in taking up arms the county's residents sent a powerful message to the king about the depth of their discontent. Although the evidence should not be pushed too far, in many ways political discourse was both orderly and disorderly.[176]

---

[172] CPR 1301–1307, 538.
[173] A. Musson, *Medieval Law in Context: The Growth of Legal Consciousness from Magna Carta to the Peasants' Revolt* (Manchester, 2001), pp. 241–242.
[174] Cf. Carpenter, *Warwickshire*, pp. 438, 606–614.
[175] Cf. Walker, *Political Culture*, p. 32; Payling, *Nottinghamshire*, p. 207.
[176] Cf. Musson, *Legal Consciousness*, p. 217.

Despite these many strands of fractiousness, however, it is not necessary to see Cornwall as constantly marred by unrestrained depravity. There is plentiful evidence that the common law operated in the county, as elsewhere in England, with the Crown deploying the central courts to help resolve disputes and protect public order. At the same time Cornish coroners, JPs, sheriff-stewards and hundredal officials can all be found indicting felons whom royal justices of gaol delivery tried at Launceston, promoting peace in the peninsula.[177] With a steady stream of Cornish litigants actually choosing to make their way to the common law tribunals, these courts and their judgments proved essential to the smooth running of county affairs.[178] It followed that folk from the whole range of county society often welcomed the intervention of the courts in their daily lives. And despite the allegations of violence and thuggery, virtually no leading proprietors died at the hands of their fellows. We would do well to remember that by their very nature the voluminous records of the courts present an image of fractiousness and conflict – cohesiveness, although no less common, has left a far lesser documentary trail.

Since public order in the county was dependent on kings, courts, lords and also a local desire for peace, the interface between law and society was a highly complex relationship. In Cornwall, it seems that a limited amount of direct action was considered acceptable in order to secure one's objectives, with this generally used in conjunction with both litigation and arbitration.[179] Undoubtedly a minority of cases involved more violence, and at the same time informal mechanisms of dispute resolution laid emphasis 'on the restoration of social peace through reconciliation rather than through punishment'.[180] With the number and variety of ties binding individuals together legion in Cornwall, such divided loyalties resulted in great pressure on both plaintiffs and defendants to effect a settlement.[181] Disputing parties could enter into a formal process of arbitration, as in 1394, for example, when the feuding John Arundell and Sir William Lambourne called on the arbitration of the priors of Bodmin and Launceston, who duly hammered out an out-of-court settlement.[182] At no point in the fourteenth century do we see the county divided into two permanently

---

[177] JUST3/120 mm. 23r–23d; JUST3/121 mm. 13r–13d; JUST3/147 mm. 38–40; JUST3/9/2 m. 3; JUST3/156 m. 42r–46r; JUST3/170 m. 11r–13r; Tyldesley, 'Local Communities', pp. 75–76.
[178] For example, KB27/214 m. 112d; KB27/252 m. 61d; KB27/254 m. 62r.
[179] Cf. Carpenter, *Warwickshire*, p. 625.
[180] Cf. Payling, *Nottinghamshire*, p. 187.
[181] Gluckman, 'Peace in the Feud', 2; Saul, 'Conflict and Consensus', pp. 47–49, 54.
[182] CRO, AR/17/1–2; A. Musson, 'Arbitration and the Legal Profession in Late Medieval England', in *Law and Legal Process: Substantive Law and Procedure in English Legal History*, ed. M. Dyson and D. Ibbetson (Cambridge, 2013), pp. 56–76.

hostile war-bands, as the network of formal and informal cross-cutting ties had the effect of undermining the potential for vendettas.

For all these reasons, fourteenth-century Cornwall was by no means plagued by perpetual anarchy. Neither were the county's inhabitants altogether unique in employing resort to violent self-help. A spectrum of lawlessness operated across the realm, with the king's subjects employing direct action in varying amounts as a result of local traditions and local standards of behaviour. It is illustrative of this that while Sussex saw low levels of violent feuding in comparison to Gloucestershire, Lancashire and Cheshire in contrast were renowned for their disorderly natures.[183] Although Cornwall may well have been more lawless than some shires, Cornish violent self-help resulted in neither outright war nor endless chaos. Legality and illegality also emerge as tightly intertwined, with the county's place in the kingdom greatly influencing the maintenance of Cornish peace.[184]

Taken together, what should we make of the final tumultuous years of the earldom? While it was never all-embracing, the power of lordship was nonetheless highly pervasive. Through the combined actions of Cornwall's royal lordship and government, the whole range of local society was drawn firmly into realm. Proving themselves neither passive nor inarticulate in these years, the county's residents by turns petitioned these lords and violently resisted their machinations. Although many of the final years of the earldom's rulership were ineffectual at best and predatory at worst, Edward III and John of Eltham had together set about restoring faith in the lordship. If the institution of lordship could not be exercised effectively by one person alone, it was still powerfully moulded by the personality of those who enjoyed the dignity. With so many royally appointed lords holding the earldom in quick succession, the high politics of the realm were of grave concern in Cornwall.

---

[183] Saul, *Sussex*, p. 73; Walker, *Political Culture*, p. 20; Barraclough, *Cheshire*, p. 24; P. H. W. Booth, 'Taxation and Public Order: Cheshire in 1353', *Northern History*, 12 (1976), pp. 16–31.

[184] Cf. Musson, *Legal Consciousness*, pp. 241–242.

6

The Black Prince and his Duchy, 1337–76

Edward III's hardnosed pragmatism and sense of the dignity of the royal family were to prove the curtain raiser to a remarkable era in the history of Cornwall's turbulent lordship. In March 1337 he chose to elevate the earldom to the first dukedom in England, vesting the title upon his son and heir, Edward of Woodstock, better known as the Black Prince.[1] By virtue of this act, the king had the effect of binding the duchy and the Crown together. Since he was only seven at the time of his investiture, the boy-duke necessarily relied on his council to manage the lordship on his behalf.[2] As one of the first acts of the new regime, his chief steward, one James Woodstock, undertook an exhaustive survey of all ducal prerogatives, recording gross income of £4,526 10s. 6¼d.[3] The new administration sought to boost revenues, pressing on with John of Eltham's reforms and retaining many of his officials.[4] John Moveroun was one such who continued as constable of Launceston Castle, from 1338 serving the duke as receiver in Cornwall while holding many other ducal and regnal positions. His twin lordly-royal mandates demonstrate how the king's household and that of his son worked together to establish the duke's nascent lordship.

---

[1] *CChR 1327–1341*, 399–400, 436–437; he received the stannaries minus 1,000 marks yearly, *CCR 1337–1339*, 49; in 1342 he received wool customs, *CChR 1341–1417*, 12–13; *RESDCornwall*, 5–6.
[2] See, R. Barber, *Edward, Prince of Wales and Aquitaine: A Biography of the Black Prince* (London, 1978); D. Green, *The Black Prince* (Stroud, 2001); D. Green, *Edward the Black Prince: Power in Medieval Europe* (Harlow, 2007); M. Jones, *The Black Prince* (London, 2017).
[3] *RESDCornwall*, 88–92; *CS*, lviii.
[4] SC6/816/11.

Edward III even renewed the stannary charter 'at the request' of Duke Edward, whom the county had no doubt lobbied.[5]

The imposition of the new lordship, however, was by no means frictionless. At one point father and son quarrelled over the payment of customs in the peninsula.[6] More significantly, however, the new duke is found clashing with his new subjects. In c. 1338 the Commons of Cornwall requested that Edward III order the duke and his council, along with the treasurer and chancellor of England, to replace Sir Robert Beaupel as sheriff.[7] While Beaupel supposedly held insufficient lands in the peninsula, these complaints represent an attempt by the commonalty to impress the importance of their opinions upon their new master. It seems that they enjoyed some success, with Henry Trethewey being appointed sheriff-steward in 1340, Trethewey being both a Cornishman and a diligent administrator.[8] Neither king nor duke wished to antagonise their Cornish subjects, and yet both sought to govern effectively.

At the same time that he created the new lordship, Edward III decided to open hostilities with France, and the county found itself on the frontline. To secure both his realm and his son's duchy, in July 1338 the king appointed a new peace commission containing four local lords and James Woodstock. Just a month later he added a further seven Cornishmen whom he empowered to hear and determine cases as well as oversee the county's defences.[9] During these years the king also greatly needed income for the war, but popular resistance to his many subsidies had the effect of reducing tax yields. The king blamed his ministers, some of whom he fired, by 1340 provoking a major political crisis when he clashed with Archbishop Stratford about his diligence in collecting royal dues, not least those relating to wool.[10] In Cornwall, the government arrested all six wool collectors, among them William Trelawny, so as 'to punish such delinquents in an exemplary manner'.[11] Ducal actions at this time, however, were just as significant as those of the king. For the better management of the lordship, in 1342 the duke's council decided to separate the stewardship and shrievalty; Trethewey continued to hold the latter post, while the prince appointed to the former his clerk, a certain Hugh de Berewyk.[12]

---

[5] *CChR 1341–1417*, 12.
[6] *CCR 1343–1346*, 78.
[7] SC8/193/9648.
[8] SC6/816/11–13.
[9] *CPR 1338–1340*, 279; *CCR 1337–1339*, 509; *CPR 1338–1340*, 139, 141, 146; Michael Trenewith the elder had been added in the meantime; Ormrod, *Edward III*, pp. 109–110; for disorder, *CPR 1338–1340*, 150, 486; JUST1/1422 mm. 111r–119r; SC8/241/12049.
[10] Ormrod, *Edward III*, pp. 212–246.
[11] *CPR 1338–1340*, 502–503; *CPR 1340–1343*, 26, 118, 314; *CCR 1339–1341*, 436; *CFR 1337–1347*, 285, 295.
[12] DCO 1–3.

Replacing Trethewey with William Chaumpernoun a year later and then appointing Thomas atte Fenne of Tregorrick sheriff in 1344, the ducal council showed an apparently great concern to find the right men for these offices.

Acting as a backdrop to these changes in personnel was the war with France. On his return from campaigning in Brittany, Edward III turned his attention once again to public order.[13] To this end, in Cornwall he appointed to the county bench two Cornish proprietors and the ducal servants Trethewey, Berewyk and John Dabernon of Bradford, Devon, the feodary and escheator.[14] It seems that Cornish lawlessness was a particular concern to the king and the prince. In 1343, for example, the Crown launched an investigation at the prince's behest into fifty-five people 'and others' who had carried away wreck of the sea, smuggled, resisted ducal ministers and broken seigniorial parks.[15] Naming gentlemen, burgesses, priors and Bishop Grandisson himself, the list reads like a Cornish 'Who's Who'. Over the next few years the investigations launched by father and son reportedly found that 'piracy' was rife in Cornish waters and that local gentlemen had usurped 'divers stannaries' by force, compelling the tinners to work as virtual slaves.[16] This list marks the arrival of a new and vigorous lordship that enjoyed the king's full support.

Such efforts, however, did not distract either prince or king from the great royal enterprise in France. In 1346 Edward heavily defeated the French army at Crécy and the sixteen-year-old prince won his spurs, symbolically attaining his majority.[17] The survival of many of the prince's letters from these years allow for a detailed study of his lordship, revealing that he kept his subjects fully abreast of his successes and that he and his council took a keen interest in Cornwall.[18] Removing Berewyk from the stewardship in 1346, the prince instead appointed his bachelor and chief steward, one Sir Edmund Kendale.[19] In November 1347, however, he chose to recombine the stewardship and shrievalty, placing both under the charge of Thomas atte Fenne.[20] As household men enhanced ducal authority, Dabernon, Moveroun, Trethewey and Thomas Fitz Henry, the havener, are to be found diligently performing their duties.[21] So as to maximise the dues from the lordship, in 1346 the prince replaced Moveroun as receiver

---

[13] Ormrod, *Edward III*, pp. 259–260.
[14] *CPR 1343–1345*, 394, 396, 399.
[15] *CPR 1340–1343*, 582–583; *CPR 1343–1345*, 66.
[16] *CPR 1338–1340*, 488; *CPR 1340–1343*, 449, 454, 553–554; *CPR 1343–1345*, 71, 74–75, 77, 401, 413–414.
[17] Froissart, *Chronicles*, p. 92.
[18] *RBP*, i, 15; *CPR 1345–1348*, 123.
[19] DCO 3; *RBP*, i, 5, 13.
[20] *RBP*, i, 141; DCO 4, records Kendale accounting.
[21] SC6/812/3; *RBP*, i, 4–5, 10, 15, 45.

with Sir John Pirier, his clerk and chief receiver.[22] The receivership experienced considerable changes in personnel, with Tideman de Lymbergh, the prince's Hanseatic merchant, holding this post from late 1347. Although he relied on his attorney in the south west, a certain John Conyng, Lymbergh enjoyed direct connections with the king.[23] Retaining Justice William Shareshull in his service, the prince had this important 'man of law' sit on his council, serve on the county bench and adjudicate over the Cornish assize.[24] On coming of age the prince had decided to pack the duchy's hierarchy with a cadre of his own men, only two of whom hailed from west of the Tamar.

Combined with the peace commission of 1346, on which Cornishmen such as Sir John Arundell enjoyed a place, the prince's retainers set about moulding the peninsula to their employer's will. Launching another series of investigations, including into the theft of the prince's Castilian armour in Falmouth, the king once again mobilised the royal government in his son's favour.[25] At this time royal justices even examined Cornwall's ministers for corruption and empanelling jurors of 'bad report'.[26] The prince's assertiveness inevitably prompted some complaints, and in 1347 Cornwall's residents are to be found grumbling about the numbers of 'under-bailiffs and others who meddle in the prince's name'.[27] Yet, while balancing the demands of lordship with those of tenants was no easy task, the prince's rulership was surprisingly well accepted in the county. In tandem with this assertion of his might, the prince garnered the peninsula's wealth. In 1346 he announced that he would employ Lymbergh to buy all Cornish tin, and in due course he would lease the stannaries to Lymbergh for 3,500 marks annually.[28] Running 'a tight ship', the prince pursued outstanding debts with vigour, investigated thoroughly the leasing of conventionary lands and forced the havener to pay for wine that he had sold without licence.[29] Although Dabernon was generally assiduous, the prince ordered him to 'make a better inquisition' on the lands of one tenant, Sir Thomas Prideaux.[30] The prince expected the duchy to pay its way, but even so he did not resort to extortion. His care for the county is underlined by his pardoning of manorial fines following the outbreak of the Black Death.[31] His stands out as pragmatic munificence, however, as these dues were to prove uncollectable.

[22] DCO 3; *RBP*, i, 92.
[23] DCO 3–4; SC6/812/3; *RBP*, i, 9–10, 106.
[24] *RBP*, i, 106, 135.
[25] *CPR 1348–1350*, 61, 74, 157, 247, 518, 593.
[26] *CPR 1345–1348*, 388.
[27] *RBP*, i, 151.
[28] *RBP*, i, 9–10, 26–27, 32, 66; *CPR 1345–1348*, 373; *PROME*, iv, 420.
[29] *RBP*, i, 32, 64, 82–83, 91; SC6/812/3.
[30] *RBP*, i, 136–137.
[31] *RESDCornwall*, 102–105.

The year 1349 saw fresh administrative change, with the prince appointing his butler, one John Skirkbeck, as sheriff-steward. It seems that Fenne had succumbed to the plague, having failed to keep up with his accounts.[32] A mere six months later, however, the ubiquitous Dabernon appears holding the posts of sheriff-steward, feodary, escheator and constable of Trematon and Tintagel Castles, all alongside that of JP.[33] The king had renewed the county bench 'by bill of the prince' himself, removing nearly all Cornishmen in favour of Moveroun, Skirkbeck and Dabernon. Household men were to be the favoured instruments of the prince's lordship. This had been the case ever since 1346, and was to become especially apparent from 1349 onwards. While the plague rendered collecting the duchy's dues all the more difficult, the prince's responses to the changes wrought by the Black Death were 'remarkable both in their wisdom and foresight'.[34]

Embarking on thirteen years of meticulous oversight, the prince was to reach the effective age of his majority in 1349. In ruling the duchy and other lordships, however, he had to delegate many powers of day-to-day administration to his subordinates. It follows that his council enjoyed a great deal of authority, with its lawyers and men of experience serving as the lordship's chief policy-making body. In association with the chief steward and receiver, the councillors directed local administrators 'within closely defined limits', although officials in the locality still provided a constant stream of advice.[35] More significantly still, the prince himself is to be found governing the duchy actively until 1363, with as many as 15 per cent of lordly instructions including a personal authorisation warrant.[36] It may be unwise, however, to press too far the distinction between the prince and his administrators, as he took care to verse these men, appointing them to further his own ambitions and priorities.[37]

The household men were to prove crucial to the assertion of the prince's rulership over the Cornish peninsula. Dabernon stood pre-eminent among them, holding virtually all his numerous offices until 1354, and surrendering only the keepership of Tintagel.[38] Skirkbeck instead served as Tintagel's castellan and acted as controller of the stannaries, while John Kendale held the receivership

[32] *RBP*, ii, 7, 13, 29–30, 96.
[33] SC6/817/1 m. 19r; DCO 5; *RBP*, ii, *passim*.; Dabernon also held Exeter Castle and Dartmoor Chase.
[34] *RESDCornwall*, 116.
[35] *CPR 1345–1348*, 123; M. Sharp, 'The Household of the Black Prince', in *Chapters in the Administrative History of Medieval England*, ed. T. F. Tout, 6 vols (Manchester, 1920-33), v, pp. 289–400 at 382–388; *RESDCornwall*, 43–45; for example, *RBP*, ii, 159.
[36] *RBP*, ii, *passim*; the figures fluctuated, with fewer – sometimes nearly none – while he campaigned.
[37] Cf. Walker, *Lancastrian Affinity*, p. 31; Carpenter, *Warwickshire*, p. 371.
[38] SC6/817/1 m. 19r; SC6/817/3 m. 13r; *RBP*, ii, 14.

at the same time as overseeing Restormel.[39] The prince also retained Fitz Henry in the office of havener and, with his father's backing, employed Shareshull on many judicial commissions west of the Tamar.[40] The county's sons still held a place in local administration, however, regularly collecting royal taxes, while a few, Sir Reginald Botreaux among them, found a place on the Cornish bench.[41]

Running a formidably forceful regime, the prince worked all these men hard. One of them, Skirkbeck, felt the full force of his master's exactitude when he was commanded to 'labour more diligently' and 'painstakingly'.[42] Ordering Dabernon to certify the council 'plainly' regarding Cornwall's parkers 'and which of them has least knowledge of what belongs to his office', the prince exhorted him to 'conduct himself well' in all things.[43] To secure his prerogative rights, the prince pursued outstanding debts with vigour and protected his physical assets in the county, even ordering the arrest of 'swine' found trampling in the moat of Launceston Castle.[44] He had all the financial actions of his officials recorded in the ministers' accounts, which he subsequently had thoroughly audited.[45] As part of this process, the prince empowered his auditors to supervise ducal lands, hear complaints and even remove nefarious officials, reporting all this activity back to him. Although the maintenance of the lordship required constant vigilance, these efforts throughout the 1350s to manage the county discouraged corrupt activities.[46]

Not simply demanding and receiving due diligence, the prince also rewarded it, for example granting does caught in 'his parks of Cornewaille' to Skirkbeck, Fitz Henry, Kendale and Dabernon.[47] It was Dabernon himself who received the most magnificent gift, when the prince granted him the manor of Calstock for a yearly rent of just four marks, the lands having yielded as much as £39 in 1337.[48] Dabernon was loaded with rewards in this way as part of a policy to raise this most loyal official to the pinnacle of south-western society as a pillar of princely authority. As the prince received homage from numerous Devonian gentlemen, retained the Courtenays themselves and at times enjoyed Devon's judicial profits, his power had spread throughout south-western England, with Cornwall forming the focus and centre of his rulership.[49]

[39] *RBP*, ii, 6, 9.
[40] *CPR 1350–1354*, 285.
[41] *CPR 1343–1345*, 399; *CPR 1350–1354*, 285; *CPR 1358–1361*, 345.
[42] *RBP*, ii, 24.
[43] *RBP*, ii, 7, 14.
[44] *RBP*, ii, 2, 4–5, 9, 26–27, 30–31, 48–49, 55–56.
[45] SC6/817/1–2; *RBP*, ii, 5; *RESDCornwall*, 46–47.
[46] *CPR 1350–1354*, 24; *RBP*, ii, 6–7, 9–10, 12–13, 59; KB27/363 *Rex* m. 22r; JUST1/1445 mm. 51r–56r; JUST1/1448 mm. 83r–100r.
[47] *RBP*, ii, 15.
[48] *RBP*, ii, 23; *CS*, 107.
[49] *RBP*, ii, 26, 155, 157, 196.

The vigour and alertness of the prince's lordship are both illustrated by his response to a quarrel that erupted in 1350 between his father and John de Grandisson, the bishop of Exeter. Before we turn to these events, however, it is necessary to consider the implications of Grandisson's long episcopate for the county. A cultured and civilised man, he had succeeded the short-lived James Berkeley at Exeter in 1327 and was to prove an active and enlightened diocesan.[50] He was enthroned in August 1328 and was evidently unhappy at the condition of his see, in one of his letters bemoaning its state of disarray.[51] Accordingly, he sacked Treiagu as steward and appointed in his place another local proprietor, John Billioun.[52] While Grandisson naturally enjoyed considerable sway to west of the Tamar, he made the fatal mistake of usurping some ducal rights.[53] In 1350 Edward III, annoyed by this and also disagreeing with the bishop over certain appointments to benefices, confiscated his temporalities and in this way virtually eliminated his power.[54] At this point the prince stepped in, ordering the archdeacon of Cornwall 'on his peril' to cease 'attending not so much to the salvation and correction of souls as to the levying and collection of great sums of money'.[55] In this way, ducal and regnal authorities come across as mutually supporting, with the greater freedom that came with the prince's majority making him a more effective enforcer of both.

Table 4: The Black Prince's Cornish Itinerary of 1354

18 August	Launceston Castle
24 August to 2 September	Restormel Castle
5 September	Launceston Castle

Sources: *RBP*, ii, 62–70; he also visited Tintagel, *RBP*, ii, 120–121.

Sending endless instructions to the county, the prince received equally frequent calls on his grace from the peninsula's inhabitants. On one occasion he actually made the journey down to Cornwall, which none of his fourteenth-century predecessors had done. He travelled west in 1354 and he was met at the Tamar by a Cornish landowner, John Killigrew, clad in 3s. 4d. worth of new grey cape, who by custom had to carry 'with the prince at the prince's

---

[50] A. Erskine, 'John Grandison', *ODNB*, xxiii, pp. 266–268.
[51] *Reg.Grandisson*, i, 179–180.
[52] *Reg.Grandisson*, i, 236, 553.
[53] *Reg.Grandisson*, ii, 840–841; *CS*, 139–140; *RBP*, i, 33.
[54] *CPR 1348–1350*, 462, 587; C. Whatley, 'Temporalities Be Taken: Edward III, Unruly Ecclesiastics and the Fight for the Benefices of Exeter, 1337–60', *Fourteenth Century England, VIII*, ed. J. S. Hamilton (Woodbridge, 2014), pp. 59–82.
[55] *RBP*, ii, 9.

entry into Cornewaille'.⁵⁶ Surrounded by his lavish household, the prince then established himself in the freshly renovated Restormel Castle, one of the most impressive manifestations of lordly power in the peninsula: awe was to form the keynote.

While in Cornwall, the prince received homage and fealty from John Ingepenne, John le Jeu, John Killigrew, John Nansladron and Warin Vautort, along with some landowners from Devon.⁵⁷ The great and the good of the two counties performed this act of obedience and the prince entertained them sumptuously.⁵⁸ Regranting Helston's and Liskeard's charters to the benefit of his dignity and treasury, in this way he asserted his power over Cornish burgesses too.⁵⁹ The prince displayed his largesse through the giving of many gifts and the righting of numerous wrongs in the peninsula.⁶⁰ He even sought to harness the efficacy of prayer to his rulership, paying the chaplain William Pruet an extra 16s. 4d. 'to stay for life at the hermitage within the park of Restormel to sing masses there for the prince's ancestors, and the prince' himself.⁶¹ Projecting his majesty and mastery to all, the prince did everything expected of him.

At the same time the prince made adjustments to the duchy's personnel. After serving as sheriff-steward for four years, escheator for eleven and feodary for sixteen, Dabernon resigned all his commissions, shifting his interests to Devon where he was to serve as sheriff.⁶² The prince therefore appointed Robert de Eleford, one of his yeomen, to the sheriff-stewardship and nominated Skirkbeck as feodary and escheator, on top of his other commissions.⁶³ Although 'for certain causes' the prince had stripped the receivership from Kendale, he soon restored him to office.⁶⁴ Almost certainly at the request of his son, the king issued a new peace commission at this time dominated by justices and ducal men.⁶⁵ For the better enforcement of royal-ducal peace, the king and the prince had Shareshull, John Wingfield and Richard de Stafford sit in Cornwall on a general oyer and terminer commission known as a commission of trailbaston. All three travelled to the peninsula in 1354–5, where they levied over 1,200 fines for disorders committed against the peace, yielding over £178.⁶⁶

---

56   *RBP*, iii, 168; *RBP*, ii, 69.
57   *RBP*, ii, 62–63, 67–68.
58   *RBP*, ii, 68–69.
59   CRO, BHEL/454; BLIS/2–3; *RBP*, ii, 63.
60   *RBP*, ii, 63–65, 75–76.
61   *RBP*, ii, 63.
62   *RBP*, ii, 69, 84; *Sheriffs*, 35; he retained Trematon Castle.
63   *RBP*, ii, 62, 66; SC6/817/4 m. 13v; *CFR 1347–1356*, 444.
64   *RBP*, ii, 65, 67.
65   *CPR 1354–1358*, 123.
66   JUST1/122/1–2; JUST1/123; JUST1/128/1–2; *CPR 1354–1358*, 120; *RBP*, ii, 86.

On the prince's departure from the county, the local administration settled into a fairly stable rhythm. During these years, however, England and France were moving closer to war again.[67] In July 1355 the prince arrived in Plymouth, where he stayed for two months before sailing for Aquitaine, with the duchy covering expenses of £1,000.[68] Since his attentions were soon to be consumed elsewhere, the prince removed all the stannary bailiffs and John de Horsham, the bailiff of Powdershire, on charges of negligence, also having the king renew the previous peace commission.[69] Distributing another tranche of gifts, the prince rewarded those loyal to him and secured their continuing diligence.[70] With the duchy administration galvanised and his fleet now ready for him, he set sail in September on an expedition which would become celebrated for his victory over the French at Poitiers.[71]

In May 1357 the prince returned from France with his illustrious prisoner the French king in tow and peace negotiations began.[72] In Cornwall, the prince removed Eleford from the sheriff-stewardship in October, later imprisoning him in Launceston Castle for his misdemeanours and debts of over £600.[73] The prince then reappointed Dabernon, who was to serve his master diligently until 1369.[74] While he also retained Kendale in his posts, in 1358 the prince was 'amazed and moved with anger' as Kendale was accused of leaking secret correspondence; and if it happened again he 'would have him so chastised that others [would] take future warning'.[75] Asserting his mastery over his subordinates, we find the prince criticising Skirkbeck for having 'hitherto failed to certify anything thereon' concerning a ducal commission, 'at which the prince marvels greatly'.[76] As household men were to continue leading Cornwall, the prince granted extra posts to those with proven track-records and removed those of negligible worth.[77] To support his efforts, between 1354 and 1370 the king regularly renewed the commissions of trailbaston in the county.[78] So long as these commissions worked hard – investigating assaults, murders and false

[67] Ormrod, *Edward III*, pp. 339–340.
[68] *RBP*, ii, 77, 80, 86; Barber, *Prince of Wales*, pp. 114–116.
[69] *RBP*, ii, 80–81; *CPR 1354–1358*, 227.
[70] *RBP*, ii, 82.
[71] Froissart, *Chronicles*, pp. 120–145.
[72] Froissart, *Chronicles*, pp. 167–168; Barber, *Prince of Wales*, p. 152.
[73] JUST1/124 mm. 2d–3r, 5r; *RBP*, ii, 155.
[74] SC6/817/6 m. 2v; *RBP*, ii, 125.
[75] *RBP*, ii, 150.
[76] *RBP*, ii, 113.
[77] *RBP*, ii, 164, 171; DCO 13.
[78] *CPR 1354–1358*, 120; *CPR 1358–1361*, 70; *CPR 1364–1367*, 444; *CPR 1367–1370*, 136; *RBP*, ii, 135, 146, 154, 168; also, *CPR 1358–1361*, 68.

metal in tin ingots and levying many fines, some of over £100 apiece – the king and the prince together were able to curb Cornish lawlessness.[79]

During these years revenue was a major concern for the prince and his administration – and the income from the stannaries in particular. As the prince was 'greatly astonished' at the decline in the level of tin income, Dabernon had to attend to coinages personally.[80] The prince went on to bemoan the collapse in profits, summoning both Dabernon and Kendale to London to explain.[81] In the same year he employed his own tinners and later sold a great part of the coined tin to London pewterers, before writing to Ghent and Bruges concerning the safe passage of tin-trading vessels.[82] While he was able to micro-manage his lordship from afar through his many lordly officers, the massive plague visitation of 1348–9 made his task more difficult. The prince's drive for money was to a large extent driven by his need to raise revenue to pay for military campaigning.[83] Despite King John's capture, peace remained elusive and in 1359 Edward III and the prince embarked upon one last big expedition, the Rheims Campaign, which was intended to deliver a knockout blow against the French, but which was to end without a major success.[84] Despite the inconclusiveness of the expedition, the two sides agreed on a draft treaty at Brétigny which was to usher in a decade of peace. Creating his son the first and only prince of Aquitaine in 1362, Edward III then entrusted the prince with a new and heavy responsibility.[85] Later in 1363 he was to sail to his new principality from Plymouth, but he was first to undertake his second itinerary to Cornwall in eight years. His movements are well documented.

Table 5: The Black Prince's Cornish Itinerary of 1362–3

24 August to 18 September	Restormel Castle
23 September	Liskeard Manor
26 September	Plympton
24 November to 5 January	Restormel Castle
18 February to 10 April	Restormel Castle
20 May to 8 June	Plympton, on June 8 he was aboard Ship in Plymouth Haven

Sources: *RBP*, ii, 192–204; *RBP*, iii, 454–458; *RBP*, iv, 465–501.

[79] JUST1/128/1 mm. 5r–6d; JUST1/123; JUST1/124; JUST1/127 m. 1r; *RBP*, ii, 132, 153, 158.
[80] *RBP*, ii, 149.
[81] *RBP*, ii, 155–156.
[82] *RBP*, ii, 157–158, 170, 162–163, 165.
[83] *RBP*, ii, 166–169; *CCR 1360–1364*, 98.
[84] Barber, *Prince of Wales*, pp. 158–169.
[85] Barber, *Prince of Wales*, pp. 175–179.

Although the prince stayed in Restormel over Christmas 1362, the visit was a private affair without the pomp of 1354.[86] All the same, he found the time to replace two stannary bailiffs and see that the Cornish bench now comprised John Dabernon and Cornish gentlemen rather than professional justices.[87] While aboard his flagship, he granted Dabernon yet more lands as he had served his master so well.[88] The close supervision that had characterised the prince's lordship to this point, however, was to wane after 1363. Now that he had responsibility for a principality in south-west France, the many problems of that territory consumed his attentions, leaving him less and less time to administer Cornwall.[89] Previously so voluminous, his register now becomes greatly condensed and contains no personal authorisation warrants. This was because the prince increasingly delegated the duchy's running to his council.

We should be wary of seeing too abrupt a shift of policy after the prince's departure, however, as although a change had undoubtedly taken place, few personnel were to be moved.[90] It was not until September 1365 that the council replaced John Kendale as receiver at his 'own request on account of his inability', employing his kinsman Richard Kendale instead.[91] From 1362 on, the county was left more to run its own affairs. Even though the king renewed the commission of trailbaston in 1367, royal justices were no longer appointed to the Cornish bench. Father and son both realised that without unremitting supervision they could not continue to manipulate or overrule local power structures.[92] The register of the prince's correspondence ends suddenly in 1365, throwing the administrative history of the duchy thereafter in comparative darkness. What little we know of the prince's appointments and policies in these years, however, tends to reinforce this picture of his growing distance from Cornish affairs.[93] As time went on, the prince was increasingly distracted by the Castilian civil war between the pro-English Peter the Cruel and his brother, Henry of Trastamara, the Valois candidate. Although the prince crushed Trastamara at the battle of Nájera in 1367, the campaign cost him his health and he was never to fully recover.[94] In the light of all this, it is no surprise that the maintenance of a continuous, direct relationship between the prince and his Cornish subjects grew harder and harder.

---

[86] *RBP*, ii, 198, 202.
[87] *RBP*, ii, 201; SC6/817/8 m. 23v; DCO 15; *CPR 1361–1364*, 65, 207.
[88] *RBP*, ii, 203.
[89] Barber, *Prince of Wales*, pp. 208–225; Ormrod, *Edward III*, pp. 420–421.
[90] *RBP*, ii, 204–215; SC6/817/8–10; DCO 17; E101/263/13; *CPR 1361–1366*, 303.
[91] *RBP*, ii, 213.
[92] *CPR 1364–1367*, 444; *CCR 1364–1368*, 390–391.
[93] *CPR 1377–1381*, 209.
[94] Barber, *Prince of Wales*, pp. 192–206; Ormrod, *Edward III*, pp. 436–442.

The duchy officials themselves were also beginning to show their age. By 1367 Dabernon had served the prince for at least thirty years, with the 'great and arduous business' of ducal rule forming the leitmotif of his career.[95] But although he was the prince's south-western retainer-in-chief, he could not go on forever. In 1368 he composed his will and he had died by late 1369, leaving his executors and widow, one Joan, to account for 1368–9.[96] On his death the king tried to nominate Sir Richard Sergeaux to the shrievalty, but the prince quickly disabused both of the idea.[97] Instead, he appointed a certain Richard Seck in Dabernon's stead, although in 1371 he replaced him with William Cranewell, his yeoman and a former clerk to the chamberlain of North Wales.[98] During these years the prince is also found substituting his receiver, Richard Kendale, for the local powerbroker Ralph Trenewith, employing as feodary one Henry Cokyn of Lostwithiel too.[99] Yet Cokyn did not hold his new post for long, and from 1369 the Cornishman Henry Nanfan added this office to his responsibilities in the duke's manors.[100] The king and prince also oversaw a surprisingly rapid turnover of the county bench. Whereas the 1367 commission consisted of two duchy men and three proprietors, that of 1369 comprised two justices, Dabernon, Skirkbeck, and seven Cornishmen, with Sir John l'Ercedekne and John Trevarthian prominent.[101]

This batch of appointments marks the end of the long period of stability that had characterised the prince's rulership of the county. What was happening was that, although some of the prince's household staff were still involved, local Cornishmen were coming to the fore again after a gap of twenty years. Across the realm more generally, in the 1360s we find 'local establishments' successfully reasserting control of local office-holding. In Cornwall, then, on the one hand, the prince was accommodating the commonalty's growing expectations of self-regulation as part of a change in policy that sought to harness local power to his rulership. On the other, this political volte-face came about because he lacked the time and energy to enforce his will though assertive 'outsiders' as fully as he once had.

In 1369 England and France found themselves at war again, Charles V being intent on undoing the dramatic concessions that his father had been forced to make in 1360. Unfortunately for Edward III, Charles was a skilful opponent.[102] The ailing prince tried to hold onto Aquitaine, but his growing

---

[95] *CCR 1369–1374*, 29–30.
[96] DCO 18; *Cornish Wills*, 31–35.
[97] *CFR 1368–1377*, 147; *CCR 1369–1374*, 271.
[98] SC6/818/1 m. 18r; *Sheriffs*, 21; SC6/818/4 m. 8r.
[99] DCO 18; SC6/818/1.
[100] SC6/818/4 m. 9r.
[101] *CPR 1364–1367*, 434; *CPR 1367–1370*, 266.
[102] Ormrod, *Edward III*, pp. 498–523.

illness weakened his authority in the principality and in 1371 he resigned his commission.[103] In that year he returned to England with his energies spent and his health broken. Although there would be no return to the policy of close supervision in Cornwall, there is some evidence that he showed a little interest in the personnel of the county's sheriff-stewardship.[104] In 1375 he replaced Cranewell with Sir Richard Sergeaux, who was the first Cornishman to hold this post since 1349, but a retainer of his since at least 1368. Appointing yet more Cornishmen to shire-franchisal administration in these years, the prince employed the lawyer Robert Tresilian on both the county bench and directly in the duchy.[105]

As the rolling trailbaston commission came to an end in this period, it was inevitable that the county's peace suffered. It is illustrative of the times that from 1368 onwards the court of king's bench repeatedly summoned some forty-one Cornishmen to appear for 'diverse transgressions', while in 1371 royal investigations into the breaching of ducal maritime prerogatives and assaults on officials were to name over 300 malefactors.[106] In these years the commonalty were also concerned with hundredal racketeering and the growing tensions between stannary-men and others in the county.[107] To try to combat the disorder, the Crown made numerous alterations to the county bench, with new appointments in 1370, 1375 and 1376, along with subsequent additions to these tribunals. The county's sons now dominated the bench, folk such as Sir Ralph Carminow and Sir John Hamley, so that 'outsiders' were less prominent than in the earlier years of the prince's rule.[108] Neither the infirm prince nor the geriatric king had the energy to quash the growing lawlessness, a powerful testament to their twin declines. Without close supervision of the duchy the proper channels of redress were diminished, prompting all in the county to look to their own resources.

Nationally, growing tensions found their outlet in the Good Parliament of 1376, the sessions of which afforded the most vocal expression of the discontent growing at the end of Edward's long reign.[109] While tradition has it that the Black Prince was a covert supporter of the parliamentary Commons during these events, this view has since been discredited and there is no evidence that

---

[103] Froissart, *Chronicles*, pp. 175–180; Barber, *Prince of Wales*, pp. 209–227; Ormrod, *Edward III*, pp. 506–514.
[104] SC6/818/4.
[105] SC8/333/E1038.
[106] KB27/431 *Rex* m. 22r; KB27/433 *Rex* m. 6r; KB27/451 *Rex* m. 20r; *CPR 1370–1374*, 170–173.
[107] SC8/102/5080; *PROME*, v, 347.
[108] *CPR 1367–1370*, 418; *CPR 1370–1374*, 388, 397; *CPR 1374–1377*, 139, 141, 310, 313.
[109] Ormrod, *Edward III*, pp. 550–558; also, G. Holmes, *The Good Parliament* (Oxford, 1975).

he influenced Cornwall's returns.[110] The prince had been fit enough to attend the opening of parliament, but another bout of sickness was to strike him down in May. He died on 8 June 1376.[111]

*

Leaving an indelible mark on Cornwall, the prince's lordship, however, neither stands out as wholly beneficent nor even completely benign. His heavy reliance on 'outsiders' in no small part excluded county proprietors from their traditional place of local authority. Indeed, Sir Richard Sergeaux was the only Cornishman to appear in the 1368 muster of his household.[112] At times the prince's assertiveness and financial exactions drew down the ire of the commonalty. Cornish complaints in 1347 about the 'under-bailiffs and others who meddle in the prince's name' are a clear sign of dissatisfaction with the weight of ducal rule at this time. His demands also led to complaint in 1356, when the commonalty again made 'great clamour' as he owed them 'a great sum of money' for purveyances.[113] Neither did the prince brook local alternative or opposition to his will, for example forbidding Sir John Trevaignon and Sir John Arundell from accompanying him on campaign because of their 'outrageous and offensive' bearing.[114]

Despite frictions of this sort, however, there was no such thing as perpetual acrimony between the prince and the commonalty. On the contrary, he engaged extensively with the county's residents, a point best evidenced by the dozens of surviving petitions that Cornishmen and women sent to him, calling for his intervention in their disputes.[115] All these people had faith in his judgements, and in responding to their entreaties he attracted much goodwill in the county. Taking a close interest in the county, the prince kept in close and continuous contact with the peninsula's residents through his numerous officers. While most of these administrators, as have seen, were 'outsiders', many went on to acquire Cornish wives and lands that helped to make these agents of lordly authority more acceptable to the county.[116] And for all his assertiveness, the prince responded to the commonalty's increasing demands

---

[110] D. Green, 'Politics and Service with Edward the Black Prince', in *Age of Edward III*, pp. 53–68 at 65; Holmes, *Good Parliament*, pp. 134–135.

[111] D. Green, 'Masculinity and Medicine: Thomas Walsingham and the Death of the Black Prince', *Journal of Medieval History*, 35 (2009), pp. 34–51; Froissart, *Chronicles*, p. 193.

[112] E101/29/24; Cf. D. Green, 'Edward the Black Prince and East Anglia: An Unlikely Association', *Fourteenth Century England, III*, ed. W. M. Ormrod (Woodbridge, 2004), pp. 83–98.

[113] *RBP*, ii, 103; also, *PROME*, iv, 420.

[114] *RBP*, ii, 9–10.

[115] Below, p. 178, 212–213.

[116] Below, Chapter 10.

for self-regulation in the 1360s and 1370s. He also led some twenty-four Cornish gentlemen to war, in this way winning their loyalty both on the battlefield and back at home.[117]

Since the wellbeing of the lordship ranked high in his priorities, the prince's rulership proved to be relatively responsive and by no means relentlessly predatory. When buying Cornwall's tin, for example, he agreed on a price of 22*d*. per foot after 'being informed... that thereby the estate of the poor people will be very much relieved'.[118] After many people had hidden the metal in 1351 to avoid tax, the prince even chose to reduce fines for this misdemeanour on account of 'the present bad times and the poverty of the said persons'.[119] Two years later, we find him ordering the removal of the coinage to Lostwithiel unless this was ruinous to poor tin-workers 'whose estate the prince would not wish to worsen'.[120] Having a highly developed sense of right, at times the prince was 'greatly exercised in his conscience'.[121] When in the 1340s Lymbergh appeared to be becoming Pessagno redivivus, the prince quickly forbade his interfering with tin-weights which, he said, 'he greatly dislikes, not only because of the dishonour which might attach to [the prince], but because of the damage and loss of the commonality'.[122]

Protecting his subjects and respecting legal process, the prince's goodwill was spread across the whole range of Cornish society. It is illustrative of this that in 1357 he excused customary fines owing to the 'hard years... of late', and after a storm had battered the peninsula Dabernon pardoned rents 'in accordance with the charge which the prince gave.... by word of mouth'.[123] As John Hatcher has written, the prince's 'estates were often governed with a degree of benevolence that far exceeded the feudal obligations of a lord to his tenants, and with a spirit of charity pitifully wanting in the administration of many ecclesiastical estates at this time'.[124] Until 1363 the lordship stood near the heart of the prince's personal concerns and was treated accordingly. He offered the county vigorous government in the interests of both the common good and the highest revenues, with both strands interrelated.

It is also worth considering the prince's promotion of peace, although any assessment must remain impressionistic. While the longstanding factors undermining public order to west of the Tamar continued during the prince's tenure, in contrast to the final years of the earldom his lordship helped to

---

[117] Appendix II.
[118] *RBP*, i, 26.
[119] *RBP*, ii, 18.
[120] *RBP*, ii, 48.
[121] *RBP*, i, 5.
[122] *RBP*, i, 71.
[123] *RBP*, ii, 133, 189.
[124] *RESDCornwall*, 127.

re-establish order.¹²⁵ With his father's backing, the prince employed numerous practices to quash local disorder. A case in point is his treatment of Sir John l'Ercedekne, a freebooter of the first order. After several episodes of disorder in which l'Ercedekne assaulted numerous people with what was called his 'confederacy', staged a prison break from Launceston and twice received pardons on account of his military service, the prince confiscated his estates and forced him to pay large fines in annual instalments.¹²⁶ So substantial were these sums that in the 1360s l'Ercedekne asked to be excused payment on grounds of poverty. The prince often employed debt to cripple malefactors, among them such other gentlemen-criminals as John Trevarthian and Nicholas Wamford, in this way securing their future compliance.¹²⁷

The prince's 'open-house' policy towards petitions proved significant too. As many folk took advantage of this point of contact, the prince was able to forestall much violence by brokering agreements whereby both parties might 'be appeased in the best manner possible'.¹²⁸ Here especially we see how he became the accepted arbiter of justice in the county. Within the ranks of his officials, the prince readily identified strong-arm tactics and dismissed or admonished those who were guilty of them. One such case is to be found in 1355, when he retired John de Horsham, the bailiff of Powdershire, after it had come to light that Horsham had not only been negligent, but had also violently breached the peace on at least five occasions.¹²⁹ Believing in constant, careful supervision, in 1358 the prince even ordered Justice Shareshull to 'observe how the prince's ministers demean themselves towards the prince and the common people'.¹³⁰ So it was that the prince actively promoted local peace, being aided in this by a king who was conscientious in his governance of the realm.

The prince had a powerful incentive to ensure the establishment of order, however, not least the fact that the justice dispensed yielded an income from fines. Neither does his record on law and order stand altogether unblemished. Although he punished his receiver, one John Kendale, for mendacious behaviour, he still allowed him to remain in office. Kendale went on to take advantage of his post to reoffend repeatedly, violently seizing tinning and landed assets.¹³¹ The prince could never succeed in stamping out all disorder in

---

[125] Above, p. 132.
[126] JUST1/123 m. 1r; JUST1/122/1 m. 12r; KB9/9 mm. 28, 34–35; *CPR 1334–1338*, 457; *CCR 1339–1341*, 629; *CPR 1340–1343*, 439; *CPR 1343–1345*, 66, 401; *CPR 1345–1348*, 113, 180, 494; *CPR 1350–1354*, 171; *RBP*, ii, 16–17, 19–21, 32–34, 45, 167–168, 179.
[127] *RBP*, ii, 158–159, 169; JUST1/123.
[128] *RBP*, ii, 19.
[129] JUST1/128/1 m. 5r; *RBP*, ii, 20, 28–29, 80–81, 85.
[130] *RBP*, ii, 135.
[131] *RBP*, ii, 109; JUST1/122/2 m. 1r; JUST1/128/1 mm. 1r, 3r; JUST1/1476 m. 74d.

the county because his lordship was never all-powerful.[132] This point is worth emphasising, as Cornwall's inhabitants were still guilty of committing many disorders even during the greatest years the prince's tenure. Indeed, after his departure for Aquitaine in 1363 the prince was no longer able to deal with disorder so effectively. Twenty years of close supervision could not altogether expunge a 'culture of violence'. His sometimes intrusive lordship may actually have contributed in some degree to generating disorder by disrupting local conventions. 'Peace' formed a more subjective concept than at first it seems and the prince inevitably enforced order for reasons beyond altruism.

We may well wonder what the commonalty of Cornwall made of the prince. In governing so assertively he risked his rulership becoming overbearing and divisive, yet in many ways his iron fist in a velvet glove approach seemed to work. And while quarrels arose between him and the county's residents, their scarcity is more noteworthy than their occurrence. In contrast to south-west England, however, the prince's mode of government was to provoke discontent in parts of Aquitaine, Cheshire and the Welsh Marches: why?[133] Unlike the autonomy that the Gascons had long enjoyed, Cornwall was a land thoroughly conditioned to assertive lordly-royal governance. The absence of a resident great lord left the Cornish gentry more susceptible to princely blandishments, so that no tensions erupted with the ambitions of other noblemen, as in Aquitaine or the March of Wales. More important still was the character and rulership of the prince himself, the sheer force of his personality. He genuinely strived to provide justice in the county, answering petitioners, policing lawbreakers and wooing leading Cornishmen with gifts.[134] While he set about collecting as much money as he could, a powerful sense of reciprocity between him and the commonalty still emerges. Since Edward III consistently supported his son's lordship with the full force of the royal government, the prince, the king and the commonalty stand out as tightly interconnected, earning the prince the fidelity of his Cornish subjects and drawing them closely into the political mainstream of the realm. With Charles V seizing every opportunity to undermine the prince in Aquitaine, events in south-western France again contrast with those in south-western England. Yet perhaps the best that we can say of the prince's lordship in Cornwall is that it worked, not that it was perfect. No government is flawless.

---

[132] Cf. Walker, *Lancastrian Affinity*, pp. 235, 261.
[133] Barber, *Prince of Wales*, pp. 209–215; Barraclough, *Cheshire*, p. 23; Morgan, *Cheshire*, pp. 101–102; Davies, *March of Wales*, pp. 269–273; G. Pépin, 'Towards a New Assessment of the Black Prince's Principality of Aquitaine: A Study of the Last Years (1369–1372)', *Nottingham Medieval Studies*, 50 (2006), pp. 59–114; Jones, *Black Prince*, pp. 271–276, 324–334.
[134] *RBP*, ii, 15.

7

Richard of Bordeaux: Duke of Cornwall and King of England, 1376–99

With the Black Prince dead, in June 1376 his only surviving son, Richard of Bordeaux, the future Richard II, inherited most of his father's many titles.[1] By the terms of the creation of the duchy in 1337, however, the lordship of Cornwall returned to the hands of the king, the aged and bereft Edward III. In July the Crown appointed Sir Hugh de Segrave as steward of all the prince's former lordships while his executors surveyed their value.[2] Soon after bestowing on Richard two thirds of the duchy estates and profits, the king granted the young duke's mother, the widowed Princess Joan of Kent, the profits of the remaining portion of the lordship.[3] For the better management of her prerogatives, Joan chose to employ as her receiver in Cornwall the well-connected Sir William Brantingham, a relative of the bishop of Exeter. She also had the Crown sue out commissions of oyer and terminer to investigate grievances of hers, including one in 1383, after 'divers fishermen' had avoided paying customs in her lordship.[4] Exercising no little influence across the kingdom, the princess's 'supplication' in 1381 even prompted Richard II to expand Brantingham's commission to that of receiver of all Cornwall and Devon.[5] On Joan's death in 1385, however, all her lands reverted to Richard himself.

---

[1] This discussion owes a great debt to Tyldesley's 'Local Communities' and builds on my 'Politics and Society in Richard II's Cornwall: A Study in Relations between Centre and Locality', *JRIC* (2013), pp. 23–48.
[2] *CPR 1374–1377*, 293, 374–376; C47/9/57; *RESDCornwall*, 136–137.
[3] *CCR 1374–1377*, 421, 407–408; *CPR 1374–1377*, 374–377; R. Barber, 'Joan *suo jure* countess of Kent, and princess of Wales and Aquitaine', in *ODNB*, xxx, pp. 137–139.
[4] *CPR 1381–1385*, 357.
[5] *CPR 1385–1389*, 297.

Rather more significantly, in June 1377 Richard of Bordeaux ascended to the throne of England as Richard II.[6] As a result, the duchy came to be vested directly in the Crown, remaining the childless king's personal preserve for the rest of his reign. Although during his minority the boy-king's rulership depended on a series of perpetual councils rather than a formal regency, the government still had the accounts of the lordship surveyed and deposited in the exchequer. At the same time it granted annuities from the duchy to a variety of royal dependents, among them one Rocelin de Ostery, a servitor to Richard who received the office of constable of Restormel.[7] Stepping into the shoes of the late king's former ministers and officers, many of the Black Prince's most long-standing retainers gained a significant place in government under the new king. In Cornwall, a good number of the old administrators were retained in office, notably both the prince's steward and receiver, Sir Richard Sergeaux and Ralph Trenewith respectively. Yet a change had undoubtedly taken place, for Richard, a child with a whole realm which he had to learn to rule, could devote little time to his Cornish lordship. Accordingly, he farmed out some of his manors in the peninsula, including Helstone-in-Trigg, which in 1377 he granted to his first tutor, Sir Richard Abberbury.[8] To secure the local acceptance of the new king's rulership, Richard's government sought to draw a greater proportion of the Cornish gentry into the magistracy. To this end, it chose to separate the offices of sheriff and steward, for the rest of the reign replacing the sheriff annually in line with practices elsewhere while retaining the stewardship as a private prerogative.

For all this activity, however, Richard's reign started inauspiciously in the far south west. In 1378 Castilian forces actually launched raids on the county, prompting the commonalty to beseech the king to defend them and their homes.[9] Neither had the final years of the prince's tenure been altogether happy, plagued as they were by his ill-health and increasing disorder in the county. The latter was now exacerbated by the absence of close personal rulership. Although the feud between the families of Sergeaux, on the one hand, and Carminow and Trevarthian, on the other, was rooted in the division of the Champernoun inheritance between John Sergeaux and Sir Ralph Carminow in the 1350s, it came to a head in these febrile early years of the reign.[10] To judge from the evidence of an anonymous petition of c. 1377, the Sergeauxs made the first move. Among other lawless things, Sir Richard had supposedly used his powers as sheriff in 1375–6 to protect criminals and attack the Trevarthians.[11] It

[6] See, N. Saul, *Richard II* (New Haven and London, 1997).
[7] For example, *CPR 1377–1381*, 131.
[8] *RESDCornwall*, 137.
[9] *PROME*, vi, 89–90.
[10] SC8/38/1867; *RBP*, ii, 57; Tyldesely, 'Local Communities', pp. 136–140.
[11] SC8/38/1868.

seems that John Sergeaux's skulduggery, however, was on an altogether more ambitious scale. Sir Ralph and William Carminow alleged that, while serving as sheriff in the following year, John Sergeaux had 'gathered a great number of armed men... by colour of his office' to assault the Carminow estates, causing over £1,000 of damage.[12] Employing felons, indicted by none other than Sir Ralph himself, John supposedly led further assaults on his enemies, including William Carminow.[13]

With their authority and property so flagrantly attacked, it is unsurprising that the Carminows and Trevarthians responded in kind. Sir Ralph Carminow's révanche saw him first secure the appointment of the Cornish lawyer John Penrose to investigate the activities of Sir Richard and John Sergeaux.[14] At the same time Sir Ralph and William Carminow set about breaking the Sergeauxs' dominance in local office. Achieving no small measure of success, Sir Ralph headed the county bench from 1376, finding a place there for his firm ally John Trevarthian. Both groups now struggled for mastery of these posts. In his capacity as sheriff, in 1377 John Sergeaux oversaw the election of Sir Richard Sergeaux as an MP. Once in Westminster, the latter then secured the issue of a new peace commission on which he himself sat, wasting no time in bringing proceedings against Trevarthian. Sir Ralph Carminow's riposte saw him head yet another reissue of the county bench in early 1378, although Sir Richard soon had him ejected, sitting again as a JP himself. Despite being outmanoeuvred on the county's peace commissions, in 1378 Sir Ralph managed to secure the shrievalty for himself. On attaining this powerful position, he launched yet another attack on the Sergeaux affinity. After an affray at Bodmin, Sir Ralph arrested one of Sir Richard's supporters, a certain Odo Resgerens, before handing him over to the prior of Bodmin who then allegedly had his servants beat him.[15] Inevitably, Sir Richard Sergeaux was to strike back and in 1380 he secured the issue of yet another royal commission to arrest Penrose, the prior of Bodmin, and other Carminow supporters, having them sent to the Marshalsea.[16] Rumbling on, the dispute only grew less heated after 1386 for the simple reason that Sir Ralph died in this year.[17]

In contrast to the assaults on Edward II's ministers in the 1310s and 1320s, which emerged in no small part from his predatory regime, the violence of the late 1370s and early 1380s arose from the Crown's inability to supervise the far south west closely. The young king simply did not yet have the personal authority necessary to enforce peace, and so the Cornish gentry naturally took

[12] SC8/38/1867; SC8/38/1869.
[13] Tyldesley, 'Local Communities', p. 136.
[14] SC8/38/1866; below, pp. 246–248; *CCR 1377–1381*, 110.
[15] Tyldesley, 'Local Communities', p. 138.
[16] *CPR 1377–1381*, 569.
[17] *CCR 1381–1385*, 560.

'matters into the own hands'. And yet it should be noted that these truculent Cornishmen still chose to employ the apparatus of regnal and seignorial government to further their vendetta, a testament to the increasing pervasiveness of the royal-lordly administration. We may well wonder whether this feud was actually exceptionally violent or just exceptionally well documented.

The government was by no means ignorant of the disturbances, initiating an investigation into all the king's ministers in the county for corruption.[18] As part of this process, in July 1377 the Crown stripped Sir Richard Sergeaux of the stewardship, replacing him with the Cornish lawyer Robert Tresilian, and at the same time it appointed as receiver the prosperous tin-merchant Roger Juyl.[19] When Tresilian was appointed to the office of pusine justice of the king's bench in 1378, however, the king nominated Sir John Kentwood to the stewardship.[20] He did so because Kentwood, who was a Berkshire man, had enjoyed an impressive career in the service of his father, the Black Prince. For the next decade Kentwood was to serve on nearly every major commission in his new county, supervising everything from the peninsula's defences to the value of beached whales. Since Sir William Brantingham was serving as receiver from 1381, both leading duchy offices were now held by household men whom the Crown expected to defend its interests. Turning its attention to the county bench, the government issued a new commission in February 1381 that excluded every local gentleman and instead contained four 'outside' lawyers and justices, among them Robert Bealknap, the chief justice of the common pleas.[21] All these measures were designed to restore peace and effective governance to the peninsula.

Soon after this, however, national politics again intruded upon Cornish affairs. As a rejuvenated France threatened the realm, the government was in desperate need of money. To this end, the council levied a series of three poll taxes across the kingdom. Proving deeply unpopular, these levies saw so many Cornish folk avoid paying that almost two-thirds of the county's eligible taxpayers 'vanished' between the 1377 and 1381 issues.[22] The poll taxes were universally resented, forming the main short-term cause of the Great Revolt that convulsed all England in 1381.[23] Although no specific rising occurred in Cornwall, the local gentry seized the opportunity presented to them violently to furthering their own agendas. After being 'informed by his friends that certain traitors of Essex and Kent had risen against the king', Sir William Botreaux

[18] *CFR 1377–1383*, 127.
[19] *CFR 1377–1383*, 7.
[20] *CFR 1377–1383*, 269.
[21] *CPR 1377–1381*, 572–573.
[22] *The Poll Taxes of 1377, 1379 and 1381*, ed. C. C. Fenwick, 3 vols, Records of Social and Economic History, n.s. 27, 29, 37 (Oxford, 1998–2005), i, p. 80.
[23] See, *The Peasants' Revolt of 1381*, ed. R. B. Dobson, 2nd Edition (London, 1983).

allegedly gathered together some 'eighty traitors' who then assaulted Sir Ralph Carminow's lands and sought to 'slay' his servants.[24] It seems very likely, however, that Botreaux was actually campaigning in Portugal at this time, as his wife Elizabeth later claimed in her petition to parliament that sought his exoneration.[25] These fictitious crimes were instead part of a long-running dispute over the ownership of Trembethow manor, which Botreaux had recovered at law from John Trevarthian and John Penrose in the previous year. Having lost the initial case, Trevarthian and Penrose had secured this false indictment and led an assault on Trembethow, attacking Botreaux's tenant Richard Eyr in the process.

Naturally enough, Eyr turned to violent self-help himself, allegedly mobilising 'a large band of men in manner of war' who then beheaded a number of the king's lieges.[26] Not content with this action, he supposedly raised a further 300 supporters who attacked the lands of the prior of Bodmin, an assault partly related to the Sergeaux–Carminow–Trevarthian feud. Eyr was one of Sir Richard Sergeaux's dependents. Supposedly 'counselling and procuring' Eyr to lead the latter attack, the lawyer John Tremayne had himself 'gathered' together yet another 'band of armed men to aid the rebels… in manner of war', riding to murder John Treglosek. We see here how disturbed conditions across the realm provided convenient cover for the furtherance of private quarrels in Cornwall, although many of these allegations may not actually have been true. Some measure of lawlessness still spread fluidly across south-western England, however, prompting the government to issue a commission in 1382 to numerous royal justices and county gentlemen:

> To arrest all homicides, robbers and insurgents now more usually present in the counties of Somerset, Dorset, Devon and Cornwall, as well as their maintainers and notorious suspects, and deliver them to the gaol of the county in which their offence was committed, as it seems that they escape from one county into another.[27]

Faced with such a serious challenge to the established order, the Crown nominated as many as fourteen men to the county bench in March 1382, including Chief Justice Tresilian, the steward John Kentwood and landed gentlemen such as Otto Bodrugan.[28] Attempting to harness the stabilising influence of the nearest temporal and spiritual magnates to its cause, the government also included on the commission Thomas Brantingham, the bishop of Exeter, and

---

[24] *CIM 1377–1388*, 101.
[25] SC8/277/13838; *CIM 1377–1388*, 101–102.
[26] *CIM 1377–1388*, 102.
[27] *CPR 1381–1385*, 136.
[28] *CPR 1381–1385*, 142.

Edward Courtenay, the earl of Devon. All these proprietors – lay, spiritual, gentle and noble alike – then employed both their private clout and royal commissions to re-establish peace. Yet despite their best efforts, the county's law and order was undermined by the absence of either a resident nobleman in Cornwall or a duke who took a keen interest in the peninsula from afar. It is illustrative of the problem that in 1382 Sir John Trevarthian and his supporters supposedly seized a Spanish vessel in Mount's Bay, one already arrested by the havener for the king.[29] On the same day, a Portuguese ship had the misfortune to sail into the bay, whereupon Trevarthian allegedly compelled 'the master by force and threat of death' to gift all its cargo to him, among these items being nine swords and a cannon.[30] The king was aware that all remained far from well to west of the Tamar, something shown by the fact that in these years he charged royal justices and duchy staff with investigating the 'concealment of divers lands, tenements, wardships, marriages, reliefs, forfeitures, escheats, goods and chattels, wreck of the sea and other things'.[31]

In the 1380s Richard's growing age and assertiveness began to make themselves felt in Cornwall, as they did in the rest of the realm. From 1382 the king increasingly packed the royal household with his own supporters, foremost among them Robert de Vere, the earl of Oxford. Granting annuities from his Cornish revenues to household men as diverse as Sir Philip Courtenay and Sir Thomas Trivet, who received £100 apiece per annum, the king mobilised the county's resources to the advantage of the court.[32] He also made many gifts of land in the peninsula, as for example in 1382, when he bestowed the manors of Climsland and Liskeard on his queen, Anne of Bohemia.[33] When Princess Joan's Cornish estates returned to Richard's hands in 1385, he soon granted them away to men such as Nicholas Sarnsfield, his standard-bearer.[34] In this way, Richard farmed out most of the duchy's Cornish manors. The king also made many appointments of his own household men to key offices in the county, such as his esquire, Richard de Hampton, who from 1386 jointly held both the havenership and Tintagel Castle with the royal butler John Slegh.

Dissatisfaction with Richard's increasingly partisan rule generated tensions which led to a major political crisis in England in the years 1386–8. In the so-called 'Wonderful Parliament' of 1386, the king's opponents, chief among them the duke of Gloucester and the earl of Arundel, forced Richard to dismiss his councillors and imposed on him a continual council which was charged

[29] CPR 1381–1385, 249, 286.
[30] CIM 1377–1388, 129.
[31] CPR 1381–1385, 283.
[32] CPR 1377–1381, 456–457; CPR 1385–1389, 43.
[33] CCR 1389–1392, 273.
[34] CPR 1385–1389, 17, 18, 22; Syllabus of Rymer's Foedera, ed. T. D. Hardy, 3 vols (London, 1869–85), i, 509.

with reforming the royal finances. Faced with this affront to his majesty, the king summoned judges from across the realm to whom he put a series of questions about the legality of the lords' actions.[35] Hearing news of this, the Lords Appellant, as they were to become – the duke of Gloucester and the earls of Arundell, Warwick, Derby and Nottingham – knew that they had to fight to defend themselves. After prevailing in battle at Radcot Bridge in December 1387, the Lords 'appealed' (prosecuted) in the so-called 'Merciless Parliament' of February 1388 many of the king's leading supporters, including Robert de Vere, Michael de la Pole and Sir Robert Tresilian.

Such kingdom-wide political disturbances had major repercussions for the far south west. In May 1388 the Appellants appointed Sir John Kentwood as steward of the lands in Cornwall, Devon and Somerset of de Vere, Tresilian, John Cary and others forfeited in parliament.[36] While de Vere's Cornish estates were few in number, Tresilian had amassed a great deal of land in the county with the profits of his legal expertise. Kentwood soon after presented Tresilian's 'charters, writings, rolls, and memoranda' to the justices of assize at Launceston, who then used them as evidence for people suing for the recovery of land.[37] It seems that the judge had passed many false judgments in order to expand his estates.[38] The Appellants sold off the bulk of these lands to just three buyers: John Hawley of Dartmouth, Sir Humphrey Stafford and the prior of Launceston.[39] The disgraced 'man of law' John Cary also held some property in the county. Delivering nearly 700 marks of Cary's money to Kentwood, the prior of Launceston took advantage of this for his own purposes.[40] While the confiscations were going on, the Cornish gentry seized the opportunity to revive old feuds. Sir Richard Sergeaux, for example, took advantage of his appointment as sheriff in 1388 to present to the king's bench indictments relating to John Trevarthian from 1383, outlawing Trevarthian in the county court soon after.[41]

In order to secure the local enforcement of their programme of reform across the realm, the Appellants turned their attention to the personnel of Cornwall's government. To this end, in 1387 they oversaw the appointment of a new county bench that double its size to twelve members, with the earl of Devon the most striking addition – indeed, the earl led this tribunal.[42] While

---

[35] Saul, *Richard II*, pp. 173–175; A. Goodman, *The Loyal Conspiracy: The Lords Appellant under Richard II* (London, 1971).
[36] *CPR 1385–1389*, 446.
[37] *CPR 1385–1389*, 493.
[38] Below, pp. 248–249.
[39] *CPR 1385–1389*, 531; *CPR 1388–1392*, 11, 126, 156.
[40] *CPR 1385–1389*, 502, 547.
[41] Tyldesley, 'Local Communities', p. 157.
[42] *CPR 1385–1389*, 385.

the Courtenays hardly stood out as the most prominent of the king's adversaries, the earl's appointment as a JP aimed to attach this noble family and their south-western influence to the Appellants' cause. To further their position west of the Tamar, the Appellants dismissed Sir William Brantingham, who had been the receiver since 1381, replacing him with a certain Robert Thorley, who had connections with the duke of Gloucester. Expecting full compliance with their rule, the Appellants had the ministers' accounts thoroughly audited and ordered a major survey of the king's possessions in the county.[43] Later the Appellants launched yet another investigation into concealments and general skulduggery 'since the coronation', as they put it, charging leading proprietors such as Sir William Botreaux along with the duchy steward Sir John Kentwood with leading this wide-ranging enquiry.[44] After a decade in office, however, Kentwood was relieved of his duties in November 1388, his place being taken by Sir Philip Courtenay. The exact reasons behind his dismissal remain unclear, but it was obviously a product of these tumultuous years. In the summer compelling 'the gentlest and ablest' Cornishmen to take an oath to 'keep the peace' and 'maintain them to the death against every man without exception', the Appellants took care to exact the obedience of the whole range of county society.[45]

Throughout this time Richard had patiently endured the humiliation of having to bow to the will of the Appellants. Determined to restore the supremacy of the Crown, however, he declared himself of age in 1389 and announced his desire to govern his realm effectively. In Cornwall, as elsewhere, the king took a close interest in the membership of the county bench, making alterations to its personnel on four occasions between November 1389 and December 1390. Although local gentlemen and lawyers, such as Sir Richard Sergeaux and John Tremayne, remained prominent, Richard ensured that royal interests were represented by the presence of central court justices. Instructing members of the county bench 'to busy themselves' in their office, the king had professional justices supervise the rolls of indictment from across the realm.[46] Until the end of the reign, Richard also had the visiting justices of assize take recognizances, generally of around £200–300, for 'good behaviour' from leading Cornish proprietors.[47] With the aim of asserting his rulership and promoting peace in the peninsula, the king was instrumental in appointing many commissions of oyer and terminer to investigate disorderly behaviour that arose.[48]

---

[43] *CPR 1385–1389*, 318, 378.
[44] *CPR 1385–1389*, 165–166.
[45] *CCR 1385–1389*, 406.
[46] *CCR 1389–1392*, 40, 252–253.
[47] Tyldesley, 'Local Communities', pp. 173, 181–183.
[48] *CPR 1391–1396*, 237.

To give a more secure basis to his rule in the localities, from the late 1380s Richard set about establishing a magnate-style royal affinity, a body of retainers whom he could count on to implement his will. As part of this policy, he recruited into his household the Cornishmen John Chenduyt, John Treverbyn, John Trevarthian the younger and Mark and John Michelstow.[49] Chenduyt, Treverbyn and Trevarthian held lands in the peninsula, while the Michelstows had maritime interests. Richard aimed to tie the local influence of all these powerbrokers closely to his Crown. He also oversaw the plantation of 'new men' into the county, John Colshull foremost among them. A London vintner and common councillor who had enjoyed close connections with the royalist mayor Nicholas Brembre, Colshull married Emmeline, the widow of Sir Robert Tresilian, and through this match acquired extensive estates across Cornwall. Made a mere five months after Tresilian's death in 1388, almost certainly with the king's blessing, if not his active encouragement, the match saw Richard soon after grant to Colshull the diamonds and so on that Tresilian had acquired 'for [Colshull's] good service... and in consideration of his having taken the said [Emmeline] to wife'.[50] Through this marriage, Richard had succeeded in introducing one of his loyal supporters into the highest echelons of Cornish society, duly making him a king's esquire and in 1392 appointing him to the duchy stewardship.[51] Becoming locally influential, Colshull acquired a place on the county bench at this time and served twice as sheriff before 1399.

In the 1390s the local importance of the duchy was to lead to a steady increase in royal influence over Cornwall. In the course of the decade, two minor royal esquires were appointed to take charge of castles in the county, Henry Kirkestede of Trematon and William Corby of Launceston, whose wife had been Richard's childhood nurse. A few years later Robert Thorley, who by 1396 had been wooed by Richard and recruited into the royal affinity, was nominated to the constableship of Restormel. For the better management of his many lordly-royal prerogatives, in 1395 the king appointed the Cornishman Sir Henry Ilcombe as escheator. Richard expected all these loyal dependents to labour diligently in his service, securing the royal position in the peninsula.

The king had yet grander ambitions for the duchy estates. Before 1389 as we have seen he had granted them out piecemeal to his supporters. After this date, however, he used them to establish John Holand, the earl of Huntingdon, as the mightiest landholder in the south west. As part of this policy, in 1389 he appointed Holand as guardian of Tintagel Castle, three years later granting

---

[49] *CPR 1388–1392*, 398; *CPR 1391–1396*, 190, 569; *CPR 1396–1399*, 293; Saul, *Richard II*, pp. 265–269; see, C. Given-Wilson, *The Royal Household and the King's Affinity: Service, Politics and Finance in England, 1360–1413* (New Haven and London, 1986).
[50] *CCR 1385–1389*, 627.
[51] *CPR 1391–1396*, 32.

him and his wife the manors of Trematon, Calstock and Saltash.[52] Richard made many other grants to the couple in both Cornwall and Devon; in 1395, for example, he bestowed on them the manors of Tewington, Moresk and Tintagel, along with the boroughs of Bossiney and Trevailly (Trevena?).[53] The king's aim was to elevate Holand and his family to a position of supremacy from which they could enforce the royal writ throughout the region. He was seeking to compensate for the absence of a prince of Wales and duke of Cornwall who in a different realm would have supported the Crown locally and nationally with the full force of his lordship. Holand's power was indeed to spread throughout Cornwall and Devon. It is illustrative of this that he gave employment in his new estates to Cornishmen such as Geoffrey Penriche and John Lanhergy, his 'adherents' as they were termed, while leading seven county proprietors to war, among them Sir Henry Ilcombe, and retaining John Trenarake 'for life'.[54] To provide himself with a base of suitable splendour in the south west, in 1388 Holand embarked on the rebuilding of Dartington Hall in Devon.[55] Decorating this building with images of the white crowned and chained hart, Richard's personal emblem, he constructed this residence as a 'hymn of gratitude' to the king, a home worthy of Richard's foremost representative in south-western England.[56]

From 1389 onwards, Richard's policies had exercised considerable influence on the county, altering the very workings of its society. While disorder still occurred, with the elder and younger William Talbot in 1393 leading a private assault on Trematon Castle, the king and his supporters succeeded in supervising the county more closely in these years.[57] In 1397, however, Richard's sudden act of arresting the former three senior Appellant Lords brought to a sharp end this period of relative political stability.[58] The king chose to imprison the earl of Warwick in Tintagel Castle as part of this change in his style of kingship, granting his manors in Cornwall to John Holand.[59] There are signs that the Cornishman Richard Trenode was even involved in the royally sanctioned murder of the duke of Gloucester in Calais.[60] With his former adversaries removed, Richard embarked on one of the greatest restructurings of the medieval English peerage ever undertaken. As part of this process, he

---

[52] *CPR 1385–1389*, 537; *CPR 1391–1396*, 102.
[53] *CPR 1391–1396*, 600; *CPR 1396–1399*, 22.
[54] *CIM 1399–1422*, 55–56; *CPR 1399–1401*, 255; A. Emery, *Dartington Hall* (Oxford, 1970), pp. 43–44; Appendix II.
[55] Emery, *Dartington Hall*, pp. 42–43, 96–99.
[56] Cf. Saul, *Richard II*, p. 244.
[57] *CPR 1391–1396*, 357, 604; *CCR 1392–1396*, 372.
[58] Saul, *Richard II*, pp. 366–404.
[59] *CPR 1396–1399*, 360–361; *CCR 1396–1399*, 161.
[60] *CPR 1401–1405*, 227.

raised Holand to the rank of duke of Exeter, a title recognising and proclaiming his might in the south west. This, however, did not prevent the chronicler Thomas Walsingham contemptuously placing Holand among the *duketti*, the little dukes.[61]

In the remaining two years of the reign Exeter headed the commission of the peace in Cornwall, a position that ratified his dominance in the county. Richard also rewarded Holand's supporters with posts, as for example in 1397, when he appointed as controller of the stannaries one Thomas Shelley, Holand's steward and a king's esquire, expanding his commission to that of steward of the duchy in 1398. By this point, the lordships of the king and the duke of Exeter were tightly intermeshed. At the same time as appointing Holand as admiral of the west, Richard granted the havenership to the duke of Aubermarle, another of his loyal supporters. To secure the collection of the duchy's dues, the king employed one John Copelston as receiver of Cornwall, Copelston having previously served as escheator. The deposition articles were to state that Richard had manipulated the appointment of sheriffs, and it is significant in this connection that in 1397 we find his ally John Colshull holding this office, although his term was not extended beyond one year. While the king threatened his 'wrath' to secure payments from the burgesses of Lostwithiel and Bodmin, those of Liskeard 'freely and of their own accord' lent Richard 10 marks at this time.[62] Although Cornwall did not come to form the 'inner citadel' of the kingdom, as did Cheshire after 1397, with Richard's extensive recruiting of its archers and his buttressing of its palatinate administration, the Cornish peninsula had held an integral place in Richard's schemes ever since 1389.[63] Sparing the county the 'blank charters' that he imposed on many other shires compelling them to submit 'themselves and their goods to the king's pleasure', he displayed his confidence in the loyalty of his Cornish subjects.[64]

Events in the rest of the realm, however, were to show that the foundations of this brave new Ricardian polity were built on sand. Returning in 1399 from exile in France to reclaim the Lancastrian inheritance of which Richard had deprived him, Henry Bolingbroke, John of Gaunt's son, found a realm dissatisfied and a king absent in Ireland. Supporters quickly flocked to his banner and in September he was able to set aside Richard and take the throne for himself.[65] Even before Richard's formal deposition, 'on the advice of the duke of Lancaster', that is, the new king-to-be, the government appointed John Wynter to the stewardship of Cornwall.[66] A thoroughgoing Lancastrian, Wynter was made

---

[61] Saul, *Richard II*, pp. 381–382; Walsingham, *Chronica Maiora*, ii, pp. 102–103.
[62] Elliott-Binns, *Medieval Cornwall*, p. 100; CPR 1396–1399, 179; CCR 1396–1399, 520.
[63] Saul, *Richard II*, pp. 393–394.
[64] Saul, *Richard II*, p. 388.
[65] See C. Given-Wilson, *Henry IV* (New Haven and London, 2016).
[66] CPR 1396–1399, 595.

constable of Restormel later in 1399. Henry's promotion of Wynter to these offices was made with the aim of securing Lancastrian power in the far south west. The new king soon replaced John Holand on the county bench with the royal justice William Rikhill, removing Ilcombe from the escheatorship too. Henry IV even issued instruction to leading Cornish proprietors 'to bring to the attention of all the king's lieges' in the county his intention to 'observe… the common wealth and laws and customs of the realm'.[67]

On Bolingbroke's seizure of the throne his eldest son, Henry of Monmouth, the future Henry V, became duke of Cornwall. As part of his lordly rights, Monmouth assumed the shrievalty in October 1399, appointing Sir John Arundell of Lanherne as his deputy a month later. Although there would be no return to the fused shrievalty-stewardship of the Black Prince's day, the new duke came to exercise a great deal of influence over this office in particular and the county in general. To support his son's lordship, the new king granted him the right to levy all debts owed to the Crown in Cornwall and launched investigations into dilapidations in the duchy.[68] Since a new duke was now overseeing the county, however, John Holand found his possession of the duchy estates looking increasingly untenable. In late 1399 his fears were realised when the escheator received royal instruction to seize his manors in the county.[69] It was this perhaps which spurred the earl, as he was reduced to being, into action.

In January 1400 Holand and a group of other of the former king's close associates planned to restore Richard to the throne. Henry, however, quashed the attempted coup, the so-called Epiphany Rising, which had planned to seize the king himself. It was some five days later that a certain Geoffrey Penriche, the bailiff of Trematon, arrived in Saltash with his armed supporters in an attempt to incite the burgesses to rise 'against King Henry'.[70] Although Penriche allegedly threatened to behead 'divers men of the town because they would not go and ride' against the king, he found little support in Saltash and had to content himself with seizing 6 marks from 'la comyn box' and three tuns of red wine before riding for London.[71] Investigations into those who had risen with the earl were to name a few other Cornishmen, including John Lanhergy and Nicholas Bromford, 'who were consenting and assistant to the earl in his treason… as far as in them lay'.[72] There is evidence that the prior of Launceston was another supporter of the 'zeurl of Huntyngdon', but the absence from this list of any other leading local proprietors stands as testament to the lack of

[67] CPR 1401–1405, 126; Proceedings and Ordinances of the Privy Council, 10 Richard II–33 Henry VIII, ed. H. Nicolas, 7 vols (London, 1834–7), i, p. 163.
[68] CPR 1399–1401, 61, 348, 373, 544.
[69] CCR 1399–1402, 22–23; CIM 1399–1422, 58.
[70] CIM 1399–1422, 57–58.
[71] CIM 1399–1422, 51.
[72] CIM 1399–1422, 56.

support that Holand and his royal master enjoyed in Cornwall.[73] The roots of lordship grew slowly.

After the rising, the Crown assumed control of the duchy manors that had been in Holand's keeping.[74] A process of administrative upheaval followed, and it was only in 1404 that Henry IV restored the whole estate to his son.[75] It seems, however, that Monmouth's appointment in 1402 of Sir John Arundell as steward of Cornwall 'for life' formed part of the process whereby the young duke assumed the governance of his own lordship.[76] Arundell was someone he came increasingly to rely on, holding the stewardship until as late as 1430. 'Good Prince Hal', as Shakespeare was to call him, turned sixteen in 1404, taking greater control of the duchy as a result and being petitioned often by Cornwall's residents.[77] A powerful agent of Lancastrian rule, he governed more with the grain of the county than Richard had. In 1413 he was to ascend to the throne as Henry V, once again uniting the duchy with the Crown.[78]

*

The key instrument connecting Cornwall to the ebb and flow of national politics, the duchy had remained vested in the Crown throughout Richard II's turbulent reign. Many Cornish folk can be found taking advantage of this link with the sovereign, among them John Russell, 'the king's bondsman', who in 1388 complained that John Hirde had recovered a tenement 'without due process' in the manor court of Tintagel.[79] Exercising his direct lordly-royal rulership over the peninsula, Richard responded by having the sheriff and escheator investigate. The very same direct royal lordship, however, generally emerges as less exacting than that of men such as the Black Prince. With a whole kingdom to rule, Richard could spare Cornwall little time, an absence of assertive personal rulership that contributed to the revival of disorder in the late 1370s. As Richard was later to call on John Holand to mediate his royal writ in the peninsula, the king realised that he alone could not govern the county as forcefully as he wished. Here especially we see the paradox of direct royal lordship, which at one and the same time connected Cornwall closely to the Crown while proving less assertive than that of an active magnate who enjoyed the king's full backing.

As the history of fourteenth-century Cornwall shows, lordship was a fine art that required sound delegation, constant supervision and good relations

---

[73] *CIM 1399–1422*, 56, 59.
[74] *CPR 1399–1401*, 313; *CFR 1399–1405*, 35.
[75] Tyldesley, 'Local Communities', pp. 195–197.
[76] *CPR 1401–1405*, 42.
[77] Below, p. 212–213.
[78] Tyldesely, 'Local Communities', pp. 198–224.
[79] *CPR 1385–1389*, 474; also, SC8/258/12867; *CCR 1389–1392*, 504.

with dependents and kings alike. The lord – whether the king or someone in his place – stood at the centre of all these responsibilities, providing direction and momentum to his lordship. It is illustrative of this that whereas Piers de Gaveston's inabilities had seen the earldom slide into confusion and chaos, the force of the Black Prince's character brought the most effective personal lordship to Cornwall. Although we should shrink from terming any of these regimes 'good', the theory of good lordship being too shot through with contradictions ever to be achievable in practice, the contrasting rulerships of these great lords stand as testament to the importance of personal agency to the institution of lordship.

While the influence of Cornwall's relative remoteness on the operation of its lordship should not be dismissed altogether, as lords were advised to look upon their estates often and then 'suche as serve you' will 'endevoure to doe the better', the royal character of the earldom-duchy helped to spread the king's authority into the furthest corners of the county.[80] For over forty years between 1300 and 1422 the king himself held the lordship, while the royal status of Queen Isabella, John of Eltham, the Black Prince, Princess Joan and Prince Henry resulted in the earldom-duchy remaining a conduit for kingly authority during their tenures. We have seen how the Crown consistently afforded the full force of its administration to these royally appointed lords, granting them access to its institutional memory and launching judicial commissions to support these loyal lieutenants of the king.[81] The actual officials of the lordship and the Crown are often found overlapping, with men such as Chief Justice Shareshull serving as both a regnal judge and a ducal councillor. Creating an enduring personal and institutional bond between Cornwall and the rest of the kingdom, the earldom-duchy and the Crown were inexorably linked and mutually buttressing.

Having underlying faith in the rule of their lord and master, the county's residents engaged with their earls, dukes and kings in sundry ways across the century. A great many Cornishmen and women are to be found inviting these lords to personally intercede in disputes of theirs and even when the lordship sank into decline these same folk chose to employ violent self-help to send a powerful statement concerning the depth of their discontent. Through both conflict and co-operation, these rich and varied interactions helped to mesh the whole range of local society into the political mainstream. So it was that the exercise of royal lordship pulled Cornwall towards greater integration with the wider realm, spreading awareness of the county's status as a clearly defined part of the kingdom of England.

---

[80] *Walter of Henley*, pp. 342–343; Cf. Harriss, *Shaping the Nation*, p. 30.
[81] For example, *RBP*, iv, 284; *CChR 1341–1417*, 12.

III

Connectivity: Cornwall and the Wider Realm

Communication, Movement and Exchange: Connectivity Frameworks

Although there can be little doubt that fourteenth-century Cornwall possessed a historical and cultural identity of its own, it is equally clear that the county also depended on the place that it held in the wider realm. Cornwall actually fitted into the mesh of the kingdom through a rich and varied range of links that constituted a form of Cornish connectivity. It was Peregrine Horden's and Nicholas Purcell's study of the Mediterranean that first gave the idea of historical connectivity wide currency, the co-authors conceptualising this sea and its hinterland 'of intense topographical fragmentation' as being overlaid by an interconnected 'kaleidoscope of human micro-ecologies'. In this sense connectivity 'describes the way micro-regions cohere, both internally and with one another' in this large, interdependent area by '*potentially* all-around... nearly frictionless communication and movement'.[1]

In the case of later medieval England, however, a slightly different conceptual structure needs to be sketched from that applicable to the Mediterranean.[2] While maritime connections undoubtedly proved important to a kingdom surrounded by the sea, the movement by land of people, goods and ideas brought about by the needs of the Crown, warfare, lordship, commerce, the law and the Church were equally significant. Growing yet denser across the later middle ages, connections transcending Cornwall come across as ubiquitous. Careerists formed 'social bridges', who can be seen as linking the county's

---

[1] P. Horden and N. Purcell, *The Corrupting Sea: A Study of Mediterranean History* (Oxford, 2000), pp. 123–172; P. Horden, 'Situations Both Alike? Connectivity, the Mediterranean, the Sahara', in *Saharan Frontiers: Space and Mobility in Northwest Africa*, ed. J. McDougall and J. Scheele (Bloomington and Indianapolis, 2012), pp. 25–38 at 27–29; P. Horden, 'Afterword', *Postmedieval: A Journal of Medieval Cultural Studies*, 7 (2016), pp. 565–571.
[2] P. Horden, 'Introduction: Towards a History of Medieval Mobility', in *Freedom of Movement*, pp. xvii–xxxiv; W. R. Childs, 'Moving Around', in *Social History of England*, pp. 260–275.

inhabitants to a web of contacts across the realm and beyond.[3] Such personal, communicative and structural networks helped to bind the peninsula into a concentric circle of connections that imbued the realm with substance while sustaining many sub- and supra-kingdom solidarities. Spreading awareness of the county's place in a rich matrix of loyalties, connectivity disseminated a consciousness of Cornish integration that actually sharpened notions of Cornishness in the peninsula itself.

---

[3] For social networks, Carpenter, *Warwickshire*, pp. 281–346; A. Barabási, *Linked: The New Science of Networks* (Cambridge, MA, 2002).

8

Sovereign Kings and Demanding Subjects: Regnal Connectivity

At the centre of the hub of all pan-English interactions was the person and office of the king himself. The Crown reached out physically and symbolically to every corner of the realm through the king's highways, a physical network that bound England together.[1] Proclaiming and encouraging interactions, the 'royal road' in Cornwall was a monumental testament to the county's many connections east of the Tamar. Even on those rare occasions when parts of the route were 'obstructed by force', as they allegedly were in c. 1295, when Ranulph Giffard, Joan his mother and other malefactors were accused of committing diverse highway banditries, everyone was aware that this royal road linked them and their peninsula to the king himself.[2] After all, county folk went so far as to claim that highway robbery of this sort was not only a 'hindrance' in Cornwall, but that it was costing Edward I a full two marks each year.

Emerging as no passive entity, the Crown actively deployed administrators across the kingdom in the defence of its interests. It follows that royal government introduced a striking profusion of 'outsiders' into Cornwall. For example, the king is often found dispatching sergeants-at-arms to the county who served as his 'eyes and ears' in the locality.[3] During the course of their duties these officials closely supervised government in Cornwall, reporting back to their master about conditions in the far south west. It seems that at times they engaged in activities beyond their official business, something suggested by the

---

[1] Childs, 'Moving Around', pp. 263–264; cf. Horden and Purcell, *Corrupting Sea*, p. 128.
[2] *PROME*, ii, 80.
[3] *CCR 1346–1349*, 412; R. Partington, 'Edward III's Enforcers: The King's Sergeants-at-Arms in the Localities', in *Age of Edward III*, pp. 89–106.

fact that in 1361 the sergeant William Walklett owed £60 to one Michael Ude of St Columb Major.[4] The Crown is found sending other employees to Cornwall on an even more *ad hoc* basis, as in 1316 for example, when the London goldsmith John de Castleare travelled there on what was termed Edward II's 'business'.[5] Numerous royal clerks also made their way to the peninsula, especially those who oversaw royal mineral rights in the south west. The controllers of the king's silver and lead mines in Cornwall and Devon, among them Thomas de Swavesey of Cambridgeshire, managed the extraction of ore and investigated new metalliferous deposits.[6] Royal administration depended on the movement of officials, people whose influence radiated widely as a result of their commissions from the king.

It is striking that Cornishmen are to be found in positions of royal employment, something which indicates that they had settled far from their native county. Numerous royal messengers hailed from the peninsula, for example, with Odo de Cornubia whose origins are betrayed by his name active in places as distant as Chester and Sandwich.[7] Other Cornish careerists were to achieve more exalted positions in the royal administration, John Urban of Helston and Southfleet, Kent amongst them. Urban made his fortune in tin and sat several times in parliament for Helston, bringing him to the Crown's attention. He went on to serve as lieutenant to the admiral of England and rose to the office of royal diplomat, treating with the duke of Burgundy and the Flemish towns on behalf of Henry IV and Henry V.[8] His appointments indicate that Crown employment gave this Cornishman the opportunity even to have a role in international affairs. In his will of 1420 Urban asked to be buried in Southfleet Church in Kent.[9] At the same time, however, he remembered many people and places west of the Tamar, including the 'poor people' of Cornwall, to whom he left no fewer than 200 marks.

Another Cornishman, one Hugh Treganon, served Edward III in a more personal capacity. This man first appears as a king's sergeant and purveyor of the officer of baker, but was later appointed usher and doorkeeper of his chamber.[10] Enjoying close personal connections with the king, Treganon held

---

[4] C131/12/13.
[5] CPR 1313–1317, 519.
[6] CCR 1296–1302, 433; CPR 1338–1340, 101; CPR 1340–1343, 564; CCR 1343–1346, 406; cf. S. Rippon, P. Claughton and C. Smart, *Mining in a Medieval Landscape: The Royal Silver Mines of the Tamar Valley* (Exeter, 2009).
[7] M. C. Hill, *The King's Messengers, 1199–1377: A List of all Known Messengers, Mounted and Unmounted, who Served John, Henry III, and the First Three Edwards* (Stroud, 1994), pp. 137, 36.
[8] HOP, iv, 690–692.
[9] *Cornish Wills*, 54–56.
[10] CPR 1330–1334, 8, 86, 89, 369; CCR 1330–1333, 489; CCR 1343–1346, 107.

this post until his death in 1343. 'In consideration of his long service', Treganon received royal grants from York to London, including the portership of the archbishop of Canterbury's palace.[11] He never forgot his Cornish roots, however, and neither did his master, for in 1331 Edward granted him the lease of the manors of Helston and Moresk in Kerrier.[12] Although Treganon had engineered the appointment of his kinsman, a certain Serlo Treganon, as a yeoman of the royal buttery in 1343, Serlo's untimely death in 1350 cut short this promising career.[13] A trickle of Cornishmen can be found serving their king in capacities of this kind, including Sir Robert Beaupel (deputy larderer), Sir Ralph Botreaux (royal diplomat) and Sir John Arundell (vice-admiral of England), as the Crown's magnetising influence enveloped every corner of the kingdom.

For all the importance of these super-connected Cornish careerists, it was actually the offices of local administration that formed the more permanent framework for the movement of people into and out of the county. In order to enforce his writ, the king regularly dispatched to the peninsula trusted royal appointees, among them officials as varied as justices and escheators. It is illustrative of this that throughout the 1380s Sir Robert Bealknap, the chief justice of the common pleas, served on the quorum of the county bench, influencing local affairs and forming a personal point of contact between the county and the wider realm. Drawing a considerable body of Devonians into Cornish administration, the Crown appointed such folk as the lawyer John Copelston to the escheatorship and receivership in the duchy in the 1390s. At the same time a steady flow of Cornishmen can be shown to have held office in Devon, such as the sheriff John Kendale. A great many people had to move around to keep the government running.

These royal officials formed a potent network of information and influence. From scions of leading local lineages through prominent 'outsiders' and right down to obscure Cornish folk, the hundreds of men who held office in fourteenth-century Cornwall helped to connect the king to all his subjects in the far south west. Even the lowliest royal appointee served in some sense as a representative of his king, for others viewed such local administrators as the local personifications of royal power.[14] Across the century the local office-holders were actually to grow in number, drawing a greater proportion of the Cornish gentry into the magistracy.[15] This expansion both broadened and deepened interactions between government and the whole range of the county's populace,

---

[11] *CPR 1340–1343*, 392, 458; *CPR 1330–1334*, 369, 487; *CPR 1334–1338*, 108.
[12] *CFR 1327–1337*, 261–262.
[13] *CPR 1343–1345*, 12; *CIPM*, ix, 284.
[14] Harriss, *Shaping the Nation*, p. 9.
[15] Above, Chapter 2.

binding the realm even more tightly together. When the thousands of royal writs sent to these office-holders and the many temporary commissions issued by the Crown are also considered, investigating local grievances and national concerns alike, the degree of connectivity becomes quite striking.

Emerging in the late-fourteenth century, the king's affinity, an affinity of shire knights, helped to further these interactions. From the late 1380s Richard II set about recruiting leading provincial men into his service, in Cornwall retaining John Chenduyt, John Treverbyn, John Trevarthian the younger and Mark and John Michelstow.[16] Such retained proprietors came to form a social bridge between the county and the court, with Treverbyn employing his place in the latter to secure a pardon for Thomas Kendale's skulduggery in the former.[17] After seizing the throne, it is no surprise that Henry IV continued recruiting from the gentry with the result that Sir John Arundell of Lanherne assumed the role of his Cornish retainer-in-chief.[18] Although the Arundells had already been of consequence in the fourteenth century, they rose to ascendency partly as a result of this Lancastrian connection. Sir John 'the magnificent' was appointed steward of Cornwall in 1402, a position that he retained until as late as 1430. During this time Sir John served as a royal powerbroker under three kings, furthering interactions between Cornwall and the court while overseeing the aggrandisement of his family.[19] Other Cornishmen too benefited from royal largesse. One of them, John Nanfan (d. 1458), served as an esquire of the body to Henry VI, a governor of the Channel Islands and the sheriff of both Cornwall and Worcester. He naturally grew fat on royal grants, acquiring the manor of Birtsmorton, Worcestershire, to supplement his Cornish estates.[20] Drawing the peninsula closely into the kingdom, all these careerists linked 'the household and court to the outlying regions of the realm'.[21]

Since royal regulation was 'seen as the essence of government', the enforcement of the law was one of the main responsibilities of a king and an essential strand of regnal connectivity.[22] Even the hundredal court of Penwith, near Land's End, heard cases *contra pacem domini regis*, reminding us that in Cornwall the peace was the king's peace.[23] Across the fourteenth century the scope

---

[16] *CPR 1388–1392*, 398; *CPR 1391–1396*, 190, 569; *CPR 1396–1399*, 293; Saul, *Richard II*, pp. 265–269; see, Given-Wilson, *King's Affinity*.
[17] *CPR 1388–1392*, 398.
[18] Ormrod, *Political Life*, p. 21.
[19] *HOP*, ii, 58–61; Harriss, *Shaping the Nation*, p. 27.
[20] *CPR 1441–1446*, 315; *Cornish Wills*, 75, 235; *Victoria County History of Worcestershire*, ed. W. Page, 4 vols (London, 1901–26), iv, p. 31.
[21] Saul, *Richard II*, p. 268.
[22] Harriss, *Shaping the Nation*, pp. 10–11; below, Chapter 12.
[23] 'Three Courts', pp. 181–182, 194.

and scale of royal justice was to expand greatly, rendering the king's power all the more apparent. Legal prerogatives created many personal contacts too, for the simple reasons that royal justices often itinerated to the county and while there interacted with people from the whole range of local society. One case of this kind is to be found in the eyre of 1302, when Justice Berwick enquired about the local practice of neifs marrying out of their manor and proclaimed 'on behalf of the king' that 'no man be so bold or so daring as to ill-treat any one who purposes to sue another for trespass committed against him'.[24] Hearing many cases for the Crown, in 1302 for example, these justices adjudicated over a dispute between Sir Thomas l'Ercedekne and Sir Ralph Bloyou, on the one hand, and Sir Henry Bodrugan, on the other. The case turned on Bodrugan's allegation that l'Ercedekne had, after 'a long conversation' in his 'inn' with Bloyou, come 'with force and arms' with Bloyou and their followers to the Bodrugan residence, forcibly seizing his ward.[25] Although the judgment is not recorded, suits of this sort left all the king's subjects in little doubt about the length of his judicial reach.

With the Crown at times prosecuting people from across the realm for 'arraying themselves in warlike manner', among them 'a great number of evildoers' who in 1405 allegedly attacked the lands of Thomas Lychebarwe near Redruth and planned many other 'mischiefs', it was the king himself who defined the legitimate and illegitimate use of force within his realm.[26] In contrast to the position in France and the Marches of Wales, there was no such thing as the right to private war in England.[27] Indeed, it was the king himself who held monopoly rights on the making of war and peace, with war waged under his authority alone.[28] It followed that it was also the king who raised armies and navies, with this very act standing out as an assertion of his sovereignty. More practically, in drawing together soldiers and sailors from across the realm, and it should be noted here that many thousands of Cornishmen fought in the wars of the fourteenth century, the Crown also brought into being a multitude of pan-English personal connections that helped to draw the far south west into the realm.[29] Since all these folk campaigned for the king, risking their lives for his military ambitions, all this activity spread awareness of Cornish integration throughout the ranks of the peninsula's fighting men and the whole range of county society. In both theory and practice, the regnal act of war served to bind the realm together.

[24] YB 30 & 31 Edward I, pp. 84, 164.
[25] YB 30 & 31 Edward I, pp. 106-111.
[26] CCR 1402-1405, 463
[27] Cf. Kaeuper, *Justice*; Davies, *March of Wales*, pp. 217-281.
[28] Harriss, *Shaping the Nation*, p. 85.
[29] Below, chapter 9.

England's fiscal machinery yielded further centripetal strength to the kingdom, largely because the Crown was to levy royal taxes regularly in this period.[30] Subsidy collectors often itinerated to and around the peninsula as Cornwall's residents were subject to the same obligation to contribute to parliamentary taxation as the residents of every other shire.[31] For the collection of the 1327 lay subsidy alone, the county's two chief tax collectors, Sir Robert Bilkemore and Sir Richard Huish, nominated two or three sub-taxers in each parish, drawing over 400 Cornishmen into the service of the Crown.[32] Spreading awareness of the king's fiscal might throughout the whole range of local society, these folk then raised juries of parishioners who valued the goods of their fellows and had over 6,000 men and women contribute financially to 'the defence of the kingdom against the Scots'. When it is remembered that a whole customs service also collected the king's dues, the all-pervasiveness of royal money-raising is rendered yet clearer.[33] As taxation touched all Cornish folk, so it made them contributors to the common good of both the county and the kingdom alike.[34] Fiscal considerations were also to create another, perhaps unlikely, point of contact between the king and his south-western subjects. When times were hard, it might be necessary to petition for relief from the burden of tax. In c. 1380, for example, the subsidy collector Thomas Collan beseeched Richard II to excuse the parish of Lanteglos-by-Fowey and others their tax liabilities after a Castilian raid had supposedly crippled these areas.[35]

As a result of all this governmental activity, the Crown created and sustained a thick web of personal and structural ties that bound the realm together. With force if necessary, the king employed every royal office-holder west of the Tamar to defend his royal rights there. Here, especially, the importance of these officials and ultimately of the king himself was brought sharply into focus, reminding Cornwall's residents of their place in the kingdom. After the government had imprisoned Sir John Petit in the Tower in 1339 for debts accruing from his tenure as sheriff-steward, for example, Petit can have been left in little doubt that the king held administrators accountable for their time in office.[36] Every Cornishman and woman would have had some experience of the royal administration, with the Cornish-language *Ordinalia* even having

---

[30] W. M. Ormrod, 'England in the Middle Ages', in *The Rise of the Fiscal State in Europe, c. 1200–1815*, ed. R. Bonney (Oxford, 1999), pp. 19–52.

[31] The Crown excused tinners parliamentary subsidies, above, pp. 8–9.

[32] CPR 1327–1330, 173; E179/87/7; E179/87/37.

[33] For instance, E122/113/55; see, E. M. Carus-Wilson and O. Coleman, *England's Export Trade, 1275–1547* (Oxford, 1963).

[34] Harriss, *Shaping the Nation*, p. 66; Ormrod, "Common Profit".

[35] SC8/40/1954.

[36] CCR 1339–1341, 169; CPR 1350–1354, 81.

King David refer to 'the Clerk of my Privy Seal' (*mab-lyen ov sel pryve*) for their entertainment.[37]

For all these coercive powers, however, the Crown did not simply impose government on a resentful folk in the county. By the fourteenth century the peninsula's residents are generally found welcoming the presence of the royal administration, often inviting the king's involvement in their affairs. There is plentiful evidence that proprietors sought positions in local government, for such posts provided the means to secure greater power and standing in Cornwall itself. While Henry Trewinnard, for instance, did not hail from a leading lineage, his seat on the county bench throughout the 1350s and 1360s made him a man of importance in the county. Cornish knights similarly sought such appointments, valuing the influence that they bestowed. We can see this as no fewer than eight scions of the family of Carminow held office in the fourteenth century, providing this dynasty with a sustained say in county affairs. One of the most active members of the family, Sir Ralph Carminow, sat on the county bench on some ten occasions, represented Cornwall in three parliaments and held the shrievalty in 1378–9. Service of this kind made him all the more mighty, and in the 1380s he remodelled his manor house at Carminow in St Mawgan-in-Meneage to match his pretensions and proclaim them in stone.[38] In this way, the gentry depended on such positions for self-aggrandisement while the Crown relied on local proprietors for the effective enforcement of the royal writ. Since the growing number of office-holders furthered this reciprocity, Cornish gentlemen and the king emerge as strikingly and increasingly interdependent.

Belief in the Crown's efficacy, however, stretched far beyond propertied society. This point is evident from *Beunans Meriasek*, in which the character of St Meriasek himself can be found articulating notions of royal government derived from Cornwall's shared experience of regnal rulership:

Welcome here, royal liege,	*Welcum omma lych ryall*
As you are head and principal	*del ogh pen ha princypall*
Over us altogether	*dreson ny ol yn tyan*
Worthy to receive reverence	*worthy rag cawas reuerens*
Because of your governance	*drefen agis governens*
Ruled are we, great and small.	*rewlys on brays ha byan.*[39]

The residents of Cornwall as a whole depended on the royal writ, calling upon the king through judicial commissions, petitions and the like, with entreaties seen most clearly in parliament.

---

[37] *Cornish Drama*, i, OM, line 2600.
[38] *Reg.Brantingham*, ii, 586.
[39] *Beunans Meriasek*, lines 252–257.

Table 6: Petitions Submitted by the Residents of Cornwall, 1300–1420

Year	Individual named petitioners			Institutional petitions (e.g. the priory of Bodmin)			Common petitions (e.g. from towns and hundreds)			Common petitions from the county commonalty			No named petitioner		
	KC	PC	ED	KC	PC	ED	KC	PC	ED	KC	PC	ED	KC	PC	ED
1300–10	14	–	–	1	–	–	5	–	–	2	–	–	7	–	–
1310–20	12	–	–	2	–	–	5	–	–	6	–	–	–	–	–
1320–30	9	–	1	3	–	–	2	–	–	4	–	–	1	–	–
1330–40	5	–	–	3	–	–	3	–	–	1	–	–	1	–	–
1340–50	1	–	–	–	–	–	–	–	–	1	–	–	–	–	–
1350–60	2	–	32	–	–	–	–	–	3	–	–	–	–	–	–
1360–70	1	–	5	–	–	–	–	–	–	1	–	–	1	–	–
1370–80	8	–	19	–	–	1	1	–	2	3	1	2	5	–	–
1380–90	30	6	–	–	–	–	1	–	–	1	–	–	1	–	–
1390–1400	3	–	1	–	–	–	–	–	–	2	–	–	–	–	–
1400–10	1	5	4	–	–	–	1	–	–	–	1	–	–	–	–
1410–20	1	–	–	–	–	–	1	2	–	1	–	–	–	–	–
Totals	87	11	62	9	–	1	19	2	5	22	2	2	16	–	–

Key: KC relates to petitions submitted to the king and his council; PC refers to petitions sent to the Parliamentary Commons; ED relates to petitions submitted to the earl-duke.

Sources: SC8; *RBP*, ii; *PROME*; these figures represent the survival rates of petitions rather than the totality submitted, especially for those supplications sent to the earl-duke. A further four petitions submitted to the king originated from too wide a possible date range to be included in the table.

By the fourteenth century it was parliament that formed the focal point for the political life of the entire realm. Yet it was only in the period between 1290 and the late 1320s that the Lower House, the Commons, achieved real prominence. Forging the Commons into a more coherent force, kings and magnates increasingly called on the knights and burgesses to validate and publicise their policies during these years.[40] Parliament's power was only to grow stronger in the century after 1320 as the Lower House gained a pre-eminent position in the passing of legislation, serving as the instrument through which kings sought consent for taxation and legitimacy in general.[41] Like every county, Cornwall sent two knights of the shire to this increasingly assertive body, but the high density of parliamentary boroughs in the peninsula resulted in as many as fourteen Cornish spokesmen sitting in a typical assembly.[42] Although the tally of returns is incomplete, the names of as many as 500 MPs returned from Cornwall have come down to us. While parliamentarians attended for many reasons, most of which are now lost, each was invested with the authority to speak for his locality in the greatest debating chamber in the realm.[43]

Enjoying a disproportionately large voice in the parliamentary Commons, Cornwall's residents submitted a steady stream of petitions articulating a mixture of their complaints and requests. As many as 172 supplications of this sort sent to the king, council and parliament survive from between 1300 and 1420, another list that is no doubt incomplete.[44] A few matters of complaint, however, can be touched on here. In 1315, for instance, Katherine Giffard twice called on the king's grace: in the first instance, requesting remedy after Sir William Millburn had corruptly administered one of her manors for some six years before selling it to a 'stranger'; and, in the second, seeking restitution after Lawrence of Cornwall and 'others unknown' had allegedly attacked her property in Helston, seizing £200 of goods along with sixteen silver spoons.[45] Responding in each case, the auditors of the petitions in parliament granted Giffard a writ to have 'the contents of the petitions heard and determined' and enrolled this answer in the official parliamentary record. There is evidence that people from a wide cross-section of county society made such supplications, with the burgesses and tenants of the borough and manor of Helston, for example, complaining that the sheriff-steward had continued distraining them for a fifteenth, even though they had already paid the eighth penny of

---

[40] Maddicott, *English Parliament*, pp. 335–342.
[41] Harriss, *Shaping the Nation*, pp. 66–71.
[42] Above, p. 23–25.
[43] See, M. V. Clarke, *Medieval Representation and Consent* (New York, 1964).
[44] Cf. W. M. Ormrod, 'Introduction: Medieval Petitions in Context', in *Medieval Petitions*, pp. 1–11.
[45] *PROME*, iii, 60.

their goods to the king.[46] Since the endorsement recorded that the barons of the exchequer were 'to do justice on the contents of the petition', the House facilitated a dialogue between the king and all his Cornish subjects.[47]

More to the point, the county commonalty itself employed common petitions on no fewer than twenty-four occasions. One such petition was submitted in 1315, when the peninsula's residents complained that Antonio Pessagno's manipulation of the stannaries had resulted in over 2,500 of the county's 3,000 tin workers abandoning their trade:

> [Therefore] the moors will be closed and... harm beyond estimate will come to the king, and his people of the same country will be destroyed... [as] the said Anthony through his merchants has taken from them by extortion £6,000 in these two and a half years.... [and] through the said tin the people of the said country used to be provided with cloth, wine, iron, salt and other merchandise, in respect of which nothing now arrives....[48]

Since the county requested the king's intervention in matters ranging from justice (1315) to defence (1378 and 1405), tin, the matter raised here, was by no means Cornwall's only concern.[49] While common petitions could veil sectional interests, matters of tax, tin and war affected the whole range of the peninsula's populace. It is inconceivable that at these times the county's parliamentarians would not have combined to lobby for such all-embracing interests. Many of these supplications actually arose from universal concerns drawing the county and kingdom together, with county MPs expressly linking Cornwall's interests with those of the wider realm and the Crown responding to their concerns. So it was that a two-way discourse sustained political communication, with the demands of subjects playing just as significant a role in spurring the government to action as royal ambitions.[50]

By gathering together the great and good of the realm, parliament inevitably performed an essential role in the transmission of information. The government typically had statutes and other royal *acta* approved in parliamentary assemblies announced in sessions of the county court, while gossip circulated whenever members returned home.[51] MPs have always needed their expenses

---

[46] *PROME*, iii, 61.
[47] From early in Edward III's reign the government only had 'public' business enrolled, Dodd, *Justice and Grace*, p. 89.
[48] *PROME*, iii, 99–100.
[49] *PROME*, iii, 100; *PROME*, vi, 89–90; SC8/102/5068; Dodd argues that SC8 ('Ancient Petitions') were mainly presented in parliament, G. Dodd, 'Parliamentary Petitions? The Origins and Provenance of the "Ancient Petitions" (SC 8) in the National Archives', in *Medieval Petitions*, pp. 12–46.
[50] Dodd, *Justice and Grace*, pp. 47, 50, 319.
[51] Maddicott, *English Parliament*, p. 370.

to be paid and constituents have always had to meet these, being made only too aware thereby of their collective representation in the House. As parliament provided the opportunity for complaint to be made to the king himself, it follows that the House also afforded the sovereign a 'worm's eye view' of his kingdom. We find just such a case in 1315, when Lostwithiel's members argued that the coinage of tin should be returned to their town, as its relocation to Bodmin had resulted in 'a great quantity of tin' being 'carried secretly by sea and by land'.[52] With the endorsement recording the king's order to re-establish Lostwithiel's staple, this request evidently fell on receptive ears.

Naturally enough, while in the House Cornish representatives could be found interacting with their fellow MPs. In 1414, for example, Cornwall and Devon together submitted a petition concerning cloth duties which the king promised 'to consider... further'; while back in 1380 Cornwall, Devon, Dorset, Hampshire, Kent, Norfolk, Suffolk and Sussex had all combined to complain about the destruction caused by Richard II's soldiers.[53] With parliament summoned on an increasingly regular basis, the Crown – albeit inadvertently – brought into being an 'experienced body of MPs' who perceived themselves as 'principal lobbyists for the kingdom's welfare'.[54] As a result, the Commons developed an increasingly corporate, self-confident personality, which the petitioning lexicon came to reflect.[55] Whereas in 1300 Cornwall's representatives had submitted petitions addressed to the king and his council, a century later petitioners often requested that the parliamentary Commons intercede on their behalf.[56] Such was the growing influence of parliament that the commonalty of the entire realm can often be found lobbying the king, notably concerning the operation of local administration and the policing of lawlessness.[57] Shaping and thwarting royal policy, parliament increasingly came to guide the king's government while nurturing and enlarging 'a politically aware public'.[58] A remarkable number of Cornish spokesmen were privy to these debates about humdrum events and high-flown politics alike.

Yet despite the extraordinary edifice of England's government, with its deep, pervasive roots, we would do well not to overstate its strengths. This is a point perhaps best demonstrated by the paradox of petitioning. On the one hand, calls on the king's grace provide evidence of Cornish belief in royal power and the length of the king's reach; while, on the other, they lay bare the limitations of a government that had failed to correct the abuses which had prompted

---

[52] *PROME*, iii, 69–71.
[53] *PROME*, ix, 105–106; *PROME*, vi, 165–166.
[54] Dodd, *Justice and Grace*, p. 132.
[55] Maddicott, *English Parliament*, p. 277; Ormrod, *Edward III*, pp. 454–455.
[56] *PROME*, viii, 491; Dodd, *Justice and Grace*, p. 154.
[57] Saul, *Gloucestershire*, pp. 106–147; Walker, *Lancastrian Affinity*, p. 256.
[58] Maddicott, *English Parliament*, p. 374.

these supplications in the first place. It is important to remember that as the Crown was dependent on the voluntary services of the gentry to fill offices in the shires, its power could never be absolute. Royal and comital-ducal government also emerge as tightly tied together in Cornwall, with the county's residents choosing to petition both the king and earl-duke to affect change in the peninsula.

While medieval England did not form a unitary state, the royal government still created a strikingly interlocked kingdom in which 'national' concerns overlapped with 'local' interests. The distinctive and yet still integral place that Cornwall held within England's political culture is no better demonstrated than in *Bewnans Ke*, where in one scene the character of the bishop crowns Mordred as king of Britain, announcing:

The Crown of Britain I shall set	*Curyn Bretayn me a set*
upon your head in the name of Paul.	*war the ben in hanaw Paul.*
The laws you will faithfully uphold	*An lahys te a lel-syns*
and the rights of all your subjects,	*ha guyer the ol the wostoyth,*
the rights of the church as many as they are,	*guyryow eglos myns del ens,*
and the estates as formerly,	*ha statys kepar ha kyns,*
as is right for a good king.	*the vightern da del degoyth.*[59]

Rendering a version of the English coronation oath into Middle Cornish, this drama drew on themes understood by its Cornish-speaking audience, evidencing the pan-English political lexicon that these folk shared with their fellows from across the realm.[60] Together, constant co-operation, conflict and discourse between the king and his subjects forged and sustained the kingdom.[61] Such connections spread awareness of royal power and Cornish integration throughout the whole range of county society, with John Trevisa in no doubt that, as he put it, 'Cornwayle is in Engelond'.[62] Undergirding intra-English connectivity and the realm itself, regnal government stood at the heart of all kingdom-wide interactions.

---

[59] *Bewnans Ke*, lines 3103–3108.
[60] See, A. Spencer, 'The Coronation Oath in English Politics, 1272–1399', in *Political Society*, pp. 38–54.
[61] Cf. Reynolds, *Kingdoms*, pp. 330–331; Watts, *Polities*, pp. 201–286.
[62] Trevisa, trans., *Polychronicon*, ii, p. 91.

9
Pillagers with Long Knives: Military Connectivity

Of the many links generated by the Crown, military connectivity was one of the most potent. As they forged England into a 'war state', the three Edwards with their bellicose ambitions mobilised the people and resources of their realm on a scale that dwarfed anything attempted by their predecessors.[1] Inevitably, Cornwall was drawn into the war effort. Between the battles of Falkirk in 1298 and Agincourt in 1415 there were no fewer than 452 instances of named Cornish men-at-arms and mounted archers fighting in major royal expeditions.[2] Yet there were wide variations in the degree of participation. While no fewer than twenty-seven Cornishmen served at Crécy-Calais, for example, only two enlisted in 1373 to go with John of Gaunt on his 'great march'.

The changing demands of war greatly influenced the nature and scale of Cornish military service. While the large Falkirk and Bannockburn campaigns drew about eighteen gentlemen to Scotland, the smaller armies operating north of the border in the 1330s were more poorly attended. The Hundred Years' War was to result in a dramatic expansion of the county's service. In 1340 some eight Cornishmen served at Sluys-Tournai, but just two years later twice that number fought in Brittany, a campaign for which the peninsula was more conveniently sited.[3] With some twelve Cornishmen contesting the

---

[1] For the best introductions, A. Ayton, *Knights and Warhorses: Military Service and the English Aristocracy under Edward III* (Woodbridge, 1994); Bell et al., *The Soldier*; H. Hewitt, *The Organization of War under Edward III, 1338–62* (Manchester, 1966); for recent studies, N. A. Gribit, *Henry of Lancaster's Expedition to Aquitaine, 1345–46: Military Service and Professionalism in the Hundred Years' War* (Woodbridge, 2016); *Military Communities in Late Medieval England: Essays in Honour of Andrew Ayton*, ed. G. P. Baker, C. L. Lambert and D. Simpkin (Woodbridge, 2018).
[2] Appendix II.
[3] Bell et al., *The Soldier*, pp. 233–234.

field at Poitiers, the county was well placed for expeditions to Aquitaine too. From 1369 royal demands for troops grew more regular, as 'the Edwardian War was intermittent; the Caroline War (1369–89) unremitting'.[4] In a war which favoured the county's strong military-maritime tradition, England and France increasingly fought for command of the sea routes. It is illustrative of this that the earl of Arundel's 'cruising war-fleets' of 1387 and 1388 contained as many as fifty-six Cornish men-at-arms and archers. Since England and France increasingly drew other kingdoms into this phase of the war, in 1386 some nine Cornishmen campaigned with John of Gaunt in his bid for the Castilian throne. In these years Princess Joan can even be found paying her steward an addition £13 6s. 8d. for raising recruits to fight in France and Spain.[5] With twenty-three Cornish gentlemen contesting the field at Agincourt, the county's soldiery also showed their willingness to enlist in the Lancastrian phase of the war in the fifteenth century.

Yet when the peninsula's contribution is set against that of other counties, Cornish military service begins to look more modest. Although precisely comparable figures remain hard to come by, it seems that the Gloucestershire gentry were often better represented on campaigns.[6] The men of Cheshire and Lancashire made the largest contribution of all. It has been argued that there were few years when fewer than 500 of their number were in arms – during some, the Crown mobilised thousands.[7] Such a relatively smaller showing by Cornish men-at-arms can be explained in a number of possible ways. First, the Cornish gentry were simply less numerous than their peers in Gloucestershire and so were bound to be more sparsely represented. And, second, it is clear that the absence of a resident great lord limited opportunities for service. Combined with the exceptional stature of the earl-duke, this absenteeism resulted in the county's non-resident magnates looking to Cornwall comparatively little as they could recruit men of greater standing from elsewhere. Both Piers de Gaveston and John of Eltham served in Scotland, for instance, and yet their retinues of 1310–11 and 1336 contained no leading Cornishmen.[8] Mobilising no fewer than twenty-four local proprietors over the course of fifteen years, a greater number than any of his predecessors, the Black Prince was exceptional.

While the nearest resident noble dynasty, the Courtenay earls of Devon, marshalled as many as fifty-nine Cornishmen across the century, the point still stands that the nature of lordly settlement was weighted against the county's service. It is also clear that Cornwall's martial tradition itself was divided

---

[4] J. Palmer, *England, France and Christendom, 1377–99* (London, 1972), p. 1.
[5] SC6/813/1; *RESDCornwall*, 145.
[6] Saul, *Gloucestershire*, pp. 48–52, 270–292.
[7] Bennett, *Cheshire and Lancashire*, p. 174.
[8] C71/4 m. 11; E101/19/36.

between land and sea, splitting the peninsula's resources between these two modes of war. This had the effect of further reducing the number of county folk who served in the king's armies. As the peninsula actually held a place on the frontline of the war at sea, this compelled the government to leave a considerable body of gentlemen to garrison Cornwall, a 'land by the seacoast, where a fleet of ships could easily touch and perils thereby arise'.[9] While all these factors reduced the scale of Cornish soldiering, very considerable numbers of county folk still chose to serve their king in war.

To make full sense of these figures, however, our sources call for some further analysis. Until 1369 horse inventories and *restauro equorum* accounts provide invaluable information; with the former constituting an initial appraisal of the army's warhorses, and the latter comprising lists of horses lost on campaign.[10] Yet these documents relate only to the men-at-arms and not the infantry and, more seriously, not all of them have survived. By way of partial compensation we can turn to the enrolled protections and letters of attorney, but these too present problems. Again, they lean heavily towards gentle society and may only show an intention to serve, not actual performance.[11] We find an example of such intentions in 1384, when the Crown rescinded the Cornishman Walter Hall's protection as he 'tarried' in London rather than serving in Brest.[12] More significant still is the degree to which protections under-assess military service. Although costing a mere 2s. to enrol, lists of protections are grossly incomplete and decline even further after 1369.[13] From this date, muster rolls came to replace the horse inventories of old. Commanders sent their copies of these rolls in to the exchequer to claim expenses at the end of campaigns, listing the soldiers who served with them and their rates of pay. While muster rolls provide a view of a large cross-section of the army, many do not survive, including those relating to the Black Prince's final years and Richard II's Scottish and Irish campaigns.[14] Our sources afford but a partial picture of the total military service performed.

The information recorded in these records presents even more challenges than might be supposed. While individual names are noted, the parts of the country whence these men hailed usually are not. It is easy enough to identify those gentry with distinctively Cornish names: Bodrugan, l'Ercedekne and so on. Others, however, including the Arundells, Bassets, Ingepennes,

---

[9] *CFR 1319–1327*, 300; this was also connected to Edward's and Isabella's fraught relationship.
[10] Ayton, *Warhorses*, pp. 49–50.
[11] Ayton, *Warhorses*, p. 158.
[12] *CPR 1381–1385*, 471.
[13] Saul, *Gloucestershire*, p. 48; Ayton, *Warhorses*, pp. 156–160; Bell et al., *The Soldier*, p. 5.
[14] Bell et al., *The Soldier*, pp. 10–11.

Lambournes, Peverells and Mohuns are excluded from the present analysis for fear of confusing the Cornish branches of these families with those who shared these surnames but resided elsewhere in England. This methodology necessarily has the drawback of potentially excluding many Cornishmen. As toponymic surnames have typically been used to identify sub-gentry servicemen, the names of a great many Cornishmen that were not so distinctive have been excluded from our total as well. Identifying many more knights than the lesser gentry and freemen who served with them, our figures remain incomplete.

Gentlemen would generally have been accompanied on campaign by their own personal retinues, which these documents rarely record. Although Sir William Botreaux sought a protection for his retinue (*pro comitiva*) for the Rheims Campaign, neither the names nor numbers of those who served with him are noted. In 1370 it is known from another source that he served at this time with a retinue of ten men-at-arms and an unspecified number of archers, but from no document do we learn the names of these companions.[15] Some retinues were substantial, and in 1387 that of John Treverbyn included a company of as many as nineteen men-at-arms, twenty archers and ten miners, many of whom hailed from Cornwall.[16] In the great majority of cases, however, no such information is available. Our list of Cornish combatants therefore greatly under-assesses the county's contribution. In an attempt to rectify this, we can employ a multiplier; assuming that just five men accompanied each named gentleman, our total is increased to some 2,000 Cornish soldiers. While every possible multiplier is fraught with dangers, a figure of this sort does at least provide a sense of the scale of Cornish soldiering.

Even this enlarged figure, however, excludes county and urban levies. In the first half of the century especially, the government often employed commissions of array to raise foot soldiers and archers from Cornwall. It is illustrative of this that in 1322 Edward II ordered county administrators to raise no fewer than 500 footmen 'clad in one uniform' for his Scottish expedition.[17] Four years later, the king instructed local officialdom to mobilise as many as 650 men and in 1337–8 Edward III arrayed another 500 Cornish archers.[18] Later in the century, in 1382–3 alone, the government instructed county officialdom to provide 200 crossbowmen and 100 other archers.[19] These figures naturally represent government intent rather than actual fact, and in 1322

---

[15] C76/37 m. 2; *Catalogue des Rolles Gascons, Normans et François...*, ed. T. Carte, 2 vols (London, 1743), ii, p. 73; *Issue Roll of Thomas de Brantingham, A.D 1370*, ed. F. Devon (London, 1835), pp. 461, 486.
[16] E101/40/33 m. 19; *HOP*, iv, 659–660.
[17] *CPR 1321–1324*, 93, 96; also, *CCR 1330–1333*, 488; C76/12 m. 26; C61/36 m. 14.
[18] C61/36 no. 169; C61/49 no. 428; *The Gascon Rolls project 1317–1468*, http://www.gasconrolls.org/en/ (accessed 7 March 2019).
[19] C76/67 m. 15.

only 200 men served of the 500 who should have been raised, while county levies become less frequent later in the century.[20] All the same, royal orders of this sort resulted in hundreds, if not thousands more of the county's sons fighting for their king. With Sir John Arundell of Lanherne commanded 'to induce' 105 archers to serve in Normandy in 1421, the Lancastrians relied on commissions of array too.[21] The county's boroughs also provided troops, and in 1346 Edward III mobilised as many as fifty-one Cornish townsmen.[22] All told, *thousands* of Cornishmen are likely to have served in royal wars between 1298 and 1415.

Since war was an expensive and often family business, knightly lineages naturally formed the backbone of the county's military personnel. Sir William Bodrugan, for example, fought at both Crécy and Poitiers, his father and grandfather, Sir Otto and Sir Henry Bodrugan respectively, having served in Scotland and Aquitaine before him. Perhaps owing their very titles to good military service, less prominent knights such as Sir John Trevaignon also proved regular campaigners. As Edward I wished 'to show special favour' to Robert Giffard, who was imprisoned in Launceston Castle for an alleged murder, in 1298 he granted him permission to stay at the king's pleasure in Scotland 'with horse and arms' before standing trial.[23] Military service was by no means confined to armigerous society, however, for many Cornish folk from the murky world of the sub-gentry chose to fight for the king, among them the archer Opy Penpole and John Raulyn of Truro. The full range of county society was represented on the many battlefields that the kings of this period were to contest.

The waging of war brought about a most remarkable movement of the county's militarily eligible, with Cornishmen fighting in fields as far flung as Aquitaine, Brittany, Castile, Flanders, Ireland, Normandy, Portugal and Scotland. In campaigning for their king, these folk also forged links with some of the greatest noblemen and captains of their day. We find that military service strengthened the relationship between the county and the Black Prince, with Cornish knights such as John Sergeaux serving him on multiple occasions. As troop-raising was one of the most important interfaces between the earl-duke and his subjects, it is unsurprising that in both *Bewnans Ke* and *Beunans Meriasek* the character of the duke of Cornwall commanded soldiers 'as becomes a worthy lord'.[24] Yet the earl-duke emerges as by no means the only magnate to

---

[20] *CCR 1318–1322*, 645.
[21] *CPR 1416–1422*, 386–387.
[22] *Crécy and Calais, from the Original Records in the Public Record Office*, ed. G. Wrottesley (London, 1898), pp. 68, 71.
[23] *CCR 1296–1302*, 167.
[24] *Bewnans Ke*, lines 1258–1273, 1383–1384; *Beunans Meriasek*, lines 2258, 2296–2298, 2303.

employ Cornishmen, for involvement in warfare connected members of the county elite to lords and commanders as varied as Reginal de Cobham, Henry, earl of Lancaster, and Edward of Norwich, duke of York.

While some Cornishmen were simply 'hired guns', others were much more closely connected to their captains. Looking after the interests of one John Lynyen of Cornwall, who had served with him in France in 1345, the earl of Lancaster successfully petitioned for a charter of pardon for Lynyen and his wife, Sybil, after they had appropriated 'goods and jewels' from her mother.[25] Involvement in warfare created a web of interpersonal connections, linking the county's residents into national networks of patronage, clientage and communication. During campaigns, Cornish soldiers interacted with their betters, peers and inferiors alike over issues as diverse as marching order and the distribution of victuals, serving in retinues and armies raised from many English shires. Although it remains nearly impossible to penetrate far into the *mentalité* of these men, great victories such as Crécy, Poitiers and Agincourt would have helped to create an *espirit de corps*, a shared sense of soldiering experience and military-regnal solidarity.[26] Every campaign was fought in the name of the king and so had the effect of binding all parts of the realm together.

Many Cornishmen enjoyed distinguished careers, with military service forming a major attraction for the careerists who sought to participate in these expeditions. John Treverbyn was one such who served in the king's wars, in 1382 fighting 'at his own expense… well armed, furnished and arrayed as pertains to a gentleman in the king's company'.[27] As Treverbyn became a king's esquire and the bailiff of Winchelsea, involvement in warfare opened the door to royal service in peacetime.[28] It also opened the door to office and greater landholding in Cornwall itself, for Treverbyn went on to represent the county in three parliaments in the 1390s. Another careerist gentleman, John Trelawny, used his military service at Agincourt and thereafter to climb high from his notably minor means.[29] In 1419, at the king's camp at Gisors, Henry V granted him a £20 annuity from the stannaries and later, after he had returned to England with the king, he was elected to serve in the two parliaments of 1421.[30] According to a tradition recorded in the nineteenth century, the west gate of Launceston had once displayed the effigy and arms of Henry V, along with the inscription:

---

[25] SC8/254/12666; SC8/254/12667; *CPR 1348–1350*, 548.
[26] A. Bell, *War and the Soldier in the Fourteenth Century* (Woodbridge, 2004), pp. 3–4.
[27] *CPR 1381–1385*, 160; *CFR 1383–1391*, 26–27.
[28] *CPR 1385–1389*, 439.
[29] *HOP*, iv, 645; Tyldesley, 'Local Communities', pp. 205–206.
[30] *CPR 1422–1429*, 9.

He that will do aught for mee,
Let him love well Sir John Tirlawnee.[31]

Naturally enough, some of the county's leading lords also won local advancement though involvement in warfare. In 1300, for example, Sir Thomas l'Ercedekne began his career by serving the king in Scotland and, having by that means brought himself to the king's notice, was able to secure appointment as sheriff-steward of Cornwall. Such was Edward II's faith in l'Ercedekne that in 1324 he dispatched him to Aquitaine on 'some difficult business', appointing him envoy 'to receive into the king's peace all those of the duchy who have rebelled against the king and adhered to the French'.[32] It seems that l'Ercedekne performed diligently, keeping state secrets while travelling around south-western France to enforce Edward's rulership.

However, calls to arms might either be resisted or end in misfortune. Although in his youth l'Ercedekne had gained from military service, it was to cost him dear in 1314 when he was captured at Bannockburn and had to pay a ransom to secure his release.[33] Tensions could also occur under the pressures of war, with Froissart recording Edward III's fury in the aftermath of Crécy, for:

> among the English there were pillagers and irregulars, Welsh and Cornishmen armed with long knives, who went out after the French... and, when they found any in difficulty, whether they were counts, barons, knights or squires, they killed them without mercy.[34]

Whether or not these events actually happened remains unclear, for Froissart was given to embellishing his stories. Nonetheless, the military activities of the Cornishman Sir Henry Ilcombe were less than exemplary. Ilcombe served with the earl of Cambridge on his ill-fated expedition to Portugal in 1381, which ended ignominiously with the English being shipped home in Castilian galleys.[35] On his return to England, Cambridge claimed that seventeen men, Ilcombe chief among them, had contributed to this debacle by 'rebelling'. It was not until 1385 that Ilcombe managed to secure a pardon for this, through the auspices of the countess of Cambridge.[36] Here we see how war created many powerful bonds, some of which were far from positive.

---

[31] J. Polsue, *A Complete Parochial History of the County of Cornwall...*, 4 vols in 2 (1867–72), iii, p. 89.
[32] C61/36 no. 162, 165, 176–177, 204, 212–213, 291, 398; *Gascon Rolls project*.
[33] Phillips, *Pembroke*, p. 75; *Annales Londonienses* mistakenly claims that he was slain, *Chronicles of the Reigns of Edward I and Edward II*, ed. W. Stubbs, 2 vols, Rolls Series (London, 1882–3), i, p. 231.
[34] Froissart, *Chronicles*, p. 93.
[35] P. E. Russell, *The English Intervention in Spain and Portugal in the time of King Edward III and Richard II* (Oxford, 1955), pp. 343, 372.
[36] *CPR 1381–1385*, 256, 534; *HOP*, iii, 472–474.

A few Cornishmen are recorded as perishing on campaign, including Sir John Hamley and Sir John Dauney who both lost their lives at Crécy.[37] The majority, however, returned home after the fighting. As homecomings resulted in the campaigner regaling his family and friends with tales of life in the field, of battles fought, hardships endured and of lords and kings seen in distant lands, the passage of men generated major flows of news. Some Cornishmen came back brutalised by conflict, as did the soldiers of the demobilised affinity of Sir Henry Bodrugan, who together committed crimes on their return to the county in 1302.[38] Many Cornish criminals also received pardons on account of their military service, not least the four who in 1336 served in a 'felons' company' in Scotland.[39] Other county soldiers sought to commemorate their martial might on sumptuous tombs. After fighting in Scotland with Edward of Caernarfon himself, for example, Sir Ranulph Blanchminster immortalised this service in a grand military freestone effigy in Stratton Church.[40] Geoffrey St Aubyn (d. c. 1429) similarly chose to be depicted splendidly armed and armoured on his brass in Crowan, having campaigned for the king in 1381.[41] Adorning their local churches with memorials that proclaimed in brass and stone their contribution to the royal war effort, 'old Cornish soldiers' helped spread awareness of the county's campaigning prowess.

The wars of this period were actually to introduce a remarkable variety of people into the peninsula. One of the best examples of this is be found in 1360, when Edward III commanded that the arrayers in Gloucestershire and Worcestershire march their forces to the 'seaward parts' of Cornwall, Devon, Dorset and Somerset.[42] An important military staging-post, Cornwall saw many retinues embark from its shores in the course of the Hundred Years' War. In 1364, for instance, the Black Prince dispatched 'certain men-at-arms, archers, and Welsh footmen' from the peninsula, with retinues of this sort requiring 'housing and lodging within Cornwall' while waiting to sail to war.[43] Troops also landed in Cornwall, with Buckingham's army, for example, arriving back in the Fal estuary from Brittany in 1381.[44] Ten years previously, John of Gaunt had set sail from La Rochelle to Fowey with two Castilian princesses

[37] *Crécy and Calais*, p. 280.
[38] *CPR 1301–1307*, 63.
[39] C71/15 m. 16; Ayton, *Warhorses*, p. 146.
[40] M. Downing, *Military Effigies of England and Wales*, 4 vols (Shrewsbury, 2010), i, p. 89.
[41] W. Lack, H. M. Stuchfield, and P. Whittemore, *The Monumental Brasses of Cornwall* (London, 1997), pp. 27–28.
[42] *CCR 1360–1364*, 98.
[43] *RBP*, ii, 211; C61/101 no. 95; *Gascon Rolls project*.
[44] E101/39/8 m. 1r; J. W. Sherborne, 'Indentured Retinues and English Expeditions to France, 1369–1380', *EHR*, 79 (1964), pp. 718–746 at 733; *CCR 1385–1389*, 548; *CCR 1389–1392*, 260–261.

and leading English and Gascon captains.[45] Others arrived under less happy circumstances, and in 1345 it seems that the 'fury of the sea' had driven some 600 Welshmen onto the Scilly Isles where they stayed for twenty days, allegedly causing £500 of damage.[46] We find the king and earl-duke introducing many veterans to the lands west of the Tamar, with the Black Prince even granting Saltash ferry to William Lenche as compensation or reward for Lenche having lost an eye at Poitiers.[47] None in the county can have failed to appreciate the scale and significance of war, nor the degree to which Cornwall had contributed to this great pan-English enterprise.

Confining our attention solely to the Cornish men-at-arms and mounted archers who served in the king's war, however, would be a grave mistake, as there were also thousands of mariners who fought for their king.[48] With only a small permanent navy of a few ships, fourteenth-century governments instead called on the realm's merchant shipping to serve in the country's fleets. The king depended on the ancient right of impressment to form these flotillas, a complex process which in its simplest form involved dispatching royal officials, chiefly sergeants-at-arms, from port to port with the power to arrest ships and crews for royal service. For the better management of these resources, the Crown typically divided the realm into two great admiralty bailiwicks, the northern and southern (often referred to as western) admiralties. As Cornwall remained a constant fixture on the itineraries of the latter's officials, between 1297 and 1418 a veritable armada of 521 Cornish ships and 8,090 sailors sailed under the king's command.[49]

The county's naval service was greatly influenced by the nature and location of such fleets, however, for technological limitations meant that medieval squadrons could only ever enjoy 'a measure of local control for the limited time and limited area' of their operation.[50] Fought far from the county's waters, the Scottish Wars saw only about thirteen Cornish vessels sail in the king's flotillas from 1297. In 1303, for instance, Edward I ordered that between them Bodmin, Fowey, Looe, Lostwithiel, Polruan, Porthpean and Saltash provide just two ships to serve against the Scots. Since the peninsula was conveniently

---

[45] J. Sumption, *Divided Houses: The Hundred Years' War, III* (London, 2009), p. 120.
[46] *CPR 1343–1345*, 494.
[47] *RBP*, ii, 98–99.
[48] For the best introductions, J. W. Sherborne, 'The Hundred Years' War. The English Navy: Shipping and Manpower 1369-1389', *Past and Present*, 37 (1967), pp. 163–175; C. L. Lambert, *Shipping the Medieval Military: English Maritime Logistics in the Fourteenth Century* (Woodbridge, 2011); N. A. M. Rodger, *The Safeguard of the Sea: A Naval History of Great Britain, I, 660–1649* (London, 1997); more broadly, S. Rose, *Medieval Naval Warfare, 1000–1500* (London and New York, 2002).
[49] Appendix III.
[50] C. F. Richmond, 'The War at Sea', in *The Hundred Years' War*, ed. K. Fowler (London, 1971), pp. 96–121 at 99.

sited for expeditions to France, it is no surprise that the Hundred Years' War was to result in a great expansion of Cornwall's naval contributions. In 1337 alone no fewer than twenty-one of the county's ships and 495 mariners sailed in a squadron guarding the English coast. It was nine years later, in 1346, that Edward III amassed the biggest armada of the century, with Cornwall providing a little under a tenth of the total force, some seventy ships and 1,289 sailors. As the war turned increasingly after 1369 on who controlled the sea, so the peninsula's long maritime tradition came increasingly to the fore. Raising fleets in nearly every year from 1370, the Crown called on the service of 152 Cornish ships and 1,899 sailors in the decade as a whole. With seven Cornish ships and 310 mariners sailing in 1387 and 1388, the county's sons were well represented in these cruising war-fleets too. Even after a truce was agreed in 1389, Richard II is to be found impressing some twenty-nine vessels for his Irish expeditions of 1395 and 1399. And once the war was renewed in the fifteenth century, in 1416 alone Henry V indentured some sixteen ships to support his ambitions in France.

Yet as ever, we must subject our sources to some careful scrutiny. While evidence of the county's fourteenth-century naval service survives in a near unbroken series of payrolls listing the vessels impressed and the pay that seafarers received, these documents often name ships and mariners who sailed under the king's command on multiple occasions. Such 'double counting' has the effect of inflating the number of individual Cornishmen who served at sea. On the other hand, as many as 187 shipmen are named on only one occasion, suggesting that the Crown drew on a wide cross-section of the county's shipping and manpower.[51] It should also be noted that in 138 cases we possess only the names of the impressed ship and shipmaster, and sometimes not even these, with no evidence at all for crew sizes. To allow for this underassessment, we can tentatively employ another multiplier. If we assume that just fifteen men sailed on each of these 138 ships, then our overall figure for the county's naval servicemen might be increased by some 2,070 to 10,160.

In addition to these 'great fleets', Cornish sailors were also involved in many smaller expeditions and supply flotillas. In 1324, for example, Edward II ordered the sheriff to prepare 'a good ship sufficiently furnished with mariners and other necessities' for Sir Thomas l'Ercedekne's passage to Aquitaine.[52] There is evidence that the Black Prince often transported in 'ships from the parts of Cornewaille... whiting, sheaves of arrows, and all other things which have been purveyed'.[53] He also sent troops overseas in these vessels, as in 1352 for

---

[51] Thirty-three served the Crown twice, eleven thrice, eleven four times, two on five occasions and one each in six, seven and eight fleets.
[52] *CCR 1323–1327*, 248; also, *CPR 1340–1343*, 28; Sumption, *Divided Houses*, p. 310.
[53] *RBP*, ii, 160.

example, ordering that Sir Walter de Bentele and his company take ship from Fowey to Brittany.[54] Throughout the war, Cornish craft can be found shipping troops and supplies, conveying ambassadors and patrolling the Channel both formally and as 'pirates'.[55] Such was the scale of the county's service that in 1378 the Commons of Cornwall complained that the peninsula's mariners, 'who constitute a large part of their power to defend their lands against their enemies', have been 'taken abroad on various expeditions by force of the commissions of our lord the king, to the great damage and injury of the community of the said duchy'.[56] Many thousands of Cornishmen served in the war at sea, and certainly thousands more than fought on *terra firma*.[57]

So many mariners and ships from Fowey sailed under the king's command that the town ranked among the realm's leading ports for the scale of its naval contributions. We see this between 1363 and 1388, when Fowey consistently provided more ships to the king than either Southampton or Winchelsea, and sometimes more than Bristol or Great Yarmouth.[58] It was Dartmouth, however, that made the largest contribution of all English ports.[59] Although between 1320 and 1400 ships from Kent sailed in the service of the Crown on as many as 490 occasions, during which time some 465 Cornish vessels served the king, the contribution of Kentish ports declined markedly after 1360, in contrast to Cornwall's sustained service thought the fourteenth century and beyond.[60] At some 78 tons the average tonnage of Cornish ships emerges as entirely typical of English harbour towns, with William Symond's eighteen-ton *Cog John* of Fowey the smallest vessel impressed by the Crown and William Rogeroun's 240-ton *Gracedeu* of Fowey the largest.[61]

But on which Cornish ports in particular did the Crown call? Inevitably, Fowey provided more ships and sailors than any other settlement from west of the Tamar, some 326 and 4,974 respectively. East and West Looe together

---

[54] RBP, ii, 32, 165.
[55] E101/37/25; CCR 1389-1392, 260-261; *The Navy of the Lancastrian Kings: Accounts and Inventories of William Soper, Keeper of the King's Ships, 1422-1427*, ed. S. Rose, The Navy Records Society, 123 (London, 1982), p. 212; Walsingham, *Chronica Maiora*, i, p. 289; CPR 1377-1381, 12; CCR 1399-1402, 239; below, p. 298-300.
[56] PROME, vi, 89.
[57] Cf. Sherborne, 'English Navy', p. 175.
[58] S. J. Drake, '"The Gallaunts of Fawey": a Case Study of Fowey during the Hundred Years' War, c. 1337-1399', *Historical Research*, 90 (2017), pp. 296-317 at 304-305.
[59] M. Kowaleski, *Local Markets and Regional Trade in Medieval Exeter* (Cambridge, 1995), pp. 29-30.
[60] Cf. A. Ayton and C. Lambert, 'A Maritime Community in War and Peace: Kentish Ports, Ships and Mariners, 1320-1400', *Archaeologia Cantiana*, 134 (2014), pp. 67-103 at 71-73, 89-91.
[61] Tonnages should only be regarded as a guide; cf. Ayton and Lambert, 'Kentish Ports', p. 75.

came in a distant second, with 102 ships and 1,385 sailors to their credit, while a series of other ports, including Padstow, Saltash and even Penryn, supplied a few ships for royal service. Judging from the evidence of a payroll of 1338–40, in which John Polruan's modestly named *Cog John* of Polruan was listed as originating from Fowey, 'Fowey' actually included ships from Polruan, Lostwithiel and many places along the river Fowey.[62] While it in no way diminishes Cornwall's overall naval service, the practice of assigning ships to 'head ports' obscures the contribution of smaller coastal settlements. It seems that crews were recruited from right around the Cornish coast and from no small distance inland, with arrayers in the county sending men whom they had mobilised under their royal commissions of array to serve on these impressed vessels.[63] Believing that Bodmin was a sea-port because of the shipping interests of its burgesses, in 1339 the admiral of the west demanded four ships of war from the inland borough.[64] When the ships were not forthcoming, he had the mayor imprisoned. It was only after an inquisition found that Bodmin stood 'six or more leagues from the sea' that the admiral withdrew these demands and freed the major. All this activity drew many thousands of Cornishmen into the king's service.

It is also worth considering the identities of some these seafarers. None of them served the Crown so often as the eight-times impressed Peter Godesgate of Fowey, who assisted the king throughout the 1370s on as many as four different ships. The great preponderance of these shipmen, however, were like Roger Mares of Mousehole and John Spanell of Padstow, who sailed in the king's fleets once only. The war at sea could form a major draw for some careerists at least, Richard and Mark Michelstow of Fowey among them.[65] Although Richard Michelstow had enjoyed a successful commercial career, he was to achieve particular prominence as a result of his naval service, not least to the Black Prince. Contributions of this sort enabled Michelstow by the 1360s to establish himself both as one of Fowey's leading burgesses and a landed gentleman. Following him into the gentry, Michelstow's son Mark became an esquire who fought as a man-at-arms in the war-fleets of 1387 and 1388. A man of significant landed and maritime resources, Mark was later appointed a 'pirate admiral' searching for Henry IV's enemies at sea. With a certain James Treverbyn arresting shipping for the Crown in the 1370s and the government appointing Sir Robert Beaupel admiral of the West back in 1343, other ambitious Cornishmen too found employment in the administration of the king's fleets.[66]

---

[62] E101/21/7 m. 3r; also, *CPR 1358–1361*, 320; *CPR 1388–1392*, 84.
[63] Lambert, *Maritime Logistics*, p. 184; *Foedera*, i, 462.
[64] *CCR 1339–1341*, 196.
[65] Drake, 'Michelstow Family'.
[66] *Issue Roll of Thomas de Brantingham*, pp. 274–276; *CCR 1343–1346*, 1, 56.

At times, however, the war at sea left mariners facing significant costs. Ships could be lost or damaged while in royal service, as was the *Michel* of Fowey for example, which was sunk by Edward III's 'command in the haven of Calais'.[67] Even if vessels were not crippled in action, naval service itself hollowed-out trading time and shipping profits. It is was as a result of this that in 1357 Matthew de Cornwaille petitioned the Black Prince, complaining that his sixty-ton vessel 'on its first voyage was arrested for the prince on his going to Gascony, was delayed there a great while, and when he returned to England was again arrested for the duke of Lancaster, so that he sold it because of the delay'.[68] With little in the way of compensation paid to shipmasters before the introduction of tuntyght in 1380, impressment was 'in effect' an extra tax on the maritime population of the realm.[69] Mariners also faced the very real threat of capture during the course of hostilities, and in c. 1380 it was alleged that sailors from the settlements of the Fowey were 'imprisoned for ransom in Spain, Normandy, and France'.[70] It follows that seafarers sometimes resented and resisted the demands of the Crown. On one occasion in 1342 the sailors of some twenty-three Cornish ships, along with others from across England, were so dissatisfied that they abandoned Edward III at Brest.[71] Naval activity of this sort disrupted maritime trade too or, as the havener put it in 1338–9, 'boats hardly dare to go to sea because of the war at sea'.[72]

Yet for all the costs incurred, many benefits could also accrue from involvement in hostilities.[73] Since the government paid over £3,500 in the 169 instances when the wages received by Cornish mariners are recorded, those who served the king earnt 'hard cash' for shipping services rendered.[74] Sailors could also profit from capturing enemy ships, as in 1387 for example, when the Crown divided the thousands of tuns of wine seized at Cadzand among the combatants, including eighty-three of the county's sons.[75] Regularly hiring Cornish

---

[67] *RBP*, i, 84; also, E101/24/8.
[68] *RBP*, ii, 115–116.
[69] Sherborne, 'English Navy', 165, 174–5; A. Saul, 'Great Yarmouth and the Hundred Years War in the Fourteenth Century', *Bulletin of the Institute of Historical Research*, 52 (1979), pp. 105–115 at 111.
[70] SC8/40/1954.
[71] CCR 1343–1346, 129–131; also, SC1/34/119a.
[72] *HA*, 137.
[73] Cf. M. Kowaleski, 'Warfare, Shipping, and Crown Patronage: the Impact of the Hundred Years War on the Port Towns of Medieval England', in *Money, Markets and Trade in Late Medieval Europe: Essays in Honour of John H. A. Munro*, ed. L. Armstrong, I. Elbl and M. Elbl (Leiden, 2007), pp. 233–254.
[74] Cf. Ayton and Lambert, 'Kentish Ports', 84; Saul, 'Great Yarmouth', 111.
[75] T. K. Moore, 'The Cost-Benefit Analysis of a Fourteenth-Century Naval Campaign: Margate/Cadzand, 1387', in *Roles of the Sea in Medieval England*, ed. R. Gorski (Woodbridge, 2012), pp. 103–124.

shipping to support his war efforts, the Black Prince is often found granting 'gifts' of custom exemptions to shipmasters and paying them handsomely for their efforts. In 1359 he assigned as much as £60 to John Tegyn, the master of the *Cog Johan* of Fowey, 'as a recompense for his great labours and expenses in coming from the parts of Gascony to England in the prince's company'.[76] Emerging as neither entirely bankrupting nor wholly beneficial, the war at sea exercised great influence on the peninsula, right down to the 269 Cornish ship's boys who served in royal fleets.

The naval aspects of the king's wars formed a powerful force for connectivity, bringing about many interactions between shipmen and others from across the realm. For the formation of the fleet, the Crown regularly dispatched royal sergeants-at-arms to the county, men such as John Clyfton and James Treverbyn. Journeying to Cornwall in 1370 with a clerk, a guard of two archers and a chest containing 5,000 marks of wages, Clyfton and Treverbyn were drawn into interaction with numerous mariners and many other people besides.[77] Since these officials served as representatives of the king, no Cornish sailors could have been ignorant of their English subjecthood. Once they were impressed, these mariners were then compelled to sail to major embarkation points, among them Plymouth and Sandwich. During these times, the crews involved intermingled with seafarers and soldiers from across the realm.[78] Interactions continued at sea, as admirals commanded and consulted 'the captaines and the masters of the ffleete' about everything from sailing order to the division of prizes.[79]

More significantly still, the war at sea created many points of contact between the county, the Crown and the earldom-duchy. The Black Prince, for example, often called on the naval service of 'sure mariners of Cornewaille', who he said served him 'well and faithfully'.[80] Service of this sort was to bring the prince closer to his Cornish subjects. Fostering another strand of interaction, Edward III summoned representatives from the county's ports to the maritime councils that he called to 'inform the king and his council upon the state of the shipping of the realm of England'.[81] Royal demands of this kind helped to foster kingdom-wide maritime concerns, so that even the fifteenth-century *Libelle of Englysche Polycye* appreciated the county's contribution to English sea-power:

---

[76] *RBP*, iv, 283; *RBP*, ii, 141; also, *CPR 1391–1396*, 568.
[77] *Issue Roll of Thomas de Brantingham*, pp. 272–273.
[78] For example, *CPR 1361–1364*, 415.
[79] *Monumenta Juridica: The Black Book of the Admiralty*, ed. T. Twiss, 4 vols, Rolls Series (London, 1871–6), i, pp. 14–27.
[80] *RBP*, iv, 18; *RBP*, ii, 98.
[81] *CCR 1343–1346*, 360; M. Oppenheim, 'Maritime History', in *The Victoria County History of the County of Cornwall, I*, ed. W. Page (London, 1906), pp. 475–511 at 479.

To fortefye anone he [Edward III] dyd devyse
Of Englysshe townes iij., that is to seye
Derthmouth, Plymmouth, the thyrde it is Foweye.[82]

Despite Froissart's disparaging comments about the 'bloody and murderous' nature of 'sea-fights', the sea was an essential theatre of war that created much connectivity in its own right.[83] Yet it is surely a mistake to treat land and maritime campaigns as completely separate. Armies depended on maritime logistics for their supply and transport, and in practice there was much overlap between the two modes of war. If we were to combine the two sets of figures for Cornish service on land and at sea, we would find that in 1346 alone some 1,500 men were drawn into royal service and that over the century-and-a-quarter between 1297 and 1418 considerably in excess of 10,000 fought for the king. Such figures place Cornwall's martial contribution closer to that of the military-powerhouses of Cheshire and Lancashire than that of Gloucestershire. While it did not amount to 'total war', all this participation had the effect of pulling the county towards greater integration with the wider realm.

Since its coastline formed part of the frontline of the war with France and her allies, the Cornish peninsula felt the impact of war acutely. We see this on 6 April 1338, when the government sent a warning that 'the enemy have invaded the realm' with 'a great fleet and perpetrated burnings, homicides, robberies and many other crimes both on land and at sea, and are now at sea coming towards Cornwall to commit similar wickedness and crimes'.[84] It seems that at this time French and Castilian freebooters did indeed harry the county's shipping and fishermen and went on to attack some of its coastal settlements.[85] To judge from the wording of Bishop Grandisson's letter allowing the monks of Tywardreath, near Fowey, to retreat inland temporarily because of the attacks 'of pirates' (*piratarum*), the raids at this time were made by a force less committed than the French flotilla that sacked Southampton.[86] All the same, enemy activity was highly worrying to both the county commonalty and the government alike.[87] Forty years later, in 1378, the St Albans-based chronicler Thomas Walsingham despaired that 'the French were ranging over the open sea, and

---

[82] *Libelle*, chapter 1 heading, lines 215–218.
[83] Froissart, *Chronicles*, p. 64.
[84] C61/50 no. 87; *Gascon Rolls project*.
[85] *Chronicon Galfridi le Baker de Swynebroke*, ed. E. M. Thompson (Oxford, 1889), pp. 63–64; *HA*, 153.
[86] *Reg.Grandisson*, ii, 870–871. The monks faced other problems too; cf. M. Hughes, 'The Fourteenth-Century French Raids on Hampshire and the Isle of White', in *Arms, Armies and Fortifications in the Hundred Years War*, ed. A. Curry and M. Hughes (Woodbridge, 1994), pp. 121–143; C. Platt, *Medieval Southampton: the Port and Trading Community, 1000–1600* (London, 1973), pp. 109–110.
[87] *CPR 1338–1340*, 279.

freely burning the villages of Cornwall, like Fowey and certain others, without resistance'.[88] This raid formed part of a three-pronged Franco-Castilian campaign targeting English territory on both sides of the Channel. Seeking both tax exemptions and the Crown's intervention in local defence, residents from settlements around the Fowey were soon to complain that their ships had been 'well nigh annihilated by galleys and the enemy landing there'.[89] It seems that Truro also suffered at this time, for in 1379 its burgesses claimed that between them 'pestilence and hostile invasion' had left the town 'almost uninhabited and wholly wasted'.[90]

It is from 1405, however, that the most detailed account of an assault on medieval Cornwall survives. In this year, Don Pero Niño's squadron of three Castilian galleys and two French ships raided the south coast of England, sacking a town named 'Chita' in the peninsula.[91] On arriving off the Cornish coast, they 'made their way to the shore with the tide, up a river' and 'drew into land' by Chita, a sheltered but unfortified town of around 300 souls. After Niño's forces had landed and fought a 'rough fight', the 'English were driven in and many among them killed or taken'. Actually occupying Chita, the captain then:

> commanded that the standards and the men-at-arms should remain in good array outside the town, so that they should not be surprised if the English came up in greater force, and that the oarsmen and crossbowmen should enter the city to sack it, the ones fighting the others plundering. When everything had been carried off he set fire to the town and burnt it all: all this was done in the space of three hours. The trumpet sounded: everyone went back on board and the galleys set out again, taking with them two sailing ships.

Pelting the Castilians with 'a hail of stones and arrows', the English rallied at the river's mouth, but the squadron escaped and later attacked Dartmouth. Lightning-quick raids of this sort presented a serious challenge to security, although this force suffered some losses, for the chronicler of these deeds recorded that Sir Guillaume de Chastel died 'as a good knight should, waging war in Cornwall'.[92]

---

[88] Walsingham, *Chronica Maiora*, i, pp. 234–237.
[89] *CCR 1377–1381*, 388; SC8/40/1954; Cf. Saul, *Richard II*, pp. 31–34.
[90] *CPR 1377–1381*, 208.
[91] *The Unconquered Knight: A Chronicle of the Deeds of Don Pero Niño, Count of Buelan, by his Standard-Bearer Gutierre Diaz de Gamez (1431–1449)*, trans. J. Evans (London, 1928), pp. 115–117; Chita's identity remains unclear, for the name is corrupted and the description could fit Fowey, Helford, or Looe.
[92] *Unconquered Knight*, p. 150; Chastel actually died attacking Dartmouth, Given-Wilson, *Henry IV*, p. 239.

Even in the years when the county was not assaulted, Cornwall's residents lived in near constant fear of enemy activity. At times this could grow into apoplexy, as in 1379 for example, when it was alleged in the king's bench that while serving as a JP and head of the commission of array itself some seven year earlier, Sir Richard Sergeaux had conspired with 'emissaries of the king of Spain' to launch an assault on Fowey in exchange for the safety of his own lands.[93] Sergeaux later secured an acquittal, but not until after the government had imprisoned him in the Marshalsea. As France and her allies often tested Cornish defences, the government's concerns are perhaps understandable. In 1404, for example, local levies in Falmouth had to drive off a French force that was destined to support the Welsh Revolt, and Elizabeth Treffry was left to repel 'the French out of her house [Place Manor, Fowey] in her housebandes absence' during Henry VI's reign.[94] No Cornishman or woman can have been ignorant of the influence that war exercised over their lives.

In the light of all this, it is no surprise that the peninsula's defences were of pressing concern to the king, the earl-duke and the commonalty alike. Across Cornwall, a series of customary conventions sought to mobilise local men in the cause of county security. One such traditional defence held the eighty-eight parishes around Fowey and Polruan responsible 'in time of war' for providing 160 archers 'day and night' from 1 May to the end of August each year for the protection of these settlements.[95] More to the point, the county's inhabitants are often to be found calling on the king to defend them, and it was usual for the king to respond positively because it was in his interest to do so.[96] Since Cornwall held an integral place on the sea routes to English lordships in Aquitaine, Ireland and Wales, the county's occupation by the French would have menaced English interests in these areas. A force of French soldiers in the county would have threatened the realm itself, not least because Cornwall formed a significant source of revenue and shipping resources. As the defence of his subjects, the Cornish among them, was one of main duties of a king, royal concern for county security was assured.

For all these reasons, the peninsula held an integral place in a 'national' defensive network that aimed to protect the county in particular and the realm in general. To counter enemy activity, the Crown issued commissions of array regularly in the county which nominally mobilised every Cornishman between sixteen and sixty able to bear arms. For the better management of these forces,

---

[93] *HOP*, ii, 506–507; Tyldesley, 'Local Communities', pp. 133–134.
[94] *Chronique du Religieux de Saint-Denys, 1380–1422*, ed. M. Bellaguet, 6 vols (Paris, 1839–52), iii, pp. 224–225; Given-Wilson, *Henry IV*, p. 239; Leland, *Itinerary*, i, p. 204; *Three Fifteenth-Century Chronicles...*, ed. J. Gairdner, Camden Society, n.s. 28 (Westminster, 1880), p. 166.
[95] *CCR 1377–1381*, 388; also, *CPR 1301–1307*, 538.
[96] Drake, 'Fawey', 306.

before 1375 the government placed the 'maritime lands' of the realm, a 'belt of land running parallel to the coast' between six and twelve leagues deep, under the command of 'keepers of the maritime land'.[97] Knights such as Philip de Columbers and Hugh Courtenay held this position in 1338, commanding forces that arrayers had raised in the counties of Cornwall, Devon, Dorset and Somerset.[98] Serving as actual arrayers at this time were the ducal servant James Woodstock and four Cornishmen, as this royally mobilised home-guard sought to defend the whole south west.

By 1375, however, the Crown held the arrayers themselves responsible for raising and commanding these county levies, with commissions growing in size accordingly. This much is shown by the Crown's activities during 1385–6, when it appointed as county arrayers the duchy steward Sir John Kentwood and as many as thirteen other proprietors, including Sir Richard Sergeaux.[99] Exhorting these office-holders 'to array all men-at-arms, armed men, and archers who live in that county, and arm all able-bodied men, both those who have the wherewithal to arm themselves and those who have not', the king commanded them to lead their forces 'to the sea coast and other places where danger threatens'. Arrayers were to distrain those who through 'feebleness of body' could not fight, making even these folk contribute to those 'who labour in the defence of the realm'.

This county-level activity was meshed tightly with the work of urban bailiffs and the actions of lordly officers. A regular stream of letters was sent to the bailiffs of the Cornish towns, ordering them to 'make ready' the defences of these boroughs 'as far as possible'.[100] To deny the French easy prizes, the government was especially concerned to ensure that the bailiffs permit vessels to sail only if they were properly armed. The duke proved just as active as the king in securing 'the safety of his duchy of Cornewaille and the people of the country in this time of war'.[101] We can see this in 1359, when the prince commanded that all the county's castles be made ready, especially that at Tintagel, which he bemoaned was 'utterly without a garrison'.[102] He attached to this instruction a statement to focus minds in the peninsula, having it written that he was 'in the parts of France in furtherance of the war, and knows not how the future may turn out or what perils may arise in his absence'.

---

[97] J. R. Alban, 'English Coastal Defence: Some Fourteenth-Century Modifications', in *Patronage, the Crown, and the Provinces in Later Medieval England*, ed. R. A. Griffiths (Gloucester, 1981), pp. 57–78 at 59, 69–70.
[98] *CPR 1338–1340*, 134, 139.
[99] *CPR 1381–1385*, 588.
[100] Drake, 'Fawey', 307–308; *CPR 1338–1340*, 279.
[101] *RBP*, ii, 9.
[102] *RBP*, ii, 166; also, *CPR 1381–1385*, 427, 600; *CPR 1388–1392*, 95.

All this 'local' action formed part and parcel of the defensive structures of the country as a whole. While they were discharging their duties as arrayers in Cornwall, for example, Kentwood and Sergeaux also served 'as principal captains and leaders of men-at-arms, armed men, hobelars, and archers in the south of England', joining no lesser office-holders than William Courtenay, the archbishop of Canterbury and Nicholas Brembre, the mayor of London.[103] Around the same time, when it gave orders that beacons be 'placed in the accustomed spots to warn people of the coming of the enemy', the Crown created a direct visual line of communication connecting the whole realm together.[104] In this way, the peninsula's place in a 'national' *Garde de la Mer* led to thousands, and probably tens of thousands, more Cornishmen contributing to the interrelated defence of their county and kingdom. Even Cornish children were supposedly trained 'in the use of arms and archery'.[105]

None of this, however, is to suggest that the government oversaw some comprehensive 'grand strategy' for defence. On the contrary, the fact that we find the king and earl-duke issuing so many instructions about Cornish security suggests that commands of this sort were often ineffectual. There were times, such as in 1380, when all that the Crown could do was urge local proprietors 'to remain upon their lands'.[106] Neither were many Cornish settlements fortified. Fowey, for example, was only walled on the 'se cost' and perhaps not even there.[107] We may well wonder whether in practice violent storms and dangerous rocks were Cornwall's best defences. Yet at no point did the county's residents invite the French to free them from the 'yoke of English oppression'; quite the reverse, in fact, for they linked their own security strongly with that of the kingdom at large.[108] Viewing the fortification of Fowey as one of Edward III's great triumphs, *The Libelle of Englysche Polycye* was to emphasise Cornwall's role in collective English security.[109]

The wars of the fourteenth century profoundly influenced the governance of England, not only by drawing knights who served in local administration to join in the king's campaigns against his adversaries, but also in driving the expansion of the royal administration. Since taxes were generally levied for the prosecution of war, the military needs of the age in no small part drove the growth in scale and intensity of government in this period. Also significant was the practice of purveyance, or compulsory requisitioning. Although according to the Statute of Purveyors of 1362 the Crown was only able to

---

[103] *CPR 1385–1389*, 80; Froissart, *Chronicles*, pp. 306–307.
[104] *CPR 1381–1385*, 588.
[105] Froissart, *Chronicles*, p. 58.
[106] *CPR 1377–1381*, 455.
[107] Leland, *Itinerary* i, p. 323.
[108] *PROME*, vi, 89–90.
[109] *Libelle*, lines 215–218.

requisition goods for the needs of the royal household, before this date goods were regularly taken at below marked price.[110] The three Edwards exploited the right of purveyance in the peninsula to the full, collecting thousands of quarters of grain, hundreds of tins of wine and thousands of fish.[111] In 1329, for example, Edward III was moved to investigate how Sir Thomas l'Ercedekne had purveyed many goods in the county, among them 300 quarters of oats from 'divers men'.[112] l'Ercedekne had then paid for their freightage onto a 'small ship' in Falmouth which transported these supplies to a 'great ship' in Fowey, Richard Rohan's *Seint Saviour Cog*, the latter vessel then sailing this cargo to Scotland for 'the king's use in war'.

After the creation of the duchy, however, demands made in the name of the king were replaced by those in the name of his son, the duke. Naturally enough, Cornwall proved essential to the prince's war efforts and during his long tenure he purveyed all the aforesaid victuals, along with carts, arrows, baggage-horses, 150,000 nails, 'clayes and bridges' for horse transportation and a host of other things.[113] Following the prince, in 1394 Richard II even ordered the arrest of ten south-western 'fishing vessels and ten master fishermen with the necessary crews, nets, and other tackle' to fish for him off the coast of Dublin.[114] With tinners contributing to siege warfare and county 'workmen and carpenters' helping construct a 'new ship' for the Black Prince, Cornish expertise made an invaluable contribution to the war effort.[115] Mobilising the county's resources, the king and the earl-duke together set the peninsula on a war-footing.[116]

Another way in which the organisation of war contributed to connectivity was through the dispatch of regular royal instructions to shire administrators. In 1297, for example, Edward I is found proclaiming the making of peace, while twice in the 1320s his son is found doing the same.[117] In 1337 at a meeting that he had summoned at Lostwithiel, Edward III even ordered county administrators to 'lay before' the men of Cornwall 'the king's intention in regard to the safety of the realm'.[118] Victories regularly merited proclamation too. The Black Prince chose to publish news of his triumphs, sending county administrators 'news

---

[110] *Statutes of the Realm*, i, pp. 371–373; J. R. Maddicott, *The English Peasantry and the Demands of the Crown, 1294–1341* (Oxford, 1975), pp. 15–20.

[111] *CPR 1292–1301*, 242, 344; *CPR 1301–1307*, 419; C71/4 m. 3; C71/6 m. 6; *CPR 1321–1324*, 93; *CCR 1330–1333*, 16, 19.

[112] *CIM 1307–1349*, 269.

[113] *RBP*, ii, 10, 77, 94, 105, 110, 112–113, 124, 155, 167, 205, 207, 208; *Foedera*, i, 381.

[114] *CCR 1392–1396*, 364, 405–406; *CCR 1381–1385*, 285; *CPR 1391–1396*, 529.

[115] *RBP*, ii, 150.

[116] Cf. Morgan, *Cheshire*, p. 114.

[117] *CCR 1296–1302*, 78; *CCR 1318–1322*, 678; *CCR 1323–1327*, 385.

[118] *CPR 1334–1338*, 503.

of the prince's successful expedition and arrival before Calais', while giving commands urgency by linking them to the demands of war.[119] Since the prince smuggled into an order for purveyance in 1355 a reference to 'John, who calls himself king of France' having 'broken the covenants... drawn up at Calais... for which reason war has broken out', instructions of this kind could serve as vehicles for royal propaganda.[120] The war was also fought in the pulpits of England, as Edward III, the Black Prince, Richard II, Henry IV and Henry V all repeatedly instructed the bishops of Exeter to organise prayers, processions and public thanksgivings for their successes, while having the course of the conflict announced in Cornish churches.[121] Ridings on St George's feast day gained popularity in the peninsula after Agincourt, no doubt because all these efforts impressed upon the county's collective memory the scale of Cornwall's contribution to the war effort.[122]

Yet communications do not emerge as one-directional. The county's residents themselves sent many petitions and complaints to the king and earl-duke concerning the course of hostilities. For example, in 1378 the Commons of Cornwall petitioned Richard II in a state of apoplexy, stating that:

> they are greatly harassed and beladen with great troubles on account of the war with the enemies overseas on all sides and from year to year... and now, in this present year, come galleys from Spain, burning all the ships, boats and towns which are in the ports and along the coasts of the sea, and the said enemies have put to grievous ransom a great part of the said duchy, for want of strength and power to resist the aforesaid enemies. And the said enemies threaten to return next season to the said duchy with an even greater force, and seize and claim the said land as their own, and trouble the said commons forever.[123]

The king's reply to the petition, to 'provide and ordain a remedy', enrolled on the Parliament Rolls, was matched by firm action in 1380, when he dispatched the duchy steward to supervise the defences of Fowey and Polruan.[124] War set in motion a constant dialogue in both directions.

Taken together, the waging of war exercised a profound material and psychological effect on Cornwall. An act of royal policy, war formed a 'continuum of service, binding king, magnates, and gentry into the prosecution of consensual

---

[119] *RBP*, i, 15, 66.
[120] *RBP*, ii, 77, 166.
[121] *Reg.Grandisson*, ii, 1173–1174, 1190–1191, 1200–1201; *Reg.Brantingham*, i, 186–187, 190–191, 199, 201–203, 299–300, 342–344, 432; ii, 639–640; *Reg.Stafford*, 128–129.
[122] Processions held by guilds of St George to celebrate his feast day, *Early English Drama*, p. 412.
[123] *PROME*, vi, 89–90; also, SC8/35/1714.
[124] *CCR 1377–1381*, 388.

war'.[125] Victory helped encourage feelings of national pride, strengthening fellow-feeling between Englishmen.[126] Defeat was also an 'energising force' that prompted collective action in the realm, while a common enemy bound the Cornish and their king together in resistance to the foe.[127] Serving as a force for 'national unity' and an agent of connectivity, warfare accelerated the making of ties of association and the creation of lines of communication in Cornwall and across the realm.[128]

[125] Harriss, *Shaping the Nation*, pp. 85–86, 175–178; Bell et al., *The Soldier*, pp. 260, 241.
[126] Harriss, *Shaping the Nation*, p. 86.
[127] Ormrod, *Political Life*, p. 108.
[128] Cf. Bell et al., *The Soldier*, p. 241.

10

Formidable Lords and True Tenants: Lordly Connectivity

Warfare introduced a great many Cornishmen into the glamorous circle of the fighting nobility, and it was only natural that in peacetime demobilised Cornish soldiers should further their interests by profiting from these connections. Although he held no lands in the county, Aymer de Valence, the earl of Pembroke, twice influenced the personnel of the earldom, securing the sheriff-stewardship for two of his retainers, Sir Roger Ingepenne of Berkshire and Sir Thomas l'Ercedekne. Both Ingepenne and l'Ercedekne had fought alongside the earl, which helped recommend them to him for peacetime employment. Across the century, the Courtenay earls of Devon raised as many as fifty-nine fighting men from Cornwall. It is therefore no surprise that a few Cornish gentlemen, Richard Kendale and John Tregorrek among them, appeared as retainers on Edward Courtenay's livery roll of 1384–5. As the family held some lands to west of the Tamar, they employed a certain John Isaak as receiver in Cornwall and Devon, Isaak having sat in parliament for Truro and Helston in 1364–5.[1] Just after the Great Revolt, the Crown came to recognise the family's influence by appointing Earl Edward to the Cornish bench. Since the earls of Warwick owned three manors in Cornwall, they too employed local men to look after their interests. In the 1390s, for example, the lawyer Roger Trewythenick is found serving as their steward locally, and on one occasion the family 'made representations' to the Black Prince about their villeins.[2] Magnate connections of this kind helped to widen the county's horizons. Richard Germyn even wrote to his employer, one William Stoner: 'as

---

[1] BL, Add. Roll 64320; 64317; 64323; *MPs*, 174; M. Cherry, 'The Courtenay Earls of Devon: The Formation and Disintegration of a Late Medieval Aristocratic Affinity', *Southern History*, 1 (1979), pp. 71–97.
[2] *HOP*, iv, 662; *RBP*, ii, 72.

to your tenaunts in Cornwale, thei be as trew unto you as y can understand as any tenauntes that ye have'.[3]

Many lords from east of the Tamar held estates in the peninsula, fostering ties with key local landowners and officials to ensure their better protection. It is illustrative of this that in 1400 the bailiff of the Devonian Sir John Dinham paid the sheriff of Cornwall 6s. 8d. for a writ served against the tenants of Blisland.[4] Back in 1313, Sir John Wylinton of Gloucestershire had leased to Sir Thomas l'Ercedekne the lands and wardship of John Arundell of Lanherne, prerogatives that had come into his hands as Arundell held part of the manor of Conerton by knight's service of Wylinton.[5] A decade later, the king was to dispatch to Cornwall one John de Leicester to seek out Christiana, late the wife of Edward Wylinton, because she was supposedly 'an idiot from birth'.[6] Edward II aimed to seize her lands, as was his right, but John Carminow and nine others allegedly took her out of Leicester's 'hands by force and arms, and led her away whither they wished' in an attempt to retain control of her estates. Despite occasional frictions, these lords generally depended on the royal administration to manage their distant patrimonies. We find just such a case in 1344, when the Devonian Henry Pomeroy sued one Richard atte Wyne for having failed to render account for his time as Pomeroy's reeve of Tregony.[7]

For all the importance of these landed connections, however, it was the earl-duke himself who was the most powerful agent of lordly connectivity. The county's royal lordship provided a personal link between Cornwall and one of the foremost men of the kingdom. Yet the earl-duke was a figure of national importance who sought to exercise power in the realm at large, through the maintenance of close personal contact with the king himself. Relying on the structures of both the royal administration and his own lordship to govern the county, he rarely visited or resided in the peninsula. The semi-royal nature of the lordship magnified this interdependence, with the Crown supporting comital-ducal government with its full arsenal of powers. Inevitably, this overlap of lordly and royal authority was most apparent when the king held the county directly, as he did for over forty years between 1300 and 1422. Edward I, for instance, can be found appointing royal officials to key posts in Cornwall, granting the custody of Restormel and Penlyn parks to one Roger de Troye, a yeoman of his daughter, Mary.[8] Awarding Liskeard Park to a certain John de Bristol in 1331, Edward III likewise took advantage of the opportunity

[3] *Stonor Letters*, ii, p. 120.
[4] CRO, AR/2/463 m. 1.
[5] CRO, AR/4/347.
[6] CCR 1323–1327, 65.
[7] CPR 1343–1345, 199.
[8] CPR 1301–1307, 65.

presented to him when he held the lordship.[9] Bristol enjoyed close connections with the king's sister, Joan, Queen of Scotland.

As he introduced many royal dependents into Cornwall, Richard II's twenty-two-year tenure of the county was to be of greater significance than that of his grandfather. One of the most prominent of Richard's 'incomers' was his father's former retainer, Sir John Kentwood of Berkshire, who he appointed duchy steward. During his time in Cornwall, Kentwood built connections with many leading gentlemen and acquired a share of the manor of Rosecraddoc with Sir Henry Ilcombe and others, an agreement witnessed by Sir William Botreaux, Sir Warin l'Ercedekne and the like.[10] Since many folk in the county had faith in Kentwood after he had represented them in parliament, Sir Ralph Carminow was to leave him 100s. in his will and appoint him an executor.[11] Yet Kentwood was only one of numerous 'outside' royal-ducal officials, from bailiff-errants to haveners, who interacted with the whole range of the county's populace.

While royal tenure of the lordship would naturally draw the county into national affairs, the earldom-duchy itself played a major role in creating connectivity. In employing John Dabernon as sheriff-steward of Cornwall for some sixteen years, for example, the Black Prince raised this Devon-born man to the pinnacle of county society. The prince granted him estates to match his status and Dabernon acquired yet more Cornish property by spending his rewards of office.[12] Leading gentlemen, among them Thomas Carminow and Sir William Botreaux, can be found calling regularly on him as a trusted witness and his son, Matthew, sat as an MP for Lostwithiel.[13] In his will of 1368, Dabernon left goods to many people and institutions in the county and appointed as an executor none other than the local lawyer John Tremayne, who had married his daughter.[14] Back in 1361, Dabernon had gone out of his way to secure the employment of his kinsman, another John Dabernon, as duchy parker of Lanteglos and Helsbury. This John was to retain a position in the peninsula until the 1390s, having acquired tinning interests.[15] While Dabernon senior's field of influence extended widely, his integration into the county was clearly the result of his own ambitions.

An exacting discipline, lordship depended on the movement around the country of personnel. It is illustrative of this that a retainer of Henry of

---

[9] *CPR 1330–1334*, 163.
[10] CRO, ME/529; ME/44.
[11] *Cornish Wills*, 40.
[12] *RBP*, i, 99, 102; *RBP*, ii, 23; *CFR 1347–1356*, 221; *FF*, i, 362, 370, 386–387.
[13] CRO, AR/37/12; AR/1/890; RP/6/8; *CCR 1346–1349*, 359; *CCR 1369–1374*, 86.
[14] *Cornish Wills*, 31–35.
[15] *RBP*, ii, 182; JUST1/1476 m. 77r; E101/263/19, 24, 28; CRO, WM/349; CF/2/215/35; *CPR 1391–1396*, 263.

Monmouth, one Thomas Jayet of East Anglia, is to be found serving as controller of the stannaries and employing the Cornishman Thomas West as his servant.[16] Not every 'outside' official, however, sought to ingratiate himself with the county's residents. As there is no evidence of his interactions over sensitive issues such as property transactions, John Wynter, steward from late 1399 to early 1402, seemingly developed little affinity with Cornwall. Many lordly officials can be shown to have taken a close interest in their bailiwicks, however, and in 1364 the Black Prince appointed his servant, one John Cook, to the office of bailiff-errant 'as a reward for his great labours'.[17] Some of these folk relied on local attorneys, as did John de Bakton, a yeoman of the prince's buttery, who from 1351 to 1355 deputised the post of bailiff of Blackmore to a certain John Ridel.[18] Appointments such as these created a constant influx of loyal retainers into the county. The earl-duke sometimes farmed out whole manors, so that Sir Neil Loring (d. 1386), the Black Prince's chamberlain and a Founder Knight of the Order of the Garter, held the manors of Calstock and Trematon during the 1370s.[19] A few 'outsiders' arrived under duress, and to support his lordship elsewhere in 1346 the prince imprisoned the Welshman Sir Howe ap Gronou in Launceston Castle, 'not allowing anyone to speak with him in private'.[20]

The main key to gaining a permanent place in Cornish society, however, lay in marriage, a point made by Sir Roger Ingepenne's career as sheriff-steward. During his brief tenure of office, he oversaw the betrothal of his nephew and heir, another Roger Ingepenne, to one Joan, daughter and heiress of the Cornishman Sir John Halton.[21] With the lineage that he established remaining a knightly presence in Cornwall for decades to come, Ingepenne had succeeded in grafting his nephew onto county society.[22] Emulating Ingepenne's success in the late 1380s, the London vintner John Colshull served as duchy steward and acquired the hand of one Emmeline, heiress to the Huish estates in Cornwall and widow of Justice Sir Robert Tresilian. By 1450 the lineage that he had founded held the honour of being the second wealthiest in the county.[23] Through marriage, these 'incomers' were able to secure a lasting place in the peninsula for themselves and their families.

[16] *HOP*, iii, 492; *CPR 1416–1422*, 30.
[17] *RBP*, ii, 209.
[18] *RBP*, ii, 80–81, 111.
[19] *CPR 1377–1381*, 209.
[20] *RBP*, i, 37, 110.
[21] CRO, AR/1/250; AR/1/279–283.
[22] C47/2/41/5; *FA*, i, 208–218; *RBP*, ii, 198.
[23] *HOP*, iii, 633–635; E179/87/92.

With so many small towns in the county, the earl-duke naturally took care to ensure that his urban interests were well looked after.[24] The case of the Kendales illustrates how lordly agents were used in urban society. Despite John Kendale hailing from as far off as Westmorland, on John of Eltham's recommendation Edward III appointed him constable of Restormel Castle. As Kendale went on to serve the Black Prince as receiver from 1348 until 1365, he was able to exploit this position of influence in the duchy to secure properties for himself and his family.[25] After seventeen years of service, however, he chose to yield his post to a kinsman of his, one Richard Kendale. Richard's busy public career saw him audit the duchy accounts in 1377–8, represent three boroughs in parliament, sit on the county bench and serve as escheator and sheriff of both Cornwall and Devon. Naturally enough, he still found the time to serve his own interests, acquiring Cornish estates, trading in fish and serving the Courtenays.[26] Richard became a man of significance, employing a certain Walter Bole as receiver and extending his residence at Treworgy so grandly that he had to relocate a hundred perches of footpath.[27] He was not the only Kendale to be active, however, for John Kendale's son, another John, is to be found holding land with his father in Penlyn, trading in tin and engaging in a little 'piracy'. Since he also held the mayoralty of Lostwithiel on three occasions and twice represented the borough in parliament, salt-water thievery proved no bar to public office. On his death before March 1403, his son, Stephen, succeeded him, sitting as an MP for Lostwithiel in 1417.[28] Becoming thoroughly Cornish gentlemen, the Kendales went on to hold a position of prominence under the Tudors.[29]

But what of lordship's role in transferring Cornishmen to east of the Tamar? With so many officials drawn from the earldom of Chester and the duchy of Lancaster to buttress the power of their masters elsewhere in the realm, these lordships formed major sources of administrative manpower.[30] In sharp contrast to the north west, however, in the south west the earl-duke made little effort to mobilise Cornwall's 'human resources'. A rare example is afforded by the Black Prince's employment of William de Cornewaille as a yeoman and sergeant-at-arms in Berkshire, for none of Cornwall's lords, from Earl Richard to Henry of Monmouth, looked to the county as a recruiting ground for administrative careerists elsewhere.[31] Yet Cornwall was not unique in providing few such men, for the Derbyshire gentry were likewise little called-upon

[24] Cf. Walker, *Lancastrian Affinity*, p. 190.
[25] DCO 1, 6; CRO, RP/6/7; WM/11–12; *FF*, i, 344–345, 392–393; *RBP*, ii, 100.
[26] SC6/818/7 m. 1r; CRO, WM/17; ME/44; *FF*, i, 394–395; *CPR 1364–1367*, 32, 406.
[27] *CPR 1388–1392*, 33; *CPR 1377–1381*, 427.
[28] DCO 18; *CPR 1381–1385*, 285; *HOP*, iii, 513–515.
[29] *Carew*, 137v.
[30] Bennett, *Cheshire and Lancashire*, pp. 204–215.
[31] *RBP*, iv, 181; for Earl Richard, Page, 'Barons' War', 27.

for posts in officialdom outside their own shire.[32] The earldom-duchy instead formed one of the chief sources of patronage in Cornwall itself, a principal employer of the local gentry and budding administrators alike.

Holding seigniorial office actually provided one of the main means of securing pre-eminence in the county itself. It was Sir William Botreaux's service as sheriff-steward in the 1320s and 1330s, for example, which crucially added to his local power, enabling him to lay the foundations for his son to ascend into the parliamentary peerage. To Sir William, good lordship meant profit, power and advancement. In much the same way, Sir Richard Sergeaux was a retainer of the Black Prince who went on to serve as sheriff and steward, enjoy a seat on the Cornish bench and represent the county in no fewer than ten parliaments between 1361 and 1390.[33] Since Sergeaux can be found employing his appointments to advance his feud with the Carminows and Trevarthians, lordly office-holding enabled him to grow mighty indeed. From these examples we can see how the earldom-duchy was tightly intertwined with the workings of county society.

Indeed, lordship could raise those of humble origins to leading local positions. Although Henry Trethewey did not hail from a leading lineage, this drawback failed to diminish his ambitions. His employment as sheriff-steward by John of Eltham and the Black Prince actually established him as one of the greatest men in the county. Cornish gentlemen, among them Sir Otto Bodrugan and Sir Roger Carminow, accordingly sought him as a trusted witness to their deeds.[34] For the aggrandisement of himself and his family, Trethewey managed to secure the post of bailiff-errant for his kinsman, one William Trethewey, and acquired property in his own right. Purchasing what were termed 'many lands' with over £600 of ducal money, Trethewey and his greed, however, were later to draw down the ire of the Black Prince.[35] The prince therefore investigated Trethewey's assets with a view to seizing them.

Similarly rising in status as a result of lordly service, Henry Nanfan was also of humble stock. He is first to be found serving as under-bailiff of Kerrier Hundred in 1344, holding the post of bailiff of Helston-in-Kerrier between 1349 and 1370, the only paid manorial bailiff in the duchy. Nanfan evidently had some administrative abilities and so promotion was to follow, when in 1362 the prince granted him the hundred of Penwith and in 1371 appointed him feodary.[36] Auditing Princess Joan's accounts and those of Richard II in 1382 and 1383 respectively, Nanfan remained a steadfast official even after the prince's

---

[32] Wright, *Derbyshire*, p. 63.
[33] The prince rarely granted posts to Cornishmen who had distinguished themselves in war, unlike John of Gaunt, Walker, *Lancastrian Affinity*, pp. 78–79.
[34] CRO, AR/1/204; AR/1/305; ME/646; ME/381; ME/386; RP/6/7; CCR 1346–1349, 359.
[35] *FA*, i, 209; *FF*, i, 359; *RBP*, ii, 4, 30.
[36] *RBP*, ii, 197; SC8/333/E999.

death.³⁷ In the course of his long life many leading Cornishmen were to seek Nanfan's services as a witness, and in 1369 he served as feoffee to Sir William Botreaux himself.³⁸ Representing three Cornish boroughs in parliament and attaining a seat on the county bench from 1373 to 1380, Nanfan's public career was no less impressive. Naturally enough, none of these duties distracted him from his own enrichment, and to this end he amassed property and acquired tinning interests for himself and his family.³⁹ Both Nanfan and Trethewey used lordship to secure the status and wealth that otherwise would have been denied them by birth.

Each of these lordly office-holders, whether Cornishmen or 'outsiders', acted as a point of contact between the county's residents, their lords and pan-English networks of association. Nonetheless, connections did not necessarily imply the existence of amity. Fighting constantly to prevent the erosion of seigniorial rights, these officials could often be brought into conflict with the peninsula's inhabitants. Coercive power was still to spread an appreciation of Cornish integration, however, as the lordly revenue-raising mechanisms of coinage duty on tin, prise of wine from ships and feudal incidents on land affected nearly everyone. Yet, Cornishmen still sought out seigniorial posts, requesting lordly intervention in their affairs because they had underlying faith in the rule of their lord and master. A powerful sense of reciprocity between the commonalty and the lordship emerges, one that simultaneously spread awareness of the county's many connections to east of the Tamar.

To support his rulership, the earl-duke sent a constant stream of officials into the peninsula on a temporary basis. In 1351, for instance, the Black Prince ordered his retainers in Cornwall to prepare for the arrival of his auditors.⁴⁰ This annual event resulted in the regular dispatch of comital-ducal-royal clerks to the county, officials whom the prince empowered to audit his accounts, examine and remove ministers and even hear complaints from his subjects.⁴¹ Four or five yet more senior seigniorial officials, including the receiver-general or steward-in-chief themselves, had to travel to the far south west to oversee each Cornish assession; while in 1354–5 Chief Justice Shareshull and other high-ranking judicial and ducal men levied over 1,200 fines on the prince's behalf.⁴² Influencing the lives of thousands of the county's residents, the lordship's immense potential for money-raising is made apparent.

The earldom-duchy drew many people out of Cornwall on temporary commissions too. A good example of this is to be found in 1359, when the prince

---

[37] SC6/818/9; *CPR 1381–1385*, 303.
[38] *CCR 1369–1374*, 86; CRO, ME/606.
[39] *RESDCornwall*, 247; *RBP*, ii, 101, 156, 157–158; *FF*, i, 369–370; CRO, EN/36–38.
[40] *RBP*, ii, 5.
[41] *RESDCornwall*, 46–47; *RBP*, ii, 91–92, 117; SC8/333/E1021; SC6/820/3 m. 7.
[42] *RBP*, i, 64; *RBP*, ii, 136; *RESDCornwall*, 54; JUST1/123; above, p. 142.

summoned Dabernon and Kendale to London to explain the reasons behind declining tin revenues; while another comes from c. 1375, when Sir Robert Tresilian requested expenses for travelling twice from London to Cornwall on the command of the prince's council.[43] As comital-ducal officials in the county had to render account to the central office in person, this obligation involved regular itineraries back and forth, while the prince sometimes purchased household supplies from the peninsula.[44] In his capacity as feudal overlord he often summoned leading Cornish gentlemen to London to perform homage, in 1346 even ordering his officials to have Sir John Dauney's heiress, one Maud, brought to his manor at Kennington 'as quickly as possible, doing what courtesy they can to the damsel's mother'.[45]

Lordship sustained a constant two-way flow of people and information, a point perhaps best-illustrated by petitioning. As many as sixty-five petitions sent by the county's residents to their earl-duke have come down to us, this being the way in which the Cornish made their voice heard.[46] It was almost certainly the case, however, that county folk lobbied their earl-duke many hundreds of times between 1300 and 1422, with most of their supplications now lost. This much is suggested by the fact that while in some years no evidence of petitioning remains, as many as nineteen petitions from Cornwall survive in a file sent to the prince in 1375–6.[47] When we look across the century as a whole, we find that there were peaks in petitioning in the 1310s and 1320s which point to a period of tension, as the county's residents often raised concerns at this time about lordly-kingly government. In much the same way, the forty or more supplications made in the 1370s and 1380s reveal the county's disturbed condition in these years. Yet even during the 1350s, when the Black Prince was governing Cornwall assertively, county folk made at least thirty-two entreaties to him. This was because the interface created by petitioning between the earl-duke and his Cornish subjects was of enduring importance.

A few surviving requests can be touched on here as illustrative of the kinds of matters raised. Collective supplications are not uncommon, as in 1375–6 for example, when the people of Cornwall petitioned the Black Prince for a ducal writ to repair storm-damaged buildings.[48] Individuals also made many entreaties to him, Michael Petit for example, beseeching him to return his

---

[43] *RBP*, ii, 155–156, 207; SC8/333/E1038.
[44] *RBP*, ii, 22, 152; *RBP*, iv, 18.
[45] *RBP*, ii, 23–24; *RBP*, i, 15–16.
[46] Above, p. 178; cf. A. Musson, 'Lordship and Petitioning'; C. Rawcliffe, 'The Great Lord as Peacekeeper: Arbitration by English Noblemen and their Councils in the Later Middle Ages', in *Law and Social Change in British History*, ed. J. A. Guy and H. G. Beale (London, 1984), pp. 34–54.
[47] SC8/333/E996–E1101.
[48] SC8/333/E1020.

estates, these having been confiscated on account of Petit's criminality.[49] More remarkable still are the many petitions from the sub-gentry. We find that poor fishermen, tinners and tenants sent in their tales of woe, as did freemen accused of having villein blood, while the lesser folk (*petitz gentz*) of Landrake even complained about the payment of feudal dues.[50] Having all these supplications enrolled in his register, the prince ordered his ministers in Cornwall 'to consider the contents of the enclosed' petitions 'and to do right and reason therein'. Following one letter of entreaty from Reynold Trenansaustel concerning a 10s. debt and the arrest of his nag, the prince replied 'marvelling greatly that... such poor folk are importuning him and his council so much, bringing their suits to him from such distant parts and upon such petty matters', but he still 'charged the steward to do right to all his subjects'.[51]

Evidently lordship provided a direct line of communication to one of the greatest men in England, one which the Cornish exploited to the full. Engaging with seigniorial government and seeking to influence its policies, these folk actively invited lordly intervention in the locality. This is shown clearly by the events of 1356, when the residents of Cornwall made what was called a 'great clamour' because the prince had not paid them for purveyed goods, prompting him to assign no less than 500 marks for these items.[52] Petitioning enabled the county's inhabitants and their earl-duke to keep in constant, close communication throughout the later middle ages. Lords as varied as Queen Isabella and Henry of Monmouth were lobbied by Cornishmen and women, with, for example, the Dinhams' bailiff in the county in 1401 speaking to the future Henry V's council at Launceston.[53] Facilitating a constant dialogue in both directions, the points of contact between the county's lords, their officials and the populace at large emerge as rich and varied.

Such was the significance of the earl-duke to Cornish life that he gained a prominent place in the county's collective imagination, appearing as a character in some Cornish-language miracle plays. In *Bewnans Ke*, for example, the duke's character announced that 'I am Cador, duke of Cornwall./ No man can ever bear my wrath'.[54] Enjoying a yet more prominent role in *Beunans Meriasek*, the character of the duke proclaimed his lordship 'from the Tamar to Land's End'.[55] Throughout this drama he is found issuing lordly commands to his officials, who themselves had parts in the play, and defending the county

---

[49] SC8/333/E1073.
[50] *RBP*, ii, 19, 35–36, 97, 129, 131, 178.
[51] *RBP*, ii, 22.
[52] *RBP*, ii, 103.
[53] CRO, AR/2/463 m. 6r; SC8/333/E1111; SC8/333/E1116.
[54] *Bewnans Ke*, lines 1263–1264.
[55] *Beunans Meriasek*, lines 2205–2299.

from the tyrannical King Teudar, who sought to 'crush' the 'duke of Cornwall and all his folk... just like grains of sand'.[56]

All Cornwall's residents understood that they were the subjects of their earl-duke, a perception connecting them to a wider world of high politics and high chivalry.[57] Lordly castles and parks, such as those at Tintagel and Restormel, loomed over them as physical manifestations of these connections. Interweaving the county into pan-English networks of association, comital-ducal-royal lordship was a major force for connectivity, social mobility and integration. We see this in *Beunans Meriasek*, which drew on ideas current in Cornwall about the interlinked nature of great lordships and the Crown by having the character of the duke of Brittany state that he was 'raised from royal blood', ruling as 'the nearest to the high sovereign' of whose 'lineage right truly am I'.[58] In this way, royal lordship helped spread an awareness of Cornwall's distinctive place in the realm among the whole range of county society.

---

[56] *Beunans Meriasek*, lines 2397–2399.
[57] Elliott-Binns, *Medieval Cornwall*, p. 166.
[58] *Beunans Meriasek*, lines 1–5.

11

Gold, Tin and Terrible Ale: Commercial Connectivity

In the later middle ages Cornwall's diversified economy profited the county's lords and commoners alike, linking them into pan-English credit, exchange and personal networks.[1] Cornishmen and women are to be found trading in commodities as diverse as feathers, fish, cloth and, most significantly, tin, with deals of this sort creating much connectivity.[2] Since tin was so valuable, it is small wonder that leading gentlemen from dynasties as diverse as the Bodrugans and the l'Ercedeknes paid coinage duty on hundreds of thousands of pounds (lbs) of the metal in the first half of the fourteenth century alone.[3] In 1306-7 the landed widow Margery Treverbyn presented as much as 15,000 lbs of tin for coinage. Some local proprietors owned the tin workings themselves, among them Sir Richard Sergeaux, who in 1391 jointly held one such site named 'Tye'.[4] With the absence of urban economic muscle in the county encouraging gentry involvement in this industry, tin could significantly augment local lordly income. By the fifteenth century, however, it was rarer for leading proprietors to engage as directly as this in the tin trade, although men such as John Bolenowe, a gentleman from Camborne, dealt in unspecified 'merchandise'.[5] Whatever the reasons behind the retreat, Cornish lords perennially enjoyed the prerogative of toll tin and were not above involvement in trade.

---

[1] Above, pp. 4-6.
[2] For example, *CCR 1343-1346*, 334-335.
[3] E101/260/25 mm. 5-6, 9; E101/261/1 mm. 4-7; E101/260/20 m. 20; E101/261/11 mm. 2, 5; E101/262/21 mm. 6-7; Cf. P. Nightingale, 'Knights and Merchants: Trade, Politics and the Gentry in Late Medieval England', *Past and Present*, 169 (2000), pp. 36-62 at 38, 60.
[4] *CPR 1388-1392*, 398.
[5] C241/219/1-2, 25, 70.

Some gentlefolk relied on income from the metal to rise yet higher in the ranks of society, Michael Trenewith the elder and younger amongst them. Both Michaels traded extensively in tin, using the resultant wealth to acquire more expansive estates and lend money to people as diverse as Sir John Hamley and the obscure John Ycca.[6] Although both father and son regularly employed violence to further their positions, a Michael Trenewith still acquired a place on the county bench from 1338 to 1344 and represented Cornwall in parliament. Tinning interests enabled the elder and younger Trenewith to secure for their family a position of prominence in the county for the rest of the century. It is illustrative of this that one Ralph Trenewith is found serving as duchy receiver in the 1370s and making a good marriage, when he acquired the hand of Joan Bodrugan, one of Otto Bodrugan's heiresses. Ralph and Joan's son, a certain William Trenewith, was to inherit a considerable portion of the Bodrugan estate, in turn taking a place in the highest echelons of Cornish society and the Bodrugan name itself.[7]

Just as remarkable are the crop of prominent merchant and master tinners – those who traded tin, as opposed to labouring tinners who extracted the metal – who did not hail from leading local lineages; in each generation new men of this sort are found rising to the fore. Gerard de Villiers of Lostwithiel was one such. In 1302–3 he presented 179 thousandweights of tin for coinage, one of the largest amounts ever recorded in the hands of a single person.[8] As he also served as one of Earl Edmund's merchants, commerce raised him to a position of importance.[9] In the next generation, Thomas Goldsmith of Bodmin was to maintain a lively interest in tin, coining 4,704 lbs of this metal in 1332–3 alone. Although the routes by which these men established themselves in trade remain obscure, by 1337–8 commerce had enabled Goldsmith to accumulate sufficient financial and social capital to represent his home town in parliament.[10] Despite his equally obscure roots, by 1327 Roger Blake had become the second richest man in Bodmin, having made his fortune in trading tin. Being 'in great need of money both for his concerns where he is and in England', in 1346 the Black Prince himself called on Blake for a £100 loan.[11] Blake had sat for Bodmin in 1320 and it was naturally the case that his son, John, followed him into both the tinning business and the House, before the latter's tragic suicide in 1350.[12] The operations of these master tinners could be on a considerable scale indeed. By 1357 it seems that Abraham Lesteymour (le Tinner) had for

---

[6] *RBP*, ii, 30–31; *FF*, i, 291–292.
[7] *HOP*, ii, 269–271; iv, 650.
[8] E101/260/20 mm. 4–6; E101/261/1 mm. 2–4, 7–10; Hatcher, *Tin*, p. 79.
[9] *CPR 1292–1301*, 153; *FF*, i, 221.
[10] C241/121/230; E101/262/25; *MPs*, 119.
[11] E179/87/37 m. 5; *RBP*, i, 8; Hatcher, *Tin*, pp. 79–80.
[12] *MPs*, 59, 130.

some time been employing as many as 300 men on six different tinning sites, with these workings allegedly having produced so much waste that they were silting up the haven of Fowey.[13]

The Crown generated one of the best lists to come down to us of the county's mercantile elite, when in 1392 it fined some forty-seven 'merchants of Cornwall' no less than £200 for exporting tin 'without repairing' to the staple.[14] Thomas Bere of Bodmin was among those listed and he is known to have maintained a considerable interest in this lucrative trade. Coining over 10,500 lbs of tin in 1394, Bere also held property in Bodmin and represented his home town in three parliaments.[15] Others fined include John Megre and John Foll, whose interests in this metal took them both to London. Many of these merchants, however, handled other commodities besides tin. One such trader was Odo Ude, who also had shipping concerns, trading in salt and owing customs dues in Fowey in 1401–2.[16] Since the government had conceded a series of export licences in 1364 for cloth and fish, including one for example to Nicholas Cardrew of Mousehole, county merchants clearly dealt in many commodities.[17] Just as Cornwall's economy was diversified, so too were the interests of its traders.

Evidently commerce, especially that involving tin, raised some Cornish merchants and gentlemen to positions of wealth and power. Yet it seems that the majority of those who grew fat on the profits of trade originated from the 'middling sort' or better. The Scarlet family can stand as a case in point. Appearing in the pardon of 1392, Oliver Scarlet a decade earlier had been named as one of thirty-three malefactors who had captured a Portuguese vessel.[18] Commerce was typically a family affair, with Oliver's kinsman, a certain Adam Scarlet, coining tin during Edward I's reign, and one William Scarlet trading in the middle of the century.[19] There is evidence that William handled commodities as diverse as armour and butter, but tin appears to have been his speciality. In 1342 the Black Prince even accused him, along with Michael Trenewith the elder and younger, of violently usurping diverse stannary districts and forcing the tinners to work as virtual slaves.[20] It is important not to exaggerate the case for seeing involvement in trade as a path to upward mobility. Even though thousands of labouring tinners extracted tin, in the early fourteenth century between one- and two-thirds of all the metal coined was registered in

[13] *RBP*, ii, 109–110; Lostwithiel was probably suffering at this time.
[14] *CPR 1391–1396*, 263.
[15] *HOP*, ii, 196–197; E101/263/26 m. 7.
[16] *CPR 1381–1385*, 285; E122/113/3; *FF*, ii, 1–2.
[17] *CPR 1361–1364*, 496.
[18] *CPR 1381–1385*, 142.
[19] E101/260/20 mm. 2, 6–7.
[20] *CCR 1343–1346*, 334–335; *CPR 1340–1343*, 553–554.

the names of just ten persons yearly.[21] While master tinners could make great profits, grinding poverty characterised the lives of the majority of labouring tinners. Yet it is worth noting that 'the immensely rich tin merchants of the early fourteenth century had no counterparts in the mid-fifteenth'.[22] In the longer term the industry acted as something of a leveller, perhaps because of the risks inherent in investing in tin workings that often failed.

For all these challenges, however, tinning interests bound together Cornwall and London, the greatest city in medieval England. Stipulating that tin had to be presented on specific days in a number of towns for tax purposes, the stannary charters created coinage sessions that in the sixteenth century came to form important market places for Cornishmen and Londoners alike.[23] However, the coinage rolls, which list those who presented tin to be taxed at these sessions, provide little evidence for such interactions in the later middle ages. A few Londoners perhaps attended, including Reginald Thunderlegh, but such visits were a rarity.[24] Instead, the medieval tin industry depended on an intricate web of credit, as John Hatcher has demonstrated.[25] Tin dealers, mainly Londoners and aliens, advanced money to merchant or master tinners in anticipation of future production. Generally wealthy Cornishmen, the master tinners, subsequently lent these funds along with their own money to the labouring tinners who actually extracted the metal, with the tin itself used as security. In the late-sixteenth century London and alien merchants are said to have advanced as much as £10,000–£40,000 annually.[26]

Once this metal had been extracted, processed and coined the merchants then transported a great part of it to London or Southampton, in some sense the capital's out-port. It is illustrative of this that in 1423–4 traders aimed to ship some 2,254 pieces of tin directly to London, a cargo comprising nearly half the county's annual output.[27] Such was the importance and antiquity of this trade that by the fifteenth century a 'weyhouse' stood in Walbrook Ward, London, to which Cornish merchants and others delivered 'tynne of Cornewayle'.[28] Considerable amounts of this metal were then exported in their ingot form from the City, with the Venetians representing a particularly ready market in the

---

[21] Hatcher, *Tin*, p. 52.
[22] Hatcher, *Tin*, p. 69.
[23] Lewis, *Stannaries*, pp. 150–151; *Carew*, 14r.
[24] E101/260/20 mm. 1–2; *CPR 1292–1301*, 522.
[25] Hatcher, *Tin*, pp. 51–55.
[26] Hatcher, *Tin*, p. 53.
[27] Hatcher, *Tin*, pp. 137–141.
[28] C1/70/77; *LBK*, 342–343.

fifteenth century, but little evidence remains of Cornishmen dealing directly with alien merchants in London.[29]

Tin also proved essential to the production of pewter, an alloy for which London was renowned and for which there was much demand. Emerging as a significant craft in the mid-fourteenth century, the London pewterers in little more than a hundred years held a place 'just outside the magic circle of twelve livery companies'.[30] As early as 1360 we find a certain William Peudrer (Pewterer) of London striking an agreement with the Black Prince on behalf of his fellow pewterers to 'willingly come to the next coinage after Easter to buy a great part of the tin', paying 'promptly for the coinage thereof if the prince would assist him with boats for carrying the tin'.[31] It is estimated that by 1400 London pewterers were producing 15–20 tonnes of pewter annually, a figure which was to rise to an exceptional 90 tonnes by 1466–7 and represented hundreds of thousands of items.[32] Since the City's pewter was of the highest quality, Londoners then traded items of this sort throughout England and far overseas; often purchased by Hanseatic merchants, by 1480–1 this metal ranked among London's biggest export earners.[33]

Cornwall and the capital were strikingly interdependent, for what is clear is that hundreds of Londoners relied on thousands of Cornish tinners. Tensions abounded within the tin trade, however, for labouring tinners, master tinners, tin dealers and pewterers all sought to maximise their profits at the expense of those who produced and handled the metal. Inevitably, this exploitation resulted in much rancour. And just as inevitably, the level of tin output greatly influenced the scale of connections forged. The Black Death and subsequent plague visitations had a catastrophic effect on tin production and, although output had risen to new highs by the end of the fourteenth century, yields fell every year from 1414 until their nadir in the 1460s.[34] Yet despite the many ups and downs of the trade, every person who handled this metal was interconnected because tinning still remained 'big business'.

Analysis of the tin trade reveals Cornwall as a county by no means economically isolated from the rest of the realm, a point made even more forcefully by the study of debt patterns. Although the certificates of debt which survive in the chancery records provide the basis for the following discussion, as a source

---

[29] *The Views of the Hosts of Alien Merchants, 1440–1444*, ed. H. Bradley, London Record Society, 46 (Woodbridge, 2012), *passim*.; Hatcher, *Tin*, p. 143.
[30] J. Hatcher and T. C. Barker, *A History of British Pewter* (London, 1974), pp. 38, 80.
[31] *RBP*, ii, 170.
[32] R. F. Homer, 'Tin, Lead and Pewter', in *English Medieval Industries: Craftsmen, Techniques, Products*, ed. J. Blair and N. Ramsay (London, 1991), pp. 57–80 at 73.
[33] *Views of the Hosts*, pp. 3, 87, 118; *The Overseas Trade of London: Exchequer Customs Accounts 1480–1*, ed. H. S. Cobb, London Record Society, 27 (Bristol, 1990), p. xxxv.
[34] Hatcher, *Tin*, pp. 90–91, 162.

they are by no means without their limitations. Such records arose from the Statutes of Acton Burnell (1283), Merchants (1285) and the Staple (1353) that the government designed and drafted to facilitate the quick recovery of mercantile debt. Establishing that bonds or recognizances be drawn-up between the two parties transacting business, the Statute of the Staple made provision for debts to be formally registered before the mayor and clerk of the staple in designated towns across the realm.[35] If the debtor defaulted, the creditor could then employ these written instruments immediately to seize their person or goods in the borough where these debts had been registered. If the person or chattels of the debtor remained beyond the town's jurisdiction, however, the creditor 'could deposit a certificate of the debt in chancery which would authorise the issue of process for the imprisonment of the debtor and seizure of their chattels' anywhere in the realm.[36]

Whatever may be their inadequacies, we are largely dependent on the debt certificates because the recognizance rolls of the staple courts, on which were recorded every debt enrolled in the staple, rarely survive.[37] We can therefore only see the cases where the creditor failed to recover his loan, with no way of assessing what proportion of the total these 'bad debts' represented.[38] The reason for which these debts were actually incurred is also rarely recorded, leaving us with little more than the overall figure. By the late fourteenth century it seems that non-merchants were widely employing these bonds to ensure the performance of contracts.[39] The amounts recorded present yet more problems, as they perhaps include a penal bond. And actually taking a case to Westminster, where most people registered the cases studied herein, was an expensive undertaking limited to a wealthy few.[40] While we must bear these caveats in mind, such debt-based evidence reveals a rich network of connections.

Between 1330 and 1430 some seventy-one cases of debt involving Cornish people and Londoners have come down to us. In these seventy-one certificates, fifty Londoners are found advancing over £5,000 globally to 108 Cornishmen and women.[41] The body of lenders is drawn from a whole range of companies. Until the 1370s mercers predominated, but from approximately

---

[35] *Statutes of the Realm*, i, pp. 332–343; J. L. Bolton, *Money in the Medieval English Economy, 973–1489* (Manchester, 2012), pp. 73, 202–203, 276–277.
[36] Kowaleski, *Exeter*, p. 213.
[37] P. Nightingale, 'Monetary Contraction and Mercantile Credit in Later Medieval England', *EcHR*, 43 (1990), pp. 560–575 at 565.
[38] Bolton, *Money*, pp. 276–277.
[39] M. M. Postan, *Medieval Trade and Finance* (Cambridge, 1973), pp. 38–39; Bolton, *Money*, pp. 277–278; Kowaleski, *Exeter*, pp. 212–213.
[40] Bolton, *Money*, pp. 278–279.
[41] C131 and C241, studied directly and through Nightingale's detailed catalogue; counting cases brought on multiple occasions just once.

this date fishmongers and grocers are found rising to prominence. At the same time a few members of other companies made an appearance, the likes of the goldsmiths, armourers and tailors.[42] Ranging from £500 down to as little as £4, the amounts recorded were equally varied: seventeen cases involved sums of £100 or more; fourteen cases fell within the £40–£90 bracket; the rest were less than £30.[43] Most metropolitan merchants appear only once, although a number of them had multiple interests in the county. In the 1340s, for instance, the mercer Richard Causton brought four cases to chancery concerning Cornish debtors, while his kinsman Nicholas is recorded bringing a further two. No doubt to spread the risk, many City merchants jointly lent money.

But with whom were these Londoners dealing? Predictably enough, scions of leading local lineages are often found appearing. A certificate of 1343 appears to suggest that Sir John Hamley, Sir John l'Ercedekne, Sir John Petit and Sir John Treiagu had formed a syndicate that probably dealt in tin and owed £400 to the mercers Adam Frauncey and Richard Causton.[44] The county's merchants are well represented in the certificates too; and in 1347, for example, a consortium of five of them, including John Scarlet of Bodmin and Nicholas Pieres of Lostwithiel, are found owing £20 to the Londoner Simon Frauncey.[45] Some Cornishmen actually went into partnerships with metropolitan merchants, acting as agents in the locality. One such trader was Thomas Goldsmith of Bodmin, whose collaborations with the London fishmongers John de Gildesburgh and Richard Sumli' were made apparent in 1346, when together they sued Michael Trenewith the younger and Michael Wastel for no fewer than 28,000 lbs of coined tin.[46]

On the one hand, debts could form part of a 'complex web of reciprocal ties that supported social relationships as well as facilitating exchange'.[47] Merchants usually conducted trade with 'a known circle of contacts'; for example, the London Goldsmith John Cary approached the widow of Simon Yurle of Launceston and reported Yurle 'for a true man and good paier'.[48] On the other hand, debt could often result in bitterness. Richard Carew, admittedly writing in the sixteenth century, was to denounce the 'cutthroate and abominable dealing' whereby Londoners made 'excesive gaine[s]'.[49] He was to rail against metropolitan credit reducing Cornishmen to 'pettie chapmen', but at times

---

[42] C241/157/144; C241/176/25; C241/178/7.
[43] The largest, C241/118/272; the smallest, C241/113/69.
[44] C241/118/288.
[45] C241/123/140.
[46] C241/121/230.
[47] Kowaleski, *Exeter*, p. 204.
[48] Bolton, *Money*, p. 291; *HOP*, iv, 940.
[49] *Carew*, 14r–15v.

Londoners failed to recover their dues.[50] Radiating outwards, the influence of debt made the family, acquaintances and tenantry of debtors – along with local officialdom itself – only too aware of commercial connections to east of the Tamar.[51] After the Londoner Richard Causton had seized the lands of Sir John Treiagu to cover his dues, for instance, the Black Prince himself came to hear of these events.[52] There can be little doubt that provincial and metropolitan merchants both interacted and intersected, as competition and co-operation characterised commercial connectivity.

Although we will never know the reason why most of these debts were incurred, and some may not even have been concerned with commercial arrangements, tin almost certainly loomed large, as four certificates specifically relate to debts arising from trade in this metal.[53] There is plenty of evidence, however, that Cornish commerce did not depend on tin alone. As the cloth industry in the east of the county developed from the late-fourteenth century, so London grocers developed an interest in this commodity.[54] The county's fisheries also expanded in this period, with metropolitan fishmongers purchasing Cornish fish for the sustenance of the City.[55] Londoners sometimes sourced grain and other food stuffs from the peninsula too, while a considerable trade in hides carried on between the two regions.[56] Such interconnected markets saw merchants from within and without Cornwall endlessly transport goods from the county to the capital.

Since London formed the hub of inter-regional English trade, it was commonplace for Cornishmen and women to make purchases in the capital. Folk from the county often acquired textiles from the City, for instance, as London's Blackwell Hall rose to pre-eminence among English cloth marts.[57] Setting and supplying the fashions for the entire kingdom, London held a place at the centre of conspicuous consumption in England.[58] And following the latest trends, the Arundells of Lanherne made many purchases in the City; in 1443, for instance, John Arundell obtained 7¼ yards of crimson cloth directly from

---

[50] *Carew*, 15v; for example, C241/195/25.
[51] For instance, C131/33/11.
[52] *RBP*, i, 5–6.
[53] C241/117/162; C241/119/235; C241/121/226; C241/121/230; also, *CPMR 1364–1381*, 187.
[54] *RESDCornwall*, 169–170; *CPR 1461–1467*, 502; *CPR 1467–1477*, 432.
[55] Kowaleski, 'South-Western Fisheries'.
[56] *CPR 1313–1317*, 447; *HA, passim.*; cf. J. A. Galloway, 'One Market or Many? London and the Grain Trade of England', in *Trade, Urban Hinterlands and Market Integration, c. 1300–1600*, ed. J. A. Galloway (Loughborough, 2000), pp. 23–42; D. Keene, 'Changes in London's Economic Hinterland as Indicated by Debt Cases in the Court of Common Pleas', in *Urban Hinterlands*, pp. 59–81.
[57] C. Barron, *London in the Later Middle Ages: Government and People 1200–1500* (Oxford, 2004), pp. 53–54; *Overseas Trade of London*, pp. 93, 162–163.
[58] Barron, *London*, pp. 76–83.

Lucchese merchants in the capital, and in 1466–7 the family acquired livery cloth from the City for their retainers.[59] The Arundells were even to cover costs for 'lechecraft at London' and 'leche crafte paid to a surger'.[60] Leading Cornish residents also procured fashionable funerary monuments from the capital, including those of the cassocked Thomas Awmarle in Cardinham, the armigerous Thomas de Mohun in Lanteglos-by-Fowey and the splendidly garbed Lady Margery Arundell in Anthony; William Treffry of Fowey even requested one 'like unto a tomb which lieth on M[aster] Browne in the Crutched Friars of London'.[61]

Such varied two-way exchanges saw people move constantly to and fro between Cornwall and the capital. It follows that the Arundells' receiver met expenses incurred 'for schoyng when my master went to London' and that the family owned an inn in Peter Lane, near Paul's Wharf, which perhaps served as their London base.[62] Mobility of this kind did not remain the preserve of knights alone, however, as Cornish merchants were in the habit of frequently travelling to the City. It is illustrative of this that one Robert Borlas, a merchant, had thirty-nine pieces of tin 'cariide oute of Cornwall yn to the citee of London' in the fifteenth century; while back in 1367 the Cornishmen John Nichol and Andrew Bakere had both been in the capital trading in wine when the government arrested them on suspicion of murdering a Welshman.[63] It seems that commerce also took Thomas Randyll to the capital, where in 1480 he is recorded as carrying cloth from London to Fowey on two horses, while many Cornishmen can be shown to have transported goods into and out of the City by sea.[64] It is certainly worth remembering that all those who registered debts in London had to journey to the City to do so.[65] And where people travelled, so too did news: '[in Cornwall]', as Richard Carew was to write, 'the Marchant unfoldeth his packe of strange newes, which either he brought with him from London... or forged by the way, telling what great likelyhood there is of warres [and] what danger of Pirates at Sea'.[66] In this way, London formed 'a clearing-house for news and views' from across the realm and beyond.[67]

---

[59] *Views of the Hosts*, p. 76; H. Douch, 'Household Accounts at Lanherne', *JRIC* (1953), pp. 25–32 at 27; CRO, AR/2/1235/3.
[60] CRO, AR/2/935/12.
[61] Lack et al., *Brasses of Cornwall*, pp. 1–2, 16–17, 67–68; *Cornish Wills*, 118.
[62] CRO, AR/2/1244 m. 2; AR/1/941–2; AR/2/1229.
[63] C1/70/77; *CCR 1364–1368*, 368.
[64] *Overseas Trade of London*, p. 99; below, p. 287.
[65] Nightingale, 'Knights and Merchants', 40.
[66] *Carew*, 14r.
[67] M. Bennett, 'The Plantagenet Empire as "Enterprise Zone": War and Business Networks, c. 1400–50', in *Plantagenet Empire*, pp. 335–358 at 356.

Some Cornishmen and women can be shown to have made their wills while they were staying in London. For example, Christine Batyn of Launceston (d. 1393–4) composed her testimony while visiting or living in the City with her daughter and son-in-law.[68] John Foll (d. 1407), a Cornish tin merchant with longstanding connections with London, composed his testimony while staying with the London pewterer William Buxton; he requested burial in the collegiate church of St Thomas of Acre in Cheapside, next to his wife, Joan.[69] Perhaps having resided in the City for a time, John Reynold of Bodmin (d. 1413) similarly wished to be interred in the church or the cemetery of the Friar Preachers of London.[70] Although visiting Cornishmen and women often attached themselves to friaries, hospitals and colleges in the capital, as these institutions were well geared to accommodating 'strangers', the larger point to emerge is that Cornish folk were a continuing presence in the City. Some even chose to settle in London and found families, among them the metropolitan draper William Botreaux (d. c. 1440), who was of Cornish gentry stock.[71] Perhaps content just to visit London when necessary while governing their patrimonies, few proprietors permanently established themselves in the City. It quickly becomes apparent, however, that Cornishmen of lesser means were more enterprising.

Naturally enough, examples are found of Cornishmen being admitted into the Worshipful Company of Pewterers.[72] Although John Megre hailed from Truro, his remarkable career saw him establish himself as a pewterer in London. Coining 20,000 lbs of tin in 1392 alone, Megre five years later was to acquire property in Lombard Street, London, while sitting in parliament for Truro.[73] He enjoyed no small measure of success as a pewterer, in 1418 pledging as much as £50 to Henry V.[74] Yet despite his metropolitan achievements, he always retained his links with Cornwall, not least in the county's tin.[75] Megre's will of 1419 shows that he considered himself a naturalised Londoner, while remembering numerous people and institutions in the far south west, leaving money for a seven-year chantry in St Mary's Church in Truro.[76] A 'Cornyshman' of Fowey, John Dogowe held a similarly leading role in the internal tin trade, in his case from the 1430s to the 1460s. In recognition of his

---

[68] LMA, DL/C/B/004/MS09171/001 f. 309r; *Cornish Wills*, 42, 213.
[69] E101/263/19 m. 2; E101/263/24 m. 8; LMA, DL/AL/C/002/MS09051/001 f. 183; *Cornish Wills*, 43–44, 226.
[70] LMA, DL/C/B/004/MS09171/002 f. 254r; *Cornish Wills*, 49, 240.
[71] *CPR 1436–1441*, 333.
[72] C241/173/33; C241/195/25.
[73] E101/263/19 m. 9; *HOP*, iii, 711–712.
[74] *LBI*, 203.
[75] C241/193/115.
[76] *HW*, ii, 422; *Cornish Wills*, 50–52.

prominence, the pewterers admitted him to the freedom of their company in 1452, with promotion following when in 1460 they appointed him warden.[77] Regularly 'fetcht[ing] tynne' from Cornwall, in 1491 the pewterers even paid 'for ale whanne the Cornysshe men were at our halle, iij d'.[78]

More unexpected perhaps are the many Cornish-born skinners who resided in the capital. This connection is partly to be explained by the fact that many hides and furs were produced in Cornwall itself. Although the skinners were not the wealthiest London guild, they came to hold an increasingly ascendant position in their lucrative trade.[79] Many Cornishmen joined their ranks, amongst them the skinner Michael Trewethenek, called 'Cornwaille', who almost certainly originated from the west of the Tamar.[80] He died in 1385, having enjoyed a successful commercial and civic career during which he had served as a common councillor for Cornhill.[81] William Olyver's life was yet more impressive. Hailing from Truro, Olyver was to represent his native town in the parliaments of 1381 and 1382.[82] His Cornish origins, however, did not prevent him establishing himself in the City of London, where Walbrook Ward repeatedly elected him alderman; he even drafted City legislation and in 1392 attended Richard II when the latter stripped London of its liberties.[83] Olyver rose to significance in the skinners too, serving as their warden from 1385.[84] Developing many connections in the City, in 1390 Olyver found six fellow Londoners, including four skinners, to mainprise him under pain of 1,000 marks after the government had imprisoned him in the Tower for an alleged assault.[85]

A long document, Olyver's will of 1396 reveals his accumulation of wealth and loyalties. His wish to be buried in St Stephen's Walbrook demonstrates his integration into the City's parochial life; back in 1371 he had served as a churchwarden in London, but he had never forgotten Cornwall. He actually bequeathed money to St Clement's near Truro and remembered the children of his brother, one Laurence Polwhile.[86] In the course of his busy career, Olyver had also found the time to develop links with his fellow Cornishmen

---

[77] GL, CLC/L/PE/D/002/MS07086/001 f. 6r; Hatcher, *Tin*, p. 138; C. Welch, *History of the Worshipful Company of Pewterers of the City of London*, 2 vols (London, 1902), i, p. 45.
[78] GL, CLC/L/PE/D/002/MS07086/001 f. 101r.
[79] E. M. Veale, *The English Fur Trade in the Later Middle Ages* (Oxford, 1966), pp. 78–80.
[80] *HW*, ii, 289.
[81] *CPMR 1381–1412*, 86; *LBH*, 238.
[82] *FF*, ii, 23–24; *MPs*, 207, 212.
[83] *LBH*, 213, 235, 304, 362, 393, 409; *CPR 1391–1396*, 130.
[84] *LBH*, 262.
[85] *CCR 1389–1392*, 200, 286.
[86] LMA, DL/C/B/004/MS09171/001 ff. 384v–385r; *HW*, ii, 324; *CPR 1370–1374*, 61–62.

in the capital. We can see this from his bequest of the sum of 20 marks for her marriage to Sarah Tregollas, the daughter of another Cornish-born skinner in London, a certain Thomas Tregollas (d. 1394). While Thomas had sat for Truro in the parliament of 1380 and bequeathed 20s. to 'my fraternity, that is of Mary at Truro', he wished to be buried in a St Martin's in London and appointed Olyver supervisor of his testimony.[87] Olyver left a further 40s. to his apprentice, one John Trethewey, who evidently had Cornish origins and did much business in both regions.[88] Since he too had become a naturalised Londoner, Trethewey's own will of 1433 remembered St Stephen's Walbrook.[89] Another Trethewey, this time Robert, also established himself as a metropolitan skinner, in 1445 making yet another bequest to St Stephen's Walbrook, and so too did Isabel Trethewey.[90]

Other Cornishmen, too, established themselves as London skinners. Ralph Skynnard (d. 1429), for example, probably hailed from Cornwall but, like the others, made his fortune in the capital. Amassing money from his success in trade and prominence in civic administration, where he had served as an alderman, he left 100s. to John Touker of Liskeard and bequeathed over 1,000 marks to his wife.[91] Another skinner, Hugh Trethowen, had a name suggestive of Cornish birth or ancestry, and the register of the Skinners' Company Fraternity is peppered with others: John and Thomas Tregoll, Nicholas Tretherbyn, John Trewyns, John Trerys, Thomas Fowey and John Trewynard among them.[92] A certain Reginald Treskewys, citizen and skinner of London, even went to law concerning his Cornish 'enheritance', while another metropolitan skinner, one Thomas Lansew (d. 1477), bequeathed his 'lyvelode' in Cornwall to his sister's daughter.[93] We can see how Cornish-born skinners in the capital retained links with their natal county, drawing yet more of their compatriots to the 'big smoke'.

For all these skinners, however, the Cornish were just as prominent in the Worshipful Company of Brewers. One John Tregole (d. 1412), for example, to judge from his name could claim to be a Cornishman, as could William Trenewyth and John Tregoys.[94] Bequeathing money to a St Stephen's in Cornwall

---

[87] *MPs*, 203; LMA, DL/C/B/004/MS09171/001 f. 338r; my thanks to Caroline Barron for these references; *CCR 1389–1392*, 312.
[88] *CPR 1413–1416*, 208; *CPMR 1413–1437*, 16, 182; *LBI*, 140.
[89] LMA, DL/C/B/004/MS09171/003 f. 353v.
[90] LMA, DL/C/B/004/MS09171/004 ff. 172v, 207v.
[91] LMA, DL/C/B/004/MS09171/003 ff. 211v–212v; *LBI*, 284.
[92] LMA, DL/C/B/004/MS09171/003 f. 126r; GL, CLC/L/SE/A/004A/MS31692 ff. 5v–6r, 13v, 14r, 24r.
[93] C1/11/483; LMA, DL/C/B/004/MS09171/006 f. 201v; *Cornish Wills*, 205–206.
[94] LMA, DL/AL/C/002/MS09051/001 f. 272v; DL/C/B/004/MS09171/002 f. 240v; DL/C/B/004/MS09171/003 f. 23r.

'where I was born', the citizen and brewer William Longe (d. 1431) definitely hailed from the county; as did John Polgwest (d. 1437), who remembered St Keverne Church in the Lizard 'where I was taken up from the holy font'.[95] The appropriately named Ralph Hoppy (d. 1446) similarly bequeathed money to St Erth 'where I originated', and one Thomas Bere (d. 1450) held property in Launceston.[96] A John Basset was likewise to leave money and goods to his heir, one John Hoplyn of Cornwall, and his peers Richard Trevethek and Richard Newlyn, to judge by their names, were probably Cornishmen too.

City records note yet more London brewers whose names suggest Cornish origins, such as Henry Trebolans, John Tregelowe, Michael Tregeneon, Michael Treys and John Penverne.[97] Other London brewers, including John Treloskan and John Trerise, had interests in the county, suggesting that they too hailed from Cornwall.[98] Receiving their company's livery and attending fraternity feasts in London, Henry Trebolans, Ralph Hoppy, Michael Trerys, Reynold Trelowe and many other Cornish-born brewers can be shown to have played an integral role in the brewers' guild.[99] One of them, Henry Trebolans, contributed 7s. to the rebuilding of the brewers' hall and actually went on to attain the mastership of the Company in the early years of Henry VI's reign.[100] Such links probably did not develop from a specific taste for Cornish ale, however, as some thought that it would make you 'kacke, also to spew'.[101] Instead, brewing probably represented an entry-level craft for the Cornishmen of modest means who travelled to London seeking their fortunes.

By no means confined to these three trades, Cornish folk can be found in many City companies. Michael Haryes (d. 1489), for example, originated from St Columb Major but became a London draper; and another City draper, a certain John Newlyn, may be taken on the evidence of his name and interests in Cornish property to have hailed from the peninsula.[102] One Robert Trenerth, who was apprenticed into the London mercers and by 1428 had risen to the beedlery of the company, originated in Cornwall and retained his connections there, trading in tin and representing three county boroughs in parliament.[103] Although apprenticeship could provide many Cornishmen with an entrée into London, arrangements of this sort could not be counted on to always

---

[95] *Cornish Wills*, 202–203; LMA, DL/C/B/004/MS09171/003 f. 481v.
[96] LMA, DL/C/B/004/MS09171/004 f. 198v; DL/C/B/004/MS09171/003 f. 152v; DL/C/B/004/MS09171/005 ff. 17v, 256v–257r, 287v; *Cornish Wills*, 204.
[97] *LBI*, 233–235.
[98] *CPR 1422–1429*, 29; C1/45/292.
[99] GL, CLC/L/BF/A/021/MS05440 ff. 5v, 7r, 283r–283v, 310v, 312v–313r, 317r.
[100] GL, CLC/L/BF/A/021/MS05440 ff. 25r, 86v, 106r, 153r.
[101] Boorde, *Knowledge*, p. 122.
[102] *Cornish Wills*, 206; LMA, DL/C/B/004/MS09171/004 f. 162r; C1/6/111.
[103] *HOP*, iv, 648–649; C131/228/9; also, *CCR 1396–1399*, 385.

run smoothly. The unlucky John Thomas of Cornwall, for example, had been apprenticed for eight years to the London tailor John Davy, but on the latter's death was passed on to another draper, a certain Henry Goof.[104] Withdrawing 'to the privileged place of Westminster' in 1430, Goof left Thomas to be turned over to a third tailor to complete his term. Despite occasional problems of this sort, the Cornish who settled in London became fully integrated into its civic society, not gathered together in a single street, ward, or company.

Cornishmen do not emerge as the only inward migrants pouring into London. Employing place-name evidence, Peter McClure has charted the scale of migration to the City from the rest of England to show that London was a city made up of migrants.[105] Local and regional migration to London was indeed commonplace. In the years around 1400, for example, a cluster of Liverpool merchants established themselves in the capital, and from the mid-fifteenth century Cheshire and Lancashire men are found rising to prominence in the City.[106] Despite originating in Coventry, the Tate family climbed high in the capital after being apprenticed into the mercery trade there. Between 1485 and 1500 two Tate brothers served as aldermen of London, while three Tates achieved the mayoralty on four occasions, the family's success drawing in other Coventry folk: 'the Tate effect'.[107] We have noted how 'the Olyver effect' in the skinners and 'the Cornish effect' in London more generally saw those county folk ensconced in the capital ease the passage to the City for their acquaintances. With towns forming nodes in inter-urban networks, many of the folk who settled in London hailed from the boroughs of their native county. No urban monopoly existed in commercial contacts, however, for connections stretched across the peninsula and the sea formed an important medium of exchange.

Yet, if many county folk established themselves in London, it was often the case that they did not neglect or forget their origins. Some even chose to define themselves as 'Cornyshmen', while others forged links with their fellow compatriots in the City.[108] Although craft loyalties often determined such connections, at times Cornish sentiments proved more potent than City associations. We find one such case in 1411, when John Megre and William Trigillowe of Cornwall, along with the London brewers John Trigillowe and Henry Bedell, made a bond for the management of a deceased Londoner's property.[109] While few became 'merchant princes', a considerable cohort of Cornishmen and

---

[104] *CPMR 1413–1437*, 238–239; also, *CPR 1401–1405*, 80,
[105] P. McClure, 'Patterns of Migration in the Late Middle Ages: The Evidence of English Place-Name Surnames', *EcHR*, 32 (1979), pp. 167–182.
[106] Bennett, *Cheshire and Lancashire*, pp. 124–127.
[107] A. Sutton, *A Merchant Family of Coventry, London and Calais: The Tates, c. 1450–1515* (London, 1998), p. 11.
[108] *CCR 1402–1405*, 362; *CPMR 1381–1412*, 302.
[109] *CPMR 1381–1412*, 310.

women thrived in the capital while retaining their links to the far south west. In moving to London, these folk both exploited and contributed to the City's resources and mercantile networks.[110] A Cornish-born 'citizen and inhabitant of London', Ralph Trenewith, for example, certainly mobilised his City connections to good effect. Along with four other Londoners, in 1363–4 he had the mayor write a letter to the admiral of France and 'other justices of the good towns' in Normandy.[111] He did so because Norman 'seamen' had alleged seized their ship sailing from Cornwall to the capital with 360 pieces of white tin, before distributing these plundered wares along the French coast. If compensation to Trenewith and his associates was not forthcoming, the mayor threatened to take the case before the king 'and obtain a remedy by others means'.

Of all the Cornish to establish themselves in London, however, Dame Thomasine Percyval, 'the maid of Week', that is Week St Mary, perhaps stands out the most. Richard Carew was to record that Thomasine Bonaventure, as she was then, was out 'in her girlish age' in the county when a passing London merchant 'saw her, heeded her, liked her, begged her of her poor parents, and carried her to his home' in the City.[112] Although it seems that she was actually of gentle origins, probably introduced into London through her well-connected brother, one Richard Bonaventure, Thomasine first appears in the City as the wife of Henry Galle (d. 1466). Having faith in her abilities, Galle in his will of 1466 attempted to leave his commercial concerns to Thomasine. She did indeed 'keep the business going', in 1467 passing it on to her second husband, another tailor named Thomas Barnaby. While it is unclear how soon after Barnaby's death in 1467 she married her third husband, a certain John Percyval (d. 1503), he was yet another tailor who was to rise to the mayoralty of the City. A talented woman, Thomasine aided John with the running of his business, trading alone after his death and endowing a grammar school in her native Week St Mary with the profits of her remarkable life. There can be little doubt that these many Cornish careerists were important points of contact between county and City.

For all the rich connections between Cornwall and the capital, however, the peninsula was no London satellite. There is evidence that the county's residents traded with a host of cities and regions, some in England and some further afield, the sea linking the peninsula to many lands.[113] Naturally enough, Cornish merchants exported tin to northern France, Flanders and beyond,

---

[110] Cf. Bennett, 'Enterprise Zone', p. 356.
[111] *Calendar of Letters from the Mayor and Corporation of the City of London, c. 1350–1370*, ed. R. R. Sharpe (London, 1885), pp. 95–96.
[112] *Carew*, f. 119; M. Davies, 'Thomasine Percyvale, 'The Maid of Week', (d. 1512)', in *Medieval London Widows 1300–1500*, ed. C. M. Barron and A. F. Sutton (London, 1994), pp. 185–208.
[113] Below, Chapter 14.

with this metal also drawing Italian banking houses to the peninsula.[114] In 1325, for example, Sir Thomas l'Ercedekne was recorded as owing 120 marks to three Florentine merchants, while seven years later Edward III granted the Bardi one of the keys to the chest in which the stamp of tin itself was kept.[115] The county also enjoyed many links with other areas of England. In 1368, for instance, Richard Ledhed of Bodmin is to be found indebted to two merchants of Salisbury.[116] Elsewhere in the realm, Cornishmen and Bristolians began process in chancery on five occasions between 1330 and 1430, while Thomas Catour of Breage (d. 1458) remembered one 'Ricard Trynwyche of Bristol, pewterer' in his will.[117] Although not always legally, county merchants and others can also be found trading tin in Gloucester.[118] Yet Cornishmen are conspicuous by their absence from another Midlands city – Coventry – reminding us that we should neither overplay the scale of connections to other parts of the realm nor the integrated nature of the medieval English economy.[119]

Inevitably, commercial links with Exeter were more significant than those with more distant regional centres. Some Exeter merchants, for example, advanced money to their western neighbours, as did Henry Westover in 1383 to Laurence Tremur of Cornwall.[120] The city is often found admitting to its freedom Cornishmen such as John Russel of Bodmin, who had served an apprenticeship that family members and acquaintances had presumably organised.[121] The county's merchants appear to have maintained a presence in the city, although they are sometimes found behaving violently, as for example in 1318, when an alleged assault within its bounds on John Tavistock by John le Seler of Bodmin and eight others prompted a government investigation.[122] Since dozens of debts were enrolled in Exeter between Cornish gentlemen, merchants and clergymen, the staple court there acted as a significant draw to county folk.[123] Considerable bonds linked the two areas, but Exeter was too small and too distant from Cornwall to serve as a provincial capital for the south west. This much is shown by the fact that of the seventy-four chancery certificates enrolled in the 1390s relating to Cornwall, only one details a debt between a Cornishman and a man of Somerset; six recorded dealings between

---

[114] Hatcher, *Tin*, pp. 53, 92–93, 110–111; C131/174/4.
[115] *CCR 1323–1327*, 531, 571; *CCR 1330–1334*, 255–256.
[116] C131/19/36.
[117] *Cornish Wills*, 84.
[118] *CCR 1313–1318*, 42.
[119] *The Statute Merchant Roll of Coventry, 1392–1416*, ed. A. Beardwood, Dugdale Society, 17 (London, 1939), *passim*.
[120] C241/171/78.
[121] *Exeter Freemen, 1266–1967*, ed. M. M. Rowe and A. M. Jackson, DCRS, Extra Series I (Exeter, 1973), pp. 4–48; Kowaleski, *Exeter*, p. 86.
[122] *CPR 1317–1321*, 286.
[123] Kowaleski, *Exeter*, p. 279; for instance, C241/146/6.

Cornishmen and Londoners; ten show Cornish and Devonian agreements; while the remaining fifty-seven were concerned with intra-county interactions. Since deeply localised agreements greatly outnumbered recognizances, commerce within the peninsula is likely to have been even more significant than these figures suggest.[124]

It is helpful to think of England as a country made up of distinct economic regions, resulting from localised supply, demand and transport networks.[125] With land prices and industries varying across the peninsula, even Cornwall as a whole did not form a single market.[126] A good example of this economic regionalism is to be found in 1320, when Cornwall and Devon submitted a joint petition alleging that merchants sold wine for 6*d*. a gallon in Exeter and 8*d*. a gallon elsewhere in these counties, but that in London it cost a mere 4*d*.[127] Yet the fact that both counties possessed information about the cost of wines in London suggests that regional markets existed neither in isolation nor in ignorance of each other. The nature of markets actually depended on the commodities traded, and the tin trade made for a strong connection between Cornwall and the commercial hub of London. Across England, a 'flourishing' network of trade and credit bound together an intricate series of marts, ranging from London through county towns such as Lostwithiel and right down to villages. All Cornwall's main urban centres were also entwined with their hinterlands, while the tin industry enveloped both urban and rural parts in the county.[128] In this way, local, regional, national and international commerce were interwoven. A number of scholars have argued that the English economy grew increasingly integrated in the changed world created by the Black Death and successor plagues, and both Cornwall and London increased their share of the realm's wealth.[129] As hillsides and even churchyards were excavated in the name of commerce, the tin workings gouged into the county's landscape formed potent reminders that there was no such thing as Cornish autarky.[130]

In point of fact, commercial connections relied on the administrative framework that covered the whole realm. Underpinning many transactions,

---

[124] Cf. R. H. Britnell, 'Urban Demand and the English Economy, 1300–1600', in *Urban Hinterlands*, pp. 1–21 at 4.

[125] Harriss, *Shaping the Nation*, p. 272; J. Hatcher and M. Bailey, *Modelling the Middle Ages: The History and Theory of England's Economic Development* (Oxford, 2001), p. 155; J. L. Bolton, *The Medieval English Economy, 1150–1500* (London, 1980).

[126] *RESDCornwall*, 258–259.

[127] *PROME*, iii, 389.

[128] Harriss, *Shaping the Nation*, pp. 271–272; Kene, 'Economic Hinterland', p. 71.

[129] R. H. Britnell, *The Commercialisation of English Society, 1000–1500* (Cambridge, 1993), pp. 155–203; P. Nightingale, 'The Growth of London in the Medieval English Economy', in *Progress and Problems in Medieval England*, ed. R. H. Britnell and J. Hatcher (Cambridge, 1996), pp. 89–106.

[130] *RBP*, ii, 122, 178.

credit was only so widely available because creditors possessed the legal instruments required to record and recover debts; and without these they would have been far more reticent to lend.[131] In this way, royal statutes were essential to English commerce. Since the king's officials enforced contracts made under its auspices, the royal government rendered this legislation more effective. It follows that the Crown's establishment of staple towns greatly influenced and benefited English commerce. We can see this in 1327, when the government ordered that the staples of hides, tin, wools and woolfells in England should be held at Bristol, Exeter, Lincoln, London, Newcastle-upon-Tyne, Norwich, Winchester and York; with the staple for 'tin of Cornwall' at Lostwithiel and Truro; and that for 'tin of Devonshire' at Ashburton.[132] Royal licences for staples, fairs and boroughs helped to nourish commercial centres, while the Crown's policing and maintenance of highways encouraged trade between these market places.[133]

Together, the king, the earl-duke and Cornwall's residents sought to manage the county's wealth. This becomes especially apparent when we consider how the Black Prince and 'the mayor and good men of the town of Lostwithiel' combined forces to lobby Edward III for 'a seal for the recognisances of debt pursuant to the statute merchant'.[134] Establishing just such a staple in 1341, the king placed the 'larger piece' of the seal in the custody of the mayor and the 'smaller piece' in the charge of a clerk appointed by him and his heirs. Accordingly, in 1357 the prince is found employing one William de Bakton, a yeoman of his buttery, as 'clerk of the statute within the duchy of Cornewaille'.[135] Bakton's task was to enforce law and business agreements in the Cornish peninsula with royal, seigniorial and urban administrations alike. The prince actually helped to draw Cornwall into the commercial mainstream by himself taking part in the selling of tin to London pewterers and others.[136] All this activity reduced internal trade barriers, minimising transaction costs and fostering pan-English interactions.[137]

With so many lucrative deals struck, coinage was essential to English commerce. In contrast to the position in France, centralised minting was the norm in England and the Crown tightly controlled minting centres. Such monetary standardisation meant that English coinage provided a standard measure of

---

[131] Bolton, *Money*, p. 208.
[132] CPR 1327–1330, 98–99.
[133] Britnell, *Commercialisation*, pp. 16–18, 160–161; Bolton, *Money*, p. 23; *Markets and Fairs*, i, pp. 76–85.
[134] CPR 1340–1343, 223.
[135] RBP, ii, 111.
[136] RBP, ii, 170.
[137] Cf. Kowaleski, *Exeter*, pp. 179–221; Galloway, 'Grain Trade', p. 23.

value, a common unit of reckoning and exchange across the realm.[138] Bearing the image of the king as a guarantee of their weight and fineness, coins also possessed symbolic value that projected the sovereignty and majesty of the monarch.[139] The money in peoples' hands helped the realm to cohere, affording a constant reminder to people of their status as English subjects.[140] For the entertainment of their audiences, even the Cornish-language dramas had characters reckon values in pounds, nobles and pennies.[141] When one currency operated in the realm, the Crown naturally wished to introduce standardised weights and measures.[142] In this connection it is worth noting that in 1315 the commonalty of Cornwall petitioned Edward II requesting standardisation in accordance with Magna Carta, claiming that his officials and many folk were employing 'other measures and weights than are used elsewhere in the realm'.[143] Ten years later, Edward was to have the nine weights used for weighing tin committed to the mayor and sheriffs of London 'to agree with the king's standard of London', these tin-weights having become 'broken... by reason of their age', use and falsification.[144] The county's residents welcomed the introduction of national standards into their peninsula here, and as the century went on the Crown responded by passing more economic legislation.[145]

Whenever the county felt that its tinning and other commercial interests had been compromised, it launched a vociferous political defence of them. We find such an instance in the 1390s, when Cornish MPs complained that the removal of the staple for tin from Lostwithiel to Calais was 'to the very great loss of our lord the king and destruction of all the commons of the said county'.[146] All those who had commercial concerns to west of the Tamar – sundry Cornish folk, merchants from across the realm, the earl-duke and the king himself – helped to politically and economically draw Cornwall into the kingdom. This is shown by the fact that in 1346 the merchants and Commons of the whole realm lent their voice to a petition requesting that the king restrain the tinning policies of Tideman de Lymbergh.[147] Claiming in 1391 that 'in Cornwall there accrues a great commodity of the kingdom of England, that is tin', the

---

[138] Bolton, *Money*, pp. 20–21, 56–57, 240–241.
[139] Bolton, *Money*, pp. 20–21, 34.
[140] S. Piron, 'Monnaie et Majesté Royale dans le France DU 14ᵉ Siècle', *Annales Historie, Sciences Sociales*, 51 (1996), pp. 325–354 at 325–327.
[141] *Cornish Drama*, i, PC, lines 505, 3144; *Bewnans Ke*, lines 1169, 1211–1212, 2451; *Beunans Meriasek*, line 1464.
[142] Bolton, *Money*, pp. 28–30; Britnell, *Commercialisation*, pp. 173–174.
[143] *PROME*, iii, 101.
[144] *LBE*, 203–204; *CIM 1307–1349*, 211; *CCR 1323–1327*, 300.
[145] Cf. A. Musson and W. M. Ormrod, *The Evolution of English Justice: Law, Politics and Society in the Fourteenth Century* (Basingstoke, 1999), pp. 52–53, 89–96.
[146] *PROME*, vii, 217–218, 269–270.
[147] *PROME*, iv, 420.

parliamentary Commons were articulating views that circulated widely; even the fifteenth-century *Libelle of Englysche Polycye* referred to 'oure Englysshe commodytees, woole and tynne'.[148] Everyone knew that Cornwall was a major contributor to the common profit.

Since there were factors that weighed on the other side, however, neither the strength of government nor the integrated nature of the English economy should be overstressed. Especially in the mid-fourteenth century and from c. 1375 to c. 1415, bullion shortages challenged the monetised economy.[149] On numerous occasions the king is found investigating both the circulation of counterfeit coinage in Cornwall and the discrepancies in local weights and measures.[150] In 1390 the Crown even investigated John Kendale for having 'counterfeited the die of the king's seal for the statute merchant in Lostwithiel' and, just as seriously, the 'dies of the king's money'.[151] And while Cornish MPs petitioned for the defence of the tin industry, their fellows often employed violent self-help to bring about change more quickly. Nonetheless, the many interlinked strands of commercial connectivity, from networks of exchange and social interaction through to political considerations arising from trade, helped Cornwall cohere with the rest of England.

---

[148] *PROME*, vii, 217–218; *Libelle*, lines 89–90.
[149] Bolton, *Money*, pp. 163–164, 233–240.
[150] *CCR 1296–1302*, 412–413; *CFR 1327–1337*, 491; *CPR 1345–1348*, 170, 182, 307; *Carew*, 54r–54v; Bolton, *Money*, p. 30.
[151] *CPR 1388–1392*, 360.

12

Lawless Judges and Litigious Cornishmen: Legal Connectivity

Royal jurisdiction was to play a vital role in integrating England politically, for the law formed the essence of government and was a major force for connectivity.[1] Enjoying a virtual monopoly on criminal proceedings across the kingdom, the Crown's judicial agencies reached to the furthest corners of Cornwall in a standard (common) form.[2] In sharp contrast to the position in parts of Wales, where distinct Welsh and English judicial systems prevailed, the common law regarded all Cornishmen and women as English.[3] In Cornwall the peace was the king's peace, symbolically drawing the county into the realm.

Across the fourteenth century the scope of both statute and common law greatly expanded throughout England. Royal courts increasingly drew pleas concerning debt into their competence, while the king passed and enforced a burgeoning number of statutes. Statute law came to regulate spheres of life which had never before fallen within the purview of royal justice, among these wage levels.[4] Unsurprisingly, procedural and institutional changes were to match these developments. In the thirteenth century the eyre had formed one of the main instruments of royal government, the justices visiting each county every seven years or so and, once there, hearing all cases concerning that

---

[1] For the best introductions, see J. H. Baker, *An Introduction to English Legal History*, 4th Edition (Bath, 2002); Musson and Ormrod, *English Justice*; A. L. Brown, *The Governance of Medieval England, 1272–1461* (London, 1989), pp. 100--140; Harriss, *Shaping the Nation*, pp. 47–58.
[2] Musson and Ormrod, *English Justice*, p. 1; Harriss, *Shaping the Nation*, p. 41.
[3] Cf. Davies, *March of Wales*, pp. 158–161, 302–318; for instance, YB 11 Edward II, 113–114; YB 12 & 13 Edward III, 70–73; YB 2 Richard II, 94–100; for year books, P. Brand, *Observing and Recording the Medieval Bar and Bench at Work: The Origins of Law Reporting in England* (London, 1999).
[4] Musson and Ormrod, *English Justice*, pp. 89–96, 147–157.

locality.[5] Since the eyre collapsed under its own weight in the early-fourteenth century, however, the Crown had to find new mechanisms of enforcing its legal prerogatives. The solution it alighted upon involved the justices of the peace. In the years before 1330 the keepers of the peace had possessed only modest authority, but by the 1360s their successors, the justices of the peace, had amassed considerable judicial powers. It followed that the range of responsibilities that the Crown devolved to these local officers greatly increased.[6] These local agents, however, never achieved a monopoly on the local dispensation of justice. Bringing with them national practices and precedents in both civil and criminal matters, the central court justices who sat on commissions of assize and gaol delivery in the provinces and on the quorum of each county bench closely supervised the local magistracy.[7] In this way, the Crown and the shires together forged a remarkably integrated system of royal jurisdiction across the realm, a more pervasive 'national' legal culture.[8]

While such developments helped to weld England into a more coherent juridical entity, in practice, the workings of the law were greatly tempered by the customs and traditions of particular localities. Three main legal traditions took root in England in the middle ages: common law, canon law and customary law.[9] The common law, as we have already noted, consisted of a standardised body of pan-English judicial customs authorised by the king himself. Canon law, by contrast, was composed of papal decretals and Roman civil-law traditions regulating clerical conduct and cases concerning morality. The most amorphous of the three, customary law consisted of a range of localised practices interpreted in accordance with local 'custom' or convention. As elsewhere in the realm, Cornwall contained a striking variety of courts in which these many different types of laws were pleaded, a point made apparent by considering the workings of just a few of these tribunals.

At the local staple court at Lostwithiel, for example, Cornishmen and women could register debts so as to secure repayment, the recognizances sealed there empowering the creditor, if necessary, to pursue the debtor through the joint action of this tribunal and the chancery.[10] Also sitting at Lostwithiel and adjudicating over business deals and interactions arising overseas or below the tide mark, the admiralty's tribunal in Cornwall came to enjoy considerable sway over the county's commercial and maritime affairs.[11] Back on land

---

[5] Baker, *Legal History*, p. 16; Crook, 'Later Eyres'.
[6] Above, pp. 25–28; Musson and Ormrod, *English Justice*, pp. 50–54, 74.
[7] For instance, JUST1/1330 mm. 1–49r; JUST1/1476 mm. 68r–82r.
[8] Musson and Ormrod, *English Justice*, pp. 53, 73–74.
[9] Musson, *Legal Consciousness*, pp. 9–10.
[10] For example, C241/219/1.
[11] *Select Pleas in the Court of the Admiralty: The Court of the Admiralty of the West (AD 1390–1404) and The High Court of the Admiralty (AD 1527–1545)*, ed. R. G. Marsden,

but remaining with commercial litigation, the peninsula's numerous borough courts were similarly involved in the enforcement of mercantile law and traders' customs.[12] Although institutions of this sort exercised jurisdiction over many Cornish towns, in Fowey, for example, the manorial court remained the chief judicial organ, overseen by the prior of Tywardreath.[13] At the same time as implementing the customary law of the manor of Fowey, this local tribunal enforced the prior's seigniorial rights of assize of bread and ale. Manorial courts of this sort administered each manor to west of the Tamar, regulating the lives of their inhabitants in accordance with village customs and by-laws; the courts at Lanhadron and Gready, for example, are to be found adjudicating over matters as varied as Odo Watte's defamation of Robert Parov as a 'false harlot' and John Tyrell's grinding of black tin in the local mill 'to the serious damage of the lord's tenants'.[14]

Hearing many cases, hundredal tribunals enjoyed a wider-ranging judicial and geographic jurisdiction than those of the manor. We see this in 1333, when the hundredal court at Penwith investigated numerous cases of trespass and debt-detinue from across the large Penwith peninsula at the tip of Cornwall.[15] In some sense hundreds may be seen as constituting the nexus where manorial and royal jurisdictions intersected, for twice a year the sheriff undertook his tourn in which hundredal justice was supervised by an officer of the Crown. The sheriff also convened the county court on behalf of the king, the earl-duke and the commonalty, a tribunal which adjudicated over outlawries and more substantial pleas than those dealt with by the hundreds.[16] Outside the regular system, the earl-duke exercised a form of equitable jurisdiction in his council, one on which the county's residents are often found calling.[17] One such supplicant was John Coulyng, who in 1353 sought the Black Prince's intervention during a dispute with Sir John Beaupel over the ownership of a tin mine. Commanding his ministers to investigate Coulyng's claims that during the feud one of his brothers had been murdered and his house burnt down, the prince had this petition enrolled in his register as a formal record. Beyond even the earldom-duchy's competences stood a whole hierarchy of ecclesiastical courts,

---

2 vols, Selden Society, 6, 11 (London, 1894–7), i, pp. xlix–l, 1–2; below, pp. 296–297, 301.

[12] Cf. Musson, *Legal Consciousness*, p. 11.
[13] *Quo Warranto*, p. 109; S. J. Drake, 'Pirates and Pilchards: the Wealth and Peopling of Fowey during the Hundred Years War', *JRIC* (2015), pp. 23–44 at 24–26.
[14] CRO, ART/2/3 mm. 2–3; ART/2/341; P. R. Hyams, 'What did Edwardian Villagers understand by 'Law'?', in *Medieval Society and the Manor Court*, ed. Z. Razzi and R. Smith (Oxford, 1996), pp. 69–102; L. Bonfield, 'What did English Villagers means by Customary Law?', *idem.*, pp. 103–116.
[15] 'Three courts', p. 181; above, pp. 35–36.
[16] SC2/161/74 mm. 1–11; above, pp. 47–48.
[17] *RBP*, ii, 51; above, pp. 212–213.

ultimately stretching up to the pope himself.[18] Especially in relation to civil pleas, this jurisdictional complexity renders the Crown's ascendancy less absolute than it at first appears.

Possessing officials, procedures and precedents of their own, each of these jurisdictions in some sense constituted its own legal system. Yet no court in fourteenth-century Cornwall enjoyed full jurisdictional finality, a point which becomes apparent when considering the stannaries. By ancient tradition each stannary bailiwick was headed by a bailiff whose task it was to enforce the customary law of tinners. Edward I had enshrined this convention in a charter of 1305 which, among other things, had freed tinners from local manorial justice.[19] Accordingly, the stannary courts exercised a civil and minor criminal jurisdiction over debts, detinue, replevin and 'any plea or quarrel' arising within their bounds.[20] These courts, however, did not remove tinners from 'pleas of life, land, and limb', the essence of royal justice. In 1312, for instance, when a couple of tinners, William Brondel and Gilbert de Talgarrek, were hauled before the king's justices on a plea of theft, the men claimed that as tinners they could only be tried in stannary courts, even producing a copy of the stannary charter to prove their case.[21] As tinning officials did not enjoy the determining power in criminal cases, however, they were only able to indict criminal tinners before turning them over for trial by royal justices of gaol delivery.[22] Peace in the stannaries belonged to the king, who at times can be found prosecuting corrupt tinning officials themselves.[23]

Since the stannary courts did not enjoy jurisdiction over criminal cases, it is not altogether surprising that they held no complete monopoly on civil tinning pleas either. Some tinners, such as John Zeke of Roche for example, might register their debts in staple courts and yet later be pursued in chancery by their creditors, as Zeke was in 1399, for the 4,000 lbs of white tin that he owed to Thomas Amarle and Henry Richard of Bodmin.[24] Even though sundry folk could claim to be tinners, the stannaries could never serve as a separate Cornish jurisdiction because the competence of these tribunals was simply too narrow. In 1337 the stannary courts yielded a mere £17 in fines.[25] The

[18] Below, p. 274.
[19] CChR 1300–1326, 53–54; Lewis, *Stannaries*, pp. 39, 158–159; R. R. Pennington, *Stannary Law: A History of the Mining Law of Cornwall and Devon* (Newton Abbot, 1973), pp. 72–101; Hatcher, *Tin*, p. 48.
[20] PROME, v, 347–348; *Les Reports des Cases en Ley: En le Cinque an du Roy Edward le Quart Communement Appelle Long Quinto* (London, 1680), pp. 34–35; Hatcher, *Tin*, pp. 48, 52; SC2/156/26.
[21] JUST1/109 m. 6r.
[22] JUST/3/120 m. 23r; CPR 1385–1389, 461–462.
[23] For example, KB9/9 m. 39.
[24] C241/188/105.
[25] CS, lvi.

Commons of Cornwall were in no doubt that the stannaries existed within the king's grace, even if at times tinning courts operated beyond their jurisdictional bounds. This is shown by the fact that in 1376 the county commonalty petitioned Edward III through parliament requesting that he investigate the 'customs and usages' of the stannary-men, who had allegedly been causing 'oppressions... by colour of their franchise'.[26] The king responded by having the fact that tinners remained subject to his jurisdiction in pleas of 'life, land, and limb' enrolled in the Parliament Rolls themselves.

While no court in the county held anything like monopoly powers, local practices and tribunals could still prove significant. The eyre rolls of 1284 and 1302, for example, show that Cornwall enjoyed the special right to sue without writ in cases of mesne and dower.[27] In the bustling port of Fowey, the manorial court played an essential role in regulating the town's collective life by investigating such matters as small debts, loose pigs and drunken brawls, even hearing of the way in which Joan and her daughter, another Joan, were living 'suspiciously with great expense and no income'.[28] In 1459, however, when Hanys Dutyshman drew a sword on John Scote, jurors from Fowey chose to present him to the king's justices.[29] One hundred and fifty-seven years earlier, in the *Quo Warranto* proceedings of 1302, the prior of Tywardreath in Fowey and all Cornwall's leading proprietors had secured royal confirmation of their liberties, accepting the king's overarching jurisdiction while defending their local prerogative rights.[30]

When we turn from civil to criminal jurisdiction, we find that a far higher degree of integration with the wider realm was achieved, with a unified criminal justice system operating across the entire country. In the course of the fourteenth century the bench of JPs in Cornwall was to gain in stature and importance, bringing the king, the earl-duke and the commonalty together in the enforcement of the law. Supervising criminal justice across the peninsula, the justices of gaol delivery tried at Launceston felons indicted before the county's sheriff-stewards, coroners, peace commissioners and hundredal officials alike.[31] As the Crown linked together the circuits of gaol delivery with those of assize, the latter hearing civil pleas and cases of title to land, all this activity had the effect of drawing royal criminal and civil justice to west of the Tamar.[32] Across the fourteenth century, in fact, public demand resulted in a 'relentless growth in the scope and scale of civil actions undertaken in the

---

[26] *PROME*, v, 347–348.
[27] 'Three Courts', p. 173.
[28] CRO, ART/2/1 mm. 1–13, 7.
[29] CRO, ART/2/1 m. 10.
[30] *Quo Warranto*, pp. 108–111.
[31] JUST3/120 m. 23; JUST3/121 m. 13; JUST3/156 mm. 42–46.
[32] Cf. Musson, *Public Order*, pp. 95, 109–110, 121.

royal courts'.[33] It was gentle society that most enjoyed the luxury of choosing in which court to sue, but a large and growing number of sub-gentry folk can be found bringing cases before the assizes and common pleas, as even the lowliest peasant was drawn into 'the common law ambit' by everything from litigation to jury service.[34] Since the royal courts kept all 'lesser authorities within the procedural and jurisdictional bounds of the law', and the king himself retained the right to administer justice outside the regular system, England, Cornwall included, played host to an integrated hierarchy of tribunals.[35] Across the realm royal sovereignty stood out as transcendent, with the *Quo Warranto* proceedings affording evidence of the length of the king's judicial reach and his role as the judge of last resort in Cornwall.

In practice, England's legal culture was even more complex than a brisk survey of the outlines of its structure would suggest. As the king possessed no proper police force, the enforcement of justice depended on the voluntary co-operation of the local gentry. Yet unpaid gentlemen in general and those resident in Cornwall in particular had a penchant for lawlessness, undermining the local peace. A culture of violence influenced the operation of the king's tribunals in the peninsula, not least as litigants often chose to employ both direct action and the law to bring pressure on their adversaries.[36] Sometimes the many overlapping jurisdictions in the county are also to be found in opposition, as in 1351 for example, when the Black Prince commanded his steward to continue investigations into 'piracy', despite the defendant having obtained a writ in 'the king's chancery on wanton allegations' to halt enquires.[37] In every way, local traditions, the local impact of lordship and the local workings of society had the effect of tempering the direct impact of the law. Even allowing for this, however, the point still stands that a system of remarkably pervasive royal jurisdiction operated in the county and across the realm. With the king generally launching investigations in response to complaints made by his subjects, Cornishmen and women themselves invited the law's involvement in their disputes.

Since the law came to regulate more and more aspects of everyday life, the Crown's legal omnipresence increasingly impinged on the legal consciousness of Cornwall's residents.[38] No free person in the county could be ignorant of the importance of due process and documentation, a situation attested to by their regular purchase of royal charters, the care taken over the drawing-up and

[33] Musson and Ormrod, *English Justice*, p. 127.
[34] Hyams, '"Law"?', p. 75; Bonfield, 'Customary Law', p. 113; for example, *YB 30 & 31 Edward I*, 154–155.
[35] Baker, *Legal History*, pp. 98, 143.
[36] Above, pp. 127, 129, 131–132.
[37] *RBP*, ii, 12–13.
[38] Musson, *Legal Consciousness*, pp. 18, 89, 101, 217.

preservation of deeds and the careful affixation of legally binding seals to such documents.[39] A good example of this comes from 1386, when Oliver Wysa, sensitive to the need to have his document attested by someone whose seal would be widely recognised, asked the dean of Eastwivelshire to attach his seal to an indenture leasing out the hundred of Eastwivelshire because his own seal remained 'unknown to many'.[40] As numerous men were typically to witness each agreement, legal documents helped to propagate an appreciation of the law's scope and significance. In 1302 one Ralph Arundell attached such importance to his muniments that, after Sir Roger Ingepenne had stolen them, he went to the trouble of bringing a plea before the justices to secure their recovery.[41]

Recourse to the king's courts was to lay bare the essential functions of the law, for many Cornishmen and women can be shown to have called on royal tribunals to secure a settlement of their disputes, not least in such sensitive cases as title to land.[42] From the 1330s, when they regularly requested the appointment of commissions of oyer and terminer to investigate grievances of theirs, the peninsula's residents invited yet more royal intervention in county affairs. We find just such an instance in 1343, when one Matilda, the widow of Sir Thomas l'Ercedekne, sought three commissions of this kind to investigate the theft of her cattle and assaults on her 'men and servants'.[43] At the same time as introducing a wide cross-section of Cornish society to the niceties of the law, the array of royal tribunals depended for their working on the participation of magistrates and jurors drawn from the locality.

Indeed, the expansion of local officialdom across the century extended the magistracy, broadening and deepening legal knowledge among the county's landed populace. With the king levying a £20 fine on the sheriff Sir William Talbot for his failure to deliver a prisoner to the court of common pleas, the government could hold Cornishmen to account for the enforcement of royal justice.[44] Even malefactors cannot have been entirely ignorant of the fact that the peace belonged to the king, for they were risking heavy punishments at the hands of his justices. After being indicted for the murder of John Trefurthken in 1344, for example, John, the son of John Arundell, and eight others knew that to avoid royal justice they had no alternative but to flee the county and 'lie low' elsewhere.[45] Legal knowledge was widespread enough for the Cornish-language *Ordinalia* plays to employ the terminology of the law for the

---

[39] CRO, BLAUS/44; AR/4/415; *Markets and Fairs*, i, pp. 76–85.
[40] CRO, CY/1929.
[41] KB27/171 m. 63d.
[42] *FF, passim.*
[43] *CPR 1343–1345*, 181.
[44] *CPR 1396–1399*, 141.
[45] *CPR 1343–1345*, 393.

entertainment of their audiences. In the *Origo Mundi*, for example, King David rewarded his messenger with a charter (*chartour*) for lands in Carnsew and elsewhere, while later in the play the character of the bishop issued an order to take seizin (*sesa*) of Bosanath in Mawnan.[46] The second play, *Passio Christi*, even parodied the workings of the law. In this drama, a courtroom wrangle takes place in which Pilate passes judgment on criminals, and although the jailor and his servant 'bring out the thieves', the officials themselves clashed about wages and service agreements.[47] To detain his recalcitrant employee, the jailor, supposedly the worst master west of Trigg, then employed a writ of *capias*. Sometimes co-operating with legal process and sometimes subverting and even lampooning it, Cornwall's residents were nonetheless at every point absorbing a legal consciousness.

As a result of all these legal developments, Cornish perceptions of the law evolved and generally became more positive. Whereas in 1233, for example, the Cornish had fled into the woods to avoid an eyre, in 1315 the county commonalty petitioned Edward II to keep 'his peace in accordance with his oath', as 'many serious trespasses' supposedly went unpunished.[48] Since local expectations of law and order had grown in the meantime, by 1315 the commonalty were keen to seek out royal intervention and the king responded by endorsing the petition with a promise to dispatch justices to the peninsula. Across the later middle ages Cornwall's residents grew increasingly litigious, so that by the sixteenth century they would supposedly 'try the Law... for waggyng of a straw'.[49] It follows that both royal ambitions and 'consumer demand' between them drove the expansion of regnal justice and jurisdiction in the peninsula. John Trevisa took great satisfaction in fourteenth-century Cornwall being 'i-ruled by the lawe of Engelond', a condition that he viewed as vital in securing the county's place in the kingdom.[50] Protecting the traditions underpinning collective identity, laws formed an essential aspect of a medieval people. Writing of the Anglo-Irish, R. R. Davies has argued that their 'use of English law was a triumphant affirmation of their Englishness, of their sense of belonging to a greater English community'; much the same can be said to hold true for the inhabitants of every English shire, Cornwall amongst them.[51] Forging a juridical England, the law was a potent bonding agent which in practice and imagination manufactured unity within the realm.

[46] *Cornish Drama*, i, OM, lines 2311–2312, 2766–2769.
[47] *Cornish Drama*, i, PC, lines 2231–2268; G. J. Betcher, 'Translating a Labour Dispute in the Cornish *Ordinalia* within a Legal Context', *Fourteenth Century England, I*, ed. N. Saul (Woodbridge, 2000), pp. 89–102.
[48] *Annales Monastici*, iii, p. 135; *PROME*, iii, 100–101.
[49] Boorde, *Knowledge*, p. 122; Chynoweth, *Tudor Cornwall*, pp. 278–306.
[50] Trevisa, trans., *Polychronicon*, ii, p. 91.
[51] Davies, 'Laws and Customs', 5.

With both the legal system and the law itself moulded by the actions of practitioners, it is worth considering the role of personal agency' in the development of a legal consciousness. Since Cornwall was included in the south-western assize circuit, every time the assize justices visited the county they brought with them their legal expertise and the accumulations of years of experience on the bench. Among the justices who visited the peninsula was Sir William Shareshull, a man who played a key role in shaping the workings of the judicial system in the middle years of the century.[52] Issuing demands on behalf of their king and listening to claims and counter-claims, the justices can be found interacting with Cornishmen and women grand and modest alike.[53] No one in Cornwall could fail to recognise their power, nor the fact that these men were the personifications of royal justice. Acting as a point of contact between the county and the Crown, the assize justices also informed the king about conditions in the peninsula, providing him with a 'worm's eye view' of the far south west. With the introduction of a quorum of central court justices onto the county bench, the Crown was able to bring yet more men of law into the peninsula, including Henry de Perchay, the chief baron of the exchequer and a justice of the common pleas, who was to sit on the Cornish bench throughout the 1370s.

Inevitably, Cornishmen and women interacted with justices at hearings at Westminster itself. A good example is afforded by a case in 1324, when one William Blundel is found bringing a suit to the king's bench *in persona* against Michael Trenewith the elder, Trenewith having allegedly assaulted him *contra pacem et contra forma statuta*.[54] Sometimes incidents of violence were committed actually in the presence of the justices. We see this in 1380, when Isabel Mohun brought a case of abduction against Sir Henry Ilcombe, who again assaulted her and those who rushed to her aid, all within sight of the justices of the common pleas.[55] If litigants were unwilling or unable to travel, they could instead employ a professional attorney to plead on their behalf. Many Cornish folk chose to employ this latter option, with attorneys such as John Mark making handsome livings as a result.[56] Information also travelled; attorneys communicated with their clients about the course of cases, while courts sent writs regarding trials and judgments to the sheriff who then

---

[52] For instance, JUST1/1445 m. 51r; Putnam, *William Shareshull*; A. Musson, 'Centre and Locality: Perceptions of the Assize Justices in Late Medieval England', in *Law, Governance, and Justice: New Views on Medieval Constitutionalism*, ed. R. W. Kaeuper (Leiden, 2013), pp. 211–242.
[53] *YB 30 & 31 Edward I*, 74–78, 84–85, 240–241.
[54] KB27/254 m. 85r, although this was subsequently crossed through.
[55] *HOP*, iii, 472–474.
[56] KB27/227 m. 73r.

returned suspected criminals under guard.[57] With Cornish gentlemen and lawyers such as John Tremayne, Thomas Tregora and Robert Cary mainprising folk as varied as Roger Snell of Winchester, Philip Smith of Surrey and John Windsor of London, the law helped to tie the county into national networks of connectivity.[58]

When we turn from the workings of the courts to the personnel who staffed them, it is important to remember that no clear distinction can be maintained between the justices of the central courts and the justices or pleaders who heard cases locally. There are numerous examples of Cornish men of law who went on to forge successful careers at the centre. At the peak of the fourteenth-century legal profession stood the serjeants-at-law, the men who held a monopoly on pleading at the bar in the common pleas, the busiest court in England.[59] By Edward III's reign the serjeants had grown into a fraternity known as the order of the coif, identified by the wearing of a distinctive attire. In the fourteenth century no fewer than five Cornishmen can be identified as attaining this prestigious dignity: John Penrose, John Tremayne, Robert Tresilian, John Trevaignon and Simon Trewythosa.[60]

Our first serjeant, Simon Trewythosa, took the coif in 1332. Although his origins are obscure, his abilities were evidently sufficient to enable him both to establish a busy practice in Cornwall, for clients as eminent as Sir John Petit, and at the same time periodically to represent the county in parliament.[61] In due course he became a trusted royal servant, in 1336 advising on legal matters 'touching the king' himself.[62] Naturally enough, Trewythosa also looked after his own interests, acquiring lands in Cornwall and Somerset and lending some 500 marks to Richard, Lord Grey of Codnor.[63] In contrast to Trewythosa's modest background, John Tremayne hailed from an established Cornish legal and parliamentary dynasty.[64] Sitting on the county bench for nearly twenty years, Tremayne took a keen interest in the government of Cornwall. He, too, established a successful legal practice which attracted prominent local gentlemen, among them the Bodrugans, and drew clients from outside the county. Tremayne went on to sit in parliament for Truro in 1388, suggesting that many

---

[57] For example, *SCKB*, iii, 150.
[58] *CCR 1381–1385*, 43–44; *CCR 1385–1389*, 466; *CCR 1392–1396*, 48.
[59] See, J. H. Baker, *The Order of the Serjeants at Law: A Chronicle of Creation, with Related Texts and an Historical Introduction*, Selden Society, Supplementary Series 5 (London, 1984).
[60] Baker, *Serjeants*, pp. 530, 541.
[61] *CPR 1330–1334*, 581; CRO, ME/1245.
[62] *CCR 1333–1337*, 677; Baker, *Serjeants*, p. 541.
[63] *FF*, i, 300, 321–323; *CCR 1337–1339*, 124; *CIPM*, viii, 156; *CCR 1339–1341*, 286; *CFR 1337–1347*, 141.
[64] *HOP*, iv, 646–648.

esteemed his advocacy. Less than eight months later the City of London was to appoint him a common serjeant, subsequently promoting him to the capital's recordership. Tremayne's career continued to blossom even after he had landed this plum position, as in 1401 he took the coif and by 1404 he held a prominent place on Henry IV's council. While the law had raised both these men to positions of power, the three Cornishmen whom the king appointed to the judicial bench were to rise yet further still. These were John Penrose, Robert Tresilian and John Trevaignon.

Probably hailing from the minor gentry, John Trevaignon was the first Cornishman to be called to the rank of serjeant, back in 1313.[65] His busy career saw him sit on numerous judicial commissions and debate complex points of law with his fellows.[66] Trevaignon rose through the ranks too, being appointed a king's serjeant in 1329 and serving on the king's behalf in places as diverse as Kent and Cornwall.[67] Although his knowledge of the Cornish peninsula proved especially indispensable, not all his investigations ran smoothly. In 1332 Edward III had appointed Trevaignon to investigate 'oppressions' by some of his father's ministers in the county, including Sir John Treiagu. Perhaps in response, Treiagu and twenty-six other malefactors then assembled 'a great mob, mounted and on foot' which allegedly assaulted Trevaignon's house at Great Gothers, near St Dennis.[68] It was claimed that during this assault the wrongdoers had abducted Trevaignon's wife, one Joan, imprisoned and threatened to murder his servants and destroyed his property, all while he was engaged elsewhere on the king's service. Trevaignon, however, was to have his revenge. A royal inquisition found Treiagu guilty of the assault and imprisoned him, with Trevaignon then refusing to accept damages allegedly 'in order to vex' Treiagu 'by a long imprisonment'.[69]

In 1334 Trevaignon reached the peak of his career when he was appointed to the bench of the common pleas itself.[70] He sat in the court for only a short time, however, as he died a year later.[71] In the course of his career, Trevaignon had acquired lands in west Dorset and he is commemorated by a freestone effigy in Trent church near Sherborne in that county, on which he is depicted wearing the coif, the symbol of his office and the source of his success.[72] Trevaignon

---

[65] Baker, *Serjeants*, p. 541.
[66] *CPR 1313–1317*, 582, 596; *YB 11 Edward II*, 47–52; *CPR 1324–1327*, 238–239.
[67] *CPR 1327–1330*, 351; *CCR 1333–1337*, 155; *CCR 1327–1330*, 476–477; *CPR 1330–1334*, 133, 198, 348.
[68] *CPR 1330–1334*, 350.
[69] *CFR 1327–1337*, 357.
[70] *CPR 1334–1338*, 12.
[71] JUST1/1418 m. 20r; *CPR 1334–1338*, 69, 72, 201.
[72] *FA*, iv, 342–343; N. Saul, *English Church Monuments in the Middle Ages: History and Representation* (Oxford, 2009), pp. 277–278.

had never forgotten his natal county, however, as he went out of his way to acquire properties in Cornwall and can be found suing in the county court, with his kinsmen a continuing presence west of the Tamar.[73] As Trewythosa and Trevaignon had actually sat on commissions together, it is quite possible that Trevaignon sponsored his fellow Cornish 'man of law'.[74]

Our next serjeant, the redoubtable John Penrose, was probably a kinsman of Sir Vivian Penrose and, like Trevaignon, was of minor gentry stock.[75] Penrose was to begin his career as a local lawyer too, sitting on the county bench throughout the late 1370s. Yet despite his appointments, he was by no means fastidiously law-abiding. On the contrary, he formed a close alliance with John Trevarthian and Sir Ralph Carminow, two well-known law breakers.[76] In 1381 Lady Elizabeth Botreaux alleged that all three were 'enemys' of her husband, Sir William, having procured a false indictment for his treason while he fought on campaign in Portugal. At this time Penrose also led an assault on Botreaux's manor of Trembethow, which the latter had recovered from him at law, while indicting for treason one of Botreaux's tenants, a certain Richard Eyr, before dispatching people to kill him.[77]

Since the Eyrs held a place in the affinity of the Sergeaux family, it is unsurprising that Penrose is found drawn into the long and violent feud which broke out at this time between the Sergeauxs, on the one hand, and the Trevarthians and Carminows on the other. Back in 1377 the Carminows had secured Penrose's appointment to hear an assize of *novel disseisin* against Sir Richard Sergeaux, no doubt to humble their joint foe.[78] In 1378, however, Sir Richard struck back in his capacity as justice of the peace by having Penrose indicted for a felony.[79] Later in this same year Penrose himself gained a place on the county bench, hearing allegations of Sergeaux's treason and other felonies. The tables were turned once again in 1380, when the king commanded Penrose to appear in chancery from 'day to day upon warning' under penalty of £100, before imprisoning him in the Marshalsea.[80] Scenting victory, in 1383 Botreaux and Sergeaux combined forces to bring about the arrest of Penrose and twenty-five others for a felony committed in Surrey.[81] Although Penrose secured his release from gaol in London soon after, this proved to be a bruising affair.[82]

---

[73] FF, i, 284, 293, 310–312, 315; SC2/161/74 m. 2; HOP, iv, 657.
[74] CPR 1330–1334, 581; CCR 1339–1341, 286.
[75] CPR 1385–1389, 394.
[76] Tyldesley, 'Local Communities', pp. 22–23.
[77] SC8/277/13838.
[78] Tyldesley, 'Local Communities', pp. 136–138; above, pp. 153–156.
[79] CCR 1377–1381, 126.
[80] CCR 1377–1381, 374; CPR 1377–1381, 569.
[81] CPR 1381–1385, 352.
[82] CCR 1381–1385, 412.

Penrose's willingness to indulge in lawless behaviour had thus been made clear. Yet remarkably in 1385 the king himself gave him employment, appointing Penrose to the county bench and promoting him to the influential post of justice of the king's bench in Ireland.[83] Still his behaviour raised questions, however, and in 1386 he withdrew from Ireland without leave; two years later the government imprisoned him in the Tower.[84] Collectively standing surety to secure his release, his fellow serjeants-at-law nonetheless chose to rally round him.[85] Neither did Penrose's thuggery form a bar to further office-holding, for in 1389 the king once again appointed him to the county bench. Even more extraordinarily, in 1391 Richard II raised him to the rank of puisne justice of the king's bench in England, granting him lavish robes and an additional yearly income of 50 marks for his troubles.[86]

On attaining one of the highest offices in the land, Penrose once again turned his energies to quashing the Sergeauxs. To this end, he adjudicated over a case brought by Peter Trelewith (Trevarthian's man) alleging that William Eyr (Sergeaux's man) had encouraged Trelewith to murder Penrose himself in London.[87] Under the combined scrutiny of the chief justices of the king's bench and common pleas, along with the chief baron of the exchequer, the chancellor, treasurer and many more ministers, Trelewith admitted that he had been put up to bringing this false charge by Penrose, his brother, one Josse Penrose and a certain Alan St Just. On hearing this, the king once again imprisoned Penrose in the Tower, dispatching Josse to the Marshalsea and St Just and Trelewith to the Fleet, where the latter remained incarcerated for 'almost a year'. This time leading Cornishmen, among them Sir John Arundell of Lanherne, stood mainprise for the mendacious judge, to the tune of 500 marks.[88] Even this made little dent in Penrose's career, however, as in the following year he was appointed a justice in the royal lordship of Haverford in South Wales.[89] Considering his previous record, it is unsurprising that his judgments were soon called into question and that he never again sat as a judge after 1393.[90]

Throughout his life Penrose had set about acquiring estates in Cornwall, working closely in this with his brother, Josse.[91] Being a man of law, he was only too happy to turn to the courts to protect his hard-earnt and hard-won

---

[83] *CPR 1381–1385*, 534; *CPR 1385–1389*, 8, 80; Baker, *Serjeants*, p. 530.
[84] *CCR 1385–1389*, 534; *CPR 1388–1392*, 93; *SCKB*, vii, xii.
[85] *CCR 1385–1389*, 629.
[86] *CPR 1388–1392*, 364, 374.
[87] *SCKB*, vii, xii–xiii, 77–80; Tyldesley, 'Local Communities', p. 23.
[88] *CCR 1389–1391*, 271, 376; *CCR 1392–1396*, 2–3.
[89] *CPR 1391–1396*, 56.
[90] *CPR 1391–1396*, 359, 445, 523.
[91] *CCR 1389–1392*, 289, 351; *FF*, i, 402–403; ii, 2–3, 23, 36.

properties.[92] He can even be shown to have built up a small retinue of local supporters, in 1391 granting Peter Trelewith a tenement 'for his good service'.[93] To secure his interests, he made a point of propagating connections with other Cornish lawyers. When in Ireland, for example, he appointed as his attorney one Andrew Borlas, who oversaw a busy practice himself from the 1380s and had the expertise required to defend Penrose's estates; and in 1391 the Helston-based lawyer Roger Trewythenick was one of the men who stood mainprise for him.[94] Also making a good marriage in the county, Penrose acquired the hand and lands of one Joan Giffard, whose considerable dowry was confirmed to him by her brother after her death in 1392.[95] Penrose's career emphasises the intertwined nature of law and lawlessness, which together tied the county into the kingdom's legal culture.

It was Sir Robert Tresilian, however, who was the Cornishman to enjoy the most glittering legal career of all.[96] Although the man hailed from Cornwall, he is first recorded in the 1350s as providing legal advice in Oxfordshire and Berkshire. He for long retained his interests in the peninsula, however, in 1368 sitting as an MP for the county and from 1370 until his death serving nearly continuously on the Cornish bench. The Black Prince himself gave him employment in the duchy from at least 1375.[97] Tresilian's career continued to blossom when he was created serjeant-at-law in 1376, and just one year later Richard II retained him as a king's serjeant and nominated him as steward of the duchy.[98] Further promotion was to follow when in 1378 the king raised him to the rank of puisne justice of the king's bench, dubbing him a banneret. He continued as a puisne judge until 1381 when he was appointed to succeed Chief Justice Cavendish, who had been murdered by the rebels in the Great Revolt. Holding a place among the foremost men of the kingdom, Tresilian then played an integral role in suppressing the revolt. He also became involved in England's febrile politics, acting as a key judicial ally of the king. On 13 February 1388, Richard II's adversaries sentenced Tresilian to death *in absentia* for his role in the sympathetic answers which the judges gave to Richard's questions about the prerogative in 1387, a few days later discovering him wearing a disguise in Westminster and dragging him off to hang at Tyburn. Although it had cost him his life, Tresilian had served as 'one of the principal architects of the "high" doctrine of the royal prerogative'.

---

[92] For instance, *YB 7 Richard II*, 44–46.
[93] *CCR 1389–1392*, 357.
[94] *HOP*, ii, 295; *CPR 1381–1385*, 352; *CCR 1389–1392*, 376.
[95] *CCR 1389–1392*, 536–537.
[96] L. Leland, 'Robert Tresilian', *ODNB*, lv, pp. 317–319.
[97] SC8/333/E1038.
[98] Baker, *Serjeants*, p. 541.

Yet for all his involvement in national affairs, Tresilian always remembered his natal county. He grew fat on the profits of his profession, investing much of this money in Cornish lands which he then defended with legal duress and physical force.[99] Being a man 'on the make' he also procured a good marriage, winning the hand of Emmeline Huish, who brought with her a substantial inheritance in Cornwall. Creating a web of Cornish dependents to further his interests, Tresilian ensured that one John Bodilly, his Cornish clerk and receiver, secured the keepership of the rolls of the king's bench itself. Tresilian perhaps supported his colleague Penrose as well, for the latter can be found mainprising him in 1385 when he leased Penwith.[100] Naturally enough, he developed connections with many Cornish lawyers, including Pascoe Polruddon and John Tregoose, all of whom promoted his aggrandisement while lining their own pockets.[101] Tresilian's towering ambitions had greatly influenced the workings of Cornwall and the wider kingdom, with the obit celebrated in the county on the anniversary of his death recording that 'Robert Tresilian, knight, chief justice of England, was attainted in the Parliament of the year 11 Richard 2 and was hung at Tyburn'.[102]

Looking beyond this elite group of serjeants and judges, there were many more Cornishmen who pursued legal careers. In the early-fourteenth century the law was less fully professionalised than it was to become later, when it drew in a wider body of practitioners.[103] Attorneys were active in the Cornish eyre of 1302, for instance, but they are all unnamed, as are those who in 1333 pleaded in the county court.[104] It actually remains difficult to identify men of law at this time. One possible candidate is Henry Trethewey, the sheriff-steward, whose legal training is suggested by his extensive involvement in officialdom. It is surely a mistake to regard judicial appointments outside Westminster as separate branches of the legal profession, as all these men were responsible for enforcing the laws. There can be little doubt, however, that across the century the legal profession was to expand and gain in definition. While initially only observing and taking notes from the serjeants, the apprentices-at-law emerged during this period and acquired the right to practice – aside from in the common pleas – forming a distinct group by the fifteenth century. At the

---

[99] CRO, SN/59; WM/16–17; R/569; *FF*, i, 393–394, 395–396, 410, 413–414, 416–417; ii, 17, 19–20; *CIM 1387–1393, passim.*; SC8/76/3770; SC8/54/2695; *CPR 1385–1389*, 541–542; *CPR 1389–1392*, 55.
[100] *HOP*, ii, 268–269; *CFR 1383–1391*, 90.
[101] *HOP*, iv, 106, 643–644.
[102] *TCO*, 33, 338.
[103] J. H. Baker, *The Legal Profession and the Common Law: Historical Essays* (London, 1986), pp. 75–98; N. Ramsay, 'What was the Legal Profession?', in *Profit, Piety*, pp. 62–71.
[104] *YB 30 & 31 Edward I*, 162; SC2/161/74 mm. 1–11.

local level, a body of apprentices came to exist which overlapped with their central court colleagues, handling the most prestigious local cases. Growing into what we would now term 'county solicitors', a much larger group of lawyers also developed below these provincial apprentices. Such national-level developments can be traced at the local level in Cornwall.

In the early years of the century it is possible to spot some Cornishmen who were to emerge onto the national stage later beginning their careers locally. One such figure was John Trenda, who originated from west of the Tamar and pleaded in the central courts on behalf of Cornish clients, including Eude of Treres in 1313.[105] Serving as an attorney for Cornishmen and Londoners alike, John Trellan also built up a busy practice at these tribunals and even counted the Botreaux family among his clients.[106] Since Cornish gentlemen regularly pursued their quarrels with one another in both the local and central courts, the disorderly ways of the county elite provided many lawyers with a good living. William Polgas, for example, while serving as Sir William Botreaux's attorney in the 1360s, acquired a place on the county peace sessions so as better to defend the interests of his employer. Enjoying solid reputations for their counsel, Cornish lawyers can be found representing folk from across England.[107]

The duchy administration formed another important source of employment for the county's lawyers, albeit not one that was always prompt in payment. Complaining in 1359 that 'although he has been the prince's attorney and has sued for him before the justices of "traillebaston" in their sessions in the counties, hundreds and courts of those parts for four years, to the prince's great advantage, he has not had any reward', John Trevenour of Fowey resorted to a bitterly worded petition to make his point.[108] In spite of somewhat tardy payment, one John Tremayne, a kinsman of the John Tremayne whom we have already met, made a handsome living providing legal advice and administrative 'know-how' to the duchy.[109] The Black Prince so appreciated his work that he granted him many gifts 'as a reward for his labours'.[110] Tremayne was a busy man whose advocacy many esteemed, chief among them Bishop Grandisson and Sir William Botreaux; serving the latter as a feoffee, he also sat in parliament for the county on no fewer than eleven occasions. In the cause of 'feathering his own nest', Tremayne invested the profits of his expertise in land and made a good match when he acquired the hand of a certain Isabel, the

---

[105] *YB 6 & 7 Edward II*, 14–15.
[106] *YB 11 Edward II*, 22–26, 47–52, 190–192.
[107] For example, *CCR 1381–1385*, 43–44.
[108] *RBP*, ii, 164.
[109] *RBP*, ii, 54, 98, 135, 169, 185; *RBP*, iv, 185, 351.
[110] *RBP*, ii, 212, 215, 116.

daughter of John Dabernon, onetime sheriff-steward of Cornwall.[111] His legal talents made his fortune, elevating the Tremaynes to new heights.

Since it was such a profitable profession, the law provided many Cornishmen with a good living. By the 1370s Cornish lawyers are to be found sitting frequently in parliament for the county's boroughs, no doubt because their expertise made them effective lobbyists for their constituents while their interests in the central courts resulted in them covering some of their own expenses.[112] Accordingly, the *History of Parliament* volumes allow for a case study of those county lawyers who sat in the House between 1386 and 1421, naming over thirty Cornish parliamentarians who were also men of law. One such lawyer was Stephen Bant, who was to sit for three boroughs in eight parliaments between 1377 and 1388 and build a busy legal practice in the assizes at Launceston, with his reputation resulting in Cornish litigants paying him to conduct their affairs in the central courts. Holding a regular place as a pleader at the latter, he came to be recognised by the government in 1410, when he was appointed a justice of assize in Cornwall itself.[113] John Cork started his career in characteristic fashion too, later being appointed to the escheatorship and to the local quorum in 1426.[114] Nonetheless, he did not always operate within the bounds of the law. Allegedly assaulting, binding and robbing John Fursdon, despite Fursdon having served as his fellow parliamentary burgess, Cork was supposedly of such 'grete porte and maytenaunce in his contree' that Fursdon had to take his case to chancery.

A close connection with the local landholding class undoubtedly helped a man to develop his legal practice. This much is shown by the lawyer Otto Tregonan, who built his livelihood on serving the legal needs of landed proprietors such as the Prideauxs and went on to hold the offices of JP and coroner before 1439.[115] Another lawyer, John Syreston, actually had marriage links with the Bodrugans and Sergeauxs, mobilising these connections to aid his busy career in the local and central courts, where he represented clients as eminent as Sir John Arundell of Lanherne.[116] Growing rich on the fees that he earnt, Syreston invested much of this money in Cornish land and tin while serving as under-sheriff and representing numerous towns in parliament. The appeal of the law could run within families, and it seems that the brothers John and Thomas Treffridowe both chose it as their profession.[117] In the mid-fifteenth century, however, the career that stands out most is that of Sir Nicholas

---

[111] *Cornish Wills*, 223; *HOP*, iv, 646–648.
[112] Tyldesley, 'Local Communities', pp. 44–46, 57–59.
[113] *HOP*, ii, 116.
[114] *HOP*, ii, 660–661.
[115] *HOP*, iv, 642–643.
[116] *HOP*, iv, 556–557.
[117] *HOP*, iv, 641–642.

Aysshton (d. 1466), probably a Lancastrian man in origin.[118] While nothing is known of his family background, he seems to have ended up settling in Cornwall and making his home at Callington in the east of the county. After an active career in advocacy, he was appointed to the bench in 1444 and was employed as a trier of petitions in both Henry VI's reign and Edward IV's. For all his activities at Westminster, he never forgot Cornwall and by his death was referred to as 'lord of a part of the town of Callington'. Also rebuilding Callington Church, he was buried there and commemorated by a fine brass depicting him clad in his robes of office.

What lessons can we take from the careers of these Cornish lawyers? It is striking that so many of them 'cut their teeth' at the Launceston assizes, using that forum as a pathway to gaining recognition later in the central courts. Evidently no clear distinction can be made between 'central' and 'local' justices and agencies, their personnel emerging as increasingly intertwined and interchangeable. These tribunals formed a lasting point of contact between local and central justices, forging a kingdom-wide legal system which sustained, and was sustained by, a highly mobile and surprisingly expansive cohort of legal practitioners. As a result, all these men of law were important agents of connectivity who in both practice and imagination helped to integrate the county into the kingdom.

It is equally clear that the law raised these careerists to positions of wealth and power, both to the east and west of the Tamar. Those who attained the coif stand out as pre-eminent, for despite their relatively humble backgrounds each of them developed a thick web of contacts across the realm to support their pretentions. Lesser lawyers were also significant. Although these men hailed chiefly from the 'middling sort', the law enabled them to overlap and intermingle with established gentry. It is illustrative of this that after a legal career in which he had attained a seat on the county bench and sat in parliament for Helston on a dozen occasions, Roger Trewythenick's achievements were commemorated by a brass of the gentlemanly sort in Sithney Church.[119] After making his fortune at the law, John Tregoose chose to proclaim his achievements in a residence so grand that even seventy years after his death William Worcestre noted that there stood 'a tower in the parish of St Columb once of John Tregoose esquire'.[120] Serving as a major force for social mobility, the law was to alter the very workings of local society. On the one hand, Cornish lawyers could provide formal and informal mechanisms of dispute resolution which helped to keep the peace, as in 1455 for example, when Justice Aysshton and Chief Justice Fortescue arbitrated a dispute between Henry Bodrugan and

---

[118] *HOP*, ii, 90–93; Lack et al., *Brasses of Cornwall*, pp. 13–14; *Cornish Wills*, 85.
[119] *HOP*, iv, 662; Lack et al., *Brasses of Cornwall*, pp. 155–156.
[120] *HOP*, iv, 643–644; Worcestre, *Itineraries*, pp. 22–23.

John Arundell.[121] On the other, the presence of so many legal men encouraged litigiousness, if not outright disorder, prompting disorderly Cornishmen and women to call on their expertise to circumvent punishment.

While influential in the county, locally important lawyers were not a phenomenon unique to Cornwall. Successful men of law from right across the realm can be found investing their wealth in wide estates and handsome residences, while also commissioning sumptuous tombs immortalising their professional expertise and social status.[122] Michael Bennett has drawn attention to the valuable employment provided by the law to the men of the north west.[123] Yet he has also shown that most of those folk who pursued legal careers in Cheshire and Lancashire did not hail from leading local lineages. By virtue of the fact that few county lawyers were the sons of knights, the Cornish evidence confirms the picture that he has drawn. Nevertheless, we have seen how Cornishmen excelled at the law in a way that surpassed even the well-connected careerists of the north west. This was partly because in contrast to the palatinates, with their localised courts, Cornwall held a permanent place on the gaol delivery and assize circuits and sent many cases and practitioners to central tribunals. All this legal activity drew the county firmly into the common law ambit, with these same Cornish cases and practitioners informing the workings of the wider English legal system.

The question remains of what training these Cornish lawyers could have received. Unfortunately, the answer is by no means clear. It is likely to have been the case that an informal legal training was available locally through novice lawyers observing tribunals in the county and noting down process and precedents, akin to what the apprentices did in the central courts. In the lower echelons of the legal profession, clerks and scriveners were probably trained 'on the job' by their predecessors in the earldom-duchy, the county and its boroughs.[124] It was in this period, however, that the Inns of Chancery and Court emerged as training centres. Based on the western outskirts of the City of London, these places served initially as hostelries for lawyers attending the central courts, but by the mid-fifteenth century had come to form a *studium publicum*.[125] Although the extent to which they provided legal training before this date remains unclear, Cornishmen certainly attended these institutions.

---

[121] CRO, AR/3/314.
[122] A. Musson, 'Legal Culture: Medieval Lawyers' Aspirations and Pretensions', *Fourteenth Century England, III*, ed. W. M. Ormrod (Woodbridge, 2004), pp. 16–30; Saul, *Church Monuments*, pp. 269–289.
[123] Bennett, *Cheshire and Lancashire*, pp. 195–198.
[124] Cf. K. L. Bevan, 'Clerks and Scriveners: Legal Literacy and Access to Justice in Late Medieval England' (Unpubl. Univ. Exeter PhD, 2013), pp. 31–32, 203–207, 217–218.
[125] P. Brand, *The Making of the Common Law* (London, 1992), pp. 57–75; Musson and Ormrod, *English Justice*, p. 30.

In 1397, for example, John Trerys and Peryn Dunioun were both said to have been dwelling in the 'New Inn' of the Strand when they were indicted for a trespass.[126] The Inns were later to assume the position of 'the third university of England', and profiting from their expertise more than sixty Cornishmen attended them between 1440 and 1550.[127] We should not focus entirely on the Inns, however, for legal knowledge was widely diffuse in later-medieval England. Emerging as a potent force of connectivity, the 'lawe of Engelond' tied Cornwall tightly into the legal system, culture and networks of the kingdom.

---

[126] *CCR 1396–1399*, 117.
[127] J. H. Baker, *The Men of Court 1440 to 1550: A Prosopography of the Inns of Court and Chancery and the Courts of Law*, 2 vols, Selden Society, Supplementary Series 18 (London, 2012), *passim*.

13

God and Cornwall: Ecclesiastical Connectivity

Operating on a level simultaneously local, national and international, the Church was a unique institution that formed one of the premier engines of social and geographic mobility across Western Christendom.[1] At one and the same time Cornwall held a place in the diocese of Exeter, the *Ecclesia Anglicana* and the wider Catholic Church, with these many ties all contributing to connectivity. While the Church created an enduring personal link between the county and a leading spiritual lord in the person of the bishop of Exeter, only one of the bishops appointed to the see in this period actually hailed from the south west and that was Walter de Stapeldon, who came from just across the Tamar in Devon.[2] A very active diocesan, he ordained no fewer than 836 priests, 865 deacons and 813 subdeacons, making an impressive six formal visitations of the archdeaconry of Cornwall and three partial journeys.[3] Bishop Stapeldon was a force to reckoned with in the affairs of the peninsula.

In contrast to Stapeldon's relatively local origins, Bishop Grandisson, his successor but one, was of distant Savoyard extraction, but he too itinerated

---

[1] For the best introductions, see E. Duffy, *The Stripping of the Altars: Traditional Religion in England, c. 1400–c. 1500* (New Haven and London, 1992); Harriss, *Shaping the Nation*, pp. 310–351; P. Heath, *Church and Realm, 1272–1461: Conflict and Collaboration in an Age of Crisis* (London, 1988); R. N. Swanson, *Church and Society in Late Medieval England* (Oxford, 1989); B. Thompson, 'Locality and Ecclesiastical Polity', in *Political Society*, pp. 113–145; also, D. J. Cawthron, 'The Episcopal Administration of the Diocese of Exeter in the Fourteenth Century: with Special Reference to the Registers of Stapeldon, Grandisson and Brantingham' (Unpubl. Univ. London MA, 1951).

[2] Cf. R. G. Davies, 'The Episcopate', in *Profession, Vocation and Culture in Later Medieval England*, ed. C. H. Clough (Liverpool, 1982), pp. 51–89.

[3] *Reg.Stapeldon*, 547–560; Buck, *Finance and the Church*, p. 61.

around Cornwall.[4] In a dialogue with the parishioners of St Buryan in 1336, Grandisson communicated with them 'through the medium of his own voice', although his words needed to be translated into Cornish for a minority of monoglot Cornish-speakers.[5] Despite such linguistic challenges, the bishop still received oaths of loyalty from the parishioners and confirmed 'innumerable' children while in the far west of the county. There is evidence that Grandisson was a conscientious diocesan who felt a high degree of affinity with his see, in his will bequeathing money to the infirm in the diocese and even remembering the Cornish landholder Ranulph Blanchminster.[6] More prosaic considerations also linked these bishops to the county's residents. In 1389, for example, Bishop Brantingham is found taking action in chancery to recover £400 from Sir Robert Tresilian, Henry Giffard and John Tregorrek, while in the following year he received homage from John Trevenour *pro terris et tenementis*.[7] The bonds between a bishop, his see and its people emerge as many-faceted.

More often than not, however, the bishop delegated episcopal powers of day-to-day administration to his subordinates in the diocese. Many of these officials originated from outside the south west, as did the bishops they served. One 'outsider' was Robert le Petit, bishop of the Irish see of Clonfert, whom Bishop Stapeldon appointed in 1324 to perform his sacramental duties while he was engaged on government business in London.[8] It was the archdeacon of Cornwall who served as the chief minister in the peninsula's normal parochial administration, acting as the 'bishop's eye'.[9] The archdeacon's duties involved the enforcement of the bishop's instructions and the maintenance of parochial property, with the proper worship of God forming the keynote of what was referred to as his 'great labours'.[10] Only one early-fourteenth century archdeacon was a Cornishman by birth: William Bodrugan, who died in 1308.[11] All the others were 'outsiders'. Adam de Carleton, for instance, was a former royal chaplain who hailed from Huntingdonshire and held the office of archdeacon for over thirty-five years.[12] Unhappy with his post, he was finally to obtain release from it in 1347, when the Yorkshireman and royal chaplain John St Paul replaced him. For the better management of his archdeaconry, the archdeacon

---

[4] *Reg.Grandisson*, iii, 1524–1532.
[5] *Reg.Grandisson*, ii, 820–821.
[6] *Reg.Grandisson*, iii, 1551–1555.
[7] C131/205/50; *CCR 1389–1392*, 269–270; *Reg.Brantingham*, ii, 696–697.
[8] *Reg.Stapeldon*, 384, Stapeldon was treasurer of England at this time.
[9] Cawthron, 'Diocese of Exeter', p. 68.
[10] *Reg.Grandisson*, ii, 957–958.
[11] *Reg.Stapeldon*, 12.
[12] *CPR 1307–1313*, 33; *CPR 1345–1348*, 364; *Reg.Grandisson*, ii, 957–958.

at times itinerated around the county and regularly employed his own staff.[13] Among the latter, the Devonian Richard Chuddele is found serving as an official here in the 1320s.

The smallest units of the diocese, Cornish parishes played host to a surprising number of incomers. For the sake of analysis, let us consider the geographic origins of the rectors and vicars of some twenty-two of these between 1307 and 1419, roughly a tenth of the total.[14] An attempt has been made to include parishes from across Cornwall, while the ownership of advowsons has also weighed on the selection process, with patrons as diverse as the king, the earl-duke, the gentry and the Religious included. Even though episcopal registers, the source of these names, can at times prove incomplete, the lists that we possess name no fewer than 180 churchmen instituted in this period. Based on the evidence of their surnames and subsequent careers, it seems that at least fifty-one originated from east of the Tamar and probably more. Instituted to Lesnewth in 1331, John Cooke of Exeter was joined by 'outsiders' such as John Ipswich of Suffolk and William Wykeham of Hampshire (later bishop of Winchester).[15] Although non-Cornish ecclesiastics more often held richer parishes than poorer ones, it seems that around a quarter of parochial incumbents hailed from east of the Tamar. At every level Church administration depended on the movement of personnel.

Since many of the 'incomers' appointed to Cornish livings held benefices in other parts of the realm, however, we may well wonder whether the majority of them ever crossed the Tamar. Some privileged pluralists can be shown to have appointed proxies to perform their pastoral duties. Although in 1356, for example, the Black Prince nominated his clerk, one John de Gurmuncestre of Huntingdonshire, to the parish of Creed, Gurmuncestre relied on a local proxy, a certain John Grampound.[16] Non-residence was a matter of perennial concern to the ecclesiastical authorities, and the list of pluralist clerks in his see that Bishop Grandisson had compiled in 1366 named as many as thirty-eight men who also held benefices elsewhere.[17] Although some of these clerks merely hunted out rich livings for their own enrichment, others, while absentee, were

---

[13] *Reg.Brantingham*, i, 427, 478; *CPR 1350–1354*, 101.
[14] Redruth and Zennor (Penwith); Gwennap, Ruan Major and St Keverne (Kerrier); Creed, Fowey and Truro (Powdershire); St Columb Major and St Wenn (Pydarshire); Blisland, Bodmin and St Kew (Triggshire); Lesnewth and Tintagel (Lesnewth); Launcells and Week St Mary (Stratton); Menheniot and Rame (Eastwivelshire); Lanreath, Liskeard and St Neot (Westwivelshire); cf. M. Page, 'The Ownership of Advowsons in Thirteenth-Century Cornwall', *DCNQ*, 37 (1992–6), pp. 336–341.
[15] *Reg.Grandisson*, iii, 1285–1286; *Reg.Stapeldon*, 250.
[16] *RBP*, iv, 188; *Reg.Grandisson*, iii, 1441.
[17] *Reg.Grandisson*, iii, 1257–1262.

concerned about the quality of their proxies.[18] It is almost certainly the case that many more of these non-resident incumbents visited their parishes than may at first appear, for it was common for high-ranking churchmen to lead peripatetic lives.[19]

Connections between pluralists and their parishes could indeed prove significant to both parties. For example, we find the chancellors of Exeter Cathedral, John Snetysham (d. 1448) and John German (d. 1460), both bequeathing liturgical items to St Newlyn East, a rectory which was attached to their office.[20] Thomas Lynton (d. 1388) the rector of Creed was also the rector of Cliffe, near Rochester, a canon of St George's, Windsor, and sometime dean of the chapel royal.[21] Nonetheless, he still had sufficient attachment to his distant Cornish benefice to bequeath to it a set of vestments.[22] Parishioners, too, understood that through their parish they were connected to a far wider world. Thomas Catour of Breage (d. 1458), for example, chose to appoint as his executor the monk Richard Whitchurche, keeper of the blood of our lord Jesus Christ in Hailes Abbey, Gloucestershire, because this was the house that held the advowson of his local church, sometimes sending monks to oversee the parish.[23] In the reign of Henry IV, the parishioners of Saltash went so far as to complain to the dean and college of Windsor, who held the right of presentment, that their vicar, a certain John Crewkerne, was a deaf drunkard who had 'never expounded the gospels nor had he shown any other good example to his parishioners'.[24] Regardless of residency and despite the distances involved, the links maintained between parishioners, presenters, proxies and incumbents emerge as rich and varied.

It is not surprising that Cornwall's collegiate churches provided ecclesiastics with yet another entrée into the county, a point made by considering the church of St Buryan. Although this ancient minster in 1291 was served by a dean and three canons, in the mid-fourteenth century the Crown and the duchy secured the right of appointment to its canonries.[25] In this way, St Buryan was transformed into a royal free chapel, with the office of dean coming to be a

---

[18] *Reg. Stafford*, 162.
[19] D. Lepine, '"Loose Canons": The Mobility of the Higher Clergy in the Later Middle Ages', in *Freedom of Movement*, pp. 104–122 at 105–106, 111–115.
[20] *Cornish Wills*, 204.
[21] N. Saul, 'Servants of God and Crown: the Canons of St George's Chapel, 1348–1420', in *St George's Chapel, Windsor, in the Fourteenth Century*, ed. N. Saul (Woodbridge, 2005), pp. 97–115 at 102–103, 108.
[22] *Cornish Wills*, 199.
[23] *Cornish Wills*, 83–84; SC8/224/11165; *CPR 1327–1330*, 8.
[24] A. K. B. Evans (A. K. A. Roberts), 'Litigation for Proprietary Rights: the case of the Obstinate Vicar', in *St George's Chapel*, pp. 117–134.
[25] Orme, *Religious Houses*, pp. 163–171; also, G. Oliver, *Monasticon Dioecesis Exoniensis* (London, 1846).

lucrative benefice for men in royal and ducal favour. One such person was the Frenchman John de Maunte, who had served as a chaplain to Queen Margaret, Edward I's second wife, and through her patronage came to hold the post of dean.[26] From 1337 it became standard practice for royal clerks of English birth to hold the deanery, men such as Edward III's administrator Thomas de Crosse and Richard II's confidant and the dean of St Stephen's, Westminster, Nicholas Slake.[27] In his will made in 1438 at Hereford, where he held a canonry in the cathedral, the former dean of St Buryan, one William Lochard, remembered its poor parishioners and entrusted his soul to 'almighty God, the blessed Mary his mother, St Ethelbert, St Thomas of Hereford, St George, St Anne, [and] St Buryan' herself.[28] The inscription on his brass, formerly in Hereford Cathedral and now lost but known to us from antiquarian sources, recorded his office as dean of St Buryan, and this Cornish saint held a place among those holy men and women represented in the orphreys of his cope.[29]

If the college at St Buryan served as a means through which to introduce royal clerks into the county, then Glasney College at Penryn performed much the same function for the bishop of Exeter's own clerks. Bishop Walter Bronescombe had founded the college back in 1265, with Exeter Cathedral serving as its model.[30] He found sufficient endowment to provide for thirteen canons, and 'the presence of a body of secular canons able to operate freely in the world... gave the bishop posts to distribute in Cornwall and provided him with people to do administrative and pastoral duties there'.[31] It follows that the bishop's own men are often to be found holding the office of provost itself. Having served as Bishop Grandisson's registrar before being appointed to the archdeaconry of Leicester, William Doune (d. 1361), for example, chose to leave 40s. to Glasney's fabric in part because this house played such an important role in diocesan government.[32]

Not merely an administrative or intercessory centre, Glasney College in many ways acted as a sub-cathedral for the western part of the diocese. According to the college's foundation charter, the canons were to observe 'the laudable, approved, and approvable customs' of Exeter Cathedral itself.[33] Connections radiated outwards. The college held the right to presentment in

---

[26] *CPR 1301–1307*, 122; *CPR 1317–1321*, 140; *Reg.Grandisson*, i, 53, 59, also known as Matthew Boileau.
[27] *CPR 1334–1338*, 492; *CPR 1391–1396*, 529.
[28] *Cornish Wills*, 203.
[29] W. Lack, H. M. Stuchfield and P. Whittemore, *The Monumental Brasses of Herefordshire* (Colchester, 2008), pp. 105–106.
[30] Orme, *Religious Houses*, pp. 244–262.
[31] Orme, *Religious Houses*, p. 246.
[32] *Cornish Wills*, 198.
[33] Orme, *Religious Houses*, p. 246.

many western parishes, allowing its canons a considerable say over religious provision in this area. We see this in 1417–18, when Bishop Stafford granted a certain William Olyver licence to preach in Glasney and 'all churches in the diocese appropriated thereto'.[34] The bishops of Exeter are often to be found authorising the canons to hear confessions and preach throughout Cornwall, for Glasney was a powerhouse of prayer and administrative know-how.[35] The college is even the suggested place of origin for some of Cornwall's miracle plays, which were penned to promote orthodox beliefs among the laity.

When we turn from the seculars to the regulars, we see that Cornwall's monasteries played a significant role in introducing 'new men' into the peninsula. With a yearly income of at least £100, the Augustinian priory at Bodmin held the honour of being the wealthiest house west of the Tamar.[36] Although the majority of those who were appointed to the office of prior were Cornishmen, such as John de Kilkhampton, who oversaw the priory from 1310 to 1349, one Henry Canterbury whose name suggests origins in the south-east is found holding the post of sub-prior in 1403.[37] In contrast to Bodmin Priory, Tywardreath, near Fowey, was a Benedictine priory whose mother house lay in distant Angers. It was naturally the case that until the 1370s Frenchmen such as William de Bouges held the office of prior.[38] After this time, however, Englishmen are found rising to prominence, the king having taken this alien priory into his hands on account of the war with France.[39] As St Michael's Mount was similarly held by Mont St Michel, French priors often oversaw the Mount.[40] This was another alien house, however, and so Richard II had it in his gift to present Richard Auncell of Tavistock to the priory in 1385 and Henry V was to grant the Mount to Syon Abbey when he dissolved the alien priories.[41] The county's monasteries can even be found introducing laymen into Cornwall, through the grant of corrodies – lifetime allowances of food, clothing and shelter – to 'outsiders' such as Gilbert Trumpour (Trumpeter, a minstrel) at the request of the king and earl-duke.[42]

There were also two mendicant houses in the county, a Franciscan House in Bodmin and a Dominican Friary in Truro.[43] Many friars were drawn

[34] *Reg.Stafford*, 114, 236; *Reg.Brantingham*, i, 273–274.
[35] *Reg.Stafford*, 112–114; *Reg.Grandisson*, i, 422–423.
[36] Orme, *Religious Houses*, pp. 139–154.
[37] *Reg.Stapeldon*, 49; *Reg.Stafford*, 26.
[38] Orme, *Religious Houses*, pp. 284–296; *Reg.Stapeldon*, 481; *Reg.Grandisson*, ii, 695–696.
[39] *Reg.Stafford*, 359.
[40] Orme, *Religious Houses*, pp. 228–240.
[41] *CPR 1385–1389*, 62; Orme, *Religious Houses*, p. 233.
[42] *CCR 1318–1323*, 706; *RBP*, ii, 208–209; grants could be resisted, *CCR 1364–1368*, 327.
[43] Orme, *Religious Houses*, pp. 155–159, 281–284.

into Cornwall from further afield by their duties: Raymond de Bordigla, for instance, was ordained at Bodmin in the 1420s but to judge from his name probably came from overseas. Other friars hailed from elsewhere in England, including the Devonian Martin Halcombe, whose rebellious behaviour in Cornwall prompted Bishop Brantingham to launch an investigation.[44] Many friars were men of distinction, however, John Somer perhaps most notably. Somer was an astronomer of repute who had served as warden of the priory of Bodmin some time before 1380, from that date holding a place in Oxford's Convent and composing a *Kalendarium* for Princess Joan herself.[45] Preaching, teaching and hearing confessions made by the meek and mighty alike, these mendicants travelled around the whole county.[46]

There can be little doubt that Cornish posts formed part of the rich harvest of preferment at the disposal of the higher English clergy. Although many churchmen of mean substance were introduced into the peninsula, those who were really to prosper required patrons.[47] This is a point illustrated by the fact that Henry IV instituted as many as twenty incumbents to county institutions in the course of his thirteen-year reign.[48] Introductions, however, did not necessarily result in amity. Some of the most waspish assessments of Cornwall originated from incoming churchmen, with a number of priests seeking to exchange their benefices on the excuse that they could not speak Cornish.[49] For the greater part of the time, however, the clergy and laity in the peninsula were to be found co-operating for the glory of God. Some 'outside' churchmen felt a real affinity with the county, including William Doune, who bequeathed to the priory of Launceston a silver cup on which was sculpted a 'scutcheon of my father', an heirloom to forever inspire Cornish prayers for his immortal soul.[50]

But what about those Cornishmen whom the Church drew out of the peninsula in its wider service? Since the county formed part of the see of Exeter, it was commonplace for Cornish clergymen to find employment elsewhere in the diocese. Some of them were appointed to rectories and vicarages in Devon. Of greater importance, however, than the country parsons were the clerics who made their careers in the chapter of Exeter Cathedral.[51] No fewer than twenty Cornishmen are known to have sat in the chapter between 1300 and 1455, with at least twenty-five minor clergymen from the county joining

---

[44] *Reg.Brantingham*, i, 410–412, 418–419, 428–429.
[45] L. R. Mooney, 'John Somer', *ODNB*, li, p. 559.
[46] *Reg.Grandisson*, i, 420–421, 558; Worcestre, *Itineraries*, pp. 84–87, 92–93, 98–99.
[47] Cf. R. W. Dunning, 'Patronage and Promotion in the Late-Medieval Church', in *the Crown and the Provinces*, pp. 167–180.
[48] *Reg.Stafford*, 128.
[49] For example, *Reg.Stapeldon*, 219; *Reg.Grandisson*, ii, 910.
[50] *Cornish Wills*, 198.
[51] For example, *Reg.Stapeldon*, 510.

them, chiefly as vicars choral.[52] Among the latter was John Forn, who served as a vicar choral in the 1380s, despite being disciplined for having played with a piece of wood while with lay people in the cathedral cemetery.[53] Many of these men also held benefices to west of the Tamar, the dean and chapter holding the right of presentment to as many as eleven parishes in the county.[54] Exeter Cathedral played an important role in the life of the peninsula, taking boys and men from across the diocese to train in a highly organised system of worship, before sending many of them to minister in the parishes.[55]

Just as Exeter Cathedral did, so the colleges of the two universities of Oxford and Cambridge drew young people out of the county and sent both them and other graduates into it as incumbents of churches.[56] Most students from Cornwall went to study at Oxford, as Cambridge was so much further away. It was in recognition of Oxford's importance that in 1314 Bishop Stapeldon chose to found Stapeldon Hall there, reserving four places for scholars from the archdeaconry of Cornwall and endowing the foundation with the tithes of Gwinear.[57] Over time, Stapeldon's foundation came to be known as Exeter College; and of the 330 fellows known to have served there between 1318 and 1500, roughly a quarter hailed from west of the Tamar.[58] Nicholas Orme has shown that between 1180 and 1540 no fewer than 407 of the county's sons received places at Oxford Colleges.[59] At any one time around two-dozen Cornishmen resided in the university, these men in some sense forming a 'provincial society transplanted', with their presence recognised in 'Cornwall Lane' that ran beside Exeter College.[60]

Yet the avenues through which a young person might secure an education in Cornwall and thence a place at Oxford remain obscure. Some educational provision was provided in the county, for a grammar school was established at Launceston by 1342 and tuition of a kind was available from the county's

---

[52] D. Lepine, 'The Origins and Careers of the Canons of Exeter Cathedral, 1300–1455', in *Religious Belief and Ecclesiastical Careers in Late Medieval England*, ed. C. Harper-Bill (Woodbridge, 1991), pp. 87–120 at 93; N. Orme, *The Minor Clergy of Exeter Cathedral: Biographies, 1250–1548*, DCRS, n.s. 54 (Exeter, 2013), *passim*.
[53] Orme, *Minor Clergy*, p. 125.
[54] Orme, *Minor Clergy*, p. 18.
[55] Orme, *Minor Clergy*, p. 19.
[56] J. Catto, 'Masters, Patrons and the Careers of Graduates in Fifteenth-Century England', *The Fifteenth Century, I: Concepts and Patterns of Service in the Later Middle Ages*, ed. A. Curry and E. Matthew (Woodbridge, 2000), pp. 52–63.
[57] Buck, *Finance and the Church*, pp. 101–102, 110; J. R. Maddicott, *Founders and Fellowship: The Early History of Exeter College Oxford 1314–1592* (Oxford, 2014), pp. 26–27.
[58] Maddicott, *Exeter College*, p. 86.
[59] N. Orme, 'The Cornish at Oxford, 1180–1540', *JRIC* (2010), pp. 43–82.
[60] Orme, 'Oxford', 53; Maddicott, *Exeter College*, p. 86.

monasteries, friaries and gentry households.[61] Sometimes Cornishmen of modest means might attract the attentions of the bishops of Exeter. In 1333, for example, the executors of Bishop Stapeldon set aside money for a number of poor scholars, including half a mark for one William de Polmorva, a poor scholar at Oxford.[62] Valuing education, the mendicant orders can be shown to have sponsored the study of some eleven Cornish scholars, while four monks from monastic houses in the county attended university with the financial backing of their communities.[63] A route more frequently followed involved the use of parochial resources, however, as 'study often followed the acquisition of a post rather than proceeding it'.[64] Since the registers of the bishops of Exeter are littered with licences for non-residence to allow for incumbents to pursue their studies, the practice of studying at Oxford after obtaining a benefice emerges as quite widespread.

Family traditions and connections might also play a role in securing a university education, as in the case of the Mertherderwas of Camborne. After graduating from Oxford as a doctor of civil law and being appointed to the principalship of Bull Hull, Reginald Mertherderwa (d. 1448) bequeathed some money to his brother, a certain Thomas – who likewise studied at Oxford and held a prebend at Glasney.[65] He also remembered his relative Pascow Noel, alias Trewens, another Oxford-educated Cornishman who went on to oversee Bull Hall. Despite being joined by numerous local gentlemen, it seems that most of those Cornishmen who attended university originated from the 'middling sort', among them men such as Thomas Tomyowe, the son of a merchant from St Columb Major.[66] Education enabled all these folk to 'better their lot'. It is illustrative of this that Reginald Mertherderwa's will made specific mention of the heraldic arms which he had inherited or acquired, requesting that they and the insignia of a doctor of law be placed on his tomb slab as an eternal testament to his achievements.[67]

However they may have reached Oxford, some of these Cornishmen were men of distinction who rose high in academia. John of Cornwall, alias Brian, was a grammarian at Oxford in the 1340s whom John Trevisa was to claim 'chaunged the lore in gramer scole and construccioun of Frensche in to Englische'; Cornwall probably composed a major work on grammar, the *Speculum*

---

[61] Orme, 'Oxford', 51–52; see, N. Orme, *Education in the West of England, 1066–1548* (Exeter, 1976).
[62] *Reg.Stapeldon*, 577.
[63] Orme, 'Oxford', 49.
[64] Orme, 'Oxford', 44.
[65] *Cornish Wills*, 76–79; BRUO, ii, 1266–1267, 1361–1362.
[66] Orme, 'Oxford', 48–50.
[67] *Cornish Wills*, 76.

Grammaticale.⁶⁸ Another active teacher from the county, John Gascoigne, has left lecture notes on canon law from c. 1365 and may also have written a tract condemning John Wycliffe, the *Contra Wicleffum*.⁶⁹ William Penbegyll attended Exeter College from 1399 to 1409 and served there in the office of rector, all while composing a series of tracts on logic, including the *Universalia*.⁷⁰ Probably writing the *Determinaciones Trevellys*, William Trevelles was yet another academic from Cornwall who, in his case, held a fellowship at Queen's College in 1361–8.⁷¹ A few Cornishmen at least stand out as prolific scholars, with John Trevisa composing original pieces and proving a masterly translator who rendered numerous works into Middle English, including the *Polychronicon* and perhaps even the Wycliffite bible itself.⁷² Across the fourteenth century some fifteen Cornish scholars earned seventeen doctorates, including William de Heghes (medicine), John Bloyou (civil law), Michael Sergeaux (civil and canon law) and John Landreyn (medicine and theology).⁷³

Not simply thinkers or teachers, some of these folk went on to attain senior positions in university administration. Strikingly, William de Polmorva, Ralph Redruth and Walter Trengoff were each to serve as chancellor of Oxford in 1350–2, 1391–3 and 1419–21 respectively.⁷⁴ Between 1300 and 1540 as many as twenty halls are recorded as having Cornish principals at some point, a number on multiple occasions, indicating the important role that the county's sons played in the university's collective life.⁷⁵ Richard Tryvytlam, a Cornish-born friar and alumnus of the university, even composed the *De laude universitatis Oxonie* in praise of Oxford.⁷⁶ A third, that is twenty-three, of the rectors at Exeter College were Cornishmen, and although Robert Trethewey's lax management in the 1350s led to his ousting, William Palmer (c. 1420–34), a kinsman of the onetime mayor and MP for Launceston, John Palmer, was a rector of renown, building a tower that still bears his name.⁷⁷

Many Oxford-educated Cornishmen went on to gain high office in the Church, with some at least returning to their native diocese. After his time at university, for instance, Walter Giffard of Lanivet (d. 1322) served as archdeacon of Barnstaple and chancellor of Exeter Cathedral from 1314 until his

---

[68] *BRUO*, i, 490; Trevisa, trans., *Polychronicon*, ii, pp. 159–161.
[69] *BRUO*, ii, 745.
[70] *BRUO*, iii, 1455.
[71] *BRUO*, iii, 1899–1900.
[72] *BRUO*, iii, 1903–1904; Fowler, *John Trevisa*; J. Beal, *John Trevisa and the English Polychronicon* (Turnhout, 2012), pp. 1–23, 145.
[73] Orme, 'Oxford', 57.
[74] *BRUO*, iii, 1492–1493, 1561, 1896.
[75] Orme, 'Oxford', 53–54.
[76] Rigg, *Anglo-Latin Literature*, pp. 273–274.
[77] Maddicott, *Exeter College*, pp. 72–73, 86–87, 117–118.

death.[78] He was not alone in 'going back west', for Stephen Penpel of Cornwall was another who served as archdeacon of Exeter in the 1360s and his nephew, one Ralph Tregrisiow, appeared as a canon of Exeter by 1366, vicar general of the bishop by 1373 and dean by 1384.[79] The local diocese of Exeter, however, was by no means the limit of Cornish ambitions. We see this as Penpel went on to serve as dean of Wells, while Tregrisiow acted as an advocate of the court of Canterbury in 1373. Despite his illegitimacy, Michael Sergeaux (d. 1397) was an able advocate, speaking in the court of Canterbury in 1382 and holding the deanery of Arches from 1393.[80] A man of ability, he went on to serve as the archdeacon of Dorset and the chancellor of the archbishop of Canterbury himself. Another of the county's sons who attended Oxford, one John Waryn (d. 1442), later attained the archdeaconship of Barnstaple and the keeping of the spiritualities of Exeter and Bath and Wells. He also served as the auditor of the archbishop of Canterbury's cases, finding employment afterwards as the official and vicar of the bishop of Rochester.[81] Education provided the means for all these men to enter the charmed circle of the higher clergy, the *sublimes et literati*, with its rich rewards across the realm.[82]

The service of these Cornishmen in the Church overlapped with both their academic careers and duties to the Crown. Finding employment as a king's clerk in the admiralty, for example, Michael Sergeaux also enjoyed connections with the office of the privy seal and accompanied John of Gaunt himself on diplomatic missions to France. Henry V similarly involved William Bray (d. 1437) in international diplomacy, employing him to assist with negotiations with the Burgundians and Genoese on his behalf.[83] A busy man, Bray also served as commissary general of John, earl of Huntingdon, the admiral of England. Ralph Tregrisiow emerges as another quill-pusher who sat in the courts of admiralty and constable, advising Richard II on the papal schism while still finding time to lecture in Oxford. Enjoying a wide range of plum posts, William de Polmorva (d. 1362) served as chancellor of Oxford, archdeacon of Middlesex, a canon of St George's, Windsor, a royal clerk and, not least, confessor to Queen Philippa herself.

Although it was not until the fifteenth century that a Cornishman was to sit on England's episcopal bench, no fewer than four of the county's sons were then to be appointed to bishoprics in the reigns of Henry VI and Edward IV: John Arundell, Walter Lyhert, John Stanbury and Michael Tregury. Having

---

[78] BRUO, ii, 763.
[79] BRUO, iii, 1454–1455, 1893; *Cornish Wills*, 46–48.
[80] BRUO, i, 377–378.
[81] BRUO, iii, 1996.
[82] Cf. V. Davies, 'Preparation for Service in the Late Medieval English Church', *Patterns of Service*, pp. 38–51.
[83] BRUO, i, 252–253.

held a fellowship at Exeter College in the 1420s, John Arundell (d. 1477) served as Henry VI's chaplain and physician, leading the team of doctors who ministered to the king when his mental health collapsed in 1453. By way of reward, Henry raised him to the rank of bishop of Chichester five years later.[84] John Stanbury (d. 1474) was a Carmelite friar and an outstanding scholar who hailed from Morwenstow in the north-east of the county.[85] Naturally enough, Henry VI choose this learned man as his confessor some time before 1440 and elevated him to the bishopric of Bangor in 1448, translating him to Hereford in 1453. Henry's queen, Margaret of Anjou, also gave employment to Cornishmen. Despite being only a miller's son from Lanteglos-by-Fowey, Walter Lyhert (d. 1472) served as confessor to the earl of Suffolk and after that performed the same function for the queen herself. In 1446 he was rewarded with the bishopric of Norwich, later attaining a place on the council.[86] Margaret likewise had Michael Tregury of St Wenn (d. 1471) employed as a chaplain to the royal couple.[87] Appointing him the first rector of the university of Caen in 1439, the king raised him to the archbishopric of Dublin a decade later. The good connections they made proved essential to furthering the careers of these 'super-connected churchmen', with attendance at Oxford making it possible for its graduates to be integrated into pan-English learning and patronage.

While graduates and careerists from the far south west acquired new ideas and benefices across the land, they generally never forgot their origins. Employing Cornish officials, among them James Halap, and leaving 40s. to the parish of St Creed, near Grampound, 'where I originated', Ralph Tregrisiow was just one who remembered the county of his birth.[88] Archbishop Tregury was even to bequeath his soul to Archangel Michael, 'deservedly venerated in my native Cornish land', and pay for William Wise to go on pilgrimage to St Michael's Mount.[89] Since it was one Robert Bracy of Fowey who in 1478 recounted Bishop Lyhert's local origins to William Worcestre, 'local boys done good' were definitely remembered in the county.[90]

A knowledge of liturgical practices could enter Cornwall through these personal connections. An example of this is that Tregrisiow chose to bequeath to the church of Tregony the great missal that had belonged to his uncle Stephen Penpel, while leaving his law books to his kinsmen or to 'abler scholars or

---

[84] BRUO, i, 49–50, 323; C. Whittick, 'John Arundell', ODNB, ii, pp. 578–579.
[85] A. Rhydderch, 'John Stanbury', ODNB, lii, pp. 91–92.
[86] Worcestre, Itineraries, pp. 106–107; R. J. Schoeck, 'Walter Lyhert', ODNB, xxxiv, pp. 862–864.
[87] A. F. Pollard, rev. V. Davis, 'Michael Tregury', ODNB, lv, pp. 269–270.
[88] Cornish Wills, 46–48; Reg.Stafford, 276.
[89] Cornish Wills, 89–90.
[90] Worcestre, Itineraries, pp. 106–107.

clerks of the facility of law from the county of Cornwall'.[91] Artistic styles could be introduced into the county in this way. The Oxford-educated John Waryn (d. 1426), for instance, commissioned an avant-garde brass at Menheniot, the church over which he presided from 1411, on which he was depicted as a cadaver with the Latin epitaph: 'I am what you will be… and I was what you are'.[92] We also find that the movement of personnel across the Tamar provided a means for the introduction of heresy. Laurence Stephen (d. 1423) was an early devotee of John Wycliffe who returned to Cornwall to preach his views, something that Bishop Brantingham forbade.[93] There is no evidence that Lollardy and non-conformity took root in the county, however, and quite possibly the large number of Oxford graduates appointed to Cornish benefices helped to secure the local faithful for orthodoxy. When he had founded Stapeldon Hall, Bishop Stapeldon had intended to establish a '*cursus honourm* of study at the hall and subsequent return to a west country parish', so that his diocese would be forever staffed with trained priests providing the laity with the means to redemption.[94] Exeter College-educated Cornishmen often followed this 'Stapeldonian ideal', and we find that around half the county's sons who graduated from Oxford as a whole returned to minister in the peninsula of their birth.[95]

The movement of clerks and personnel more generally in and out of the county had the effect of contributing to connectivity. Bishop Grandisson even composed a letter recommending his chef to the prior of Launceston, Henry Schene having learnt his trade in 'distant parts'.[96] Many churchmen spent their lives 'on the move'; Tregrisiow, for example, who oversaw Exeter Cathedral as dean, requested burial in either St Creed or St Cuby 'if it happened' that he should die in Cornwall.[97] Indeed, Archbishop Courtenay himself itinerated around the county during his visitation of 1384.[98] Naturally enough, incumbents resident in the far south west often journeyed beyond the county's boundaries too. One such churchman was Robert Luke, who combined his holding of Ludgvan with a busy medical practice outside the county, while another, a certain Andrew Lanvyan (d. c. 1430), held the rectory of Lanivet at the same time as serving as an ecclesiastical lawyer in London.[99] The frequent

[91] *Cornish Wills*, 47.
[92] *Cornish Wills*, 60–62, 251; there were two John Waryns, P. Cockerham and N. Orme, 'John Waryn and his Cadaver Brass, formerly in Menheniot Church, Cornwall', *Transactions of the Monumental Brass Society*, 19 (2014), pp. 41–56.
[93] BRUO, iii, 1772; *Reg.Brantingham*, i, 480–481.
[94] Maddicott, *Exeter College*, p. 45.
[95] Maddicott, *Exeter College*, p. 178; Orme, 'Oxford', 58.
[96] *Reg.Grandisson*, i, 187–188.
[97] *Cornish Wills*, 46
[98] Orme, *Religious Houses*, p. 281.
[99] BRUO, ii, 1176; *Reg.Grandisson*, i, 292; *Cornish Wills* 64–66; also, CPR 1381–1385, 533; *Reg.Stafford*, 25.

visits of pilgrims to cult centres in the county also contributed to the fostering of connectivity. We see this in 1362, when Exeter College entertained a party of presumed pilgrims from Gwinear and John Peeche of London planned to go 'very soon' to St Michael's Mount.[100] It was William Worcestre, however, who was the most famous of all these travellers, meeting county notables and noting down Cornwall's many saints on his way to the Mount in 1478.[101]

The question remains of how all this activity managed to situate the county within its diocese, the *Ecclesia Anglicana* and the wider Catholic Church. The fact that Cornwall formed one archdeaconry within a bigger see in no way diminished local practices and saints' cults.[102] It is clear, however, that the diocese of Exeter brought together the whole south west in one large unit. Insofar as their actions created a perpetual movement of people and parchment, the bishops of Exeter helped to bestow coherence on the region itself. In Cornwall, the clergy and laity are often found requesting episcopal involvement in their affairs, with the 'strong and noble' (*stout ha gay*) bishop even appearing as a character in the county's miracle plays.[103] All this helped to establish notions of collective diocesan concerns. An episode that occurred in Oxford in the 1430s helps to show this. Although it was the custom for students from certain parts of the realm to hold feast days during which they celebrated a mass in the university church of St Mary the Virgin, in 1436, on the feast of St Peter's Chair, the south-western scholars chose to break with this tradition. In an act of rebelliousness, the Cornish and Devonian students took a statue of St Peter from another church and placed it on the altar of the priory church of St Frideswide, celebrating mass there instead.[104] When the chancellor forbade this breach of etiquette, those involved 'showed their defiance by parading at night in arms'. St Peter stood out as the patron saint of Exeter diocese, around whom all the folk of the see could rally.

At the other end of the spectrum, Cornwall held a place in a wider Christendom. Indeed, it was an article of faith that all those who lived under the grace of the Church formed a universal moral and spiritual society.[105] To some extent Christendom also comprised a fiscal and juridical entity, with Cornish parishes, for example, paying Peter's Pence to the Apostolic See and the

---

[100] Maddicott, *Exeter College*, p. 130; *RBP*, iv, 332; N. Orme, *Medieval Pilgrimage: With a survey of Cornwall, Devon, Dorset, Somerset and Bristol* (Exeter, 2018).
[101] Worcestre, *Itineraries*.
[102] *Reg.Grandisson*, i, 585.
[103] For example, *Cornish Drama*, i, OM, line 2685.
[104] *Epistolae Academicae Oxon...*, ed. H. Anstey, 2 vols (Oxford, 1898), i, pp. 133–135; Orme, 'Oxford', 60–61.
[105] A. Black, *Political Thought in Europe, 1250–1450* (Cambridge, 1992), pp. 87–92; for the 'end' of Christendom, M. Greengrass, *Christendom Destroyed: Europe 1517–1648* (St Ives, 2014); my thanks to Mark Whelan for his advice on this subject.

Roman courts exercising some form of appellate jurisdiction.[106] In 1317 Pope John XXII even launched an investigation into one David de Truro, who had 'falsely styled' himself a papal nuncio so as to extract money from religious houses across southern England.[107] As the office and person of the pope created an institutional and personal focal point for all the faithful, so nuncios and diocesans working in the pontiff's name acted as his local personifications.[108] Spreading awareness about the extent of their integration into this great Christian commonwealth, on occasion Cornish churchmen and laymen alike can be found requesting the pontiff's involvement in their affairs.[109] In a most sensitive case, in 1371 Sir Ralph Carminow received papal dispensation to remain married to his wife, Catherine, despite the fact that they were related in their third and fourth degree of kindred.[110] A two-way discourse between the Church authorities and the faithful helped to sustain Cornwall's place in a wider Christendom.

The opportunities presented by the universal Catholic Church prompted numerous journeys into and out of the peninsula. It is illustrative of this that the Cornishmen John Nans and Thomas Tomyowe both attained doctorates in law from fifteenth-century Bologna, with Nans going on to serve as rector of the two universities there in 1481 before joining the household of Cardinal Hadrian.[111] Some churchmen from the county made their way to the Curia itself, bringing cases there concerning benefices and the like.[112] At the same time papal provisions can be seen introducing 'outsiders' into the peninsula, amongst them Walter Dolbeara, a member of the household of Boniface IX himself, who was provided to Glasney College.[113] It was far more common

---

[106] *Reg.Stapeldon*, 128–129, 313; *Reg.Grandisson*, i, 343–344, 351–352, 360, 408–409, 439; *Reg.Brantingham*, i, 3–8, 221, 300, 324–326, 395–400; *Reg.Stafford*, 29–30; W. E. Lunt, *Financial Relations of the Papacy with England to 1327* (Cambridge, MA, 1939), pp. 3–30; idem, *Financial Relations of the Papacy with England, 1327–1534* (Cambridge, MA, 1962), pp. 1–54.

[107] *Calendar of Entries in the Papal Registers: Papal Letters 1305–1342*, ed. W. H. Bliss, HMSO (London, 1895), pp. 148–149.

[108] For example, *Papal Letters 1305–1342*, p. 503.

[109] For example, *Calendar of Entries in the Papal Registers: Papal Letters 1362–1404*, ed. W. H. Bliss and J. A. Twemlow, HMSO (London, 1904), p. 376; *Calendar of Entries in the Papal Registers: Petitions to the Pope 1342–1419*, ed. W. H. Bliss, HMSO (London, 1896), p. 40.

[110] *Papal Letters 1362–1404*, p. 166; also, *Calendar of Entries in the Papal Registers: Papal Letters 1396–1404*, ed. W. H. Bliss and J. A. Twemlow, HMSO (London, 1904), p. 140; *Supplications from England and Wales in the Registers of the Apostolic Penitentiary, 1410–1503*, ed. P. D. Clarke and P. N. R. Zutshi, 3 vols, The Canterbury and York Society, ciii–cv (Woodbridge 2012–15), i, pp. 62–63.

[111] *BRUO*, ii, 1336; iii, 1883–1884.

[112] For example, *Reg.Stapeldon*, 279, 324; *Reg.Stafford*, 237.

[113] *Papal Letters 1362–1404*, p. 346

for Englishmen to seek papal provision to Cornish benefices, however – churchmen such as Roger Strandeby, a clerk to the archbishop of York, who petitioned the pontiff for a prebend at Crantock.[114] Such connections helped to bestow the idea of Christendom with inter-personal reality.

Accepting their place in this universal society, Cornishmen and women responded favourably to papal calls to crusade. Many county folk opened their purses to assist these pan-Christian projects, as in 1401, for example, when they contributed to an indulgence helping Emperor Manuel II Palaeologus defend Constantinople from the Turkish Sultan.[115] Some Cornishmen actually took the cross itself, with crusading in many cases a family or household affair. Receiving royal licence in 1390 to travel to the Roman court and then on to Jerusalem with 'five servants, six horses and other equipage' in order 'to fulfil his vow', Sir William Botreaux was one of those who partook in the later crusades.[116] Just two years later his son was to fight alongside the Teutonic Knights against the pagan Lithuanians.[117] Although Cornish crusaders were a relatively scarce commodity, these collective Christian endeavours exercised a considerable pull on the peninsula's residents, with one of the county's saints, St Meriasek, seeking to be 'a knight of God' to resist paganism.[118] In this way, the idea of Christendom was spread across Cornwall. Yet for all the centripetal force of this universal society, in the county and across the kingdom the degree to which notions of the *Ecclesia Anglicana* came to mediate belief in a wider Christian commonwealth is more striking still.[119]

Institutionally a point of contact between Cornwall and the wider life of the English Church was provided by the meetings of convocation which the king summoned periodically in each province when requesting taxation. The bishop of Exeter always received a personal summons to such gatherings and so too did the archdeacon of Cornwall and the county's leading priors.[120] The lower clergy also possessed a voice in convocation, with two of their number from each diocese typically elected to speak for their fellows, amongst them

---

[114] *Petitions to the Pope 1342–1419*, p. 5.
[115] *Reg.Stafford*, 358; Lunt, *Papacy, 1327–1534*, pp. 549–557.
[116] *CPR 1388–1392*, 324; C66/331 m. 10r; also, N. Orme and O. J. Padel, 'Cornwall and the Third Crusade', *JRIC* (2005), pp. 71–77; T. Guard, *Chivalry, Kingship and Crusade: The English Experience in the Fourteenth Century* (Woodbridge, 2013).
[117] *CPMR 1381–1412*, 183.
[118] *Beunans Meriasek*, line 352; also, *CPR 1321–1324*, 391; *CPR 1330–1334*, 69; C76/64 m. 6r.
[119] Ruddick, *English Identity*, p. 261; Thompson, 'Ecclesiastical Polity', pp. 144–145.
[120] Heath, *Church and Realm*, pp. 50–51, 85–88; leading churchmen could send proctors to represent their interests, *Reg.Grandisson*, ii, 766; *Reg.Brantingham*, i, 319, ii, 675; *Reg.Stafford*, 67–68; *Records of Convocation*, ed. G. Bray, 20 vols, Church of England Record Society (Woodbridge, 2005–6), iii, pp. 109, 131–132, 318–320.

from Cornwall Ralph Tregrisiow in 1373.[121] Clerical proctors were sometimes just as vocal and articulate as the bishops, and in 1328–9 Bishop Grandisson's register records a series of their protests, some of these relating to ecclesiastical liberties.[122] Sometimes the bishop is found making complaints to the king himself, as in 1337, for example, when Grandisson informed Edward III that his clergymen were unwilling to respond to royal demands because of the dangers posed by enemy attacks on the coast.[123] Informal lobbying of this sort reinforced demands made in convocation and complaints raised by clergymen in parliament. As one of the lords spiritual, the bishop of Exeter received a regular personal summons to parliament, while at the same time proctors representing the interests of the lower clergy could sit in the House.[124] At times we find these ecclesiastical spokesmen complaining vociferously. With royal summonses to parliament thought to undermine clerical privilege, however, the two convocations were to rise to prominence as the forum in which the clergy made their demands of the Crown, granting subsidies in return.[125]

Since ensuring the solvency of the Crown was one of the duties of a Christian commonwealth, the English Church more often than not acquiesced in the king's requests for funding through taxation. Royal rhetoric from Edward II's reign onwards constantly emphasised the fact that the Crown was levying clerical taxes for the combined defence of the king, kingdom and English Church.[126] During the reigns of the first two Edwards it was common for the pope to levy his own taxes on clerical incomes as well, conceding a considerable proportion of these funds to the king.[127] After 1330 exchanges of this sort ceased because the king negotiated directly with English convocations.[128] It follows that the levying of sums agreed in convocation resulted in local ecclesiastics serving as tax collectors under the command of their bishop, but in the broader service of the Crown. We see this in 1334, when Edward III requested

---

[121] *Records of Convocation*, iii, pp. 376–377; *Reg.Brantingham*, i, 319.
[122] *Reg.Grandisson*, i, 446–448.
[123] *Reg.Grandisson*, i, 300–301.
[124] *Records of Convocation*, iii, p. 353; *Proctors for Parliament: Clergy, Community and Politics c. 1248–1539*, ed. P. Bradford and A. K. McHardy, 2 vols, The Canterbury and York Society, cvii–cviii (Woodbridge, 2017–18).
[125] A. K. McHardy, 'The Representation of the English Lower Clergy in Parliament during the Fourteenth Century', in *Sanctity and Secularity: The Church and the World*, ed. D. Baker, Studies in Church History, 10 (Oxford, 1973), pp. 97–107 at 107; J. H. Denton and J. P. Dooley, *Representatives of the Lower Clergy in Parliament, 1295–1340* (Woodbridge, 1987); W. M. Ormrod, *The Reign of Edward III: Crown and Political Society in England, 1327–1377* (London, 1990), pp. 140–142.
[126] Heath, *Church and Realm*, p. 88; Ruddick, *English Identity*, pp. 199–200.
[127] Heath, *Church and Realm*, pp. 63, 85–86.
[128] Ormrod, 'England in the Middle Ages', p. 30; Thompson, 'Ecclesiastical Polity', pp. 142–143.

that the priors of Launceston and Tywardreath dispatch funds from the clerical subsidy 'graciously granted to the king [on account of] their love for him', as the Scots were 'doing all the harm they could'.[129] At times these churchmen could require more formal backing, as in 1398 for instance, when the king had to grant the prior of Bodmin a writ of aid as 'divers ecclesiastics' resisted paying.[130] In the early 1330s the government even had the prior of Launceston investigate abuses in collecting a lay subsidy.[131] Official rhetoric increasingly linked together lay taxation and the English Church, with 'the defence of the realm and of the church of England' featuring prominently in the parliamentary summons of 1372.[132]

Sharing many interests, the Crown and the Church were together engaged in the collaborative business of government and law enforcement. At the time of the Great Revolt, for example, the king appointed Bishop Brantingham to the bench in the counties of his diocese, as other prelates were in theirs, while the same bishop promulgated an excommunication for those who breached royal manors in Cornwall.[133] Spreading awareness of the degree to which royal and ecclesiastical might overlapped, in 1410 Bishop Stafford even received the oaths of the county's JPs.[134] Back in 1297 Edward I had drawn the physical structures of the Church into the royal war effort, ordering the keepers of the sea-coasts to ring bells on sighting the enemy.[135] Since St Michael's Mount stood as was said 'in the peril of the sea', the Crown held the prior responsible for the fortlet attached to his house and by extension the defence of west Cornwall.[136] Churchmen also helped to oversee the organisation of war, for in 1348 Edward III instructed the archdeacon to supervise the county's defences as 'pirates' threatened its ports and fisherman.[137] Regularly arraying men-at-arms, archers and clergymen themselves *pro defensione Ecclesie et Patrie*, in 1418 alone the bishop of Exeter raised as many as 204 men and 1,201 archers from across his see.[138] In a variety of ways these diocesans can be seen serving as local representatives of the king.

Across the realm, the Crown employed the Church in the shaping of public opinion. Requesting prayers for 'events of national importance', the kings of this period saw that a sizeable proportion of the populace was informed about

---

[129] CCR 1333–1337, 355–356; Reg.Stafford, 342–343.
[130] CPR 1396–1399, 401.
[131] CPR 1334–1338, 40.
[132] CCR 1369–1374, 462.
[133] CPR 1381–1385, 142, 248; Reg.Brantingham, i, 448.
[134] Reg.Stafford, 69; also, CPR 1321–1324, 15.
[135] CCR 1296–1302, 74.
[136] CCR 1323–1327, 183; SC8/194/9651; CPR 1338–1340, 99.
[137] Reg.Grandisson, iii, 1547–1548.
[138] CPR 1358–1361, 404–405; Reg.Brantingham, i, 271, 421–422; Reg.Stafford, 303.

war and peace by their local priest.[139] There is evidence that every king appealed for prayers and processions in Cornwall for their success over their French, Scottish and Spanish adversaries.[140] Other occasions besides prompted public devotional offerings, among them the processions that Edward III ordered for the deliverance of the realm from pestilence and Henry V's prayers for 'fine weather'.[141] In this way, the parish came to serve as the mouthpiece of the king, with the efficacy of prayer and the legitimising power of the Church harnessed to the royal cause. In offering 'state prayers', Cornishmen and women believed that they were actively contributing to the success of their realm, and this must have helped to foster a sense of shared belonging which encouraged the county's residents to view England as a collective moral unit.[142] Together, the Crown and the English Church expounded a 'national political theology'.[143]

In point of fact, royal government depended on the involvement of Churchmen. The episcopal bench in particular was by the fourteenth century packed with royal ministers. Connecting Cornwall closely to the high politics of the realm, Bishops Stapeldon, Brantingham and Stafford all held office under the Crown. Many county ecclesiastics attained leading positions in the royal administration too, being 'bound by common discipline and a common ethos of service to Crown and Church'.[144] This was no Cornish peculiarity, as Michael Bennett has identified the many clerks from the north west who achieved prominence in the service of both institutions.[145] Precisely for this reason there can be little doubt that clerical servants were integral to the administration of England, integrating the Church into the structures of the kingdom and promoting ideas of Gallicanism.[146]

Deployment of the apparatus of royal government proved equally essential to the achievement of the work of the spiritual arm. The Church relied on the king's peace for its ministry because in England the Crown stood at the heart of the criminal justice system. It is illustrative of this point that the priors of Bodmin and Launceston both brought cases before the king's bench concerning transgressions, with the prior of Bodmin even obtaining an oyer and terminer commission in 1345 to investigate the townsmen of Bodmin who had

---

[139] A. K. McHardy, 'Liturgy and Propaganda in the Diocese of Lincoln during the Hundred Years War', in *Religion and National Identity*, ed. S. Mews, *Studies in Church History*, 18 (Oxford, 1982), pp. 215–227 at 217.
[140] For example, *Reg.Stafford*, 128–129.
[141] *Reg.Grandisson*, ii, 1069–1071; *Reg.Stafford*, 129.
[142] Cf. Ruddick, *English Identity*, pp. 270, 273.
[143] *CCR 1369–1374*, 462; Ruddick, *English Identity*, pp. 199–200, 258–259, 282.
[144] Harriss, *Shaping the Nation*, p. 311.
[145] Bennett, *Cheshire and Lancashire*, pp. 150–161, especially 156–157.
[146] Swanson, *Church and Society*, pp. 98–103.

'several times besieged the priory'.[147] As one of the realm's great landholders, the Church naturally depended on the king's peace to run its estates, and the bishop's steward in Cornwall could indict criminals for trial before the royal justices.[148] Clergymen also employed the royal administration to register and recover debts, and in 1348 we find that the archdeacon of Cornwall had the £25 6s. that he was owed by Sir William Bodrugan, Henry Trethewey and Walter Kent enrolled in the chancery so as to secure repayment.[149]

While the operation of two distinct legal systems within the realm could result in tensions, in many ways the spiritual and secular courts were complementary, with the Courts Christian concerned chiefly with issues of clerical conduct and morality, and the royal courts concerned with criminal and civil matters.[150] In a typical case, in 1334 the bishop's court sat in Bodmin Church and heard how Jullans Treganhay, 'a notorious married man', had had an adulterous liaison with Matilda, the widow of Sir Thomas l'Ercedekne.[151] Although cases concerning marriage accounted for much of their business, the Church Courts were also concerned with issues of legitimacy and could issue dispensations to those who had been born out of wedlock.[152] Since bastardy was of significance to an individual's secular legal status, such investigations and judgments might, if appropriate, be later reported to the king.[153] Testamentary business likewise fell within the Church's competence, so that wills were proved before Church officials and executors pursued debts owed to the deceased through these courts.[154] Excommunication stood out as one of the most potent weapons in the arsenal of the spiritual courts, but if an excomunicant remained unreconciled after forty days these individuals could be turned over to the secular arm.[155] Bishop Brantingham handed over a number of clerics to the king in the 1380s, after episcopal punishments had failed to bring them to heel.[156] So it was that the Crown relied on the Church to regulate marriage and morality, while the Church relied on the Crown to police malefactors.

---

[147] For example, KB27/269 Roll of Attorneys; KB27/234 m. 90r; *CPR 1343–1345*, 572, 577.
[148] For example, JUST3/156 m. 46d.
[149] *CCR 1346–1349*, 589.
[150] R. H. Helmholz, *The Oxford History of Laws, I: The Canon Law and Ecclesiastical Jurisdiction from 597 to the 1640s* (Oxford, 2004), pp. 206–243.
[151] *Reg.Grandisson*, ii, 758–759; Cawthron, 'Diocese of Exeter', pp. 217–261.
[152] *Reg.Grandisson*, ii, 822; Swanson, *Church and Society*, p. 141; C. Donahue, Jnr, *Law, Marriage and Society in the Later Middle Ages* (Cambridge, 2008), pp. 34–41, 64, 71, 223.
[153] *Reg.Stafford*, 345.
[154] B. L. Woodcock, *Medieval Ecclesiastical Courts in the Diocese of Canterbury* (Oxford, 1952), p. 85.
[155] Heath, *Church and Realm*, p. 27.
[156] *Reg.Brantingham*, i, 437, 446, 488; *Reg.Stafford*, 292.

Such an intertwining of ecclesiastical and secular government afforded the commonalty of Cornwall a constant reminder of the king's power over the *Ecclesia Anglicana*. When there was a vacancy in the see of Exeter, for instance, every king took the opportunity to pack diocesan offices with royal servants.[157] At these same times the king took the temporalities of the bishopric into his hands, appointing royal officials to manage the episcopal estates.[158] During the minorities of tenants-in-chief, the Crown could also appoint to benefices owned by these proprietors, as Edward II did in 1309, when he presented Nicholas Carleton to the church of Duloe because 'the lands and heir' of Sir Henry Bodrugan were in royal hands.[159] None in the county can have been ignorant of the king's position as patron paramount, and even the *Ordinalia*, *Origo Mundi*, was infused with notions of a monarchical Church. In this Cornish-language drama, the character of King Solomon himself consecrated a bishop by bestowing on this prelate 'the first benefice' that came into his hands, so that he would be 'faithful' in royal service.[160]

In Edward III's reign periodic seizure of the alien priories provided yet another reminder of royal might. The king was to take the priories of Tywardreath and St Michael's Mount into his hands in 1338, granting the lands and incomes of these institutions to local gentleman and royal clerks.[161] Enhancing the power of the Crown, seizure served to weaken the links between these houses and the continent.[162] It also provided local monks and gentry with a vested interest in eroding connections overseas, now that they were receiving the profits of these institutions themselves. All this helped to bring about the denization of these houses. Indeed, the new focus on aliens in the fourteenth century served to sharpen perceptions of 'national' identity. Repeatedly instructing Bishops Grandisson, Brantingham and Stafford to compile lists of non-denizens beneficed in their diocese, the Crown also ordered the sheriff to command aliens to present themselves to chancery.[163] The marking out of aliens, and the associated sharpening definition of 'otherness', underlined the

---

[157] *CPR 1327–1330*, 247; *CPR 1391–1396*, 565.
[158] *CPR 1367–1370*, 408.
[159] *CPR 1307–1313*, 195.
[160] *Cornish Drama*, i, OM, lines 2611–2616.
[161] *CFR 1337–1347*, 46, 70, 78, 84, 165, 167, 178, 447–448; *CPR 1338–1340*, 99; *CFR 1347–1356*, 97–98, 314; *CFR 1368–1377*, 25.
[162] Swanson, *Church and Society*, pp. 17–18.
[163] *Reg.Grandisson*, i, 57–60; ii, 760, 763–764; *Reg.Brantingham*, i, 193–195; *Reg.Stafford*, 2; *CCR 1337–1339*, 171; *CCR 1343–1346*, 85; *CCR 1346–1349*, 47; A. K. McHardy, 'The alien priories and the expulsion of aliens from England in 1378', *Studies in Church History*, 12, *Church Society and Politics*, ed. D. Baker (Oxford, 1975), pp. 133–141; A. K. McHardy, 'The Effects of War on the Church: the Case of the Alien Priories in the Fourteenth Century', in *England and her Neighbours, 1066–1453: Essays in Honour of Pierre Chaplais*, ed. M. Jones and M. Vale (London, 1989), pp. 277–295.

fact that the Cornish occupied a place in an English Church and realm, in the sense that they were to identify 'the enemy in their midst'.

In the face of this assertive kingly policy to the Church, royal power increasingly came to mediate papal influence in England. Edward III's two Statutes of Provisors (1351) and Praemunire (1353) in particular sought to regulate the pontiff's authority, with the former limiting papal provision to benefices and the latter curtailing the ability of Englishmen to appeal to the Curia.[164] Proclaiming 'the Englishness of the English Church', these statutes are emblematic of the king's growing influence over the religious affairs of the realm.[165] With the perceived threat of Lollardy, the Church called more and more on royal aid to defend orthodoxy, while the schism that erupted in 1378, for as long as it lasted, diminished papal prestige and increasingly thrust the king into the position of deciding on religious matters.[166] Contemporaries took it for granted that the Church would fracture along 'national' lines, or at least kingly ones, with all England – Cornwall included – choosing one loyalty, but Scotland and Gaelic Ireland choosing another.

Drawing the Crown and the Church yet closer together, Henry V vigorously set about quashing heretics. To this end, he ordered Bishop Stafford to preach sermons 'for the extirpation of sedition, schism, and heresy, specially of that execrable pest – Lollardy', a demand never before made by an English king.[167] Henry had assumed the role of arbiter of orthodoxy, reinforcing the role of the spiritual and temporal arms in the lives of the laity.[168] Even before his reign, in 1402 the 'poor parishioners' of Liskeard, Linkinhorne and Talland had petitioned through parliament for restitution after the priory of Launceston had ceased paying for three perpetual vicars.[169] The supplications of these 'poor parishioners' prompted Henry IV to pass new legislation regulating the appropriation of vicarages across the realm, showing how parliament's increasing criticisms of the spiritual arms spurred the king to action.[170]

Despite all this, however, we should be mindful of the fact that the Church formed a major institution in its own right. Since the papacy was to remain a powerful force in the lives of the faithful, papal power made itself felt in

---

[164] *Statutes of the Realm*, i, 316–318, 329; Heath, *Church and Realm*, pp. 125–133.
[165] Given-Wilson, *Henry IV*, p. 354.
[166] H. Kaminsky, 'The Great Schism', in *NCMH*, pp. 674–696; M. Harvey, 'Ecclesia Anglicana, cui Ecclesiastes noster Christus vos prefecit: the Power of the Crown in the English Church during the Great Schism', in *Religion and National Identity*, pp. 229–241.
[167] *Reg.Stafford*, 129.
[168] J. Catto, 'Religious Change under Henry V', in *Henry V: The Practice of Kingship*, ed. G. L. Harriss (Oxford, 1985), pp. 97–115.
[169] *PROME*, viii, 203–204.
[170] Ormrod, *Reign of Edward*, pp. 124–127, 144; Heath, *Church and Realm*, pp. 264–265; Given-Wilson, *Henry IV*, pp. 348–365.

England, sometimes giving rise to conflicts. One such quarrel arose in 1350, when Edward III granted the post of archdeacon of Cornwall to his clerk, a certain William Cusance, a nomination that set in motion twenty years of acrimony during which the king seized the temporalities of the bishopric. Bishop Grandisson refused to admit Edward's candidate, and in 1349 the pope had reserved the post for one John Harewell, causing yet more tension; the clergymen who sought this office did so relentlessly and bitterly.[171] It was only in 1371 that the case was finally settled, after Grandisson's death.[172] The Cusance episode is illustrative of the tensions latent between 'Church' and 'State', with frictions also inherent within each entity.[173] Although Cornwall's soaring church towers could proclaim in stone the intertwined power of the Church, the Crown and the gentry, while also forming centres of parochial activity, they could just as easily stand as testament to the many different local, national and international pressures weighing on the Church. And yet while Grandisson clashed with Clement VI and Edward III, it should be said that Bishops Stapeldon, Brantingham and Stafford lent their full support to every king from Edward II to Henry V. The rarity of conflict is more remarkable than its occurrence, as bishops, popes, lords and kings collaborated for the great preponderance of the time.

For all the points of potential friction, in many ways the king served as steward of the Church in England, emphasising the inextricable involvement of the *Ecclesia Anglicana* in the political and social life of the realm. Many clerics believed that the English Church should pay royal taxes for the 'defens of the comyn profit', as a 'national' political theology propounded the idea that England formed a moral community under the leaderships of its Church and messianic king as much as a political and territorial entity.[174] Even in the far south west, John Trevisa viewed Cornwall's inclusion in the episcopal jurisdiction of the West Saxons as essential in securing the peninsula's place in the fourteenth-century realm.[175] Serving increasingly as an intellectual, institutional and personal pan-English bonding agent, the *Ecclesia Anglicana* formed a potent force for connectivity that integrated the county into the kingdom.

---

[171] *CPR 1348–1350*, 462, 587; J. le Neve, 'Archdeacons in Cornwall', in *Fasti Ecclesiae Anglicanae, 1300–1541*, compil. J. M. Horn, 12 vols (London, 1962–7), ix, pp. 15–17; Whatley, 'Temporalities be Taken', 69–72, 80.
[172] *CPR 1370–1374*, 78, 98.
[173] Thompson, 'Ecclesiastical Polity', pp. 130, 145.
[174] J. Trevisa, cited in Beal, *John Trevisa*, pp. 16–18; Ruddick, *English Identity*, pp. 304–307.
[175] Trevisa, trans., *Polychronicon*, ii, p. 121.

14

Of Shipmen, Smugglers and Pirates: Maritime Connectivity

While journeying to St Michael's Mount in 1478, William Worcestre was to note that there were '147 havens within the space of 70 miles' from the Tamar down to Penzance.[1] In Cornwall, the points of access to the sea were many, especially on the south coast with its numerous estuaries. Sundry folk therefore exchanged a rich and varied range of goods and ideas across the county's seas.[2] Tin was by far Cornwall's most valuable export, being shipped both legally and illicitly in large volumes.[3] Also prominent among county cargoes was fish, while goods as varied as hides, foodstuffs, wool and narrow cloths were sent overseas too.[4] Many Cornish seafarers resembled John Scarlet and Stephen Pole of Fowey, who in 1344 loaded their vessel with:

> 375 pieces of tin, worth £240
> 17 dickers of hides, worth £8 10s.
> 1,707 stones of cheese, worth £100

---

[1] Worcestre, *Itineraries*, pp. 32–33.
[2] Horden and Purcell, *Corrupting Sea*, pp. 123–172; for the best introductions, Carus-Wilson and Coleman, *England's Export Trade*; I. Friel, *The Good Ship: Ships, Shipbuilding and Technology in England 1200–1520* (London, 1995); I. Friel, 'How Much did the Sea Matter in Medieval England (c. 1200–c. 1500)?', in *Roles of the Sea*, pp. 167–185; R. Gorski, 'Roles of the Sea: Views from the Shore', in *Roles of the Sea*, pp. 1–23; R. Unger, *The Ship in the Medieval Economy 600–1600* (London, 1980); R. Ward, *The World of the Medieval Shipmaster: Law, Business and the Sea c. 1350–c. 1450* (Woodbridge, 2009).
[3] M. Kowaleski, 'Coastal Communities in Medieval Cornwall', in *The Maritime History of Cornwall*, ed. H. Doe, A. Kennerley and P. Payton (Exeter and London, 2014), pp. 43–59; W. R. Childs, 'Overseas Trade and Shipping in Cornwall in the Later Middle Ages', in *Maritime History of Cornwall*, pp. 60–71.
[4] *CPR 1361–1364*, 496.

54 bacon hogs, worth £10 12*d*.
57 stone of butter, worth 66*s*. 8*d*.
Cloth of diverse colour, beds, and armour, worth £30
6 sacks of feathers, worth £6.[5]

In exchange, Cornish sailors can be found importing wine from Bordeaux, iron from Spain, salt from Brittany and a host of other commodities besides. Although Fowey stood out as the county's pre-eminent port, Looe, Padstow and Saltash also enjoyed significant shipping resources, while a multitude of coves and creeks played host to vessels.[6]

Not simply a source of shipping, the peninsula and its ports also held an integral place in a chain of coastal contacts that at its most expansive linked together the Baltic and the Mediterranean. Long journeys in this period were made of a series of short sails between safe havens, a point made by the Abbot of Tavistock in c. 1300, when he complained that his lands on the Scilly Isles were exposed to ships 'passing between France, Normandy, Spain, Bayonne, Gascony, Scotland, Ireland, Wales, and Cornwall'.[7] The county's increasingly well-developed port structures, such as the quay at Mousehole 'for common traffic of ships and boats, both of the king's lieges and of foreigners', proclaimed Cornwall's contribution to growing networks of seagoing connectivity.[8]

Even though the rugged north coast was comparatively poor for shipping, as Hayle, Padstow and St Ives formed the only reasonable harbours on this long lee-shore, the county still contributed to connectivity in the Irish-Celtic Seas. In 1371–2, for example, the sheriff investigated the circulation of Scottish coinage in the peninsula, suggesting that there was some exchange between Cornwall and this northerly kingdom.[9] Further to the south, it seems that there was more sustained contact with Wales. We see evidence of this in that the havener regularly noted the presence of Welsh ships docking in Cornish ports, while county vessels were often listed as landing wine in Beaumaris, Haverford and elsewhere.[10] Profiting from these many connections, in 1347 one Thomas Cook of Fowey even sold a vessel in Haverford west of Swansea.[11] Links with ports on Ireland's eastern coast, not least Dublin, were yet more substantial.[12]

---

[5] *CCR 1343–1346*, 334–335.
[6] Kowaleski, 'Coastal Communities', p. 44.
[7] SC8/75/3720.
[8] *CPR 1391–1396*, 247; C143/416/4; for the 'Havener's Hall' in Fowey, Leland, *Itineraries*, i, pp. 203, 323; CRO, CA/B46/6; cf. Ward, *Medieval Shipmaster*, p. 183.
[9] E122/189/150.
[10] *HA*, 72, 147, 177; E. A. Lewis, 'A Contribution to the Commercial History of Medieval Wales', *Y Cymmrodor*, 24 (London, 1913), pp. 86–188.
[11] *RBP*, i, 77–78; also, SC8/301/15035; *CPR 1401–1405*, 510.
[12] *CPR 1364–1367*, 32; *HA*, 214; *Calendar of Ancient Records of Dublin*, ed. J. T. Gilbert, 18 vols (Dublin, 1889–1922), i, p. 16.

Naturally enough, seafarers from these two lands could co-operate, as in 1349 for example, when four Irishmen chartered the *Seint Michel* of Mousehole to carry furs to Flanders.[13] The sea helped to sustain a rich range of connections, with Cornish fishermen regularly salting their cargoes in seasonal fishing stations in Ireland.[14] At the same time many Irish folk 'crossed in various ways' to Cornwall and not a few chose to stay on, with an anonymous petition of 1381–2 claiming that to escape the disorderly region of Munster 'many of the king's subjects have fled to Bristol and Cornwall'.[15] The poll tax levied in 1440 on first generation immigrants across the realm found that no fewer than seventy-six Irishmen and women resided west of the Tamar, with 'the toun' of Padstow supposedly 'ful of Irisch men'.[16]

Table 7: Cornwall's Assessment in the 1440 Alien Subsidy

Nationality	Householders	Non-Householders	Total
Breton	10	21	31
Channel Islanders	1	1	2
'Dutch'	12	6	18
Fleming	2	-	2
French	12	5	17
Gascon	4	1	5
Irish	39	37	76
Norman	4	12	16
Portuguese	3	1	4
Scottish	2	1	3
Unidentified (including seven women)	72	72	151
Total			325

Source: *England's Immigrants 1330–1550*, http://www.englandsimmigrants.com/, version 1.0 (accessed 21 November 2017), citing E179/87/78.

Just as significantly, the sea was to bind the county to other English regions further north or east on this watery expanse. There is evidence that Cornish mariners voyaged to Chester on a regular basis, carrying wine and other goods

---

[13] *CCR 1349–1354*, 25–26.
[14] T. O'Neil, *Merchants and Mariners in Medieval Ireland* (Dublin, 1987), pp. 33–35.
[15] *A Calendar of Irish Chancery Letters, c. 1244–1509, Patent Roll 49 Edward III*, ed. P. Crooks, https://chancery.tcd.ie/document/patent/49-edward-iii/206 (accessed 27 March 2019); SC8/118/5889.
[16] Leland, *Itineraries*, i, p. 179.

there to trade, while these same folk can be found transporting tin to Gloucester, much further to the south.[17] Although the Crown kept no record of English coasting trade, we know that around a tenth (some fourteen) of the vessels that arrived in Bristol in 1437–8 hailed from ports such as St Ives and Fowey, carrying with them tin, fish and cloth.[18] It seems that people often travelled and moved between these two areas. In 1387, for example, one Thomas Cornwale whose origins are revealed by his name was found to hold property in Bristol, and some sixty years earlier a certain William de Bristol had resided in Lelant.[19] In c. 1331 Rayner de Befori of Bristol found an even more permanent place in the county, his body being 'taken in a small boat to Cornwall and buried there' after he had died of natural causes off the Cornish coast while voyaging to Gascony.[20]

Perhaps the most remarkable example of connectivity across these seas comes from the Cornish assize of 1337.[21] At one stage in the proceedings of a case about disputed property, the attorneys of David, the son of Ivo de Estkes, had failed to attend the tribunal to plead on his behalf, leaving him in default. So as to preserve his lands, David sought to explain their absence by recounting how in July 1337 these men, Roger de Penrose and Robert, son of Reginald de Trewyvyan, had set sail from Cornwall on pilgrimage to the shrine of St Thomas Cantilupe at Hereford. A storm had overtaken their vessel, however, driving them out to the *altum mare* and eventually to Whitehaven in Cumberland. On landing there, the luck of these men worsened further when their unfamiliar speech resulted in their imprisonment as Scottish spies. It later transpired that this tall tale was simply a ruse to subvert justice, but the fact that the authorities believed it credible enough to summon a jury at Carlisle to investigate underlines the scale of marine interconnection.

All these voyages helped to forge a rich network of ties throughout the Irish-Celtic Seas and their hinterlands, with mariners from across this area by turns co-operating and competing with each other.[22] These waters, however, were by no means self-contained. This is a point made apparent by events in 1446, when the Bristolian Robert Sturmy transported 26,000 lbs of tin from 'Bristol to Pisa', metal that had already been shipped to Bristol by Cornishmen

---

[17] *Chester Custom Accounts, 1301–1566*, ed. K. P. Wilson, The Record Society of Lancashire and Cheshire, cxi (Liverpool, 1969), *passim.*; *CCR 1313–1318*, 42.
[18] *Bristol Town Duties*, ed. H. Bush (Bristol, 1828), pp. 17–25.
[19] *The Great Red Book of Bristol*, ed. E. W. Veale, 4 vols, Bristol Record Society, 4, 8, 16 and 18 (Bristol, 1933–53), i, pp. 209–210; *The Overseas Trade of Bristol in the Later Middle Ages*, ed. E. M. Carus-Wilson, Bristol Record Society, 7 (London, 1937), pp. 122–124, 222; E179/97/7 m. 1v; C241/190/21.
[20] SC8/292/14600.
[21] Brand, 'Travails of Travel', pp. 215–216.
[22] For example, *CPR 1377–1381*, 360–361.

and others.[23] Stretching out into the western seas, the county formed a nodal point in these long-distance trade routes. A good example of this is to be found in 1358, when the Black Prince ordered that if 'any ships freighted with wines or other wares for the city of Chester put into port in Cornwall on account of storms at sea, the havener is to allow them to proceed to the said city without paying custom for any wares'.[24] In 1388 Hanseatic merchants even put into Penryn 'to hire a steersman of more skill', as 'by lack of skill the 'lodesman' dared not steer the ship on the high sea towards Ireland'.[25] In this way, international trade and more localised *cabotage* came together in ways that were mutually supporting.

From all this activity we can see that Cornish seafarers were linked into a wide web of transmarine contacts, with wine one of the many commodities that they shipped.[26] Wendy Childs has shown that in the years around 1300 between seven and fifteen county vessels arrived in Bordeaux annually, constituting around 1 per cent of the entire wine fleet.[27] As the peninsula was less exposed to the privations of long voyages to Bordeaux than ports in the south-east, it is not surprising that by the 1370s some ten to fourteen Cornish ships were carrying 600–700 tuns of wine a year, comprising around 7 per cent of the fleet. By 1448–9 the county's vessels had achieved yet greater prominence still, representing some 15 per cent of the fleet (twenty-four ships) that transported 1,862 tuns of wine. Some sailors then carried the wine back home, among them Richard Michelstow of Fowey, who in the 1350s docked in both Fowey and Padstow with this valuable cargo.[28] Actually sailing far and wide, the county's wine-traders made great profits from shipping this commodity to every port from Chester right round to London.[29] In exchange, folk such as John Boswens carried cloth, fish, grain and many other goods down to Bordeaux, with this reciprocal trade significant enough to prompt a few Gascons at least to sail directly to Cornwall to do business.[30]

[23] *Overseas Trade of Bristol*, p. 84.
[24] *RBP*, ii, 146–147; also, SC8/41/2022; SC8/113/5649; *CCR 1354–1360*, 368; *CCR 1389–1391*, 258.
[25] *CCR 1385–1389*, 364–365.
[26] See, M. K. James, *Studies in the Medieval Wine Trade* (Oxford, 1971).
[27] Childs, 'Shipping in Cornwall', p. 64.
[28] *HA*, 226, 251; also, *RBP*, i, 82.
[29] *Chester Custom Accounts*, p. 23; *CPR 1345–1348*, 104; Childs, 'Shipping in Cornwall', pp. 61, 63; *The Local Custom Accounts of the Port of Exeter, 1266–1321*, ed. M. Kowaleski, *DCRS*, n.s. 36 (Exeter, 1993), *passim.*; *The Port Books of Southampton, 1427–1430*, trans. and ed. P. Studer, Southampton Record Society, 15 (Southampton, 1913), p. 18.
[30] *CPR 1361–1364*, 496; *CPR 1364–1367*, 6–7, 11, 32; *HA*, 181; *RBP*, ii, 175, 183; *CPR 1350–1354*, 358; James, *Wine Trade*, pp. 79, 175.

Wine-traffic from many lands put in to Cornish harbours, sheltering on the voyage from Gascony to markets further along the English coast or even further afield still. Since wine ships owed customs in the first port in which they called, whether or not they disgorged their cargoes, the havener's accounts provide evidence for just how many vessels anchored in the county while on this journey.[31] Although some wine was 'secretly landed by night', we know that between 1338 and 1356 no fewer than eighty-seven ships were to touch in Fowey and that a further seventy-five were to arrive in Falmouth.[32] Vessels also landed in the county on their outward journey to Bordeaux, among them the *Marget Cely* of London, which in 1488 docked in Fowey for two weeks on the voyage to Gascony, purchasing 'yerbes' (vegetables) and bread while in port.[33] Creating much connectivity, the county played many roles in the wine trade. A few Cornishmen actually settled in Gascony, including William Penzance of Bordeaux and William Cornish of Bayonne, while in c. 1401 Henry of Monmouth shipped as many as 50,000 pieces of tin down to Bordeaux 'in order to buy wine' for his household.[34]

Further to the south, Cornish mariners seized the opportunity presented to them to gain a share of the growing maritime pilgrimage routes to Santiago de Compostela.[35] Especially in Jubilee years, when the feast of St James fell on a Sunday, shipmen can be found seeking royal licence to transport pilgrims on special voyages to this prominent shrine. The permission received in 1394 by one Richard Robyn of Fowey, master of the *George*, 'to embark four-score pilgrims, take them to Santiago in Galicia to perform their vows, and bring them back to England' is entirely typical.[36] Of the 284 vessels known to have received licences of this sort between 1390 and 1460, no fewer than sixty-three hailed from Cornwall, with Fowey the third most important embarkation point in England.[37] William Wey, who in 1456 set sail from Devon on pilgrimage to Compostela, even noted that 'it was commonly said':

Be the man ne'er so hard,
He'll quake by the beard
Ere he pass Lizard.[38]

---

[31] *HA*, 27–32, 250.
[32] *CPR 1343–1345*, 194; *RBP*, ii, 127, 147; *CPR 1334–1338*, 389; *HA*, 167–168, 273–274.
[33] A. Hanham, *The Celys and Their World: An English Merchant Family in the Fifteenth Century* (Cambridge, 1985), pp. 390–391.
[34] C61/63 no. 36; C61/98 no. 63; C61/109 no. 104; *Gascon Rolls project*.
[35] C. M. Storrs, *Jacobean Pilgrims from England to St James of Compostella, from the Early Twelfth to the Late Fifteenth Century* (Santiago de Compostela, 1995).
[36] *CPR 1391–1396*, 362.
[37] Childs, 'Shipping in Cornwall', p. 66.
[38] W. Wey, *The Itineraries of William Wey*, ed. and trans. F. Davey (Oxford, 2010), p. 212.

As Cornish gentlemen and shipmen themselves sailed on this pilgrimage, such devotional journeys added yet more traffic to this sacred marine way.[39]

In the light of connections between the two peninsulas of Cornwall and Iberia, it is not surprising to find mariners of Spanish extraction landing in the county. This was because Castilians controlled nearly all Anglo-Spanish commerce until the early fourteenth century, the goods they brought including figs, lambskins and good-quality iron to sell, and purchasing fish and tin in exchange.[40] While the intermittent hostilities between England and Castile could disrupt such traffic at times, trade carried on under truces and safe-conducts for the understandable reason that potential profits might often outweigh the risks.[41] Portuguese merchants repeatedly landed in the county too, not least because their king enjoyed a more cordial relationship with the English Crown than his Castilian counterpart. Although some of these seafarers docked in the county to trade, as did the sailors of two ships in 1338, most sought to use the peninsula's ports as anchorages connecting them to their overseas markets.[42] It is illustrative of this that in 1371 a 'tempest' was said to have driven into Falmouth four Portuguese ships cruising home laden with merchandise, showing how the county's ports helped to facilitate long-distance exchange.[43]

To judge by the evidence of a chancery case from the 1390s, it was commonplace for county traders to purchase 'various merchandise from different parts of the English coast' to trade in Brittany.[44] In return, Cornish seafarers often acquired salt to sell back home, the processing of fish being dependent on this commodity.[45] Demand in the peninsula for Breton cloth, not least for sails, encouraged yet more exchange, while the shared heritage of the Cornish and Breton languages helped underpin these agreements linguistically.[46] One Odo Ude of Fowey is even found owning a ship of Guérande in Brittany, which traded salt in the 1380s and was captained by John Geer of that land.[47] Naturally enough, Bretons sailed regularly to Cornwall to sell their wares and at least a few chose to stay on, with the government investigating in the 1380s

---

[39] *Parliamentary Writs*, ii part 2, p. 655; *CPR 1367–1370*, 46.
[40] E122/39/6; *HA*, 142, 181, 191, 227; W. R. Childs, *Anglo-Castilian Trade in the Later Middle Ages* (Manchester, 1978), p. 30.
[41] For example, *HA*, 153; *CPR 1401–1405*, 238, 276; *CPR 1381–1385*, 249.
[42] *CPR 1338–1340*, 142–143; *CPR 1396–1399*, 367.
[43] The sheriff arrested these ships, C47/2/46/1-5; *CPR 1370–1374*, 160; *CCR 1369–1374*, 270–271.
[44] *West Country Shipping*, p. 5, this voyage resulted in acrimony.
[45] A. R. Bridbury, *England and the Salt Trade in the Later Middle Ages* (Oxford, 1955), pp. 116, 121; Childs, 'Shipping in Cornwall', p. 65.
[46] Padel, 'Where was Middle Cornish Spoken?', 30–31.
[47] *CPR 1381–1385*, 285.

and 1390s a number of the county's residents who had Breton ancestry.[48] One such migrant was John Breton's father, a certain William, who had been born in Brittany but had acquired nearly £14 of property in Bodmin, having 'born himself faithfully therein as a denizen and true Englishman'.[49] Although trade was to diminish as the French exerted greater control over fifteenth-century Brittany, the two peninsulas remained tied together by complex maritime, linguistic and social networks.[50]

Further east in the Channel, a lively trade carried on between Cornwall, Normandy, the Channel Islands and the Low Countries.[51] It seems that commerce with the Low Countries was of particular prominence, so that sailors from the county carried tin, hides, foodstuffs and many other tradable items to this densely populated land.[52] A petition to the Black Prince in 1357 from 'some merchants of Cornwall' even claimed that county traders in Flanders had been 'in great peril of their bodies', as blowers of tin had made 'many pieces of tin in the middle of which they have put false metal'.[53] Despite such dirty dealings, vessels from the Low Countries regularly arrived in the peninsula and in 1440 no fewer than twenty 'Dutchmen' and Flemings were found residing west of the Tamar.[54] By 1460 one John Browne of Flanders had even established himself as a householder and goldsmith of Fowey.

With the sea in this sense forming an enabling space, it was possible for the Cornish peninsula to enjoy connections with yet more distant lands. A few county seafarers can be found landing in King's Lynn, for example, with its strong links throughout the North Sea.[55] In the late 1430s it seems that the *Nicholas* of Saltash journeyed as far as Norway as part of a small fleet of cod fishermen and traders, while other Cornish vessels sailed to distant Iceland.[56] Further east, after unloading one cargo in London in 1439, the crew of the *Marie* of Fowey sailed to the Baltic with another; and to the south, there is evidence that vessels from the county shipped many commodities from Lisbon and Andalucía.[57] With the opening of direct sea-routes between the

---

[48] HA, 239–241; SC1/55/94; CCR 1381–1385, 380; CPR 1388–1392, 2; CPR 1396–1399, 241; CCR 1396–1399, 494.
[49] CPR 1388–1392, 2.
[50] Childs, 'Shipping in Cornwall', p. 65; *Beunans Meriasek*, lines 9–11, 118–134, 588–589.
[51] For example, HA, 159; SC1/43/10.
[52] CCR 1296–1302, 15; CCR 1343–1346, 334–335; CCR 1385–1389, 196.
[53] RBP, ii, 132; also, SC8/98/4896.
[54] HA, 176–178, 273.
[55] E210/8466; *The Making of King's Lynn: A Documentary Survey*, ed. D. M. Owen, Records of Social and Economic History, n.s. 9 (London, 1984), p. 366.
[56] CPR 1436–1441, 232, 234, 235; CPR 1446–1452, 523; Childs, 'Shipping in Cornwall', p. 66.
[57] Childs, 'Shipping in Cornwall', p. 66, citing E122/73/12 m. 22; *Overseas Trade of London*, pp. 17, 71.

northern seas and the Mediterranean in the fourteenth century, Cornwall came to hold an important position in an even more expansive network of maritime settlements.[58] For example, the manual compiled between 1332 and 1345 by Francesco Balducci Pegolotti shows how it was common practice for the Bardi to ship Cornish tin out to Bruges and then on to Florence, Venice and Constantinople, at times hiring county craft for cross-Channel services.[59] Vessels from distant lands could dock in the peninsula itself, as for example did a Genoese carrack and crew in 1379, the latter then warehousing 'twelve bails of spice' in Fowey.[60]

The county's many links overseas cannot be doubted, and yet we should not overlook the fact that maritime connectivity simultaneously bound the peninsula to the rest of England too. Since Devon was only a short sailing distance away, it is unsurprising that seafarers from these two shires can be found interacting. There is evidence that Cornish traders often sailed to Dartmouth, Plymouth and Teignmouth to do business, among them for example William Treverugh, who in 1364 exported as many as 30,000 'hakes' from Plymouth and Mousehole.[61] Shipping links of this sort naturally created many personal contacts, some of which one William de Fowey was to activate in 1304–5 when he chartered space on the *Andru* of Dartmouth to carry wine to Exeter.[62] In the first quarter of the fourteenth century alone, ships from Looe, Lostwithiel, Polruan and Saltash arrived in Exeter carrying commodities as varied as salt and brass-ware, with all these voyages tying together the two most south-westerly counties of England.[63]

By no means confined to neighbouring Devon, maritime connectivity along the English coast stretched right to the south-eastern counties. In 1403–4, for instance, the *Michel* of Mount's Bay docked in Melcombe, while merchants from Poole travelled regularly to Cornwall to purchase fish landed there.[64] Since seagoing links supported many social interactions, it is natural enough to find one John Estcote of Fowey in the 1350s employing as receiver a certain Phillip Bagge of Shoreham in Sussex.[65] In an initiative to bring hunger relief

---

[58] Cf. Bolton, *English Economy*, pp. 287–288.
[59] F. B. Pegolotti, *La Practica della Mercatura*, ed. A. Evans (Cambridge, MA, 1936), pp. 214, 245, 262, 381; *HA*, 147–148; *CCR 1339–1341*, 414, 473; *CCR 1337–1339*, 317, 578; Hatcher, *Tin*, pp. 93–94.
[60] *CCR 1377–1381*, 186; also, E122/40/13 m. 1; *CCR 1377–1381*, 187; cf. M. Kowaleski, '"Alien" Encounters in the Maritime World of Medieval England', *Medieval Encounters*, 13 (2007), pp. 96–121.
[61] *CPR 1364–1367*, 11; C241/176/69; *HA*, 197, 149; *CPR 1361–1364*, 496; C1/1494/30; CRO, ME/774; *HA*, 39, 177, 212.
[62] *Port of Exeter*, p. 91.
[63] *Port of Exeter*, pp. 15–16, 77, 109, 129, 158, 196–197; *HA*, 37.
[64] E122/102/30 m. 1; *HA*, 45, 87.
[65] *CPR 1358–1361*, 438; *SCKB*, iii, 149–152.

to the county, in 1365 John Rous shipped some fifty quarters of wheat in the *Margaret* of Northfleet, Kent, for the 'succour of the king's people' in Cornwall, who were 'suffering greatly from scarcity of corn'.[66] Exchanges with Southampton were especially prominent, with no fewer than sixteen county vessels, from Perranporth right round to Landulph, sailing there in 1427–30 with cargoes of slate, tin, wheat, wine and fish.[67] As Southampton's role in the internal tin trade was so significant, the burghal authorities established a 'tinne howse' to which all this metal had to be delivered.[68] After landing their precious cargo there, Cornish and non-Cornish merchants alike, among them John Dogowe of Fowey, carted hundreds of pieces of tin to Reading and thousands to London.[69]

It was inevitable that the Cornish would enjoy many maritime links with London, the greatest city and port in England. Since the capital formed the largest food market in the realm, profits could be made freighting fish and grain from the peninsula to keep the City in victuals.[70] The county's ships and seafarers regularly sailed to London, including the wool-bearing *William* of Fowey in 1380–2; while others can be found transporting commodities as diverse as sugar and hides, typically carrying out cloth, the capital's leading export.[71] Once again, however, tin stands out as the single most valuable item exchanged. Although poorly documented, this trade was worth thousands of pounds yearly and to regulate it a 'weyhouse' stood in London.[72] The scale of intra-English coasting, which in Exeter accounted for as much as 70 per cent of all shipping traffic, should not be underestimated.[73]

What, then, do these many seagoing links tell us about the nature of maritime connectivity? Evidently vessels and mariners from within and without Cornwall both coasted and sailed overseas interchangeably, carrying cargoes owned by county folk and 'outsiders' alike.[74] Anchoring in many havens while on such voyages, ships left and collected goods and people on the way, with

---

[66] *CPR 1364–1367*, 134; also, *HA*, 148–149, 238, 274; SC8/208/10357; *CCR 1369–1374*, 53.
[67] *Port Books of Southampton, 1427–1430*, pp. 16, 18, 32–33, 34, 57, 62–63, 66, 68, 74, 94–96, 98.
[68] *The Oak Book of Southampton of c. 1300*, trans. and ed. P. Studer, 3 vols, Southampton Record Society, 10, 11, 12 (Southampton, 1910–11), i, pp. 146–147.
[69] *The Brokage Book of Southampton 1443–1444*, ed. O. Coleman, 2 vols, Southampton Record Society, 4, 6 (Southampton, 1960–1), i, pp. xxxi–xxxii, 15, 274; *Port Book of Southampton for 1435–36*, pp. 44–45; *RBP*, ii, 170; cf. *English Inland Trade 1430–1540: Southampton and its Region*, ed. M. Hicks (Oxford, 2015).
[70] Kowaleki, 'South-Western Fisheries'; *HA*, 43; *CPR 1313–1317*, 447, 458.
[71] E122/71/4 mm. 3r, 4v; *CCR 1385–1389*, 191–192; *Overseas Trade of London*, pp. 17, 71, 93–94, 140, 162–163; *HA*, 148, 160, 190, 250.
[72] C1/70/77; *LBK*, 342–343; Hatcher, *Tin*, p. 137; *CCR 1399–1402*, 354–355.
[73] *Port of Exeter*, p. 31.
[74] *HA*, 160; *Port of Exeter*, p. 196; *Port Book of Southampton for 1435–36*, pp. 44–45; *Overseas Trade of London*, p. 71.

the mutinous sailors of the *Mary* of Kinsale hailing from places as diverse as Cornwall and Gascony.[75] All these voyages and seafarers together created zones of interaction more than they did narrow shipping lanes.[76] Expertise acquired from more modest voyages actually proved essential to the commanding heights of commerce, for Cornish pilots who had learnt their trade on smaller-scale crossings were later to be employed by wealthy Hansards and Londoners alike to guide their vessels to safety.[77] In this way, 'local' and 'international' trade were intertwined, with the county's enterprising mariners gaining a growing share of late-medieval England's shipping.[78]

It is also clear that maritime connectivity created and sustained a rich web of personal connections. To support their seagoing activities, ship-owning families such as the Michelstows of Fowey, the Maynhers of Tregony and the Slugges of Saltash propagated a wide variety of contacts across the realm and beyond.[79] Since vessels had to be sailed and crewed, it naturally followed that thousands of Cornishmen came to enjoy maritime links. Even port-side dockhands and residents interacted with the many seafarers who landed in the county, while navigable rivers helped to carry the sea littoral and 'sailortown culture' deep into the peninsula.[80] As a result, sundry folk, among them Sir William Botreaux and Thomas Goldsmith of Bodmin, a merchant, are to be found hiring vessels and owning shares in the ships themselves.[81] An important strand of interaction, the ship-share system linked together men from across the county and throughout England. This much is shown by events in 1295, when Walter Droys of Truro, Lambert of Whith (Lostwithiel?) and Jeel of Devon sold to one Walter Hobbe of Bristol a half-share in a ship that they jointly owned.[82] The sea nourished all these connections in a process greatly widening Cornish horizons.

When we turn from dealings of this sort to the more fractious aspects of maritime life, we find an equally rich range of interactions. By seeking out well-hidden paths along which to deliver their contraband, for example,

---

[75] *CCR 1302–1307*, 38–39; *CFR 1356–1368*, 60; *CIM 1392–1399*, 101–102.
[76] Cf. Horden and Purcell, *Corrupting Sea*, pp. 138–140.
[77] For example, C1/43/275–8.
[78] Cf. Kowaleski, 'Crown Patronage', pp. 249–250.
[79] Drake, 'Michelstow Family'; *HA*, 39; Childs, 'Shipping in Cornwall', p. 63.
[80] Ward, *Medieval Shipmaster*, pp. 48–68; for example, CRO, ART/2/1/2; *CCR 1399–1402*, 475; for 'sailortowns', B. Bevan, 'The Resilience of Sailortown Culture in English Naval Ports, c. 1820–1900', *Urban History*, 43 (2016), pp. 72–95.
[81] E122/113/3, many of these men had simply chartered vessels; *CCR 1339–1341*, 196; E101/41/31 m. 7; C47/2/49/20; *CPR 1381–1385*, 405; cf. M. Kowaleski, 'The Shipman as Entrepreneur in Medieval England', in *Commercial Activity, Markets and Entrepreneurs in the Middle Ages: Essays in Honour of Richard Britnell*, ed. B. Dodds and C. Liddy (Woodbridge, 2011), pp. 165–182.
[82] *PROME*, ii, 14–16, the presumed date is 1295.

smugglers exploiting the peninsula's rugged coast created yet more points of contact with the sea. In 1387, to cite one not untypical instance, the king was informed that despite not having paid customs, 'a great number of merchants... have many times laden merchandise in divers ports and other places in Cornwall called "crykes" and taken it to foreign parts'.[83] The high value to volume ratio of tin rendered the metal ideally suited for toll avoidance, with the result that the government was forever seeking to prevent local knights and merchants shipping it illegally.[84] Despite these efforts, however, in 1414 the parliamentary Commons complained that:

> certain merchants, both people from the Islands of Jersey and Guernsey and other merchants from the regions of Brittany and Guyenne, buy in various places in Cornwall unsmelted tin ore, and they take and carry it to be sold in various regions of France, Normandy, Brittany, Guyenne and elsewhere, rather than at the [Calais] staple. And also, various other merchants, both denizen and foreign, buy and send smelted tin, called shotted tin, out of the realm, to the regions of Flanders, Holland, Zeeland and other regions overseas.[85]

After being cast into 'pocket tin' for ease of transport, most of the metal was shipped out of the county without paying customs dues and a 'secret staple' even operated in Guernsey.[86] Although successful smuggling produced no customs ledgers, rendering it invisible to us, the government was concerned that Cornwall's illicit traders were handling not only tin but also commodities as varied as wool and wine.[87] Inevitably, smugglers depended on complex networks of informers, sailors, distributors and consumers alike, all of whom had maritime interests.

Another strand of marine interconnectedness was wrecking, which was inexorably linked to Cornwall's treacherous shores, fierce storms and shipping activities.[88] A good example of this comes from 1318, when the cables of a Portuguese ship that had anchored in Padstow parted, 'casting ashore' the vessel and its cargo.[89] Although the crew made it to land, invalidating claims to wreck

---

[83] *CCR 1385–1389*, 305; cf. J. B. Blake, 'Medieval Smuggling in the North-East: Some Fourteenth-Century Evidence', *Archaeologia Aleiana*, Fourth Series, 43 (1965), pp. 243–260.
[84] Coinage duty, not customs dues, prompted smuggling, Hatcher, *Tin*, p. 6; *CPR 1343–1345*, 66, 71, 74; *CPR 1345–1348*, 309; *CPR 1370–1374*, 170–173; *CPR 1388–1392*, 268; *CPR 1391–1396*, 263.
[85] *PROME*, ix, 108–109; SC8/23/1142.
[86] *PROME*, viii, 468; Hatcher, *Tin*, pp. 6, 110–111.
[87] *CCR 1292–1301*, 480–482; *CPR 1340–1343*, 364; *RBP*, i, 45.
[88] *HA*, 23–27.
[89] *CPR 1317–1321*, 169, 403.

of the sea that rested on the fact that ships could be adjudged wrecked only if no man, dog, or cat escaped alive, John Carminow and many others allegedly carried away all their goods and wares. A trickle of shipwrecked mariners arrived in the county under such inauspicious circumstances, among them a Breton crew whose ship had been overcome by a storm and who then 'fell in with a man who saved himself from some wreck', who, 'so far as they could comprehend his language', they believed to be a Venetian galley oarsman.[90] Some Cornishmen perhaps helped a few ships on their way, as did for example Nicholas Wamford the younger in 1342, when in Weymouth he boarded the *Trinity* of Fowey and cut its 'cables and cords' so that the tide washed the vessel ashore.[91] There is little evidence of deliberate wrecking, however, and none of false lights being used to lure ships onto the rocks, a myth of later centuries.[92] Most wrecking actually took the form of beach harvest, with ships carrying 'goods and merchandise of great value' often 'wrecked on sands' in the peninsula.[93] In an attempt to secure the resultant profits the original owners, the king, the earl-duke, local lords and lesser folk could certainly quarrel, but in pressing their rights all these people were still engaging with the marine.[94]

Perhaps the most fractious activity at sea, piracy, nonetheless represented the continuation of water-based redistribution 'by other means'.[95] Since pirates depended on the world of trade to sell their stolen wares, lawful exchange and seagoing thievery were tightly intertwined. The links between commerce and salt-water robbery were even closer than we might suppose, however, as the 'vicious pirate and the peaceful trader' were often one and the same person at different times.[96] Because technological limitations meant that no polity could command the waves with formal fleets, the sea formed an extra-jurisdictional space, a lawless watery frontier within which marcher laws, customs and the right to reprisal operated. It follows that trade under arms was an accepted type of commercial interaction and border warfare, so that mariners from across Christendom engaged interchangeably in theft and trade.[97]

---

[90] *State Papers, Venetian*, p. 312.
[91] *CPR 1340–1343*, 449.
[92] Cf. C. Pearce, *Cornish Wrecking 1700–1860: Reality and Popular Myth* (Woodbridge, 2010), pp. 11, 21, 69; *HA*, 61–62.
[93] *CPR 1391–1396*, 653–654.
[94] For example, CRO, AR/15/1; *HA*, 87–88, 90–91, 100, 166, 194, 222.
[95] Horden and Purcell, *Corrupting Sea*, p. 158.
[96] Rodger, *Safeguard of the Sea*, p. 115.
[97] N. A. M. Rodger, 'The Law and Language of Private Naval Warfare', *The Mariner's Mirror*, 100 (2014), pp. 5–16 at 7; Drake, 'Fawey', 314; C. R. Backman, 'Piracy', in *A Companion to Mediterranean History*, ed. P. Horden and S. Kinoshita (Chichester, 2014), pp. 172–183; F. L. Cheyette, 'The Sovereign and the Pirates, 1332', *Speculum*, 45 (1970), pp. 40–68; T. K. Heebøll-Holm, 'Law, Order and Plunder at Sea: a Comparison of England and France in the Fourteenth Century', *Continuity and Change*,

Even the language of medieval piracy was ambiguous. Actually having few moral or legal overtones, the Latin word *pirata* simply described a type of sea-fighting.[98] It was not until 1536 that the government was to define piracy as a crime, and as late as the 1660s that it began to employ the term 'privateer' for state-sanctioned attacks. Such legalistic terms are ill-suited to medieval piracy. We should think instead of water-borne larceny, salt-water raids and private maritime predation, with direct action often employed without social stigma. Violence was routinely practised at sea, and not surprisingly because violence had an integral place in the workings of medieval society at large. Neither 'unlimited maritime mayhem' nor a gratuitous blood-thirsty pursuit, as it has sometimes been characterised, salt-water raiding instead formed part of a system of mutual reprisals.[99] While it may have forced changes in the pattern of redistribution, sustained seagoing thievery in the Channel actually bears testament to the range of exchanges across this expanse of water.[100]

There can be little doubt that Cornish seafarers had a penchant for 'piracy'. Providing many anchorages from which ships could sail forth to seize their prey, the peninsula's jagged coastline played a key role here. Combined with the wealth of passing trade, the skill of the county's sailors and Cornwall's many connections overseas, the long coastline provided the basis for a significant and growing 'pirate industry'. Until the mid-fourteenth century most commercial sea-fights took place near the coast or in the county's ports themselves. In a not untypical case, in 1346, after the vessel of John Vanas of Kampen in the Low Countries had landed in the peninsula, it was alleged that county folk 'horribly cast out' his crewmen and seized the ship.[101] Across the century and into the next, however, seagoing thieves were to prowl an ever-growing arc of salt water. In 1434, for example, John Michelstow of Fowey was said to be cruising off Portugal arrayed in manner of war as the captain of a great ship, the *Edward*, and in conjunction with a barge and crew of no fewer than 200

---

32 (2017), pp. 37–58; T. K. Heebøll-Holm, *Ports, Piracy and Maritime War: Piracy in the English Channel and the Atlantic, c. 1280–c. 1330* (Leiden, 2013); M. Pitcaithly, 'Piracy and Anglo-Hanseatic Relations, 1385–1420', in *Roles of the Sea*, pp. 125–145; E. S. Tai, 'The Legal Status of Piracy in Medieval Europe', *History Compass*, 10/11 (2012), pp. 838–851.
[98] Rodger, 'Private Naval Warfare'; *Documents Relating to Law and Custom of the Sea*, ed. R. G. Marsden, The Navy Records Society, 49–50, 2 vols (London, 1915–16), i, pp. 99–100.
[99] D. G. Sylvester, 'Communal Piracy in Medieval England's Cinque Ports', in *Noble Ideals and Bloody Realities: Warfare in the Middle Ages*, ed. N. Christie and M. Yazigi (Brill, 2006), pp. 163–176 at 167; Kingsford, *Prejudice and Promise*, p. 78; cf. Heebøll-Holm, *Maritime War*, pp. 20–21; C. Richmond, 'Royal Administration and the Keeping of the Seas, 1422–85' (Unpubl. Univ. Oxford D.Phil, 1963), pp. 7–8.
[100] Cf. Horden and Purcell, *Corrupting Sea*, p. 157.
[101] *CPR 1345–1348*, 110.

men.[102] Capturing a Genoese carrack near Cape St Vincent, Michelstow had the crew 'put ashore in Portugal in a destitute condition on the plea that they were "Sarasenes", though they were not'. He then sailed their ship to Fowey, before distributing its cargo throughout south-western England.

A formidable bunch, Cornish salt-water bandits can be found preying on ships from Brittany, Castile, Flanders, France, Genoa, Ireland, Portugal, the cities of the Hanseatic League and even from other English ports, sometimes in the most violent way.[103] A good example of maritime disorder comes from 1346, after a storm had driven a wine-ship from Brussels into St Ives Bay.[104] Hearing of this happening, more than sixty armed Cornishmen, among them Richard Johan of Fowey, allegedly arrived in two ships to plunder the vessel, overcoming the crew in short time. In desperation, the men of Brussels offered a local customs collector some fifteen tuns of wine if he could secure the return of their ship. When approached by this office-holder, however, the plunderers held a 'conference' about what to do and then 'hoisted the sail of the ship and feloniously fled to the parts of Wales'. Despite cutting-out raids of this sort being commonplace, the identities of malefactors were often hard to obtain. We see this again in 1346, when 'certain men of England in two ships and a barge' were allegedly to have seized a Castilian wine-vessel.[105] Luckily for the owners, John Peritz and Domyngus Aynes, they were ashore on their affairs, as the unnamed Englishmen entered their ship by armed force. Once aboard, they supposedly proceeded to kill 'all the men and mariners in the ship except John's son, who had hidden himself among the tuns through fear of death, and so escaped alive by the aid of men entering the ship when it reached the port of Fowey'.

Even when the names of alleged malefactors were forthcoming, punishments were by no means always effective. In 1338, for instance, it was alleged that one John Lamborne and others had forcibly entered two Portuguese ships and 'carried away' their goods, delivering these stolen items to certain men of Fowey and Mousehole.[106] For this, the government had Lamborne arrested, but he soon after broke from prison and escaped. In much the same way, in 1382 over thirty Cornishmen, including Oliver Scarlet of Fowey, allegedly 'captured off the English coast' a Portuguese barge worth 3,900 francs, placing the crew in chains.[107] Although the government ordered the wrongdoers to pay

---

[102] *CPR 1429–1436*, 355.
[103] *CPR 1381–1385*, 285 *CPR 1313–1317*, 94, 301, 313, 490, 538; *CCR 1385–1389*, 364–365; *CCR 1318–1322*, 110–111; *CCR 1355–1360*, 653–654; *CCR 1369–1374*, 447; *CPR 1317–1321*, 283; SC8/279/13913.
[104] *CPR 1345–1348*, 115.
[105] *CCR 1346–1349*, 11, 22, some hailed from Plymouth.
[106] *CPR 1338–1340*, 130, 142.
[107] *CPR 1381–1385*, 142.

compensation of £200, later in the year only £50 of this was forthcoming.[108] In 1311 Edmund de Trevelwythe had even claimed that ten Cornishmen, among them none other than his business partner, one John Stonhard, had commandeered his vessel in Fowey and then sailed it 'beyond the seas', wounding and imprisoning him in Lostwithiel during the theft.[109]

Although they themselves often lived by the sword, the county's mariners found that they by no means always enjoyed the upper hand. It is illustrative of this that in 1337 one William Collan of Truro petitioned the king 'as he was lately plundered of diverse goods and merchandise... by pirates of Flanders'.[110] There is evidence that Cornishmen sometimes lost out to French, Castilian and even English freebooters.[111] In 1350, for instance, 'on the high sea off the coast of Cornwall by Lizard', as many as five ships from Bristol, Chester and Plymouth allegedly seized the vessel of one Adam Scarlet of Fowey, appropriating its £1,200 cargo of grain and tin.[112] More seriously still, back in the 1310s a feud had erupted between the men of Fowey, Lostwithiel and Polruan on the one hand, and those of the Cinque Ports on the other.[113] It seems that the Cornishmen had helped to arrest some Portsmen who had attacked a ship from Great Yarmouth that was docked in Fowey itself. Seeking revenge for their fellows, many Portsmen supposedly lay in wait near these Kentish harbours, threatening the county's seafarers with 'capture and death'. Passing into myth, the fact that 'Fawey men had victorie' over the Cinque Ports 'and therapon bare their armes mixt with the armes of Rye and Winchelsey' was still a matter of local pride in the sixteenth century.[114]

Raiders from many lands can be found roving the seas surrounding the county, landing their captured wares in the peninsula's harbours and 'pirate entrepôts'. In 1327, for example, some Basque sailors had supposedly seized a ship near Brittany, selling its 240-tun cargo of wine in Fowey for £4 a tun before re-christening the vessel the *Despensere* to avoid detection.[115] Such lucrative skulduggery naturally depended on the aid of local accomplices, with co-operative predation itself commonplace.[116] Cornishmen often pooled their resources 'in manner of war' with both their fellow county mariners and

---

[108] *CCR 1381–1385*, 72.
[109] *CPR 1307–1313*, 424–425, 537.
[110] *CCR 1337–1339*, 24–25, 116; SC8/50/2455.
[111] *CCR 1343–1346*, 334–335; *CCR 1346–1349*, 79.
[112] *CPR 1348–1350*, 593.
[113] *CPR 1317–1321*, 557; cf. Sylvester, 'Communal Piracy'.
[114] Leland, *Itinerary*, i, pp. 203–204.
[115] *CPR 1327–1330*, 168; *CPR 1401–1405*, 227.
[116] For example, *CPR 1338–1340*, 494; *West Country Shipping*, pp. 21–22.

with seafarers from every port from Bristol to Great Yarmouth.[117] The sailors of Fowey and Dartmouth in particular chose to work together to plunder vessels.[118] One of the most striking examples of this sort of collective thievery comes from 1385–6, when Genoese merchants alleged that after their vessel had been driven by a storm into a Breton port, 'certain Englishmen [by] main force took the said goods and carried them off to Dartmouth'.[119] As many as eight English ships fought in this major sea-fight, three each from Fowey and Dartmouth.

Since the county's seafarers succeeded in seizing so many vessels and cargoes, it was naturally the case that networks of raiders and traders then redistributed the stolen wares – from large quantities of alum to hundreds of tuns of wine – to folk throughout the peninsula.[120] Pilfered goods often passed along even more extended chains of contact, with cargoes plundered by the county's water-borne thieves appearing in the possession of men from Plymouth, Dartmouth, the Cinque Ports and even Wales.[121] We see an example of this in 1360, when John Thomas' *Savoie* of Fowey, along with ships from Great Yarmouth, Weymouth and even Bayonne, captured two wine-vessels from Sluys and Spain near Portland.[122] Landing in Southampton, the raiders then sold their ill-gotten wine to many burgesses there, although subsequent investigations found that '30 tuns were drunk and wasted among the mariners of the ships before they left port'. As maritime larceny could prove so lucrative, it was inevitable that leading Cornish townsmen and gentlemen often received a share of the stolen cargoes, probably having interests in the ships involved. Some of these folk actually engaged in the act of seagoing thievery itself, including Sir John Trevarthian and John Kendale, the mayor of Lostwithiel.[123] A great deal of gentle and mercantile money backed these ventures.

Where goods moved, so too did people. Stolen wares had to be coasted to other ports across the realm, while maritime malefactors themselves roved the sea in search of their prey before being welcomed back in Cornwall as 'friends'.[124] The county's growing reputation for maritime predation drew in folk from far and wide, among them the 'Dutchman' Hankyn Selander. In the

---

[117] *CCR 1377–1381*, 413; *CPR 1327–1330*, 467, 556–557; *CPR 1377–1381*, 360–361; *CIM 1348–1377*, 153–154.
[118] For example, *CCR 1360–1364*, 120; *CPR 1364–1367*, 147; *CPR 1405–1408*, 60; *West Country Shipping*, pp. 9–12; cf. J. Appleby, 'Devon Privateering from Early Times to 1668', in *The New Maritime History of Devon*, ed. M. Duffy et al., 2 vols (London, 1992–4), i, pp. 90–97.
[119] *CPR 1385–1389*, 165, 320.
[120] *CPR 1388–1392*, 267, 274; *CCR 1389–1391*, 487; *CCR 1385–1389*, 227.
[121] *CPR 1345–1348*, 115; *CPR 1354–1358*, 56.
[122] *CIM 1348–1377*, 153–154.
[123] *CPR 1381–1385*, 249, 257, 259, 286; *CPR 1385–1389*, 165; *CPR 1388–1392*, 212.
[124] *CPR 1416–1422*, 425.

1430s and 1440s he was regularly to be found cruising off the Cornish coast, boarding vessels and throwing their letters of safe conduct overboard before claiming these ships as his own.[125] After capturing crews, raiders often shipped home prisoners so as to collect ransoms for the release of these folk, a practice that brought about yet more mobility.[126] Cornishmen themselves could be captured, however, and on occasion evidently in some numbers, with the result that in 1380 Bishop Brantingham was moved to issue an indulgence for south-western mariners imprisoned by 'French pirates'.[127] Such activities did not amount to a fully fledged trade in people. A petition from Henry IV's reign, however, claimed that during a land dispute in Wiltshire, a certain John Rolves of Gloucestershire had first tried to hide Robert Chamberlain's heiress, one Agnes, in a nunnery in Wales, but after she had refused to become a nun he then 'sent her to Cornwall', to Helston, 'and sold her to the Bretons'.[128] Ransoming formed both a significant source of profit and an accepted hazard of life at sea.[129]

Whether it did so peacefully or violently, seagoing thievery had the effect of linking Cornwall to distant lands, and in so doing it formed yet another strand of connectivity. Local knights, merchants, fishermen and many others made it their 'seasonal avocation', with 'piracy' wearing the face of respectability as a type of commercial enterprise.[130] While some maritime predation simply arose from opportunism, other cases almost certainly occurred during commercial disputes with overseas traders. This is how the peninsula could form a centre of legal shipping and illegal raids at one and the same time. Indeed, county seafarers did not systematically murder their victims. It was probably the case that most of the deaths which occurred happened during the capture of a vessel, for once the crew had surrendered they were generally imprisoned for later ransom or release.[131] This much is suggested by events in 1418, when the captors of a Castilian crew freed their prisoners 'without ransom, as is the custom between the men of Spain and the men of Devon and Cornwall'.[132] With waterborne larceny having a common code of ethics, it was no blood-sport.

---

[125] Drake, 'Pirates and Pilchards', 41–42.
[126] For example, *CPR 1381–1385*, 142; *CPR 1388–1392*, 214; *Royal and Historical Letters during the Reign of Henry the Fourth...*, ed. F. C. Hingeston, Rolls Series, 2 vols (London, 1860–1965), i, p. 127.
[127] *Reg.Brantingham*, i, 433; also, *CPR 1401–1405*, 499.
[128] SC8/33/1637.
[129] Kowaleski, "'Alien' Encounters', 120.
[130] Cf. R. I. Burns, 'Piracy as an Islamic–Christian Interface in the Thirteenth Century', *Viator*, 11, (1980), pp. 165–178.
[131] Cf. Heebøll-Holm, *Maritime War*, pp. 52–53.
[132] *CIM 1399–1422*, 312–313; cf. Kowaleski, "'Alien' Encounters', 117–121.

'Piracy' remains a vexed subject, however, not least because of the many complex customs and courts that were involved in seeking to regulate maritime violence. Since the common law was ill-equipped to deal with cases of this kind, in the early-fourteenth century local courts, especially in boroughs, often handled suits of prize and 'piracy' under the auspices of the law merchant and the *Rôles d'Oléron*, an international customary law regulating the conduct of sailors.[133] Lacking as they did criminal jurisdiction, these courts dealt with 'piracy' as civil suits of damages and debt, awarding restitution of lost property or monetary compensation to the plaintiff.[134] The records of these tribunals in Cornwall are scanty, but there is evidence that the earldom-duchy's marine courts sometimes came to judgments regarding what were termed 'trespasses' at sea.[135]

If denied redress in tribunals local to the theft, however, a dissatisfied plaintiff could either petition his own king or the king of the defendant for restitution. In 1337 Mounfrere of Seville is found doing the latter, when he called on Edward III's grace after John le Carpenter of Lostwithiel, the bailiff of the sea, had allegedly refused to arrest the malefactors who had plundered his vessel.[136] Increasingly keen to intervene in cases of maritime predation, the king himself enjoyed ultimate responsibility for the division of prizes.[137] To this end, the Statute of the Staple in 1353 stipulated that if any goods seized at sea were landed in an English port, the victim could, on proof of ownership, be delivered of his property 'without making other suit at the common law'.[138] For the better enforcement of this legislation, across the fourteenth century the Crown developed the courts of the admiralty. Concerned with 'contact made between merchant and merchant, or merchant and mariner, overseas or within the tide mark', these specialised tribunals came to exercise jurisdictional powers amounting to flexible equity.[139] While the admiralty courts, one

---

[133] R. G. Marsden, 'The Vice-Admirals of the Coast', *EHR*, 22 (1907), pp. 468–477 at 468–469; Heebøll-Holm, 'Plunder at Sea', 40–45.
[134] T. Heebøll-Holm, 'The Origins and Jurisdiction of the English Court of Admiralty in the Fourteenth Century', in *Courts of Chivalry and Admiralty in Late Medieval Europe*, ed. A. Musson and N. Ramsay (Woodbridge, 2018), pp. 149–170 at 156; A. F. Sutton, 'The Admiralty and Constableship of England in the Later Fifteenth Century: the Operation and Development of these Offices, 1462–85, under Richard, Duke of Gloucester and King of England', in *Chivalry and Admiralty*, pp. 187–214 at 192.
[135] *RBP*, i, 25; *HA*, 41–43.
[136] SC8/295/14728; *CPR 1334–1338*, 443.
[137] C. J. Ford, 'Some Dubious Beliefs about Medieval Prize Law', in *Chivalry and Admiralty*, pp. 215–236.
[138] *PROME*, v, 76–77; *Statutes of the Realm*, i, p. 338; Kingsford, *Prejudice and Promise*, p. 79; Heebøll-Holm, 'Plunder at Sea', 51–52.
[139] Ward, *Medieval Shipmaster*, pp. 28–47.

of which was to sit in Lostwithiel, heard many cases of prize and maritime disorder, nearly all their records have unfortunately perished.[140]

If turned away altogether by a foreign prince, dissatisfied seafarers could then petition their own monarch to either seize the goods of the raiders' fellow countrymen or request a letter of marque. In 1344 after French freebooters had seized their vessel, for example, and having been 'utterly refused' remedy by Philip VI of France, William Scarlet and Stephen Pole of Fowey duly approached Edward III.[141] In response to their initiative he arrested hundreds of pounds of French goods in Exeter, London and Sandwich as compensation for their losses. Working on much the same principle, letters of marque empowered victims themselves forcibly to secure compensation from 'the fellow-townsmen or subjects' of a foreign prince.[142] Such documents formed part of marcher law – that is holding whole commonalties responsible for individual crimes and recognising rights to prize, reprisal and retaliatory violence.[143] Yet despite professing to be concerned with private quarrels, these letters often covered political motives as the sea played host to many competing jurisdictions.[144] Medieval letters of marque were actually only conceded in times of peace; in war, all enemy ships were fair game. Even in peacetime, however, government-sanctioned reprisals often faded into self-determined retaliation and counter-raids.[145]

As a result of these many customs and procedures, along with the chance survival of documentation, the royal investigations that have come down to us provide evidence only of a small proportion of salt-water larceny. Such enquiries are generally concerned with the commanding heights of theft, with many less valuable and less deadly incidents being dealt with locally. Little evidence of the latter cases remains, but their presence necessarily makes water-borne banditry a far more humdrum activity than it first appears. We may also wonder about the truth of royal commissions, for plaintiffs often exaggerated levels of skulduggery in order to secure the most compensation.[146] More significantly still, the Crown only involved itself in cases of maritime predation when it chose. Royal justice was firmly closed to enemy seafarers.

---

[140] But see the cases heard in chancery, *West Country Shipping, passim.*; cf. M. Beilby, 'The Profits of Expertise: the Rise of the Civil Lawyers and Chancery Equity', in *Profit, Piety*, pp. 72–90.
[141] *CCR 1343–1346*, 334–335; cf. Heebøll-Holm, *Maritime War*, pp. 155–159.
[142] Rodger, 'Private Naval Warfare', 6–7; *PROME*, ix, 200–202.
[143] For a Cornish example, C47/28/7/26; for a threat of letters against Cornish seafarers, SC8/269/13408.
[144] Tai, 'Status of Piracy', 841–842.
[145] D. A. Gardiner, 'The History of Belligerent Rights on the High Seas in the Fourteenth Century', *Law Quarterly Review*, 48 (1932), pp. 521–546; Cheyette, 'Sovereign and the Pirates', 56–57.
[146] For example, *CCR 1381–1385*, 72.

All sea-thefts were grounded in private self-interest. Yet although the Crown attempted to police diplomatically embarrassing incidents, cases committed by Englishmen against enemy shipping did not usually merit restitution as they served the king's purposes of harrying the foe with minimal expense to the exchequer.[147] Turning a blind eye to raids of this sort, the government chose not to initiative investigations into these attacks because they formed a legitimate part of war. While the king certainly did not exercise complete control over the redoubtable seafarers of Cornwall, or anywhere else for that matter, there can be little doubt that 'piracy' formed an essential part of royal policy, especially during the Hundred Years' War. We can see this in 1338, near the beginning of the long conflict, when Edward III made a point of investigating attacks on 'merchants of Spain, Portugal, Catalonia, the duchy of Aquitaine and other lands and places *in friendship with the king* [my italics]'.[148] Inquiries into assaults on French merchantmen, however, are conspicuously absent throughout the war. It is illustrative of this that in 1320, before the opening of hostilities, Edward II had launched an investigation into the Cornishmen who had allegedly seized a French wine-vessel, killing the crew 'and throwing them into the sea'.[149] In time of war some sixty-five years later, however, Richard II chose to issue no commissions enquiring into the west-country seafarers who had attacked French shipping amassed at Sluys to invade England, sinking at least four vessels and capturing four more.[150] Neither did he pursue those mariners from Fowey and Dartmouth who in 1388 captured twenty-five French ships 'of varying sizes, with full cargoes of wine', returning home unscathed.[151] The king's studied inactivity arose from the fact that these salt-water raids made an invaluable contribution to English sea-power.

All the polities of western Christendom sought in some measure to manage maritime violence. Foreign princes and powers certainly wrote to the king of England from time to time requesting compensation for Cornish attacks on their subjects, among them the duke of Brittany, the king of Portugal and the cities of both Flanders and the Hanseatic League.[152] During periods of peace, even the French king can be found addressing demands for restitution to the English Crown.[153] In much the same way, the county's mariners regularly

---

[147] Cf. C. J. Ford, 'Piracy or Policy: The Crisis in the Channel, 1400–1403. The Alexander Prize', *Transactions of the Royal Historical Society*, Fifth Series, 29 (1979), pp. 63–78.
[148] *CPR 1338–1340*, 68–69.
[149] *CPR 1317–1321*, 538.
[150] Sumption, *Divided Houses*, p. 543; Drake, 'Fawey', 314.
[151] *The Westminster Chronicle 1381–1394*, ed. and trans. L. C. Hector and B. F. Harvey (Oxford, 1982), pp. 376–377.
[152] SC1/34/159; SC1/55/94; E30/1271 mm. 22, 26; SC8/116/5780.
[153] For example, *CPR 1327–1330*, 556–557.

requested that the king correspond with overseas rulers on their behalf. After their ship had allegedly been attacked in 1346 by two Castilian vessels using 'armed power', for example, with some of their crewmen perishing and their £2,000 cargo seized, Thomas Lewyn and Richard Broun of Fowey approached Edward III for aid. [154] In response to their petition he then threaten the king of Castile to 'cause the speedy complement of justice to be done', otherwise 'it would behove [him] to provide another remedy'.

With the king forming the fountain head of English justice, he was obliged to investigate attacks by his subjects on allied, neutral and denizen shipping alike when they were brought to his attention.[155] In 1365, for instance, the sheriff and sub-admiral arrested some 920 quintals of iron landed in Fowey 'because of a suspicion they had by reason of certain speeches' that Englishmen had stolen this Spanish cargo.[156] To get to the bottom of such cases, the government regularly took inquisitions 'by good and sufficient seamen and merchants' in the peninsula.[157] The earl-duke was sometimes moved to launch investigations of his own, as in 1347 for example, after the master and mariners of Thomas Cook's *Michel* of Fowey had allegedly seized Flemish goods.[158] As it was reported that the cargo was 'stolen in the prince's lordship and by his subjects', putting him 'in great peril', the Black Prince commanded the havener to enquire into this case with a view to putting the ship on dry land. All this activity brought many seafarers into direct contact with the government, which was taking the opportunity to define legal and illegal maritime theft for its political advantage.

Far from trying to supress all maritime violence, the king actually rewarded those seafarers who attacked his 'enemies of France' by allowing them to retain the spoils of war.[159] With the Crown often receiving a share of the profits and even licensing shipmen to 'go to sea… for the destruction of the king's enemies… and the safety of the realm', across the century the government was to develop a more coherent policy of directing water-borne attacks against targets of its choosing.[160] So it was that the Crown succeeded in drawing into its service many English sea-raiders, the Cornish in their vanguard, to extend royal power over 'the open space of the sea and the commercial space of the ship'.[161]

---

[154] *CCR 1346–1349*, 79.
[155] For example, *CCR 1318–1323*, 110–111; *CPR 1340–1343*, 306–307.
[156] *CCR 1364–1368*, 102–103.
[157] For example, *CCR 1343–1346*, 210, 458.
[158] *RBP*, i, 77–78, 98; SC1/54/56.
[159] For example, *CPR 1413–1416*, 36.
[160] For example, *CPR 1401–1405*, 457; Ford, 'Piracy or Policy?'; Ford, 'Prize Law'; *RBP*, ii, 163.
[161] Tai, 'Status of Piracy', 842; *Documents Relating to Law and Custom of the Sea*, pp. 115–118; Richmond, 'Keeping of the Seas', pp. 110, 173, 186; Cheyette, 'Sovereign and

Henry IV in particular turned to private naval syndicates, fighting a pirate war with France from 1400 to 1403.[162] To this end, he appointed Mark Michelstow of Fowey as one of his principal pirate admirals, empowering him to captain a flotilla of three barges based in Fowey and Falmouth that were 'searching for the king's enemies at sea'.[163] Michelstow was a potent government agent, in 1402 alone capturing no fewer than ten Gallic vessels and seizing numerous enemy cargoes found in neutral ships.[164] Such 'pirate patrols' enabled the Crown to make a virtue out of the necessity for direct action at sea, in this way more sharply defining the right and wrong forms of seagoing disorder in relation to its geopolitical imperatives and the learned law.[165]

Even those seadogs whom the Crown licensed could exceed the terms of their contracts, however, among them Mark Michelstow, who in 1402 was summoned before the council 'under pain of the king's wrath' for seizing numerous Spanish ships.[166] With the county's formidable salter-water raiders often enjoying the protection of local powerbrokers, they could regularly operate with impunity, encouraging yet more skulduggery.[167] Violence and self-help abounded at sea, in some sense rendering Cornish ports frontier towns and the whole peninsula a marcher land.[168] At times fear of reprisals could reach such heights that seafarers simply refused to put to sea.[169] The St Albans-based Thomas Walsingham even recounted how in 1379 the crew of a Cornish barge hoped to 'make gains of their own [from] the enemy' after keeping the sea for the king.[170] While voyaging home, however, they were intercepted by Flemings who then proceeded to kill every Cornishman aboard. 'Seeing that our men must perish', one Cornish boy jumped aboard the Flemish ship and concealed himself in its hold, only emerging three days later after the vessel had docked in an English port. Shouting for aid, he ensured that the ship was confiscated for the king's service. At the same time as being a violent and disorderly activity, salt-water larceny formed both an extension of commercial interactions and an increasingly Crown-sanctioned enterprise, one governed by a whole range of customs which often brought about the overlap of formal and informal

---

the Pirate', 46–47, 54.
[162] Ford, 'Piracy or Policy?'; Given-Wilson, *Henry IV*, pp. 202–205, 455–458; J. Sumption, *Cursed Kings: The Hundred Years' War, IV* (London, 2015), pp. 89–95.
[163] *CPR 1401–1405*, 133; Drake, 'Michelstow Family'.
[164] Ford, 'Piracy or Policy?', 72.
[165] Cf. Ford, 'Prize Law', pp. 216–218.
[166] *CCR 1402–1405*, 24.
[167] For example, *West Country Shipping*, pp. 80–84.
[168] Drake, 'Fawey', 314; *CPR 1330–1334*, 497; *CPR 1350–1354*, 24; cf. Cheyette, 'Sovereign and the Pirates', 58; Sylvester, 'Communal Piracy', pp. 169, 171, 174; Heebøll-Holm, *Maritime War*, p. 8.
[169] *RBP*, ii, 162–163.
[170] Walsingham, *Chronica Maiora*, i, pp. 289–293.

seakeeping. So it was that Cornish seafarers were pirates, patriots and traders in turn, potent agents of connectivity.

It is also worth considering how the maritime aspects of royal and lordly government added to the web of ties between Cornwall and the rest of the kingdom. To manage his seagoing prerogatives, for example, the earl-duke created and staffed an entire office, the havenership. Collecting the prise of wine and overseeing the local marine courts, the havener helped spread awareness of the lordship's power, so that even 'poor fishermen' looked to the earl-duke's judgments.[171] Since the king also sought to govern the county's seagoing population, he is regularly found despatching customs officials down west and Edward II even sent 'spies' to watch over Cornish ports.[172] The rise of the admiralty was to prove especially significant in this context. From modest beginnings, by the 1360s this office had come to enjoy wide-ranging powers over maritime life.[173] As Cornwall held a place in the southern (western) admiralty, the staff of the office were increasingly active in the county arresting malefactors and so on.[174] Sitting in Lostwithiel, its local court developed into the most important tribunal in the peninsula for maritime suits.[175] Across the century the admiralty drew some 10,000 county seafarers into the royal fleets, often giving employment to Cornishmen such as Sir John Arundell of Lanherne, whom in 1418 we find holding the post of vice-admiral of England.[176] It formed a lasting point of contact between Cornwall and wider realm.

More than any other office, the admiralty proclaimed royal sovereignty over the sea.[177] Every king from Edward I onwards employed the lofty title *seignur le roi de la mare* or some such variant, with these assertions perhaps finding their greatest champion in the anonymous author of the fifteenth-century *Libelle of Englyshe Polycye*.[178] Exhorting 'alle Englande to kepe the see enviroun

---

[171] *RBP*, ii, 129.
[172] *CCR 1296–1302*, 316–317; *CFR 1319–1327*, 146–147; E122/113/55; N. S. B. Gras, *The Early English Customs Service* (Cambridge, MA, 1918); M. H. Mills, 'The Collectors of Customs', in *The English Government at Work: II, Fiscal Administration*, ed. W. A. Morris and J. R. Strayer (Cambridge, MA, 1947), pp. 168–200, especially 175, 192; *CCR 1323–1327*, 132.
[173] Ward, *Medieval Shipmaster*, pp. 27–47; Marsden, 'Vice-Admirals'; Heebøll-Holm, 'Court of Admiralty', p. 164; D. Simpkin, 'Keeping the Seas: England's Admirals, 1369–1389', in *Roles of the Sea*, pp. 79–102.
[174] *CCR 1364–1368*, 103; *CCR 1369–1374*, 52; *CCR 1377–1381*, 60; *CCR 1381–1385*, 384–385; *CPR 1401–1405*, 67; *Black Book of the Admiralty*, i, pp. xvii–xxi, 3–87.
[175] For example, C47/6/7, translated in *Pleas in the Court of Admiralty*, pp. 1–17, 149–165; *HA*, 41–43.
[176] Above, pp. 173, 191.
[177] Cf. Cheyette, 'Sovereign and the Pirates', 45, 51, 54; Heebøll-Holm, 'Plunder at Sea', 46.
[178] *PROME*, v, 260–261; *Pleas in the Court of Admiralty*, i, xxx–xxxv; Rodger, *Safeguard of the Sea*, pp. 78–79; Heebøll-Holm, *Maritime War*, pp. 185–190.

and namelye the narowe see', the poet argued that the king should 'be lorde of the see aboute'.[179] He also believed that mastery of the narrow sea belonged to 'alle Englyshe menne', with the king and his subjects – Fowey in particular was named – engaged in the collaborative business of ruling this salt-water domain for the common good.[180] Imagined sovereignty, on the one hand, and the growth of royal marine government, on the other, together had the effect of propagating pan-English seafaring concerns. In 1378 Cornwall's parliamentarians articulated such sentiments when they petitioned the king about the county's defences 'and in the same petition they prayed for all the marches of the sea throughout the kingdom'.[181] Spreading awareness of the many seagoing interests that Cornwall shared with the rest of England, of the peninsula's place in the realm, maritime connectivity at the same time linked the county firmly to a wider Europe. The sea formed a most remarkable medium of interchange.

---

[179] *Libelle*, chapter 1 heading and line 858; S. Sobecki, *The Sea and Medieval English Literature* (Cambridge, 2008), pp. 145–160.
[180] *Libelle*, chapter 1 heading, lines 215–218.
[181] *PROME*, vi, 89–90.

Connecting Cornwall

If we attempt to draw these various strands together, one important point to emerge is how strongly interlinked was each and every one of these 'forms' of connectivity. Let us consider the case of the Sergeaux family of Colquite near Bodmin. Sir Richard Sergeaux served many times on royal commissions in Cornwall, representing the county in no fewer than ten parliaments.[1] Along with his kinsman, John, he sailed to France and fought there for the Black Prince, who showed his appreciation of his services by rewarding him with seigniorial office at home. A forceful character, Sir Richard tenaciously defended his patrimony in both the local and central courts, while finding the time to engage in the extraction, selling and shipping of tin. The Sergeauxs put their landed, mineral and marine resources to good effect.[2] Sir Richard married well twice, the first time securing the hand of a Bodrugan heiress and then after her death marrying Philippa, the illegitimate granddaughter of the earl of Arundel. Taking care to sponsor the education of their gifted illegitimate sons, the family saw Michael Sergeaux, who took holy orders, rise to a clerkship in the admiralty and later to the deanery of Arches itself.

Sir Richard's deathbed grant of 1393 bore witness to his wealth of good connections. In an agreement made in London and witnessed by William, Lord Botreaux and Guy Mone, the subsequent keeper of the privy seal and bishop of St Davids, he charged his two kinsmen Michael and John Sergeaux, along with Edward Courtenay, the earl of Devon, and Thomas Arundel, the archbishop of York, to dispose of his goods in accordance with his wishes. Sir Richard's estates were later to pass to his daughters, one of whom, Alice, was to marry the earl of Oxford, while another, Elizabeth, was already betrothed to the Essex lawyer Sir William Marny. From all this activity we can see that the Sergeauxs' experience corresponds to Ranulph Higden's characterisation of his fellow Englishmen as restless and ambitious, endlessly travelling in search of riches elsewhere.[3] Indeed, the Latin words of this Cheshire monk are made all the

---

[1] *HOP*, ii, 506–507.
[2] Sir Richard's father exported wool, *HA*, 216.
[3] Trevisa, trans., *Polychronicon*, ii, pp. 168–170; Bennett, *Cheshire and Lancashire*, p. 5.

more compelling when it is remembered that they were rendered into Middle English by none other than John Trevisa, an Oxford-educated Cornishman in the service of the baronial Berkeleys of Gloucestershire. Cornish connectivity created a grand arc, a whole greater than the sum of its parts.

Throughout this discussion we have been concerned chiefly with the geographical movements of an elite social group. It is clear that the shire establishment provided generations of highly mobile men who ranged far and wide across England and beyond. Having many friends in high places, leading Cornish lineages possessed the means to cultivate profitable contacts. Networking ran in their very blood and upbringing, as 'careerism bred careerism'.[4] Some families, however, including the Carminows, proved more adept at forging good connections than others, among the latter perhaps the Soors, who seemingly developed few contacts outside the county. Since Sir Robert Tresilian rose from relative obscurity to serve as chief justice of the king's bench, 'new men' could sometimes gain a place in the charmed circle of the interconnected elite. Yet few folk were suddenly 'raised from the dust' in this way, a more common experience being for ambitious men to build upon the achievements of their forebears. The lineages of Michelstow, Nanfan, Tremayne and Trenewith illustrate this point well. In the fourteenth century Richard Michelstow, Henry Nanfan, John Tremayne and Michael Trenewith the elder all raised their families to significance through lordly service, office-holding, commerce, the law, war and advantageous marriage. It was left to their successors to achieve greatness: Mark Michelstow was to serve as one of Henry IV's 'pirate admirals'; John Nanfan was to attain the governorship of the Channel Islands under Henry VI; another, John Tremayne, came to hold a place on Henry IV's council; and William Trenewith was to take the Bodrugan name, along with a leading position in Cornwall.[5] As these families raised their social stock they grew increasingly geographically mobile, forging more expansive networks that enabled them to climb yet higher still, a virtuous circle. In this way, social status and geographic mobility directly correlated.

That being so, mobility did not remain the preserve of the leading lineages alone. Firstly, many underlings followed where the elite led: knights depended on the prowess of their retinues; lawyers relied on the writings of scriveners; merchants required carters to transport their wares; churchmen had porters carry their liturgical tomes; and shipmen depended on the skill of their crews. It is illustrative of these connections that in 1326 Edward II is found ordering the sheriff of Derbyshire to despatch 'sixty of the strongest and most suitable workmen of that county' to work in his Cornish mines.[6] More significantly

---

[4] Bennett, *Cheshire and Lancashire*, p. 161.
[5] Above, pp. 174, 194, 210–211, 216, 244–245, 250–251.
[6] *CCR 1323–1327*, 478.

still, there is plentiful evidence that people of lesser means travelled in pursuit of their own interests, so that many of Cornwall's less wealthy residents were surprisingly mobile.

After establishing themselves east of the Tamar, some county folk assumed the surname 'Cornwaille', 'de Cornubia', or one of its variants.[7] At first glance this practice provides the perfect opportunity for the scholar to study the whole topic of Cornish migration, but there are problems with the evidence of personal names. Some people bearing Cornish-sounding names may have been the descendants of county folk, not directly Cornish themselves, while at the same time the bastard progeny of Earl Richard of Cornwall shared the appellation 'Cornewall'.[8] Nonetheless, the prevalence of those named 'de Cornubia' remains conveniently suggestive of the levels of Cornish mobility: with soldiers, sailors, chancery clerks, lordly bailiffs, London aldermen, MPs, merchants, royal messengers, archdeacons, Oxford dons, cathedral chancellors and many more people from across the realm bearing this badge of identity.[9] While some of these men and women had no connection to the county, many of them can be shown as hailing from the peninsula. In some sense forming a medieval Cornish diaspora, these people and their shared name 'de Cornubia' stand as testament both to the county's distinctiveness and its integration.

We have probably only scratched the surface of connectivity between Cornwall and the wider realm, as it is likely that much material remains to be discovered. Indeed, evidence of only the merest fraction of late-medieval Cornwall's connections has survived the passage of time. For both these reasons, there can be little doubt that a truly remarkable degree of communication and movement existed in an age that had yet to witness digital technology or mass transport. Although some people lived out their whole lives within the county's boundaries, *many thousands* of Cornishmen and women ranged widely across England and beyond in this period. At the same time a multitude of 'outsiders' established themselves in the county, while messengers carried an endless flow of letters, writs and petitions in both directions across the Tamar. One of the best examples of these sorts of interactions is to be found in William Worcestre's writings, where he noted that he had carried news and personal correspondence from one Piers Carde, a Helston-born mariner living in Great Yarmouth, to Cornish folk as varied as the provost of Glasney and the mercer John Emond of Helston.[10] Through the agency of Worcestre, Carde promised Emond 'that he would see him at Helston about the feast of John

---

[7] Elliott-Binns, *Medieval Cornwall*, pp. 56–57.
[8] *HOP*, ii, 661–663; S. J. Payling, 'John Cornewall', *ODNB*, xiii, pp. 446–447.
[9] C71/6 m. 8r; E101/16/39 m. 1; *RBP*, ii, 115–116; *CPR 1292–1301*, 242; *CCR 1296–1302*, 96, 310, 501; *RBP*, iv, 185; *LBH*, 44, 102, 138; *HW*, ii, 289; PROB11/3/383; C241/147/135; C131/28/22; Hill, *Messengers*, p. 137; *BRUO*, i, 489–491.
[10] Worcestre, *Itineraries*, pp. 102–103.

the Baptist' and at the same time another Helston resident, one John Sadler, 'recommended himself' to Carde 'to send to him concerning his health'. Such travel, migration and communication all created a thick web of ties.

When considering Cornwall's connections, it becomes apparent that they were in some ways very similar to the nearly frictionless communication and movement that characterised the Mediterranean.[11] By land and sea, a great many Cornishmen and women chose to travel far and wide in pursuit of their interests. Itineraries and migrations across the kingdom, however, were more often constrained and directed by local structures and networks than those in the Middle Sea. In some sense systems of patronage can be said to have underpinned the whole edifice of connectivity in England, with patrons seeking talented men from right across the country in order to profit from their expertise. The king and the earl-duke brought about many introductions into the peninsula for precisely this reason, while these same lords regularly despatched the county's sons beyond the shire of their birth in the cause of royal-lordly enrichment. Yet as Cornish careerists actively went in search of patrons, the agency behind these reciprocal arrangements emerges as multi-polar and multi-directional.

Perhaps the relative poverty of Cornwall prompted some folk to travel. There is little sense that the peninsula's residents sought connections out of desperation, however, not least because Cornwall was by no means unique among English provincial districts in possessing such a rich body of careerists. Michael Bennett has demonstrated the way in which the north west formed a recruiting-ground for soldiers, administrators and the like, with these men then deployed across the realm to buttress the power of their patrons.[12] A. J. Pollard has likewise outlined the ways in which the north east saw its sons travel south on legal, commercial and political business.[13] Studies of other parts of the realm would undoubtedly reveal many more connections of this sort. In considering connectivity across the kingdom, we may also wonder about the influence that the Black Death exercised on these links. Although the plague killed off many people and contacts, those who survived increasingly had the resources required to travel and network. Higher mortality rates actually increased the rate of changeover in personnel, with around half of Cornwall's benefices requiring new priests in the aftermath of the massive plague visitation of 1349 alone.[14] So many deaths and new appointments must have accelerated the tempo of connectivity. All told, an extraordinary and growing number of people – at least in relative terms – from every locality

---

[11] Cf. Horden and Purcell, *Corrupting Sea*, pp. 123–172; Horden, 'Afterword', 565, 570.
[12] Bennett, *Cheshire and Lancashire*, pp. 108–235.
[13] Pollard, *North-Eastern England*, pp. 22–27.
[14] *RESDCornwall*, 293–294.

of England began moving around, interacting with their fellow countrymen from all corners of the kingdom.

These sorts of personal interactions played an essential role in binding England together, forging the realm into a unit of common human endeavour. Interpersonal contacts from across the kingdom intersected in places as varied as parliament, convocation, the royal court and household, Oxford University, military campaigns on land and at sea, the central law courts and London – with its commercial, political and legal clout. It follows that the pan-English personal networks in which the county's residents held an integral place were both rich and varied, being created and sustained by a plurality of 'agents', both Cornish and non-Cornish, mighty and modest. Such networks did not prove static, however, as people constantly forged new links and endlessly left old ones unravel. Neither might all connections be considered equal. A Cornishman in the king's affinity, for example, was bound to play a more important role in binding the kingdom together than an impecunious London-based Cornish brewer. Nonetheless, the range of countrywide cross-ties was both dense and tightly woven. Fashioning an intra-English cultural and political milieu, the ties brought together people from all across the realm in co-operation and competition. Some parts of the county clearly enjoyed better connections than others, but connectivity was a phenomenon common to the entire peninsula. Many Cornish careerists can be shown to have returned to the county of their birth after making fame and fortune, bringing with them newly acquired ideas and wealth that made the peninsula a more varied and dynamic place. All these personal links helped to establish the kingdom as a shared social and political space, a polity of interdependent people.

The governmental structures of the realm strengthened, and were strengthened by, these interpersonal links. Through fostering universal English concerns, royal 'regulation, taxation, troop-raising, and representation' linked Cornwall firmly to the rest of the kingdom.[15] Activities and structures such as these stood as triumphant affirmations of English unity and common purpose, creating a more politically aware public. As the century went on, the scale and intensity of government only grew: the statute book thickened; the jurisdiction of the royal courts expanded; the number of local office-holders burgeoned; and kings more regularly tapped their kingdom's wealth. All this activity encouraged the increasing assertiveness of parliament, the instrument through which the Crown sought legitimacy. Together, these developments had a potent integrative effect, strengthening the sinews of government and multiplying the points of contact between the king and his subjects. Combined with the gravitational pull of the court, along with personal loyalty to

---

[15] Cf. Watts, *Polities*, pp. 201–285; Reynolds, *Kingdoms*, pp. 250–331.

the king himself, these structures helped to mesh the county into the kingdom's pervasive connectivity.

The range of connections, however, should not be seen as an imposition on a recalcitrant Celtic people in Cornwall. By the fourteenth century the peninsula's inhabitants had long been habituated to the king's government, generally welcoming the royal administration and being regarded as English by their sovereign. Across the century, the hundreds of petitions that the county's residents drafted to the king and his many responses to these supplications bear testament to well-placed Cornish confidence in the efficacy of royal power. Here especially we see how Cornishmen and women were enthusiastic recipients of royal government, with the Crown an equally willing and responsive provider of rulership in the peninsula. Seeking themselves to influence 'national' policy, the county's MPs are often found lending support to common petitions concerning the overall direction of royal activity. A two-way discourse forged and sustained political communication, with the demands of subjects playing just as significant a role in bestowing the realm with substance as royal impositions. In levying taxes, for instance, the king was exercising his sovereignty, but in paying subsidies the inhabitants of Cornwall, and the realm at large, were to hold the Crown responsible for the wise employment of these funds. We find Cornishmen often seeking appointments to local royal offices too, for the simple reason that kingly power and local muscle proved interdependent. In many ways the binary division of 'centre' and 'locality' dissolves, for the county's sons often established themselves in the centre, while central power was in the habit of shaping and moulding the locality.[16] Connectivity instead welded England into a single system, one to which kings and subjects alike shared a commitment.

Yet despite all this, the Crown was never to achieve total ascendancy in Cornwall or anywhere else for that matter. Many power structures existed in the far south west, with the earldom-duchy, gentry lordships, urban governments and the like all enjoying great sway over county affairs. There can be little doubt that a significant notion of Cornwall itself weighed on the considerations of all those who resided west of the Tamar, while maritime exchanges and the international Church linked these same folk to a far wider world. With many overlapping agents and jurisdictions, the exercise of power comes across as fragmented in both the county and the wider realm. Local society even retained a place for violent self-help, for while Cornishmen may have registered debts in chancery, for example, many were only too happy to send around the 'heavies' to secure their will. Neither did county folk perpetually embrace these many

---

[16] For a helpful discussion of centre and locality, J. W. Armstrong, 'Centre, Periphery, Locality, Province: England and its Far North in the Fifteenth Century', in *Plantagenet Empire*, pp. 248–272.

links and associations, with the result that sundry Cornish interests came to moderate the impact of royal rulership in the far south west.

All these powerbrokers, structures and sentiments, however, more often than not underpinned the overarching framework of the realm. While it is clear that the earldom-duchy greatly nuanced Cornish perceptions of the kingdom, through its institutions it also drew royal authority to the far south west. We have seen how regnal government, lordly administration and local power structures generally coalesced as overwhelmingly interdependent, rendering the peninsula part and parcel of the wider realm while simultaneously bestowing coherence upon Cornwall itself. Even when connections were resented and resisted by the county's residents, these folk were left only too aware that they lived a by no means self-contained existence, that their interests and identities were nested in a rich matrix of associations. A pan-English political and cultural milieu therefore came to overlap with local customs and practices, by turns influencing and being influenced by these traditions. Tied together by connectivity, the kingdom of England formed a highly varied unit of co-ordination and dialogue.

Running through all these strands of experience was the world of imagination. Propagating notions of Englishness, the cohesive and coercive workings of connectivity spread awareness of the king's government, politics and personnel, of the realm's unifying forces. No Cornishman or woman can ever have been ignorant of the place that each held in the kingdom, with John Trevisa writing unequivocally that 'Cornwayle is in Engelond'.[17] The structures and networks of the realm together fostered an idea of England, one permeating right down through the social strata. Imagined solidarity, on the one hand, and structural and interpersonal reality, on the other, both helped to pull the kingdom together. Connectivity and identity were interlinked, for encounters between residents from every part of England laid bare the integration of all these people into a wider realm. Recognition of the county's incorporation into the kingdom did not diminish a sense of Cornishness in the peninsula, for links beyond the Tamar sharpened notions of Cornwall as a most distinctive place within a wider hierarchy of loyalties.

None of this is to write an apologia for the beneficent effects of government. All government is flawed, while at the same time expectations of government always move ahead of its ability to deliver, these twin strands prompting perpetual complaint and endless reform: politics. Later-medieval England was certainly an imperfectly ruled realm, riddled with local rivalries, quarrels and faction fights. Contrasting ideas of theocratic kingship and representational government rendered the delicate task of governing all the more difficult.[18]

---

[17] Trevisa, trans., *Polychronicon*, ii, p. 91
[18] Harriss, *Shaping the Nation*, pp. 3–5.

Indeed, across the later middle ages the expansion of government itself generated diverse tensions that could manifest themselves in protest, violence and even rebellion by folk from all ranks of society. And yet every Englishman and woman, the Cornish most definitely among them, had a powerful interest in the continuation of the realm. This was because, for all its limitations, the kingdom served as the best arbiter of their intertwined 'local' and 'national' concerns. Together, the king and his subjects had succeeded in creating a tightly interlinked polity, a kingdom of common interest that enjoyed legitimacy by virtue of forming an integrated but by no means unitary whole. It was connectivity that helped link together the many inhabitants and regions of this varied medieval realm, within and without Cornwall spreading awareness of the county's integration while sharpening notions of Cornishness itself.

Conclusion: Cornish Otherness and English Hegemony?

It is a fact universally acknowledged that medieval Cornwall was a county quite unlike any other. Distant from the political and social heartlands of England, lamented as 'the very ends of the earth' by its bishops, overseen by a powerful lordship and inhabited by men and women who at times were labelled an 'obdurate folk', believing that their county formed 'a large land long ago bearing the name of a kingdom', Cornwall was viewed as somewhere curiously distinctive by many contemporaries and historians alike. The county's leading lineages, bearing names the like of which you find nowhere else, among them Bodrugan, Carminow and l'Ercedekne, exercised great influence over Cornish affairs, not least through office-holding in the peninsula. By the fourteenth century, when royal government had come to reach out into the entire realm, Cornwall ranked as one of the country's great seigniorial enclaves. Together, myths, saints, government and lordship were to endow the name and notion of Cornwall with authority in the minds of its inhabitants. Combined with the continued currency of the local Cornish language and the circulation of chivalric literature that marked out the county as historically different, the land of King Arthur, it is not difficult to explain the trope of Cornish otherness.

Yet, despite the peninsula forming a remote and idiosyncratic corner of the kingdom, the county most emphatically still held a place in the realm of England. In this respect, the position of Cornwall contrasted sharply with that in parts of Ireland and Wales, where power remained fractured and an English elite attempted to rule over people whom blood, birth, administration and law regarded as inferior.[1] Since the king's writ always extended to west of the Tamar, constitutionally Cornwall did not even correspond to an English palatinate, which enjoyed the status of a liberty. Indeed, the common law regarded all Cornishmen and women as English; Cornwall's residents like those of every other county paid parliamentary subsidies for the common good; the county possessed a substantial voice in the parliamentary Commons; the king directly

---

[1] Cf. R. Frame, 'Ireland'; Davies, *Wales 1064–1414*, pp. 283–285, 391–392, 419–421.

appointed nearly all local government officials; and Cornishmen owed military service for the defence of the realm. Many thousands of county folk can be found serving and thriving elsewhere in the kingdom, while a multitude of 'outsiders' established themselves in the peninsula, with the result that connectivity was to act as a powerful integrative force.

To understand Cornwall and its place in the English polity, however, it is necessary to consider the nature of England itself. While Cornwall, with a cultural and historical identity of its own, fits ill into a 'Merrie England' of cricket and vicars and endless summers filled with warm beer, it needs to be recognised that such a monolithic, unvariegated and unchanging entity has actually never existed. As countries are 'not laid up in heaven', England was neither pre-ordained nor final in its form.[2] By the fourteenth century the people of England believed in – even assumed – their kingdom's coherence, but that kingdom still contained a kaleidoscope of structures and sentiments. Ranulph Higden's *Polychronicon* went so far as to contrast the 'mylde' men of the South with the cruel men of the North, a stereotype invested with administrative reality by northern and southern ecclesiastical provinces and royal escheatries.[3] That being so, North and South still played host to many smaller regions, from the 'North Country' to the West Midlands, and to expansive dioceses.[4] The Crown also divided the kingdom into a network of counties, among which there was no such thing as a 'typical' shire. Devon, Northumberland and Warwickshire, for example, were dominated by resident nobles, while Gloucestershire and Bedfordshire only ever had magnates of the second rank. With a greater or lesser number of knights enjoying estates of quite different size and character, the society and collective life of each and every shire can be shown to have varied markedly. And while the *Descriptio Norfolchiae*, with its depiction of Norfolk's dim-witted and drunken inhabitants, suggests that a notion of this county existed in peoples' minds, Warwickshire, less sharply defined and internally divided between forest and cultivated lands, left no such clear impression.[5]

Inevitably, sub-county localism was a major force too within each and every one of these shires. In Kent, for instance, topographical variations between Weald, marshland, arable and so on helped to create areas of quite different character.[6] Stretching longitudinally, the coherence of Sussex was undermined

---

[2] Davies, *First English Empire*, p. 54.
[3] Trevisa, trans., *Polychronicon*, ii, pp. 162–163, 167–168; Jewell, *North-South Divide*.
[4] Walker, *Political Culture*, p. 73; Hilton, *West Midlands*; Armstrong, 'Centre, Periphery'.
[5] Cherry, 'Courtenay Earls'; Bennett, *Cheshire and Lancashire*, pp. 68–69; Saul, *Gloucestershire*, pp. 2–4; Liddy, *Durham*, pp. 174–235; Carpenter, *Warwickshire*, pp. 25–34; Virgoe, 'East Anglia', pp. 225–228; Ruddick, *English Identity*, p. 83.
[6] A. Everitt, *Continuity and Colonization: The Evolution of Kentish Settlement* (Leicester, 1986), pp. 43–65.

by the fact that its main lines of communication ran north to south.[7] As Alan Everitt has written: 'England is one of the most varied countries in the world in its landscape', and from these 'contrasting countrysides' we see 'something of the diversity of the historic communities of England'.[8] We should avoid blunt environmental determinism, for associations within the realm played just as significant a role in shaping England's social and political dynamics. Sundry solidarities can be found operating in every part of the kingdom, from liberties, hundreds and hamlets through to manors, parishes and gentry affinities. The boroughs and cities strewn across the land also exercised significant influence within their walls and throughout their respective hinterlands. Regions and regional associations, moreover, could both wax and wane. The Courtenays and Beauchamps, for example, succeeded in welding together Devon and Warwickshire respectively for a time, only for such creations to collapse during family minorities.[9]

In sharp contrast to the voluminous archives of the royal administration, however, much of the documentation arising from these many regions and local rulerships has long since disappeared. Fostering the illusion that the king enjoyed a natural omnipresence in his unitary realm, the mere fact of the survival of the Crown's archive perpetuates the seductive fiction of the awesome power of the medieval state. In reality, however, the kingdom contained many authorities beyond that of the king's administration, with spiritual and temporal lordships also playing a role. While it was rare for lordships to coalesce around great territorial blocks in England, across the land lords ranging in wealth and dignity from mighty dukes down to petty esquires enjoyed power over their retainers and tenants alike. During the course of the Great Revolt, the rebels even demanded 'that no lord should have lordship... except for the king's own lordship'.[10] England, the so-called 'matron of many regions', comprised an ever-shifting, overlapping and infinitely complex mosaic of solidarities, structures and sentiments.[11]

When we turn from these diverse powerbrokers and localities to consider the country as a whole, we find that England was still bound together by the mighty apparatus of royal government. For the great preponderance of the time the Crown and the other authorities of the realm actually emerge as intertwined and reciprocal. It is illustrative of this mutuality that earls and knights, although deriving their status from inherited estates or titles, depended on the favour of the royal administration to secure their patrimonies. At the same

---

[7] Saul, *Sussex*, pp. 58–60.
[8] Everitt, *Kentish Settlement*, p. 348.
[9] Cherry, 'Courtenay Earls', 75, 94–97; Carpenter, *Warwickshire*, pp. 393–401.
[10] *The Anonimalle Chronicle, 1333–1381*, ed. V. H. Galbraith (Manchester, 1927), p. 147.
[11] *Wright's Political Songs*, ed. Coss, p. 262.

time the Crown relied on these lords to carry its government into the localities, appointing them to commissions and the like. In this way, royal and lordly muscle became tightly interwoven. Although points of friction undoubtedly existed, rendering the kingdom no easy place to rule, with both mighty and modest subjects at times employing violence and rebellion to affect political change, the fourteenth-century expansion of the royal administration generally served to enhance the authority of all these groupings. Nobles and gentry increasingly came to view themselves as essential partners in government with the Crown, while growing governmental demands augmented the coherence of both the wider kingdom and individual shires.

On the one hand, therefore, England formed a much-governed and densely interconnected polity, with its practical and imagined coherence sustained by the interdependent interests of kings and subjects alike. On the other, the royal administration by no means obliterated 'private' structures of power. Quite the reverse, in fact, for the Crown depended on lordships great and small to carry its government into the country's many regions, just as the lordships and localities themselves relied on the Crown to promote and protect their own interests. Connectivity was to weld them all together not into a nation state but into a kingdom, in which the brokerage of power and the use of direct action formed essential parts of political life. And although Cornwall was perhaps more distinctive than any other area of the realm, all parts of the kingdom were at one and the same time both distinctive and integrated: with no long-term tension between these two strands and no hegemonic England to which Cornwall was annexed.

For all its idiosyncrasies, by no stretch of the imagination could Cornwall be said to have constituted a land apart, subjugated by an outside colonial elite. On the contrary, the Crown administered the peninsula as an integral part of England, with the county's distinctive royal lordship furthering this integration. Since connectivity resulted in the peninsula's residents contributing to every sphere of the kingdom's collective life, so these many processes of interaction had the effect of drawing the county firmly into the realm. Cornwall was not somehow diminished by holding a place in England, for notions of Cornishness and Englishness interacted in the county itself, mutually strengthening these strands of identity. We have seen how Cornish contemporaries believed that their peninsula simultaneously formed 'a large land' existing 'since the time of King Arthur', 'a schere of Engelond' and 'oon of the chief parties of this Bretayne'. Such overlapping loyalties can be seen to reconcile the contradiction lying at the heart of Cornish history and identity, with fourteenth-century Cornwall rendered all the more remarkable by its integration into a wider realm.

Epilogue: Contesting Cornwall

There can be little doubt that the notion of Cornwall remains contested to this day. Within and without its boundaries, sundry folk reimagine the peninsula as both a shire of England and a Celtic nation, fiercely debating contemporary Cornish identity and the county's place in the British Isles. The history of Cornwall itself forms one of the most disputed strands of this struggle for Cornishness, with the so-called 'Kernowsceptic' and 'Kernowcentric' interpretations of the county's past vying for dominance.[1] Arguing that an Imperial England subverted Cornwall's nationhood and forever regarded its Celtic people as a conquered alien other, the Kernowcentric school of thought holds that the history of Cornwall is entirely separate from that of England.

Although few medievalists are yet to subscribe to this 'Grand Kernowcentric Narrative', the medieval past forms an integral part of the latter's discourse.[2] It was the alien Anglo-Saxons, after all, who conquered Cornwall back in the 800s. While preserving the peninsula's separate administration and identity, in 1337 Edward III at the same time gave it a special status in the kingdom by raising it to a duchy. 'A little government of its own', the 'Celtic Duchy' supposedly fostered an 'aura of semi-independence' securing Cornish autonomy.[3] As the duke of Cornwall also oversaw the stannaries, this special constitutional settlement removed the peninsula from the mainstream of the realm. Combined with the county's extreme remoteness, such a political and social structure is said to have given rise to 'feudal anarchy'.[4] In this narrative, the Cornish are said to have formed a subjugated people much like the Welsh and Irish, with language marking out their alterity.[5] Inaugurated by the Anglo-Saxon conquest

---

[1] B. Deacon, *Cornwall: A Concise History* (Cardiff, 2007), pp. 1–3; Philip Payton's *Modern Cornwall* and *Cornwall* form the two most prominent Kernowcentric accounts.
[2] But see Chynoweth's dismissal of, as he terms it, 'The Theory of Cornish Distinctiveness', *Tudor Cornwall*, pp. 21–31; cf. A. M. Kent, 'Mending the Gap in the Medieval, Modern and Post–Modern in New Cornish Studies: "Celtic" Materialism and the Potential of Presentism', *Cornish Studies*, n.s. 20 (2012), pp. 13–31.
[3] Payton, *Modern Cornwall*, pp. 47–48.
[4] Payton, *Cornwall*, pp. 104–105.
[5] Payton, *Cornwall*, p. 87.

of the far south west, this first great phase of peripherality was finally brought crashing down by the centralising might of the Tudors, irrevocably dragging Cornwall out of its glorious isolation. Such Kernowcentricity is fast on the way to forming the new orthodoxy.[6]

As we have seen, however, virtually none of this was actually the case. Although the county's residents may be said to have enjoyed a distinctive identity of their own, they were not regarded as a separate people by the king or anyone else. On closer inspection even the peninsula's isolation emerges as nothing of the sort, with thousands of its folk 'on the move'. Perhaps more significantly still, the construct of a coherent Cornwall standing perpetually opposed to a monolithic England obscures the workings of these two highly varied and strikingly interlinked entities, county and kingdom. While a rich range of myths, saints' cults and even the Cornish language itself flourished in the peninsula, Cornwall simultaneously held a place in the wider realm. Belief in one's Cornish credentials by no means precluded a range of more localised self-perceptions and a simultaneously wider sense of Englishness, with these many identities nested and interdependent. In this way, later medieval Cornwall remained highly distinctive while at the same time holding an integral place in the kingdom.

Although academic debates about the distant past may seem esoteric, the county's history continues to exercise great influence on its present. In an age of localism and devolution, on the one hand, and the homogenising forces of globalisation and social media, on the other, a sense of Cornishness has become of pressing concern to many of the peninsula's inhabitants.[7] When combined with fears about overdevelopment, it is not hard to explain why the trope of a 'vanishing Cornwall' is both commonplace and emotive.[8] In recent years attempts have even been made to rename Cornwall itself as Kernow or the Duchy, with this shift in nomenclature showing that both a great deal is in a name and that the collective identity it fosters is subject to endless renegotiation. The revival of the Cornish language with the establishment of the Gorsedh Kernow (Cornish Gorsedd) in 1928 and the rise of Cornish Nationalism have galvanised views of Cornwall as a separate nation.[9] Founded in 1951, Mebyon Kernow (Sons of Cornwall) by the 1970s had come to form a political party in its own right, campaigning for the administrative recognition of Cornwall as one of the nations of the British Isles. Although Cornish Nationalism has struggled to make political headway, as a national mould fits

[6] For example, Stoyle, *West Britons*.
[7] For example, R. Dickinson, 'Meanings of Cornishness: A Study of Contemporary Cornish Identity', *Cornish Studies*, n.s. 18 (2010), pp. 70–100; J. Willett, 'Cornish Identity: Vague Notion or Social Fact?', *Cornish Studies*, n.s. 16 (2008), pp. 183–205.
[8] It is also of some antiquity, see D. du Maurier, *Vanishing Cornwall* (London, 1967).
[9] Cf. P. Clark, 'Celtic Tradition and Regional Discontent: Cornish Nationalism Revisited', *Cornish Studies*, n.s. 21, (2013), pp. 288–320.

ill with the county's complex self-perceptions, there can be little doubt that Cornishness remains a powerful force to this day.

A shared past is essential to a sense of Cornishness in the present. Certain historical events, among these the Anglo-Saxon conquest of the peninsula and the fate of Michael Joseph in 1497, have all entered the county's collective consciousness.[10] In nationalist rhetoric especially, they have come to epitomise the clash between Celtic Cornwall and Anglo-Saxon England that continues still. The county's medieval past has become highly political, with charters, chronicles and miracle plays used to argue for present constitutional, cultural and linguistic autonomy. There are profound dangers, however, in marshalling Cornish history to make a political case for its present. By emphasising separatism to establish the legitimacy of independence, the national history of Cornwall risks marginalising the peninsula's rich and varied interactions with the rest of the realm. These too formed an integral part of Cornish history and identity. It also risks reducing centuries of change to a single static narrative of Cornwall against England, when in reality Cornishness and Englishness have often overlapped and have been endlessly reimagined both east and west of the Tamar. At the same time, such a national construct threatens to obscure the peninsula's varied self-perceptions in favour of an artificially constructed sense of pan-Cornishness. While perhaps lacking the romance of a narrative that sees Celtic Cornwall conquered by an Imperial England before finally returning to its natural state of independence, the peninsula's existence as a place simultaneously integrated, distinctive and highly varied has for long underpinned its remarkable nature. A history of Cornwall that does not take this into account risks imposing ideas on the past that threaten to refashion the notion of Cornwall in the present.

For all these points of contention, the fact that so many interpretations of Cornwall struggle for pre-eminence stands as a testament to the strength of feeling that the peninsula elicits in both its people and its historians. With its sharply contrasting granitic moorland and sub-tropical valleys, wild windswept headlands and sheltered creeks, the county's many landscapes have a role to play in determining how people respond to it. When combined with a rich array of local myths and customs, a complex and engaging history and an endlessly reimagined range of identities, it is no surprise that Cornwall is somewhere whose history and Cornishness itself is worth contesting. Yet the many contrasting aspects of Cornwall surely deserve to be studied, debated and discussed at length and for their own sake, and not forced into reductive narratives of relentless repression, national destiny, or quiet homogenisation.

[10] For example, *Cornwall: One of the Four Nations of Britain*, ed. W. C. H. Rowe and E. R. Nute (Cornwall, 1996, revised 2012); J. Angarrack, *Our Future is History: Identity, Law and the Cornish Question* (Padstow, 2002).

Appendix I: Cornwall's Office-Holders, c. 1300–c. 1400

The names of Cornish gentlemen who hailed from leading lineages have been standardised, but for those outside the ranks of the elite the original spelling has been preserved. The careers of those folk that began before 1300 or continued after 1405 have been excluded for reasons of space, as have the names of parliamentary burgesses who held no other posts in the county. For ease of use, the name of each main office has also been standardised.

First Name	Surname	Offices Held	Source
John	Aet, de	Coroner until 1319	*CCR 1318–1322*, 162

Notes: John de Aet perhaps hailed from the Alet family of Mudgeon in St Martin-in-Meneage, with the form of his name here corrupted (*TCO*, 34, 52).

First Name	Surname	Offices Held	Source
John	Aldestow, de	Parliamentary Burgess for Lostwithiel, 1326	*MPs*, 75
		Knight of the Shire, 1329–30	*MPs*, 89
		Knight of the Shire, 1330	*MPs*, 91
		Knight of the Shire, 1331–2	*MPs*, 95
		Knight of the Shire, 1336	*MPs*, 111
		Parliamentary Burgess for Liskeard, 1337	*CCR 1337–1339*, 114
		Parliamentary Burgess for Helston, 1337	*CCR 1337–1339*, 114
		Knight of the Shire, 1338	*MPs*, 121
		Justice of the Peace, 15 July 1352–December 1354	*CPR 1350–1354*, 285

		Justice of the Peace, 16 December 1354–December 1355	*CPR 1354–1358*, 123
		Justice of the Peace, 10 December 1355–February 1358	*CPR 1354–1358*, 227
		Justice of the Peace, 10 February 1362–March 1364	*CPR 1361–1364*, 207

Notes: John de Aldestow appears to have been a lawyer, serving as Sir Otto Bodrugan's attorney in 1331 and performing the same function for Bishop Grandisson in 1343 (*CPR 1330–1334*, 69; *CPR 1343–1345*, 32); he held some lands in the county (*FF*, i, 300–302, 316–317); and served on numerous commissions (*CPR 1343–1345*, 581; *CPR 1350–1354*, 24).

Thomas	Alger	Havener, April 1313–September 1314	*CPR 1313–1317*, 34

Notes: Thomas Alger was a yeoman of Edward II's chamber (*CPR 1313–1317*, 34; *CFR 1307–1319*, 167).

Sir John	Arundell	Justice of the Peace, 3 August 1338–July 1344	*CPR 1338–1340*, 139, 146
		Knight of the Shire, 1340	*MPs*, 130
		Knight of the Shire, 1343	*MPs*, 136
		Justice of the Peace, 10 November 1344–December 1346	*CPR 1343–1345*, 396

Notes: By 1300 the Arundell family seat lay at Lanherne; during the fourteenth century there were as many as three John Arundells alive concurrently, however, and it remains unclear whether the same John Arundell served as an MP and JP (Fox and Padel, *Arundells of Lanherne*, pp. xv–xvi); a John Arundell served repeatedly as a tax collector and commissioner of array (*CPR 1338–1340*, 279, 502; *CCR 1339–1341*, 437) but this may also represent the service of more than one individual.

John	Arundell the Elder	Coroner until 1360	*CCR 1360–1364*, 65
Sir John	Arundell	Knight of the Shire, 1397	*HOP*, ii, 58–61
		Justice of the Peace, 27 February 1397–November 1397	*CPR 1396–1399*, 97
		Justice of the Peace, 12 November 1397–February 1399	*CPR 1396–1399*, 237
		Knight of the Shire, 1397	*HOP*, ii, 58–61
		Sheriff of Cornwall, 3 November 1399–October 1400	*Sheriffs*, 21
		Justice of the Peace, 28 November 1399–February 1400	*CPR 1399–1401*, 557

		Justice of the Peace, 16 February 1400–May 1401	CPR 1399–1401, 557
		Justice of the Peace, 16 May 1401–March 1403	CPR 1399–1401, 557
		Steward of Cornwall, 16 February 1402–February 1430	CPR 1401–1405, 42
		Sheriff of Cornwall, After Easter 1402–October 1402	Sheriffs, 21
		Justice of the Peace, 14 March 1403	CPR 1401–1405, 516
		Knight of the Shire, January 1404	HOP, ii, 58–61
		Knight of the Shire, October 1404	HOP, ii, 58–61

Notes: Sir John Arundell's father died in 1375 and was followed in quick succession by Sir John's two elder brothers; Sir John inherited his father's estates while still a minor, proving his age before August 1388; he raised his family to new heights, supposedly being called 'the magnificent' (HOP, ii, 58–61; Fox and Padel, *Arundells of Lanherne*, pp. xvii–xviii).

Robert	Arundell	Coroner until 1385	CCR 1381–1385, 547
Robert	Aspel, de	Justice of the Peace, 22 July 1330–February 1331	CPR 1327–1330, 567

Notes: Robert Aspel served as Queen Isabella's chief steward; Edward III also appointed him steward of Isabella's lands south of the Trent after he had confiscated these estates from his mother (CFR 1327–1337, 215–216; CPR 1330–1334, 23).

John	Asshenden	Havener, 1376–7	Campbell, 'Haveners', 115–116.
John	Aston, de	Escheator of Cornwall and Devon, 12 December 1382–June 1383	Escheators, 31
		Escheator of Cornwall and Devon, 11 November 1384–December 1386	Escheators, 31
		Escheator of Cornwall and Devon, 30 November 1387–November 1388	Escheators, 31

Notes: John de Aston probably came from North Devon; he was a lawyer who sat in parliament for Dartmouth, Barnstaple and Leominster (HOP, ii, 79–80).

Duke Edward	Aumerle, of	Havener, 17 October 1397–November 1399	CPR 1396–1399, 259

| John | Auternon | Coroner until 1384 | CCR 1381–1385, 465 |

Notes: A John Auternon sat five times as a parliamentary burgess for Helston between 1329 and 1340 (*MPs*, 89, 91, 95, 106, 130) but his connection with this John is unclear.

Sir Richard	Bakhampton	Knight of the Shire, 1328	*MPs*, 83
		Steward of Cornwall, 1336?	*RBP*, ii, 42; *RESDCornwall*, 236
		Justice of the Peace, 12 April 1336–July 1336	*CPR 1334–1338*, 287
		Justice of the Peace, 15 July 1336–July 1338	*CPR 1334–1338*, 357
		Knight of the Shire, 1340	*MPs*, 132

Notes: Sir Richard Bakhampton served as John of Eltham's steward in Cornwall (*CPR 1334–1338*, 235–236); the exact dates of his tenure are unclear, however; he probably hailed from Wiltshire (*FF*, i, 301–302); but evidently had connections with Cornwall – or at least developed them – with his son, William Bakhampton, holding land in the county (DCO 2, 6; *RBP*, ii, 42, 97; *RESDCornwall*, 70–71, 236–237).

| John | Barber, le | Constable of Tintagel Castle, 1291–1306? | SC6/811/5 m. 4r |

Notes: John le Barber was appointed constable for life in 1291 (E372/152B m. 9r; SC6/811/5 m. 4r; *CPR 1301–1307*, 454; Spreadbury, *Castles in Cornwall*, p. 32).

| Reynold | Barber, le | Constable of Restormel Castle, 1312–13 | *CFR 1307–1319*, 148 |

Notes: Reynold le Barber was a citizen of London; he was perhaps a kinsman of John le Barber.

| Sir William | Basset I | Knight of the Shire, 1332 | *MPs*, 98 |
| | | Knight of the Shire, 1334 | *MPs*, 104 |

Notes: The Basset family seat lay in Tehidy, near Camborne; Sir William Basset I was only a child of five on his father's death (*CIPM*, iv, 175; Vivian, *Visitations*, pp. 17–18); he married Joan, the daughter of Sir William Botreaux; he died on 16 October 1334, leaving a son, Thomas Basset (*TCO*, 33, 236).

| Sir William | Basset II | Justice of the Peace, 14 December 1381–March 1382 | *CPR 1381–1385*, 85 |
| | | Justice of the Peace, 9 March 1382–June 1382 | *CPR 1381–1385*, 142 |

		Justice of the Peace, 21 December 1382–February 1385	*CPR 1381–1385*, 248

Notes: Sir William Basset II was probably the son of Thomas Basset and grandson of Sir William Basset I (*TCO*, 33, 236; cf. Vivian, *Visitations*, pp. 17–18); a Thomas Basset left a minor as his heir in 1353 (*RBP*, ii, 56); in 1379 he received a chapel licence for Tehidy and Carn Brea (*Reg. Brantingham*, i, 394–395).

Sir Robert	Bealknap	Justice of the Peace, 20 February 1381–December 1381	*CPR 1377–1381*, 572–573
		Justice of the Peace, 8 February 1385–July 1387	*CPR 1381–1385*, 502, 503
		Justice of the Peace, 16 July 1387–July 1388	*CPR 1385–1389*, 385

Notes: Sir Robert Bealknap served as chief justice of the common pleas in 1374-88 (*CPR 1374–1377*, 3).

Sir William	Beauchamp	Sheriff of Cornwall, Mich. 1329–January 1331	*Sheriffs*, 21
		Steward of Cornwall, Mich. 1329–January 1331	*Sheriffs*, 21
		Constable of Launceston Castle, before 1331	*CFR 1327–1337*, 222
		Constable of Tintagel Castle, Mich. 1329–January 1331	*Sheriffs*, 21; *CCR 1313–1318*, 298

Notes: Sir William Beauchamp was a relative of the earls of Warwick; he had held the constableship of Southampton Castle (*CFR 1327–1337*, 205) and served as sheriff of Worcester (*CPR 1317–1321*, 46); he was a bachelor to Edward II (*CFR 1319–1327*, 70, 137; *CPR 1317–1321*, 575; *CPR 1321–1324*, 65, 428; *CPR 1324–1327*, 14, 105, 119); but later transferred his loyalties to Queen Isabella; he held Tintagel Castle by dint of the stewardship (*CCR 1313–1318*, 298).

Baldwin	Beaupel	Knight of the Shire, 1319	*MPs*, 57

Notes: The Beaupels held considerable lands in the south west, in 1330–1 receiving a chapel licence for St Tudy while celebrating obits for numerous family members (*Reg. Grandisson*, i, 602; *TCO*, 33, 144).

Sir John	Beaupel	Parliamentary Burgess for Launceston, 1328	*MPs*, 83
		Justice of the Peace, 25 November 1349–July 1352	*CPR 1348–1350*, 383

Notes: It is unclear if the same Sir John Beaupel sat for Launceston and served as a JP; Sir John Beaupel was a bachelor of the Black Prince (*RBP*, ii, 86; *TCO*, 33, 144).

Sir Robert	Beaupel	Sheriff of Cornwall, 29 September 1338–Mich. 1340	SC6/816/12 m. 11v; *Sheriffs*, 21
		Steward of Cornwall, 29 September 1338	SC6/816/12 m. 11v; *Sheriffs*, 21

Notes: Sir Robert Beaupel served as a deputy king's larderer (*CCR 1337–1339*, 500, 559); he held land in Devon and Cornwall (*FA*, i, 390, 410, 413, 415–416, 418–420; *CCR 1339–1341*, 646); and was active in Devonian administration (*CPR 1343–1346*, 1, 56); by 1352 he was in arrears for his time in Cornish office (*RBP*, ii, 27).

John	Bedewynde	Receiver of Cornwall, March 1312	*CCR 1307–1313*, 457
		Sheriff of Cornwall, 20 July 1312–Mich. 1313	*CFR 1307–1319*, 140; *Sheriffs*, 21
		Steward of Cornwall, 20 July 1312–Mich. 1313	*CFR 1307–1319*, 140; *Sheriffs*, 21

Notes: John Bedewynde was one of Edward II's clerks (*CCR 1307–1313*, 457).

Sir Robert	Bendyn	Constable of Trematon Castle, 1322–3	E389/62 m. 1r
		Knight of the Shire, 1326–7	*MPs*, 75

Notes: Sir Robert Bendyn (or Beudyn) enjoyed an income of £40 p.a. and was returned to a Great Council in 1323–4 (*Parliamentary Writs*, ii part 2, p. 655).

Hugh	Berewyk, de	Steward of Cornwall, 1342–6	DCO 1–3; *Duchy Servants*, 382; *RBP*, i, 5
		Justice of the Peace, 20 July 1344–November 1344	*CPR 1343–1345*, 394, 399
		Justice of the Peace, 10 November 1344–December 1346	*CPR 1343–1345*, 396

Notes: Hugh de Berewyk was clerk of the market in the household of the Black Prince (*CPR 1338–1340*, 187).

John	Berie	Escheator of Cornwall and Devon, 3 December 1386–November 1387	*Escheators*, 31
John	Beville I	Knight of the Shire, 1375–6	*MPs*, 193
		Knight of the Shire, 1378	*MPs*, 199
		Knight of the Shire, 1379–80	*MPs*, 203

| | | Sheriff of Cornwall, 1 November 1381–November 1382 | *Sheriffs*, 21 |
| | | Sheriff of Cornwall, 20 October 1385–November 1386 | *Sheriffs*, 21 |

Notes: The Bevilles were a longstanding fixture in Cornwall (*TCO*, 33, 339); John Beville I's estates were based around Woolston in Poundstock, but his activities are difficult to disentangle from those of his son (*HOP*, ii, 221–222).

John	Beville II	Constable of Trematon Castle, before April 1380–December 1381	*CPR 1377–1381*, 455
		Justice of the Peace, 26 May 1380–February 1381	*CPR 1377–1381*, 513
		Knight of the Shire, 1386	*HOP*, ii, 221
		Justice of the Peace, 16 July 1387–July 1388	*CPR 1385–1389*, 385
		Justice of the Peace, 4 July 1388–July 1389	*CPR 1385–1389*, 545
		Sheriff of Cornwall, 1 December 1396–November 1397	*Sheriffs*, 21

Notes: John Beville II's career spanned nearly forty years; during his early life it is hard to differentiate him from his father (*HOP*, ii, 221–222).

Sir Reginald	Beville	Knight of the Shire, 1295	*MPs*, 4
		Knight of the Shire, 1297	*MPs*, 7
		Knight of the Shire, 1298	*MPs*, 8
		Knight of the Shire, 1300–1	*MPs*, 13
		Justice of the Peace, 10 May 1300–December 1307	*CPR 1292–1301*, 516
		Knight of the Shire, 1306	*MPs*, 21
		Knight of the Shire, 1309	*MPs*, 30

Notes: Sir Reginald Beville held considerable lands in the county (*FA*, i, 201, 205, 207); he served on numerous commissions, including that of taxer in 1295 (*CPR 1292–1301*, 171); in 1309–10 he received a chapel licence for Galowras in Goran and Woolston in Poundstock (*Reg.Stapeldon*, 299).

William	Beville	Parliamentary Burgess for Truro, 1371	*MPs*, 185
		Justice of the Peace, 8 February 1385–February 1385	*CPR 1381–1385*, 502
		Justice of the Peace, 16 July 1387–July 1388	*CPR 1385–1389*, 385
		Justice of the Peace, 4 July 1388–July 1389	*CPR 1385–1389*, 545

Notes: In 1377–8 William Beville received a chapel licence for Lanner (*Reg. Brantingham*, i, 386); his son, Alexander Beville, died on 17 September 1400 (*TCO*, 33, 144).

Sir Robert	Bilkemore	Escheator of Cornwall, Somerset, Dorset and Devon, 10 December 1325–February 1327	*CFR 1319–1327*, 369; *Escheators*, 134
		Sheriff of Cornwall, Easter 1327–Mich. 1329	*CFR 1327–1337*, 222; *Sheriffs*, 21
		Steward of Cornwall, Easter 1327–Mich. 1329	*CFR 1327–1337*, 222; *Sheriffs*, 21
		Constable of Restormel Castle, Easter 1327–Mich. 1329	*Sheriffs*, 21
		Escheator South of the Trent, 1327–32	*Escheators*, 134
		Sheriff of Cornwall, 18 January 1331–February 1331	*Sheriffs*, 21
		Steward of Cornwall, 18 January 1331–February 1331	*Sheriffs*, 21
		Constable of Launceston Castle, January 1331–February 1331	*CFR 1327–1337*, 222
		Constable of Trematon Castle, 13 April 1331	*CFR 1327–1337*, 247–248
		Constable of Tintagel Castle, 13 April 1331	*CFR 1327–1337*, 247–248
		Constable of Restormel Castle, January 1331–February 1331	*Sheriffs*, 21

Notes: Sir Robert Bilkemore hailed from Bedfordshire (*CCR 1327–1330*, 94, 563); but acquired lands in Cornwall (JUST1/1426A m. 23r); he served as a taxer in Cornwall and guardian of the temporalities of Exeter (*Reg. Grandisson*, i, 37; *CPR 1327–1330*, 173, 250); he was deputy chief butler to the king (*CPR 1327–1330*, 417); and later served as a justice in North Wales (*CPR 1334–1338*, 122).

| John | Billioun I | Knight of the Shire, 1324 | *MPs*, 71 |

		Knight of the Shire, 1326–7	MPs, 75
		Knight of the Shire, 1328 and 1328–9	MPs, 87
		Justice of the Peace, 21 March 1332–July 1335	CPR 1330–1334, 294, 296, 348, 496

Notes: John Billioun I held considerable lands in the county (*FF*, i, 359–360; *Maclean*, i, 385–391); he served on numerous commissions in Cornwall (*CPR 1327–1330*, 215, 433; *CPR 1330–1334*, 207, 449; *CPR 1334–1338*, 443; *CPR 1348–1350*, 157); but was summoned before the king for his contempt in collecting wool taxes (*CFR 1337–1347*, 295, 305; *CCR 1341–1343*, 506); he served as Bishop Grandisson's Cornish steward (*Reg.Grandisson*, i, 236, 553); it seems that Billioun was dead by 1351 (*RBP*, ii, 2); although there were two John Billiouns active at this time (*CCR 1337–1339*, 114; *Maclean*, iii, 359–361).

John	Billioun	Parliamentary Burges for Helston, 1351–2?	MPs, 150
John	Billioun II	Justice of the Peace, 17 February 1358–March 1361	CPR 1358–1361, 68

Notes: John Billioun II might have been the son of John Billioun I; in 1351 the Black Prince sold his wardship to Sir Walter de Wodeland for £50 (*RBP*, ii, 2; *FF*, i, 359–360); but another John Billioun was also active at this time (*CCR 1337–1339*, 114; *Maclean*, iii, 359–361).

Richard	Birton, de	Justice of the Peace, 15 July 1352–December 1354	CPR 1350–1354, 285
		Justice of the Peace, 16 December 1354–December 1355	CPR 1354–1358, 123
		Justice of the Peace, 10 December 1355–February 1358	CPR 1354–1358, 227
		Justice of the Peace, 17 February 1358–March 1361	CPR 1358–1361, 68

Notes: Richard de Birton sat regularly as a justice of assize in Cornwall (For example, JUST1/1448 m. 83r).

Roger	Blacolvesle, de	Receiver of Cornwall, 1324	CFR 1319–1327, 302
		Justice of the Peace, 22 July 1330–February 1331	CPR 1327–1330, 567
		Controller of the Coinage of Tin, 1331	CPR 1330–1334, 54

Notes: Roger de Blacolvesle served initially as Edward II's clerk, transferring his loyalties to Queen Isabella and then to Edward III (*CPR 1330–1334*, 54); he served on numerous commissions in the county (*CPR 1330–1334*, 207); and was a prebendary at Glasney College (*CPR 1350–1354*, 186).

| Sir John | Blanchminster | Knight of the Shire, 1373 | MPs, 190 |

Notes: The Blanchminsters were a longstanding feature of Cornwall, holding extensive lands in the peninsula and exercising lordship over the Scilly Isles (*FA*, i, 208–218; *FF*, i, 97, 276–277, 308–309); the family also possessed estates in Yorkshire, holding office in both counties (*CPR 1330–1334*, 133, 136, 287; *CPR 1338–1340*, 505); Sir John Blanchminster was the son of Sir Ranulph Blanchminster (*TCO*, 33, 237); he was retained by the earl of Salisbury (*CCR 1369–1374*, 220–221).

Sir Ranulph	Blanchminster	Knight of the Shire, 1314	MPs, 46
		Justice of the Peace, 12 April 1336–July 1336	*CPR 1334–1338*, 287
		Justice of the Peace, 15 July 1336–July 1338	*CPR 1334–1338*, 357
		Justice of the Peace, 6 July 1338–August 1338	*CPR 1338–1340*, 139

Notes: Sir Ranulph Blanchminster served as a taxer in Cornwall (*CFR 1337–1347*, 286, 295); he married Eleanor, daughter of Sir Mauger St Aubyn; it seems that he died in 1348; he left a son, Sir John (*CFR 1347–1356*, 70; *Cornish Wills*, 27–30; *TCO*, 33, 237).

Sir Ralph	Bloyou	Knight of the Shire, 1328 and 1328–9	MPs, 87
		Justice of the Peace, 2 November 1333–July 1335	*CPR 1330–1334*, 496
		Knight of the Shire, 1335	MPs, 106
		Knight of the Shire, 1335–6	MPs, 108
		Justice of the Peace, 26 July 1335–April 1336	*CPR 1334–1338*, 209
		Justice of the Peace, 6 July 1338–August 1338	*CPR 1338–1340*, 139
		Justice of the Peace, 3 August 1338–July 1344	*CPR 1338–1340*, 139

Notes: The Bloyous were long-established in Cornwall, holding land in Dorset too (*CPR 1334–1338*, 77, *Maclean*, iii, 152–154; *TCO*, 33, 189); Sir Ralph Bloyou served on numerous commissions in Cornwall (*CPR 1330–1334*, 440); in 1331 he received a chapel licence for St Endellion (*Reg.Grandisson*, ii, 627); Edward III granted him the keeping of St Michael's Mount (*CFR 1337–1347*, 46); he also served the king overseas (*CPR 1330–1334*, 180); he died on 22 May 1341 leaving no male issue but a wife, Marieria, the daughter of Sir William Botreaux I (*CFR 1337–1347*, 229; *TCO*, 33, 189).

Reginald	Bloyou	Parliamentary Burgess for Liskeard, 1369	*MPs*, 181

Notes: Reginald Bloyou was probably related to Ralph Bloyou, although not in the direct male line.

Richard	Bloyou	Parliamentary Burgess for Lostwithiel, 1393	*HOP*, ii, 265

Notes: Richard Bloyou may have been related to Ralph Bloyou (*HOP*, ii, 265).

Walter	Bloyou	Parliamentary Burgess for Bodmin, 1384	*HOP*, ii, 265–266
		Parliamentary Burgess for Liskeard, September 1388	*HOP*, ii, 265–266
		Parliamentary Burgess for Truro, 1390	*HOP*, ii, 265–266

Notes: Walter Bloyou traded tin in Bodmin and Truro (*HOP*, ii, 265–266).

Walter	Bluet	Knight of the Shire, 1343	*MPs*, 136

Notes: Walter Bluet is an obscure character, but it seems that he married Johanna, daughter and heiress of Sir Peter Nanskoyk (*Maclean*, iii, 152–153).

Richard	Bodennel	Coroner until 1389	*CCR 1385–1389*, 591
Sir Henry	Bodrugan	Knight of the Shire, 1306–7	*MPs*, 24

Notes: The Bodrugans were 'an ancient, eminent, and opulent' Cornish family (*Maclean*, i, 548); Sir Henry Bodrugan served Edward I militarily in Gascony and Scotland (*CPR 1301–1307*, 63); and was active in county administration (*CCR 1296–1302*, 381, 389, 395); he died in 1309 leaving a son, Otto, aged '18 or more' (*CIPM*, v, 64–66).

Sir Otto	Bodrugan I	Knight of the Shire, 1323–4	*MPs*, 69
		Justice of the Peace, 14 June 1327–November 1327	*CPR 1327–1330*, 90

Notes: Sir Otto Bodrugan I was the son of Sir Henry Bodrugan; in 1322 he rebelled against Edward II (SC6/1146/21; *CIM 1307–1349*, 124–125); despite this, in 1325 he travelled to Gascony in the king's service (*CPR 1324–1327*, 109); in 1326 Queen Isabella granted him the keeping of Lundy Island (*CFR 1319–1327*, 425); he married Margaret, the daughter of Sir William Chaumpernoun, and died on 6 September 1331, with his body lying in Monte Pessulano 'in the cloister of the brothers' (*CIPM*, vii, 275–278; *CPR 1330–1334*, 174, 196; *TCO*, 33, 190); his eldest son, Henry, died on 15 October 1331 and so the family estates passed to Otto's second son, William.

Otto	Bodrugan II	Knight of the Shire, 1369	MPs, 181
		Justice of the Peace, 2 October 1369–January 1370	CPR 1367–1370, 266
		Justice of the Peace, 28 January 1370–December 1375	CPR 1367–1370, 418
		Justice of the Peace, 4 March 1378–August 1378	CPR 1377–1381, 48
		Sheriff of Cornwall, 5 November 1379–October 1380	Sheriffs, 21
		Justice of the Peace, 14 December 1381–March 1382	CPR 1381–1385, 85
		Justice of the Peace, 9 March 1382–June 1382	CPR 1381–1385, 142
		Justice of the Peace, 21 December 1382–May 1384	CPR 1381–1385, 248
		Knight of the Shire, 1384	MPs, 219
		Justice of the Peace, 20 May 1384–February 1385	CPR 1381–1385, 428

Notes: Otto Bodrugan II was the youngest son of Otto Bodrugan I (Whetter, *Bodrugans*, pp. 4, 101); in 1372 he received a chapel licence for Bodrugan in Gorran (*Reg.Brantingham*, i, 267).

Sir William	Bodrugan I	Knight of the Shire, 1336–7	MPs, 113
		Justice of the Peace, 3 August 1338–July 1344	CPR 1338–1340, 146
		Justice of the Peace, 21 March 1361–3	CPR 1361–1364, 65

Notes: Sir William Bodrugan I was the second son of Otto Bodrugan I, receiving his inheritance in 1333 (CCR 1333–1337, 59); he was a trusted witness and tax collector (CCR 1337–1339, 387; CFR 1356–1368, 46); he married Juliana, the daughter of Sir John Stonor; he died on 28 March 1362 (*TCO*, 33, 190; Whetter, *Bodrugans*, p. 43).

William	Bodrugan II	Parliamentary Burgess for Helston, 1384	MPs, 219
		Parliamentary Burgess for Launceston, February 1388	HOP, ii, 269
		Knight of the Shire, 1401	HOP, ii, 269
		Sheriff of Cornwall, 6 October 1402–October 1403	Sheriffs, 21

Notes: William Bodrugan II was the illegitimate son of Otto Bodrugan II, with his inheritance giving rise to a great deal of litigation; his nephew was another William Bodrugan, making it difficult to separate their careers; circumstantial evidence suggests that William II served as both sheriff and MP (*HOP*, ii, 269–270).

William	Boneface	Coroner until 1370	*CCR 1369–1374*, 122
John	Bosewyns	Coroner until 1380	*CCR 1377–1381*, 400, 411
		Justice of the Peace, 20 May 1384–February 1385	*CPR 1381–1385*, 428
Sir Ralph	Botreaux	Knight of the Shire, 1404	*HOP*, ii, 313

Notes: The Botreaux family held extensive lands across the south west (*FA*, i, 208–218); Sir Ralph Botreaux, however, was a younger son who could rely on inheriting little; he was connected to Henry IV, perhaps explaining his knighthood and his role as an ambassador to Flanders and France (*HOP*, ii, 313).

Sir Reginald	Botreaux	Justice of the Peace, 20 November 1327–May 1329	*CPR 1327–1330*, 156
		Justice of the Peace, 26 October 1329–July 1330	*CPR 1327–1330*, 431
		Knight of the Shire, 1331	*MPs*, 94
		Justice of the Peace, 6 July 1338–August 1338	*CPR 1338–1340*, 139
		Justice of the Peace, 20 July 1344–November 1344	*CPR 1343–1345*, 394, 399
		Justice of the Peace, 10 November 1344–December 1346	*CPR 1343–1345*, 396

Notes: Sir Reginald Botreaux was Sir William Botreaux I's firstborn son (*CPR 1317–1321*, 584); he attended a Great Council in 1323–4 as a knight (*Parliamentary Writs*, ii part 2, p. 655); he died in 1349 or 1346 (*CIPM*, ix, 154; *TCO*, 33, 236).

Sir William	Botreaux I	Knight of the Shire, 1304–5	*MPs*, 18
		Justice of the Peace, 17 March 1308–March 1312	*CPR 1307–1313*, 54
		Constable of Launceston Castle, March 1312	*CCR 1307–1313*, 454
		Justice of the Peace, 20 March 1312–April 1314	*CPR 1307–1313*, 473
		Justice of the Peace, 13 April 1314–June 1314	*CPR 1313–1317*, 107

Justice of the Peace, 5 June 1314–June 1316	*CPR 1313–1317*, 122
Justice of the Peace, 18 June 1320–June 1327	*CPR 1317–1321*, 459
Sheriff of Cornwall, Mich. 1321 (sworn in 18 May 1323)–September 1324	*Sheriffs*, 21
Steward of Cornwall, Mich. 1321–September 1324	*Sheriffs*, 21
Constable of Restormel Castle, Mich. 1321–September 1324	*Sheriffs*, 21
Constable of Tintagel Castle, 17 December 1325	*CPR 1324–1327*, 202
Justice of the Peace, 14 June 1327–November 1327	*CPR 1327–1330*, 90
Sheriff of Cornwall, 10 February 1331–July 1333	E389/64 m. 1r; *Sheriffs*, 21
Steward of Cornwall, 10 February 1331–July 1333	SC6/811/18 m. 1r; *Sheriffs*, 21
Constable of Launceston Castle, 10 February 1331–July 1333	SC6/811/18 m. 1r; *CFR 1327–1337*, 200, 222, 232
Constable of Restormel Castle, 10 February 1331–July 1333	*Sheriffs*, 21
Justice of the Peace, 26 July 1335–April 1336	*CPR 1334–1338*, 209
Justice of the Peace, 12 April 1336–July 1336	*CPR 1334–1338*, 287
Justice of the Peace, 15 July 1336–July 1338	*CPR 1334–1338*, 357
Justice of the Peace, 3 August 1338–July 1344	*CPR 1338–1340*, 146
Justice of the Peace, 18 December 1346–November 1349	*CPR 1345–1348*, 232

Notes: In 1302 Sir William Botreaux I received the lands of his father, another William (*CFR 1272–1307*, 455); he served often in Cornwall's administration (*CPR 1317–1321*, 349, *CPR 1321–1324*, 251, *CPR 1324–1327*, 55); he died in 1349 (*CIPM*, ix, 156; *CP*, ii, 241–242); although the lands of a William Botreaux were taken into the king's hands on his death in 1340 (*CFR 1337–1347*, 195; *Maclean*, i, 634–635; *TCO*, 33, 236); circumstantial evidence suggests that Sir William I held all the above offices.

| Sir William | Botreaux II | Justice of the Peace, 26 May 1380–February 1381 | *CPR 1377–1381*, 513 |
| | | Justice of the Peace, 4 July 1388–July 1389 | *CPR 1385–1389*, 545 |

Notes: Sir William Botreaux II was probably born on 28 September 1337, the son and heir of William Botreaux I, although there is some confusion as two William Botreauxs were active at this time (*TCO*, 33, 100, 236); he definitely gained the Botreaux estates in 1359; he was personally summoned to parliament between 1367 and 1390, being Lord Botreaux (*CP*, ii, 241–242); he died in 1391; his son, another William Botreaux, was twenty-four on his father's death, being summoned by writ to parliament before his death in 1395 (*CIPM*, xvii, 185–187; *CP*, ii, 242).

Walter	Botyler	Justice of the Peace, 23 February 1376–July 1376	*CPR 1374–1377*, 310
Roger	Bradeston	Constable of Trematon Castle, 1339	SC6/816/12 m. 2v
Thomas	Brantingham, Bishop of Exeter	Justice of the Peace, 9 March 1382–June 1382	*CPR 1381–1385*, 142
		Justice of the Peace, 21 December 1382–February 1385	*CPR 1381–1385*, 248
Sir William	Brantingham	Princess Joan's Receiver in Cornwall, 1381	SC6/818/9 m. 1v
		Receiver of Cornwall, 17 September 1381–December 1387	*CFR 1377–1383*, 267; *CPR 1385–1389*, 297

Notes: Sir William Brantingham's actual relationship to other members of his prestigious family cannot be established (*HOP*, ii, 338–341); he was connected to the Black Prince's widow, Princess Joan (*CPR 1385–1389*, 297).

| Walter | Bray | Havener, 1373–6 | DCO 19; *CPR 1374–1377*, 293 |

Notes: Walter Bray may have been related to the family of Bray of St Cleer and Lanlivery who sat often in parliament (Vivian, *Visitations*, p. 54; *TCO*, 33, 278; 34, 8; *HOP*, ii, 343; *MPs*, 32, 39, 43, 45, 48, 73).

William	Brenchesle	Justice of the Peace, 15 July 1389–November 1389	*CPR 1388–1392*, 136
		Justice of the Peace, 10 November 1389–June 1390	*CPR 1388–1392*, 138
		Justice of the Peace, 28 June 1390–December 1391	*CPR 1388–1392*, 342, 344
		Justice of the Peace, 15 December 1391–February 1393	*CPR 1388–1392*, 525

		Justice of the Peace, 28 February 1393–June 1394	CPR 1391–1396, 292
		Justice of the Peace, 18 June 1394–February 1397	CPR 1391–1396, 436
		Justice of the Peace, 27 February 1397–November 1397	CPR 1396–1399, 97
		Justice of the Peace, 12 November 1397–February 1399	CPR 1396–1399, 237
		Justice of the Peace, 26 February 1399–November 1399	CPR 1396–1399, 436
		Justice of the Peace, 28 November 1399–February 1400	CPR 1399–1401, 557
		Justice of the Peace, 16 February 1400–May 1401	CPR 1399–1401, 557
		Justice of the Peace, 16 May 1401–March 1403	CPR 1399–1401, 557
		Justice of the Peace, 14 March 1403	CPR 1401–1405, 516

Notes: William Brenchesle was a Kentishman; he served as a justice of assize in Cornwall from 1389 and sat as a justice of the common pleas from May 1398 (Tyldesley, 'Local Communities', p. 95).

| Richard | Breton | Bailiff-Errant, 1386 | CPR 1385–1389, 138 |

Notes: Richard Breton served as a yeoman of Richard II's chamber.

| Sir Guy | Brian | Justice of the Peace, 10 February 1370–December 1375 | CPR 1367–1370, 422 |

Notes: Sir Guy Brian served as a royal diplomat and admiral of the west, rising to the baronage in the process (J. L. Gillespie, 'Guy Brian', ODNB, vii, pp. 540–541); his appointment as a JP was probably connected to his role as admiral.

| William | Brightelegh | Escheator of Cornwall and Devon, 8 June 1383–November 1383 | Escheators, 31 |

Notes: William Brightelegh was a Devonian who died in 1401 (CIPM, xviii, 151).

Sir William	Broun	Knight of the Shire, 1373	MPs, 190
		Justice of the Peace, June 1373?	
		Justice of the Peace, 6 December 1375–July 1376	CPR 1370–1374, 388
		Justice of the Peace, 4 July 1376–July 1377	CPR 1374–1377, 139
			CPR 1374–1377, 313

		Justice of the Peace, 2 July 1377–December 1377	*CPR 1377–1381*, 45
		Justice of the Peace, 14 December 1381–March 1382	*CPR 1381–1385*, 85
		Justice of the Peace, 9 March 1382–June 1382	*CPR 1381–1385*, 142
		Justice of the Peace, 21 December 1382–February 1385	*CPR 1381–1385*, 248

Notes: Sir William Broun was an assessor of the 1379 poll tax (*CFR 1377–1383*, 144).

Matthew	Bryt	Coroner until 1383	*CCR 1381–1385*, 199
Peter	Burdet	Constable of Launceston Castle, 18 February 1301–March 1312; and 1313–33?	*CPR 1292–1301*, 573; *CCR 1333–1337*, 30, 140

Notes: Peter Burdet was a yeoman of Edward I; it seems that he held the constableship of Launceston again after 1312, although the date of his second appointment remains unclear; he was probably reappointed soon after 1312 (*CCR 1313–1318*, 4).

Ralph	Burdet, son of Peter	Constable of Launceston Castle, November 1329?	*CPR 1327–1330*, 455

Notes: Ralph Burdet was the son of Peter Burdet; he served Queen Isabella and Edward II, being granted the reversion of the constableship on his father's death; it seems likely, however, that he never acted.

William	Burleston, de	Escheator of Cornwall, 24 November 1394–November 1395	*Escheators*, 31

Notes: William Burleston represented several Devonian boroughs before attaining the escheatorship (Tyldesley, 'Local Communities', p. 128).

Richard	Calwar	Havener, 9 January 1331	*CPR 1330–1334*, 43

Notes: Richard Calwar was a yeoman and sergeant of Edward III's buttery.

Walter	Carburra	Coroner until 1365	*CCR 1364–1368*, 97

Notes: Walter Carburra held land in the county, for the Black Prince 'borrowed' 102 oaks from him (*RBP*, ii, 185); earlier in the century, John, Roger, Robert and William Carburra had sat repeatedly as parliamentary burgesses for Bodmin (*MPs*, 18, 30, 39, 43, 45, 57, 95, 106, 124).

Sir John	Carminow I	Justice of the Peace, 18 May 1329–July 1330	*CPR 1327–1330*, 431
		Justice of the Peace, 16 February 1331–February 1332	*CPR 1330–1334*, 137

	Constable of Restormel Castle, April 1331–November 1331	*CPR 1330–1334*, 106
	Constable of Trematon Castle, April 1331–November 1331	*CPR 1330–1334*, 106

Notes: The Carminows owned extensive lands in Cornwall, having settled in the peninsula by at least the twelfth century; there were two branches of the family active in the 1300s, however, with the brothers Sir John Carminow I and Sir Oliver Carminow heading separate branches of this house after the death of their father, Sir Roger Carminow (d. 1309) (Vivian, *Visitations*, pp. 72–75; *TCO*, 33, 190); Sir John Carminow I died on 2 December 1341, after having served as keeper of the royal forests, parks, woods and warrens in Cornwall (*CFR 1327–1337*, 249, 277, 288; *TCO*, 33, 190); his eldest son, Walter, succeeded him as a minor (*CPR 1330–1334*, 242, 261; *Maclean*, iii, 151–152).

John	Carminow II	Knight of the Shire, 1348	MPs, 145
		Justice of the Peace, 12 February 1367–July 1368?	*CPR 1364–1367*, 434

Notes: It seems that John Carminow II was the younger son of Sir Oliver Carminow (Vivian, *Visitations*, p. 73); but a John Carminow also hailed from the junior branch of the family.

Sir Oliver	Carminow	Knight of the Shire, 1313	MPs, 43
		Justice of the Peace, 12 February 1332–March 1332	*CPR 1330–1334*, 286
		Justice of the Peace, 21 March 1332–November 1333	*CPR 1330–1334*, 294, 296, 348
		Justice of the Peace, 3 August 1338–July 1344	*CPR 1338–1340*, 146
		Steward of Cornwall, 8 November 1336 (did not account)	*Sheriffs*, 21
		Sheriff of Cornwall, 8 November 1336 (did not account)	*Sheriffs*, 21
		Constable of Launceston Castle, 8 November 1336	*CFR 1327–1337*, 500

Notes: Sir Oliver Carminow was the son and heir of Sir Roger Carminow (d. 1309), hailing from the senior branch of the family; Sir Thomas l'Ercedekne was returned to parliament in 1313, but expenses record that Sir Oliver sat for the county instead; he died on 23 December 1343 (*TCO*, 33, 191; *RBP*, i, 13).

Sir Ralph	Carminow	Justice of the Peace, November 1373?	*CPR 1370–1374*, 388
		Justice of the Peace, 4 July 1376–July 1377	*CPR 1374–1377*, 313

		Justice of the Peace, 2 July 1377–December 1377	CPR 1377–1381, 45
		Justice of the Peace, 4 March 1378–August 1378	CPR 1377–1381, 48
		Sheriff of Cornwall, 25 November 1378–November 1379	Sheriffs, 21
		Justice of the Peace, 26 May 1380–February 1381	CPR 1377–1381, 513
		Justice of the Peace, 14 December 1381–March 1382	CPR 1381–1385, 85
		Justice of the Peace, 9 March 1382–June 1382	CPR 1381–1385, 142
		Justice of the Peace, 21 December 1382–February 1385	CPR 1381–1385, 248
		Knight of the Shire, 1383	HOP, ii, 489–490
		Knight of the Shire, 1384	HOP, ii, 489–490
		Justice of the Peace, 8 February 1385–July 1387	CPR 1381–1385, 502–503
		Knight of the Shire, 1386	HOP, ii, 489–490

Notes: Sir Ralph Carminow was the son and heir of Sir Walter Carminow and the nephew of Sir Oliver Carminow; he died in 1386 (*HOP*, ii, 489–490; *Cornish Wills*, 39–40, 218–219; *TCO*, 33, 191).

| Sir Roger | Carminow | Knight of the Shire, 1299–1300 | MPs, 10 |

Notes: A Sir Roger Carminow died in 1339, although the Sir Roger who sat as an MP in 1299–1300 was probably the head of the family who died in 1309 (Vivian, *Visitations*, pp. 72–75; *TCO*, 33, 191).

| Sir Thomas | Carminow | Knight of the Shire, 1363 | MPs, 172 |
| | | Justice of the Peace, 10 July 1368–October 1369 | CPR 1367–1370, 195 |

Notes: Sir Thomas Carminow was the son of Sir Roger Carminow (d. 1339) of the elder branch of the family; he was born on 14 April 1336 and died on 20 August 1369, having married Elizabeth, the daughter of Sir Ralph Beaupel, and having had a son also named Thomas (*TCO*, 33, 101, 191; Worcestre, *Itineraries*, 36, 220).

| Sir Walter | Carminow | Knight of the Shire, 1336 | MPs, 111 |

Notes: Sir Walter Carminow was the son of John Carminow I of the junior branch of the family (*CPR 1330–1334*, 242; Vivian, *Visitations*, pp. 72–75; *TCO*, 33, 190); he married Alice, daughter of Stephen de Tynten; he was dead by 1347? (*RBP*, i, 122).

William	Carminow	Justice of the Peace, 14 June 1327–November 1327	*CPR 1327–1330*, 90
John	Cary	Parliamentary Burgess for Launceston, 1362	*MPs*, 169
		Parliamentary Burgess for Launceston, 1364–5	*MPs*, 174
		Justice of the Peace, 1373	*CPR 1370–1374*, 388
		Justice of the Peace, 6 December 1375–July 1376	*CPR 1374–1377*, 139
		Justice of the Peace, 20 February 1381–December 1381	*CPR 1377–1381*, 572–573
		Justice of the Peace, 23 June 1382–December 1382	*CPR 1381–1385*, 194
		Justice of the Peace, 20 December 1382–December 1382	*CPR 1381–1385*, 251
		Justice of the Peace, 16 July 1387–July 1388	*CPR 1385–1389*, 385

Notes: John Cary hailed from Devon and went into the law; he held land in Launceston; he had close connections with the Black Prince and Princess Joan; Richard II appointed him chief baron of the exchequer in 1386 (A. Goodman, 'John Cary', *ODNB*, x, pp. 433–434).

William	Cary	Escheator of Cornwall and Devon, 10 December 1376 (did not account)	*Escheators*, 31
		Justice of the Peace, 20 February 1381–December 1381	*CPR 1377–1381*, 572–573
		Justice of the Peace, 23 June 1382–December 1382	*CPR 1381–1385*, 194

Notes: William Cary was probably related to John Cary (Vivian, *Visitations*, p. 79).

Sir John	Cassy	Justice of the Peace, 4 July 1388–July 1389	*CPR 1385–1389*, 545

Notes: Sir John Cassy was chief baron of the exchequer from May 1389 (*CPR 1388–1392*, 29).

Sir Henry	Chaumpernoun	Knight of the Shire, 1311	*MPs*, 32
		Justice of the Peace, 13 April 1314–June 1314	*CPR 1313–1317*, 107

		Justice of the Peace, 5 June 1314–June 1316	*CPR 1313–1317*, 122
		Justice of the Peace, 14 June 1316–June 1320	*CPR 1313–1317*, 482
		Justice of the Peace, 18 June 1320–June 1327	*CPR 1317–1321*, 459

Notes: The Chaumperouns held extensive estates in Cornwall and Devon (*FA*, i, 208–218, 345–372); Sir Henry Chaumpernoun was the son of William Chaumpernoun I, receiving his lands in 1305 (*CFR 1272–1307*, 511); he served on many commissions in Cornwall and Devon; Edward II summoned him to a Great Council in 1323–4 (*Parliamentary Writs*, ii part 2, p. 655); he was dead by 1330 (*CFR 1327–1337*, 160).

William	Chaumpernoun II	Knight of the Shire, 1338–9	*MPs*, 124
		Sheriff of Cornwall, Mich. 1343–Mich. 1344	*Sheriffs*, 21
		Justice of the Peace, 20 July 1344–November 1344	*CPR 1343–1345*, 394, 399
		Justice of the Peace, 6 December 1345–December 1346	*CPR 1345–1348*, 35
		Justice of the Peace, 18 December 1346–November 1349	*CPR 1345–1348*, 232
		Knight of the Shire, 1351–2?	*MPs*, 150

Notes: William Chaumpernoun II was the son of Sir Henry Chaumpernoun (*CFR 1327–1337*, 160); he served on numerous commissions in Cornwall and Devon, but failed to account as sheriff of Devon when appointed (*CFR 1337–1347*, 320); a number of family members were active at this time (*TCO*, 33, 145, 188).

John	Chaunceler	Coroner until 1331	*CCR 1330–1333*, 345

Notes: John Chaunceler resided in Raginnis in Paul; he married Alice, the daughter of John Enisworgi of St Columb Major; he died on 1 January 1331 (*TCO*, 34, 6).

Thomas	Chaunceler	Knight of the Shire, 1315–16	*MPs*, 50
Richard	Chelmswick	Steward of Cornwall, 26 February 1397–August 1398	*CPR 1396–1399*, 82

Notes: Richard Chelmswick was an esquire of Richard II; he accompanied Henry Bolingbroke to Prussia and sat as an MP for Shropshire (*HOP*, ii, 538–539).

Edmund	Chelreye	Justice of the Peace, 10 July 1368–October 1369	*CPR 1367–1370*, 195

| | | Justice of the Peace, 26 October 1369–January 1370 | *CPR 1367–1370*, 266 |
| | | Justice of the Peace, 28 January 1370–December 1375 | *CPR 1367–1370*, 418 |

Notes: Edmund Chelreye was a man 'learned in the law', serving as a serjeant-at-law and sitting as a justice of assize (*CCR 1369–1374*, 59; *CCR 1364–1368*, 73).

| John | Chenduyt | Knight of the Shire, 1395 | *HOP*, ii, 539–540 |
| | | Knight of the Shire, 1404 | *HOP*, ii, 539–540 |

Notes: The Chenduyts probably originated from Hertfordshire, but a branch of the family were established in Cornwall by the thirteenth century; John Chenduyt inherited the family estates in or before 1386; Richard II retained him as an esquire (*HOP*, ii, 539–540); in 1400 Chenduyt received a chapel licence for Molingey in St Austell (*Reg.Stafford*, 273).

| Sir James | Chuddleigh | Escheator of Cornwall and Devon, 8 December 1391–October 1392 | *Escheators*, 31 |
| Ralph | Clegher | Coroner until 1351 | *CCR 1349–1354*, 283 |

Notes: The Clegher family hailed from Mullion; Ralph Clegher was the son and heir of Oger Clegher, who died in 1349, and Joan, the daughter of Odo Sacheville (*TCO*, 34, 52).

| Richard | Clerc | Bailiff-Errant, 1360?–December 1361 | *RBP*, ii, 171, 185 |

Notes: The Black Prince ordered the removal of Richard Clerc from office in 1360 because of his negligence; the prince later reinstated him in consideration of his 'long service', but again removed him in 1361.

Walter	Clopton	Justice of the Peace, 6 December 1375–July 1376	*CPR 1374–1377*, 139
		Justice of the Peace, 4 July 1376–July 1377	*CPR 1374–1377*, 313
		Justice of the Peace, 2 July 1377–December 1377	*CPR 1377–1381*, 45
		Justice of the Peace, 18 December 1377–March 1378	*CPR 1377–1381*, 48
		Justice of the Peace, 4 March 1378–August 1378	*CPR 1377–1381*, 48
		Justice of the Peace, 12 August 1378–May 1380	*CPR 1377–1381*, 301

		Justice of the Peace, 26 May 1380–February 1381	*CPR 1377–1381*, 513
		Justice of the Peace, 20 February 1381–December 1381	*CPR 1377–1381*, 572–573
		Notes: Walter Clopton was a serjeant-at-law by 1377 and chief justice of the king's bench from 1388 (Tyldesley, 'Local Communities', p. 96).	
Henry	Cokyn	Feodary, 1369–71	SC6/818/1 m. 19r
		Notes: Henry Cokyn hailed from Lostwithiel (*FF*, i, 408–409); he served as reeve of Lostwithiel Manor in 1359–60 (DCO 13); in 1366 he allegedly deprived Richard Cosyn of a tenement in Lostwithiel (JUST1/1476 m. 72v).	
Thomas	Collan	Coroner until 1388	*CCR 1385–1389*, 413
		Notes: Thomas Collan was involved in collecting the 1380 poll tax, having strong links with Polruan (SC8/40/1954).	
John	Colshull	Knight of the Shire, 1391	*HOP*, ii, 633–635
		Justice of the Peace, 15 December 1391–February 1393	*CPR 1388–1392*, 525
		Steward of Cornwall, 24 February 1392–February 1397	*CPR 1391–1396*, 32
		Sheriff of Cornwall, 18 October 1392–November 1393	*Sheriffs*, 21
		Justice of the Peace, 28 February 1393–June 1394	*CPR 1391–1396*, 292
		Knight of the Shire, 1394	*HOP*, ii, 633–635
		Justice of the Peace, 18 June 1394–February 1397	*CPR 1391–1396*, 436
		Knight of the Shire, 1397	*HOP*, ii, 633–635
		Justice of the Peace, 20 February 1397–November 1397	*CPR 1396–1399*, 97
		Sheriff of Cornwall, 3 November 1397–October 1398	*Sheriffs*, 21
		Justice of the Peace, 12 November 1397–February 1399	*CPR 1396–1399*, 237
		Justice of the Peace, 26 February 1399–November 1399	*CPR 1396–1399*, 436
		Knight of the Shire, 1399	*HOP*, ii, 633–635

		Justice of the Peace, 28 November 1399–February 1400	*CPR 1399–1401*, 557

Notes: John Colshull was a London vintner who had served on the City's Common Council (*LBH*, 234–235); his marriage to Emmeline, heiress to the Huish fortune and Sir Robert Tresilian's widow, implanted him in Cornwall (*HOP*, ii, 633–635); he was also connected to Richard II, serving as his esquire (*CPR 1391–1396*, 32); he died in 1413.

John	Colyn	Justice of the Peace, 20 May 1384–February 1385	*CPR 1381–1385*, 428
		Sheriff of Cornwall, 18 November 1387–December 1388	*Sheriffs*, 21
		Sheriff of Cornwall, 18 November 1391–October 1392	*Sheriffs*, 21

Notes: In 1379 John Colyn received a chapel licence for Boscarne in Bodmin and elsewhere (*Reg.Brantingham*, i, 392).

Thomas	Colyn	Parliamentary Burgess for Launceston, 1402	*HOP*, ii, 640
		Coroner until 1409	*CCR 1405–1409*, 440

Notes: Thomas Colyn was the son of John Colyn (*HOP*, ii, 640).

John	Cook	Bailiff-Errant, 12 May 1364–78	*RBP*, ii, 209

Notes: John Cook was the Black Prince's servant, being granted the office of bailiff-errant and a daily salary of 2*d*. as a reward for his service.

John	Copelston	Parliamentary Burgess for Launceston, 1364–5	*MPs*, 174
		Escheator of Cornwall and Devon, 24 October 1392–October 1394	*Escheators*, 31
		Receiver of Cornwall, 30 November 1398	*CFR 1391–1399*, 286

Notes: The Copelstons were a Devonian family of lawyers (Tyldesley, 'Local Communities', pp. 12–13).

William	Corby	Constable of Launceston Castle, before April 1380–after 1401	*CPR 1377–1381*, 454; *CPR 1399–1401*, 407

Notes: William Corby's wife, Agnes, had been Richard II's nurse (*CPR 1385–1389*, 51); he was an esquire of Richard II (*CIPM*, xvi, 40).

Thomas	Corhorta	Bailiff-Errant, 1362	*Duchy Servants*, 310

John	Cornewaille	Justice of the Peace, 26 February 1399–November 1399	*CPR 1396–1399*, 436
Walter	Cornewall/Cornubia, de	Knight of the Shire, 1312	*MPs*, 37
		Coroner until 1313	*CCR 1307–1313*, 521

Notes: Walter de Cornubia died in 1313, leaving a twenty-six-year-old son, William, as heir to his manor of Branel (*CIPM*, v, 208).

Edward	Courtenay, Earl of Devon	Justice of the Peace, 9 March 1382–June 1382	*CPR 1381–1385*, 142
		Justice of the Peace, 21 December 1382–February 1385	*CPR 1381–1385*, 248
		Justice of the Peace, 16 July 1387–July 1388	*CPR 1385–1389*, 385
		Justice of the Peace, 4 July 1388–July 1389	*CPR 1385–1389*, 545
Sir Philip	Courtenay	Steward of Cornwall, 15 November 1388–February 1392	*CPR 1385–1389*, 525

Notes: Sir Philip Courtenay was the fifth son of Sir Hugh Courtenay, 2nd Earl of Devon (*HOP*, ii, 670–673); he held numerous royal offices, saw much military service and sat in the parliamentary Commons for Devon on some eight occasions.

| Roland | Coykyn, de | Knight of the Shire, 1307 | *MPs*, 27 |

Notes: Roland Coykyn held some land in Cornwall; it seems that he hailed from Somerset (*FA*, i, 200).

William	Cranewell	Justice of the Peace, 30 May 1370–December 1375	*CPR 1367–1370*, 422
		Steward of Cornwall, 6 May 1371–October 1375	SC6/818/4 m. 8r; *Sheriffs*, 21
		Sheriff of Cornwall, 6 May 1371–July 1375	SC6/818/4 m. 8r; *Sheriffs*, 21
		Justice of the Peace, 1373	*CPR 1370–1374*, 388

Notes: William Cranewell was a yeoman of the Black Prince who served as chamberlain to the clerk of North Wales (*RBP*, iii, 355; *RBP*, iv, 469; *CCR 1369–1374*, 264, 270); he died in 1376 (*Cornish Wills*, 36–39, 222).

| William | Crishile | Constable of Tintagel Castle, May 1398 | *CCR 1396–1399*, 264 |

John	Croghard	Knight of the Shire, 1334	MPs, 104
		Receiver of the Stannaries, before 1345	CCR 1343–1346, 669

Notes: In 1333 John Croghard (or Crouchard) brought a plea of debt before the county court (SC2/161/74 m. 4v); in 1352 he is recorded as having served as receiver of Cornwall (RBP, ii, 30); he was actually receiver of the stannaries of Cornwall; he died leaving debts of over £1,700 (CCR 1343–1346, 669).

Thomas	Curthuhir, de	Coroner until 1367	CCR 1364–1368, 325, 331
Sir Stephen	Cusyngton	Justice of the Peace, 26 June 1373?	CPR 1370–1374, 388
		Constable of Launceston Castle, 1375	Reg.Brantingham, i, 152
		Justice of the Peace, 6 December 1375–July 1376	CPR 1374–1377, 139
John	Dabernon	Feodary, before 1338–September 1354	SC6/816/11 m. 16r
		Escheator of Cornwall, 26 January 1343–54	Escheators, 30
		Justice of the Peace, 10 November 1344–December 1346	CPR 1343–1345, 396
		Justice of the Peace, 18 December 1346–November 1349	CPR 1345–1348, 232
		Justice of the Peace, 25 November 1349–July 1352	CPR 1348–1350, 383
		Steward of Cornwall, 23 February 1350–August 1354	DCO 5; SC6/817/1 m. 19r; Sheriffs, 21
		Sheriff of Cornwall, 23 February 1350–Mich. 1354	DCO 6; Sheriffs, 21
		Constable of Trematon Castle, 1350–69	SC6/817/1 m. 19r; RBP, ii, 9
		Constable of Tintagel Castle, before 11 June 1351–July 1351	RBP, ii, 9, 14
		Justice of the Peace, 15 July 1352–December 1354	CPR 1350–1354, 285
		Steward of Cornwall, 26 August 1357–69	RBP, ii, 125; SC8/817/6 m. 2v
		Sheriff of Cornwall, Mich. 1357–69	Sheriffs, 21

	Justice of the Peace, 17 February 1358–March 1361	*CPR 1358–1361*, 68
	Steward of the Prince's Stannary, 13 July 1359	*RBP*, ii, 159
	Justice of the Peace, 21 May 1361–May 1364	*CPR 1361–1364*, 65
	Justice of the Peace, 8 May 1364–February 1367	*CPR 1361–1364*, 528
	Justice of the Peace, 12 February 1367–July 1368	*CPR 1364–1367*, 434
	Justice of the Peace, 10 July 1368–October 1369	*CPR 1367–1370*, 195
	Justice of the Peace, 26 October 1369?	*CPR 1367–1370*, 266
	Justice of the Peace, 28 January 1370?	*CPR 1367–1370*, 418

Notes: John Dabernon hailed from Bradford, Devon; he became the Black Prince's south-western retainer-in-chief, serving on many commissions in Cornwall and Devon; he died in 1369 (*Cornish Wills*, 31–35, 223).

Matthew	Dabernon	Parliamentary Burgess for Bodmin, 1362	*MPs*, 169
		Parliamentary Burgess for Lostwithiel, 1362	*MPs*, 169
		Parliamentary Burgess for Bodmin, 1364–5	*MPs*, 174
		Parliamentary Burgess for Lostwithiel, 1364–5	*MPs*, 174
		Parliamentary Burgess for Liskeard, 1368	*MPs*, 179
		Parliamentary Burgess for Lostwithiel, 1368	*MPs*, 179

Notes: Matthew Dabernon was the son of John Dabernon (*Cornish Wills*, 35).

Thomas	Daumarle	Controller of the Stannaries, 1334	*CPR 1330–1334*, 493

Notes: Thomas Daumarle was one of Edward III's clerks.

William	Daumarle	Keeper of Launceston Gaol, 1334	*CPR 1330–1334*, 493

Notes: William Daumarle served as a yeoman of Edward III.

| Sir John | Dauney | Justice of the Peace, 6 July 1338–August 1338 | CPR 1338–1340, 139 |
| | | Justice of the Peace, 3 August 1338? | CPR 1338–1340, 139 |

Notes: Sir John Dauney (or Alento) served on numerous commissions in Cornwall and Devon (CPR 1334–1338, 448); in 1330 he received a chapel licence for Portloe (Reg.Grandisson, i, 590); he died at Crécy in 1346 (CFR 1337–1347, 478; RBP, i, 119, 130); Edward III assigned his widow, Sibyl, some of his lands in Cornwall, Devon and Somerset (CIPM, ix, 66–68).

| Stephen | Derenford | Receiver of Cornwall, 6 December 1387–February 1388 | CFR 1383–1391, 164 |

Notes: Stephen Derenford hailed from Plymouth.

Laurence	Dynisel	Coroner until 1298	CCR 1296–1302, 146
Robert	Eleford, de	Justice of the Peace, 15 July 1352–December 1354	CPR 1350–1354, 285
		Steward of Cornwall, 18 August 1354–August 1357	RBP, ii, 62; DCO 7–11
		Sheriff of Cornwall, 18 August 1354–Mich. 1357	RBP, ii, 62; DCO 7–11; Sheriffs, 21
		Justice of the Peace, 16 December 1354–December 1355	CPR 1354–1358, 123
		Justice of the Peace, 10 December 1355–February 1358	CPR 1354–1358, 227

Notes: Robert de Eleford was a yeoman of the Black Prince (RBP, ii, 62); he also served as the earl of Pembroke's general attorney (CCR 1341–1343, 527); he sat on many commissions in Cornwall.

| Henry | Erth, de | Constable of Trematon Castle, 1337–9 | CPR 1334–1338, 383 |

Notes: Henry de Erth had served as John of Eltham's standard bearer at Berwick.

John	Everard	Escheator of Cornwall, Devon, Somerset and Dorset, 29 November 1323–December 1325	Escheators, 134
John	Fareway	Coroner until 1394	CCR 1392–1396, 197, 327
Thomas	Fenne, atte	Sheriff of Cornwall, Mich. 1344–July 1349	DCO 4; Sheriffs, 21
		Steward of Cornwall, 5 November 1347–July 1349	RBP, i, 141

Constable of Tintagel Castle, 1348–9

Notes: Thomas atte Fenne, sometimes Van, had obscure origins; he was attacked in his home in Tregorrick and held some land in the county (*CPR 1343–1345*, 390; *FF*, i, 347–348); it seems that in 1346 he served as deputy escheator to John Dabernon (*CPR 1345–1348*, 145); he was a man of some means, losing a white horse on campaign worth 100s. (*Norwell*, p. 309); during his tenure as sheriff-steward the two offices were divided, and although he was again appointed steward in 1347, Sir Edmund Kendale, his predecessor, appeared as steward in the ministers' accounts for 1348–9 (DCO 4); Fenn died in 1349, leaving considerable debts (*RBP*, ii, 96, 7, 12, 13, 29–30, 85).

Sir John	Ferrers	Justice of the Peace, 6 December 1345–December 1346	*CPR 1345–1348*, 35
		Justice of the Peace, 18 December 1346–November 1349	*CPR 1345–1348*, 232
		Justice of the Peace, 25 November 1349–July 1352	*CPR 1348–1350*, 383

Notes: The Ferrers were a Devonian family who held some land in Cornwall (*FA*, i, 208–218).

John	Ferrers	Coroner until 1347	*CCR 1346–1349*, 226
Martin	Ferrers	Justice of the Peace, 12 August 1378–May 1380	*CPR 1377–1381*, 301
		Justice of the Peace, 26 May 1380–February 1381	*CPR 1377–1381*, 513
		Justice of the Peace, 15 July 1389–November 1389	*CPR 1388–1392*, 136
		Justice of the Peace, 10 November 1389–June 1390	*CPR 1388–1392*, 138
		Justice of the Peace, 28 June 1390–December 1391	*CPR 1388–1392*, 342
		Justice of the Peace, 15 December 1391–February 1393	*CPR 1388–1392*, 525
William	Ferrers	Knight of the Shire, 1314–15	*MPs*, 48
Sir Thomas	Fichet	Knight of the Shire, 1384	*MPs*, 222

Notes: The Fichets held the manor of Boconnion (*Maclean*, ii, 42–43); in 1353 Sir Thomas Fichet granted all his lands in Somerset to the Black Prince for life and to his executors for five years after his death (*RBP*, iv, 104–105); John of Gaunt later retained him (Tyldesley, 'Local Communities', p. 153).

Thomas	Fitz Henry 'Havener'	Havener, 12 February 1337–73	CFR 1337–1347, 4

Notes: Thomas Fitz Henry was appointed havener on a posthumous promise of John of Eltham (*CFR 1337–1347*, 4); he served the Black Prince diligently for over thirty years; he was no longer havener in 1373 (DCO 19).

Nicholas	Fitz Herbert	Controller of the Stannaries, 1386–after 1391	*CPR 1385–1389*, 107, 248; *CCR 1389–1392*, 385

Notes: Nicholas Fitz Herbert was one of Richard II's clerks.

Sir William	Fitz Water	Knight of the Shire, 1376–7	*MPs*, 195
		Sheriff of Cornwall, 1 November 1383–November 1384	*Sheriffs*, 21

Notes: Sir William Fitz Water was an assessor of the 1379 poll tax (*CFR 1377–1383*, 144); in 1381 he received a chapel license for St Veep (*Reg. Brantingham*, i, 452); he died on 10 May 1385, leaving an eleven-year-old son, Thomas (*CIPM*, xvi, 43–44).

Richard	Fleming	Coroner until 1343	*CCR 1343–1346*, 198
Thomas	Ford	Parliamentary Burgess for Bodmin, 1368	*MPs*, 179
		Parliamentary Burgess for Bodmin, 1369	*MPs*, 181
		Coroner until after 1406	*CCR 1399–1402*, 457; *CCR 1405–1409*, 43

Notes: There may have been two Thomas Fords.

Robert	Frenssh	Escheator of Cornwall and Devon, 29 November 1402	*Escheators*, 31

Notes: Robert Frenssh hailed from Devon, having contacts with Totnes (Tyldesley, 'Local Communities', p. 129).

Henry	Fulford	Justice of the Peace, 1 May 1401–March 1403	*CPR 1399–1401*, 557
Thomas	Galy	Joint Havener, 30 August 1395–October 1397	*CPR 1391–1396*, 620
James	Gerveys	Parliamentary Burgess for Bodmin, 1363	*MPs*, 172

		Parliamentary Burgess for Helston, 1363	*MPs*, 172
		Justice of the Peace, 15 July 1389–November 1389	*CPR 1388–1392*, 136
		Justice of the Peace, 18 June 1394–February 1397	*CPR 1391–1396*, 436

Notes: James Gerveys is wrongly named John in the 1394 peace commission; it remains unclear if he sat as a burgess or not (Tyldesley, 'Local Communites', p. 91; Vivian, *Visitations*, p. 175); the Gerveys, however, had a long tradition of sitting for boroughs (*MPs*, 54, 57, 59, 121, 130, 163, 166, 199); in 1374 he received a chapel licence for Constantine (*Reg.Brantingham*, i, 332, 359; *Reg.Stafford*, 275).

| Thomas | Gevely | Constable of Trematon Castle, 1315–May 1316 | SC6/811/15 m. 1r; *CCR 1313–1318*, 254 |

Notes: Thomas Gevely fought in Scotland and engaged in lawlessness in Cornwall (SC8/76/3756).

| Sir Richard | Giffard | Knight of the Shire, 1300–1 | *MPs*, 13 |

Notes: The Giffards were 'of high antiquity' in Cornwall (*Maclean*, ii, 151–154).

Sir Robert	Giffard	Knight of the Shire, 1299–1300	*MPs*, 10
		Knight of the Shire, 1306	*MPs*, 21
		Justice of the Peace, 24 December 1307–March 1308	*CPR 1307–1313*, 30
		Justice of the Peace, 17 March 1308–March 1312	*CPR 1307–1313*, 54
		Justice of the Peace, 13 April 1314–June 1314	*CPR 1313–1317*, 107
		Justice of the Peace, 5 June 1314–June 1316	*CPR 1313–1317*, 122
		Justice of the Peace, 14 June 1316–June 1320	*CPR 1313–1317*, 482
		Justice of the Peace, 18 June 1320–June 1327	*CPR 1317–1321*, 459

Notes: Sir Robert Giffard served Edward I militarily in Scotland and Gascony; he held numerous commissions in Cornwall (*CPR 1292–1301*, 373, 613; *FA*, i, 195, 197).

| Nicholas | Giffard | Parliamentary Burgess for Liskeard, 1306–7 | *MPs*, 24 |

		Knight of the Shire, 1325	MPs, 73

Notes: Nicholas Giffard received his rights in 1312 (*Maclean*, ii, 152); he married Isabel, the daughter of Sir Richard Huish; he died on 25 March 1334, leaving a son, John (*TCO*, 33, 191).

Sir Peter	Gildesburgh, de	Controller of the Stannaries, 1340–7	*CPR 1340–1343*, 72, 459; *RBP*, i, 71

Notes: Sir Peter Gildesburgh was clerk to Edward III; he served as the Black Prince's chief receiver and pesage of tin in Cornwall (*RBP*, i, *passim*.; *CPR 1340–1343*, 459).

Richard	Glenyan	Justice of the Peace, 4 July 1388–July 1389	*CPR 1385–1389*, 545
		Justice of the Peace, 12 November 1397–February 1399	*CPR 1396–1399*, 237
		Justice of the Peace, 26 February 1399–November 1399	*CPR 1396–1399*, 436
		Justice of the Peace, 28 November 1399–February 1400	*CPR 1399–1401*, 557

Notes: In 1397 Richard Glenyan received a general chapel licence for the diocese (*Reg.Stafford*, 275)

Peter	Glynn, de	Coroner until 1338	*CCR 1333–1337*, 270

Notes: Peter de Glynn was perhaps a younger son of the Glynn Family (Vivian, *Visitations*, pp. 178–179).

Sir John	Grenville	Sheriff of Cornwall, 11 November 1394–November 1395	*Sheriffs*, 21
		Justice of the Peace, 1 May 1401–March 1403	*CPR 1399–1401*, 557
		Justice of the Peace, 14 March 1403	*CPR 1401–1405*, 516
		Sheriff of Cornwall, Mich. 1404–Mich. 1406	*Sheriffs*, 21

Notes: Sir John Grenville hailed from North Devon but had interests in Cornwall (Tyldesley, 'Local Communities', p. 120; *HOP*, iii, 235–236).

Henry	Guldeford	Havener, March 1324	*Havener's Accounts*, p. 320

Notes: Henry Guldeford served as Queen Isabella's valet (*Havener's Accounts*, p. 320).

Andrew	Hamley	Knight of the Shire, 1328	MPs, 85
		Parliamentary Burgess for Launceston, 1335	MPs, 106

		Parliamentary Burgess for Helston, 1335	*MPs*, 106
		Knight of the Shire, 1337–8	*MPs*, 119

Notes: The Hamleys were 'of great antiquity' in Cornwall (*Maclean*, ii, 540–553); Andrew Hamley was the son of Osbert Hamley I (*MPs*, 106).

Sir John	Hamley I	Sheriff of Cornwall, 1 February 1337 (accounted from Christmas 1336)–September 1338	*Sheriffs*, 21
		Steward of Cornwall, 1 February 1337–September 1338	*Sheriffs*, 21
		Constable of Launceston Castle, 1 February 1337–September 1338?	*CFR 1337–1347*, 2

Notes: Sir John Hamley I inherited considerable lands in the county from his father, Osbert Hamley I (*FA*, i, 198, 205, 215; *FF*, i, 159, 300; *TCO*, 33, 191); he served on numerous commissions (*CPR 1338–1340*, 502; *CPR 1340–1343*, 154; *CCR 1337–1339*, 509); and was keeper of the fortlet of St Michael's Mount (*CPR 1338–1340*, 99); he died at Crécy in 1346 (*CFR 1337–1347*, 479; *TCO*, 33, 191); in 1347 his widow, Margaret, the daughter of Walter de Ydlis, was assigned some of his lands by Edward III, but the king retained the bulk of them to cover his debts (*CIPM*, ix, 66).

John	Hamley II	Parliamentary Burgess for Helston, 1355	*MPs*, 157
		Parliamentary Burgess for Liskeard, 1355	*MPs*, 157
		Parliamentary Burgess for Lostwithiel, 1355	*MPs*, 157
		Parliamentary Burgess for Truro, 1355	*MPs*, 157
		Knight of the Shire, 1357	*MPs*, 159
		Knight of the Shire, 1360	*MPs*, 163
		Parliamentary Burgess for Bodmin, 1360–1	*MPs*, 166
		Parliamentary Burgess for Helston, 1360–1	*MPs*, 166
		Knight of the Shire, 1362	*MPs*, 169
		Justice of the Peace, 4 July 1376–July 1377	*CPR 1374–1377*, 313
		Justice of the Peace, 2 July 1377–December 1377	*CPR 1377–1381*, 45

Notes: The family tree of the Hamleys is somewhat confused and it is unclear if John Hamley II sat in all these parliaments or not.

Osbert	Hamley I	Parliamentary Burgess for Bodmin, 1309	*MPs*, 30
		Coroner until 1328	*CCR 1327–1330*, 249

Notes: Osbert Hamley I married Margaret, the daughter of Ralph Glynn; Hamley died on 20 January 1332, leaving a son, John Hamley I (*TCO*, 33, 191).

Osbert	Hamley II	Justice of the Peace, 4 March 1378–August 1378	*CPR 1377–1381*, 48
Richard	Hampton, de	Constable of Tintagel Castle, 15 February 1377–January 1386	*CPR 1377–1381*, 169
		Havener, 22 March 1378–January 1386	*CPR 1377–1381*, 169
		Joint Constable of Tintagel Castle, January 1386–January 1389	*CPR 1385–1389*, 97
		Joint Havener, 5 January 1386–December 1388	*CPR 1385–1389*, 97

Notes: Richard Hampton served as Richard II's esquire (*CCR 1381–1385*, 2); he lost office after saying 'rebellious words', being reinstated at the supplication of Simon de Burley (*CPR 1381–1385*, 371).

Peter	Hatton	Receiver of Cornwall, 10 October 1399	*CPR 1399–1401*, 10
John	Hawley	Escheator of Cornwall and Devon, 12 December 1390–December 1391	*Escheators*, 31
		Receiver of Cornwall, 20 December 1390	*CFR 1383–1391*, 342

Notes: John Hawley was a notorious 'pirate' of Dartmouth; he acquired lands in Cornwall through the agency of marriage (*HOP*, iii, 328–331).

Sir John	Herle	Sheriff of Cornwall, 7 November 1393–November 1394	*Sheriffs*, 21
		Justice of the Peace, 18 June 1394–February 1397	*CPR 1391–1396*, 436
		Justice of the Peace, 20 February 1397–November 1397	*CPR 1396–1399*, 97
		Justice of the Peace, 12 November 1397–February 1398	*CPR 1396–1399*, 237
		Justice of the Peace, 26 February 1398–November 1399	*CPR 1396–1399*, 436

		Justice of the Peace, 28 November 1399–February 1400	CPR 1399–1401, 557

Notes: Sir John Herle was of Northumberland and Worcestershire extraction; his marriage to Margaret, a co-heiress of William Chaumpernoun, implanted him into Cornish society (Tyldesley, 'Local Communities', p. 120); in 1396 he received a general chapel licence for the diocese (*Reg. Stafford*, 276).

John	Holand, Earl of Huntingdon	Constable of Tintagel Castle, 6 January 1389	CPR 1385–1389, 537
		Constable of Trematon Castle, 25 June 1392	CPR 1391–1396, 102
		Justice of the Peace, 20 February 1397–November 1397	CPR 1396–1399, 97
		Justice of the Peace, 12 November 1397–February 1399	CPR 1396–1399, 237
		Justice of the Peace, 26 February 1399–November 1399	CPR 1396–1399, 436
Sir Richard	Huish I	Knight of the Shire, 1307	MPs, 27
		Justice of the Peace, 24 December 1307–March 1308	CPR 1307–1313, 30
		Knight of the Shire, 1311	MPs, 32
		Knight of the Shire, 1314	MPs, 45
		Steward of Cornwall, 4 November 1315–May 1316	SC6/811/14 m. 1r; SC6/811/16
		Sheriff of Cornwall, 4 November 1315–May 1316	SC6/811/14 m. 1r; *Sheriffs*, 21
		Constable of Restormel Castle, 1315–16	*Sheriffs*, 21, CCR 1313–1318, 298
		Havener, September 1315–May 1316	CFR 1307–1319, 262
		Knight of the Shire, 1325?	MPs, 73

Notes: The Huishs held estates in Cornwall and Devon (*FA*, i, 208–218); in 1303 Sir Richard I received the lands of his father, another Sir Richard Huish (d. 1297) (CCR 1302–1307, 13; TCO, 33, 145); he held numerous commissions in Cornwall (CPR 1313–1317, 49, 474; CPR 1317–1321, 96, 349); he died in 1330–1 (CFR 1327–1337, 244).

Sir Richard	Huish II	Knight of the Shire, 1331	MPs, 94

		Justice of the Peace, 12 February 1332–March 1332	*CPR 1330–1334*, 286
		Justice of the Peace, 21 March 1332–November 1333	*CPR 1330–1334*, 294, 296, 348
		Justice of the Peace, 26 July 1335–April 1336	*CPR 1334–1338*, 209
		Knight of the Shire, 1336–7	*MPs*, 113
		Justice of the Peace, 3 August 1338–July 1344	*CPR 1338–1340*, 146
		Knight of the Shire, 1352	*MPs*, 152

Notes: Sir Richard Huish II received his father's lands in 1331, although the family tree is somewhat confused (*CFR 1327–1337*, 244; *TCO*, 33, 145); he served on many commissions in the county (*CPR 1330–1334*, 358; *CPR 1338–1340*, 146); in 1332 a Richard Huish received a chapel licence for Raphael in Lansallos and Tremadart in Duloe (*Reg.Grandisson*, ii, 653); he died in 1369 (*CIPM*, xii, 347–348).

Robert	Hull	Escheator of Cornwall and Devon, 10 February 1377–November 1377	*Escheators*, 31
		Justice of the Peace, 15 July 1389–November 1389	*CPR 1388–1392*, 136
		Justice of the Peace, 10 November 1389–June 1390	*CPR 1388–1392*, 138
		Justice of the Peace, 28 June 1390–December 1391	*CPR 1388–1392*, 342, 344
		Justice of the Peace, 28 February 1393–June 1394	*CPR 1391–1396*, 292

Notes: Robert Hull held land in Cornwall, Devon and Somerset; he sat in parliament for several Devonian boroughs (Tyldesley, 'Local Communities', p. 130).

William	Hureward	Knight of the Shire, 1323–4	*MPs*, 69
John	Hustyng', de	Coroner until 1369	*CCR 1369–1374*, 14
Thomas	Hyde, de la	Sheriff of Cornwall, Easter 1296–June 1312	SC6/811/3 m. 1r; SC6/811/11 m. 1r; *Sheriffs*, 21
		Steward of Cornwall, Easter 1296–June 1312	SC6/811/3 m. 1r; SC6/811/11 m. 1r
		Constable of Tintagel Castle, before 1306–March 1312	E372/152B m. 9r; SC8/53/2638

		Constable of Restormel Castle, March 1312–October 1312	CCR 1307–1313, 454
		Justice of the Peace, 20 March 1312–April 1314?	CPR 1307–1313, 473
		Justice of the Peace, 5 June 1314?	CPR 1313–1317, 122

Notes: Thomas de le Hyde was a Staffordshire-man; it seems that despite the gaps in his career suggested by the *L&IS*, he held the stewardship continuously to 1312; he served on many commissions, among them keeper of the coinage of tin (*CPR 1301–1307*, 127, 202, 456; *CFR 1272–1304*, 493; *CPR 1307–1313*, 23); he held the constableship of Tintagel from at least 1306 and possibly from 1300, John le Barber perhaps being his deputy (E372/152B m. 9r; SC6/811/5 m. 4r; *CPR 1301–1307*, 454); Hyde's final appointment as a JP and tax collector (*CPR 1307–1313*, 521; *CPR 1313–1317*, 122) may instead have been his son, with whom he shared a name; Hyde senior died in 1314, having acquired some lands and wardships in the county (CRO, AR/1/971; ME/333; *FF*, i, 226–227; *CIPM*, v, 276; *CPR 1307–1313*, 523; *CFR 1307–1319*, 162, 215); it was his son who in 1317 sold land in Tintagel while retaining land in La Hyde, Staffordshire (C143/128/18; JUST1/1368 m. 19v).

Sir Henry	Ilcombe	Knight of the Shire, 1388	*HOP*, iii, 472–474
		Knight of the Shire, 1395	*HOP*, iii, 472–474
		Coroner until 1395	CCR 1392–1396, 445
		Escheator of Cornwall, 18 November 1395–November 1399	*Escheators*, 31
		Parliamentary Burgess for Lostwithiel, 1402	*HOP*, iii, 472–474

Notes: Sir Henry Ilcombe had a remarkable career which saw him fight overseas and engage in much lawlessness at home (*HOP*, iii, 472–474).

| Sir Roger | Ingepenne, de | Sheriff of Cornwall, 1 October 1302 (did not account) | SC6/816/9; *Sheriffs*, 21 |
| | | Steward of Cornwall, 1 October 1302 (did not account) | SC6/816/9 |

Notes: Sir Roger Ingepenne was of Berkshire origin (A. R. Ingpen, *An Ancient Family: A Genealogical Study showing the Saxon Origin of the Family of Ingpen* (London, 1916), pp. 76, 82, 86–87); he served as Earl Edmund's steward in 1285–8 (*Sheriffs*, 21); Edward I appointed him sheriff-steward in 1302, but removed him from office and prosecuted him for his lawlessness (*CPR 1301–1307*, 122; KB27/171mm. 63d–64r; *SCKB*, iv, lxxiii); he was a retainer of the earl of Pembroke (*CPR 1307–1313*, 105, 581); he rented and owned some Cornish lands (CRO, AR/1/279–283), later granting these to his nephew and heir, Roger Ingepenne Junior, who had married Joan, daughter and heiress of Sir John Halton of Halton in St Dominick (Ingpen, *Ingepen*, pp. 87–88; *FA*, i, 206, 349, 352; C143/51/21; *CIPM*, vii, 260–261; *Maclean*, ii, 25–27, 43); Sir Roger was dead by 1306 (*CFR 1272–1307*, 536).

Roger	Juyl	Receiver of Cornwall, 1377–81	SC6/818/7 m. 1v; *CFR 1377–1383*, 7
		Escheator of Cornwall and Devon, 25 October 1381–December 1382	*Escheators*, 31
		Escheator of Cornwall and Devon, 1 November 1383–November 1384	*Escheators*, 31
		Parliamentary Burgess for Truro, 1391	*HOP*, iii, 506

Notes: Roger Juyl was probably the son of John Juyl, who represented Bodmin in 1371 and 1381; Roger was a prosperous tin merchant (*HOP*, iii, 506–508).

Ralph	Kayl I	Coroner until 1373	*CCR 1369–1374*, 501

Notes: The Kayls were long-established in Cornwall; Ralph Kayl I was the son of Henry Kale and Joan, the daughter of Trustram Boswer (*TCO*, 33, 279); he was dead by 1385.

Ralph	Kayl II	Parliamentary Burgess for Truro, 1402	*HOP*, iii, 509

Notes: Ralph Kayl II's was the son of Ralph Kayl I; he had extensive tin interests (*HOP*, iii, 509).

John	Kelerioun	Coroner until 1409	*CCR 1405–1409*, 450
Sir Edmund	Kendale	Steward of Cornwall, 1346–November 1347	DCO 3; *RBP*, i, 5

Notes: Sir Edmund Kendale was a bachelor of the Black Prince who served as steward of all the prince's lands (DCO 4; *RBP*, i, 5, 13; Sharp, 'Black Prince', p. 432); although Thomas atte Fenn was appointed steward in 1347, Kendale still appeared in this role in 1348–9 (DCO 4; *RBP*, i, 141).

John	Kendale I	Constable of Restormel Castle, 12 February 1337–65?	*CPR 1334–1338*, 383
		Receiver of Cornwall, 1348–September 1365	DCO 4; SC6/817/1 m. 1r

Notes: The Kendales originated from Westmorland; Edward III appointed John Kendale I constable and parker of Restormel on a posthumous promise of John of Eltham (*CPR 1334–1338*, 383); in 1348 he held the receivership jointly with John de Portes, perhaps under the supervision of 'Tideman de Lymbergh (DCO 4); he was also keeper of 'Tywardreath 'castle' (*RBP*, ii, 87); in 1365 he requested that he be removed from office because of his inability, asking that his kinsman Richard Kendale be appointed in his stead (*RBP*, ii, 213).

John	Kendale II	Parliamentary Burgess for Lostwithiel, January 1397	*HOP*, iii, 513
		Parliamentary Burgess for Lostwithiel, September 1397	*HOP*, iii, 513

Notes: John Kendale II was the son of John Kendale I and went on to serve as mayor of Lostwithiel (*HOP*, iii, 513–514).

Richard	Kendale	Parliamentary Burgess for Lostwithiel, 1364–5	*MPs*, 174
		Receiver of Cornwall, 30 September 1365–8	*RBP*, ii, 213
		Parliamentary Burgess for Launceston, 1369	*MPs*, 181
		Escheator of Cornwall and Devon, 26 November 1377–October 1381	*Escheators*, 31
		Parliamentary Burgess for Liskeard, 1379–80	*MPs*, 203
		Justice of the Peace, 23 June 1382–December 1382	*CPR 1381–1385*, 194
		Justice of the Peace, 20 December 1382–December 1382	*CPR 1381–1385*, 251
		Sheriff of Cornwall, 11 November 1384–October 1385	*Sheriffs*, 21

Notes: Richard Kendale was a kinsman of John Kendale I, although the pedigree in Vivian's *Visitations* is not reliable; he held office in Devon as well.

Sir John	Kentwood	Steward of Cornwall, 26 August 1378–November 1388	*CPR 1377–1381*, 269
		Knight of the Shire, 1378	*HOP*, iii, 517
		Justice of the Peace, 28 August 1378–May 1380	*CPR 1377–1381*, 301
		Justice of the Peace, 26 May 1380–February 1381	*CPR 1377–1381*, 513
		Knight of the Shire, 1380	*MPs*, 206
		Knight of the Shire, 1381	*MPs*, 207
		Justice of the Peace, 14 December 1381–March 1382	*CPR 1381–1385*, 85

	Justice of the Peace, 9 March 1382–June 1382	*CPR 1381–1385*, 142
	Justice of the Peace, 23 June 1382–December 1382	*CPR 1381–1385*, 194
	Justice of the Peace, 20 December 1382–February 1385	*CPR 1381–1385*, 348, 251
	Justice of the Peace, 8 February 1385–July 1387	*CPR 1381–1385*, 502, 503
	Justice of the Peace, 16 July 1387–July 1388	*CPR 1385–1389*, 385
	Justice of the Peace, 4 July 1388–July 1389	*CPR 1385–1389*, 545

Notes: Sir John Kentwood was a Berkshire-man who had served the Black Prince; he sat on many commissions in Cornwall for over a decade (*HOP*, iii, 517–519).

Alan	Kernek, de	Coroner until 1324	*CCR 1323–1327*, 237

Notes: Alan de Kernek was the son of Sir Oger de Kernek (d. 1292) and Alice, the daughter of John Soor (*TCO*, 33, 100, 144); he died on 27 February 1324.

Ralph	Kernek, de	Coroner until 1320	*CCR 1318–1323*, 176
John	Keynes	Escheator of Cornwall and Devon, 30 November 1388–November 1390	*Escheators*, 31

Notes: John Keynes hailed from Devon (Tyldesley, 'Local Communities', p. 121).

Henry	Kirkestede	Constable of Trematon Castle, 2 December 1381–June 1392	*CPR 1381–1385*, 56
		Constable of Trematon Castle, 15 June 1402	*CCR 1399–1402*, 535–536

Notes: Henry Kirkestede was an esquire of Richard II who later shifted his loyalty to Henry IV; he held the post of parker of Trematon and Liskeard (*CPR 1399–1401*, 87); in 1387 he is mistakenly called John (*CPR 1385–1389*, 395).

John	Knyveton	Joint Havener, 30 August 1395–October 1397	*CPR 1391–1396*, 620
John	Lambourne	Knight of the Shire, 1327	*MPs*, 78

Notes: John Lambourne held some lands in the county (*FF*, i, 288); in 1345 he served with the earl of Lancaster in France (*CPR 1345–1348*, 190); he died on 21 March 1352, leaving a son, William (*TCO*, 33, 145).

Sir William	Lambourne	Knight of the Shire, 1376–7	MPs, 195
		Knight of the Shire, 1383	CPR 1381–1385, 428
		Justice of the Peace, 20 May 1384–February 1385	MPs, 217
		Knight of the Shire, 1388	HOP, iii, 544
		Justice of the Peace, 15 July 1389–November 1389	CPR 1388–1392, 136
		Knight of the Shire, 1390	HOP, iii, 544
		Knight of the Shire, 1399	HOP, iii, 544
		Justice of the Peace, 16 February 1400–May 1401	CPR 1399–1401, 557
		Justice of the Peace, 16 May 1401–March 1403	CPR 1399–1401, 557
		Justice of the Peace, 14 March 1403	CPR 1401–1405, 516

Notes: Sir William Lambourne was the son of John Lambourne (*TCO*, 33, 145); in 1348 he assaulted John Dinham's park at Carn Brea (*CPR 1348–1350*, 74); he had an active career in county administration (*HOP*, iii, 544–545); his brother, John, died in 1349 (*TCO*, 33, 145); in 1372 Sir William received a chapel licence for Lamborn in Perranzabuloe and Trerice (*Reg.Brantingham*, i, 267; *Reg.Stafford*, 277).

William	Langbrok	Receiver of Cornwall, 13 August 1398	CFR 1391–1399, 279

Notes: William Langbrok was a clerk (*CFR 1391–1399*, 279).

William	Ledes	Controller of the Stannary of Cornwall and Devon, 1395	CFR 1391–1399, 168
Sir John	l'Ercedekne	Knight of the Shire, 1332	MPs, 98
		Knight of the Shire, 1335–6	MPs, 108
		Justice of the Peace, 26 October 1369–January 1370	CPR 1367–1370, 266

Notes: The l'Ercedekne family seat lay at Ruan Lanihorne; Sir John l'Ercedekne was the son and heir of Thomas, Lord l'Ercedekne; he was twenty-five on his father's death in 1331 (*CIPM*, vii, 253–254; *CP*, i, 187); he sat on numerous commissions, but was more notable for his lawlessness; he married Cecilia, heir to Jordan de Haccomb in Devon (*TCO*, 33, 189); Sir John died in 1377; his eldest son, Stephen, soon followed him, leaving his second son, Sir Warin, to inherit (*CIPM*, xv, 29; *TCO*, 33, 189).

Sir Michael	l'Ercedekne	Knight of the Shire, 1382–3	*MPs*, 214
		Knight of the Shire, 1390	*HOP*, ii, 45
Odo	l'Ercedekne	Constable of Trematon Castle, March 1312–15?	*CCR 1307–1313*, 454
		Knight of the Shire, 1313	*MPs*, 43
		Knight of the Shire, 1318	*MPs*, 54
		Knight of the Shire, 1319	*MPs*, 57

Notes: Odo l'Ercedekne was probably the brother of Sir Thomas l'Ercedekne; he held some lands in the county (*FF*, i, 263); he may have held Trematon Castle in 1318 (*CPR 1317–1321*, 291).

Sir Thomas	l'Ercedekne	Knight of the Shire, 1304–5	*MPs*, 18
		Justice of the Peace, 17 March 1308–March 1312	*CPR 1307–1313*, 54
		Justice of the Peace, 20 March 1312–April 1314	*CPR 1307–1313*, 473
		Constable of Tintagel Castle, March 1312–August 1314	SC6/811/11 m. 1r; *CCR 1307–1313*, 454
		Knight of the Shire, 1312–13	*MPs*, 39
		Sheriff of Cornwall, Mich. 1313–November 1314	SC6/811/12 m. 1r; *Sheriffs*, 21
		Steward of Cornwall, Mich. 1313–November 1314	SC6/811/12 m. 1r
		Knight of the Shire, 1314–15	*MPs*, 48
		Knight of the Shire, 1321	*MPs*, 62
		Justice of the Peace, 20 November 1327–May 1329	*CPR 1327–1330*, 156
		Knight of the Shire, 1328	*MPs*, 83
		Justice of the Peace, 18 May 1329–July 1330	*CPR 1327–1330*, 431
		Knight of the Shire, 1330	*MPs*, 91

Notes: Sir Thomas l'Ercedekne received the lands of his father, Odo, in 1290 (*Maclean*, iii, 254–255; *FF*, i, 211, 260–261); he served on many commissions in Cornwall, also having a penchant for lawlessness; there may have been two Thomas l'Ercedeknes alive concurrently; from 1321–5 the king summoned Sir Thomas to parliament by writ, making him Lord l'Ercedekne (*CP*, i, 186–187); he died in 1331 (*CIPM*, vii, 253–254; *TCO*, 33, 189), leaving his son, John, as his heir.

Sir Warin	l'Ercedekne	Knight of the Shire, 1380	*MPs*, 206
		Knight of the Shire, 1382	*MPs*, 210
		Sheriff of Cornwall, 24 November 1382–November 1383	*Sheriffs*, 21
		Knight of the Shire, 1382	*MPs*, 212

Notes: Sir Warin l'Ercedekne was the second son of Sir John l'Ercedekne; he was active in county administration but died without male issue before 1402 (*CP*, i, 188).

Robert	Lestre	Knight of the Shire, 1324	*MPs*, 71
		Parliamentary Burgess for Helston, 1326–7	*MPs*, 75
		Knight of the Shire, 1329–30	*MPs*, 89
		Knight of the Shire, 1338–9	*MPs*, 124

Notes: Robert Lestre held land in Cornwall (*FF*, i, 273, 316); he served as a tax collector (*CFR 1337–1347*, 158).

John	Lewis, clerk	Under-constable of Tintagel Castle for John Holand, 4 November 1397	*CPR 1396–1399*, 267
Thomas	Leygrave	Havener, May 1317–March 1324	*CFR 1307–1319*, 329
Sir Neil	Loring	Constable of Trematon Castle, 29 January 1372–after March 1378	*CPR 1377–1381*, 209

Notes: Sir Neil Loring was a chamberlain and bachelor to the Black Prince, a Founder Knight of the Order of the Garter and later one of Richard II's knights (*RBP*, ii, 94; *CPR 1377–1381*, 209).

William	London, de	Havener, January 1331	*CPR 1330–1334*, 40

Notes: William de London was a sergeant to Edward III and a tailor to Queen Philippa (*CPR 1330–1334*, 40).

Tideman	Lymbergh, de	Receiver of Cornwall, 1347–50	*RBP*, i, 92; SC6/812/3; DCO 3–4

Notes: Tideman de Lymbergh was a Hanseatic merchant who served the Black Prince (DCO 3–4; *RBP*, i, 10, 120–121; *CPR 1345–1348*, 373; SC6/812/3); in Cornwall, Lymbergh relied on his attorney, one John Coyng (DCO 4).

Sir William	Marny	Sheriff, 28 October and 4 November 1400–Mich. 1401	*Sheriffs*, 21

Notes: Sir William Marny was an Essex lawyer who married a Sergeaux heiress, introducing him into Cornwall (Tyldesley, 'Local Communities', p. 126); he died in 1414 (*CIPM*, xx, 60–61).

Thomas	Marsely	Coroner until 1379	*CCR 1377–1381*, 277

Notes: The Marsely family hailed from the Lizard; Thomas Marsely was probably the son of another Thomas Marsely (d. 1344) and Mariera, the daughter of Ralph Beville (*TCO*, 34, 52).

Roger	Martyn	Coroner until 1388	*CCR 1385–1389*, 516
John	Mattesford	Escheator of Cornwall and Devon, 12 December 1372–December 1376	*Escheators*, 31

Notes: John Mattesford was a Devonian (*CCR 1369–1374*, 250).

John	Maudeleyn	Havener, 27 December 1388–May 1389	*CPR 1385–1389*, 535
Mark	Michelstow	Justice of the Peace, 16 February 1400–May 1401	*CPR 1399–1401*, 557
		Justice of the Peace, 16 May 1401–March 1403	*CPR 1399–1401*, 557

Notes: Mark Michelstow was a shipman of Fowey who served Henry IV as a 'pirate admiral' (Drake, 'Michelstow').

John	Mohun, son of Reynold	Coroner until 1365	*CCR 1364–1368*, 129

Notes: The Mohuns were well-established at Hall and Boconnoc (*TCO*, 33, 101, 338; Worcestre, *Itineraries*, pp. 86–87).

John	Morton, de	Coroner until 1332	*CCR 1330–1333*, 372, 432
John	Moveroun	Knight of the Shire, 1335	C219/5/18; *MPs*, 106

	Constable of Launceston Castle, before November 1336–51	CPR 1334–1338, 336
	Parliamentary Burgess for Launceston, 1337–8	MPs, 119
	Receiver of Cornwall, 1338–46	SC6/816/11 mm. 1r, 5v; DCO 2–3
	Justice of the Peace, 20 July 1344–November 1344	CPR 1343–1345, 394, 399
	Justice of the Peace, 18 December 1346–November 1349	CPR 1345–1348, 232
	Controller of the Stannaries, 1347	RBP, i, 141
	Justice of the Peace, 25 November 1349–July 1352	CPR 1348–1350, 383

Notes: John Moveroun may have hailed from Essex (CCR 1343–1346, 666); he was a royal yeoman who served John of Eltham (SC6/816/11 m. 1r); he was attorney to the controller of the stannary (RBP, i, 71); he was also taker of tin and keeper of St Michael's Mount, Tywardreath, and the king's silver mines (CFR 1337–1347, 307, 70, 78, 268); from 1346 he held the posts of surveyor of the prince's parks, lieutenant of the steward, deputy receiver and controller of the stannaries (RBP, i, 5, 106, 130, 141); it seems that there were two John Moverouns active by 1345 (CCR 1334–1346, 666); Moveroun owned land in the county with Henry Trethewey (FA, i, 208–218).

Henry	Nanfan	Parliamentary Burgess for Lostwithiel, 1360–1	MPs, 166
		Parliamentary Burgess for Helston, 1363	MPs, 172
		Parliamentary Burgess for Launceston, 1363	MPs, 172
		Feodary, 1371	SC6/818/4 m. 9r
		Justice of the Peace, 12 November 1373–December 1375	CPR 1370–1374, 397
		Justice of the Peace, 6 December 1375–July 1376	CPR 1374–1377, 139
		Justice of the Peace, 18 December 1377–March 1378	CPR 1377–1381, 48
		Justice of the Peace, 12 August 1378–May 1380	CPR 1377–1381, 301

Notes: Henry Nanfan served as under-bailiff of Kerrier in 1344–5 (DCO 2); he was the salaried bailiff of Helston Manor from 1350 to 1370 (SC6/817/1 m. 19r; SC6/818/1 m. 7v; RESDCornwall, 38); and bailiff of Penwith from 1362 (RBP, ii, 197); he served as attorney for Thomas Carminow (CIPM, xvi, 254).

| John | Norbury | Havener, 1399 | CPR 1399–1401, 122 |

Notes: John Norbury was a retainer of the house of Lancaster, being appointed treasurer of England by Henry IV (*HOP*, iii, 843–846).

| Roscelin | Ostery, de | Constable of Restormel Castle, 24 January 1373–December 1398 | CPR 1377–1381, 228 |

Notes: Roscelin de Ostery was a yeoman of the Black Prince and Richard II (*CPR 1377–1381*, 228).

| Noel | Paderda | Parliamentary Burgess for Liskeard, 1379 | MPs, 201 |
| | | Coroner until 1386 | CCR 1377–1381, 261, 400; CCR 1385–1389, 43 |

Notes: Noel Paderda served as Bishop Stafford's steward in Cornwall (*Reg.Stafford*, 26, 288, 314); in 1400 Paderda and his son Thomas received a chapel licence for Paderda in Menheniot (*Reg.Stafford*, 278).

James	Park, atte	Bailiff-Errant to Princess Joan, 1379	Duchy Servants, 310
Henry	Pengersick	Knight of the Shire, 1315–16	MPs, 50
		Knight of the Shire, 1327	MPs, 78

Notes: The Pengersick family took their name from a hamlet in St Breage; Edward II summoned Henry Pengersick to a Great Council in 1323–4 (*Parliamentary Writs*, ii part 2, p. 655); a John Pengersick was to sit for Helston in the late-fourteenth century (*HOP*, iv, 46–47).

| John | Penhirgharth | Coroner in 1365 | CCR 1364–1368, 97 |

Notes: John Penhirgharth was under-bailiff of Stratton Hundred in 1348–9 (DCO 4).

| Sir Walter | Penhirhard | Knight of the Shire, 1368 | MPs, 179 |

Notes: Sir Walter Penhirhard travelled to Aquitaine from the south west in 1368 (*CPR 1367–1370*, 133).

John	Penkevelle	Coroner until 1383	CCR 1381–1385, 199
John	Penrose	Justice of the Peace, 20 May 1375–February 1376	CPR 1374–1377, 141
		Justice of the Peace, 23 February 1376–July 1376	CPR 1374–1377, 310
		Justice of the Peace, 4 July 1376–July 1377	CPR 1374–1377, 313

		Justice of the Peace, 4 March 1378–August 1378	CPR 1377–1381, 48
		Justice of the Peace, 26 June 1385	CPR 1385–1389, 80
		Justice of the Peace, 10 November 1389–June 1390	CPR 1388–1392, 138

Notes: John Penrose was a Cornish lawyer who attained the rank of justice of the king's bench, despite his lawlessness (*CPR 1388–1392*, 364); it seems that his family was of gentry stock (*TCO*, 33, 100); in 1371 he received a chapel licence for Boskenna and elsewhere (*Reg.Brantingham*, i, 247; *Reg.Stafford*, 278).

Oger	Penwore	Coroner until 1367	CCR 1364–1368, 362
Henry	Perchay, de	Justice of the Peace, 28 January 1370–May 1375	CPR 1367–1370, 418; CPR 1370–1374, 388
		Justice of the Peace, 20 May 1375–July 1376	CPR 1374–1377, 141
		Justice of the Peace, 4 July 1376–July 1377	CPR 1374–1377, 313
		Justice of the Peace, 2 July 1377–December 1377	CPR 1377–1381, 45
		Justice of the Peace, 18 December 1377–March 1378	CPR 1377–1381, 48
		Justice of the Peace, 4 March 1378–August 1378	CPR 1377–1381, 48
		Justice of the Peace, 12 August 1378–May 1380	CPR 1377–1381, 301
		Justice of the Peace, 26 May 1380–February 1381	CPR 1377–1381, 513

Notes: Henry de Perchay served as chief baron of the exchequer from 1375 and a justice of common pleas from 1377 (*CPR 1374–1377*, 170; *CPR 1377–1381*, 64).

Robert	Person	Bailiff-Errant, 24 March 1378–86	CPR 1377–1381, 156

Notes: Robert Person was a yeoman of Richard II's buttery.

Sir Antonio	Pessagno	Constable of Restormel Castle, 1313	E159/86 m. 76

Notes: Sir Antonio Pessagno was Edward II's banker (Fryde, 'Pessagno'); Restormel served as the centre of his tin-buying operations, but he probably never visited his bailiwick.

Sir John	Petit	Sheriff of Cornwall, 28 October 1334–November 1336	*Sheriffs*, 21; *CFR 1327–1337*, 422, 500
		Steward of Cornwall, 28 October 1334–Christmas 1336	*Sheriffs*, 21
		Constable of Launceston Castle, 28 October 1334–Christmas 1336	*CFR 1327–1337*, 422; *CFR 1337–1347*, 2
		Justice of the Peace, 3 August 1338–July 1344	*CPR 1338–1340*, 146
		Knight of the Shire, 1339	*MPs*, 126

Notes: The Petits were an 'eminent Cornish family' (*FF*, i, 186, 189–190; *Maclean*, i, 317; E179/87/7 m. 2r); Sir John Petit held numerous offices, including that of tax collector (*CCR 1339–1341*, 177; *CFR 1337–1347*, 52, 54, 97, 147); the king, however, later incarcerated him for falling behind on collecting dues from the sheriff-stewardship (*CCR 1339–1341*, 169); in 1330 a John Petit of Trenarth received a chapel licence for Predanack, near Mullion (*Reg. Grandisson*, i, 587–588); Sir John married Joanna, the daughter of Sir Oliver Carminow; on his death in 1362, he left a son, Michael (*TCO*, 33, 190).

Sir Michael	Petit	Coroner until 1311	*CCR 1307–1313*, 35, 313
		Knight of the Shire, 1314	*MPs*, 45
		Knight of the Shire, 1320	*MPs*, 59

Notes: It is unclear if the same Sir Michael Petit served as coroner and MP (*Maclean*, i, 317); a Sir Michael Petit died on 6 July 1326 (*TCO*, 33, 189).

James	Peverell	Knight of the Shire, 1309	*MPs*, 30
		Knight of the Shire, 1311–12	*MPs*, 37

Notes: The Peverells were well-established in Cornwall, supposedly having held a place in the county since the Norman Conquest; by the fourteenth century there were several branches of the family (*Maclean*, i, 382–383); a James Peverell died in 1314 (Worcestre, *Itineraries*, pp. 86–87).

John	Peverell	Parliamentary Burgess for Helston, 1382	*MPs*, 212
Hugh	Peverell	Justice of the Peace, 10 May 1300–December 1307	*CPR 1292–1301*, 516
Sir Hugh	Peverell	Justice of the Peace, 26 October 1369–January 1370	*CPR 1367–1370*, 266

		Justice of the Peace, 28 January 1370–December 1375	CPR 1367–1370, 418

Notes: Sir Hugh Peverell was a bachelor of the Black Prince (*RBP*, ii, 142, 148); in 1371 he received permission to celebrate mass at Rough Tor (*Reg.Brantingham*, 242); Bodmin Friary celebrated an obit for his death (Worcestre, *Itineraries*, pp. 86–87).

Thomas	Peverell	Justice of the Peace, 18 December 1377–August 1378	CPR 1377–1381, 48
		Justice of the Peace, 12 August 1378–May 1380	CPR 1377–1381, 301
		Knight of the Shire, 1379	MPs, 201
		Justice of the Peace, 14 December 1381–March 1382	CPR 1381–1385, 85
		Justice of the Peace, 9 March 1382–June 1382	CPR 1381–1385, 142
		Justice of the Peace, 21 December 1382–February 1385	CPR 1381–1385, 248
		Justice of the Peace, 16 February 1385–July 1387	CPR 1381–1385, 503
		Justice of the Peace, 4 July 1388–July 1389	CPR 1385–1389, 545
		Justice of the Peace, 15 July 1389–November 1389	CPR 1388–1392, 136
		Justice of the Peace, 10 November 1389–June 1390	CPR 1388–1392, 138
		Sheriff of Cornwall, 15 November 1389–November 1390	*Sheriffs*, 21
		Justice of the Peace, 28 June 1390–December 1391	CPR 1388–1392, 342, 344
		Justice of the Peace, 15 December 1391–February 1393	CPR 1388–1392, 525
		Justice of the Peace, 18 June 1394–February 1397	CPR 1391–1396, 436
		Justice of the Peace, 20 February 1397–November 1397	CPR 1396–1399, 97
		Justice of the Peace, 16 February 1400–May 1401	CPR 1399–1401, 557
		Justice of the Peace, 16 May 1401–March 1403	CPR 1399–1401, 557

Notes: In 1388 Thomas Peverell received a chapel licence for Egloshayle (*Reg.Brantingham*, i, 678).

Sir Thomas	Pinchbeck	Justice of the Peace, 8 February 1385–February 1385	CPR 1381–1385, 502
Notes: Sir Thomas Pinchbeck served as chief baron of the exchequer from 1388 (CPR 1385–1389, 428).				
Sir John	Pirier	Receiver of Cornwall, 1344–7	DCO 2–3; RBP, i, 92
Notes: Sir John Pirier was the Black Prince's clerk and receiver of all his lands (Sharp, 'Black Prince', pp. 327, 350–351).				
John	Poddynge	Coroner until 1393	CCR 1392–1396, 176
William	Poer, le	Coroner until 1306	CCR 1302–1307, 421, 473; CPR 1301–1307, 494
		Parliamentary Burgess for Helston, 1309	MPs, 30
		Parliamentary Burgess for Helston, 1314–15	MPs, 48
Notes: The Poer family had associations with Raginnis in Paul (TCO, 34, 7); in 1306 Willima le Poer was allegedly imprisoned on the Scilly Isles (CPR 1301–1307, 538).				
William	Polgas	Knight of the Shire, 1357–8	MPs, 160
		Justice of the Peace, 21 March 1361–March 1364	CPR 1361–1364, 65
Notes: William Polgas was probably a lawyer, serving as William Botreaux's attorney in 1364 (CPR 1361–1364, 464); and sitting on judicial commission in Cornwall (CPR 1358–1361, 67).				
Richard	Polhampton	Sheriff of Cornwall, 18 November 1314 (accounted from 16 December)–November 1315	SC6/811/13 m. 1r; Sheriffs, 21
		Steward of Cornwall, 18 November 1314–November 1315	SC6/811/13 m. 1r
Notes: Richard Polhampton hailed from Berkshire and served as sheriff of Oxford and Berkshire before his death in 1317 (CFR 1307–1319, 320, 342; CIPM, vi, 68).				
Sir John	Pomeroy, de la	Justice of the Peace, 4 March 1378–August 1378	CPR 1377–1381, 48
Notes: The Pomeroys held extensive estates in Cornwall and Devon (FA, i, 208–218); in 1376 Sir John Pomeroy received a chapel licence for Launcells and in 1389 he received another for Tregony (Reg.Brantingham, i, 377, 685).				

John	Portes, de	Joint-Receiver of Cornwall, 1348–9	DCO 4
Walter	Raynold	Controller of the Stannaries, before 1386	CPR 1385–1389, 107
Sir John	Reprenne	Justice of the Peace, 23 June 1382–December 1382	CPR 1381–1385, 194
		Justice of the Peace, 20 December 1382	CPR 1381–1385, 251

Notes: In 1402 a Richard Resprenne received a general chapel licence for the diocese (*Reg.Stafford*, 279).

John	Rescarrek'	Knight of the Shire, 1348	*MPs*, 145
Sir John	Reskymer I	Justice of the Peace, 10 May 1300–December 1307	CPR 1292–1301, 516
		Coroner in 1306	CPR 1301–1307, 482

Notes: The Reskymers were long-established in Cornwall (Vivian, *Visitations*, p. 395; *TCO*, 33, 189); Sir John Reskymer I's father was one Richard Reskymer (*FF*, i, 118, 224–225); Sir John I served on many commissions, including buying wine for Edward I's household (*CPR 1301–1307*, 456, 482); he died on 8 June 1312 (*TCO*, 33, 189).

Sir John	Reskymer II	Justice of the Peace, 20 May 1384–February 1385	CPR 1381–1385, 428
		Justice of the Peace, 16 July 1387–July 1388	CPR 1385–1389, 385
		Knight of the Shire, February 1388	*HOP*, iv, 194–195
		Knight of the Shire, September 1388	*HOP*, iv, 194–195
		Deputy Havener, 18 February 1390	CPR 1388–1392, 197
		Sheriff of Cornwall, 7 November 1390–July 1391	*Sheriffs*, 21
		Knight of the Shire, 1390	*HOP*, iv, 194–195

Notes: Sir John Reskymer II's parentage is confused, as he was supposedly the son of a certain 'Walter and Marieria'; he definitely hailed from the house of Reskymer, however, receiving the family estate in 1374 (*TCO*, 33, 189; *HOP*, iv, 194–195); he died in 1391.

| Walter | Reynold | Controller of the Stannaries, before 1386 | CPR 1385–1389, 107 |

		Escheator of Cornwall and Devon, 8 November 1401–November 1402	*Escheators*, 31

Notes: Walter Reynold was probably a Devonian, holding other offices in that county (Tyldesley, 'Local Communities', p. 131).

William	Rikhill	Justice of the Peace, 16 February 1385–July 1387	*CPR 1381–1385*, 503
		Justice of the Peace, 16 July 1387–July 1388	*CPR 1385–1389*, 385
		Justice of the Peace, 4 July 1388–July 1389	*CPR 1385–1389*, 545
		Justice of the Peace, 15 July 1389–November 1389	*CPR 1388–1392*, 136
		Justice of the Peace, 10 November 1389–June 1390	*CPR 1388–1392*, 138
		Justice of the Peace, 28 June 1390–December 1391	*CPR 1388–1392*, 342
		Justice of the Peace, 15 December 1391–February 1393	*CPR 1388–1392*, 525
		Justice of the Peace, 28 February 1393–June 1394	*CPR 1391–1396*, 292
		Justice of the Peace, 18 June 1394–February 1397	*CPR 1391–1396*, 436
		Justice of the Peace, 20 February 1397–November 1397	*CPR 1396–1399*, 97
		Justice of the Peace, 12 November 1397–February 1399	*CPR 1396–1399*, 237
		Justice of the Peace, 26 February 1399–November 1399	*CPR 1396–1399*, 436
		Justice of the Peace, 28 November 1399–February 1400	*CPR 1399–1401*, 557
		Justice of the Peace, 16 February 1400–May 1401	*CPR 1399–1401*, 557
		Justice of the Peace, 16 May 1401–March 1403	*CPR 1399–1401*, 557
		Justice of the Peace, 14 March 1403	*CPR 1401–1405*, 516

Notes: William Rikhilll was a serjeant-at-law by 1383 and a justice of the common pleas from 1389 (*CPR 1388–1392*, 43).

John	Roskier	Parliamentary Burgess for Truro, 1381	*MPs*, 207

		Parliamentary Burgess for Launceston, 1384	MPs, 219
		Parliamentary Burgess for Truro, 1384	MPs, 222
		Justice of the Peace, 10 November 1389–June 1390	CPR 1388–1392, 138
		Justice of the Peace, 28 June 1390–December 1391	CPR 1388–1392, 342
John	Rynsy	Coroner until 1386	CCR 1385–1389, 174

Notes: In 1398 John Rynsy received a chapel licence for Godolphin and Rinsey, in Breage (*Reg.Stafford*, 280).

Geoffrey	St Aubyn	Coroner until 1394	CCR 1392–1396, 315
		Sheriff of Cornwall, 17 October 1398–October 1399	*Sheriffs*, 21

Notes: The St Aubyns had held land in Cornwall since Henry III's reign (Vivian, *Visitations*, p. 437); Geoffrey St Aubyn's brass in Crowan Church survives (Lack et al., *Brasses*, pp. 27–28).

Richard	Seck	Sheriff of Cornwall, 1 May 1370 (and 21 November)–May 1371	*Sheriffs*, 21; SC6/818/1 m. 18r
		Steward of Cornwall, 1 May 1370–May 1371	SC6/818/1 m. 18r

Notes: In 1389 Richard Seck received a chapel licence for Hurdon in Launceston (*Reg.Brantingham*, i, 691).

Robert	Seliman, de	Justice of the Peace, 22 July 1330–February 1331	CPR 1327–1330, 567

Notes: Robert de Seliman held the office of escheator south of the Trent (*CFR 1327–1337*, 161).

John	Sergeaux	Sheriff of Cornwall, 26 October 1376–November 1377	*Sheriffs*, 21
		Justice of the Peace, 14 December 1381–March 1382	CPR 1381–1385, 85
		Justice of the Peace, 9 March 1382–June 1382	CPR 1381–1385, 142
		Justice of the Peace, 21 December 1382–May 1384	CPR 1381–1385, 248
		Justice of the Peace, 20 May 1384–February 1385	CPR 1381–1385, 428

Notes: With their family seat lying at Colquite, the Sergeauxs had been established in Cornwall since the start of Edward I's reign (*HOP*, ii, 506–507).

Sir Richard	Sergeaux I 'Lesine'	Justice of the Peace, 3 August 1338–July 1344	CPR 1338–1340, 146
		Knight of the Shire, 1339	MPs, 126
		Knight of the Shire, 1341	MPs, 133
		Knight of the Shire, 1355	MPs, 157
		Justice of the Peace, 21 March 1361–March 1364	CPR 1361–1364, 65

Notes: Sir Richard Sergeaux I received the lands of his father in 1308; he was only seven at the time, however, and his mother also pursued a claim to these estates (CIPM, v, 19, 83); from the late 1330s he served on many commissions in the county (CPR 1338–1340, 279; CCR 1341–1343, 506; CFR 1347–1356, 5, 15); he married Margaret, daughter and heir of John Sceneshall (TCO, 33, 190); in 1330 he received a chapel licence for Le Park in Egloshayle (Reg.Grandisson, i, 584).

Sir Richard	Sergeaux II 'Junior'	Knight of the Shire, 1360–1	MPs, 166
		Knight of the Shire, 1363	MPs, 172
		Justice of the Peace, 8 March 1364–February 1367	CPR 1361–1364, 528
		Knight of the Shire, 1364–5	MPs, 174
		Justice of the Peace, 10 July 1368–October 1369	CPR 1367–1370, 195
		Justice of the Peace, 26 October 1369–January 1370	CPR 1367–1370, 266
		Justice of the Peace, 28 January 1370–December 1375	CPR 1367–1370, 418
		Sheriff of Cornwall, 1 October 1375–October 1376	Sheriffs, 21
		Steward of Cornwall, 1 October 1375–October 1376	Sheriffs, 21
		Justice of the Peace, 6 December 1375–July 1376	CPR 1374–1377, 139
		Steward of Cornwall, 12 July 1376–July 1377	CFR 1369–1377, 355
		Knight of the Shire, 1377	MPs, 197
		Justice of the Peace, 18 December 1377–March 1378	CPR 1377–1381, 48

Justice of the Peace, 12 August 1378–May 1380	*CPR 1377–1381*, 301
Justice of the Peace, 26 May 1380–February 1381	*CPR 1377–1381*, 513
Knight of the Shire, 1381	*MPs*, 207
Justice of the Peace, 14 December 1381–March 1382	*CPR 1381–1385*, 85
Knight of the Shire, May 1382	*MPs*, 210
Knight of the Shire, October 1382	*MPs*, 212
Justice of the Peace, 9 March 1382–June 1382	*CPR 1381–1385*, 142
Knight of the Shire, 1382–3	*MPs*, 214
Justice of the Peace, 21 December 1382–February 1385	*CPR 1381–1385*, 248, 428
Justice of the Peace, 16 February 1385–July 1387	*CPR 1381–1385*, 503
Knight of the Shire, 1385	*MPs*, 225
Justice of the Peace, 16 July 1387–July 1388	*CPR 1385–1389*, 385
Justice of the Peace, 4 July 1388–July 1389	*CPR 1385–1389*, 545
Sheriff of Cornwall, 1 December 1388–November 1389	*Sheriffs*, 21
Justice of the Peace, 15 July 1389–November 1389	*CPR 1388–1392*, 136
Justice of the Peace, 10 November 1389–June 1390	*CPR 1388–1392*, 138
Knight of the Shire, 1390	*HOP*, ii, 506
Justice of the Peace, 28 June 1390–December 1391	*CPR 1388–1392*, 342
Justice of the Peace, 15 December 1391–February 1393	*CPR 1388–1392*, 525
Justice of the Peace, 28 February 1393	*CPR 1391–1396*, 292

Notes: Sir Richard Sergeaux II was the son of Sir Richard Sergeaux I; he received his father's lands after 1367 (*HOP*, ii, 506–507); he served on numerous commissions in Cornwall and was a retainer of the Black Prince from at least 1368 (E101/29/24); he died in 1393.

Sir William	Shareshull	Justice of the Peace, 20 July 1344–December 1346	*CPR 1343–1345*, 394, 399
		Justice of the Peace, 15 July 1352–December 1354	*CPR 1350–1354*, 285
		Justice of the Peace, 16 December 1354–December 1355	*CPR 1354–1358*, 123
		Justice of the Peace, 10 December 1355–February 1358	*CPR 1354–1358*, 227
		Justice of the Peace, 17 February 1358–March 1361	*CPR 1358–1361*, 68

Notes: Sir William Shareshull was a justice of assize who sat on the Black Prince's Council and later served as chief justice of the king's bench (JUST1/1422 m. 111r; *RBP*, i, 106, 135; *CPR 1354–1358, passim.*; Putnam, *William Shareshull*).

Thomas	Shelley	Controller of the Stannaries, 1397 (mistakenly named John)	*CPR 1396–1399*, 292
		Steward of Cornwall, 23 August 1398–September 1399	*CPR 1396–1399*, 409

Notes: Thomas Shelley had humble origins but became a king's esquire, owing his spectacular rise to John Holand, whom he served from 1395 (*HOP*, iv, 353–355).

John	Skirkbeck	Sheriff of Cornwall, 6 July 1349–February 1350	*Sheriffs*, 21
		Steward of Cornwall, 6 July 1349–February 1350	*Sheriffs*, 21
		Justice of the Peace, 25 November 1349–July 1352	*CPR 1348–1350*, 383
		Constable of Launceston Castle, before June 1351–after 1359	SC6/817/1 m. 19r; *RBP*, ii, 9, 166.
		Constable of Tintagel Castle, 22 July 1351–after 1365	DCO 6; *RBP*, ii, 14
		Controller of the Stannaries, 1351–9?	*RBP*, ii, 6, 152
		Justice of the Peace, 16 December 1354–December 1355	*CPR 1354–1358*, 123
		Feodary, 9 September 1354–October 1359	*RBP*, ii, 66; SC6/817/4 m. 13v
		Escheator of Cornwall, 24 November 1355–November 1361	*Escheators*, 30

		Justice of the Peace, 12 February 1367–July 1368	*CPR 1364–1367*, 434
		Justice of the Peace, 26 October 1369–January 1370	*CPR 1367–1370*, 266

Notes: John Skirkbeck was the Black Prince's butler from 1347 (*RBP*, i, 57).

John	Slegh	Joint Havener, 5 January 1386–December 1388	*CPR 1385–1389*, 97
		Constable of Tintagel Castle, 5 January 1386–January 1389	*CPR 1385–1389*, 97
		Sole Havener, before 24 May 1389–August 1395	*CCR 1385–1389*, 585

Notes: John Slegh was an esquire of Richard II (*CPR 1385–1389*, 97).

John	Son of William	Coroner until 1306	*CCR 1302–1307*, 367
Robert	Son of William	Coroner until 1329	*CCR 1327–1330*, 432
Ranulph	Spekcote	Knight of the Shire, 1341	*MPs*, 133
Sir Richard	Stapeldon	Knight of the Shire, 1314	*MPs*, 46

Notes: Sir Richard Stapeldon was the brother of Walter Stapeldon, the bishop of Exeter; in 1314 he served as a knight of the shire in Devon; he held some land in Cornwall and acquired more, in 1327 paying 13s. 4d. in tax (E179/87/7 m. 9r).

Bishop Walter	Stapeldon of Exeter	Constable of Tintagel Castle, 1326	*CCR 1323–1327*, 591; *CFR 1319–1327*, 401
Robert	Stonard	Coroner until 1365	*CCR 1364–1368*, 129
Ralph	Stonehouse, de	Justice of the Peace, 3 August 1338–July 1344	*CPR 1338–1340*, 146
James	Stonore, de	Justice of the Peace, 22 July 1330–February 1331	*CPR 1327–1330*, 567
Odo	Stor	Coroner until 1342	*CCR 1341–1343*, 439
John	Stouford	Justice of the Peace, 15 July 1352–December 1354	*CPR 1350–1354*, 285
		Justice of the Peace, 16 December 1354–December 1355	*CPR 1354–1358*, 123
		Justice of the Peace, 10 December 1355–February 1358	*CPR 1354–1358*, 227

		Justice of the Peace, 17 February 1358–March 1361	CPR 1358–1361, 68

Notes: John Stouford was a royal justice who served as a justice of assize in Cornwall (JUST1/1448 m. 83r).

John	Stour, de	Coroner until 1338	CCR 1337–1339, 297
Simon	Sudbury	Knight of the Shire, 1321	MPs, 62
David	Sulgene, de	Coroner until 1329	CCR 1327–1330, 460

Notes: The Sulgene family was of minor gentry stock (*TCO*, 34, 7).

William	Sulgene, de	Coroner until 1353	CCR 1349–1354, 533
John	Syreston	Parliamentary Burgess for Liskeard, May 1382	MPs, 214
		Parliamentary Burgess for Truro, October 1382	MPs, 212
		Parliamentary Burgess for Liskeard, 1383	HOP, iv, 556–557
		Parliamentary Burgess for Lostwithiel, 1385	MPs, 225
		Parliamentary Burgess for Lostwithiel, 1386	HOP, iv, 556–557
		Parliamentary Burgess for Bodmin, February 1388	HOP, iv, 556–557
		Parliamentary Burgess for Launceston, 1390	HOP, iv, 556–557
		Escheator of Cornwall, 26 November 1399–November 1401	Escheators, 31

Notes: John Syreston's background is obscure, but he was a lawyer by training; he was connected to the Bodrugans and Sergeauxs by marriage; he served as under-sheriff of Cornwall (*HOP*, iv, 556–557); in 1400 he received a chapel licence for Trevarthian (*Reg.Stafford*, 281).

Sir William	Talbot I	Knight of the Shire, 1379–80	MPs, 203
		Sheriff of Cornwall, 18 October 1380–November 1381	Sheriffs, 21
		Justice of the Peace, 14 December 1381–March 1382	CPR 1381–1385, 85
		Justice of the Peace, 9 March 1382–June 1382	CPR 1381–1385, 142

		Justice of the Peace, 21 December 1382–February 1385	*CPR 1381–1385*, 248
		Knight of the Shire, 1385	*MPs*, 225
		Justice of the Peace, 16 July 1387–July 1388	*CPR 1385–1389*, 385
		Justice of the Peace, 4 July 1388–July 1389	*CPR 1385–1389*, 545
		Sheriff of Cornwall, 5 August 1391–November 1391	*Sheriffs*, 21
		Sheriff of Cornwall, 9 November 1395–December 1396	*Sheriffs*, 21
Sir William	Talbot II	Knight of the Shire, 1402	*HOP*, iv, 564
		Justice of the Peace, 14 March 1403	*CPR 1401–1405*, 516
		Escheator of Cornwall and Devon, 1 December 1405	*Escheators*, 31

Notes: Sir William Talbot II was the son of Sir William Talbot I; he first appears in 1393 when he and his father were involved in an attack on Trematon Castle; he later attained a position of significance in Cornwall (*HOP*, iv, 564–565); in 1372 a William Talbot received a chapel licence for Botus Fleming (*Reg.Brantingham*, i, 267; *Reg.Stafford*, 281).

William	Talcarn	Havener, c. 1302	*Havener's Accounts*, p. 318

Notes: William Talcarn was probably from Talcarn in St Just-in-Roseland (*Havener's Accounts*, p. 318).

Sir Nicholas	Tamworth, de	Knight of the Shire, 1364–5	*MPs*, 174

Notes: Sir Nicholas Tamworth served as Captain of Calais (*CPR 1367–1370*, 331, 469); in 1365–6 he and his wife were brought before the county assize for dispossessing William Monk of land (JUST1/1473 m. 15r); in 1370 Tamworth received rights to free warren in St Winnow (*CChR 1341–1417*, 216).

Robert	Thorley	Receiver of Cornwall, 19 February 1388	*CFR 1383–1391*, 225
		Receiver of Cornwall, 27 February 1395?	*CPR 1391–1396*, 588
		Constable of Restormel Castle, 8 December 1398–October 1399	*CPR 1396–1399*, 458

Notes: Robert Thorley was initially connected to Thomas of Woodstock, but by 1396 he was serving Richard II as an esquire (*CPR 1392–1396*, 720).

Simon	Tregawore	Coroner until 1381	CCR 1381–1385, 27
William	Tregoedek	Coroner until 1334	CCR 1333–1337, 193
John	Tregoose	Parliamentary Burgess for Helston, 1379	MPs, 201
		Parliamentary Burgess for Truro, 1383	MPs, 217
		Parliamentary Burgess for Truro, 1385	MPs, 225
		Parliamentary Burgess for Truro, 1386	HOP, iv, 643
		Parliamentary Burgess for Bodmin, 1395	HOP, iv, 643
		Parliamentary Burgess for Liskeard, January 1397	HOP, iv, 643
		Coroner until 1406	CCR 1399–1402, 457; CCR 1405–1409, 169

Notes: John Tregoose was a lawyer who originated from Tregoose, near St Columb Major; he served as under-sheriff of Cornwall (*HOP*, iv, 643–644).

John	Tregorrek	Parliamentary Burgess for Helston, 1382	MPs, 212
		Justice of the Peace, 23 June 1382–December 1382	CPR 1381–1385, 194, 251
		Parliamentary Burgess for Truro, 1383	MPs, 217
		Knight of the Shire, 1384	MPs, 219
		Parliamentary Burgess for Bodmin, 1385	MPs, 225
		Justice of the Peace, 8 February 1385–February 1385	CPR 1381–1385, 502
William	Tregudek	Coroner until 1338	CCR 1337–1339, 297
Sir John	Treiagu	Parliamentary Burgess for Truro, 1304–5	MPs, 18
		Knight of the Shire, 1306–7	MPs, 24
		Knight of the Shire, 1312–13	MPs, 39

	Knight of the Shire, 1318	*MPs*, 54
	Knight of the Shire, 1320	*MPs*, 59
	Sheriff of Cornwall, Easter 1321–Mich. 1321	*Sheriffs*, 21
	Steward of Cornwall, Easter 1321–Mich. 1321	*Sheriffs*, 21
	Constable of Restormel Castle, Easter 1321–Mich. 1321	*Sheriffs*, 21
	Sheriff of Cornwall, 26 September 1324–Easter 1327	E389/63 m. 1r; *Sheriffs*, 21
	Steward of Cornwall, 26 September 1324–Easter 1327	E389/63 m. 1r; *Sheriffs*, 21
	Constable of Restormel Castle, 26 September 1324–Easter 1327	E389/63 m. 1r; *Sheriffs*, 21
	Knight of the Shire, 1327–8	*MPs*, 80
	Justice of the Peace, 8 July 1329–October 1329	*CPR 1327–1330*, 431
	Justice of the Peace, 16 February 1331–February 1332	*CPR 1330–1334*, 137
	Justice of the Peace, 12 February 1332–March 1332	*CPR 1330–1334*, 286
	Justice of the Peace, 21 March 1332–November 1333	*CPR 1330–1334*, 294
	Knight of the Shire, 1340?	*MPs*, 130

Notes: Sir John Treiagu held significant estates in Cornwall (*FA*, i, 198–204; 215, 216; E179/87/7 m. 11v); he served as Bishop Stapeldon's steward in the peninsula, receiving robes and a £10 annuity (*Reg.Stapeldon*, 392); Treiagu sat on many commission and was a knight from at least 1309 (CRO, AR 16/1); it seems that the Londoner Richard Causton gained his lands to recover a debt before 1346, with the Black Prince subsequently acquiring these for 400 marks and selling them back to Treiagu (*RBP*, i, 5–6); Treiagu married Joan, daughter of Stephen Trewithnek; he died in 1349, leaving a son, Stephen (*TCO*, 33, 237).

Reginald	Trelouthes	Coroner until 1329	*CCR 1327–1330*, 432
John	Tremayne I	Parliamentary Burgess for Helston, 1323–4	*MPs*, 69
		Knight of the Shire, 1344	*MPs*, 138

		Knight of the Shire, 1346	*MPs*, 140
		Knight of the Shire, 1354	*MPs*, 155
		Knight of the Shire, 1355	*MPs*, 157
		Knight of the Shire, 1357	*MPs*, 159
		Knight of the Shire, 1357–8	*MPs*, 160
		Knight of the Shire, 1360	*MPs*, 163
		Knight of the Shire, 1360–1	*MPs*, 166
		Knight of the Shire, 1362	*MPs*, 169
		Knight of the Shire, 1366	*MPs*, 176
		Parliamentary Burgess for Lostwithiel, 1368?	*MPs*, 179
		Parliamentary Burgess for Helston, 1368?	*MPs*, 179
		Knight of the Shire, 1369	*MPs*, 181
		Parliamentary Burgess for Lostwithiel, 1369?	*MPs*, 181

Notes: John Tremayne I was a lawyer who counted among his clients the Black Prince, Bishop Grandisson and others (*RBP*, ii, 116, *CCR 1354–1360*, 288, *CPR 1361–1364*, 126, *CPR 1361–1364*, 464); it seems that he was active until 1376, but there were as many as four 'John Tremaynes' by this time (*HOP*, iv, 646–648).

John	Tremayne, son of John Tremayne	Parliamentary Burgess for Launceston, 1344	*MPs*, 138
		Parliamentary Burgess for Launceston, 1351–2	*MPs*, 150
		Parliamentary Burgess for Bodmin, 1351–2?	*MPs*, 150
		Parliamentary Burgess for Helston, 1351–2?	*MPs*, 150
		Parliamentary Burgess for Bodmin, 1355?	*MPs*, 157

		Parliamentary Burgess for Liskeard, 1355?	*MPs*, 157

Notes: John son of John Tremayne represented Launceston in 1344 and 1351–2; he may have represented these other boroughs as well (*HOP*, iv, 647).

John	Tremayne Junior	Parliamentary Burgess for Helston, 1364–5	*MPs*, 174
		Parliamentary Burgess for Truro, 1364–5	*MPs*, 174
		Parliamentary Burgess for Liskeard, 1368	*MPs*, 179
		Parliamentary Burgess for Lostwithiel, 1368?	*MPs*, 179
		Parliamentary Burgess for Helston, 1368?	*MPs*, 179
		Parliamentary Burgess for Lostwithiel, 1369?	*MPs*, 181
		Parliamentary Burgess for Helston, 1371?	*MPs*, 185
		Parliamentary Burgess for Launceston, 1373?	*MPs*, 190
		Parliamentary Burgess for Helston, 1376–7	*MPs*, 195

Notes: John Tremayne Junior may have represented Lostwithiel in 1368 and 1369, and Launceston in 1371 and 1373 (*HOP*, iv, 647).

John	Tremayne, son of Richard	Parliamentary Burgess for Helston, 1369	*MPs*, 181
John	Tremayne II	Justice of the Peace, 12 August 1378–May 1380	*CPR 1377–1381*, 301
		Justice of the Peace, 26 May 1380–February 1381	*CPR 1377–1381*, 513
		Justice of the Peace, 9 March 1382–June 1382	*CPR 1381–1385*, 142
		Justice of the Peace, 23 June 1382–December 1382	*CPR 1381–1385*, 194
		Justice of the Peace, 20 December 1382–February 1385	*CPR 1381–1385*, 248, 251
		Justice of the Peace, 8 February 1385–July 1387	*CPR 1381–1385*, 502, 503
		Justice of the Peace, 16 July 1387–July 1388	*CPR 1385–1389*, 385

		Parliamentary Burgess for Truro, February 1388	*HOP*, iv, 646
		Justice of the Peace, 4 July 1388–July 1389	*CPR 1385–1389*, 545
		Justice of the Peace, 28 June 1390–December 1391	*CPR 1388–1392*, 342
		Justice of the Peace, 15 December 1391–February 1393	*CPR 1388–1392*, 525
		Justice of the Peace, 28 February 1393–June 1394	*CPR 1391–1396*, 292
		Justice of the Peace, 18 June 1394–February 1397	*CPR 1391–1396*, 436
		Justice of the Peace, 20 February 1397–November 1397	*CPR 1396–1399*, 97
		Justice of the Peace, 12 November 1397–February 1399	*CPR 1396–1399*, 237
		Justice of the Peace, 26 February 1399–November 1399	*CPR 1396–1399*, 436
		Justice of the Peace, 28 November 1399–February 1400	*CPR 1399–1401*, 557
		Justice of the Peace, 16 February 1400–May 1401	*CPR 1399–1401*, 557
		Justice of the Peace, 16 May 1401–March 1403	*CPR 1399–1401*, 557
		Justice of the Peace, 14 March 1403	*CPR 1401–1405*, 516

Notes: John Tremayne II was another lawyer who ran a busy practice; he attained the position of Common Serjeant and Recorder of London (*HOP*, iv, 646–648); in 1400 he and his brother, Richard, received a chapel licence for Tremayne (*Reg.Stafford*, 281).

William	Tremayne	Parliamentary Burgess for Lostwithiel, 1360–1	MPs, 166
William	Trembetheu	Coroner until 1345	*CCR 1343–1346*, 539

Notes: William Trembetheu was the son of Reginald Trembetheu of Trembethow; he married Anne, daughter of James Trefuses; he died in 1353 (*TCO*, 33, 189).

Richard	Trenaga	Coroner until 1392	*CCR 1392–1396*, 10
Henry	Trenaswethen	Coroner until 1365	*CCR 1364–1368*, 97

Notes: The Trenaswethen family were well-established in Cornwall (*TCO*, 33, 237).

John	Trenewith	Parliamentary Burgess for Truro, 1369	*MPs*, 181
		Knight of the Shire, 1371	*MPs*, 185
Michael	Trenewith (the elder?)	Knight of the Shire, 1337–8	*MPs*, 119
		Knight of the Shire, 1338	*MPs*, 121
		Justice of the Peace, 3 August 1338–July 1344	*CPR 1338–1340*, 139, 146

Notes: The lives of Michael Trenewith the elder and the younger are difficult to disentangle; both had tinning interests and a penchant for lawlessness (Hatcher, *Tin*, pp. 80–82).

Nicholas	Trenewith	Parliamentary Burgess for Bodmin, 1379–80	*MPs*, 203
		Parliamentary Burgess for Truro, September 1397	*HOP*, iv, 649

Notes: Nicholas Trenewith may have been related to Ralph Trenewith II; he served as deputy havener to Richard Hampton (*HOP*, iv, 649).

Sir Ralph	Trenewith I	Knight of the Shire, 1351–2	*MPs*, 150

Notes: Sir Ralph Trenewith I died on 12 May 1360 (*TCO*, 33, 338).

Ralph	Trenewith II	Justice of the Peace, 10 July 1368–October 1369	*CPR 1367–1370*, 195
		Justice of the Peace, 26 October 1369–January 1370	*CPR 1367–1370*, 266
		Receiver of the Cornwall, 1369–77	SC6/818/1 m. 16v; DCO 18; *CFR 1369–1377*, 355
		Justice of the Peace, 28 January 1370–June 1373	*CPR 1367–1370*, 418
		Justice of the Peace, 26 June 1373–December 1375	*CPR 1370–1374*, 388
		Justice of the Peace, 4 July 1376–July 1377	*CPR 1374–1377*, 313
		Parliamentary Burgess for Truro, January 1377	*MPs*, 195
		Justice of the Peace, 2 July 1377–December 1377	*CPR 1377–1381*, 45

		Parliamentary Burgess for Truro, October 1377	HOP, iv, 650
		Justice of the Peace, 18 December 1377–August 1378	CPR 1377–1381, 48
		Justice of the Peace, 12 August 1378–May 1380	CPR 1377–1381, 301
		Parliamentary Burgess for Truro, 1393	HOP, iv, 650
	Notes: Ralph Trenewith II was the son of Walter Trenewith and a kinsman of Ralph Trenewith I and Michael Trenewith; he held estates in the county and had tinning interests; he died before December 1393 (HOP, iv, 650–651).		
Ralph	Trenewith III	Parliamentary Burgess for Liskeard, 1395	HOP, iv, 651
	Notes: Ralph Trenewith III was the grandson of Ralph Trenewith II, receiving his grandfather's lands in 1393 (HOP, iv, 651).		
Ralph	Trenewith of Padstow	Justice of the Peace, 14 March 1403	CPR 1401–1405, 516
Stephan	Trenewith	Parliamentary Burgess for Bodmin, January 1397	HOP, iv, 651–652
Sir Robert	Tresilian	Knight of the Shire, 1368	MPs, 179
		Justice of the Peace, 28 January 1370–June 1373	CPR 1367–1370, 418
		Justice of the Peace, 26 June 1373–December 1375	CPR 1370–1374, 388
		Justice of the Peace, 6 December 1375–July 1376	CPR 1374–1377, 139
		Justice of the Peace, 4 July 1376–July 1377	CPR 1374–1377, 313
		Justice of the Peace, 2 July 1377–December 1377	CPR 1377–1381, 45
		Steward of Cornwall, 20 July 1377–August 1378	CFR 1377–1383, 7
		Justice of the Peace, 18 December 1377–March 1378	CPR 1377–1381, 48
		Justice of the Peace, 12 August 1378–May 1380	CPR 1377–1381, 301
		Justice of the Peace, 26 May 1380–February 1381	CPR 1377–1381, 513
		Justice of the Peace, 9 March 1382–June 1382	CPR 1381–1385, 142

		Justice of the Peace, 23 June 1382–December 1382	*CPR 1381–1385*, 194
		Justice of the Peace, 20 December 1382–February 1385	*CPR 1381–1385*, 248, 251
		Justice of the Peace, 8 February 1385–July 1387	*CPR 1381–1385*, 502, 503
		Justice of the Peace, 16 July 1387–8	*CPR 1385–1389*, 80, 385

Notes: Sir Robert Tresilian was a Cornish lawyer who rose to become chief justice of the king's bench; the Appellants murdered him in 1388 (Leland, 'Robert Tresilian').

Henry	Trethewey	Parliamentary Burgess for Bodmin, 1325	*MPs*, 73
		Sheriff of Cornwall, 5 July 1333–October 1334	E372/179 m. 17r; *Sheriffs*, 21
		Steward of Cornwall, 5 July 1333–October 1334	SC6/812/1
		Constable of Launceston Castle, 5 July 1333–October 1334	*CFR 1327–1337*, 364
		Justice of the Peace, 3 August 1338–July 1344	*CPR 1338–1340*, 139, 146
		Steward of Cornwall, Mich. 1340–2	*Sheriffs*, 21
		Sheriff of Cornwall, Mich. 1340–Mich. 1343	DCO 1; *Sheriffs*, 21
		Justice of the Peace, 20 July 1344–November 1344	*CPR 1343–1345*, 394, 399
		Justice of the Peace, 10 November 1344–December 1346	*CPR 1343–1345*, 396
		Justice of the Peace, 18 December 1346–November 1349	*CPR 1345–1348*, 232

Notes: Henry Trethewey's origins are obscure, although in 1327 he paid 18*d*. of tax in Lanlivery (E179/87/7 m. 12r); he held some lands in Cornwall (*FA*, i, 209; *FF*, i, 359); he enjoyed an active administrative career, serving as a tax collector (*CCR 1338–1341*, 437) and keeper of Tywardreath (*CFR 1337–1347*, 268); he was a yeoman of the Black Prince (*RBP*, ii, 37); he might have had some form of legal training.

William	Trethewey	Bailiff-Errant, 1351?	*RBP*, ii, 4, 55

Notes: William Trethewey was probably related to Henry Trethewey; he accumulated considerable debts during the course of his duties as bailiff-errant (*RBP*, ii, 55).

Henry	Treualuard	Coroner until 1379	CCR 1377–1381, 180, 182, 235
John	Treury	Parliamentary Burgess for Bodmin, 1347–8	MPs, 143
John	Trevaignon	Justice of the Peace, 8 December 1356–February 1358	CPR 1354–1358, 389
		Justice of the Peace, 12 February 1332–March 1332	CPR 1330–1334, 286, 296
		Justice of the Peace, 21 March 1332–November 1333	CPR 1330–1334, 348
		Justice of the Peace, 2 November 1333	CPR 1330–1334, 496

Notes: John Trevaignon was a Cornishman who rose to the rank of judge of the common pleas (*CPR 1330–1334*, 350; JUST1/1418 m. 20r; *CPR 1334–1338*, 12; *FF*, i, 312–313).

John	Trevarthian II	Justice of the Peace, 26 October 1369–January 1370	CPR 1367–1370, 266
		Justice of the Peace, 4 July 1376–July 1377	CPR 1374–1377, 313
		Justice of the Peace, 2 July 1377–December 1377	CPR 1377–1381, 45
		Justice of the Peace, 4 March 1378–August 1378	CPR 1377–1381, 48

Notes: The Trevarthians were well-established in Cornwall; John Trevarthian II was born on 1 February 1328, the son and heir of John Trevarthian I (*TCO*, 33, 100, 143).

Sir John	Trevarthian III 'the younger'	Knight of the Shire, 1393	HOP, iv, 657–658
		Justice of the Peace, 28 February 1393–June 1394	CPR 1391–1396, 292
		Knight of the Shire, 1397	HOP, iv, 657–658
		Knight of the Shire, 1401	HOP, iv, 657–658
		Sheriff of Cornwall, Mich. 1401–After Easter 1402	Sheriffs, 21

Notes: Sir John Trevarthian III was born on 18 October 1360, the third son and heir of John Trevarthian II and Matilda, the daughter of Sir Oliver Carminow (*TCO*, 33, 100); from 1392 Richard II retained him as an esquire (*CPR 1391–1396*, 190); it seems that he died in April 1395 (*TCO*, 33, 143; *Reg.Stafford*, 282).

Peter	Treveluargh, son of William	Constable of Tintagel Castle, August 1314–May 1316	*CPR 1313–1317*, 163; SC6/811/14 m. 1r

Notes: Peter Treveluargh held land in the county (*FF*, i, 213–214).

John	Treverbyn	Justice of the Peace, 18 December 1377–March 1378	*CPR 1377–1381*, 48
		Knight of the Shire, 1391	*HOP*, iv, 659–660
		Knight of the Shire, 1393	*HOP*, iv, 659–660
		Knight of the Shire, 1394	*HOP*, iv, 659–660

Notes: By 1388 John Treverbyn was an esquire of Richard II (*HOP*, iv, 659–660); he held numerous offices in Cornwall and elsewhere.

Henry	Trewinnard	Justice of the Peace, 15 July 1352–December 1354	*CPR 1350–1354*, 285
		Justice of the Peace, 16 December 1354–December 1355	*CPR 1354–1358*, 123
		Justice of the Peace, 10 December 1355–February 1358	*CPR 1354–1358*, 227
		Justice of the Peace, 17 February 1358–March 1361	*CPR 1358–1361*, 68
		Justice of the Peace, 21 March 1361–March 1364	*CPR 1361–1364*, 65
		Justice of the Peace, 8 March 1364–February 1367	*CPR 1361–1364*, 528
		Justice of the Peace, 12 February 1367–July 1368	*CPR 1364–1367*, 434
		Justice of the Peace, 26 June 1373–December 1375	*CPR 1370–1374*, 388

Notes: Henry Trewinnard was probably the son of Richard Trewinnard (d. 1347) and Odona, the daughter of Robert Tyrel; in 1372 Henry received a chapel licence for Trewinnard in St Erth and elsewhere (*Reg.Brantingham*, i, 267); he married Joan, the daughter of Richard Eyr, and left a son, Richard, on his death (*TCO*, 34, 52–53).

James	Trewinnard	Knight of the Shire, 1346	*MPs*, 140
William	Trewinnard	Parliamentary Burgess for Liskeard, 1351–2	*MPs*, 150
		Knight of the Shire, 1354	*MPs*, 155

		Parliamentary Burgess for Helston, 1355	*MPs*, 157
		Parliamentary Burgess for Truro, 1360–1	*MPs*, 166
		Parliamentary Burgess for Truro, 1362	*MPs*, 169

Notes: William Trewinnard mainprised the prior of Launceston (*CPR 1364–1367*, 241); he was probably related to Henry and James Trewinnard.

John	Trewoef	Coroner until 1366	*CCR 1364–1368*, 228

Notes: John Trewoef was the son of Hugh Trewoef (d.1349), and Nicola, the daughter of John Chantecler; he married Mariana, the daughter of Stephen Tregilion (*TCO*, 34, 53).

Thomas	Trewyn	Controller of the Stannaries, 1388	*CPR 1385–1389*, 382

Notes: Thomas Trewyn was one of Richard II's servants.

Stephen	Trewynt, de	Coroner until 1311	*CCR 1307–1313*, 313
Roger	Trewythenick	Parliamentary Burgess for Helston, 1381	*MPs*, 207
		Parliamentary Burgess for Helston, 1382–3	*MPs*, 214
		Parliamentary Burgess for Helston, 1383	*MPs*, 217
		Parliamentary Burgess for Helston, 1385	*MPs*, 225
		Parliamentary Burgess for Helston, 1386	*HOP*, iv, 662
		Parliamentary Burgess for Helston, February 1388	*HOP*, iv, 662
		Parliamentary Burgess for Helston, 1390	*HOP*, iv, 662
		Parliamentary Burgess for Helston, 1391	*HOP*, iv, 662
		Parliamentary Burgess for Helston, 1395	*HOP*, iv, 662
		Justice of the Peace, 20 February 1397–November 1397	*CPR 1396–1399*, 97
		Justice of the Peace, 12 November 1397–February 1399	*CPR 1396–1399*, 237

		Justice of the Peace, 26 February 1399–November 1399	*CPR 1396–1399*, 436
		Parliamentary Burgess for Helston, 1399	*HOP*, iv, 662
		Justice of the Peace, 28 November 1399–February 1400	*CPR 1399–1401*, 557
		Justice of the Peace, 16 February 1400–May 1401	*CPR 1399–1401*, 557
		Justice of the Peace, 16 May 1401–March 1403	*CPR 1399–1401*, 557
		Parliamentary Burgess for Helston, 1402	*HOP*, iv, 662
		Justice of the Peace, 14 March 1403	*CPR 1401–1405*, 516

Notes: Roger Trewythenick was a lawyer; he served as receiver of the earl of Warwick's manors in Cornwall (*HOP*, iv, 662).

Simon	Trewythosa	Knight of the Shire, 1328	*MPs*, 85
		Knight of the Shire, 1331–2	*MPs*, 95

Notes: Simon Trewythosa was a Cornish lawyer who took the coif (Baker, *Serjeants*, p. 541).

John	Tunsy	Coroner until 1387	*CCR 1385–1389*, 234
Wynand	Tyrel the younger	Havener, March 1315–May 1316	*CFR 1307–1319*, 238, 278
Richard	Tyrel	Coroner before 1372–92	*CCR 1369–1374*, 363; *CCR 1389–1392*, 422

Notes: The Tyrel family celebrated numerous obits in the county, although their landed possessions remain obscure (*TCO*, 34, 52).

John	Urban	Parliamentary Burgess for Helston, 1381	*MPs*, 207
		Parliamentary Burgess for Helston, 1382	*HOP*, iv, 690–692
		Parliamentary Burgess for Helston, 1383	*MPs*, 217
		Parliamentary Burgess for Helston, 1384	*MPs*, 222
		Parliamentary Burgess for Helston, 1385	*MPs*, 225

		Parliamentary Burgess for Helston, 1386	*HOP*, iv, 690–692
		Parliamentary Burgess for Helston, 1390	*HOP*, iv, 690–692
		Parliamentary Burgess for Truro, 1391	*HOP*, iv, 690–692
		Justice of the Peace, 28 February 1393–June 1394	*CPR 1391–1396*, 292
		Parliamentary Burgess for Helston, 1397	*HOP*, iv, 690–692

Notes: John Urban was a Helston-based merchant; his interests in tin resulted in him serving as a royal ambassador under Henry IV and V (*HOP*, iv, 690–692).

John	Vautort	Knight of the Shire, 1327–8	*MPs*, 80
Ranulph	Vautort	Constable of Trematon Castle, 1323	E389/63 m. 1r
William	Venour	Receiver of Cornwall, February 1386 (vacated the office)	*CPR 1385–1389*, 109
John	Waksham, de	Escheator of Cornwall and Devon, 11 November 1371–December 1372	*Escheators*, 31
William	Waldeshef	Havener, 1272–1300	*Havener's Accounts*, p. 318
Philip	Walwayn	Bailiff-Errant, 1398	*CPR 1396–1399*, 355

Notes: Philip Walwayn served as an esquire to Richard II.

Nicholas	Wamford, de	Justice of the Peace, 10 February 1362–March 1364	*CPR 1361–1364*, 207
		Knight of the Shire, 1366	*MPs*, 176
		Justice of the Peace, 12 February 1367–July 1368	*CPR 1364–1367*, 434
		Justice of the Peace, 10 July 1368–October 1369	*CPR 1367–1370*, 195
		Justice of the Peace, 26 October 1369–January 1370	*CPR 1367–1370*, 266
		Justice of the Peace, 28 January 1370–December 1375	*CPR 1367–1370*, 418
		Knight of the Shire, 1375–6	*MPs*, 193

	Knight of the Shire, 1377	*MPs*, 197
	Sheriff of Cornwall, 26 November 1377–November 1378	*Sheriffs*, 21
	Knight of the Shire, 1379	*MPs*, 201
	Justice of the Peace, 14 December 1381–March 1382	*CPR 1381–1385*, 85
	Justice of the Peace, 9 March 1382–June 1382	*CPR 1381–1385*, 142
	Justice of the Peace, 21 December 1382–February 1385	*CPR 1381–1385*, 248
	Sheriff of Cornwall, 18 November 1386–November 1387	*Sheriffs*, 21

Notes: In 1376 Nicholas de Wamford and Nicholas Gros received a chapel licence for Launcells and places in Devon (*Reg.Brantingham*, i, 372); Nicholas de Wamford died in 1398; his Cornish estates were then divided between his daughter, Joan, who had married one John Kaynes, and his great great grandson John Durant, whose grandmother, Eleanor, was Wamford's daughter (*CIPM*, xvii, 400).

Sir John	Whalesborough I	Knight of the Shire, 1344	*MPs*, 138
	Knight of the Shire, 1353	*MPs*, 153

Notes: The Whalesborough family were well-established in Cornwall; Sir John Whalesborough I 'died in parts beyond the sea' sometime before 1382, leaving his fifteen-year-old son, another John, as his heir (*CIPM*, xv, 258–259; *TCO*, 33, 145–146).

John	Whalesborough II	Knight of the Shire, 1402	*HOP*, iv, 822
	Justice of the Peace, 14 March 1403	*CPR 1401–1405*, 516
	Sheriff of Cornwall, 22 October 1403–Mich. 1404	*Sheriffs*, 21

Notes: Sir John Whalesborough II was born on 6 July 1346, the son of Sir John Whalesborough I and Joan, the daughter of Otto Bodrugan (*TCO*, 33, 100); in 1400 he received a chapel licence for Whalesborough in Marhamchurch and in all his other manors in the diocese (*Reg. Stafford*, 282).

William	Wichyngham	Justice of the Peace, 10 July 1368–October 1369	*CPR 1367–1370*, 195
	Justice of the Peace, 26 October 1369–January 1370	*CPR 1367–1370*, 266
	Justice of the Peace, 28 January 1370–December 1375	*CPR 1367–1370*, 418

Robert	Wisdom	Feodary, 4 October 1359–69	*RBP*, ii, 164; DCO 15
		Escheator of Cornwall, 5 November 1361–November 1371	*Escheators*, 30
		Parliamentary Burgess for Launceston, 1363	*MPs*, 172

Notes: William Wichyngham was a justice of the common pleas (*CPR 1364–1367*, 177).

Notes: Robert Wisdom was a servant of the Black Prince who served as Liskeard's Parker from 1353 (*RBP*, ii 52, 164); the prince later appointed him feodary in Cornwall, Devon, Somerset and Dorset (*RBP*, ii, 185).

| James | Woodstock, de | Justice of the Peace, 6 July 1338–August 1338 | *CPR 1338–1340*, 139 |
| | | Justice of the Peace, 3 August 1338–July 1344 | *CPR 1338–1340*, 139 |

Notes: In 1337–8 James de Woodstock served as steward of all the Black Prince's lands (Sharp, 'Black Prince', p. 439); he served as a justice of assize in Cornwall and as a judge in the central courts (JUST1/1426A m. 21r; *CPR 1338–1340*, 415).

| Alan | Wolwayn | Havener, 1308–9 | *Havener's Accounts*, p. 318 |

Notes: The Wolwayn family were a longstanding feature in Cornwall (*TCO*, 34, 6).

Sir Henry	Wylinton	Sheriff of Cornwall, 15 May 1316– Easter 1321	SC6/811/17 m. 1r; *Sheriffs*, 21
		Steward of Cornwall, 15 May 1316–Easter 1321	SC6/811/17 m. 1r
		Constable of Restormel Castle, 15 May 1316–Easter 1321	*CFR 1307–1319*, 278–279
		Constable of Tintagel Castle, 15 May 1316–Easter 1321	*CFR 1307–1319*, 278–279
		Constable of Trematon Castle, 15 May 1316–Easter 1321	*CFR 1307–1319*, 278–279
		Constable of Launceston Castle?, 15 May 1316–Easter 1321	*CFR 1307–1319*, 278–279
		Havener, 15 May 1316–July 1317	*CFR 1307–1319*, 278–279

Notes: Sir Henry Wylinton was of Gloucestershire baronial stock (*CP*, xii part 2, 642–649); he held the Cornish manors of Lanteglos-by-Fowey and Fawton, which his elder brother, John, had granted jointly to him and Christina, the widow of their other brother, Edmund (SC8/149/7409); Sir Henry served on many commissions in Cornwall; he fought against the king in 1321 (*CCR 1321–1324*, 15–16); he again sided with Edward's opponents in 1322, which cost him his life (*CCR 1318–1322*, 519, *CPR 1321–1324*, 148, 378; SC8/149/7408; SC6/1146/21); he was probably constable of Launceston Castle (*CFR 1307–1319*, 278–279).

| William | Wyncelower | Controller of the Stannaries, 1386–8 | CPR 1385–1389, 248 |

Notes: William Wyncelower was a yeoman of Richard II's chamber.

| John | Wynter | Steward of Cornwall, 29 September 1399–February 1402 | CPR 1396–1399, 595 |
| | | Constable of Restormel Castle, 5 October 1399 | CPR 1399–1401, 1 |

Notes: A thoroughgoing Lancastrian, John Wynter was appointed steward 'on the advice of the duke of Lancaster' before Richard II's formal deposition (*HOP*, iv, 929–931).

| John | Wysa | Coroner until 1392 | CCR 1389–1392, 445 |

Notes: The Wysa family held the hereditary bailiffship of the hundred of Eastwivelshire (CRO, CY/1929).

Appendix II: Cornish Men-at-Arms and Mounted Archers who served the King between c. 1298 and c. 1415

The names of Cornish gentlemen who hailed from leading lineages have been standardised, but for those outside the ranks of the elite the original spelling has been preserved. The rank of each named individual is based solely on the information relating to their specific incidence of military service.

First Name	Surname	Rank	Captain	Year	Military Service/Expedition	Reference
Odo	Ludderal	Yeoman	Walter Treverbyn	1296	Berwick	*CPR 1292–1301*, 193
Walter	Treverbyn	Knight		1296	Berwick	*CPR 1292–1301*, 193
Robert	Giffard			1298–9	Scotland	C67/14 m. 15
John	Tregor			1298–9	Scotland	C67/14 m. 17
Ranulph	Beaupel	Esquire	Hugh Courtenay	1298	Falkirk	*Falkirk*, ed. Gough, pp. 38, 208
Richard	Beaupel	Esquire	Thomas of Lancaster	1298	Falkirk	*Falkirk*, ed. Gough, p. 212
Robert	Beaupel	Esquire	Hugh Courtenay	1298	Falkirk	*Falkirk*, ed. Gough, pp. 38, 208
William	Botreaux	Esquire	John de Warenne	1298	Falkirk	*Falkirk*, ed. Gough, pp. 20, 86
Robert	Giffard	Knight		1298	Falkirk	*Falkirk*, ed. Gough, pp. 50, 236; *CCR 1296–1302*, 167
William	Lacy, de			1298	Scotland	*CPR 1292–1301*, 385

Serlo	Nansladron	Esquire	1298	Falkirk	*Falkirk*, ed. Gough, pp. 47, 87
Richard	Portilly		1298	Scotland	*CPR 1292–1301*, 363
William	Trewent	Esquire	1298	Falkirk	*Falkirk*, ed. Gough, p. 218
Simon	Trewyke, de		1298	Falkirk	*Falkirk*, ed. Gough, p. 33
Henry	Bodrugan	Knight	1299–1300	Scotland	C67/14 mm. 7, 10
Michael	Bloyou	Esquire	1300	Scotland	E101/8/23
John	Carminow	Esquire	1300	Scotland	E101/8/23
Robert	Giffard	Knight	1300	Scotland	E101/8/23
John	Hamley	Knight	1300	Scotland	E101/8/23
Richard	Huish	Esquire	1300	Scotland	E101/8/23
Thomas	l'Ercedekne		1300–1	Scotland	C67/14 m. 6
Serlo	Nansladron		1300–1	Scotland	C67/14 m. 6
Adam	Crofton, son of Ralph de		1301	Scotland	*CPR 1292–1301*, 563
Thomas	Hugun		1301	Scotland	*CPR 1292–1301*, 614; *CPR 1301–1307*, 166, 200
Stephen	Swynk		1301	Scotland	*CPR 1292–1301*, 608
Roger	Trewervenes, son of Henry de		1301	Scotland	*CPR 1292–1301*, 563
Robert	Halegod		1302	Scotland	*CPR 1301–1307*, 24
Henry	Bodrugan	Knight	1302	Scotland and Aquitaine	*CPR 1301–1307*, 63

Peter	Bodrugan	Henry Bodrugan	1302	Scotland and Aquitaine	*CPR 1301–1307*, 63
John	Bodrugan	Henry Bodrugan	1302	Scotland and Aquitaine	*CPR 1301–1307*, 63
John	Fughelere, le	Henry Bodrugan	1302	Scotland and Aquitaine	*CPR 1301–1307*, 63
Adam	Markewelle, de	Henry Bodrugan	1302	Scotland and Aquitaine	*CPR 1301–1307*, 63
Serlo	Wysa	Henry Bodrugan	1302	Scotland and Aquitaine	*CPR 1301–1307*, 63
Henry	Bodrugan	Hugh Despenser	1302–3	Scotland	C67/15 m. 8
Peter	Bodrugan	Hugh Despenser	1302–3	Scotland	C67/15 m. 8
William	Botreaux		1302–3	Scotland	C67/15 m. 4
John	Carminow		1302–3	Scotland	C67/15 m. 11
Ralph	l'Ercedekne		1303	Scotland	*CPR 1301–1307*, 115
John	Hamely		1303–4	Scotland	C67/15 m. 14
Ranulph	Blanchminster	Edward of Caernarfon	1306	Scotland	*CPR 1301–1307*, 480
Thomas	Geveley		1310	Scotland	*CPR 1307–1313*, 362
Philip	Beville	Aymer de Valence	1314	Bannockburn	C71/6 m. 5
Otto	Bodrugan	Ralph de Monthermer	1314	Bannockburn	C71/6 mm. 4, 5
Thomas	Geveley	Henry de Beaumont	1314	Bannockburn	C71/6 m. 4

Henry	Godrevy		Aymer de Valence	1314	Bannockburn	C71/6 m. 5
Odo	l'Ercedekne		Aymer de Valence	1314	Bannockburn	C71/6 m. 5
Thomas	l'Ercedekne		Aymer de Valence	1314	Bannockburn	C71/6 m. 5
John	Pican		Aymer de Valence	1314	Bannockburn	C71/6 m. 5
Michael	Trenewith		Aymer de Valence	1314	Bannockburn	C71/6 m. 5
Robert	Beaupel		Bartholomew de Badelesmere	1318	Siege of Berwick	C71/10 m. 12
John	Chyneden		Bartholomew de Badelesmere	1318	Siege of Berwick	C71/10 m. 12
Thomas	Geveley			1320	Scotland	C71/10 m. 4
John	Aignell			1322	Scotland	C47/5/10 m. 2
Reginald	Botreaux	Knight		1322	Scotland	C47/5/10 m. 2
John	Caynhes			1322	Scotland	C47/5/10 m. 2
John	Chenduyt		Thomas l'Ercedekne	1322	Scotland	CPR 1321–1324, 200
William	Cherward			1322	Scotland	C47/5/10 m. 2
Osbert	Hamley			1322	Scotland	C47/5/10 m. 2
Thomas	l'Ercedekne	Knight		1322	Scotland	CPR 1321–1324, 200
Matthew	Trenewith		Thomas l'Ercedekne	1322	Scotland	CPR 1321–1324, 200
John	Tresuhkan			1322	Scotland	C47/5/10 m. 2
Wyan	Tyrel		Thomas l'Ercedekne	1322	Scotland	CPR 1321–1324, 200
Thomas	l'Ercedekne	Knight	Ralph, Lord Basset of Draton	1323	Beyond the Sea	CPR 1321–1324, 338

Adam	Bloyou		1324	War of Saint-Sardos	E101/17/2 m. 1
Thomas	l'Ercedekne	Knight	1324	War of Saint-Sardos	C61/36 mm. 28, 40; *CPR 1324–1327*, 80
Otto	Bodrugan		1325	War of Saint-Sardos	*CPR 1324–1327*, 108, 109; *CCR 1327–1330*, 503
John	Pikard	Otto Bodrugan	1325	War of Saint-Sardos	*CPR 1324–1327*, 108
John	Harepath		1325	War of Saint-Sardos	C61/36 no. 215.1; *Gascon Rolls project*
Robert	Rithre		1325	War of Saint-Sardos	C61/36 no. 215.2; *Gascon Rolls project*
Thomas	Tregoose	John de Warenne	1325	War of Saint-Sardos	C61/36 no. 281.1.21; *Gascon Rolls project*
John	Martin the Younger		1325	War of Saint-Sardos	C61/37 no. 135; *Gascon Rolls project*
William	Stokhay		1325	War of Saint-Sardos	C61/37 no. 145; *Gascon Rolls project*
Laurence	Fantengimpis		1325	War of Saint-Sardos	C61/37 no. 157; *Gascon Rolls project*
Richard	Hodgkin		1325	War of Saint-Sardos	C61/37 no. 204; *Gascon Rolls project*
John	Son of Simon Burgess		1325	War of Saint-Sardos	C61/37 no. 234; *Gascon Rolls project*
John	Baghowe		1327	Scotland	*CCR 1327–1330*, 176

Otto	Bodrugan		Roger Mortimer	1327	Scotland	C71/11 m. 6
Nicholas	Dauney			1327	Scotland	C71/11 m. 6
Ralph	Bloyou	Knight		1331	Aquitaine	CPR 1330–1334, 154, 180
Ralph	Bloyou	Knight	Oliver de Ingham	1333	Halidon Hill	C71/13 mm. 9, 20
William	Chenduyt			1333	Halidon Hill	C71/13 m. 5
John	Trenge, de			1333	Halidon Hill	C71/13 m. 8
William	Treveshkeu			1333	Halidon Hill	C71/13 m. 12
John	Fowey			1336	Scotland	C71/15 m. 15
John	Penles, junior			1336	Scotland	C71/15 m. 16
John	Penles, senior			1336	Scotland	C71/15 m. 16
Ranulph	Trenewith, de			1336	Scotland	C71/15 m. 16
Roland	Treres			1336	Scotland	C71/15 m. 16
John	Chaumpernoun			1338	Flanders	C76/12 m. 4
Thomas	Fenne, atte			1338–40	Flanders	*William de Norwell*, p. 309; *Treaty Rolls*, ed. Ferguson, p. 150
John	Lambourne, de			1338	Flanders	C76/12 m. 4
John	l'Ercedekne			1338	Flanders	C76/12 mm. 6, 7; *Treaty Rolls*, ed. Ferguson, pp. 136, 142
Hugh	Peverell			1338	France	*Treaty Rolls*, ed. Ferguson, p. 149
Roland	Trewennard			1338	Flanders	CPR 1338–1340, 221
Ralph	Bloyou	Knight		1340	Sluys-Tournai	C76/15 m. 23
William	Botreaux	Knight	Walter Mauny	1340	Sluys-Tournai	C76/15 m. 24

Walter	Carminow		1340	Sluys-Tournai	C76/15 m. 21
Richard	Erth, de		1340	Sluys-Tournai	CPR 1338–1340, 457
James	Hamley		1340	Sluys-Tournai	C76/15 m. 22
John	l'Ercedekne		1340	Scotland and Sluys-Tournai	CPR 1338–1340, 457
Richard	Trewelone	Walter Mauny	1340	Sluys-Tournai	C76/15 m. 24
John	Whalesborough	Henry de Ferrers	1340	Sluys-Tournai	C76/15 m. 21
John	Betheware		1342	Brittany	C76/18 m. 9
Walter	Bodrugan	Hugh Courtenay	1342	Brittany	C76/17 m. 37
Richard	Channonn?		1342	Brittany	C76/18 m. 7
John	Dauney	Hugh Courtenay	1342	Brittany	C76/17 m. 37
John	Dauney	Knight Hugh Courtenay	1342	Brittany	C76/17 m. 37
Thomas	Fenne, atte		1342	Brittany	E36/204 f. 87r
John	Gayregrave		1342	Brittany	C76/18 m. 11
John	Goustard		1342	Brittany	C76/18 m. 7
Philip	Hoba		1342	Brittany	C76/17 m. 1
Roger	Leyde		1342	Brittany	C76/18 m. 2
Roger	Nansteglos		1342	Brittany	C76/18 m. 7
Hugh	Peverell	Hugh Courtenay	1342	Brittany	C76/17 m. 37
Reginald	Tredaek, de		1342	Brittany	C76/18 m. 7
Serlo	Tregonon		1342	Brittany	E36/204 f. 108v

Roger	Tresawel, de			1342	Brittany	C76/18 m. 6
John	Trevaignon		Hugh Courtenay	1342	Brittany	C76/17 m. 35
John	Welde			1342	Brittany	C76/18 m. 11
John	Whalesborough		Hugh Courtenay	1342	Brittany	C76/17 m. 37
John	Lynyen		Henry of Lancaster	1345	Aquitaine	CPR 1348–1350, 548; SC8/254/12666
John	Lambourne		Henry of Lancaster	1345	Aquitaine	CPR 1345–1348, 190
Thomas	Seyntcler	Esquire	Henry of Lancaster	1345	Aquitaine	Gribit, *Henry of Lancaster*, p. 322
Nicholas	Beaupel		Thomas de Daggeworth	1346	Brittany	E101/25/18
Hugh	Bere, de la, son of David	Knight	Hugh Despenser	1346–7	Crécy-Calais	*Crécy*, ed. Wrottesley, p. 150
John	Beville, son of Laurence		The Black Prince	1346–7	Crécy-Calais	*Crécy*, ed. Wrottesley, p. 135
William	Bodrugan	Knight	William de Bohun	1346–7	Crécy-Calais	*Crécy*, ed. Wrottesley, pp. 7, 34, 133
William	Botreaux	Knight	The Black Prince	1346–7	Crécy-Calais	*Crécy*, ed. Wrottesley, pp. 7, 33, 131
Walter	Carminow	Knight	William de Bohun	1346–7	Crécy-Calais	*Crécy*, ed. Wrottesley, pp. 34, 133
John	Dauney	Knight	The Black Prince	1346–7	Crécy-Calais	*Crécy*, ed. Wrottesley, pp. 93, 280
William	Gwenha			1346–7	Crécy-Calais	*Crécy*, ed. Wrottesley, p. 232; *CPR 1345–1348*, 500
John	Hamley	Knight		1346–7	Crécy-Calais	*Crécy*, ed. Wrottesley, p. 280
Robert	Hamley		The Black Prince	1346–7	Crécy-Calais	*Crécy*, ed. Wrottesley, p. 246
John	Hillary		Reginald de Cobham	1346–7	Crécy-Calais	*Crécy*, ed. Wrottesley, p. 228; *CPR 1345–1348*, 505

John	l'Ercedekne	Knight	Reginald de Cobham	1346–7	Crécy-Calais	*Crécy*, ed. Wrottesley, pp. 6, 33, 118, 240; *CPR 1345–1348*, 494
Hugh	Peverell	Knight	Gerard d'Lisle	1346–7	Crécy-Calais	*Crécy*, ed. Wrottesley, pp. 34, 94
Hilary	Polmorva, de		William de Bohun	1346–7	Crécy-Calais	*Crécy*, ed. Wrottesley, pp. 228, 264; *CPR 1345–1348*, 505
Thomas	Prideaux		John Trevaignon	1346–7	Crécy-Calais	*Crécy*, ed. Wrottesley, p. 130
Adam	Selk			1346–7	Crécy-Calais	*Crécy*, ed. Wrottesley, p. 220; *CPR 1345–1348*, 513
Richard	Sergeaux	Knight	Maurice de Berkeley	1346–7	Crécy-Calais	*Crécy*, ed. Wrottesley, p. 137
Matthew	Soor, le		Hugh Despenser	1346–7	Crécy-Calais	*Crécy*, ed. Wrottesley, p. 83
Serlo	Tregonan, de			1346–7	Crécy-Calais	*Crécy*, ed. Wrottesley, pp. 124, 208
John	Rauf		Earl of Northampton	1346–7	Crécy-Calais	*CPR 1345–1348*, 505
William	Trenedon, son of Walter		William de Bohun	1346–7	Crécy-Calais	*CPR 1345–1348*, 523
Michael	Trenewith the younger			1346–7	Crécy-Calais	*CPR 1345–1348*, 518
John	Trevaignon	Knight	William Kildesby	1346–7	Crécy-Calais	*Crécy*, ed. Wrottesley, pp. 37, 94
William	Trevaignon		William Kildesby	1346–7	Crécy-Calais	*Crécy*, ed. Wrottesley, p. 94
Robert	Trevaignon		William Kildesby	1346–7	Crécy-Calais	*Crécy*, ed. Wrottesley, p. 94
Richard	Trevaignon		William Kildesby	1346–7	Crécy-Calais	*Crécy*, ed. Wrottesley, p. 94
William	Warrewyk			1346–7	Crécy-Calais	*CPR 1345–1348*, 506
Oliver	Rusculian			1347	Calais	*CPR 1350–1354*, p. 37; SC8/270/13464

Roland	Penfoun		John d'Lisle	1342–7	Brittany, Calais, Aquitaine	CPR 1348–1350, 538
Ralph	Beaupel		The Black Prince	1355–7	Poitiers	Hewitt, *Expedition of 1355*, p. 197
John	Beaupel	Knight	The Black Prince	1355–7	Poitiers	Hewitt, *Expedition of 1355*, p. 197; *RBP*, ii, 86
John	Blanchminster	Knight	The Black Prince	1355–7	Poitiers	Hewitt, *Expedition of 1355*, p. 198
Otto	Bodrugan		The Black Prince	1355–7	Poitiers	Hewitt, *Expedition of 1355*, p. 198
William	Bodrugan	Knight	The Black Prince	1355–7	Poitiers	Hewitt, *Expedition of 1355*, p. 198
Richard	Huish	Knight	The Black Prince	1355–7	Poitiers	Hewitt, *Expedition of 1355*, p. 205
William	Lambourne		The Black Prince	1355–7	Poitiers	Hewitt, *Expedition of 1355*, p. 206
Hugh	Peverell		The Black Prince	1355–7	Poitiers	Hewitt, *Expedition of 1355*, p. 209
John	Sergeaux		The Black Prince	1355–7	Poitiers	Hewitt, *Expedition of 1355*, p. 200
John	Trevaignon	Knight	The Black Prince	1355–7	Poitiers	Hewitt, *Expedition of 1355*, p. 213
Robert	Trevaignon		The Black Prince	1355–7	Poitiers	Hewitt, *Expedition of 1355*, p. 213
John	Whalesborough		The Black Prince	1355–7	Poitiers	Hewitt, *Expedition of 1355*, p. 214
William	Botreaux	Knight	Guy de Brian	1359–60	Rheims	C76/37 m. 2; C76/40 m. 10; *RBP*, ii, 164; *Rot. Gascones*, ed. Carte, p. 73
Thomas	Carminow		The Black Prince	1359–60	Rheims	C76/37 m. 3
Richard	Flaunche		John of Gaunt	1359–60	Rheims	CPR 1358–1361, 506
Ralph	Giffard		The Black Prince	1359–60	Rheims	C76/37 m. 3

Thomas	Gregga			1359–60	Rheims	CPR 1358–1361, 383
Geoffrey	Hamley	The Black Prince		1359–60	Rheims	C76/37 m. 3
Roland	Penford	The Black Prince		1359–60	Rheims	C76/37 m. 3
John	Sergeaux	The Black Prince		1359–60	Rheims	C76/37 m. 3
Simon	Pengressek			1361–3	Ireland	E101/28/11 m. 4r
Ralph	Carminow	The Black Prince		1366	Aquitaine	C61/79 no. 91; *Gascon Rolls project*
Thomas	Peverel	The Black Prince		1367	Aquitaine	C61/80 no. 5; *Gascon Rolls project*
Richard	Sergeaux	The Black Prince	Knight	1367–9	Aquitaine	E101/29/24; C61/80 no. 6; C61/82 no. 148; *Gascon Rolls project*
Walter	Penhirgard			1368	Aquitaine	CPR 1367–1370, 133; Walker, *Lancastrian Affinity*, pp. 68–69
John	Beville	The Black Prince		1369	Aquitaine	C61/82 no. 148; *Gascon Rolls project*
Thomas	St Aubyn	John de Hastings		1369	Aquitaine	C61/81 no. 61, 68; *Gascon Rolls project*
Walter	Bluet	William Botreaux	Knight	1369	France	C76/52 m. 11
William	Botreaux		Knight	1369	France	C76/52 mm. 11, 12
Thomas	Botreaux	William Botreaux		1369	France	C76/52 m. 11
John	Dauney			1369	France	C76/52 m. 5
John	Hamley			1369	France	C76/52 m. 21
Thomas	Tregodeck	William Botreaux		1369	France	C76/52 m. 11

William	Tredewy	Archer		1369	Southampton, garrison	E101/29/29/no1 m. 2; *The Soldier in Later Medieval England*
William	Beville	Archer		1369	Portsmouth, garrison	E199/1/35 m. 7v; *The Soldier in Later Medieval England*
Richard	Boscaweyn	Archer		1369	Portsmouth, garrison	E101/29/32 m. 1; *The Soldier in Later Medieval England*
William	Botreaux	Knight		1370	France	*Issue Roll of Thomas Brantingham*, pp. 461, 486
Ralph	Lauwe		John of Gaunt	1370	France	CPR 1367–1370, 461
Thomas	Arundell	Archer	Lord Guy Brian	1370	Keeping the Sea	E101/30/21 m. 2; *The Soldier in Later Medieval England*
Ralph	Carminow	Knight	Lord Guy Brian	1370	Keeping the Sea	E101/30/21 m. 1; *The Soldier in Later Medieval England*
William	Fowey, de		Lord Guy Brian	1370	Keeping the Sea	E101/30/21 m. 1; *The Soldier in Later Medieval England*
John	Harry		Lord Guy Brian	1370	Keeping the Sea	C76/53 m. 20; *The Soldier in Later Medieval England*
Richard	Penrose		Lord Guy Brian	1370	Keeping the Sea	E101/30/21 m. 1; *The Soldier in Later Medieval England*
Odo	Sede		Lord Guy Brian	1370	Keeping the Sea	E101/30/21 m. 1; *The Soldier in Later Medieval England*
William	Constantyn		William de Windsor	1371	Keeping the Sea	E101/31/25 m. 2; *The Soldier in Later Medieval England*
John	Curteys		Nicholas Tamworth	1371	Calais, Garrison	C76/54 m. 14; *The Soldier in Later Medieval England*

John	Polruwan		Lord Guy Brian	1371	Keeping the Sea	E101/31/11/no2 m. 2; *The Soldier in Later Medieval England*
Thomas	St Aubyn			1371	Keeping the Sea	E101/31/11/no2 m. 1; *The Soldier in Later Medieval England*
Henry	Trensawithen		Lord Guy Brian	1371	Keeping the Sea	C76/54 m. 13; *The Soldier in Later Medieval England*
John	Beville	Knight	Ralph, Lord Basset of Drayton	1372	Naval Expedition	E101/31/39 m. 1; *The Soldier in Later Medieval England*
Nicholas	Beville		Ralph, Lord Basset of Drayton	1372	Naval Expedition	E101/31/39 m. 1; *The Soldier in Later Medieval England*
William	Botreaux	Knight	Lord Guy Brian	1372	Naval Expedition	E101/36/16 m. 1; *The Soldier in Later Medieval England*
John	Fowey		William Neville	1372	Naval Expedition	E101/32/24 m. 2; *The Soldier in Later Medieval England*
Robert	Fowey			1372	Keeping the Sea	E101/31/32 m. 3; *The Soldier in Later Medieval England*
William	Fowey			1372	Keeping the Sea	E101/31/32 m. 3; *The Soldier in Later Medieval England*
Henry	Ilcombe	Esquire	William de Salisbury	1372	Naval Expedition	E101/32/30 m. 6; *The Soldier in Later Medieval England*
Warin	l'Ercedekne	Knight	Ralph, Lord Basset of Drayton	1372	Naval Expedition	E101/31/39 m. 1; *The Soldier in Later Medieval England*
John	l'Ercedekne		Ralph, Lord Basset of Drayton	1372	Naval Expedition	E101/31/39 m. 1; *The Soldier in Later Medieval England*

Thomas	Penhergarth	Esquire	William de Salisbury	1372	Naval Expedition	E101/32/30 m. 6; *The Soldier in Later Medieval England*
Walter	Penhirgard	Knight	John of Gaunt	1372	Naval Expedition	C76/55 m. 21; *The Soldier in Later Medieval England*
William	Trenger	Archer	William Montagu	1372	Naval Expedition	E101/32/30 m. 6v; *The Soldier in Later Medieval England*
John	Treverbyn	Esquire	William Montagu	1372	Naval Expedition	E101/32/30 m. 6; *The Soldier in Later Medieval England*
Thomas	Trewennack	Esquire	William de Salisbury	1372	Naval Expedition	E101/32/30 m. 6; *The Soldier in Later Medieval England*
John	Dauney	Esquire	Edward, Lord Despenser	1372–4	Naval Expedition/France	E101/32/26 m. 2; *The Soldier in Later Medieval England*
?	Tregoys	Esquire	Edward, Lord Despenser	1372–4	Naval Expedition/France	E101/32/26 m. 1; *The Soldier in Later Medieval England*
William	Bodrugan	Esquire	Philip Courtenay	1372–3	Keeping the Sea	E101/31/31 m. 4; *The Soldier in Later Medieval England*
William	Fitz Wauter	Esquire	Philip Courtenay	1372–3	Keeping the Sea	E101/31/31 m. 4; *The Soldier in Later Medieval England*
Richard	Kylloyowe		Philip Courtenay	1372–3	Keeping the Sea	C76/56 m. 35; *The Soldier in Later Medieval England*
William	Lambourne	Esquire	Philip Courtenay	1372–3	Keeping the Sea	E101/31/31 m. 4; *The Soldier in Later Medieval England*
John	Lanwernek	Esquire	Philip Courtenay	1372–3	Keeping the Sea	E101/31/31 m. 5; *The Soldier in Later Medieval England*

Robert	Monshole	Archer	Philip Courtenay	1372–3	Keeping the Sea	E101/31/31 m. 5; *The Soldier in Later Medieval England*
Nicholas	Penbon	Archer	Philip Courtenay	1372–3	Keeping the Sea	E101/31/31 m. 5; *The Soldier in Later Medieval England*
Opy	Penpole	Archer	Philip Courtenay	1372–3	Keeping the Sea	E101/31/31 m. 5; *The Soldier in Later Medieval England*
John	Roscarrek	Esquire	Philip Courtenay	1372–3	Keeping the Sea	E101/31/31 m. 4; *The Soldier in Later Medieval England*
John	Tregeu	Archer	Philip Courtenay	1372–3	Keeping the Sea	E101/31/31 m. 4; *The Soldier in Later Medieval England*
William	Tregos	Esquire	Philip Courtenay	1372–3	Keeping the Sea	E101/31/31 m. 4; *The Soldier in Later Medieval England*
Robert	Trevanon	Esquire	Philip Courtenay	1372–3	Keeping the Sea	E101/31/31 m. 4; *The Soldier in Later Medieval England*
James	Trevanour	Esquire	Philip Courtenay	1372–3	Keeping the Sea	E101/31/31 m. 5; *The Soldier in Later Medieval England*
John	Whalesborough	Esquire	Philip Courtenay	1372–3	Keeping the Sea	E101/31/31 m. 4; *The Soldier in Later Medieval England*
Henry	Ilcombe		John of Gaunt	1373	France	*Register of John of Gaunt*, i, p. 33
John	Treyage	Archer	John of Gaunt	1373	France	E101/32/39 m. 3; *The Soldier in Later Medieval England*
John	Harfot	Chaplain	John Montfort	1373	France	C76/56 m. 12; *The Soldier in Later Medieval England*
Ralph	Jenyn		Richard Green	1373	France	C76/56 m. 30; *The Soldier in Later Medieval England*

Roger	Stronassham	John Montfort	1374	Naval Expedition	C76/57 m. 13; *The Soldier in Later Medieval England*
John	Blanchminster	Philip Courtenay	1374	Naval Expedition	E101/33/9 m. 2; *The Soldier in Later Medieval England*
Philip	Seneschall	John Blanchminster	1374	Naval Expedition	C76/57 m. 21; *The Soldier in Later Medieval England*
John	Trewonenech	John Blanchminster	1374	Naval Expedition	E101/33/9 m. 2; *The Soldier in Later Medieval England*
John	Mohun	John Blanchminster	1374	Naval Expedition	C76/57 m. 21; *The Soldier in Later Medieval England*
John	Arundell	Edmund of Langley	1374	Brittany	C76/57 m. 12; *The Soldier in Later Medieval England*
John	Boleugh	Edmund of Langley	1374	Brittany	C76/57 m. 12; *The Soldier in Later Medieval England*
William	Lambourne	Edmund of Langley	1374	Brittany	C76/57 m. 12; *The Soldier in Later Medieval England*
Robert	Cornwayle, de	Philip Courtenay	1374	Naval Expedition	E101/33/9 m. 2; *The Soldier in Later Medieval England*
Baldwin	Ilcombe		1374	France	C76/57 m. 13; *The Soldier in Later Medieval England*
Henry	Ilcombe junior		1374	France	C76/57 m. 13; *The Soldier in Later Medieval England*
Thomas	Lambourne	Philip Courtenay	1374	Naval Expedition	E101/33/9 m. 2; *The Soldier in Later Medieval England*

Vivian	Penrose		Benedict Botteshale	1374	Naval Expedition	E101/33/17 m. 2; *The Soldier in Later Medieval England*
Joce	Penrose		Benedict Botteshale	1374	Naval Expedition	E101/33/17 m. 2; *The Soldier in Later Medieval England*
Roger	Roger		Philip Courtenay	1374	Naval Expedition	C76/57 m. 22; *The Soldier in Later Medieval England*
Alan	Rospegh		Benedict Botteshale	1374	Naval Expedition	E101/33/17 m. 2; *The Soldier in Later Medieval England*
Walter	Trelewyth		Philip Courtenay	1374	Naval Expedition	C76/57 m. 22; *The Soldier in Later Medieval England*
John	Symond	Merchant	John Montfort	1374	France	C76/57, m. 13; *The Soldier in Later Medieval England*
John	Treverbyn		Edmund of Langley	1374	Brittany	C76/57 m. 12; *The Soldier in Later Medieval England*
Walter	Trelewyth		Edmund of Langley	1374	Brittany	C76/57 m. 12; *The Soldier in Later Medieval England*
Ralph	Trethern		Benedict Botteshale	1374	Naval Expedition	E101/33/17 m. 2; *The Soldier in Later Medieval England*
John	Chaumpernoun		Philip Courtenay	1375	Escort	E101/34/1 m. 2; *The Soldier in Later Medieval England*
John	Beville		Edward, Lord Despenser	1375	France	E101/34/3 m. 3; *The Soldier in Later Medieval England*
Mark	Dony		John Montfort	1375	France	C76/58 m. 25; *The Soldier in Later Medieval England*

John	Trefusis		Edmund of Langley	1375	France	E101/35/6 m. 1; *The Soldier in Later Medieval England*
Geoffrey	Tregeneth		Edward, Lord Despenser	1375	France	E101/34/3 m. 1; *The Soldier in Later Medieval England*
Edmund	Trelener		Edmund of Langley	1375	France	E101/35/6 m. 1; *The Soldier in Later Medieval England*
John	Treverbyn		Edmund of Langley	1375	France	E101/35/6 m. 1; *The Soldier in Later Medieval England*
Thomas	Trewynnack		Edmund of Langley	1375	France	E101/35/6 m. 2; *The Soldier in Later Medieval England*
William	Breton			1377	Brest, Garrison	C76/61 m. 31; *The Soldier in Later Medieval England*
Philip	Tregooz		Earl of Stafford	1377?	France	CPR 1377–1381, 411
William	Fowey	Archer	John, duke of Brittany	1377–8?	Naval Expedition	E101/42/13 m. 1; *The Soldier in Later Medieval England*
Richard	Chaumpernoun		Waryn d'Lisle	1378	Naval Expedition	E101/36/32 m. 4; *The Soldier in Later Medieval England*
Henry	Ilcombe		John Arundel	1378	Naval Expedition	C76/62 m. 14; *The Soldier in Later Medieval England*
John	Roskarrok		Aubrey de Vere	1378	Naval Expedition	E101/36/32 m. 7; *The Soldier in Later Medieval England*
John?	Treverbyn		John Arundel	1378	Naval Expedition	E101/36/39 m. 10v; *The Soldier in Later Medieval England*
Odo	Steven		John, Lord Neville	1378	Aquitaine	C61/92 m. 10; *The Soldier in Later Medieval England*

John	Man		John, Lord Neville	1378	Aquitaine	C61/92 m. 5; *The Soldier in Later Medieval England*
Thomas	Vyyyan		Aubrey de Vere	1378	Naval Expedition	E101/36/32 m. 7; *The Soldier in Later Medieval England*
Thomas	Trewennet		Richard Craddock	1379–80	Aquitaine, standing force	E101/28/27 m. 3i; *The Soldier in Later Medieval England*
Vivian	Penrose		Richard Craddock	1379	Aquitaine, standing force	E101/38/27 m. 3i; *The Soldier in Later Medieval England*
John	Treverbyn		Thomas Percy	1379	Brittany	C76/64 m. 24; *The Soldier in Later Medieval England*
Robert	Alour			1380	Brittany	C76/64 m. 7
Thomas	Giffard			1380	Brittany	C76/64 m. 7
Richard	Keche		Ralph, Lord Basset	1380	France	C76/65 m. 26; *The Soldier in Later Medieval England*
John	Lesard		Hugh Hastings	1380	Brittany	C76/64 m. 7
John	Treverbyn		Thomas de Percy	1380	Brittany	C76/64 m. 24
Gerard	Tyrell			1380	Brittany	C76/64 m. 7
Thomas	St Aubyn			1381	Aquitaine	C61/94 m. 8; *The Soldier in Later Medieval England*
Robert	Trethewey	Clerk		1380–1	The King's Service	C76/65 m. 10
William	Lambourne	Knight		1381	The King's Service	*Rot. Gascones*, ed. Carte, p. 135

Geoffrey	St Aubyn	Esquire	Edmund of Langley	1381	Overseas	C76/75 m. 10; *The Soldier in Later Medieval England*
John	Quellesbrewe (Whalesbor-ough?)		Edmund of Langley	1381	Overseas	C76/65 m. 10; *The Soldier in Later Medieval England*
William	Eyr	Esquire	Matthew Gournay	1381		C76/65 m. 11; *The Soldier in Later Medieval England*
William	Bodrugan	Knight	Matthew Gournay	1381	Portugal	C76/65 m. 3; *The Soldier in Later Medieval England*
Thomas	Bray		Matthew Gournay	1381	Portugal	C76/65 m. 13; *The Soldier in Later Medieval England*
John	Fawy			1381	Portugal	*CPR 1381–1385*, 256
Richard	Glynn			1381	Portugal	*CPR 1381–1385*, 256
Henry	Ilcombe	Knight		1381	Portugal	*CPR 1381–1385*, 179, 256, 349, 494, 534
William	Ilcombe			1381	Portugal	*CPR 1381–1385*, 179, 256, 534
Baldwin	Ilcombe			1381	Portugal	*CPR 1381–1385*, 256, 534
Henry	Pentry			1381	Portugal	*CPR 1381–1385*, 349
Robert	Trethewey	Clerk		1381	Portugal	C76/65 m. 1
John	Luke		John Roches	1381	France	C76/65 m. 14; *The Soldier in Later Medieval England*
William	Botreaux	Knight		1382	Portugal	C76/67 mm. 30, 21
John	Trevarne	Clerk		1382	Portugal	C76/67 m. 29
Thomas	Trewynnak			1382	Portugal	C76/67 m. 29

William	Bodyere	Mariner, master of ship	John Roches	1382	Keeping the Sea	C76/67 m. 25; *The Soldier in Later Medieval England*
Reginald	Martyn	Esquire		1382	Overseas	C76/67 m. 24; *The Soldier in Later Medieval England*
John	Polkessen		John Baker	1382	Keeping the Sea	E101/39/25 m. 2; *The Soldier in Later Medieval England*
John	Treverbyn	Esquire		1382	At his own Expense	CPR 1381–1385, 160
John	Jowy alia Juwy			1383	Despenser's Crusade	C76/67 m. 16; CPR 1381–1385, 265
Thomas	Forde			1383	Despenser's Crusade	C76/67 m. 17; *The Soldier in Later Medieval England*
John	Rescarek			1383	Despenser's Crusade	C76/67 m. 18; *The Soldier in Later Medieval England*
Richard	Tregnne			1383	Despenser's Crusade	C76/67 m. 16
John	Trevarthian			1383	Despenser's Crusade	HOP, iv, 657–658
Odo	Ude			1383	Despenser's Crusade	C76/67 m. 16
William	Bodyere	Mariner		1383	Cherbourg, garrison	C76/67 mm. 25, 20
Thomas	Trewynnack			1383	Keeping the Sea	C76/67 m. 29

William	Bodyere		1384	Brest, garrison	C76/68 m. 6; *The Soldier in Later Medieval England*
Walter	Hall		1384	Brest, garrison	CPR 1381–1385, 471
Alexander	Hekelyng		1384	Portugal	C76/69 m. 20; *The Soldier in Later Medieval England*
Thomas	Hekelyng		1384	Portugal	C76/69 m. 20; *The Soldier in Later Medieval England*
Henry	Ilcombe	Knight	1384	Portugal	C76/69 m. 11
William	Ilcombe		1384	Portugal	C76/69 m. 11
John	May		1384	Portugal	C76/69 m. 14; *The Soldier in Later Medieval England*
John	Tregorek		1384	Portugal	C76/69 m. 9
John	Rescarek		1385	Naval Expedition	E101/40/39 m. 2; *The Soldier in Later Medieval England*
Walter	Hall		1385	Brest, garrison	C76/69 m. 15
John	Treverbyn		1385	Keeping the Sea	C76/69 m. 4
Peter	Pollard		1385	Scottish Marches	C71/65 m. 9; *The Soldier in Later Medieval England*
Roger	Juyl		1385	Portugal	C76/69 m. 11; *The Soldier in Later Medieval England*
Walter	Hall		1385	Calais, garrison	C76/70 m. 37; *The Soldier in Later Medieval England*
Henry	Ilcombe	Knight	1386	Brest, garrison	C76/71 m. 24; *The Soldier in Later Medieval England*

William	Ilcombe		John Roches	1386	Brest, garrison	C76/71 m. 24; *The Soldier in Later Medieval England*
Thomas	Treneref		William Beauchamp	1386	Calais, garrison	C76/70 m. 36
Vivian	Penrose	Knight	Thomas Trivet	1386	Naval Expedition	C76/70 m. 13; *The Soldier in Later Medieval England*
John	Rosmilain	Esquire	Edward Courtenay	1386	Naval Expedition	E101/41/5 m 5; *The Soldier in Later Medieval England*
Martin	Symond		Thomas Trivet	1386	Naval Expedition	C76/70 m. 13; *The Soldier in Later Medieval England*
Robert	Carndon	Esquire	John of Gaunt	1386	Spain	C76/70 m. 11; *The Soldier in Later Medieval England*
Thomas	Kenegy		John Holand	1386	Spain	C76/71 m. 15; *The Soldier in Later Medieval England*
William	Lambourne	Knight	John of Gaunt	1386	Spain	*Rot. Gascones*, ed. Carte, p. 154
John	Lambourne		John of Gaunt	1386	Spain	C76/70 m. 11
John	Reskymer	Esquire	John of Gaunt	1386	Spain	C76/70 m. 20
Nicholas	Trenage		John of Gaunt	1386	Spain	C76/70 m. 11
Robert	Trevanyon		John of Gaunt	1386	Spain	C76/70 m. 20
John	Trevenour		John of Gaunt	1386	Spain	C76/71 m. 22; *The Soldier in Later Medieval England*
Philip	Trewythosa		John of Gaunt	1386	Spain	C76/70 m. 20
Richard	Forde		John Roches	1386	Brest, garrison	C76/71 m. 21; *The Soldier in Later Medieval England*

Roger	Juyl		John Roches	1386	Brest, garrison	C76/70 m. 27; *The Soldier in Later Medieval England*
John	Tresevellak		Thomas Swineburne	1386	Scottish Marches	C71/66 m. 8; *The Soldier in Later Medieval England*
William	Alet	Esquire	Edward Courtenay	1387	Naval Expedition	E101/40/33 m. 1i; *The Soldier in Later Medieval England*
John	Baak		Richard Fitzalan	1387	Naval Expedition	C76/71 m. 15; *The Soldier in Later Medieval England*
Nicholas	Baak		Richard Fitzalan	1387	Naval Expedition	C76/71 m. 15; *The Soldier in Later Medieval England*
John	Beville	Esquire	Edward Courtenay	1387	Naval Expedition	E101/40/33 m. 3; *The Soldier in Later Medieval England*
Walter	Bluet	Archer	Edward Courtenay	1387	Naval Expedition	E101/40/33 m. 3v; *The Soldier in Later Medieval England*
Nicholas	Cook	Esquire	John Treverbyn	1387	Naval Expedition	E101/40/33 m. 19; *The Soldier in Later Medieval England*
Richard	Lamelyn	Archer	Edward Courtenay	1387	Naval Expedition	E101/40/33 m. 3v; *The Soldier in Later Medieval England*
John	Launcelegron	Esquire	Edward Courtenay	1387	Naval Expedition	E101/40/33 m. 3; *The Soldier in Later Medieval England*
Warin	l'Ercedekne	Knight	Edward Courtenay	1387	Naval Expedition	E101/40/33 m. 3; *The Soldier in Later Medieval England*
Walter	l'Ercedekne	Esquire	Thomas Trivet	1387	Naval Expedition	E101/40/33 m. 7; *The Soldier in Later Medieval England*

Mark	Michelstow	Esquire	Edward Courtenay	1387	Naval Expedition	E101/40/33 m. 3; *The Soldier in Later Medieval England*
John	Penhonell	Archer	Edward Courtenay	1387	Naval Expedition	E101/40/33 m. 3; *The Soldier in Later Medieval England*
John	Queynte	Esquire	Edward Courtenay	1387	Naval Expedition	E101/40/33 m. 3; *The Soldier in Later Medieval England*
Reginald	Stratton	Archer	John Treverbyn	1387	Naval Expedition	E101/40/33 m. 19; *The Soldier in Later Medieval England*
Henry	Trechenown	Archer	Edward Courtenay	1387	Naval Expedition	E101/40/33 m. 3v; *The Soldier in Later Medieval England*
Richard	Tredeway	Archer	Edward Courtenay	1387	Naval Expedition	E101/40/33 m. 3v; *The Soldier in Later Medieval England*
Henry	Tregenawen	Esquire	Edward Courtenay	1387	Naval Expedition	E101/40/33 m. 1ii; *The Soldier in Later Medieval England*
Laurence	Tremer	Esquire	John Treverbyn	1387	Naval Expedition	E101/40/33 m. 19; *The Soldier in Later Medieval England*
John	Trescullard	Esquire	John Treverbyn	1387	Naval Expedition	E101/40/33 m. 19; *The Soldier in Later Medieval England*
Richard	Trethewey	Archer	Edward Courtenay	1387	Naval Expedition	E101/40/34 m. 1ii; *The Soldier in Later Medieval England*
John	Treverbyn	Esquire	John Treverbyn	1387	Naval Expedition	E101/40/33 m. 19; *The Soldier in Later Medieval England*
John	Trevylak	Archer	Thomas Trivet	1387	Naval Expedition	E101/40/34 m. 11; *The Soldier in Later Medieval England*

Raulyn	Trewent	Archer	Edward Courtenay	1387	Naval Expedition	E101/40/33 m. 3v; *The Soldier in Later Medieval England*
Gerard	Tyrell	Esquire	Edward Courtenay	1387	Naval Expedition	E101/40/33 m. 3; *The Soldier in Later Medieval England*
William	Vyvyan	Esquire	Piers van Busch	1387	Naval Expedition	E101/40/33 m. 20; *The Soldier in Later Medieval England*
John	Wysa	Esquire	John Treverbyn	1387	Naval Expedition	E101/40/33 m. 19; *The Soldier in Later Medieval England*
John	Treverbyn		John Roches	1388	Brest, garrison	CPR 1385–1389, 380
Nicholas	Trenewyth		William Beauchamp	1388	Calais, garrison	C76/72 m. 14; *The Soldier in Later Medieval England*
John	Bere		Richard Fitzalan	1388	Naval Service	C76/72 m. 7; *The Soldier in Later Medieval England*
John	Bloyou	Esquire	John Coupeland	1388	Naval Expedition	E101/41/5 m. 14; *The Soldier in Later Medieval England*
William	Botreaux	Knight	Edward Courtenay	1388	Naval Expedition	E101/41/5 m. 5; *The Soldier in Later Medieval England*
Walter	Hamley	Esquire	Edward Courtenay	1388	Naval Expedition	E101/41/5 m. 5; *The Soldier in Later Medieval England*
William	Kendale	Esquire	Edward Courtenay	1388	Naval Expedition	E101/41/5 m. 5; *The Soldier in Later Medieval England*
John	Kendale	Esquire	Edward Courtenay	1388	Naval Expedition	E101/41/5 m. 5; *The Soldier in Later Medieval England*
William	Lamelyn	Esquire	Edward Courtenay	1388	Naval Expedition	E101/41/5 m. 5; *The Soldier in Later Medieval England*

Michael	l'Ercedekne	Knight	Edward Courtenay	1388	Naval Expedition	E101/41/5 m. 5; *The Soldier in Later Medieval England*
Mark	Michelstow	Esquire	Edward Courtenay	1388	Naval Expedition	E101/41/5 m. 5; *The Soldier in Later Medieval England*
John	Michelstow	Esquire	Edward Courtenay	1388	Naval Expedition	E101/41/5 m. 5; *The Soldier in Later Medieval England*
John	Penpons	Esquire	John Coupeland	1388	Naval Expedition	E101/41/5 m. 14; *The Soldier in Later Medieval England*
Thomas	Penpons	Esquire	Alan St Just	1388	Naval Expedition	E101/41/5 m. 17v; *The Soldier in Later Medieval England*
Richard	Peryn	Archer	Edward Courtenay	1388	Naval Expedition	E101/41/5 m. 6; *The Soldier in Later Medieval England*
Robert	Polsheth	Archer	Edward Courtenay	1388	Naval Expedition	E101/41/5 m. 5v; *The Soldier in Later Medieval England*
Thomas	Polskoc	Esquire	Benet Cely	1388	Naval Expedition	E101/41/5 m. 17; *The Soldier in Later Medieval England*
John	Resemelyan	Esquire	Edward Courtenay	1388	Naval Expedition	E101/41/5 m. 5; *The Soldier in Later Medieval England*
John	Rosmilian	Archer	Benet Cely	1388	Naval Expedition	E101/41/5 m. 17; *The Soldier in Later Medieval England*
Alan	St Just	Esquire		1388	Naval Expedition	E101/41/5 m. 17v; *The Soldier in Later Medieval England*
John	Talbot	Esquire	Edward Courtenay	1388	Naval Expedition	E101/41/5 m. 5; *The Soldier in Later Medieval England*

John	Tregos	Esquire	Richard Fitzalan	1388	Naval Expedition	E101/41/5 m. 1; *The Soldier in Later Medieval England*
Raulyn	Treheufen	Esquire	Thomas atte Lee	1388	Naval Expedition	E101/41/5 m. 17v; *The Soldier in Later Medieval England*
Laurence	Tremere	Esquire	Benet Cely	1388	Naval Expedition	E101/41/5 m. 17; *The Soldier in Later Medieval England*
Janyn	Treuren	Archer	Benet Cely	1388	Naval Expedition	E101/41/5 m. 17; *The Soldier in Later Medieval England*
John	Treverbyn	Esquire	Benet Cely	1388	Naval Expedition	E101/41/5 m. 17; *The Soldier in Later Medieval England*
Robert	Trewen	Archer	Thomas West	1388	Naval Expedition	E101/41/5 m. 8v; *The Soldier in Later Medieval England*
Thomas	Trewent	Esquire	John Wogan	1388	Naval Expedition	E101/41/5 m. 13; *The Soldier in Later Medieval England*
John	Trewonneck	Archer	Richard Fitzalan	1388	Naval Expedition	E101/41/5 m. 2; *The Soldier in Later Medieval England*
Thomas	Trewyn	Esquire	Thomas West	1388	Naval Expedition	E101/41/5 m. 8; *The Soldier in Later Medieval England*
William	Vyvyan	Esquire	John Clavering	1388	Naval Expedition	E101/41/5 m. 13v; *The Soldier in Later Medieval England*
John	Wysa	Esquire	Edward Courtenay	1388	Naval Expedition	E101/41/5 m. 5; *The Soldier in Later Medieval England*
Roger	Ivyll		John Stanley	1389	Berwick, garrison	C71/68 m. 1; *The Soldier in Later Medieval England*

John	Hill		William Beauchamp	1389	Calais, garrison	C76/73 m. 5; *The Soldier in Later Medieval England*
John	Trevarthian junior		John Holand	1392	Overseas	C76/76 m. 9; *The Soldier in Later Medieval England*
John	Raulyn		John Holand	1393	Brittany, Brest	C76/78 m. 18; *The Soldier in Later Medieval England*
Roger	Beauchamp		John of Gaunt	1393	Aquitaine	C61/104 no. 68; *Gascon Rolls project*
William	Talbot			1394	Ireland	*CPR 1391–1396*, 482
Henry	Kyrkestede		Thomas, duke of Gloucester	1395	Ireland	*CPR 1391–1396*, 537
Stephen	Trevelowe		John Holand	1396	Brittany, Brest, garrison	C76/81 m. 12; *The Soldier in Later Medieval England*
John	Tregorreck		John Holand	1399	Calais, garrison	C76/83 m. 10; *The Soldier in Later Medieval England*
Henry	Ilcombe	Knight	John Holand	1399	Ireland	*CPR 1396–1399*, 540, 573
William	Talbot	Esquire	John Holand	1399	Ireland	*CPR 1396–1399*, 537
John	Trebost		John Haddley	1400	Scotland	E101/42/16 m. 38; *The Soldier in Later Medieval England*
Ralph	Botreaux	Knight		1401	Calais, garrison	C76/85 m. 9; *The Soldier in Later Medieval England*
Thomas	Treverak		Edward of York	1401	Aquitaine	C61/108 m. 9; *The Soldier in Later Medieval England*
Ralph	Botreaux	Knight		1402	Wales, standing force	E101/43/21 m. 1; *The Soldier in Later Medieval England*

John	Pengersek		1402	Calais, garrison	C76/86 m. 6; *The Soldier in Later Medieval England*
Thomas	Tregonan	Archer	1402–4	Narberth, garrison	E101/42/23 m. 1; *The Soldier in Later Medieval England*
Ralph	Botreaux	Knight	1404	Calais, garrison	C76/87 m. 7; *The Soldier in Later Medieval England*
John	Michelstow	Esquire	1404	Keeping the Sea	E101/43/23 m. 2; *The Soldier in Later Medieval England*
John	Symond	Merchant	1405	Aquitaine, Bordeaux	C61/111 m. 12; *The Soldier in Later Medieval England*
Thomas	Treverak		1405	Bordeaux, garrison	E101/33/8 m. 2; *The Soldier in Later Medieval England*
Richard	Henry	Clerk/Merchant	1410	Calais, March	C76/94 m. 31; *The Soldier in Later Medieval England*
John	Polmorva	Esquire	1410	Calais March	C76/93 m. 14; *The Soldier in Later Medieval England*
Michael	Treyage		1410	Calais March	C76/93 m 14; *The Soldier in Later Medieval England*
Nicholas	Bromford		1412	Overseas	C76/95 m. 21; *The Soldier in Later Medieval England*
Roland	Roche		1413	Ireland	CPR 1413–1416, 146
John	Hoigge		1413	Ireland	CPR 1413–1416, 146
John	Arundell, son of Nicholas of Trerice	Edward Courtenay	1415	Agincourt	*Forty-Fourth Deputy Keeper Report*, p. 571; C76/98 m. 11; *The Soldier in Later Medieval England*;

Philip	Basset	Esquire	William, Lord Botreaux	1415	Agincourt	*Agincourt*, ed. Nicolas, p. 376; *Forty–Fourth Deputy Keeper Report*, p. 561
John	Botreaux	Esquire	Lord John Harrington	1415	Agincourt	*Agincourt*, ed. Nicolas, p. 376
William	Botreaux	Baron		1415	Agincourt	E101/45/18 m. 3; *The Soldier in Later Medieval England*
William	Botreaux	Esquire	William, Lord Botreaux	1415	Agincourt	E101/45/18 m. 3; *The Soldier in Later Medieval England*; *Forty-Fourth Deputy Keeper Report*, p. 565
John	Chenduyt	Esquire	Henry V	1415	Agincourt	*Agincourt*, ed. Nicolas, p. 377; E101/44/30/1 m. 18; *The Soldier in Later Medieval England*
John	Colshull	Esquire		1415	Agincourt	*Agincourt*, ed. Nicolas, p. 378; *Forty–Fourth Deputy Keeper Report*, p. 563
Tristram	Curteys		Edward Courtenay	1415	Agincourt	*Forty–Fourth Deputy Keeper Report*, p. 570
Jas	Ethenenes		Nicholas de Haywood	1415	Agincourt	*Forty–Fourth Deputy Keeper Report*, p. 561
John	Lansadren	Archer	Watkin Lloyd, et al.	1415	Agincourt	E101/46/20 no. 3 m. 1; *The Soldier in Later Medieval England*
William	Moyle	Esquire	John Holand	1415	Agincourt	E101/45/18 m. 2; *The Soldier in Later Medieval England*
Thomas	Pentryth	Archer	Ralph Cromwell	1415	Agincourt	E101/45/4 m. 11; *The Soldier in Later Medieval England*
Ralph	Reskymer		Edward Courtenay	1415	Agincourt	*Forty–Fourth Deputy Keeper Report*, p. 570
Alan	St Just	Esquire		1415	Agincourt	E101/45/18 m. 4; *The Soldier in Later Medieval England*

?	St Aubyn		Thomas of Lancaster	1415	Agincourt	E101/44/30 no1 m. 2; *The Soldier in Later Medieval England*
William	Talbot	Clerk	William, Lord Botreaux	1415	Agincourt	*Forty–Fourth Deputy Keeper Report*, p. 565
William	Tregaven		Richard de Veer	1415	Agincourt	E101/46/36 m. 3; *The Soldier in Later Medieval England*
William	Trelawny		Edward Courtenay	1415	Agincourt	*Forty–Fourth Deputy Keeper Report*, pp. 569, 571
John	Trelawny	Knight		1415	Agincourt	*CPR 1422–1429*, 9; *Forty–Fourth Deputy Keeper Report*, p. 569; *HOP*, iv, 645
Michael	Trenewith		Edward, duke of York	1415	Agincourt	E101/45/19 m. 1; *The Soldier in Later Medieval England*
Thomas	Trerewne		John Holand	1415	Agincourt	E101/45/7 m. 1; *The Soldier in Later Medieval England*
John	Tretherf		Edward Courtenay	1415	Agincourt	*Forty–Fourth Deputy Keeper Report*, p. 570
Richard	Trevaga		Edward Courtenay	1415	Agincourt	*Forty–Fourth Deputy Keeper Report*, p. 570
Thomas	Treunwith		John Tiptoft	1415–17	Aquitaine, standing force	E101/48/4 m. 1; *The Soldier in Later Medieval England*

Appendix III: Cornish Ports that sent ships to Royal Fleets between c. 1297 and c. 1420

For each port: (S) relates to the number of ships; (C) records the crew size; and (T) represents the average tonnage of the vessels. The average tonnage (T) is only a loose approximation as often these figures were recorded only for a few ships. In the 'total section' at the bottom of each table, the crew size may only include the shipmasters themselves because the size of crews often went unrecorded.

		1295–1300	1300–5	1305–10	1310–15	1315–20	1320–5	1325–30	1330–5	1335–40	1340–5	1345–50	1350–5	1355–60
Bodmin	(S)	–	¼	–	–	–	–	–	–	–	–	–	–	–
	(C)	–	–	–	–	–	–	–	–	–	–	–	–	–
	(T)	–	–	–	–	–	–	–	–	–	–	–	–	–
Crantock	(S)	–	–	–	–	–	1	–	–	–	–	–	–	–
	(C)	–	–	–	–	–	–	–	–	–	–	–	–	–
	(T)	–	–	–	–	–	–	–	–	–	–	–	–	–
Falmouth	(S)	–	–	–	–	–	2	–	–	2	2	1	–	2
	(C)	–	–	–	–	–	–	–	–	93	–	27	–	35
	(T)	–	–	–	–	–	–	–	–	–	–	–	–	–
Fowey	(S)	–	2 ¼	–	1	–	7	2	–	26	12	73	–	17
	(C)	–	–	–	–	–	–	48	–	817	–	1,871	–	353
	(T)	–	–	–	–	–	90	–	–	–	–	–	–	–
Lelant	(S)	–	–	–	–	–	–	–	–	–	–	–	–	–
	(C)	–	–	–	–	–	–	–	–	–	–	–	–	–
	(T)	–	–	–	–	–	–	–	–	–	–	–	–	–

Looe	(S)	–	2 ⅓	–	1	–	2	7	–	24	10	24	–	6
	(C)	–	–	–	–	–	–	132	–	502	–	533	–	60
	(T)	–	–	–	–	–	–	–	–	–	–	–	–	–
Lostwithiel	(S)	–	¼	–	–	–	–	–	–	–	–	–	–	–
	(C)	–	–	–	–	–	–	–	–	–	–	–	–	–
	(T)	–	–	–	–	–	–	–	–	–	–	–	–	–
Mousehole	(S)	–	–	–	–	–	1	–	–	–	–	–	–	–
	(C)	–	–	–	–	–	–	–	–	–	–	–	–	–
	(T)	–	–	–	–	–	–	–	–	–	–	–	–	–
Padstow	(S)	1	–	–	–	–	1	–	–	–	–	2	–	1
	(C)	–	–	–	–	–	–	–	–	–	–	27	–	12
	(T)	–	–	–	–	–	–	–	–	–	–	–	–	–
Penryn	(S)	–	–	–	–	–	–	–	–	–	–	–	–	–
	(C)	–	–	–	–	–	–	–	–	–	–	–	–	–
	(T)	–	–	–	–	–	–	–	–	–	–	–	–	–
Polruan	(S)	–	¼	–	–	–	–	–	–	12	5	7	–	–
	(C)	–	–	–	–	–	–	–	–	344	–	146	–	–
	(T)	–	–	–	–	–	–	–	–	–	–	–	–	–
Porthpean	(S)	–	⅓	–	–	–	–	–	–	–	–	–	–	–
	(C)	–	–	–	–	–	–	–	–	–	–	–	–	–
	(T)	–	–	–	–	–	–	–	–	–	–	–	–	–

St Michael's Mount	(S)	–	–	–	–	–	1	–	–	–	–
	(C)	–	–	–	–	–	–	–	–	–	–
	(T)	–	–	–	–	–	–	–	–	–	–
Saltash	(S)	⅓	–	–	–	–	–	–	–	–	–
	(C)	–	–	–	–	–	–	–	–	–	–
	(T)	–	–	–	–	–	–	–	–	–	–
Truro	(S)	–	–	–	–	–	–	–	–	–	–
	(C)	–	–	–	–	–	–	–	–	–	–
	(T)	–	–	–	–	–	–	–	–	–	–
Total	(S)	1	6	–	2	–	15	9	–	64	–	107	–	26
	(C)*	1	6	–	2	–	15	180	–	1,756	29	2,674	–	470
	(T)⁺	–	–	–	–	–	450	–	–	–	29	–	–	–

* including shipmasters
⁺ cumulative

Cornish Ports that sent ships to Royal Fleets between c. 1360 and c. 1420

		1360–5	1365–70	1370–5	1375–80	1380–5	1385–90	1390–5	1395–1400	1400–5	1405–10	1410–15	1415–20
Falmouth	(S)	–	–	4	1	–	1	–	–	½	1	–	1
	(C)	–	–	30	32	–	7	–	–	–	–	–	–
	(T)	–	–	42	–	–	70	–	–	–	–	–	32
Fowey	(S)	14	3	64	47	5	13	–	22	3	1	–	14
	(C)	224	–	827	787	79	444	–	114	–	–	–	–
	(T)	93	–	81	69	60	115	–	111	140	–	–	107
Lelant	(S)	–	–	1	1	–	–	–	1	–	–	–	–
	(C)	–	–	–	–	–	–	–	–	–	–	–	–
	(T)	–	–	–	20	–	–	–	–	–	–	–	–
Looe	(S)	–	–	14	4	1	2	–	1	1½	2	–	–
	(C)	–	–	38	33	–	44	–	–	–	–	–	–
	(T)	–	–	–	39	20	40	–	–	80	–	–	–
Lostwithiel	(S)	–	–	2	2	–	–	–	–	½	–	–	–
	(C)	–	–	–	49	–	–	–	–	–	–	–	–
	(T)	–	–	–	20	–	–	–	–	–	–	–	–
Mousehole	(S)	–	–	1	–	–	–	–	1	–	–	–	–
	(C)	–	–	–	–	–	–	–	–	–	–	–	–
	(T)	–	–	–	–	–	–	–	–	–	–	–	–

Padstow	(S)	1	–	16	–	–	–	–	–	1	–	–	1
	(C)	–	–	–	–	–	–	–	–	–	–	–	–
	(T)	–	–	–	–	–	–	–	–	–	–	–	30
Penryn	(S)	–	–	–	–	–	–	–	–	–	–	–	1
	(C)	–	–	–	–	–	–	–	–	–	–	–	–
	(T)	–	–	–	–	–	–	–	–	–	–	–	20
Polruan	(S)	1	–	3	2	–	–	–	–	–	–	–	–
	(C)	–	–	2	60	–	–	–	–	–	–	–	–
	(T)	120	–	–	–	–	–	–	–	–	–	–	–
Saltash	(S)	–	–	2	–	–	–	–	–	2	½	–	3
	(C)	–	–	–	–	–	–	–	–	22	–	–	–
	(T)	–	–	–	–	–	–	–	–	–	–	–	–
Truro	(S)	–	–	2	–	–	–	–	–	1	–	–	–
	(C)	–	–	16	–	–	–	–	–	–	–	–	–
	(T)	–	–	70	–	–	–	–	–	–	–	–	–
Total	(S)	15	3	97	57	6	16	–	–	29	3	4	20
	(C)*	225	3	938	963	80	507	–	–	140	3	4	20
	(T)+	1,112	–	2,094	2,627	319	1,609	–	–	359	360	–	402

* including shipmasters
+ cumulative

Sources:-
1295–1300: Rodger, *Safeguard of the Sea*, p. 496; 1300–5: SC1/16/37; *CCR 1296–1302*, 438, 612; 1310–15: *CPR 1307–1313*, 353; 1320–5: BL, Add. MS 7967 f. 97r; *CCR 1318–1323*, 534 and *CCR 1323–1327*, 183, assuming that each port sent one ship; 1325–30: E101/17/3 m. 7; *CCR 1323–1327*, 610–611; 1335–40: E101/19/38 mm. 3–4; E101/19/39; E101/32/7 m. 3; *Norwell*, ed. M. Lyons et al., pp. 369–370, 372, 374; 1340–5: C47/2/35 m. 4; *CCR 1343–1346*, 129, 131; 1345–50: BL, Harley MS 3968 f. 132; Hewitt, *Organization of War*, p. 182; *RBP*, ii, 84; E101/21/35 mm. 4–6; 1355–60: E101/36/20 f. 6, the date of this document is lost, but the ships that it lists as transporting the Black Prince to Aquitaine differ from the fleets of 1362 and 1363, suggesting that this roll relates to the campaign of 1355; E101/27/10 m. 3; E101/27/19; 1360–5: *CIM 1348–1377*, 150; E101/28/9; E101/28/24 mm. 4, 6; E101/29/1 mm. 3, 6; *CPR 1361–1364*, 33, 415, assuming Padstow sent one ship; 1365–70: C61/79 no. 4; C61/81 no. 24; C61/82 no. 45; *Gascon Rolls project*, assuming Fowey sent just one ship on each occasion; 1370–5: E101/30/29 m. 5; C47/2/46/15; E101/31/23 mm. 2–3; E101/32/22; E101/33/31 m. 2; E101/676/32 m. 4; Ayton and Lambert, *Shipping, Mariners*; 1375–80: E101/36/14 m. 7; E101/36/15 m. 2; E101/42/22 mm. 8–9; E101/37/23; E101/37/25 mm. 3–4; E101/38/19 mm. 1–2; E101/42/21 mm. 2–6; E101/39/1; E101/38/30 mm. 2–3; 1380–5: E101/40/8 m. 4; Ayton and Lambert, *Shipping, Mariners*; 1385–90: E101/30/9 m. 2; E101/40/19 mm. 4, 6, 8; E101/40/21 m. 4; E101/40/36 m. 1; E101/40/40 m. 2; 1395–1400: E101/41/27 mm. 12–14, 16–17; E101/41/29 m. 1; E101/41/31 m. 7; E101/42/28 mm. 3–4; E101/42/5 mm. 14, 19, 22, 28–29, 34, 38, 43, 45, 58, 51, 56, 87, 90, 91; 1400–5: *CCR 1399–1401*, 238–240; *CPR 1401–1405*, 195; 1405–10: C47/2/49/20; 1415–20: C47/2/49/41; *Rotuli Normanniae*, ed. Hardy, p. 327; E101/49/25 mm. 3, 12, 34, 47.

Bibliography

Manuscript Sources

Kew, The National Archives

C 1	Court of Chancery, Early Proceedings
C 47	Chancery Miscellanea
C 61	Gascon Rolls
C 67	Supplementary Patent Rolls
C 71	Scottish Rolls
C 76	Treaty Rolls
C 131	Extents for Debts
C 143	Inquisitions *Ad Quod Damnum*
C 219	Parliamentary Election Writs and Returns
C 241	Certificates of Statute Merchant and Statute Staple
E 30	Treasury of Receipt, Diplomatic Documents
E 36	Treasury of Receipt, Miscellaneous Books
E 101	King's Remembrancer, Various Accounts
E 122	Particulars of Custom Accounts
E 159	Memoranda Rolls and Enrolment Books
E 179	Particulars of Account, Lay and Clerical Taxation
E 210	King's Remembrancer, Ancient Deeds, Series D
E 372	Pipe Rolls
E 389	Pipe Office, Miscellanea, New Series
JUST 1	Justices of Assize, Oyer and Terminer, etc., Rolls
JUST 3	Gaol Delivery Rolls and Files
KB 9	Indictments Files
KB 27	*Coram Rege* Rolls
PROB 11	Prerogative Court of Canterbury, Will Registers
SC 1	Ancient Correspondence of the Chancery and Exchequer
SC 2	Court Rolls
SC 6	Ministers' and Receivers' Accounts
SC 8	Ancient Petitions

London, British Library

Additional Manuscripts

MS 7967

Additional Rolls

MS 64317
MS 64320
MS 64323

Cotton Manuscripts

MS Claudius D.vi

Harleain Manuscripts

MS 1192
MS 3968

Royal Manuscripts

MS 14.C IX

London, Duchy of Cornwall Office

DCO Ministers' Accounts

London, Guildhall Library

CLC/L/BF/A/021/MS05440 Brewers' Company Memoranda Book
CLC/L/PE/D/002/MS07086/001 Pewterers' Company Wardens' Accounts
CLC/L/SE/A/004A/MS31692 Skinners' Company, Fraternity of the Blessed Virgin Mary, Register

London, London Metropolitan Archives

DL/AL/C/002/MS09051 Archdeaconry Court of London, Will Registers
DL/C/B/004/MS09171 Commissary Court of London, Will Registers

Truro, Cornwall Record Office

AR Arundell Family of Lanherne, Mawgan in Pydar
BHEL Helston Borough
BLAUS Launceston Borough
BLIS Liskeard Borough
CA Croft Andrew
CF Coode and French, Solicitors, of St Austell
CM Connock Marshall Family of Treworgey, St Cleer
CY Coryton Family of Pentillie, Pillaton

EN   Enys Family of Enys, St Gluvias
G   Gregor Family of Trewarthenick, Cornelly
ME   Edgcumbe Family of Cotehele, Calstock and Mount Edgcumbe, Maker
R   Rashleigh Family of Menabilly
RP   Rogers Family of Penrose, Sithney
SN   Trelawny Family of Coldrenick, St Germans
WM   Wynell-Mayow Family of Bray, Morval

Truro, Royal Institution of Cornwall
HA   Henderson Collection

Printed Primary Sources

The Acts and Monuments of John Foxe, ed. S. R. Cattley, 8 vols (London, 1837–41)
Aldhelm, *The Poetic Works*, trans. M. Lapidge and J. L. Rosier (Cambridge, 1985)
The Ancient Cornish Drama, ed. and trans. E. Norris, 2 vols (Oxford, 1859)
The Anglo-Saxon Chronicle, ed. D. Whitelock (London, 1961)
Annales Cambriae, A.D. 682-954: Texts A–C in Parallel, ed. and trans. D. N. Dumville (Cambridge, 2002)
Annales Monastici, ed. H. R. Luard, 5 vols, Rolls Series (London, 1864–9)
The Anonimalle Chronicle, 1333–1381, ed. V. H. Galbraith (Manchester, 1927)
Arthur: A Short Sketch of his Life and History in English Verse, ed. F. J. Furnivall, Early English Text Society, Old Series 2 (London, 1864)
Bacon, F., *The Historie of the Raigne of King Henry the Seventh...* ed. M. Kiernan (Oxford, 2012)
Beare, T., *The Bailiff of Blackmoor 1586...*, ed. J. A. Buckley (Camborne, 1994)
Beunans Meriasek: The Life of St Meriasek, Bishop and Confessor, trans. W. Stokes (London, 1872)
Bewnans Ke, The Life of St Kea: A Critical Edition with Translation, ed. G. Thomas and N. Williams (Exeter, 2007)
Boorde, A., *The First Boke of the Introduction of Knowledge*, ed. F. J. Furnivall, Early English Text Society, Extra Series 10 (London, 1870)
Bristol Town Duties, ed. H. Bush (Bristol, 1828)
The Brokage Book of Southampton from 1439-40, ed. B. D. M. Bunyard, Southampton Records Society, 5 (Southampton, 1941)
The Brokage Book of Southampton 1443–1444, ed. O. Coleman, 2 vols, Southampton Record Society, 4, 6 (Southampton, 1960–1)
Calendar of Ancient Records of Dublin, ed. J. T. Gilbert, 18 vols (Dublin, 1889–1922)
Calendar of Charter Rolls, 1226–1516, 6 vols, HMSO (London, 1903–27)
Calendar of Close Rolls, 1296–1454, 38 vols, HMSO (London, 1892–1947)
A Calendar of Early Chancery Proceedings Relating to West Country Shipping, 1388–1493, ed. D. Gardiner, Devon and Cornwall Record Society, New Series 21 (Torquay, 1976)
Calendar of Entries in the Papal Registers: Papal Letters 1305–1404, ed. W. H. Bliss, C. Johnson and J. A. Twemlow, 4 vols, HMSO (London, 1895–1904)

Calendar of Entries in the Papal Registers: Petitions to the Pope 1342–1419, ed. W. H. Bliss, HMSO (London, 1896)
Calendar of Fine Rolls, 1272–1452, 18 vols, HMSO (London, 1911–39)
Calendar of Inquisitions Miscellaneous, 1219–1422, 7 vols, HMSO (London, 1916–68)
Calendar of Inquisitions Post Mortem, 1272–1427, 20 vols, HMSO (London and Woodbridge, 1908–2003)
A Calendar of Irish Chancery Letters, c. 1244–1509, ed. P. Crooks, https://chancery.tcd.ie/ (accessed 27 March 2019)
Calendar of Letter Books of the City of London, A–L, ed. R. R. Sharpe, 11 vols (London, 1899–1912)
Calendar of Letters from the Mayor and Corporation of the City of London, c. 1350–1370, ed. R. R. Sharpe (London, 1885)
Calendar of Patent Rolls, 1292–1477, 42 vols, HMSO (London, 1893–1916)
Calendar of Plea and Memoranda Rolls, ed. A. H. Thomas and P. E. Jones, 6 vols (Cambridge, 1924–61)
Calendar of State Papers, Milan, ed. A. Hinds, HMSO (London, 1912)
Calendar of State Papers, Venetian, 38 vols in 40, HMSO (1864–1940)
Calendar of Wills Proved and Enrolled in the Court of Husting, London 1258–1688, ed. R. R. Sharpe, 2 vols (London, 1889–90)
Camden, W., *Britannia: or a Geographical Description of the Flourishing Kingdoms of England, Scotland, and Ireland...*, trans. R. Gough, 4 vols (London, 1806)
The Caption of Seisin of the Duchy of Cornwall (1337), ed. P. L. Hull, Devon and Cornwall Record Society, New Series 17 (Torquay, 1971)
Carew, R., *The Survey of Cornwall by Richard Carew*, ed. J. Chynoweth, N. Orme and A. Walsham, Devon and Cornwall Record Society, New Series 47 (Exeter, 2004)
The Cartulary of Launceston Priory: A Calendar, ed. P. L. Hull, Devon and Cornwall Record Society, New Series 30 (Torquay, 1987)
The Cartulary of St Michael's Mount, ed. P. L. Hull, Devon and Cornwall Record Society, New Series 5 (Torquay, 1962)
Catalogue des Rolles Gascons, Normans et François..., ed. T. Carte, 2 vols (London, 1743)
Catalogue of Ancient Deeds in the Public Record Office, 6 vols, HMSO (London, 1890–1915)
Chester Custom Accounts, 1301–1566, ed. K. P. Wilson, The Record Society of Lancashire and Cheshire, cxi (Liverpool, 1969)
The Chronica Maiora of Thomas Walsingham, ed. J. Taylor, W. R. Childs and L. Watkiss, 2 vols (Oxford, 2003–11)
The Chronicle of Adam Usk 1377–1421, ed. C. Given-Wilson (Oxford, 1997)
The Chronicle of Pierre de Langtoft, ed. T. Wright, 2 vols, Rolls Series (London, 1866–8)
Chronicles of the Reigns of Edward I and Edward II, ed. W. Stubbs, 2 vols, Rolls Series (London, 1882–3)
Chronicles of the Reigns of Stephen, Henry II, and Richard I, ed. R. Howlett, 4 vols, Rolls Series (London, 1884–9)
Chronicon Galfridi le Baker de Swynebroke, ed. E. M. Thompson (Oxford, 1889)
Chronique du Religieux de Saint-Denys, 1380–1422, ed. M. Bellaguet, 6 vols (Paris, 1839–52)

De Controversia in Curia Militari inter Ricardum le Scrope et Robertum Grosvenor..., ed. N. H. Nicolas, 2 vols (London, 1832)
The Cornish Lands of the Arundells of Lanherne, Fourteenth to Sixteenth Centuries, ed. H. S. A. Fox and O. J. Padel, Devon and Cornwall Record Society, New Series 41 (Exeter, 2000)
Cornish Wills, 1342–1540, ed. N. Orme, Devon and Cornwall Record Society, New Series 50 (Exeter, 2007)
Cornwall Feet of Fines, ed. J. H. Rowe et al., 2 vols, Devon and Cornwall Record Society (Exeter and Topsham, 1914–50)
The Cornwall Muster Roll for 1569, ed. H. L. Douch (Bristol, 1984)
Crécy and Calais, from the Original Records in the Public Record Office, ed. G. Wrottesley (London, 1898)
Crime, Law and Society in the Later Middle Ages, trans. and ed. A. Musson with E. Powell (Manchester, 2009)
Documents Relating to Law and Custom of the Sea, ed. R. G. Marsden, The Navy Records Society, 49–50, 2 vols (London, 1915–16)
Domesday Book, X, Cornwall, ed. C. and F. Thorn (Chichester, 1979)
Drayton, M., *The Battaile of Agincourt...* (London, 1893)
'Eine mittellateinishe Dichterfehde: *Versus Michaelis Cornubiensis contra Henricum Abrincensem*', ed. A. Hilka, in *Mittelalterliche Handschriften: Festgabe zum 60. Geburtstag von Hermann Degering*, ed. A. Bömer and J. Kirchner (Leipzig, 1926), pp. 123–154
England's Immigrants 1330–1550, http://www.englandsimmigrants.com/, version 1.0 (accessed 21 November 2017)
Epistolae Academicae Oxon..., ed. H. Anstey, 2 vols (Oxford, 1898)
Exeter Freemen 1266–1967, ed. M. M. Rowe and A. M. Jackson, Devon and Cornwall Record Society, Extra Series I (Exeter, 1973)
Fortescue, J., *De Laudibus Legum Anglie*, ed. S. B. Chrimes (Cambridge, 1942)
The Forty-Fourth Annual Report of the Deputy Keeper of the Public Records, HMSO (London, 1883)
Froissart, J., *Chronicles*, ed. and trans. G. Brereton (Harmondsworth, 1968)
The Gascon Rolls project 1317–1468, http://www.gasconrolls.org/en/ (accessed 7 March 2019)
Gazetteer of Markets and Fairs in England and Wales to 1516, compil. S. Letters, 2 vols, List and Index Society, Special Series 32–33 (Chippenham, 2003)
The Great Chronicle of London, ed. A. H. Thomas and I. D. Thornley (London, 1938)
The Great Red Book of Bristol, ed. E. W. Veale, 4 vols, Bristol Record Society, 4, 8, 16 and 18 (Bristol, 1933–53)
Hall, E., *Hall's Chronicle: Containing the History of England...* (London, 1809)
Hauvilla, J. de, *Architrenius*, trans. and ed. W. Wetherbee, Cambridge Medieval Classics 3 (Cambridge, 1994)
The Havener's Accounts of the Earldom and Duchy of Cornwall, 1287–1356, ed. M. Kowaleski, Devon and Cornwall Record Society, New Series 44 (Exeter, 2001)
History of the Battle of Agincourt, and of the Expedition of Henry the Fifth into France in 1415, ed. H. Nicolas (London, 1832)

Inquisitions and Assessments Relating to Feudal Aids, 1284–1431, 6 vols, HMSO (London, 1899–1920)
Issue Roll of Thomas de Brantingham, A.D. 1370, ed. F. Devon (London, 1835)
John of Gaunt's Register, 1372–1376, ed. S. Armitage-Smith, 2 vols, Camden Society, Third Series 20–21 (London, 1911)
The Lay Subsidy of 1334, ed. R. Glasscock (London, 1975)
Leland, J., *The Itinerary of John Leland in or about the years 1535–1543*, ed. L. T. Smith, 5 vols (London, 1907–10)
Les Reports des Cases en Ley: En le Cinque an du Roy Edward le Quart Communement Appelle Long Quinto (London, 1680)
Letters and Papers, Foreign and Domestic, of the Reign of Henry VIII, ed. J. S. Brewer et al., 23 vols in 35 (London, 1864–1920)
The Libelle of Englyshe Polycye..., ed. G. Warner (Oxford, 1926)
The Life and Campaigns of the Black Prince..., ed. and trans. R. Barber (Bury St Edmunds, 1979)
List of Escheators for England and Wales, compil. A. C. Wood, List and Index Society, 72 (London, 1971)
List of Sheriffs for England and Wales, List and Index Society, 9 (London, 1898)
The Local Custom Accounts of the Port of Exeter, 1266–1321, ed. M. Kowaleski, Devon and Cornwall Record Society, New Series 36 (Exeter, 1993)
The Local Port Book of Southampton for 1435–36, ed. B. Foster, Southampton Record Society, 7 (Southampton, 1963)
The Making of King's Lynn: A Documentary Survey, ed. D. M. Owen, Records of Social and Economic History, New Series 9 (London, 1984)
Malmesbury, W. of, *Gesta Regum Anglorum*, ed. R. Mynors, 2 vols (Oxford, 1998–9)
Malory, T., *The Works of Sir Thomas Malory*, ed. E. Vinaver, rev. P. J. C. Field, 3 vols (Oxford, 1990)
The Map of Great Britain circa A.D. 1360, Known as the Gough Map, ed. E. J. S. Parsons, with F. Stenton, *The Roads of the Gough Map* (Oxford, 1958)
Mézières, P. de, *Letter to King Richard II...*, ed. and trans. G. W. Coopland (Liverpool, 1975)
The Middle Cornish Charter Endorsement, ed. L. Toorians (Innsbruck, 1991)
Ministers' Accounts of the Earldom of Cornwall, 1296–7, ed. L. M. Midgley, 2 vols, Camden Society, Third Series 64, 68 (London, 1942–5)
De Miraculis Sanctae Mariae Laudunensis, ii, 15–16, ed. J. P. Migne, *Patrologia Latina*, 156 (1880), cols. 961–1018
The Mirror for Magistrates, ed. L. B. Campbell (Cambridge, 1938)
Modus Tenendi Parliamentum, ed. T. D. Hardy (London, 1846)
Monasticon Dioecesis Exoniensis, ed. G. Oliver (London, 1846)
Monmouth, Geoffrey of, *The History of the Kings of Britain*, trans. L. Thorpe (London, 1966)
Monumenta Juridica: The Black Book of the Admiralty, ed. T. Twiss, 4 vols, Rolls Series (London, 1871–6)
The Navy of the Lancastrian Kings: Accounts and Inventories of William Soper, Keeper of the King's Ships, 1422–1427, ed. S. Rose, The Navy Records Society, 123 (London, 1982)

Norden, J., *A Topographical and Historical Description of Cornwall* (London, 1728)
The Oak Book of Southampton of c. 1300, trans. and ed. P. Studer, 3 vols, Southampton Record Society, 10, 11, 12 (Southampton, 1910–11)
The Overseas Trade of Bristol in the Later Middle Ages, ed. E. M. Carus-Wilson, Bristol Record Society, 7 (London, 1937)
The Overseas Trade of London: Exchequer Customs Accounts 1480–1, ed. H. S. Cobb, London Record Society, 27 (Bristol, 1990)
The Parliament Rolls of Medieval England, ed. and trans. P. Brand, A. Curry, C. Given-Wilson, R. E. Horrox, G. Martin, W. M. Ormrod and J. R. S. Philips, 16 vols (Woodbridge, 2005)
Parliamentary Writs, ed. F. Palgrave, 2 vols in 4 (London, 1827–34)
The Peasants' Revolt of 1381, ed. R. B. Dobson, 2nd Edition (London, 1983)
Pegolotti, F. B., *La Practica della Mercatura*, ed. A. Evans (Cambridge, MA, 1936)
Placita de Quo Warranto, ed. W. Illingworth and J. Caley (London, 1818)
Political Poems and Songs Relating to English History, ed. T. Wright, Rolls Series, 2 vols (London, 1859–18)
The Poll Taxes of 1377, 1379 and 1381, ed. C. C. Fenwick, 3 vols, Records of Social and Economic History, New Series 27, 29, 37 (Oxford, 1998–2005)
The Port Books of Southampton, 1427–1430, trans. and ed. P. Studer, Southampton Record Society, 15 (Southampton, 1913)
Proceedings and Ordinances of the Privy Council, 10 Richard II–33 Henry VIII, ed. H. Nicolas, 7 vols (London, 1834–7)
Proctors for Parliament: Clergy, Community and Politics c. 1248–1539, ed. P. Bradford and A. K. McHardy, 2 vols, The Canterbury and York Society, cvii–cviii (Woodbridge, 2017–18)
'Receipts and Expenses in the Building of Bodmin Church A.D. 1469 to 1472', ed. J. J. Wilkinson, in *The Camden Miscellany*, viii, Camden Society, New Series xiv (London, 1875)
Records of Convocation, ed. G. Bray, 20 vols, Church of England Record Society (Woodbridge, 2005–6)
Records of Early English Drama: Cornwall, ed. S. L. Joyce and E. S. Newlyn (Toronto, 1999)
The Register of Edmund Stafford (1395–1419): An Index and Abstract of its Contents, ed. F. C. Hingeston-Randolph (London, 1886)
The Register of Edward the Black Prince, 4 vols, HMSO (London, 1930–3)
The Register of John de Grandisson, Bishop of Exeter (1327–1369), ed. F. C. Hingeston-Randolph, 3 vols (London, 1894–9)
The Register of Thomas de Brantyngham, Bishop of Exeter (1370–1394), ed. F. C. Hingeston-Randolph, 2 vols (London, 1901–6)
The Register of Walter de Stapeldon, Bishop of Exeter (1307–1326), ed. F. C. Hingeston-Randolph (London, 1892)
Return of Members of Parliament, 2 parts in 4 vols (London, 1878–91)
'The Romaunt of the Rose' in *The Riverside Chaucer*, ed. F. N. Robinson, 3rd Edition, ed. L. D. Benson (Oxford, 1988), pp. 687–767
Roscarrock, N., *Nicholas Roscarrock's Lives of the Saints: Devon and Cornwall*, ed. N. Orme, Devon and Cornwall Record Society, New Series 35 (Exeter, 1992)

Rotuli Normanniae in Turri Londinensi asservati: Johanne et Henrico quinto..., ed. T. D. Hardy (London, 1835)

Royal and Historical Letters during the Reign of Henry the Fourth..., ed. F. C. Hingeston, Rolls Series, 2 vols (London, 1860–1965)

Scotland in 1298: Documents relating to the campaign of King Edward I in that year, and especially to the Battle of Falkirk, ed. H. Gough (London, 1888)

Select Cases in the Court of King's Bench, ed. G. O. Sayles, 7 vols, Selden Society, 55, 57, 58, 74, 76, 82, 88 (London, 1936–71)

Select Pleas in the Court of the Admiralty: The Court of the Admiralty of the West (AD 1390-1404) and The High Court of the Admiralty (AD 1527-1545), ed. R. G. Marsden, 2 vols, Selden Society, 6, 11 (London, 1894–7)

The Sermons of Thomas Brinton, Bishop of Rochester (1373–1389), ed. M. A. Devlin, 2 vols, Camden Society, Third Series 85–86 (London, 1954)

Shipping, Mariners and Port Communities in 14th-Century England, ed. A. Ayton and C. Lambert (2011), http://discover.ukdataservice.ac.uk/catalogue/?sn5850665&type5Data%20catalogue (accessed 19 February 2015)

The Soldier in Later Medieval England, http://www.medievalsoldier.org/ (accessed 20 November 2015)

The Statute Merchant Roll of Coventry, 1392–1416, ed. A. Beardwood, Dugdale Society, 17 (London, 1939)

Statutes and Ordinances and Acts of the Parliament of Ireland, King John to Henry V, ed. H. F. Berry (Dublin, 1907)

The Statutes of the Realm, A. Luders et al., 11 vols (London, 1810–28)

The Stonor Letters and Papers, 1290–1483, ed. C. L. Kingsford, 2 vols, Camden Society, Third Series 29–30 (London, 1919)

Supplications from England and Wales in the Registers of the Apostolic Penitentiary, 1410-1503, ed. P. D. Clarke and P. N. R. Zutshi, 3 vols, The Canterbury and York Society, ciii–cv (Woodbridge 2012–15)

Syllabus of Rymer's Foedera, ed. T. D. Hardy, 3 vols (London, 1869–85)

'Thomas Chiverton's Book of Obits', ed. P. L. Hull, *Devon and Cornwall Notes and Queries*, 33 (1974–7), pp. 97–102, 143–147, 188–193, 236–239, 277–282, 337–341

'Thomas Chiverton's Book of Obits', ed. P. L. Hull, *Devon and Cornwall Notes and Queries*, 34 (1978–81), pp. 5–11, 52–55

Thomas Wright's Political Songs of England: From the Reign of John to that of Edward II, ed. P. Coss (Cambridge, 1996)

'Three Courts of the Hundred of Penwith, 1333', ed. G. D. G. Hall, in *Medieval Legal Records*, ed. R. F. Hunnisett and J. B. Post (London, 1978)

Three Fifteenth-Century Chronicles..., ed. J. Gairdner, Camden Society, New Series 28 (Westminster, 1880)

Treaty Rolls Preserved in the Public Record Office, ed. P. Chaplais and J. Ferguson, 2 vols (London, 1955–72)

Trevelyan Papers, ed. J. P. Collier et al., Camden Society, Old Series 67, 84 and 105 (London, 1857–72)

Trevisa, J., trans., *Polychronicon Ranulphi Higden...*, ed. C. Babington and J. A. Lumby, 9 vols, Rolls Series (London, 1865–86)

Tudor Royal Proclamations, ed. P. L. Hughes and J. F. Larkin, 3 vols (London, 1964–9)

The Unconquered Knight: A Chronicle of the Deeds of Don Pero Niño, Count of Buelan, by his Standard-Bearer Gutierre Diaz de Gamez (1431–1449), trans. J. Evans (London, 1928)

Vergil, P., *The Anglia Historia of Polydore Vergil, 1485–1537*, trans. D. Hay, Camden Society, Third Series 74 (London, 1950)

Vergil, P., *Polydore Vergil's English History: The Period Prior to the Norman Conquest*, ed. H. Ellis, Camden Society, 36 (London, 1846)

The Views of the Hosts of Alien Merchants, 1440–1444, ed. H. Bradley, London Record Society, 46 (Woodbridge, 2012)

Vita Edwardi Secundi, The Life of Edward II..., ed. W. R. Childs (Oxford, 2005)

Wales, G. of, *The Journey through Wales and the Description of Wales*, trans. L. Thorpe (London, 1978)

Walter of Henley and other Treatises on Estate Management and Accounting, ed. D. Oschinsky (Oxford, 1971)

The Wardrobe Book of William de Norwell..., ed. M. Lyon, B. Lyon and H. S. Lucas, with the collaboration of J. de Sturler (Brussels, 1983)

The Welsh Assize Roll, 1277–1284, ed. J. C. Davies (Cardiff, 1940)

The Westminster Chronicle 1381–1394, ed. and trans. L. C. Hector and B. F. Harvey (Oxford, 1982)

Wey, W., *The Itineraries of William Wey*, ed. and trans. F. Davey (Oxford, 2010)

Worcestre, W., *Itineraries*, ed. J. H. Harvey (Oxford, 1969)

Year Books 2 Richard II, ed. M. S. Arnold, Ames Foundation (Cambridge, MA, 1975)

Year Books 6 and 7 Edward II, ed. W. C. Bolland, Selden Society, 36 (London, 1918)

Year Books 7 Richard II, ed. M. J. Holland, Ames Foundation (Cambridge, MA, 1989)

Year Books 11 Edward II, ed. J. P. Collas and W. S. Holdsworth, Selden Society, 61 (London, 1942)

Year Books 12 and 13 Edward III, ed. L. O. Pike, Rolls Series (London, 1885)

Year Books 30 and 31 Edward I, ed. A. J. Horwood, Rolls Series (London, 1863)

Published Secondary Sources

Acheson, E., *A Gentry Community: Leicestershire in the Fifteenth Century, c. 1422–c. 1485* (Cambridge, 1992)

Alban, J. R., 'English Coastal Defence: Some Fourteenth-Century Modifications', in *Patronage, the Crown and the Provinces in Later Medieval England*, ed. R. A. Griffiths (Gloucester, 1981), pp. 57–78

Anderson, B., *Imagined Communities: Reflections on the Origins and Spread of Nationalism* (London, 1983)

Anderson, M. W., 'The honour of bothe courtes be nat lyke: Cornish Resistance to Arthurian Dominance in Malory', *Arthuriana*, 19 (2009), pp. 42–57

Angarrack, J., *Our Future is History: Identity, Law and the Cornish Question* (Padstow, 2002)

Appleby, J., 'Devon Privateering from Early Times to 1668', in *The New Maritime History of Devon*, ed. M. Duffy et al., 2 vols (London, 1992–4), i, pp. 90–97

Armstrong, D., 'Mapping Malory's *Morte*: the (Physical) Place and (Narrative) Space of Cornwall', in *Mapping Malory: Regional Identities and National Geographies in Le Morte Darthur*, ed. D. Armstrong and K. Hodges (Basingstoke, 2014), pp. 19–43

Armstrong, J. W., 'Centre, Periphery, Locality, Province: England and its Far North in the Fifteenth Century', in *The Plantagenet Empire, 1259-1453: Proceedings of the 2014 Harlaxton Symposium*, ed. P. Crooks, D. Green and W. M. Ormrod (Donington, 2016), pp. 248–272

——, J. W., 'Concepts of Kinship in Lancastrian Westmorland', in *Political Society in Later Medieval England: A Festschrift for Christine Carpenter*, ed. B. Thompson and J. Watts (Woodbridge, 2015), pp. 146–165

Arthurson, I., 'Fear and Loathing in West Cornwall: Seven New Letters on the 1548 Rising', *Journal of the Royal Institution of Cornwall* (2000), pp. 68–96

——, I., *The Perkin Warbeck Conspiracy 1491–1499* (Stroud, 1994)

——, I., 'The Rising of 1497: A Revolt of the Peasantry?', in *People, Politics and Community in the Later Middle Ages*, ed. J. Rosenthal and C. Richmond (Gloucester, 1987), pp. 1–19

Ayton, A., *Knights and Warhorses: Military Service and the English Aristocracy under Edward III* (Woodbridge, 1994)

——, A., and C. Lambert, 'A Maritime Community in War and Peace: Kentish Ports, Ships and Mariners, 1320–1400', *Archaeologia Cantiana*, 134 (2014), pp. 67–103

Backman, C. R., 'Piracy', in *A Companion to Mediterranean History*, ed. P. Horden and S. Kinoshita (Chichester, 2014), pp. 172–183

Baker, G. P., C. L. Lambert and D. Simpkin (eds), *Military Communities in Late Medieval England: Essays in Honour of Andrew Ayton* (Woodbridge, 2018)

Baker, J. H., *An Introduction to English Legal History*, 4th Edition (Bath, 2002)

——, J. H., *The Legal Profession and the Common Law: Historical Essays* (London, 1986)

——, J. H., *The Men of Court 1440 to 1550: A Prosopography of the Inns of Court and Chancery and the Courts of Law*, 2 vols, Selden Society, Supplementary Series 18 (London, 2012)

——, J. H., *The Order of the Serjeants at Law: A Chronicle of Creation, with Related Texts and an Historical Introduction*, Selden Society, Supplementary Series 5 (London, 1984)

Bakere, J. A., *The Cornish Ordinalia: A Critical Study* (Cardiff, 1980)

Barabási, A., *Linked: The New Science of Networks* (Cambridge, MA, 2002)

Barber, R., *Edward, Prince of Wales and Aquitaine: A Biography of the Black Prince* (London, 1978)

——, R., 'Joan *suo jure* countess of Kent, and princess of Wales and Aquitaine', in *The Oxford Dictionary of National Biography*, ed. H. C. G. Matthew and B. H. Harrison, 60 vols (Oxford, 2004), xxx, pp. 137–139

Barraclough, G., *The Earldom and County Palatine of Cheshire* (Oxford, 1953)

Barrett, R. W., *Against All England: Regional Identity and Cheshire Writing, 1195–1656* (Notre Dame, 2009)

Barron, C., *London in the Later Middle Ages: Government and People 1200–1500* (Oxford, 2004)

Barron, W. R. J., (ed.) *The Arthur of the English* (Cardiff, 1999)

Bartlett, R., 'Medieval and Modern Concepts of Race and Ethnicity', *Journal of Medieval and Early Modern Studies*, 31 (2001), pp. 39–56
Beacham, P., and N. Pevsner, *Cornwall: The Buildings of England* (New Haven and London, 2014)
Beal, J., *John Trevisa and the English Polychronicon* (Turnhout, 2012)
——, J., 'Mapping Identity in John Trevisa's English *Polychronicon*: Chester, Cornwall and the Translation of English National History', *Fourteenth Century England, III*, ed. W. M. Ormrod (Woodbridge, 2004), pp. 67–82
Beilby, M., 'The Profits of Expertise: the Rise of the Civil Lawyers and Chancery Equity', in *Profit, Piety and the Professions in Later Medieval England*, ed. M. Hicks (Gloucester, 1990), pp. 72–90
Bell, A., *War and the Soldier in the Fourteenth Century* (Woodbridge, 2004)
——, A., et al., *The Soldier in Later Medieval England* (Oxford, 2013)
Bellamy, J., *Crime and Public Order in England in the Later Middle Ages* (London, 1973)
Bennett, M., *Community, Class and Careerism: Cheshire and Lancashire Society in the Age of Sir Gawain and the Green Knight* (Cambridge, 1983)
——, M., 'The Plantagenet Empire as 'Enterprise Zone': War and Business Networks, c. 1400–50', in *The Plantagenet Empire, 1259–1453: Proceedings of the 2014 Harlaxton Symposium*, ed. P. Crooks, D. Green and W. M. Ormrod (Donington, 2016), pp. 335–358
Beresford, G. 'The Medieval Manor of Penhallam, Jacobstow, Cornwall', *Medieval Archaeology*, 18 (1974), pp. 90–145
Beresford, M., 'Dispersed and Grouped Settlement in Medieval Cornwall', *Agricultural History Review*, 1 (1964), pp. 13–27
——, M., *New Towns of the Middle Ages: Town Plantation in England, Wales and Gascony* (London, 1967)
——, M., and H. Finberg, *English Medieval Boroughs: A Hand-List* (Newton Abbot, 1973)
Betcher, G. J., 'Translating a Labour Dispute in the Cornish *Ordinalia* within a Legal Context', *Fourteenth Century England, I*, ed. N. Saul (Woodbridge, 2000), pp. 89–102
Bevan, B., 'The Resilience of Sailortown Culture in English Naval Ports, c. 1820–1900', *Urban History*, 43 (2016), pp. 72–95
Black, A., 'The Individual and Society', in *The Cambridge History of Medieval Political Thought, c. 350–c. 1450*, ed. J. H. Burns (Cambridge, 1988), pp. 588–606
——, A., *Political Thought in Europe, 1250–1450* (Cambridge, 1992)
Blake, J. B., 'Medieval Smuggling in the North-East: Some Fourteenth-Century Evidence', *Archaeologia Aleiana*, 4th Series, 43 (1965), pp. 243–260
Bolton, J. L., *The Medieval English Economy, 1150–1500* (London, 1980)
——, J. L., *Money in the Medieval English Economy, 973–1489* (Manchester, 2012)
——, J. L., '"The World Upside Down". Plague as an Agent of Economic and Social Change', in *The Black Death in England*, ed. W. M. Ormrod and P. F. Lindley (Stamford, 1996), pp. 17–78
Bonfield, L., 'What did English Villagers means by Customary Law?', in *Medieval Society and the Manor Court*, ed. Z. Razzi and R. Smith (Oxford, 1996), pp. 103–116
Booth, P. H. W., 'Taxation and Public Order: Cheshire in 1353', *Northern History*, 12 (1976), pp. 16–31

Borlase, W., *Antiquities, Historical and Monumental, of the County of Cornwall*, 2nd Edition (London, 1769)
Boutruche, R., *Seigneurie et Féodalité*, 2 vols (Paris, 1959–70)
Bradshaw, B., 'The Tudor Reformation and Revolution in Wales and Ireland: the Origins of the British Problem', in *The British Problem, c. 1534–1707: State Formation in the Atlantic Archipelago*, ed. B. Bradshaw and J. Morrill (Basingstoke, 1996), pp. 39–65
Brand, P., *The Making of the Common Law* (London, 1992)
——, P., *Observing and Recording the Medieval Bar and Bench at Work: The Origins of Law Reporting in England* (London, 1999)
——, P., 'The Travails of Travel: The Difficulty of Getting to Court in Later Medieval England', in *Freedom of Movement in the Middle Ages: Proceedings of the 2003 Harlaxton Symposium*, ed. P. Horden (Donington, 2007), pp. 215–228
Brayshay, M. (ed.), *Topographical Writers in South-West England* (Exeter, 1996)
Breeze, A., 'The Battle of Camlan and Camelford, Cornwall', *Arthuriana*, 15 (2005), pp. 75–90
——, A., '"Dylys" in the Middle Cornish Play of St Kea', *Devon and Cornwall Notes and Queries*, xli, part 1 (2013), pp. 4–6
Bridbury, A. R., *England and the Salt Trade in the Later Middle Ages* (Oxford, 1955)
Britnell, R. H., *The Commercialisation of English Society, 1000–1500* (Cambridge, 1993)
——, R. H., 'Urban Demand and the English Economy, 1300–1600', in *Trade, Urban Hinterlands and Market Integration, c. 1300–1600*, ed. J. A. Galloway (Loughborough, 2000), pp. 1–21
Brown, A. L., *The Governance of Medieval England, 1272–1461* (London, 1989)
Brown, M., *Disunited Kingdoms: Peoples and Politics in the British Isles 1280–1460* (Harlow, 2013)
Brown, P., 'Higden's Britain', in *Medieval Europeans: Studies in Ethnic Identity and National Perspectives in Medieval Europe*, ed. A. P. Smyth (Basingstoke, 1998), pp. 103–118
Buck, M. C., *Politics, Finance and the Church in the Reign of Edward II: Walter Stapeldon, Treasurer of England* (Cambridge, 1983)
——, M. C., 'Walter Stapeldon', in *The Oxford Dictionary of National Biography*, ed. H. C. G. Matthew and B. H. Harrison, 60 vols (Oxford, 2004), li, pp. 272–274
Burgtorf, J., '"With my life, his joyes began and ended": Piers Gaveston and King Edward II of England Revisited', *Fourteenth Century England, V*, ed. N. Saul (Woodbridge, 2008), pp. 31–51
Burns, R. I., 'Piracy as an Islamic-Christian Interface in the Thirteenth Century', *Viator*, 11, (1980), pp. 165–178
Burt, C., 'Local Government in Warwickshire and Worcestershire during the Reign of Edward II', in *Political Society in Later Medieval England: A Festschrift for Christine Carpenter*, ed. B. Thompson and J. Watts (Woodbridge, 2015), pp. 55–73
Bush, M., 'The Risings of the Commons in England, 1381–1549', in *Orders and Hierarchies in Late Medieval and Renaissance Europe*, ed. J. Denton (London, 1999), pp. 109–125
Cam, H. M., 'The Evolution of the Mediaeval English Franchise', *Speculum*, 32 (1957), pp. 427–442

——, H. M., *The Hundred and the Hundred Rolls: An Outline of Local Government in Medieval England* (London, 1930)
Campbell, S. M., 'The Haveners of the Mediaeval Dukes of Cornwall and the Organisation of the Duchy Ports', *Journal of the Royal Institution of Cornwall* (1962), pp. 113-144
Carpenter, C., 'Gentry and Community in Medieval England', *Journal of British Studies*, 33 (1994), pp. 340-380
——, C., *Locality and Polity: A Study of Warwickshire Landed Society, 1401-1499* (Cambridge, 1992)
Carus-Wilson, E. M., and O. Coleman, *England's Export Trade 1275-1547* (Oxford, 1963)
Catto, J., 'Masters, Patrons and the Careers of Graduates in Fifteenth-Century England', *The Fifteenth Century: I, Concepts and Patterns of Service in the Later Middle Ages*, ed. A. Curry and E. Matthew (Woodbridge, 2000), pp. 52-63
——, J., 'Religious Change under Henry V', in *Henry V: The Practice of Kingship*, ed. G. L. Harriss (Oxford, 1985), pp. 97-115
——, J., 'Written English: the Making of the Language, 1370-1400', *Past and Present*, 179 (2003), pp. 24-59
Chaplais, P., *Piers Gaveston: Edward II's Adoptive Brother* (Oxford, 1994)
Cherry, M., 'The Courtenay Earls of Devon: The Formation and Disintegration of a Late Medieval Aristocratic Affinity', *Southern History*, 1 (1979), pp. 71-97
Cheyette, F. L., 'The Sovereign and the Pirates, 1332', *Speculum*, 45 (1970), pp. 40-68
Childs, W. R., *Anglo-Castilian Trade in the Later Middle Ages* (Manchester, 1978)
——, W. R., 'Moving Around', in *A Social History of England, 1200-1500*, ed. R. Horrox and W. M. Ormrod (Cambridge, 2006), pp. 260-275
——, W. R., 'Overseas Trade and Shipping in Cornwall in the Later Middle Ages', in *The Maritime History of Cornwall*, ed. P. Payton, A. Kennerley and H. Doe (Exeter, 2014), pp. 60-71
Chynoweth, J., *Tudor Cornwall* (Stroud, 2002)
Clark, P., 'Celtic Tradition and Regional Discontent: Cornish Nationalism Revisited', *Cornish Studies*, New Series 21, (2013), pp. 288-320
Clarke, M. V., *Medieval Representation and Consent* (New York, 1964)
Cockerham, P., *Continuity and Change: Memorialisation and the Cornish Funeral Monument Industry, 1497-1660* (Oxford, 2006)
——, P., and N. Orme, 'John Waryn and his Cadaver Brass, formerly in Menheniot Church, Cornwall', *Transactions of the Monumental Brass Society*, 19 (2014), pp. 41-56
Cokayne, G. E., *The Complete Peerage...*, ed. V. Gibbs et al., 12 vols in 13 (London, 1912-59)
Contamine, P., 'The European Nobility', in *The New Cambridge Medieval History, VII, c. 1415-1500*, ed. C. Allmand (Cambridge, 1998), pp. 89-105
Cooper, J. P. D., *Propaganda and the Tudor State: Political Culture in the Westcountry* (Oxford, 2003)
Coss, P., *The Origins of the English Gentry* (Cambridge, 2003)
Cottle, B., *The Triumph of English, 1350-1400* (London, 1969)
Crook, D., 'The Later Eyres', *English Historical Review*, 97 (1982), pp. 241-268

Crooks, P., 'State of the Union: Perspectives on English Imperialism in the Late Middle Ages', *Past and Present*, 212 (2011), pp. 3–42
Crowder, C. M. D., *Unity, Heresy and Reform, 1378–1460: The Conciliar Response to the Great Schism* (London, 1977)
Curley, M. J., 'A New Edition of John of Cornwall's *Prophetia Merlini*', *Speculum*, 57 (1982), pp. 217–249
Davidson, J., *The History of Newenham Abbey* (London, 1843)
Davies, J. C., *The Baronial Opposition to Edward II* (Cambridge, 1918)
Davies, M., 'Thomasine Percyvale, "The Maid of Week", (d. 1512)', in *Medieval London Widows 1300–1500*, ed. C. M. Barron and A. F. Sutton (London, 1994), pp. 185–208
Davies, R. G., 'The Episcopate', in *Profession, Vocation and Culture in Later Medieval England*, ed. C. H. Clough (Liverpool, 1982), pp. 51–89
Davies, R. R., *Conquest, Coexistence and Change: Wales 1063–1415*, Oxford History of Wales, vol. II (Oxford, 1987)
——, R. R., *The First English Empire: Power and Identities in the British Isles, 1093–1343* (Oxford, 2000)
——, R. R., *Lords and Lordship in the British Isles in the Late Middle Ages*, ed. B. Smith (Oxford, 2009)
——, R. R., *Lordship and Society in the March of Wales, 1282–1400* (Oxford, 1978)
——, R. R., 'The Medieval State: The Tyranny of a Concept', *Journal of Historical Sociology*, 16 (2003), pp. 280–300
——, R. R., 'The Peoples of Britain and Ireland, 1100–1400: I. Identities', *Transactions of the Royal Historical Society*, 6th series, 4 (1994), pp. 1–20
——, R. R., 'The Peoples of Britain and Ireland, 1100–1400: II. Names, Boundaries and Regnal Solidarities', *Transactions of the Royal Historical Society*, 6th series, 5 (1995), pp. 1–20
——, R. R., 'The Peoples of Britain and Ireland, 1100–1400: III. Laws and Customs', *Transactions of the Royal Historical Society*, 6th series, 6 (1996), pp. 1–23
——, R. R., 'The Peoples of Britain and Ireland, 1100–1400: IV. Language and Historical Mythology', *Transactions of the Royal Historical Society*, 6th series, 7 (1997), pp. 1–23
——, R. R., *The Revolt of Owain Glyndŵr* (Oxford, 1995)
Davies, V., 'Preparation for Service in the Late Medieval English Church', *The Fifteenth Century: I, Concepts and Patterns of Service in the Later Middle Ages*, ed. A. Curry and E. Matthew (Woodbridge, 2000), pp. 38–51
Deacon, B., *Cornwall: A Concise History* (Cardiff, 2007)
Denholm-Young, N., *The Country Gentry in the Fourteenth Century: With Special Reference to the Heraldic Rolls of Arms* (Oxford, 1969)
——, N., *Richard of Cornwall* (Oxford, 1947)
——, N., *Seigniorial Administration in England* (London, 1937)
Denton, J. H., and J. P. Dooley, *Representatives of the Lower Clergy in Parliament, 1295–1340* (Woodbridge, 1987)
Dickinson, R. 'Meanings of Cornishness: A Study of Contemporary Cornish Identity', *Cornish Studies*, New Series 18 (2010), pp. 70–100
Dodd, G., *Justice and Grace: Private Petitioning and the English Parliament in the Late Middle Ages* (Oxford, 2007)

——, G., 'Kingship, Parliament and the Court: the Emergence of 'High Style' in Petitions to the English Crown, c. 1350-1405', *English Historical Review*, 129 (2014), pp. 515-548
——, G., 'Parliamentary Petitions? The Origins and Provenance of the "Ancient Petitions" (SC 8) in the National Archives', in *Medieval Petitions: Grace and Grievance*, ed. W. M. Ormrod, G. Dodd and A. Musson (York, 2009), pp. 12-46
Donahue, C., Jnr, *Law, Marriage and Society in the Later Middle Ages* (Cambridge, 2008)
Douch, H., 'Household Accounts at Lanherne', *Journal of the Royal Institution of Cornwall* (1953), pp. 25-32
Downing, M., *Military Effigies of England and Wales*, 4 vols (Shrewsbury, 2010)
Drake, S. J., '"The Gallaunts of Fawey": a case study of Fowey during the Hundred Years' War, c. 1337-1399', *Historical Research*, 90 (2017), pp. 296-317
——, S. J., 'The Michelstow Family (*per. c.* 1350-c. 1454)', in *The Oxford Dictionary of National Biography* (2016), http://www.oxforddnb.com/view/article/107361?docPos=1 (accessed 15 May, 2016)
——, S. J., 'Pirates and Pilchards: The Wealth and Peopling of Fowey during the Hundred Years War', *Journal of the Royal Institution of Cornwall* (2015), pp. 23-44
——, S. J., 'Politics and Society in Richard II's Cornwall: A Study in Relations between Centre and Locality', *Journal of the Royal Institution of Cornwall* (2013), pp. 23-48
——, S. J., 'Since the Time of King Arthur: Gentry Identity and the Commonalty of Cornwall, c. 1300-c. 1420', *Historical Research*, 91 (2018), pp. 236-254
Dryburgh, P., 'Living in the Shadows: John of Eltham, Earl of Cornwall (1316-36)', *Fourteenth Century England, IX*, ed. J. Bothwell and G. Dodd (Woodbridge, 2016), pp. 23-48
Duffy, E., *The Stripping of the Altars: Traditional Religion in England, c. 1400-c. 1500* (New Haven and London, 1992)
Dunkin, E., *The Monumental Brasses of Cornwall* (Bath, 1882)
Dunning, R. W., 'Patronage and Promotion in the Late-Medieval Church', in *Patronage, the Crown and the Provinces in Later Medieval England*, ed. R. A. Griffiths (Gloucester, 1981), pp. 167-180
Dyer, C., *An Age of Transition? Economy and Society in England in the Later Middle Ages* (Oxford, 2005)
Edson, E., *Mapping Time and Space: How Medieval Mapmakers viewed their World* (London, 1997)
Edwards, K., 'The Political Importance of the English Bishops during the Reign of Edward II', *English Historical Review*, 59 (1944), pp. 311-347
Elliott-Binns, L. E., *Medieval Cornwall* (London, 1955)
Ellis, G., *Earldoms in Fee: A Study in Peerage Law and History* (London, 1963)
Emden, A. B., *A Biographical Register of the University of Oxford to 1500*, 3 vols (Oxford, 1957-9)
——, A. B., *A Biographical Register of the University of Cambridge to 1500* (Cambridge, 1963)
Emery, A., *Dartington Hall* (Oxford, 1970)
Erskine, A., 'John de Grandison', in *The Oxford Dictionary of National Biography*, ed. H. C. G. Matthew and B. H. Harrison, 60 vols (Oxford, 2004), xxiii, pp. 266-268

Evans, A. K. B., (A. K. A. Roberts), 'Litigation for Proprietary Rights: the case of the Obstinate Vicar', in *St George's Chapel, Windsor, in the Fourteenth Century*, ed. N. Saul (Woodbridge, 2005), pp. 117–134

Everitt, A., *Continuity and Colonization: The Evolution of Kentish Settlement* (Leicester, 1986)

Faletra, M. A., 'Merlin in Cornwall: The Source and Contexts of John of Cornwall's *Prophetia Merlini*', *Journal of English and German Philology*, 111 (2012), pp. 304–338

Fletcher, A., and D. MacCulloch, *Tudor Rebellions*, 5th Edition (Harlow, 2008)

Fletcher, A. J., 'The Staging of the Middle Cornish Play *Bewnans Ke* ("The Life of St Kea")', *Yearbook of English Studies*, 43 (2013), pp. 165–173

Foot, S., *Athelstan: The First King of England* (New Haven and London, 2011)

Ford, C. J., 'Piracy or Policy: The Crisis in the Channel, 1400–1403. The Alexander Prize', *Transactions of the Royal Historical Society*, 5th Series, 29 (1979), pp. 63–78

———, C. J., 'Some Dubious Beliefs about Medieval Prize Law', in *Courts of Chivalry and Admiralty in Late Medieval Europe*, ed. A. Musson and N. Ramsay (Woodbridge, 2018), pp. 215–236

Fowler, D. C., *The Life and Times of John Trevisa* (Seattle, 1995)

Fox, H. S. A., 'Devon and Cornwall', in *The Agrarian History of England and Wales, III, 1348–1500*, ed. E. Miller (Cambridge, 1991), pp. 152–174, 303–323, 722–743

———, H. S. A., *The Evolution of the Fishing Village: Landscape and Society along the South Devon Coast, 1086–1550* (Oxford, 2001)

———, H. S. A., 'Urban Development', in *Historical Atlas of South-West England*, ed. R. Kain and W. Ravenhill (Exeter, 1999), pp. 400–407

Frame, R., 'Ireland', in *The New Cambridge Medieval History, VI, c. 1300–c. 1415*, ed. M. Jones (Cambridge, 2000), pp. 375–387

———, R., *Ireland and Britain 1170–1450* (London, 1998)

———, R., 'The Wider World', in *A Social History of England, 1200–1500*, ed. R. Horrox and W. M. Ormrod (Cambridge, 2006), pp. 435–453

Friel, I., *The Good Ship: Ships, Shipbuilding and Technology in England 1200–1520* (London, 1995)

———, I., 'How Much did the Sea Matter in Medieval England (c. 1200–c. 1500)?', in *Roles of the Sea in Medieval England*, ed. R. Gorski (Woodbridge, 2012), pp. 167–185

Fryde, E. B., 'Sir Antonio Pessagno', in *The Oxford Dictionary of National Biography*, ed. H. C. G. Matthew and B. H. Harrison, 60 vols (Oxford, 2004), xliii, pp. 859–860

———, N., *The Tyranny and Fall of Edward II, 1321–1326* (Cambridge, 1979)

Fulton, H., 'Introduction: Theories and Debates', in *A Companion to Arthurian Literature*, ed. H. Fulton (Oxford, 2009), pp. 1–11

Galloway, A., 'Writing History in England', in *The Cambridge History of Medieval English Literature*, ed. D. Wallace (Cambridge, 1999), pp. 255–283

Galloway, J. A., 'One Market or Many? London and the Grain Trade of England', in *Trade, Urban Hinterlands and Market Integration, c. 1300–1600*, ed. J. A. Galloway (Loughborough, 2000), pp. 23–42

Gardiner, D. A., 'The History of Belligerent Rights on the High Seas in the Fourteenth Century', *Law Quarterly Review*, 48 (1932), pp. 521–546

Geary, P. J., *The Myth of Nations: The Medieval Origins of Europe* (Oxford, 2002)

Gibson, S. T., 'The Escheatries, 1327–41', *English Historical Review*, 36 (1921), pp. 218–225

Gillespie, J. L., 'Guy Brian', in *The Oxford Dictionary of National Biography*, ed. H. C. G. Matthew and B. H. Harrison, 60 vols (Oxford, 2004), vii, pp. 540–541

Gillingham, J., *The English in the Twelfth Century: Imperialism, National Identity and Political Values* (Woodbridge, 2000)

Given-Wilson, C., *Chronicles: The Writing of History in Medieval England* (London, 2004)

——, C., *The English Nobility in the Later Middle Ages: The Fourteenth-Century Political Community* (London, 1987)

——, C., *Henry IV* (New Haven and London, 2016)

——, C., *The Royal Household and the King's Affinity: Service, Politics and Finance in England, 1360–1413* (New Haven and London, 1986)

Gluckman, M., 'The Peace in the Feud', *Past and Present*, 8 (1955), pp. 1–14

——, M., *Politics, Law and Ritual in Tribal Society* (Oxford, 1971)

Goodman, A., 'John Cary', in *The Oxford Dictionary of National Biography*, ed. H. C. G. Matthew and B. H. Harrison, 60 vols (Oxford, 2004), x, pp. 433–434

——, A., *The Loyal Conspiracy: The Lords Appellant under Richard II* (London, 1971)

Gorski, R., *The Fourteenth-Century Sheriff: English Local Administration in the Late Middle Ages* (Woodbridge, 2003)

——, R., 'A Methodological Holy Grail: Nominal Record Linkage in a Medieval Context', *Medieval Prosopography*, 17 (1996), pp. 145–179

——, R., 'Roles of the Sea: Views from the Shore', in *Roles of the Sea in Medieval England*, ed. R. Gorski (Woodbridge, 2012), pp. 1–23

Gransden, A., *Historical Writing in England*, 2 vols (London, 1996)

Grant, A., 'Fourteenth-Century Scotland', in *The New Cambridge Medieval History, VI, c. 1300–c. 1415*, ed. M. Jones (Cambridge, 2000), pp. 345–374

Gras, N. S. B., *The Early English Customs Service* (Cambridge, MA, 1918)

Green, D., *The Black Prince* (Stroud, 2001)

——, D., 'Edward the Black Prince and East Anglia: An Unlikely Association', *Fourteenth Century England, III*, ed. W. M. Ormrod (Woodbridge, 2004), pp. 83–98

——, D., *Edward the Black Prince: Power in Medieval Europe* (Harlow, 2007)

——, D., 'Masculinity and Medicine: Thomas Walsingham and the Death of the Black Prince', *Journal of Medieval History*, 35 (2009), pp. 34–51

——, D., 'The Military Personnel of Edward the Black Prince', *Medieval Prosopography*, 21 (2000), pp. 133–152

——, D., 'National Identity and the Hundred Years War', *Fourteenth Century England, VI*, ed. C. Given-Wilson (Woodbridge, 2010), pp. 115–130

——, D., 'Politics and Service with Edward the Black Prince', in *The Age of Edward III*, ed. J. S. Bothwell (York, 2001), pp. 53–68

Greengrass, M., *Christendom Destroyed: Europe 1517–1648* (St Ives, 2014)

Gribit, N. A., *Henry of Lancaster's Expedition to Aquitaine, 1345–46: Military Service and Professionalism in the Hundred Years' War* (Woodbridge, 2016)

Griffiths, R. A., 'The English Realm and Dominions and the King's Subjects in the Later Middle Ages', in *Aspects of Late Medieval Government and Society: Essays Presented to J. R. Lander*, ed. J. G. Rowe (London, 1986), pp. 83–105

Grundy, G. B., 'Ancient Highways of Cornwall', *Archaeological Journal*, 98 (1941), pp. 165–180

—, G. B., 'Ancient Highways of Devon', *Archaeological Journal*, 98 (1941), pp. 131–164

Guard, T., *Chivalry, Kingship and Crusade: The English Experience in the Fourteenth Century* (Woodbridge, 2013)

Halliday, F. E., *A History of Cornwall* (Letchworth, 1959)

Hamilton, J. S., *Piers Gaveston, Earl of Cornwall 1307–1312: Politics and Patronage in the Reign of Edward II* (London and Detroit, 1988)

Hanham, A., *The Celys and Their World: An English Merchant Family in the Fifteenth Century* (Cambridge, 1985)

Hanks, P., R. Coates, P. McClure et al. (eds) *The Oxford Dictionary of Family Names in Britain and Ireland*, 4 vols (Oxford, 2016)

Harding, A., 'The Origin and Early History of the Keepers of the Peace', *Transactions of the Royal Historical Society*, 5th series, 10 (1960), pp. 85–109

Harriss, G. L., *King, Parliament, and Public Finance in Medieval England to 1369* (Oxford, 1975)

—, G. L., *Shaping the Nation: England 1360–1461* (Oxford, 2005)

Harty, K. J., 'Malory and the Cowardly Cornish Knights – "'The strangest races [that] dwell next door"', *Études Anglaises*, 66 (2013), pp. 379–387

Harvey, D. C., 'Territoriality, Parochial Development and the Place of 'Community' in Later Medieval Cornwall', *Journal of Historical Geography*, 29 (2003), pp. 151–165

Harvey, M., 'Ecclesia Anglicana, cui Ecclesiastes noster Christus vos prefecit: the Power of the Crown in the English Church during the Great Schism', in *Religion and National Identity*, ed. S. Mews, Studies in Church History, 18 (Oxford, 1982), pp. 229–241

Hatcher, J., 'A Diversified Economy: Later Medieval Cornwall', *Economic History Review*, 22 (1969), pp. 208–227

—, J., *English Tin Production and Trade before 1550* (Oxford, 1973)

—, J., 'Non-Manorialism in Medieval Cornwall', *Agricultural History Review*, 18 (1970), pp. 1–16

—, J., *Plague, Population and the English Economy, 1348–1530* (London, 1977)

—, J., *Rural Economy and Society in the Duchy of Cornwall, 1300–1500* (Cambridge, 1970)

—, J., and M. Bailey, *Modelling the Middle Ages: The History and Theory of England's Economic Development* (Oxford, 2001)

—, J., and T. C. Barker, *A History of British Pewter* (London, 1974)

Heath, P., *Church and Realm, 1272–1461: Conflict and Collaboration in an Age of Crisis* (London, 1988)

Heebøll-Holm, T. K., 'Law, Order and Plunder at Sea: a Comparison of England and France in the Fourteenth Century', *Continuity and Change*, 32 (2017), pp. 37–58

—, T. K., 'The Origins and Jurisdiction of the English Court of Admiralty in the Fourteenth Century', in *Courts of Chivalry and Admiralty in Late Medieval Europe*, ed. A. Musson and N. Ramsay (Woodbridge, 2018), pp. 149–170

—, T. K., *Ports, Piracy and Maritime War: Piracy in the English Channel and the Atlantic, c. 1280–c. 1330* (Leiden, 2013)

Helmholz, R. H., *The Oxford History of Laws: I, The Canon Law and Ecclesiastical Jurisdiction from 597 to the 1640s* (Oxford, 2004)

Henderson, C., *The Cornish Church Guide and Parochial History of Cornwall* (Truro, 1925)
——, C., 'The Ecclesiastical History of the Four Western Hundreds of Cornwall, in four parts', *JRIC* (1955), 1–104; (1956), 105–210; (1958) 211–382; (1960), 383–497
——, C., *Essays in Cornish History*, ed. A. L. Rowse and M. I. Henderson (Oxford, 1935)
——, C., and H. Coates, *Old Cornish Bridges and Streams* (Truro, 1928)
Heng, G., *The Invention of Race in the European Middle Ages* (Cambridge, 2018)
Herring, P., 'Multiple Identities in Cornwall', in *Recent Archaeological Work in South-Western Britain: Papers in Honour of Henrietta Quinnell*, ed. S. Pearce (Oxford, 2011), pp. 159–167
——, P., et al., 'Later Medieval Cornwall', *Cornish Archaeology*, 50 (2011), pp. 287–314
Hewitt, H., *The Black Prince's Expedition of 1355–1357* (Manchester, 1958)
——, H., *The Organization of War under Edward III, 1338–62* (Manchester, 1966)
Hicks, M., (ed.), *English Inland Trade 1430–1540: Southampton and its Region* (Oxford, 2015)
——, M., (ed.), *The Fifteenth-Century Inquisitions Post Mortem: A Companion* (Woodbridge, 2012)
Higham, R. A., 'Castles, Fortified Houses and Fortified Towns in the Middle Ages', in *Historical Atlas of South-West England*, ed. R. Kain and W. Ravenhill (Exeter, 1999), pp. 136–143
Hill, M. C., *The King's Messengers, 1199–1377: A List of all known Messengers, Mounted and Unmounted, who Served John, Henry III and the First Three Edwards* (Stroud, 1994)
Hilton, R. H., *A Medieval Society: The West Midlands at the End of the Thirteenth Century* (London, 1966)
Holmes, G., *The Estates of the Higher Nobility in Fourteenth-Century England* (Cambridge, 1957)
——, G., *The Good Parliament* (Oxford, 1975)
Holt, J. C., *The Northerners* (Oxford, 1961)
Homer, R. F., 'Tin, Lead and Pewter', in *English Medieval Industries: Craftsmen, Techniques, Products*, ed. J. Blair and N. Ramsay (London, 1991), pp. 57–80
Horden, P., 'Afterword', *Postmedieval: A Journal of Medieval Cultural Studies*, 7 (2016), pp. 565–571
——, P., 'Introduction: Towards a History of Medieval Mobility', in *Freedom of Movement in the Middle Ages: Proceedings of the 2003 Harlaxton Symposium*, ed. P. Horden (Donington, 2007), pp. xvii–xxxiv
——, P., 'Situations Both Alike? Connectivity, the Mediterranean, the Sahara', in *Saharan Frontiers: Space and Mobility in Northwest Africa*, ed. J. McDougall and J. Scheele (Bloomington and Indianapolis, 2012), pp. 25–38
——, P., and N. Purcell, *The Corrupting Sea: A Study of Mediterranean History* (Oxford, 2000)
Hughes, M., 'The Fourteenth-Century French Raids on Hampshire and the Isle of White', in *Arms, Armies and Fortifications in the Hundred Years War*, ed. A. Curry and M. Hughes (Woodbridge, 1994), pp. 121–143
Hunnisett, R. F., *The Medieval Coroner* (Cambridge, 1961)
Hunt, R., *Popular Romances of the West of England* (London, 1903)

Hyams, P. R., 'What did Edwardian Villagers understand by "Law"?', in *Medieval Society and the Manor Court*, ed. Z. Razzi and R. Smith (Oxford, 1996), pp. 69–102

Ingham, P. C., *Sovereign Fantasies: Arthurian Romance and the Making of Britain* (Philadelphia, 2001)

Ingpen, A. R., *An Ancient Family: A Genealogical Study showing the Saxon Origin of the Family of Ingpen* (London, 1916)

Ivall, D. E., *Cornish Heraldry and Symbolism* (Perranwell, 1987)

James, M. K., *Studies in the Medieval Wine Trade* (Oxford, 1971)

Jefferson, J. A., and A. Putter, 'Introduction', in *Multilingualism in Medieval Britain (c. 1066–1520): Sources and Analysis*, ed. J. A. Jefferson and A. Putter (Turnhout, 2013), pp. xi–xxiv

Jewell, H. M., *English Administration in the Middle Ages* (Newton Abbot, 1972)

——, H. M., *The North–South Divide: The Origins of Northern Consciousness in England* (Manchester, 1994)

Johnstone, H., *Edward of Carnarvon, 1284–1307* (Manchester, 1946)

Jones, M., *The Black Prince* (London, 2017)

Jones, M., *The Creation of Brittany: A Late Medieval State* (London, 1988)

Jordan, W. C., *The Great Famine: Northern Europe in the Early Fourteenth Century* (Princeton, NJ, 1996)

Jurkowski, M., C. L. Smith and D. Crook, *Lay Taxes in England and Wales, 1188–1688* (Richmond, 1998)

Kaeuper, R. W., *War, Justice and Public Order: England and France in the Later Middle Ages* (Oxford, 1988)

Kaminsky, H., 'The Great Schism', in *The New Cambridge Medieval History, VI, c. 1300–c. 1415*, ed. M. Jones (Cambridge, 2000), pp. 674–696

Keene, D., 'Changes in London's Economic Hinterland as Indicated by Debt Cases in the Court of Common Pleas', in *Trade, Urban Hinterlands and Market Integration, c. 1300–1600*, ed. J. A. Galloway (Loughborough, 2000), pp. 54–81

Kent, A. M., 'Mending the Gap in the Medieval, Modern and Post-Modern in New Cornish Studies: "Celtic" Materialism and the Potential of Presentism', *Cornish Studies*, New Series 20 (2012), pp. 13–31

Kim, K., *Aliens in Medieval Law: The Origins of Modern Citizenship* (Cambridge, 2000)

Kingsford, C. L., *Prejudice and Promise in XVth Century England* (Oxford, 1925)

Kleineke, H., 'Why the West Was Wild: Law and Order in Fifteenth-Century Cornwall and Devon', *The Fifteenth Century: III, Authority and Subversion*, ed. L. Clark (Woodbridge, 2003), pp. 75–93

——, H., 'The Widening Gap: the Practice of Parliamentary Borough Elections in Devon and Cornwall in the Fifteenth Century', *Parliamentary History*, 23 (2004), pp. 121–135

Kowaleski, M., "Alien' Encounters in the Maritime World of Medieval England', *Medieval Encounters*, 13 (2007), pp. 96–121

——, M., 'Coastal Communities in Medieval Cornwall', in *The Maritime History of Cornwall*, ed. H. Doe, A. Kennerley and P. Payton (Exeter and London, 2014), pp. 43–59

——, M., 'The Expansion of South-Western Fisheries in Late Medieval England', *Economic History Review*, 53 (2000), pp. 429–454

―――, M., *Local Markets and Regional Trade in Medieval Exeter* (Cambridge, 1995)
―――, M., 'The Shipman as Entrepreneur in Medieval England', in *Commercial Activity, Markets and Entrepreneurs in the Middle Ages: Essays in Honour of Richard Britnell*, ed. B. Dodds and C. Liddy (Woodbridge, 2011), pp. 165–182
―――, M., 'Warfare, Shipping and Crown Patronage: the Impact of the Hundred Years War on the Port Towns of Medieval England', in *Money, Markets and Trade in Late Medieval Europe: Essays in Honour of John H. A. Munro*, ed. L. Armstrong, I. Elbl and M. Elbl (Leiden, 2007), pp. 233–254
Kurath, H., et al. (eds), *Middle English Dictionary* (Ann Arbor, MI, 1956–2001)
Labarge, M. W., *Gascony: England's First Colony, 1204–1453* (London, 1980)
Lack, W., H. M. Stuchfield and P. Whittemore, *The Monumental Brasses of Cornwall* (London, 1997)
―――, W., H. M. Stuchfield and P. Whittemore, *The Monumental Brasses of Herefordshire* (Colchester, 2008)
Lambert, B., and W. M. Ormrod, 'Friendly Foreigners: International Warfare, Resident Aliens and the Early History of Denization in England, c. 1250–c. 1400', *English Historical Review*, 130 (2015), pp. 1–24
Lambert, C. L., *Shipping the Medieval Military: English Maritime Logistics in the Fourteenth Century* (Woodbridge, 2011)
Latham, R. E., et al. (eds), *Dictionary of Medieval Latin from British Sources*, 4 vols (London and Oxford, 1975–2013)
Lavezzo, K., *Angels on the Edge of the World: Geography, Literature and English Community, 1000–1534* (London, 2006)
Leland, J., 'Robert Tresilian', in *The Oxford Dictionary of National Biography*, ed. H. C. G. Matthew and B. H. Harrison, 60 vols (Oxford, 2004), lv, pp. 317–319
Lepine, D., '"Loose Canons": The Mobility of the Higher Clergy in the Later Middle Ages', in *Freedom of Movement in the Middle Ages: Proceedings of the 2003 Harlaxton Symposium*, ed. P. Horden (Donington, 2007), pp 104–122
―――, D., 'The Origins and Careers of the Canons of Exeter Cathedral, 1300–1455', in *Religious Belief and Ecclesiastical Careers in Late Medieval England*, ed. C. Harper-Bill (Woodbridge, 1991), pp. 87–120
Lewis, E. A., 'A Contribution to the Commercial History of Medieval Wales', *Y Cymmrodor*, 24 (London, 1913), pp. 86–188
Lewis, G. R., *The Stannaries: A Study of the Medieval Tin Miners of Devon and Cornwall* (Truro, 1908)
Lewis, P. S., 'The Failure of the French Medieval Estates', *Past and Present*, 23 (1962), pp. 3–24
―――, P. S., *Later Medieval France: The Polity* (London, 1968)
Liddy, C., *The Bishopric of Durham in the Late Middle Ages: Lordship, Community and the Cult of St Cuthbert* (Woodbridge, 2008)
Lunt, W. E., *Financial Relations of the Papacy with England to 1327* (Cambridge, MA, 1939)
―――, W. E., *Financial Relations of the Papacy with England, 1327–1534* (Cambridge, MA, 1962)
Lysons, D. and S., *Magna Britannia: III, Cornwall* (London, 1814)
MacCulloch, D., *Reformation: Europe's House Divided 1490–1700* (London, 2003)

Maclean, J., *The Parochial and Family History of the Deanery of Trigg Minor*, 3 vols (London, 1873–9)
Maddicott, J. R., 'The County Community and the Making of Public Opinion in Fourteenth-Century England', *Transactions of the Royal Historical Society*, 5th series, 28 (1978), pp. 27–43
——, J. R., *The English Peasantry and the Demands of the Crown, 1294–1341* (Oxford, 1975)
——, J. R., *Founders and Fellowship: The Early History of Exeter College Oxford, 1314–1592* (Oxford, 2014)
——, J. R., *The Origins of the English Parliament, 942–1327* (Oxford, 2010)
——, J. R., *Thomas of Lancaster, 1307–1322: A Study in the Reign of Edward II* (Oxford, 1970)
Marsden, R. G., 'The Vice-Admirals of the Coast', *English Historical Review*, 22 (1907), pp. 468–477
Marshall, J. D., *The Tyranny of the Discrete: A Discussion of the Problems of Local History in England* (Aldershot, 1997)
Mattingly, J., 'The Dating of Bench-Ends in Cornish Churches', *Journal of the Royal Institution of Cornwall* (1991), pp. 58–72
——, J., 'The Medieval Parish Guilds of Cornwall', *Journal of the Royal Institution of Cornwall* (1989), pp. 290–329
——, J., 'One Game or Two? Wrestling and Hurling in Cornwall in 1700', *Journal of the Royal Institution of Cornwall* (2012), pp. 57–74
——, J., 'Stories in the Glass: Reconstructing the St Neot Pre-Reformation Glazing Scheme', *Journal of the Royal Institution of Cornwall* (2000), pp. 9–55
Maurier, D. du, *Vanishing Cornwall* (London, 1967)
McClure, P., 'Patterns of Migration in the Late Middle Ages: The Evidence of English Place-Name Surnames', *Economic History Review*, 32 (1979), pp. 167–182
McFarlane, K. B., *England in the Fifteenth Century: Collected Essays*, with an Introduction by G. L. Harriss (London, 1981)
——, K. B., *The Nobility of Later Medieval England* (Oxford, 1973)
McHardy, A. K., 'The Alien Priories and the Expulsion of Aliens from England in 1378', *Church Society and Politics, Studies in Church History, 12*, ed. D. Baker (Oxford, 1975), pp. 133–141
——, A. K., 'The Effects of War on the Church: the Case of the Alien Priories in the Fourteenth Century', in *England and her Neighbours, 1066–1453: Essays in Honour of Pierre Chaplais*, ed. M. Jones and M. Vale (London, 1989), pp. 277–295
——, A. K., 'Liturgy and Propaganda in the Diocese of Lincoln during the Hundred Years' War', in *Religion and National Identity*, ed. S. Mews, *Studies in Church History*, 18 (Oxford, 1982), pp. 215–227
——, A. K., 'The Representation of the English Lower Clergy in Parliament during the Fourteenth Century', in *Sanctity and Secularity: The Church and the World*, ed. D. Baker, *Studies in Church History*, 10 (Oxford, 1973), pp. 97–107
McIntosh, A., et al. (eds), *A Linguistic Atlas of Late Mediaeval English*, 4 vols (Aberdeen, 1986)
McKisack, M., *The Parliamentary Representation of the English Boroughs during the Middle Ages* (Oxford, 1932)

Michaud, C., 'The Kingdoms of Central Europe in the Fourteenth Century', in *The New Cambridge Medieval History, VI, c. 1300–c. 1415*, ed. M. Jones (Cambridge, 2000), pp. 735–763

Millea, N., *The Gough Map: The Earliest Road Map of Britain?* (Oxford, 2007)

Mills, M. H., 'The Collectors of Customs', in *The English Government at Work: II, Fiscal Administration*, ed. W. A. Morris and J. R. Strayer (Cambridge, MA, 1947), pp. 168–200

Mooney, L. R., 'John Somer', in *The Oxford Dictionary of National Biography*, ed. H. C. G. Matthew and B. H. Harrison, 60 vols (Oxford, 2004), li, p. 559

Moore, T. K., 'The Cost-Benefit Analysis of a Fourteenth-Century Naval Campaign: Margate/Cadzand, 1387', in *Roles of the Sea in Medieval England*, ed. R. Gorski (Woodbridge, 2012), pp. 103–124

Morgan, P., *War and Society in Medieval Cheshire, 1277–1403* (Manchester, 1987)

Morris, W. A., *The Medieval English Sheriff to 1300* (Manchester, 1927)

Murdoch, B. O., *Cornish Literature* (Cambridge, 1993)

——, B. O., 'The Cornish Medieval Drama', in *The Cambridge Companion to Medieval English Theatre*, ed. R. Beadle (Cambridge, 1994), pp. 211–239

Musson, A., 'Arbitration and the Legal Profession in Late Medieval England', in *Law and Legal Process: Substantive Law and Procedure in English Legal History*, ed. M. Dyson and D. Ibbetson (Cambridge, 2013), pp. 56–76

——, A., 'Centre and Locality: Perceptions of the Assize Justices in Late Medieval England', in *Law, Governance and Justice: New Views on Medieval Constitutionalism*, ed. R. W. Kaeuper (Leiden, 2013), pp. 211–242

——, A., 'Court Venues and the Politics of Justice', *Fourteenth Century England, V*, ed. N. Saul (Woodbridge, 2008), pp. 161–177

——, A., 'Legal Culture: Medieval Lawyers' Aspirations and Pretensions', *Fourteenth Century England, III*, ed. W. M. Ormrod (Woodbridge, 2004), pp. 16–30

——, A., *Medieval Law in Context: The Growth of Legal Consciousness from Magna Carta to the Peasants' Revolt* (Manchester, 2001)

——, A., *Public Order and Law Enforcement: The Local Administration of Criminal Justice, 1294–1350* (Woodbridge, 1996)

——, A., 'Queenship, Lordship and Petitioning in Late Medieval England', in *Medieval Petitions: Grace and Grievance*, ed. W. M. Ormrod, G. Dodd and A. Musson (York, 2009), pp. 156–172

——, A., and W. M. Ormrod, *The Evolution of English Justice: Law, Politics and Society in the Fourteenth Century* (Basingstoke, 1999)

Nance, R. M., 'Cornish Family Mottoes', *Old Cornwall*, 1, i (1925), pp. 18–21

——, R. M., 'Cornish Family Mottoes', *Old Cornwall*, 1, iii (1926), p. 29

——, R. M., 'Cornish Family Mottoes', *Old Cornwall*, 1, iv (1926), pp. 26–27

——, R. M., 'Cornish Family Mottoes', *Old Cornwall*, 1, vii (1928), pp. 27–28

Neve, J. le, 'Archdeacons in Cornwall', in *Fasti Ecclesiae Anglicanae, 1300–1541*, compl. J. M. Horn, 12 vols (London, 1962–7), ix, pp. 15–17

Neville, C. J., 'The Keeping of the Peace in the Northern Marches in the Later Middle Ages', *English Historical Review*, 109 (1994), pp. 1–25

Nightingale, P., 'The Growth of London in the Medieval English Economy', in *Progress and Problems in Medieval England*, ed. R. H. Britnell and J. Hatcher (Cambridge, 1996), pp. 89–106

——, P., 'Knights and Merchants: Trade, Politics and the Gentry in Late Medieval England', *Past and Present*, 169 (2000), pp. 36–62

——, P., 'Monetary Contraction and Mercantile Credit in Later Medieval England', *Economic History Review*, 43 (1990), pp. 560–575

O'Neil, T., *Merchants and Mariners in Medieval Ireland* (Dublin, 1987)

Oppenheim, M., 'Maritime History', in *Victoria County History of the County of Cornwall, I*, ed. W. Page (London, 1906), pp. 475–511

Orme, N., 'The Cornish at Oxford, 1180–1540', *Journal of the Royal Institution of Cornwall* (2010), pp. 43–82

——, N., *Education in the West of England, 1066–1548* (Exeter, 1976)

——, N., 'A Fifteenth-Century Prayer-Book from Cornwall: MS NLW 22253A', *Journal of the Royal Institution of Cornwall* (1999), pp. 69–73

——, N., *Medieval Pilgrimage: With a survey of Cornwall, Devon, Dorset, Somerset and Bristol* (Exeter, 2018)

——, N., *The Minor Clergy of Exeter Cathedral: Biographies, 1250–1548*, Devon and Cornwall Record Society, New Series 54 (Exeter, 2013)

——, N., 'Representation and Rebellion in the Late Middle Ages', in *Historical Atlas of South-West England*, ed. R. Kain and W. Ravenhill (Exeter, 1999), pp. 144–146

——, N., *The Saints of Cornwall* (Oxford, 2000)

——, N., *Victoria County History of Cornwall: II, Religious History to 1560* (London, 2010)

——, N., and O. J. Padel, 'Cornwall and the Third Crusade', *Journal of the Royal Institute of Cornwall* (2005), pp. 71–77

Ormrod, W. M., '"Common Profit" and "The Profit of the King and Kingdom": Parliament and the Development of Political Language in England, 1250–1450', *Viator*, 46 (2015), pp. 219–252

——, W. M., 'The Crown and the English Economy, 1290–1348', in *Before the Black Death: Studies in the 'Crisis' of the Early Fourteenth Century*, ed. B. M. S. Campbell (Manchester, 1991), pp. 149–183

——, W. M., *Edward III* (New Haven and London, 2011)

——, W. M., 'England in the Middle Ages', in *The Rise of the Fiscal State in Europe, c. 1200–1815*, ed. R. Bonney (Oxford, 1999), pp. 19–52

——, W. M., 'Introduction: Medieval Petitions in Context', in *Medieval Petitions: Grace and Grievance*, ed. W. M. Ormrod, G. Dodd and A. Musson (York, 2009), pp. 1–11

——, W. M., 'Murmur, Clamour and Noise: Voicing Complaint and Remedy in Petitions to the English Crown, c. 1300–c. 1460', in *Medieval Petitions: Grace and Grievance*, ed. W. M. Ormrod, G. Dodd and A. Musson (York, 2009), pp. 135–155

——, W. M., *Political Life in Medieval England, 1300–1450* (Basingstoke, 1995)

——, W. M., *The Reign of Edward III: Crown and Political Society in England, 1327–1377* (London, 1990)

——, W. M., 'The Use of English: Language, Law and Political Culture in Fourteenth-Century England', *Speculum*, 78 (2003), pp. 750–787

Padel, O. J., 'Ancient and Medieval Administrative Divisions of Cornwall', *Proceedings of the Dorset Natural History and Archaeological Society*, 131 (2010), pp. 211–214
——, O. J., 'The Arundells of Lanherne and their Archive', *Journal of the Cornwall Association of Local Historians*, 29 (1995), pp. 8–23
——, O. J., 'Christianity in Medieval Cornwall: Celtic Aspects', in N. Orme, *Victoria County History of Cornwall: II, Religious History to 1560* (Woodbridge, 2010), pp. 110–125
——, O. J., 'The Cornish Background of the Tristan Stories', *Cambridge Medieval Celtic Studies*, 1 (1981), pp. 53–81
——, O. J., 'Cornu-Latin treuga "griefs"', *Devon and Cornwall Notes and Queries*, 40 (2007–11), pp. 118–121
——, O. J., 'Evidence for Oral Tales in Medieval Cornwall', *Studia Celtica*, 40 (2006), pp. 127–153
——, O. J., 'Geoffrey of Monmouth and Cornwall', *Cambridge Medieval Celtic Studies*, 8 (1984), pp. 1–28
——, O. J., 'Geoffrey of Monmouth and the Development of the Merlin Legend', *Cambrian Medieval Celtic Studies*, 51 (2006), pp. 37–65
——, O. J., 'The Nature of Arthur', *Cambrian Medieval Celtic Studies*, 27 (1994), pp. 1–31
——, O. J., *A Popular Dictionary of Cornish Place-Names* (Penzance, 1988)
——, O. J., 'Slavery in Saxon Cornwall: the Bodmin Manumissions', *Kathleen Hughes Memorial Lectures*, 7 (Cambridge, 2009)
——, O. J., 'Where was Middle Cornish Spoken?', *Cambrian Medieval Celtic Studies*, 74 (2017), pp. 1–31
Page, M., 'Cornwall, Earl Richard and the Barons' War', *English Historical Review*, 115 (2000), pp. 21–38
——, M., 'The Ownership of Advowsons in Thirteenth-Century Cornwall', *Devon and Cornwall Notes and Queries*, 37 (1992–6), pp. 336–341
Page, W., (ed.), *Victoria County History of Cornwall, I* (London, 1906)
——, W., (ed.), *Victoria County History of Worcestershire*, 4 vols (London, 1901–26)
Palmer, J., *England, France and Christendom, 1377–99* (London, 1972)
Palmer, R., *The County Courts of Medieval England, 1150–1350* (Princeton, NJ, 1982)
Pantin, W. A., *The English Church in the Fourteenth Century* (Cambridge, 1955)
Partington, R., 'Edward III's Enforcers: The King's Sergeants-at-Arms in the Localities', in *The Age of Edward III*, ed. J. S. Bothwell (York, 2001), pp. 89–106
Payling, S. J., 'John Cornewall', in *The Oxford Dictionary of National Biography*, ed. H. C. G. Matthew and B. H. Harrison, 60 vols (Oxford, 2004), xiii, pp. 446–447
——, S. J., *Political Society in Lancastrian England: The Greater Gentry of Nottinghamshire* (Oxford, 1991)
——, S. J., 'Social Mobility, Demographic Change, and Landed Society in Late Medieval England', *Economic History Review*, 45 (1992), pp. 51–73
Payton, P., '"a... concealed envy against the English": a Note on the Aftermath of the 1497 Rebellion in Cornwall', *Cornish Studies*, New Series 1 (1993), pp. 4–13
——, P., *Cornwall* (Fowey, 1996)
——, P., *The Making of Modern Cornwall: Historical Experience and the Persistence of 'Difference'* (Redruth, 1992)
Pearce, C., *Cornish Wrecking 1700–1860: Reality and Popular Myth* (Woodbridge, 2010)

Pearce, S. M., 'The Cornish Elements in the Arthurian Tradition', *Folklore*, 85 (1974), pp. 145–163
Pearsall, D., 'The Idea of Englishness in the Fifteenth Century', in *Nation, Court and Culture: New Essays on Fifteenth-Century English Poetry*, ed. H. Cooney (Scarborough, 2001), pp. 15–27
Pennington, R. R., *Stannary Law: A History of the Mining Law of Cornwall and Devon* (Newton Abbot, 1973)
Pépin, G., 'Towards a New Assessment of the Black Prince's Principality of Aquitaine: a Study of the Last Years (1369–1372)', *Nottingham Medieval Studies*, 50 (2006), pp. 59–114
Peter, R., and O. B. Peter, *Histories of Launceston and Dunheved* (Plymouth, 1885)
Peters, C., *The Archaeology of Cornwall* (Fowey, 2005)
Phillips, J. R. S., *Aymer de Valence, Earl of Pembroke 1307–1324: Baronial Politics in the Reign of Edward II* (Oxford, 1972)
——, J. R. S., *Edward II* (New Haven and London, 2010)
Picken, W. M. M., *A Medieval Cornish Miscellany*, ed. O. J. Padel (Chichester, 2000)
Piron, S., 'Monnaie et Majesté Royale dans le France DU 14ᵉ Siècle', *Annales Historie, Sciences Sociales*, 51 (1996), pp. 325–354
Pitcaithly, M., 'Piracy and Anglo-Hanseatic Relations, 1385–1420', in *Roles of the Sea in Medieval England*, ed. R. Gorski (Woodbridge, 2012), pp. 125–145
Platt, C., *Medieval Southampton: the Port and Trading Community, 1000–1600* (London, 1973)
Plucknett, T. F. T., *Statutes and their Interpretation in the first half of the Fourteenth Century* (Cambridge, 1922)
Pollard, A. F., rev. V. Davis, 'Michael Tregury', in *The Oxford Dictionary of National Biography*, ed. H. C. G. Matthew and B. H. Harrison, 60 vols (Oxford, 2004), lv, pp. 269–270
Pollard, A. J., *North-Eastern England during the Wars of the Roses: Lay Society, War and Politics, 1450–1550* (Oxford, 1990)
Polsue, J., *A Complete Parochial History of the County of Cornwall...*, 4 vol in 2 (1867–72)
Pool, P. A. S., 'The Penheleg Manuscript', *Journal of the Royal Institution of Cornwall* (1959), pp. 163–228
Post, J. B., 'The Peace Commissions of 1382', *English Historical Review*, 41 (1976), pp. 98–101
Postan, M. M., *Medieval Trade and Finance* (Cambridge, 1973)
Pounds, N. G., 'The Duchy Palace at Lostwithiel, Cornwall', *Archaeological Journal*, 136 (1979), pp. 203–217
——, N. G., 'The Ports of Cornwall in the Middle Ages', *Devon and Cornwall Notes and Queries*, 23 (1947), pp. 65–73
——, N. G., 'Taxation and Wealth in Late Medieval Cornwall', *Journal of the Royal Institution of Cornwall* (1971), pp. 154–167
Powell, E., 'The Administration of Criminal Justice in Late-Medieval England: Peace Sessions and Assizes', in *The Political Context of Law*, ed. R. Eales and D. Sullivan (London, 1987), pp. 49–59
Powicke, M., *Military Obligation in Medieval England: A Study in Liberty and Duty* (Oxford, 1962)

Preston-Jones, A., and A. Langdon, 'St Buryan Crosses', *Cornish Archaeology*, 36 (1997), pp. 107–128
——, A., and P. Rose, 'Medieval Cornwall', *Cornish Archaeology*, 25 (1986), pp. 135–185
——, A., and P. Rose, 'Week St Mary: Town and Castle', *Cornish Archaeology*, 31 (1992), pp. 143–153
Prestwich, M., *Edward I* (London, 1988)
——, M., 'The Ordinances of 1311 and the Politics of the Early Fourteenth Century', in *Politics and Crisis in Fourteenth-Century England*, ed. J. Taylor and W. Childs (Gloucester, 1990), pp. 1–18
——, M., *The Three Edwards: War and State in England, 1272–1377*, 2nd Edition (London, 2003)
Pryce, H., 'British or Welsh? National Identity in Twelfth-Century Wales', *English Historical Review*, 116 (2001), pp. 775–801
Pugh, T. B., 'The Magnates, Knights and Gentry', in *Fifteenth Century England, 1399–1509: Studies in Politics and Society*, ed. S. B. Chrimes, C. D. Ross and R. A. Griffiths (Manchester, 1972), pp. 86–128
Putnam, B. H., *The Place in Legal History of Sir William Shareshull, Chief Justice of the King's Bench, 1350–1361: A Study of Judicial and Administrative Methods in the Reign of Edward III* (Cambridge, 1950)
——, B. H., 'The Transformation of the Keepers of the Peace into the Justices of the Peace', *Transactions of the Royal Historical Society*, 4th series, 12 (1929), pp. 19–48
Ramsay, N., 'What was the Legal Profession?', in *Profit, Piety and the Professions in Later Medieval England*, ed. M. Hicks (Gloucester, 1990), pp. 62–71
Rawcliffe, C., 'The Great Lord as Peacekeeper: Arbitration by English Noblemen and their Councils in the Later Middle Ages', in *Law and Social Change in British History*, ed. J. A. Guy and H. G. Beale (London, 1984), pp. 34–54
Reynolds, S., *Kingdoms and Communities in Western Europe, 900–1300*, 2nd Edition (Oxford, 1997)
——, S., 'Secular Power and Authority in the Middle Ages', in *Power and Identity in the Middle Ages: Essays in Memory of Rees Davies*, ed. H. Pryce and J. Watts (Oxford, 2007), pp. 11–22
Rhydderch, A., 'John Stanbury', in *The Oxford Dictionary of National Biography*, ed. H. C. G. Matthew and B. H. Harrison, 60 vols (Oxford, 2004), lii, pp. 91–92
Richmond, C. F., 'The War at Sea', in *The Hundred Years' War*, ed. K. Fowler (London, 1971), pp. 96–121
Riddy, F. (ed.), *Regionalism in Late Medieval Manuscripts and Texts* (Cambridge, 1991)
Rigg, A. G., *A History of Anglo-Latin Literature 1066–1422* (Cambridge, 1992)
Rippon, S., P. Claughton and C. Smart, *Mining in a Medieval Landscape: The Royal Silver Mines of the Tamar Valley* (Exeter, 2009)
Rodger, N. A. M., 'The Law and Language of Private Naval Warfare', *The Mariner's Mirror*, 100 (2014), pp. 5–16
——, N. A. M., *The Safeguard of the Sea: A Naval History of Great Britain: I, 660–1649* (London, 1997)
Rose, S., *Medieval Naval Warfare, 1000–1500* (London and New York, 2002)
Rose-Troup, F., *The Western Rebellion of 1549* (London, 1913)

Roskell, J. S., L. Clark and C. Rawcliffe (eds), *The History of Parliament: The House of Commons 1386-1421*, 4 vols (Stroud, 1993)

Rothwell, W., et al. (eds), *Anglo-Norman Dictionary* (London, 1992)

Rowe, W. C. H., and E. R. Nute (eds), *Cornwall: One of the Four Nations of Britain* (Cornwall, 1996, revised 2012)

Rowse, A. L., *The Little Land of Cornwall* (Guernsey, 1986)

——, A. L., *Tudor Cornwall: Portrait of a Society* (London, 1941)

Royle, E., 'Introduction: Regions and Identities', in *Issues of Regional Identity, in Honour of John Marshall* (Manchester, 1998), pp. 1–13

Rubin, M., 'Identities', in *A Social History of England, 1200–1500*, ed. R. Horrox and W. M. Ormrod (Cambridge, 2006), pp. 383–412

——, M., 'Small Groups: Identity and Solidarity in the Late Middle Ages', in *Enterprise and Individuals in Fifteenth-Century England*, ed. J. Kermode (Stroud, 1991), pp. 132–150

Ruddick, A., *English Identity and Political Culture in the Fourteenth Century* (Cambridge, 2013)

——, A., 'The English "Nation" and the Plantagenet "Empire" at the Council of Constance', in *The Plantagenet Empire, 1259–1453: Proceedings of the 2014 Harlaxton Symposium*, ed. P. Crooks, D. Green and W. M. Ormrod (Donington, 2016), pp. 109–127

——, A., 'Ethnic Identity and Political Language in the King of England's Domains: A Fourteenth-Century Perspective', *The Fifteenth Century*, VI, ed. L. Clark (Woodbridge, 2006)

Russell, J. C., *British Population History* (Albuquerque, 1948)

Russell, P. E., *The English Intervention in Spain and Portugal in the time of King Edward III and Richard II* (Oxford, 1955)

Saul, A., 'Great Yarmouth and the Hundred Years War in the Fourteenth Century', *Bulletin of the Institute of Historical Research*, 52 (1979), pp. 105–115

Saul, N., 'The Commons and the Abolition of Badges', *Parliamentary History*, 9 (1990), pp. 302–315

——, N., 'Conflict and Consensus in English Local Society', in *Politics and Crisis in Fourteenth-Century England*, ed. J. Taylor and W. Childs (Gloucester, 1990), pp. 38–58

——, N., 'The Despensers and the Downfall of Edward II', *English Historical Review*, 99 (1984), pp. 1–33

——, N., *English Church Monuments in the Middle Ages: History and Representation* (Oxford, 2009)

——, N., *For Honour and Fame: Chivalry in England, 1066–1500* (London, 2011)

——, N., *Knights and Esquires: The Gloucestershire Gentry in the Fourteenth Century* (Oxford, 1981)

——, N., *Richard II* (New Haven and London, 1997)

——, N., *Scenes from Provincial Life: Knightly Families in Sussex, 1280–1400* (Oxford, 1986)

——, N., 'Servants of God and Crown: the Canons of St George's Chapel, 1348–1420', in *St George's Chapel, Windsor, in the Fourteenth Century*, ed. N. Saul (Woodbridge, 2005), pp. 97–115.

Saunders, A., 'Administrative Buildings and Prisons in the Earldom of Cornwall', in *Warriors and Churchmen in the High Middle Ages: Essays presented to Karl Leyser*, ed. T. Reuter (London, 1992), pp. 195–216

Scammel, J., 'The Origin and Limitations of the Liberty of Durham', *English Historical Review*, 81 (1966), pp. 449–473

Schoeck, R. J., 'Walter Lyhert', in *The Oxford Dictionary of National Biography*, ed. H. C. G. Matthew and B. H. Harrison, 60 vols (Oxford, 2004), xxxiv, pp. 862–864

Schofield, P., 'The Arundell Estates and the Regional Economy in Fifteenth-Century Cornwall', in *Town and Countryside in the Age of the Black Death: Essays in Honour of John Hatcher*, ed. M. Bailey and S. Rigby (Turnhout, 2012), pp. 277–297

Sharp, M., 'The Household of the Black Prince', in *Chapters in the Administrative History of Medieval England*, ed. T. F. Tout, 6 vols (Manchester, 1920–33), v, pp. 289–400

Sharpe, R., 'Addressing Different Language Groups: Charters from the Eleventh and Twelfth Centuries', in *Multilingualism in Medieval Britain (c. 1066–1520): Sources and Analysis*, ed. J. A. Jefferson and A. Putter (Turnhout, 2013), pp. 1–40

Shenton, C., 'Edward III and the Coup of 1330', in *The Age of Edward III*, ed. J. S. Bothwell (York, 2001)

Sheppard, P., *The Historic Towns of Cornwall: An Archaeological Survey* (Wadebridge, 1980)

Sherborne, J. W., 'The Hundred Years' War. The English Navy: Shipping and Manpower 1369–1389', *Past and Present*, 37 (1967), pp. 163–175

——, J. W., 'Indentured Retinues and English Expeditions to France, 1369–1380', *English Historical Review*, 79 (1964), pp. 718–746

Simpkin, D., 'Keeping the Seas: England's Admirals, 1369–1389', in *Roles of the Sea in Medieval England*, ed. R. Gorski (Woodbridge, 2012), pp. 79–102

Sobecki, S., *The Sea and Medieval English Literature* (Cambridge, 2008)

Somerville, R., *History of the Duchy of Lancaster, 1265–1603*, 2 vols (London, 1953–70)

Spencer, A., 'The Coronation Oath in English Politics, 1272–1399', in *Political Society in Later Medieval England: A Festschrift for Christine Carpenter*, ed. B. Thompson and J. Watts (Woodbridge, 2015), pp. 38–54

Spreadbury, I. D., *Castles in Cornwall and the Isles of Scilly* (Redruth, 1984)

Sponsler, C., 'The Captivity of Henry Chrystede: Froissart's Chroniques, Ireland and Fourteenth-Century Nationalism', in *Imagining a Medieval English Nation*, ed. K. Lavezzo (London 2014), pp. 304–339

Spooner, B. C., 'The Giants of Cornwall', *Folklore*, 76 (1965), pp. 16–32

Spriggs, M., 'Where Cornish was Spoken and When: A Provisional Synthesis', *Cornish Studies*, 11 (2003), pp. 228–269

Stansfield, R. E., *Political Elites in South-West England, 1450–1500: Politics, Governance and the Wars of the Roses* (Lewiston and Lampeter, 2009)

Stenton, F., *The First Century of English Feudalism 1066–1166* (Oxford, 1961)

Storrs, C. M., *Jacobean Pilgrims from England to St James of Compostella, from the Early Twelfth to the Late Fifteenth Century* (Santiago de Compostela, 1995)

Stoyle, M., 'The Dissidence of Despair: Rebellion and Identity in Early Modern Cornwall', *Journal of British Studies*, 38 (1999), pp. 423–444

——, M., '"Fullye Bente to Fighte Oute the Matter": Reconsidering Cornwall's Role in the Western Rebellion of 1549', *English Historical Review*, 129 (2014), pp. 549–577

——, M., *West Britons: Cornish Identities and the Early Modern British State* (Exeter, 2002)
Stringer, K., 'States, Liberties and Communities in Medieval Britain and Ireland', in *Liberties and Identities in the Medieval British Isles*, ed. M. Prestwich (Woodbridge, 2008), pp. 5–36
Sumption, J., *Cursed Kings: The Hundred Years' War, IV* (London, 2015)
——, J., *Divided Houses: The Hundred Years' War, III* (Philadelphia, 2009)
——, J., *Trial by Battle: The Hundred Years' War, I* (London, 1990)
Sutherland, D. W., *Quo Warranto Proceedings in the Reign of Edward I, 1278–1294* (Oxford, 1963)
Sutton, A., 'The Admiralty and Constableship of England in the Later Fifteenth Century: the Operation and Development of these Offices, 1462–85, under Richard, Duke of Gloucester and King of England', in *Courts of Chivalry and Admiralty in Late Medieval Europe*, ed. A. Musson and N. Ramsay (Woodbridge, 2018), pp. 187–214
——, A., *A Merchant Family of Coventry, London and Calais: The Tates, c. 1450–1515* (London, 1998)
Swanson, R. N., *Church and Society in Late Medieval England* (Oxford, 1989)
Sylvester, D. G., 'Communal Piracy in Medieval England's Cinque Ports', in *Noble Ideals and Bloody Realities: Warfare in the Middle Ages*, ed. N. Christie and M. Yazigi (Brill, 2006), pp. 163–176
Tai, E. S., 'The Legal Status of Piracy in Medieval Europe', *History Compass*, 10/11 (2012), pp. 838–851
Tatlock, J. S. P., *The Legendary History of Britain* (1950)
Thompson, A. H., *The English Clergy and their Organization in the Later Middle Ages* (Oxford, 1947)
Thompson, B., 'Locality and Ecclesiastical Polity', in *Political Society in Later Medieval England: A Festschrift for Christine Carpenter*, ed. B. Thompson and J. Watts (Woodbridge, 2015), pp. 113–145
Todd, M., *The South West to AD 1000* (London, 1987)
Turville-Petre, T., *England the Nation: Language, Literature and National Identity, 1290–1340* (Oxford, 1996)
Unger, R., *The Ship in the Medieval Economy 600–1600* (London, 1980)
Veale, E. M., *The English Fur Trade in the Later Middle Ages* (Oxford, 1966)
Virgoe, R., 'Aspects of the County Community in the Fifteenth Century', in *Profit, Piety and the Professions in Later Medieval England*, ed. M. Hicks (Gloucester, 1990), pp. 1–13
——, R., 'The Crown and Local Government: East Anglia under Richard II', in *The Reign of Richard II*, ed. F. R. H. Du Boulay and C. M. Barron (London, 1971), pp. 218–241
——, R., 'The Parliamentary Subsidy of 1450', *Bulletin of the Institute of Historical Research*, 55 (1982), pp. 125–138
Vivian, J. L., *The Visitations of the County of Cornwall, Comprising the Heralds' Visitations of 1530, 1573, and 1620* (Exeter, 1887)
Wakelin, M. F., *Language and History in Cornwall* (Leicester, 1975)
Walker, S., *The Lancastrian Affinity, 1361–1399* (Oxford, 1990)

——, S., *Political Culture in Later Medieval England*, ed. M. J. Braddick (Manchester, 2006)
Ward, R., *The World of the Medieval Shipmaster: Law, Business and the Sea c. 1350–c. 1450* (Woodbridge, 2009)
Watts, J., *Henry VI and the Politics of Kingship* (Cambridge, 1996)
——, J., *The Making of Polities, Europe 1300–1500* (Cambridge, 2009)
——, J., 'Public or Plebs: The Changing Meaning of "the Commons", 1381–1549', in *Power and Identity in the Middle Ages: Essays in Memory of Rees Davies*, ed. H. Pryce and J. Watts (Oxford, 2007), pp. 242–260
Waugh, S. L., 'The Escheator's General Inquest: the Enforcement of Royal Lordship in the Late Fourteenth Century', in *Foundations of Medieval Scholarship: Records Edited in Honour of David Crook*, ed. P Brand and S. Cunningham (York, 2008), pp. 11–24
——, S. L., 'John of Eltham', in *The Oxford Dictionary of National Biography*, ed. H. C. G. Matthew and B. H. Harrison, 60 vols (Oxford, 2004), xxx, pp. 173–174
——, S. L., 'The Origins and Early Development of the Articles of the Escheator', *Thirteenth Century England, V*, ed. P. R. Coss and S. D. Lloyd (Woodbridge, 1995), pp. 89–113
Welch, C., *History of the Worshipful Company of Pewterers of the City of London*, 2 vols (London, 1902)
Whatley, C., 'Temporalities Be Taken: Edward III, Unruly Ecclesiastics and the Fight for the Benefices of Exeter, 1337–60', *Fourteenth Century England, VIII*, ed. J. S. Hamilton (Woodbridge, 2014), pp. 59–82
Whetter, J., *The Bodrugans: A Study of a Cornish Medieval Knightly Family* (St Austell, 1995)
White, A. B., *Self-Government at the King's Command: A Study in the Beginnings of English Democracy* (Minneapolis, 1933)
Whittick, C., 'John Arundell', in *The Oxford Dictionary of National Biography*, ed. H. C. G. Matthew and B. H. Harrison, 60 vols (Oxford, 2004), ii, pp. 578–579
Willard, J. F., et al. (eds), *The English Government at Work, 1327–1336*, 3 vols (Cambridge, MA, 1940–50)
——, J. F., *Parliamentary Taxes on Personal Property, 1290–1334: A Study in Medieval Financial Administration* (Cambridge, MA, 1934)
Willett, J., 'Cornish Identity: Vague Notion or Social Fact?', *Cornish Studies*, New Series 16 (2008), pp. 183–205
Wood, C. T., *The French Apanages and the Capetian Monarchy, 1224–1328* (Cambridge, MA, 1966)
Wood, J., 'The Arthurian Legend in Scotland and Cornwall', in *A Companion to Arthurian Literature*, ed. H. Fulton (Oxford, 2009), pp. 102–116
Woodcock, B. L., *Medieval Ecclesiastical Courts in the Diocese of Canterbury* (Oxford, 1952)
Wright, S., *The Derbyshire Gentry in the Fifteenth Century* (Chesterfield, 1983)
Young, C. R., *The Royal Forests of Medieval England* (Leicester, 1979)

Unpublished Secondary Sources

Bevan, K. L., 'Clerks and Scriveners: Legal Literacy and Access to Justice in Late Medieval England' (Unpubl. Univ. Exeter PhD, 2013)

Cawthron, D. J., 'The Episcopal Administration of the Diocese of Exeter in the Fourteenth Century: with Special Reference to the Registers of Stapeldon, Grandisson and Brantingham' (Unpubl. Univ. London MA, 1951)

Clowes, R. (compil.), *Duchy Servants* (Duchy of Cornwall Office)

Doherty, P. C., 'Isabella, Queen of England, 1296–1330' (Unpubl. Univ. Oxford D.Phil, 1977)

Drake, S. J., 'Cornwall and the Kingdom: Connectivity, Cohesion, and Integration, c. 1300–c. 1420' (Unpubl. Univ. London PhD, 2017)

Green, D., 'The Household and Military Retinue of the Black Prince', 2 vols (Unpubl. Univ. Nottingham PhD, 1998)

Kleineke, H., 'The Dinham Family in the Later Middle Ages' (Unpubl. Univ. London PhD, 1998)

Matthews, H., 'Illegitimacy and English Landed Society, c. 1285–c. 1500' (Unpubl. Univ. London PhD, 2012)

Page, M., 'Royal and Comital Government and the Local Community in Thirteenth-Century Cornwall' (Unpubl. Univ. Oxford D.Phil, 1995)

Rawlinson, K., 'The English Household Chapel, c. 1100–c. 1500: An Institutional Study' (Unpubl. Univ. Durham PhD, 2008)

Richmond, C., 'Royal Administration and the Keeping of the Seas, 1422–85' (Unpubl. Univ. Oxford D.Phil, 1963)

Tyldesley, C., 'The Crown and the Local Communities in Devon and Cornwall from 1377 to 1422' (Unpubl. Univ. Exeter PhD, 1978)

Index

Abberbury, Sir Richard, 153
Abyndon, Stephen, 119
Admiralty, the, *see* Sea
Advowsons, *see* Church
Agincourt, battle and campaign of, 183, 184, 188, 203
Albion, 86, 90
Aldhelm, 93
Amarle, Thomas, 238
Andalucía, 285
Angers, 260
Anglo-Saxons, 47, 59, 66, 69, 72, 86, 89, 92–95, 106, 277, 315, 317
Anne of Bohemia, Queen Consort of Richard II, 157
Anonymous of Calais, 85
Anthony, 223
Aquitaine, *see* Gascony
Arbitration, *see* Law
Arbroath, Declaration of, 105
Architrenius, the, 57, 97
Array, commissions of, *see* Warfare
Arthur, king, xviii, 19, 57, 58–59, 60, 61, 82, 86, 88–91, 311
King Arthur's Bed, Bodmin Moor, 60
Arthur's Quoit, Goss Moor, 60
Arundel, earl of, *see* Fitzalan
Arundel, Thomas, archbishop of York (later archbishop of Canterbury), 303
Arundell, family, 10, 15, 17, 35, 49, 62, 185, 222–223
   Joan, 55
   John, 36, 42, 54, 119, 138, 148, 206, 241
   John, 222, 253

   John, 265, 266
   Sir John of Lanherne, 31, 63, 133, 163, 164, 173, 174, 187, 247, 251, 301
   Margery, 223
   Ralph, 116, 241
   Remfrey, 17
   wife of, *see* Lanherne
Ashburton, 232
Aspel, Robert, 124
Assessionable Manors, *see* Duchy
Athelstan, King of England, 47, 72, 93–94, 95
Aubermarle, Edward, duke of, 162
Auditor, office of, *see* County-Franchise Government
Lord Audley, *see* Tuchet
Audley, Hugh, earl of Gloucester, 9
Auncell, Richard, 260
d'Avranches, Master Henry, 58, 96–97
Awmarle, Thomas, 223
Aynes, Domyngus, 292
Aysshton, Sir Nicholas, 251–252

Bagge, Phillip, 286
Bailiff-errant, office of, *see* County-Franchise Government
Bakere, Andrew, 223
Bakhampton, Richard, 24, 125
Bakton, John de, 208, 232
Baltic Sea, 4, 279, 285
Bangor, bishopric of, 266
Bannockburn, battle of, 98, 118, 120, 183, 189
Bant, Stephen, 251
Bardi, Florentine banking house, 230, 286

Barnaby, Thomas, 229
    wife of, *see* Bonaventure
Barnstaple, 264
Barons' War (1254), the, 89
Basque sailors, 293
Bassett, family, 80, 185
    Sir John, 10
    John, 227
    Sir William I, 10, 13, 122
Bath and Wells, diocese of, 265
Battaile of Agincourt, 78
Batyn, Christine, 224
Bayonne, 279, 283, 294
Bealknap, Robert, 155, 173
Beare, Thomas, 94
Beauchamp, earls of Warwick, 9, 205, 313
    Earl Thomas, 158, 161
Beaulieu Abbey, 70
Beaumaris, 279
Beaumont, Henry de, 127
Beaupel, family, 10, 17
    Sir John, 237
    Ranulph, 13
    Sir Robert, 136, 173, 194
Bedell, Henry, 227
Bedewynde, John, 48, 116, 117
Bedfordshire, 28, 123, 312
Befori, Rayner de, 281
Bennett, Michael, 253, 273, 306
Bentele, Sir Walter de, 193
Bere family,
    Thomas, 217
    Thomas, 227
Berewyk, Hugh de, 136, 137
Berkeley, baronial family, 304
Berkeley, James, bishop of Exeter, 141
Berkshire, 114, 118, 155, 205, 207, 209, 248
Berwick, John, justice, 175
Berwick-on-Tweed, 97, 125
Beudyn, Sir Robert, 13
Beunans Meriasek, 52, 53, 61, 72, 81, 82, 83, 177, 187, 213–214
Beville, family, 10, 17, 49
    Sir Reginald, 114
Bewnans Ke, 60, 70, 81, 83, 92, 94, 113, 182, 187, 213

Bilkemore, Sir Robert, 28, 123, 176
Billioun, John, 45, 141
Birtsmorton Manor, 174
Black Death, 6–7, 13, 138–139, 219, 231, 306
Blackheath, xvii, 103
Blackmore, stannary, 33, 208
    See also Stannaries
Black Prince, *see* Edward of Woodstock
Blacolvesle, Roger, 122, 124
Blake, family
    John, 216
    Roger, 216
Blanchminster, family, 15, 17
    Sir Ranulph, 10, 13, 39, 60, 131–132, 190
    Ranulph, 256
Blaunpayn, Michael, *see* Cornwall, Michael of
Blisland Manor, 206
Bloyou, family, 10, 13
    John, 264
    Sir Ralph, 10, 55
    Sir Ralph, 45, 175
Blundel, William, 243
Bodilly, John, 249
Bodmin
    church and parish, 79, 274
    friary, 6–7, 60, 260–261
    prior and priory, 17, 48, 61, 63, 133, 154, 156, 260, 272, 273
    town, xvii, 6, 17–18, 24, 27, 102, 154, 162, 181, 191, 194, 216, 217, 221, 224, 230, 238, 273, 285, 288, 303
Bodmin Moor, 60, 80
Bodrugan, family, 10, 15, 40, 45, 49, 185, 215, 244, 251, 303, 311
    Sir Henry, 55, 175, 187, 190, 275
    Henry, 252
    Joan, wife of Ralph Trenewith, 216
    Sir Otto I, 13, 55, 121, 123, 187
    Otto II, 57, 156, 210, 216
    Sir William I, 187, 274
    William II (previously Trenewith), 15, 57, 216, 304
    William, 256
Bole, Walter, 209

Bolenowe, John, 215
Bolingbroke, Henry, *see* Henry IV
Bologna, 269
Bolster, giant, 80
Bonaventure, family,
  Richard, 229
  Thomasine, wife and widow of Thomas Barnaby, Henry Galle and John Percyval, 229
Boniface IX, 269
Boniface, Elizabeth, wife of Thomas Treffry, 10, 199
Bonville, family, 15
Books, unnamed,
  of history, 60
  of law, 266–267
  see also individual named texts
Boorde, Andrew, 100, 101
Bordeaux, 5, 279, 282, 283
Bordigla, Raymond de, 261
Borlas family,
  Andrew, 248
  Robert, 223
Boroughbridge, battle of, 121
Bosanath in Mawnan, 242
Boscastle, 10, 39
Bossiney, 122
Boswens, John, 282
Botreaux, family, 10, 15, 17, 39, 49, 250
  Elizabeth, 130, 156, 246
  Sir Ralph, 130, 173
  Sir Reginald, 13, 140
  Sir William I, 13, 116, 120, 122, 124, 125, 210
  Sir William II, 155–156, 159, 186, 207, 211, 246, 250, 270, 288, 303
  William, Lord Botreaux, 130
  William, 270
  William, 224
Bouges, William de, 260
Boutruche, Robert, 111
Bracy, Robert, 266
Bradford (Devon), 22, 137
Brannel Manor, 123
Brantingham, Thomas, bishop of Exeter
  diligent diocesan, 261, 267, 274
  extracts homage from Cornish man, 256
  indulgence for captured mariners, 295
  recovers debts from Cornishmen, 256
  serves on the Cornish Bench, 156, 272
  support for the Crown, 273, 275, 277
Brantingham, Sir William, 152, 155, 159
Bray, William, 265
Breage, 230, 258
Brembre, Nicholas, mayor of London, 160, 201
Brest, 185, 195
Bretagne, Alan de, earl of Cornwall, 7
Brétigny, treaty of, 144
Breton, John, son of William, 285
Brewer, William, 65, 69
Brinton, Thomas, bishop of Rochester, 112
Bristol, 193, 230, 280, 281, 288, 293, 294
Bristol, John de, 206–207
Bristol, William de, 281
Britons, 59, 60, 86, 87, 88, 89, 93, 95
Brittany and the Bretons, 18, 70, 80, 81, 82, 84, 137, 183, 187, 193, 214, 279, 280, 284–285, 289, 290, 292, 293, 294, 295
Bromford, Nicholas, 163
Brondel, William, 238
Bronescombe, Walter, bishop of Exeter, 259
Brotherton, Thomas, 115
Broun, Richard, 299
Browne, John, 285
Bruges, 5, 144, 286
Brussels, 292
Brut Chronicle, 60, 61, 88, 92
Brutus, 57, 86, 90
Buckingham, earl of, *see* Gloucester
Burdet, Peter, 114
Burgundy, duke of, 172, 265
Buxton, William, 224

Cade, Jack, 103
Cadoc, 59, 213
Cadzand, battle of, 195
Caen, 266

Caerhays, Philip de, 128
Calais, 85, 161, 233, 289
　See also Crécy–Calais
Callington, 252
Calstock Manor, 140, 161, 208
Camblan, river and battle of, 59
Camborne, 63, 82, 215, 263
Cambridge, Edmund Langley, earl of (later duke of York), 188, 189
Cambridge, Isabella, countess of (later duchess of York), 189
Cambridge, University of, 262
Cambridgeshire, 172
Camden, William, 95, 101
Camel, river, 59
Camelford, 6, 27
Camelot, 91
Canterbury Cathedral Priory, 18
Canterbury, Henry, 260
Canterbury, officials of the archbishop of, 265
Cape St Vincent, 292
Carde, Piers, 305–306
Cardiff, 73
Cardinham,
　barony of, 12
　church, 223
Cardrew, Nicholas, 217
Carew, Sir Richard, 14, 17, 43, 55, 58, 60, 62, 71, 76, 77, 93–94, 101, 106, 221, 223, 229
Carleton, Adam de, 68, 96, 256
Carleton, Nicholas, 275
Carlisle, 281
Carminow, family, 10, 15, 17, 27, 40, 49, 59, 62, 72, 130, 153, 177, 210, 304, 311
　Joan, 15
　Sir John I, 13, 124, 206, 290
　John II, 128
　Minawe, 75
　Oliver, 13
　Sir Ralph, 23, 55, 147, 153–155, 156, 177, 207, 246, 269
　　wife of, *see* Chaumpernoun
　Sir Roger, 210
　Thomas, 207
　William, 154
Carn Brea, 10, 80
Carnedon Manor, 45
Carnsew, 242
Carpenter, Christine, 42
Carpenter, John le, 296
Carver, Richard, 98
Cary, Sir John, 158
Cary, John, 221
Cary, Robert, 244
Castile, *see* Spain
Castle-an-Dinas, 59, 61
Castleare, John de, 172
Catalonia, 298
Catour, Thomas, 230, 258
Causton, family
　Nicholas, 221
　Richard, 221, 222
Cavendish, Sir John, chief justice, 248
Caxton, William, 92
Celtic Sea, 279, 281
Celts, the, xvii, xviii, 18, 79, 106, 308, 315–316, 317
Chamberlain, family,
　Agnes, 295
　Robert, 295
Channel Islands, the, 174, 280, 285, 304
Charles V, King of France, 146, 151
Charter Fragment, 47
Chastel, Sir Guilliame de, 198
Chaucer, Geoffrey, 76
Chaumpernoun, family, 11, 15, 44, 153
　Sir Henry, 13
　Katherine, wife of Sir Ralph Carminow, 269
　Sir Richard, 13
　William, 137
Chenduyt, family, 10
　Richard, 160, 174
Cheshire, 20, 134, 151, 162, 184, 197, 228, 253, 303
　palatinate jurisdiction, 37, 38, 98, 209
Chester, 5, 172, 280–281, 282, 293
Chichester, bishopric of, 266
Childs, Wendy, 282
Chita, unidentified Cornish town, 198

Chivalry, 17, 214
Chuddele, Richard, 257
Church, the,
  administrative divisions,
    advowsons, 119, 257, 258, 262
    archdeaconry of Cornwall, 18, 46, 256–257, 272, 274, 277
    Chapel Royal, 256, 258
    chapels, 10, 46
    collegiate churches, 258–260
    see also Crantock, Glasney, St Buryan
    Exeter Cathedral, 258, 259, 261–262, 264, 265, 267
    Exeter, diocese of, 17, 44, 46, 88, 255–256, 261, 265, 268, 272, 275, 277
    parishes, 18, 46, 257–258
    royal free chapels, see St Buryan
  canon law and jurisdiction of, 122, 236, 237–238, 269, 274
    Court of Arches, 265
    Court of Canterbury, 265
  chantries, 224
  Christendom and the crusades, perceptions of, 80, 268–270
  and connectivity, 258, 261, 266–268, 270, 277
  Constance, Council of, 85
  Cornish churchmen, 264–266
  corrodies, 260
  and education, 262–263, 266
  Great Schism, the, 265, 276
  and identity, 268, 270, 275–276, 277
  as landholder, 17, 274
  Lollardy and non-conformity, 264, 267, 276
  and lordship, 54
  obits, 56, 60, 249
  orders,
    alien priories, 260, 275
      see also St Michael's Mount; Tywardreath
    friaries, 6, 223–224, 260–261
      see also Bodmin; Truro
    monasteries and priories, 17, 260
    see also Bodmin; Launceston
  pilgrimage, 101, 266, 268, 281, 283–284
  and royal government,
    convocation and parliament, 270–271
    dependence on royal government, 273–274
    king's power over, 275–276
    royal taxation of, 271–272, 277
    state prayers and public opinion, 203, 272–273
    support for royal government, 272–273
    tensions between church and state, 277
  and social mobility, 263, 265, 266
  see also Berkeley; Brantingham; Grandisson; Oxford; Stafford; Stapeldon
Cinque Ports, 293, 294
Clare, Richard de, 28
Clement VI, 277
Cliffe, 258
Climsland Manor, 157
Clonfert, bishopric of, 256
Clyfton, John, 196
Cobham, Sir Reginald, 188
Coinage duty, see Stanneries
Cokeworthy, John, 25
Cokyn, Henry, 29, 146
Collan, Thomas, 176
Collan, William, 293
Colquite, 303
Colshull, family, 15, 208
  John, 17, 31, 160, 162, 208
  wife of, see Huish
Columbers, Philip de, 200
Commerce,
  and the administrative framework of the realm, 232–233
  and coinage, 232–233
  and connectivity, 221–222, 223, 228–229, 334
  debt patterns, 218, 219–220, 222, 230–231
  and identity, 232–234

the regionalised economy, 229–231, 234
traders, gentry and non-gentry,
    215–217
see also London; Sea; Stanneries;
    Weights and Measures
Conerton Manor, 206
Connectivity,
  binds the kingdom together, 307–308
  commercial, *see* Commerce
  ecclesiastical, *see* Church
  and identity, 308–310
    see also Cornish identity
  legal, *see* Law
  link between social status and
    mobility, 304–305
  lordly, *see* Lordship
  maritime, *see* Sea
  military, *see* Warfare
  nature of, 169–170, 303–304, 305–306
  regnal, *see* Royal Government
Constance, council of, *see* Church
Constantine, emperor, 59
Constantinople, 270, 286
Contra Wicleffum, 264
Conventionary tenure, *see* Duchy of
    Cornwall
Conyng, John, 138
Cook, John, 208
Cook, Thomas, 279, 299
Cooke, John, 257
Copelston, John, 162, 173
Corby, William, 160
Corineus, 57, 60, 78, 86, 87, 88, 92, 95
Cork, 128
Cork, John, 251
Cornewaille, Matthew, 129, 195
Cornewaille, Sir William, 123
Cornewaille, William de, 209
Cornish Acres, 63, 76
Cornish Identity,
  in comparison to Northerners, 77
  in a composite realm, 99
  and connectivity, 170, 177, 182, 190,
    196–197, 203–204, 213–214, 232–233,
    242, 252–253, 268, 270, 275–276, 277,
    287–288, 301–302, 309

county community and commonalty,
    42–44, 64–65
and customs, 63, 76–77 *see also*
    naming practices; hurling; football;
    wrestling; saints
defined by blood and ethnicity, xix,
    76, 95–96
Englishness, 65–67, 94–95, 98, 102,
    106–107
gentry concern for, 64
governmental solidarities, 48–49, 72
and landscape, 70
and language, 46, 62–63, 84–86, 100
and the law, 73–74
layered nature, 43, 65, 66–67, 69, 96,
    106–107
liminality, 71
and local legends, 57–59, 61–62, 80
and lordship, 51–52, 72–73
and miracle plays, 80– 83
modern, xvii, 316–317
mythological source of, 57, 64, 86–88
and rebellion, 102, 104–106
and saints, 63, 78–79, 100–101
and the shire establishment, 49, 50
social network theory, 42
south-western regionalism, 44–45
stereotyped, 19, 70, 89–90, 96–97,
    101–102
sub-shire solidarities, 45–46
Cornish language, xviii, 18–19, 46,
    62–63, 69, 83–86, 100, 101, 256, 261,
    284–285
Cornish, William, 283
Cornubia, Odo de, 172
Cornubia, surname, 305
Cornwale, Thomas, 281
Cornwall,
  agriculture, 4–5
  duke of, *see* Edward III; Edward of
    Woodstock; Henry IV; Henry V;
    Joan of Kent; Richard II
  earl of, see Bretagne; Edmund;
    Eltham; Gaveston; Isabella; Richard;
    Edward I; Edward II; Edward III
  economy, 4

mineral wealth, 5
population, 6
settlement patterns and towns, 6
topography and climate, 3, 4, 46
Cornwall, John of, 59
Cornwall, John of, 85–86, 263–264
Cornwall, Lawrence of, 179
Cornwall, Michael of, 58, 96–97
Coroner, office of, *see* County-Franchise Government
Corpus Christi, feast of, 63
Coulyng, John, 237
County Bench, *see* County-Franchise Government; Law
County-Franchise Government,
 auditor, office of, 34–35
 bailiff-errant, office of, 34
 castellan, offices of, 33–34
 coroner, office of, 29–30
 escheator, office of, 28–29
 feodary, office of, 29, 34
 havener, office of, 32, 301
 hundreds, 8, 35–36, 46
 keeper of the tinners' gaol, 32, 34
 the MPs, 23–25, 48
 parker, office of, 34
 peace, keepers and justices of the, 25–28, 236, 272
 receiver, office of, 31–32
 sheriff, office of, 8, 21–23
 steward, office of, 22, 31
 under-sheriff, office of, 30
 weigher of tin, office of, 32, 34
 see also Lordship; Parliament; Royal Government; Stannaries; Taxation; Warfare
Courtenay, family of Devon, 15, 140, 184, 205, 209, 313
 Earl Edward, 157, 158, 205, 303
 Hugh, 120, 200
 Sir Philip, 157, 159
 William, archbishop of Canterbury, 201, 267
Courts, *see* Law
Coutances, Walter of, 57
Coventry, 228, 230

Cranewell, William, 146
Crantock, 270
Crécy–Calais, campaign of, 73, 126, 137, 183, 187, 188, 189, 190, 192, 194, 202
Creed, 257, 258, 266, 267
Crenelate, licences to, *see* Gentry
Crewkerne, John, 258
Crosse, Thomas de, 259
Crowan, 190
Cruel, Peter the, 145
Cumberland, 90, 281
Cusance, William, 277

Dabernon, family,
 Isabel, wife of John Tremayne I, 250–251
 Joan, wife of John, 146
 John, 22, 29, 34, 137, 138, 139, 140, 142, 143, 144, 145, 146, 149, 207, 212, 251
 John, junior, 207
 Matthew, 207
Dartington Hall, 161
Dartmouth, 158, 193, 197, 198, 286, 294, 298
Daundely, William, 39
Dauney family,
 Sir John, 10, 13, 190, 212
 Maud, 212
David, biblical king, 177, 242
Davies, R. R., 20, 69, 242
Davy, John, 228
De laude universitatis Oxonie, 264
Derby, earl of, *see* Henry IV
Derbyshire, 209, 304
Descriptio Norfolchiae, 312
Despenser, Hugh the elder, earl of Winchester, 117, 120, 121–122
Despenser, Hugh the younger, 120, 121–122
Determinaciones Trevellys, 264
Devizes, Richard of, 96
Devon, 3, 11, 22, 28, 29, 34, 44, 47, 50, 77, 78, 92, 96, 101, 103, 104, 119, 122, 127, 137, 140, 142, 152, 156, 161, 172, 173, 181, 190, 200, 207, 209, 231, 257, 261, 283, 286, 295, 312, 313

Devon, earl of, *see* Courtenay
Devon, Jeel of, 288
Dinham, family, 11
   John, 13
   Sir John, 206
Dogowe, John, 224–225, 287
Dolbeara, Walter, 269
Domesday Book, 47, 95
Donation of Constantine, 82
Don Quixote, 92
Dorset, 10, 28, 90, 103, 156, 181, 190, 200, 245
Dorset, archdeaconry of, 265
Doune, William, 259, 261
Drayton, Michael, 78
Droys, Walter, 288
Dublin, 202, 279
Dublin, archbishopric of, 266
Duchy (and earldom) of Cornwall,
   assessionable system and manors, 5, 125
   estates, 7
   Great Charter, 8, 37–38
   history of, 7, 8, 111
   mythology, 58
   palatinate status (or not), 37–38, 240
   physical structures, 8, 52–53
   prerogative rights, 7–9, 38
   see also Bretagne; Edmund; Edward I; Edward II; Edward III; Edward of Woodstock; Eltham; Gaveston; Henry IV; Henry V; Isabella; Joan of Kent; Richard; Richard II
'Duchy Palace', the, 8, 47, 52–53
Duloe, 275
Dumnonia, ancient kingdom, 92
Dungarth, King of Cornwall, 93
Dunioun, Peryn, 254
County Durham, 20, 64, 79
   palatinate jurisdiction, 22, 26, 37, 38, 40
Dutch, the, 280, 285
Dutyshman, Hanys, 239

East Anglia, 208
Eastwivelshire, dean of, 241
Eastwivelshire (East), hundred, 35, 241
   See also County-Franchise Government
Edmund, earl of Cornwall, 7, 53, 113, 114, 117, 216
Education, *see* Church; Oxford; Law
Edward the Elder, King of Wessex, 90
Edward I,
   employs Church for county defence, 272
   grants charter to tinners, 8, 114–115, 238
   imperial ideology, 90
   impresses Cornish ships, 191
   inherits earldom of Cornwall (1300), 7, 113
   proclaims the making of peace, 202
   recruits Cornish soldiers, 187
   responsive to county concerns, 114
   rulership in Cornwall, 113–115, 206
Edward II,
   appoints to Cornish benefices, 275
   calibrates tin weights with London standard, 233
   characterises Cornwall as remote, 71
   confiscates earldom from Queen Isabella, 122
   Cornish resentment towards, 117, 132
   Cornish resistance to in 1322, 121
   Cornish support for in 1322, 121
   deposed, 123
   disorder under, 116, 117, 118, 120, 122, 132, 154–155
   employs Sir Thomas l'Ercedekne, 189
   grants earldom to Piers de Gaveston, 115
   grants earldom to Queen Isabella, 120
   impresses Cornish ships, 192
   inherits earldom of Cornwall (1307), 115
   investigates Cornish pirates, 298
   mobilises Cornwall's resources, 117, 118–119
   proclaims the making of peace, 202
   recruits Cornish soldiers, 186–187, 190
   reliance on Bishop Stapeldon, 118–119, 122

reorganises escheatries, 28
sends officials to Cornwall, 172
sends spies to Cornish ports, 301
sends workmen to Cornwall, 304
stannary policies denounced, 48
supports Gaveston's rulership, 115–116
suspected murderers arrested, 124
Edward III,
  announces defence of Cornwall, 202
  appointments in the earldom, 124, 206, 209
  appoints to Cornish benefices, 259, 277
  clashes with the Black Prince, 136
  confiscates earldom from Queen Isabella (1330), 124
  defines tinners and tinning jurisdiction, 9, 239
  divides duchy estate between Princess Joan and Richard of Bordeaux, 31, 152
  employs the Church for the organisation of war, 272
  employs Cornishmen in household, 172–173
  enforces compensation for Cornish mariners, 297
  engages in hostilities with France, 136, 137, 144, 146–147
  establishes the duchy for the Black Prince, 7, 135, 315
  establishes the staple of Lostwithiel, 232
  fury at Cornish soldiers, 189
  grants the key to stannary chest to the Bardi, 230
  impresses Cornish ships, 192, 194
  inherits earldom (1336), 126
  inherits duchy (1376), 152
  investigates pirates, 298
  issues peace commission for the Black Prince, 27, 139
  levies clerical subsidy, 272
  minority of, 123
  outlines the French threat, 84
  promotes public order, 132, 137, 138, 245
  quarrels with Bishop Grandisson, 141, 277
  raises Cornish soldiers, 186–187
  reorganises escheatries, 28
  requests Cornish prayers, 203, 273
  rulership weakens, 147
  sends correspondence on behalf of Cornishmen, 299
  sends soldiers to Cornwall, 190
  summons Cornish representatives to maritime councils, 196
  supports John of Eltham's rulership, 125, 126, 134
  supports the Black Prince's rulership, 135–136, 137, 138, 141, 143, 151
  truce of 1347 mocked, 85
Edward IV, 252, 265
Edward of Woodstock, Prince of Wales, the Black Prince,
  agency of, 139
  aid for the knighting of, 9
  announces triumphs, 202–203
  appoints to Cornish benefices, 257
  attains majority, 137, 139
  borrows money from Cornishmen, 216
  care for the county, 138, 148, 149–150
  clashes with Edward III, 136
  clashes with Cornish subjects, 136, 138
  concern for the personnel of the duchy, 136–137
  concern about Cornish debtor, 222
  and Cornish identity, 53, 70
  correspondence with the Cornish gentry, 42, 54
  costs of his rulership, 148, 150–151
  council of, 139, 145
  the county's opinion of, 136, 151
  created duke of Cornwall (1337), 7, 135
  created prince of Aquitaine, 144
  death (1376), 148
  employs Cornishmen, 146, 209, 210–211, 248, 250, 303
  exploits quarrel with Bishop Grandisson, 141
  garners Cornwall's wealth, 138

generosity eulogised, 112
hires Cornish ships, 192–193, 195, 196
illness and return to England, 147
imprisons Welshman in Cornwall, 208
instructions regarding the collection of customs, 282
investigates piracy, 299
involvement in Cornish commerce, 232
journeys to Cornwall in 1354, 51, 88, 141–142
journeys to Cornwall in 1362, 144–145
limitations of his rulership, 150–151
organises defence of Cornwall, 200
petitioned by the County's residents, 148, 150, 212–213, 285
posthumous succession, 153
powerful rulership in Cornwall, 138, 140, 143
promotes public order, 137, 138, 143, 149–151, 217
purveyance in Cornwall, 202
recruits Cornish soldiers, 184, 185, 187
register and letters of, 137–138, 145
reliance on household men, 137–138
requests Cornish prayers, 203
rewards household men, 140, 207, 208
rulership accepted in Cornwall, 138
secures the issue of a peace commission, 27
sends veterans to Cornwall, 191
and stannary workers, 7, 128, 144, 149
supported by Edward III, 135–136, 151
supports, and is supported by, royal rulership, 164–165
Trailbaston of, 142, 143, 145, 147
uses Cornwall as military staging post, 190
victory at Nájera, 145
victory at Poitiers, 143
weakening rulership from 1363, 145–146, 147
Egbert, King of the West Saxons, 92–93
Eleford, Robert de, 142, 143
Eltham, John of, earl of Cornwall
    agency of, 125–126

campaigns in Scotland, 184
created earl of Cornwall (1328), 123
death in Scotland (1336), 125
policies and peace in the earldom, 125–126, 132, 134, 209
policies continued by Black Prince, 135
supported by Edward III, 125, 126
supports, and is supported by, royal rulership, 164–165
Emond, John, 305
English language, 18, 69, 83–84, 85, 99, 100, 104, 264, 304
Englishness, 20, 40, 65–67, 98–100, 309, 312–314
    see also Connectivity; Cornish Identity
Epistre of 1395, 98
Erth, Henry de, 125
Escheator, office of, see County-Franchise Government
Essex, 155, 303
Estcote, John, 286
Estkes, David de, son of Ivo, 281
Everitt, Alan, 313
Evor Castle, 39
Excalibur, 60
Exeter, city of, 3, 93, 105, 230, 231, 232, 257, 286, 287, 297
Exeter Cathedral, see Church
Exeter, diocese of, see Church
Exeter, duke of, see Holand, John
Eyr family,
    Richard, 156, 246
    William, 247

Falkirk, battle and campaign of, 183
Falmouth, 138, 190, 199, 202, 283, 284, 300
Famine, 119, 286–287
Fenn, Thomas atte, 137
Feodary, office of, see County-Franchise Government
Ferrers, Sir William, 13
Fisheries, see Sea
Fitzalan, earls of Arundel,
    Earl Richard, 157–158, 184

Philippa, wife of Sir Richard Sergeaux II, 303
Fitz Henry, Thomas "Havener", 32, 137
Fitz William, family,
  Elizabeth, wife of Reginald Mohun, 55
  Sir John, 55
  Robert, 13
Flamank, Thomas, xvii, 102–103
Flanders and the Flemings, 96, 98, 172, 187, 230, 280, 285, 289, 292, 293, 298, 299, 300
Fleet Prison, 247
Florence, 230, 286
Foll, family
  Joan, 224
  John, 217, 224
Football, 78
Forn, John, 262
Fortescue, Sir John, 74, 252
Fowey, 3, 4, 17–18, 55, 79, 190, 191, 193, 194, 195, 196, 197, 198, 199, 201, 202, 203, 217, 223, 224, 237, 239, 250, 260, 266, 278, 279, 281, 282, 283, 285, 286, 287, 288, 290, 292, 294, 297, 298, 299, 300, 302
Fowey, river, 194
Fowey, Thomas, 226
Fowey, William de, 286
Foweymore, stannary, 33
  See also Stannaries
France and the French, 10, 30, 49, 53, 85, 86, 96, 98, 155, 162, 175, 184, 192, 195, 197, 198, 199, 201, 229, 230, 232, 260, 273, 279, 280, 285, 289, 292, 293, 295, 297, 298, 300
  French ambassador, 105
  French language, 18, 69, 83–85, 99, 105
Fraunceys, family,
  Adam, 221
  Simon, 221
Froissart, Jean, 72–73, 189, 197
Fursdon, John, 251

Galle, Henry, 229
  wife of, *see* Bonaventure
Gannell, 62

Gascoigne, John, 264
Gascony and the Gascons, 74, 85, 98, 143, 146–147, 151, 184, 187, 189, 192, 196, 199, 279, 280, 281, 282, 283, 288, 289, 298
Gaunt, John of, duke of Lancaster, 80, 162, 183, 184, 190, 265
Gaveston, Piers de, earl of Cornwall,
  campaigns in Scotland, 184
  Edward II's support for, 115
  executed by dissident earls, 117
  exiled in 1310, but rumoured to be in Tintagel Castle, 116
  exiled to Ireland (1308), 115
  gains earldom (1307), 115
  supports, and is supported by, royal rulership, 164–165
  weakness of rulership, 115–116, 117, 132
Sir Gawain, 57
Geer, John, 284
Genoa and the Genoese, 117, 265, 286, 292, 294
Gentry,
  changing structure of, 12–14
  commemoration, 56, 60, 63
  curus honorum of local office, 49–50, 52
  definition of, 9
  distinctive Cornish attributes, 16
  employing lawyers, 250
  employment in the duchy, 210
  family extinctions, 14–15
  household chapels, 10, 55
  in the County Court, 48
  income, 14–15
  involvement in piracy, 294
  involvement in trade, 215–216
  itinerant lifestyles, 10, 55
  language of lordship, 11–12
  lawlessness, 130–131
  military service, 187
  numbers of, 9–10, 12
  office-holding, 30, 39–40, 177
  private jurisdictions, 39
  religious sympathies, 79
  residences, 10, 130

self-regulation, 50
social interactions, 17, 43, 55–56
social structure, 54–55
taking holy orders, 262–263
see also individual named families;
    Cornish identity
German, John, 258
Germyn, Richard, 19, 205
Gevely, Thomas, 127, 131
Ghent, 144
Giffard, family,
    Henry, 256
    Joan, 171
    Joan, wife of John Penrose, 248
    Katherine, 179
    Ranulph, 171
    Robert, 187
    Walter, 264
Gildesburgh, John de, 221
Gisors, 188
Glamorgan, 120
Glasney College, Penryn, 81, 259–260, 263, 269, 305
Gloucester, 230, 280–281
Gloucester, earl of, *see* Audley
Gloucester, Thomas of Woodstock, duke of (formerly earl of Buckingham), 157–158, 159, 161, 190
Gloucestershire, 11, 26, 118, 134, 184, 190, 197, 258, 295, 304, 312
Gluckman, Max, 56
Glyn Dŵr, Owain, 73, 89, 105
Glyn, family, 17
    Launcelot, 75
Godesgate, Peter, 194
Gogmagog, giant, 78
Goldsmith, Thomas, 216, 221, 288
Goof, Henry, 228
Gorsedh Kernow, 316
Goss Moor, 60
Gough Map, the, 70–71, 89
Grampound, 27, 125, 266
Grampound, John, 257
Grandisson, John de, bishop of Exeter
    active diocesan, 255–256, 259
    comments on Cornish language, 18, 84
    complains to Edward III about coastal attacks, 271
    concerned about non-resident incumbents, 257
    employs Cornishmen, 250
    laments of Cornwall, 3, 70, 71
    letter to the prior of Tywardreath, 197
    quarrels with Edward III and the Black Prince, 141, 277
    recommends his chef, 267
    support for the Crown, 275
    usurps ducal rights, 137, 141
    views on Cornish saints, 63
    will of, 256
Gready Manor, 237
Great Civil War of the Seventeenth Century, 104
Great Council (1323-4), 12
Great Gothers, 245
Great Yarmouth, 193, 293, 294, 305
Gronou, Sir Howe ap, 208
Grosmont, Henry of, duke of Lancaster, 188
Gruffudd, Llywelyn ap, 74
Guérande, 284
Guernsey, 289
Guinevere, 60
Gurmuncestre, John de, 257
Gurney, Thomas, 124
Gwinear, 262, 268
Gwycor, John, 75

Hailes Abbey, 258
Halap, James, 266
Halcombe, Martin, 261
Halidon Hill, battle of, 125
Haliwerfolc, 64
Hall, G. D. G., 36
Hall Manor, 55
Hall, Walter, 185
Halton, family,
    Joan, wife of Sir Roger Ingepenne Junior, 114, 208
    Sir John, 114, 208
Hamley, family,
    Sir John I, 190, 221

Sir John II, 147, 216
Hampshire, 17, 70, 181, 257
Hampton, Richard de, 157
Hanseatic League, 219, 282, 288, 292, 298
Harewell, John, 277
Hartland, 11
Haryes, Michael, 227
Hatcher, John, 149, 218
Hauvilla, Johannes de, 57, 71
Havener, office of, *see* County-Franchise Government
Haverford, 247, 279
Hawley, John, 158
Hayle, 279
Heghes, William de, 264
Heligan, family, 17
Helsbury Park, 207
Helston,
    manor, 173, 179, 210
    town, 24, 27, 125, 142, 172, 179, 205, 248, 252, 305-306
Helstone-in-Trigg Manor, 153
Henley, Walter of, 112
Henry II, 84
Henry III, 7, 22, 50
Henry IV, (Bolingbroke, formerly earl of Derby, then duke of Hereford), Appellant, 158
    appointments in Cornwall, 162-163
    appoints to Cornish benefices, 261
    combines escheatries of Cornwall and Devon, 29
    employs Cornish "pirates", 194, 300
    employs Cornishmen, 172, 245
    investigates rumours, 73
    legislates on appropriation of vicarages, 276
    recruits Cornishmen into the royal affinity, 174
    requests Cornish prayers, 203
    seizes the duchy estates from John Holand, 163
    seizes the throne (1399), 162-163
    supports his son, the future Henry V, 163, 164
Henry V, (Henry of Monmouth)
    appoints to Cornish benefices, 260
    arbiter of orthodoxy, 276
    ascends to the throne, 164
    employs Cornishmen on diplomatic missions, 172, 265
    gains duchy (1399), 7, 163
    impresses Cornish ships, 192
    petitioned by Cornish residents, 213
    requests Cornish prayers, 203, 273, 276
    rulership in Cornwall, 163, 164, 208, 209
    ships tin to Bordeaux, 283
    supports, and is supported by, royal rulership, 164-165
Henry V, play, 101
Henry VI, 101, 174, 252, 265-266
Henry VII, xvii, 83, 102-104
Hereford, bishopric of, 266
Hereford Cathedral, 259, 281
Hereford, duke of, *see* Henry IV
Hertfordshire, 73
Higden, Ranulph, 51, 59, 88, 303, 312
Hirde, John, 164
History of the Kings of Britain, 57, 59, 86, 88
Hobbe, Walter, 288
Holand, John, duke of Exeter (formerly earl of Huntingdon),
    loses the duchy estates, 163-164
    raised to the rank of duke of Exeter (1397), 162
    receives duchy estates, 160-161
    removed from the County bench, 163
    rises against Henry IV, 163-164
    supports Richard II's kingship, 161, 162, 164
Holand, John, earl of Huntingdon, 265
Holland, 289
Hoplyn, John, 227
Hoppy, Ralph, 227
Horden, Peregrine, 169
Horsham, John de, 143, 150
Huish, family, 11, 44
    Alice, 60
    Emmeline, wife of Sir Robert Tresilian and John Colshull, 16, 160, 208, 249
    Sir Richard, 176

476   Index

Hundreds, see County-Franchise Government
Hunting and hawking, 55, 78
Huntingdon, earl of, see Holand
Huntingdonshire, 256, 257
Hurlers Stones, Bodmin Moor, 80
Hurling and soule, 78
Hyde, Thomas de la, 22, 113, 115, 116, 117

Iceland, 285
Ilcombe, Sir Henry, 160, 161, 163, 189, 207, 243
Illogan, 63
Ingepenne, family, 15, 185, 208
   John, 142
   Sir Roger Senior, 114, 205, 208, 241
   Sir Roger Junior, 114, 208
   wife of, see Halton
Inns of Court and Chancery, see Law
Ipswich, John, 257
Ireland and the Irish, 55, 73–74, 75, 80, 85, 89, 90, 91, 95, 97, 98, 99, 105, 162, 187, 192, 199, 242, 247, 248, 276, 279–280, 282, 292, 311, 315
Irish Sea, 279–280, 281
Isaak, John 205
Isabella, Queen Consort of Edward II
   deposes Edward II, 122–123
   disorder under, 120
   gains earldom (1317), 120
   loses earldom (1324), 122,
   loses earldom (1330), 124
   petitioned by Cornish residents, 213
   rulership compared to that of Earl Richard, 113
   secures 'restitution' of the earldom (1327), 123–124
   supports, and is supported by, royal rulership, 164–165

Jayet, Thomas, 208
Jersey, 289
Jerusalem, 270
Jeu, John le, 142
Joan of Kent, Princess of Wales, 152, 157, 164–165, 184, 210, 261
Joan, Queen of Scotland, 207
Johan, Richard, 292
John, King of England, 22, 50
John II, King of France, 143–144, 202
John XXII, 269
John, Henry, 75
John, Richard, 75
Joseph, Michael, xvii, xviii, 102–103, 105, 317
Justices of the peace, see County-Franchise Government
Juyl, Roger, 29, 155

Kalendarium, 261
Kampen, 291
Keepers of the Peace, see County-Franchise Government
Kendale, Sir Edmund, 137
Kendale, family,
   John I, 32, 139, 140, 142, 143, 144, 145, 150, 173, 209, 212
   John II, 209, 234, 294
   Richard, 145, 146, 205, 209,
   Stephen, 209
   Thomas, 174
Kennington, 212
Kent, 90, 103, 155, 172, 181, 193, 245, 287, 293, 312
Kent, Walter, 274
Kentwood, Sir John, 24, 155, 156, 158, 159, 200, 201, 207
Kerrier, hundred, 35, 46, 173, 210
   see also County-Franchise Government
Kilkhampton, John de, 260
Killigrew, John, 51, 141, 142
King's Lynn, 285
Kinsale, 288
Kirkestede, Henry, 160
Kleineke, Hannes, 128
Knights' fees, see Taxation

Lacy, Edmund, bishop of Exeter, 79
Lagadek, Richard, 75
Lambourne, family, 17, 186
   John, 13, 292
   Sir William, 133

Lancashire, 22, 121, 134, 184, 197, 228, 252, 253
  palatinate jurisdiction, 22, 37, 209
Lancaster, duke of, *see* Gaunt; Grosmont
Lancaster, Thomas, earl of, 116, 118, 121
Lancastrian livery, 82
Landrake, 213
Landreyn, John, 264
Land's End, 53, 72, 213
Landulph, 287
Langarrow, 62
Langley, Edmund, *see* Cambridge
Langona, 62
Langtoft, Peter, 90-91
Lanhadron Manor, 237
Lanhergy, John, 161, 163
Lanherne, Alice de, wife of Remfrey Arundell, 17
Lanherne Manor, 17
Lanisley, 17
Lanivet, 264, 267
Lansew, Thomas, 226
Lanteglos-by-Fowey, 55, 176, 223, 266
Lanteglos Park, 207
Lanvyan, Andrew, 267
Laon, 61
La Rochelle, 190
Latin language, 69, 83, 85, 99, 100, 303
Launceston,
  castle, 33, 34, 114, 116, 125, 135, 140, 141, 143, 160, 187, 208, 213
  gaol, 33, 129
  grammar school, 262
  prior and priory, 48, 133, 158, 163, 261, 267, 272, 273, 276
  town, 3, 24, 27, 70, 133, 158, 188, 221, 224, 227, 239, 251, 252, 264
Law, the,
  arbitration, 57, 133, 252-253
  and connectivity, 243-244, 248, 252, 254
  courts, types of,
    admiralty, *see* Sea
    assize, 26, 37, 133, 138, 158, 159, 236, 239, 251, 252, 253, 281

common pleas, 155, 241, 244, 245
constable, 265
county bench, 25-28, 138, 139, 146, 147, 154, 155, 156-157, 159, 205, 236, 239, 243
county court, 8, 29, 47-48, 51, 122, 158, 237, 249
gaol delivery, 26, 35, 37, 38, 133, 236, 238, 239, 253
hundredal, 35, 174, 237
king's bench, 133, 147, 155, 158, 243, 247, 248, 249
manorial, 237, 239
staple, 220, 236
expansion of the law, 235-236, 239-240, 242
and identity, 242, 252-253
Inns of Court and Chancery, 253-254
laws, types of,
  common law, 73, 129, 133, 235, 236, 296
  customary law, 236, 237
  ecclesiastical (canon) law, *see* Church
  equity, chancery jurisdiction, 236
  equity, dispensed by the earl-duke, 38, 237, *see also* Petitioning
  maritime law, *see* Sea
  mercantile law, 220, 236-237, 296
  stannary law, *see* Stannaries
  statute law, 235
legal culture and consciousness, 236, 240-242, 248
liberties, 7, 73, 239
no separate courts for Cornish and English folk, 73, 238-239
oyer and terminer, commissions of, 31, 131, 142, 241
practitioners,
  central court justices, 26, 35, 37, 133, 155, 236, 243, 247, 307
  eyre, justices of, 94, 114, 175, 235-236, 239, 242, 249
  lawyers (attorneys), 243-244, 249-250

overlap of central and local justices, 252
sergeants-at-law, 244
Quo Warranto proceedings, 19, 73, 239, 240
and social mobility, 245, 252–253
statutes, named,
of Additions (1413), 12
of Acton Burnell (1283), 220
of Kilkenny (1366), 74
of Lincoln (1316), 36
of Merchants (1285), 220
of Praemunire (1353), 276
of Provisors (1351), 276
of Purveyors (1362), 201
of the Staple (1353), 220, 296
see also Petitioning; County-Franchise Government; Lawlessness
Lawhitton, 17
Lawlessness,
connection with lawfulness, 132
contribution to political discourse, 132
general causes, 126–128
intertwined with the law, 129, 240, 248
problems of evidence, 128, 133
specific causes in the south west, 44, 128–130
the peace in the feud, 56–57, 133–134
see also Sea; Stannaries
Ledhed, Richard, 230
Leicester, archdeaconry of, 259
Leicester, John de, 206
Leland, John, 10, 45, 47, 59, 62
Lelant, 27, 281
Le Morte d'Arthur, 91–92
Lenche, William, 191
l'Ercedekne, family, 10, 15, 17, 40, 49, 185, 215, 311
Sir John, 10, 54, 127, 146, 150, 221
Matilda, 241, 274
Odo, 116
Sir Thomas, 13, 24, 50, 116, 118, 121, 123, 126, 130, 175, 189, 192, 202, 205, 206, 230, 241, 274
Thomas, 130
Sir Warin, 15, 207

Lesnewth,
church, 257
hundred, 35
see also County-Franchise Government
Lesteymour, Abraham, 216
Lewyn, Thomas, 299
Libelle of Englysche Polycye, 97, 196–197, 201, 234, 301
Lincoln, 232
Lindsey, 90
Linkinhorne, 276
Lisbon, 285
Liskeard,
manor, 144, 157
park, 206
town, 24, 27, 129, 142, 162, 226, 276
Lithuania, 270
Little Ash, 3
Liverpool, 228
Lives of the Saints, 93
Lizard, the, 46, 227, 283, 293
Lochard, William, 259
London, xvii, 3, 4, 5, 98, 102–103, 113, 121, 127, 144, 160, 163, 172, 173, 185, 201, 212, 222, 232, 244, 245, 246, 267, 268, 283, 288, 297, 303, 307
Blackwell Hall, 222
Cheapside, 123
Cornhill, 225
Cornish purchases in, 222–223
friaries, 223, 224
Lombard Street, 224
London weights, 233
maritime links with, 218, 229, 282, 285, 287
migration to, 217, 224–228
Peter Lane, near Paul's Wharf, 223
tin weighouse in, 218
trade with, 218–219, 220, 231
travel to, 223
Walbrook Ward, 218, 225
Worshipful Company of Armourers, 221
Worshipful Company of Brewers, 226–227

Worshipful Company of Drapers, 227
Worshipful Company of Fishmongers, 221, 222
Worshipful Company of Goldsmiths, 221
Worshipful Company of Grocers, 221, 222
Worshipful Company of Mercers, 220, 227
Worshipful Company of Pewterers, 219, 224–225
Worshipful Company of Skinners, 225–226
Worshipful Company of Tailors, 221
Worshipful Company of Vintners, 17, 160, 208
London, William de, 124
Longe, William, 227
Looe, 3, 191, 193, 279, 286
Lordship,
   baronies in Cornwall, 12
   and the Church, 54
   and connectivity, 205–206, 211, 212, 214
   and identity, 72–73, 213–214
   importance to the government of the realm, 39–40, 164–165, 206, 313–314
   in urban centres, 209, 232
   lawlessness and maintenance, 126–127
   and lawyers, 250
   nature and expectations of, 111–113, 164–165, 210
   officials moving in the service of, 207–208, 211–212
   and petitioning, 212–214
   role in county society, 51–52, 210–211
   royal lordships as integrative force, 38, 164–165, 214
   and social mobility, 210–211
Loring, Sir Neil, 208
Lostwithiel, 8, 24, 27, 47, 52, 53, 146, 149, 162, 181, 191, 194, 202, 207, 209, 216, 221, 231, 232, 233, 234, 236, 286, 293, 294, 296, 297, 301
Lostwithiel, Lambert of, 288
Low Countries, the, 5, 123, 285, 291
Lucca, 223

Lucy, family, 15
Ludgvan, 79, 267
Luke, Robert, 267
Lundy Island, 123
Luscote, family, 17
Lychebarwe, Thomas, 175
Lyhert, Walter, 265, 266
Lymbergh, Tideman de, 138, 149, 233
Lynton, Thomas, 258
Lynyen, family
   John, 188
   Sybil, 188
Lyonesse, 62

Magna Carta, 114, 233
Malmesbury, William of, 93–94, 101
Malory, Sir Thomas, 91
Maltravers, John, 124
Manuel II Palaeologus, 270
Mappa Mundi, 89–90
March, earl of, *see* Mortimer
Mares, Roger, 194
Margaret of Anjou, Queen consort of Henry VI, 266
Margaret, Queen consort of Edward I, 259
Marizion, 27, 64
Mark, John, 243
Mark, King of Cornwall, 61, 91
Marny, Sir William, 303
   wife of, *see* Sergeaux
Marshalsea Prison, 126, 154, 199, 246, 247
Marsley, Henry, 18
Martyn, William, 120
Mary, daughter of Edward I, 206
Mary, Virgin, 79, 82, 259
Maugnel, Raymond, 128
Maunte, John de, 259
Mayner, family, 288
McClure, Peter, 228
McFarlane, K.B., 14
Mebyon Kernow, 316
Mediterranean Sea, 4, 169, 279, 286, 306
Megre, John, 217, 224, 228
Melcombe, 286
Melianus, 58

Menheniot, 267
Menywynnek, Roger, 130
Merlin, 59, 60, 89, 90
Mertherderwa family, 263
    Reginald, 63, 263
    Thomas, 263
Mezieres, Philippe de, 98–99
Michelstow family, 288, 304
    John, 160, 174
    John, 291–292
    Mark, 160, 174, 194, 300, 304
    Richard, 194, 282, 304
Middlesex, archdeacon of, 265
Miles, Robert, 120
Millburn, William, 179
Mining, *see* Stannaries
Minster, 78
Mirror for Magistrates, 105–106
Modus Tenendi Parliamentum, 25
Mohun, family of Dunster, 55
    John, Lord Mohun, 55
    Reginald, 55
        wife of, *see* Fitz William
Mohun, family of Lanteglos-by-Fowey, 186
    Isabel, 243
    Sir Reginald, 13, 121
    Thomas, 223
Mone, Guy, 303
Monmouth, Geoffrey of, 57–58, 59, 78, 82, 86–87, 88, 91, 101
Monmouth, Henry of, *see* Henry V
Mont St Michel, 260
Mordred, 60, 82, 182
Moresk Manor, 161, 173
Mortimer, Edmund, earl of March, 73
Mortimer, Roger, earl of March, 123, 124
Morwenstow, 266
Mount's Bay, 157, 286
Mousehole, 60, 124, 194, 217, 279, 280, 286, 292
Moveroun, John, 24, 125, 135, 137, 139
Mowbray, Thomas, earl of Nottingham, 158
Munster, region of Ireland, 280

Nájera, battle of, 145
Naming practices, 62–63, 75–76, 305
Nanfan, family, 304
    Henry, 146, 210–211, 304
    John, 174, 304
Nans, John, 269
Nansladron, family, 17
    John, 142
Newcastle-upon-Tyne, 232
Newenham Abbey, 96
New Inn, the Strand, 254
Newlyn, 60
Newlyn, John, 227
Newlyn, Richard, 227
Nichol, John, 223
Niño, Don Pero, 198
Noel, Pascow, 263
Noght, Benedict, 124
Norden, John, 62, 69, 100, 101–102
Norfolk, 181, 312
Normandy, 187, 195, 229, 279, 280, 285, 289
Normans, the, 95, 96
Northampton, John, 3
"North Country", the, 45, 312
Northern England, 91
Northfleet, 287
North Sea, 285
Northumberland, 312
Norway, 285
Norwich, 232, 266
Nottingham, earl of, *see* Mowbray

Oaths,
    coronation oath, 182, 242
    to defend the Appellants, 159
    from JPs, 272
Obits, *see* Church
Olyver, William, 225–226
Olyver, William, 260
Ordinalia, miracle plays, 12, 17, 46, 64, 80–81, 176–177, 241–242, 275
Ordinances of 1311, 116, 118
Orme, Nicholas, 262
Ormrod, Mark, 20
Ostery, Rocelin de, 153

Oxford, 261
Oxford, earl of, see Vere
Oxford, University of, 262, 264, 265, 304, 307
  Bull Hall, 263
  Exeter College (formerly Stapeldon Hall), 262, 264, 266, 267, 268
  Queen's College, 264
Oxfordshire, 17, 248
Oyer and terminer, commissions of, see Law

Padel, Oliver, 63
Paderda, Noel, 30
Padstow, 4, 45, 194, 279, 280, 282, 289
Page, Mark, 12
Palmer, family,
  John, 264
  William, 264
Paris, Matthew, 89
Parker, office of, see County-Franchise Government
Parliament,
  clerical proctors in, see Church
  Cornish concerns raised in, 65–66, 178–180
  elections, 48
  MPs attendance at, 23–25, 179
  Parliamentary Commons, 23, 25–26, 29, 30, 36, 65–66, 127, 147, 178–179, 181, 233–234, 289, 311
  Parliaments,
    1376 (Good), 147–148
    1386 (Wonderful), 157–158
    1388 Feb. (Merciless), 158
  See also County-Franchise Government; Petitioning
Parov, Robert, 237
Paul, 60
Peace, keepers and justices of the, see County-Franchise Government
Pecok, John, the elder, 119
Peeche, John, 268
Pegolotti, Francesco Balducci, 286
Pelynt, 96
Pembroke, earl of, see Valence

Penbegyll, William, 264
Pencogh, Richard, 75
Pencriche, Richard, 86
Pendragon, Uther, 91
Pengersick, Henry, 13
Penlyn, 206, 209
Penpel, Stephen, 265, 266
Penpole, Opy, 187
Penriche, Geoffrey, 161, 163
Penrose family,
  John, 154, 156, 244, 245, 246–248, 249
    wife of, see Giffard
  Josse, 247–248
  Sir Vivian, 246
Penrose, Roger de, 281
Penryn, 6, 27, 81, 130, 194, 259, 282
Penverne, John, 227
Penwith, hundred, 35, 36, 46, 174, 210, 237, 249
  see also County-Franchise Government
Penwith and Kerrier, stannary, 33, 128
  see also Stannaries
Penzance, 17, 60, 278
Penzance, William, 283
Perchay, Henry de, 243
Percyval, John, 229
  wife of, see Bonaventure
Peritz, John, 292
Perranporth, 62, 287
Perranzabuloe, 63
Perth, 125
Pessagno, Antonio, 117, 119, 132, 149, 180
Petit, John le, 256
Petit, family, 10, 13
  Sir John, 176, 221, 244
  Michael, 212
Petitioning, 179–182, 212–214
  communal, 45, 46, 53, 148, 285
  by the county, 38–39, 48, 50–51, 53, 65–67, 114, 117, 118, 122, 129, 136, 148, 180, 193, 203, 231, 233, 239, 242, 302, 308
  by individuals, 54, 123, 129, 153–154, 156, 176, 296, 299
Peudrer, William, 219
Peverell, family, 10, 49, 186

482 Index

Pewter, 219
  see also London
Philip VI, King of France, 297
Philippa, Queen consort of Edward III, 265
Phrygians, 57
Picts, the, 86
Pieres, Nicholas, 221
Pilate, Pontius, 81, 242
Pilgrimage, *see* Church
Piracy, *see* Sea
Pirier, Sir John, 138
Pisa, 281
Pistol, 101
Place Manor, Fowey, 10, 199
Plen-an-gwarry (playing place), 80
Plymouth, 143, 144, 196, 197, 286, 293, 294
Plympton, 144
Poer, William le, 30, 131–132
Poitiers, battle of, 143, 184, 187, 188, 190
Pole, Michael de la, 158
Pole, Stephen, 278, 297
Pole, William de la, earl of Suffolk, 266
Polgas, William, 250
Polgwest, John, 227
Polhampton, Richard, 118
Pollard, A. J., 306
Polmorva, William de, 263, 264, 265
Polper, John, 128
Polruan, 191, 194, 199, 203, 286, 293
Polruan, John, 194
Polruddon, Pascoe, 249
Polston Bridge, 3, 70
Polton, Thomas, 85
Polwhile, Laurence, 225
Polychronicon, 50, 66, 88, 89, 92, 264, 312
Pomeroy, family, 11, 17
  Richard, 206
Poole, 286
Port Books of Southampton, 97
Portland, 294
Portpean, 191
Portugal and the Portuguese, 156, 157, 187, 189, 217, 246, 280, 284, 289, 291–292, 298

Powdershire (Powder), hundred, 35, 142, 150
  see also County-Franchise Government
Prideaux, family, 251
  Roger, 13
  Sir Thomas, 138
Priest, Richard, 97
Prophecy of Merlin, 59
Pruet, William, 142
Purcell, Nicholas, 169
Pydershire (Pyder), hundred, 35
  See also County-Franchise Government
Pyne, John, 13

Quinel, Peter, bishop of Exeter, 77
Quo Warranto proceedings, *see* Law

Radcot Bridge, battle of, 158
Randyll, Thomas, 223
Raulyn, John, 187
Reading, 287
Rebellion, civil war,
  Epiphany Rising of 1400 (attempted), 163–164
  Great Revolt of 1381, 103, 155–156, 205, 248, 272, 313
  'Prayer Book Rebellion' of 1549, 100, 103–104
  Rising of 1497 (first), xvii, 102–103
  Rising of 1497 (second), 103–104
  Rising of 1548, 104
  see also Edward II; Richard II
Receiver, office of, *see* County-Franchise Government
Redruth, 130, 175
Redruth, Ralph, 264
Reformation, the, 100–101
Regum Anglorum, 93
Remonstrance of 1317, 105
Resgerens, Odo, 154
Reskymer, family, 10, 15, 17, 49, 62
  Roger, 13
Restormel,
  castle, 33, 52, 116, 117, 124, 140, 141, 142, 144, 145, 153, 160, 163, 209, 214
  park, 33, 142, 206

Reynold, John, 224
Rheims campaign, 144, 186
Richard, earl of Cornwall and king of the Romans, 7, 12, 22, 50, 113, 209
Richard I, 29
Richard II,
   and the Appellants, 157–159, 161
   appoints to Cornish benefices, 259, 260
   arrests Cornish fishermen, 202
   campaigns in Ireland and Scotland, 185, 192
   deposed (1399), 162–163
   disorder under, 153–155, 157, 161
   divides escheatries of Cornwall and Devon, 29
   divides shrievalty and stewardship, 23, 153
   employs Cornishmen, 247, 248, 265
   exiles John Northampton to Cornwall, 3
   grants duchy manors to John Holand, 160–161
   and the Great Revolt, 156–157
   importance of direct rulership, 164, 207
   inherits part of the duchy (1376), 7, 152
   majority rulership in Cornwall, 159, 161–162
   minority rulership in Cornwall, 153–154, 157
   overlooks Cornish piracy, 298
   reliance on the Black Prince's former retainers, 153, 210
   requests Cornish prayers, 203
   royal affinity of, 160
   strips London's liberties, 225
   tyranny, 161–162
Richard IV, *see* Warbeck, Perkin
Richard, Henry, 238
Richard, Lord Grey of Codnor, 244
Ridel, John, 208
Rikhill, William, 163
Rillaton Manor, 45
Roads, 3, 71, 171, 232
Roberd, John, 75
Robin Hood, 83
Robyn, Richard, 283

Roche, 238
Rochester, 112, 258
Rochester, officials of the bishop of, 265
Rogeroun, William, 193
Rohan, Richard, 202
Rolves, John, 295
Romaunt of the Rose, 76
Rome, 270
Roscarrock, Nicholas, 61, 79, 93, 102
Rosecraddoc Manor, 207
Rous, John, 287
Royal Government,
   fiscal machinery of, 176, *see also* Taxation
   intervention sought, 39, 177, 308, *see also* Petitioning
   and the law, 174–175, *see also* Law
   local government and the movement of personnel, 173, *see also* County-Franchise Government
   officials moving in service of, 172–174
   power and limitations of, 19–20, 176–177, 181–182, 313
   regnal solidarity and identity, 177, 182, 309
   royal affinity, 160, 174
   royal government and connectivity, 173–174, 182
   royal government and parliament, 179–182, *see also* Parliament
   war as a regnal act, 175, *see also* Warfare
   see also Church; Commerce; Lordship; Sea
Ruan Lanihorne, 10
Rusculian, Oliver, 126
Russel, John, 230
Russell, John, 164
Rye, 293

Sadler, John, 306
Saints, named, 18
   St Agnes, 80
   St Anne, 259
   St Buryan, 80, 259
   St Cuthbert, 64, 79

St Endellion, 61
St Erme (or St Hermes), 64
St Ethelbert, 259
St Fimbarrus, 79
St George, 79, 203, 259
St Illogan, 63
St James, 283
St Kea, 60, 70, 82
St Ludewan, 79
St Mabena, 79
St Madron, 63
St Mawes, 63
St Meriasek, 82, 177, 270
St Merthiana, 78
St Mylor, 58
St Peter, 268
St Petroc, 79
St Piran, 63, 64
St Silvester, 82
St Thomas Cantilupe, 259, 281
Saints, settlements, churches and
    institutions named after
St Agnes, 80
St Alban's Abbey, 18
St Albans, 197, 300
St Buryan, 18, 94, 256, 258–259
St Clement's, Truro, 225
St Colan, 27
St Columb Major, 27, 172, 227, 252, 263
St Columb Minor, 75
St Cuby, 267
St David's, bishopric of, 303
St Dennis, 245
St Dominick, 114
St Endellion, 79
St Erth, 227
St Euny, Redruth, 130
St Frideswide, Oxford, 268
St George's, Windsor, 101, 258, 265
St Germans, 27, 57
St Ives, 279, 281
St Ives Bay, 292
St Just-in-Penwith, 18, 71
St Kea, 82
St Keverne, xvii, 102, 105, 227
St Martin's, London, 226

St Mary the Virgin, Oxford, 268
St Mary's, Truro, 224, 226
St Mawes, 63
St Mawgan-in-Meneage, 177
St Michael's Mount, 62, 260, 266, 268,
    272, 275, 278
St Neot, 79
St Newlyn East, 258
St Paul's Cathedral, 123
St Stephen's Walbrook, London, 225,
    226
St Stephen's, Cornwall, 226
St Stephen's, Westminster, 259
St Thomas of Acre, London, 224
St Wenn, 266
St Aubyn, Geoffrey, 57, 190
St Colan, Odo, 36
St Just, Alan, 247
St Paul, John, 256
Salisbury, 230
Saltash,
    manor, 161
    town, 3, 27, 163, 191, 194, 258, 279, 285,
        286, 288
Sandwich, 172, 196, 297
Santiago de Compostela, 283–284
Sarnsfield, Nicholas, 157
Saul, Nigel, 47
Scarlet, family,
    Adam, 217, 293
    John, 221, 278
    Oliver, 217, 292
    William, 217, 297
Schene, Henry, 267
Scilly Isles, the, 62, 70, 80, 131–132, 191,
    279
Scote, John, 239
Scotland and the Scots, 66, 71, 85, 86, 87,
    89, 90, 92, 98, 102, 105, 114, 125, 127,
    129, 176, 183, 187, 189, 190, 191, 202,
    272, 273, 276, 279, 280, 281
Scrope, family, 59
Sea, the
    the admiralty and maritime
        government, 191, 196–197, 236, 265,
        296–297, 301

coasting trade, 280–281, 286–287
and connectivity, 279–280, 281–282, 287–288, 294–295, 300–301, 302
as enabling space, 285–286
fisheries, 5
and identity, 287–288, 301–302
maritime economy, 5
maritime law, 236–237, 296–297
pilots, 282, 288
piracy,
    causes of, 129, 291–292
    cases of, 5, 229, 292–295
    customs of, 295
    definition of, 290–291
    policing of, 292–293, 296–298, 299–300
    royal policy behind, 297–301
points of access to, 278
'sailor town culture', 288
ships, named,
    Andru, 286
    Barry, 79
    Cog Johan, 196
    Cog John, 193
    Cog John, 194
    Despensere, 293
    Edward, 291
    George, 283
    Gracedeu, 193
    Margaret, 287
    Marget Cely, 283
    Marie, 285
    Mary, 288
    Michel, 195
    Michel, 286
    Michel, 299
    Nicholas, 285
    Savoie, 294
    Seint Michel, 280
    Seint Saviour Cog, 202
    Trinity, 290
    William, 287
smuggling, 4, 5, 131, 217, 288–289
sovereignty over, 301–302
wrecking, 5, 128–129, 289–290
Seals, 62, 241

Seck, Richard, 146
Segrave, Hugh de, 152
Selander, Hankyn, 294–295
Seler, John le, 230
Seliman, Robert de, 124
Sergeaux, family, 10, 15, 17, 27, 49, 130, 153, 251, 303
    Alice, wife of Richard de Vere, earl of Oxford, 303
    Elizabeth, wife of Sir William Marny, 303
    John, 130, 153–155, 187, 303
    Michael, 264, 265, 303
    Sir Richard, I, 13, 130
    Sir Richard II, 23, 57, 130, 146, 147, 148, 153–155, 156, 158, 159, 199, 200, 201, 210, 215, 246, 247, 303
    wife of, *see* Fitzalan
Seville, Mounfrere of, 296
Shakespeare, William, 101, 164
Shareshull, Sir William, 27, 138, 140, 142, 150, 211, 243
Shelley, Thomas, 162
Sheriff, office of, *see* County-Franchise Government
Ships, named, *see* Sea
Shoreham, 286
Silver mines, 172
Sithney, 252
Skeweyk, John, 54
Skirkbeck, John, 139, 140, 142, 143, 146
Skynnard, Ralph, 226
Slake, Nicholas, 259
Slegh, John, 157
Slugge, family, 288
Sluys, 294, 298
Sluys-Tournai, campaign of, 183
Smelting, *see* Stannaries
Smith, Philip, 244
Smuggling, *see* Sea
Snell, Roger, 244
Snetysham, John, 258
Solomon, biblical king, 81, 275
Somer, John, 261
Somerset, 28, 103, 156, 190, 200, 231, 244
Soor, family, 10, 15, 17, 40, 304

John le, 13, 130
Reginald, 130
Southfleet, 172
Southampton, 193, 197, 218, 287, 294
Spain and the Spanish, 53, 60, 80, 145, 153, 157, 176, 184, 187, 189, 195, 197, 198, 199, 273, 279, 283–284, 292, 293, 294, 295, 298, 299, 300
Spannel, John, 194
Sparrowhawk, John, 73
Speculum Grammaticale, 263–264
Stafford, Edmund, bishop of Exeter,
   diligent diocesan, 260
   receives oaths of JPs, 272
   support for the Crown, 273, 275, 276, 277
Stafford, Sir Humphrey, 130, 158
Stafford, Richard de, 142
Staffordshire, 22, 113
Stanbury, John, 265, 266
Stannaries,
   administration of, 32–33, 180, 230, 233
   charter of, 8, 114–115, 136
   coinage duty and sessions, 9, 32, 144, 149, 181, 218
   concealment of tin, 149
   credit for tin, 5, 218
   definition of tinners, 9
   disorder in, 50, 102, 116, 117, 128, 132, 147, 217
   districts, 32
   gentry and others dealing in tin, 215–217
   importance of tin to Cornwall, 5
   influence of the Black Death on, 7, 219
   keeper of, 32–33
   law and courts of, 33, 73, 238–239
   of Devon, 45
   smelting, 5
   taxation of tinners, 4, 8
   tinners petition, 45
   toll tin, 16, 33, 215
   wealth of tinners, 217–218
   weighouses for tin, 218, 287
Stapeldon, Sir Richard, 119, 130
Stapeldon, Walter de, bishop of Exeter,
   active diocesan, 255
   appoints suffragan, 256
   founds Stapeldon Hall, Oxford, (later Exeter College), 262, 267
   murdered in London, 123
   sponsors education of Cornishmen, 263
   support for Edward II, 122, 273, 277
   temporal lordship in Cornwall, 119–120, 122–123, 132
   treasurer of England, 119
Statutes, *see* Law
Stephen, King of England, 7
Stephen, Laurence, 267
Steward, office of, *see* County-Franchise Government
Stoke Climsland, 27
Stoner, William, 19, 205
Stonhard, John, 293
Stonor Letters, 97
Strand, London, 254
Strandeby, Roger, 270
Stratford, John, archbishop of Canterbury, 136
Stratton,
   church, 190
   hundred, 35
   see also County-Franchise Government
Straw, Jack, 103
Sturmy, Robert, 281
Suffolk, 181, 257
Suffolk, earl of, *see* Pole
Sumli', Richard, 221
Surrey, 90, 103, 244, 246
Sussex, 103, 134, 181, 286, 312–313
Swansea, 279
Swavesey, Thomas de, 172
Symond, William, 193
Syon Abbey, 260
Syreston, John, 251

Talbot, family,
   William I "the elder", 161, 241
   William II "the younger", 161
Talcarn, William, 32
Talgarrek, Gilbert, 238

Talland, 276
Tamar, river, 3, 47, 53, 72, 93, 141, 278
Tate, family, 228
Tavener, John le, 124
Tavistock, 260
Tavistock, abbot of, 279
Tavistock, John, 230
Taxation
	alien subsidy of 1440, 280
	avoidance of, 4, 131, 155
	collectors of, 30, 176
	customs collectors, 301
	ecclesiastical, see Church
	levies on knights' fees (feudal aids), 8, 9, 14
	parliamentary tax levied in Cornwall, 4, 6, 14, 155, 176
	tin taxes, see Stannaries
Tees, river, 38
Tegyn, John, 196
Tehidy, 80
Teignmouth, 286
Teudar, folkloric tyrant, 82, 83, 94, 214
Teutonic Knights, 270
Tewington Manor, 161
Thames Valley, 16
Thomas, John, 228
Thomas, John, 294
Thorley, Robert, 159, 160
Thunderlegh, Reginald, 218
Tin, see Stannaries
Tintagel
	castle, 3, 33, 34, 58, 59, 61, 89, 116, 118, 122, 139, 157, 160, 161, 200, 214
	manor, 161, 164
Tomyowe, Thomas, 263, 269
Touker, John, 226
Tower of London, 176, 225, 247
Trastamara, Henry of, 145
Trebolans, Henry, 227
Treeures, John, 4
Treffridowe, family,
	John, 251
	Thomas, 251
Treffry, family,
	Thomas, 199

	wife of, see Boniface
	William, 223
Trefurthken, John, 241
Treganhay, Jullans, 274
Treganon family,
	Hugh, 172–173
	Serlo, 173
Tregelowe, John, 227
Tregeneon, Michael, 227
Treglosek, John, 156
Tregole, John, 226
Tregoll, family,
	John, 226
	Thomas, 226
Tregollas, family,
	Sarah, 226
	Thomas, 226
Tregonan, Otto, 251
Tregonon, Thomas, 127
Tregony
	castle, 11
	church, 266
	manor, 206
	town, 288
Tregoose, John, 249, 252
Tregora, Thomas, 244
Tregorrek, John, 205, 256
Tregorrick, 137
Tregoys, John, 226
Tregrisiow, Ralph, 265, 266, 267, 271
Tregury, Michael, 265, 266
Treiagu, Sir John, 24, 57, 119, 120, 122, 123, 124, 125, 127, 130, 141, 221, 222, 245
Trelawny family,
	John, 130
	John, 188
	William, 136
Trelewith, Peter, 247, 248
Trellan, John, 250
Treloskan, John, 227
Trelowe, Reynold, 227
Trematon
	castle, 33, 116, 118, 124, 125, 139, 160, 161
	manor, 161, 163, 208
Tremayne, family, 304
	John I, 34, 207, 250–251, 304

wife of, *see* Dabernon
John II, 156, 159, 244–245, 304
Trembethow Manor, 156, 246
Trembleath Manor, 62
Tremur, Laurence, 230
Trenansaustel, Reynold, 213
Trenarake, John, 161
Trenda, John, 250
Trenerth, Robert, 227
Trenewith, family, 10, 49, 304
    Michael the elder, 36, 216, 217, 243, 304
    Michael the younger, 216, 217, 221
    Sir Ralph I, 121
    Ralph, 32, 146, 153, 216
        wife of, *see* Bodrugan
    William, *see* Bodrugan
Trenewith, Ralph, 229
Trenewyth, William, 226
Trengoff, Walter, 264
Trenode, Richard, 161
Trent, Dorset, 245
Trent, river, 28, 124
Treres, Eude of, 250
Trerise, John, 227
Trerys, John, 226
Trerys, John, 254
Tresilian, Sir Robert, 16, 17, 31, 147, 155, 156, 158, 160, 208, 212, 244, 245, 248–249, 256, 304
    wife of, *see* Huish
Treskewys, Reginald, 226
Trethewey, Robert, 264
Trethewey family,
    Henry, 125, 136, 137, 210, 249, 274
    Isabel, 226
    John, 226
    Robert, 226
    William, 210
Trethowen, Hugh, 226
Trevaignon, family
    Joan, 245
    Sir John, 42, 54, 148, 187
    John, 124, 244, 245–246
Trevarthian, family, 10, 15, 27, 49, 130, 153, 210

John II, 130, 146, 150, 154, 156, 157, 158, 246, 247, 294
John III "the younger", 160, 174
Trevelles, William, 264
Trevelwythe, Edmund de, 293
Trevelyan family, 62
    John, 56, 96
    wife of, *see* Whalesborough
Trevena Manor, 161
Trevenour, John, 250, 256
Treverbyn, family, 55, 131
    James, 194, 196
    John, 160, 174, 186, 188
    Margery, 127, 128, 215
    Nicholas, 226
    Sibyl, 127, 131
    Sir Walter, 127
Treveri, John, 34
Treverugh, William, 286
Trevethek, Richard, 227
Trevisa, John, 51, 58, 59, 66, 71, 83–84, 85, 86, 88, 182, 242, 263, 264, 277, 304, 309
Treviur, Joan, 55
Trewethenek, Michael, 225
Trewinnard, Henry, 177
Treworgy, 209
Trewynard, John, 226
Trewyns, John, 226
Trewythenick, Roger, 205, 248, 252
Trewythosa, Simon, 244, 246
Trewyvyan, Robert de, son of Reginald, 281
Treys, Michael, 227
Triggshire (Trigg), hundred, 35, 46, 242
    see also County-Franchise Government
Trigillowe, family,
    John, 228
    William, 228
Tristan and Iseult, 61
Trivet, Thomas, 157
Troy, 57
Trumpour, Gilbert, 260
Truro,
    friary, 63, 260–261

town, 6, 24, 27, 45, 187, 198, 205, 224, 225, 226, 232, 244, 288, 293
Truro, David de, 269
Trynwyche, Richard, 230
Tryvytlam, Richard, 264
Tuchet, James, Lord Audley, 103
Tudor, royal house of, xviii, 82–83, 102, 209, 316
Turks, the, 270
Tyburn, xvii, 248, 249
"Tye", tin mine, 215
Tyes, Henry, 121
Tyldesley, Christopher, 130
Tyne, river, 38
Tynten, Sir John, 13
Tyrell, John, 237
Tywardreath, prior and priory of, 17–18, 197, 237, 239, 260, 272, 275
Tywarnhaile, stannary, 33
 see also Stannaries

Ude, family
 Michael, 172
 Odo, 30, 217, 284
Under-sheriff, office of, see County-Franchise Government
Universalia, 264
Urban, John, 172

Valence, Aymer de, earl of Pembroke, 114, 205
Vanas, John, 291
Vautort, barony of, 12
Vautort, John, 142
Venice, 218, 286, 290
 ambassador of, 21, 70
Vere, Richard de, earl of Oxford, 303
 wife of, see Sergeaux
Vere, Robert de, earl of Oxford, 157, 158
Vergil, Polydore, 70, 71, 87, 88, 101, 103
Villiers, Gerard de, 216
Vyvyan, family, 62

Wales and the Welsh, 66, 80, 87, 90, 91, 92, 94, 95, 97, 98, 105, 146, 199, 208, 279, 292, 294, 295, 311, 315

customs, 75
laws and courts, 37, 73–74, 235
Marcher Lordships, 36–37, 40, 51, 120, 151, 175
Principality of, 36–37, 40, 72
soldiers of, 73, 189, 190, 191
Welsh language, 18, 84, 85, 100
Wales, Gerald of, 84, 87, 93, 95
Walker, Simon, 64
Walklett, William, 172
Walsingham, Thomas, 97, 162, 197–198, 300
Wamford, Nicholas, 150, 290
Warbeck, Perkin, 103–104
Warfare,
 array, commissions of, 30–31, 186–187, 194, 199–200
 benefits of, 195–196
 communications, 193, 202–203
 and connectivity, 187–188, 189, 190–191, 196–197, 201, 203–204
 Cornish sailors, 190–191, 192–193, 194
 Cornish soldiers, 183–184, 188–189
 costs of, 195
 county defences, 199–202, 272
 evidence of, 185–187, 192–193
 extension of military service, 9–10, 12
 and identity, 190, 196–197, 203–204
 organisation of, 201–202, 272
 raids on the county, 197–199
 see also named expeditions
Warwick, 117
Warwick, earls of, see Beauchamp
Warwickshire, 42, 43, 312, 313
Waryn, John, 265
Waryn, John, 267
Wastel, Michael, 221
Watte, Odo, 237
Week St Mary, 229
Weights and measures, 76, 77, 218, 233, 234
Wells Cathedral, 265
West, Thomas, 208
Westminster, 20, 154, 220, 243, 248, 249, 252
Westminster, Matthew of, 94

Westmorland, 32, 209
Westover, Henry, 230
Westwivelshire (West), hundred, 35
    see also County-Franchise
        Government
Wey, William, 283
Weymouth, 290, 294
Whalesborough, family, 10, 15, 17
    Elizabeth, wife of John Trevelyan, 56
Whitchurche, Richard, 258
Whitehaven, 281
Wiltshire, 103, 295
Winchelsea, 188, 193, 293
Winchester, 232, 244
Winchester, earl of, see Despenser
Windsor, 101
    see also St George's
Windsor, John, 244
Wingfield, John, 142
Wisdom, Robert, 29, 34
Wise, William, 266
Woodstock, James, 135, 136, 200
Woodstock, Edmund of, 115
Woodstock, Thomas of, see Gloucester
Worcestershire, 174, 190

Worcestre, William, 10, 11, 47, 58, 59, 62, 71, 252, 266, 268, 278, 305–306
Wrecking, see Sea
Wrestling, 77–78
Wycliffe, John, 264, 267
Wykeham, William, 257
Wylinton, family, 11
    Christiana, 206
    Edward, 206
    Sir Henry, 118, 120
    Sir John, 206
Wyne, Richard atte, 206
Wynter, John, 162–163, 208
Wysa, Oliver, 57, 241

Ycca, John, 216
York, 173, 232
York, archbishopric of, 270, 303
York, duke of, see Cambridge
Yorkist livery, 82
Yorkshire, 17, 90, 256
Yurle, Simon, 221

Zeeland, 289
Zeke, John, 238